WORLD DEVELOPMENT REPORT 2000/2001

ATTACKING POVERTY

Cover Art

Voyage to the New World, 1999. Mixed media on wood, by Manuel Cunjamá, Mexico. The images used to open the chapters are also taken from this painting and from three others by Cunjamá: *Dialogue with the Universe, Magic Kite,* and *Looking for the Cosmic Balance.*

Manuel Cunjamá was born in 1971 in Tuxtla Gutiérrez, Chiapas. He began exhibiting his work in Chiapas in 1992. Currently, Ana Quijano Gallery in Mexico City is representing Cunjamá in traveling exhibits in the United States. Cunjamá's work is included in the collection of the World Bank art program.

In my work I seek and try to incorporate native symbols and elements that would take me to prehispanic issues and all that I consider useful to this effect I show it in my work.

I use the sun, the moon, the night, and the universe as symbols representing the worry and anxiety of the human being for the wholeness surrounding him: The infinite.
                                                                    —Manuel Cunjamá

The World Bank Art Program makes particular efforts to identify artists from developing nations and make their work available to a wider audience. The art program organizes exhibits, educational and cultural partnerships, competitions, artists' projects, and site-specific installations.

WORLD DEVELOPMENT REPORT 2000/2001

ATTACKING POVERTY

Published for the WORLD BANK

OXFORD UNIVERSITY PRESS

Oxford University Press

OXFORD   NEW YORK   ATHENS   AUCKLAND   BANGKOK
BOGOTA   BUENOS AIRES   CALCUTTA   CAPE TOWN   CHENNAI
DAR ES SALAAM   DELHI   FLORENCE   HONG KONG   ISTANBUL
KARACHI   KUALA LUMPUR   MADRID   MELBOURNE   MEXICO
CITY   MUMBAI   NAIROBI   PARIS   SÃO PAULO   SINGAPORE
TAIPEI   TOKYO   TORONTO   WARSAW

and associated companies in

BERLIN   IBADAN

Cover design and chapter openers by Tomoko Hirata.

Published by Oxford University Press, Inc.
200 Madison Avenue, New York, N.Y. 10016

Oxford is a registered trademark of Oxford University Press.

Manufactured in the United States of America
First printing September 2000

ISBN 0-19-521598-2 clothbound
ISBN 0-19-521129-4 paperback
ISSN 0163-5085

Text printed on recycled paper that conforms to the American
Standard for Permanence of Paper for Printed Library Material
Z39.48-1984.

Foreword

Poverty amid plenty is the world's greatest challenge. We at the Bank have made it our mission to fight poverty with passion and professionalism, putting it at the center of all the work we do. And we have recognized that successful development requires a comprehensive, multifaceted, and properly integrated mandate.

This report seeks to expand the understanding of poverty and its causes and sets out actions to create a world free of poverty in all its dimensions. It both builds on our past thinking and strategy and substantially broadens and deepens what we judge to be necessary to meet the challenge of reducing poverty. It argues that major reductions in human deprivation are indeed possible, and that the forces of global integration and technological advance can and must be harnessed to serve the interests of poor people. Whether this occurs will depend on how markets, institutions, and societies function—and on the choices for public action, globally, nationally, and locally.

The report accepts the now established view of poverty as encompassing not only low income and consumption but also low achievement in education, health, nutrition, and other areas of human development. And based on what people say poverty means to them, it expands this definition to include powerlessness and voicelessness, and vulnerability and fear. These dimensions of human deprivation emerged forcefully from our *Voices of the Poor* study, conducted as background for the report, which systematically sought the views of more than 60,000 men and women living in poverty in 60 countries.

These different dimensions of poverty interact in important ways. So do interventions to improve the well-being of poor people. Increasing education leads to better health outcomes. Improving health increases income-earning potential. Providing safety nets allows poor people to engage in higher-risk, higher-return activities. And eliminating discrimination against women, ethnic minorities, and other disadvantaged groups both directly improves their well-being and enhances their ability to increase their incomes.

The 20th century saw great progress in reducing poverty and improving well-being. In the past four decades life expectancy in the developing world increased 20 years on average, the infant mortality rate fell more than half, and fertility rates declined by almost half. In the past two decades net primary school enrollment in developing countries increased by 13 percent. Between

1965 and 1998 average incomes more than doubled in developing countries, and in 1990–98 alone the number of people in extreme poverty fell by 78 million.

But at the start of a new century, poverty remains a global problem of huge proportions. Of the world's 6 billion people, 2.8 billion live on less than $2 a day, and 1.2 billion on less than $1 a day. Six infants of every 100 do not see their first birthday, and 8 do not survive to their fifth. Of those who do reach school age, 9 boys in 100, and 14 girls, do not go to primary school.

These broad trends conceal extraordinary diversity in experience in different parts of the world—and large variations among regions, with some seeing advances, and others setbacks, in crucial nonincome measures of poverty. Widening global disparities have increased the sense of deprivation and injustice for many. And social mobility and equal opportunity remain alien concepts for far too many people.

Future demographic changes will add to the challenge we face in further reducing poverty. In the next 25 years roughly 2 billion people will be added to the world's population—almost all of them (an estimated 97 percent) in developing countries, putting tremendous pressure on these societies. Clearly, much must be done to reduce poverty in its multiple dimensions and to promote human freedom, today and in the years ahead.

While current and future challenges remain daunting, we enter the new millennium with a better understanding of development. We have learned that traditional elements of strategies to foster growth—macroeconomic stability and market-friendly reforms—are essential for reducing poverty. But we now also recognize the need for much more emphasis on laying the institutional and social foundations for the development process and on managing vulnerability and encouraging participation to ensure inclusive growth. And while domestic action is critical, we have also learned that global developments exert a potent influence on processes of change at national and local levels—and that global action is central to poverty reduction. We have taken a fresh look at our work through the Comprehensive Development Framework, which converges with the views and findings of this report.

Based on its analysis of ideas and experience, this report recommends actions in three areas:

- *Promoting opportunity:* Expanding economic opportunity for poor people by stimulating overall growth and by building up their assets (such as land and ed-

ucation) and increasing the returns on these assets, through a combination of market and nonmarket actions.
- *Facilitating empowerment:* Making state institutions more accountable and responsive to poor people, strengthening the participation of poor people in political processes and local decisionmaking, and removing the social barriers that result from distinctions of gender, ethnicity, race, religion, and social status.
- *Enhancing security:* Reducing poor people's vulnerability to ill health, economic shocks, crop failure, policy-induced dislocations, natural disasters, and violence, as well as helping them cope with adverse shocks when they occur. A big part of this is ensuring that effective safety nets are in place to mitigate the impact of personal and national calamities.

Advances in the three areas are fundamentally complementary—each is important in its own right and each enhances the others. Drawing on this framework, countries need to develop their own poverty reduction strategies, in a manner consistent with preservation of culture. Decisions on priorities must be made at the national level, reflecting national priorities. But action must also take place with local leadership and ownership, reflecting local realities. There is no simple, universal blueprint.

Action at the local and national levels is not enough, however. The evidence of the past decade vividly reveals the importance of global action, both to ensure that the opportunities from global integration and technological advance benefit poor people and to manage the risks of insecurity and exclusion that may result from global change. Five actions are key:

- Promoting global financial stability and opening the markets of rich countries to the agricultural goods, manufactures, and services of poor countries.
- Bridging the digital and knowledge divides, thus bringing technology and information to people throughout the world.
- Providing financial and nonfinancial resources for international public goods, especially medical and agricultural research.
- Increasing aid and debt relief to help countries take actions to end poverty, within a comprehensive framework that puts countries themselves—not external aid agencies—at the center of the design of development strategy and ensures that external resources are used effectively to support the reduction of poverty.

■ Giving a voice to poor countries and poor people in global forums, including through international links with organizations of poor people.

Public action must be driven by a commitment to poverty reduction. The public and private sectors must work together—along with civil society—both within and between countries. While we have much to learn, and while the world continues to change rapidly, the experiences reviewed in this report show that there is now sufficient understanding to make actions to reduce poverty truly effective. We are living in a time in which the efforts and issues surrounding poverty reduction are subject to great scrutiny. In the aftermath of protests and in the midst of controversy, this report offers real substance to the public debate and brings the dialogue to the foreground, where indeed the goal of a world without poverty belongs.

James D. Wolfensohn
President
The World Bank
August 2000

This report has been prepared by a team led by Ravi Kanbur (director of the team until May 2000) and Nora Lustig (deputy director until May 2000 and director since). Monica Das Gupta, Christiaan Grootaert, Victoria Kwakwa, Christina Malmberg Calvo, and Kevin Morrison served as full-time team members. Other core team members included Alice Sindzingre, Michael Woolcock, and Zainal Yusof. Major contributions to chapters were made by Homi Kharas, Aart Kraay, Peter Lanjouw, and Giovanna Prennushi as well as by Benu Bidani, William Easterly, Enrique Flores, Hélène Grandvoinnet, Richard Newfarmer, Gi-Taik Oh, and Mattia Romani. Michael Walton, in his capacity as director, Poverty Reduction, worked closely with the team throughout the process. Shanka Chakraborty and Shahin Yaqub assisted the team. Interns from the Washington Center provided other valuable assistance. The work was carried out under the general direction of Jozef Ritzen and Joseph E. Stiglitz and, in the final stages, Nicholas Stern. The World Bank Development Data Group was responsible for the Selected World Development Indicators. Bruce Ross-Larson and Meta de Coquereaumont were the principal editors of the report.

The team was advised by Anthony Atkinson, Anthony Bebbington, Nancy Birdsall, François Bourguignon, Angus Deaton, Alain de Janvry, Yujiro Hayami, Emmanuel Jimenez, Grzegorz Kolodko, Michael Lipton, Lant Pritchett, Martin Ravallion, Amartya Sen, Lyn Squire, T. N. Srinivasan, and Mariano Tommasi. Deepa Narayan led the *Voices of the Poor* study. Vinod Thomas led the *Quality of Growth* study, which complements the work of this report. Ariel Fiszbein led the organization of the consultation process. Much insight was gained from the papers and discussions at the Summer Workshop held in Washington, D.C., on 6–10 July 1999, as well as from the background papers prepared for this report. The authors, commentators, and participants, as well as the background papers, are listed in the bibliographic note. Many others inside and outside the World Bank provided helpful comments and other contributions; their names are also listed in the bibliographic note.

A wide range of consultations with academics, grassroots leaders, NGOs, private sector representatives, and policymakers were undertaken for this report, from initial outline to final draft. Thanks go to all the public institutions and civil society organizations that helped make these consultations possible, as well as the organizers and participants, whose contributions greatly enriched this report. Particular thanks go to the Bretton Woods Project and the New Policy Institute in the United Kingdom, which moderated the electronic discussion on the Web draft, and to all who submitted comments: 424 contributions were posted from 44 countries (44 percent from developing countries). Consultations were held in Argentina (Buenos Aires), Bangladesh (Dhaka), Canada (Ottawa), Chile (Santiago), Denmark (Copenhagen), Egypt (Cairo), Ethiopia (Addis Ababa), France (Paris), Germany (Berlin), Guatemala (Antigua), Hungary (Budapest), India (Ahmedabad, New Delhi), Japan (Tokyo), Malaysia (Kuala Lumpur), Morocco (Marrakech), Russia (Moscow), Senegal (Dakar), South Africa (Johannesburg), Sweden (Stockholm), the United Kingdom (Brighton, London), the United States (Boston, New York, Washington, D.C.), and Vietnam (Hanoi). Consultations were also held at and in conjunction with the International Monetary Fund, the regional development banks, and several United Nations organizations.

The preparation of background papers and the convening of several workshops were supported by the governments of Canada, Denmark, France, Germany, Japan, the Netherlands, Sweden, Switzerland, the United Kingdom, and the United States; the MacArthur Foundation; Cornell University; and the Development Policy Forum of the German Foundation for International Development. The *Voices of the Poor* study was supported by the MacArthur Foundation, Cornell University, the U.K. Department for International Development, and the Swedish International Development Cooperation Agency; and several of the country studies were partially or fully financed by the NGOs that conducted the research.

Rebecca Sugui served as executive assistant to the team, and Maribel Flewitt, Shannon Hendrickson, Khin-U Khine, Rudeewan Laohakittikul, Jimena Luna, Nelly Obias, Gracie Ochieng, Leila Search, and Robert Simms as team assistants. Maria D. Ameal served as administrative officer. Nacer Megherbi and Edith Thomas provided technical support.

Book copyediting and production were by Fiona Blackshaw, Garrett Cruce, Terry Fischer, Wendy Guyette, Daphne Levitas, Molly Lohman, Megan Klose, Jessica Saval, and Alison Strong of Communications Development. Book design, editing, and production were managed by Jamila Abdelghani, Catherine Hudson, Brett Kravitz, Nancy Lammers, Brenda Mejia, Randi Park and Betty Sun of the of the World Bank's Office of the Publisher. Artemis Zenetou, manager and curator of the World Bank Art Program, and her staff were instrumental in the use of the artwork in the book. Tomoko Hirata designed the cover and the chapter openers.

Ravi Kanbur is T. H. Lee Professor of World Affairs in the Department of Agricultural, Resource, and Managerial Economics, Cornell University, Ithaca, New York. Nora Lustig is senior advisor and chief of the Poverty and Inequality Advisory Unit of the Inter-American Development Bank. Kevin Morrison is a fellow at the Overseas Development Council. Alice Sindzingre is a researcher at the Centre National de la Recherche Scientifique (CNRS) in Paris and an associate researcher at the Centre d'Etude d'Afrique Noire (CEAN) in Bordeaux. Zainal Yusof is deputy director general of the Institute of Strategic and International Studies (ISIS) in Kuala Lumpur, Malaysia. The World Bank is grateful to the six institutions for making possible their participation in the preparation of the report.

The many contributors to the report may not endorse every viewpoint or assertion in it, and they bear no responsibility for any errors that remain.

Contents

Part III Empowerment

Part IV Security

Part V International Actions

Boxes (continued)

Figures

Tables

Definitions and data notes

The countries included in regional groupings in this report are listed in the Classification of Economies table at the end of the Selected World Development Indicators. The income groupings in the main text of the report are based on 1998 GNP per capita estimates, while those in the Selected World Development Indicators are based on 1999 GNP per capita estimates (see the Classification of Economies table). The thresholds for the income classifications and the differences between the 1998 and 1999 classifications of countries may be found in the introduction to the Selected World Development Indicators. Group averages reported in the figures and tables of the main text are unweighted averages of the countries in the group unless noted to the contrary.

In addition to the changes in income classifications, recent revisions to data in the Selected World Development Indicators may result in differences with the data in the main text (see the introduction to the Selected World Development Indicators).

The use of the word *countries* to refer to economies implies no judgment by the World Bank about the legal or other status of a territory. The term *developing countries* includes low- and middle-income economies and thus may include economies in transition from central planning, as a matter of convenience. The terms *developed, industrial,* or *rich* coun-

tries may be used as a matter of convenience to denote the high-income economies.

Aggregate poverty measures in the report are often based on the "$1 a day" poverty line. This line is equal to $1.08 a day in 1993 purchasing power parity terms (for further explanation see box 1.2 in chapter 1).

Dollar figures are current U.S. dollars, unless otherwise specified. *Billion* means 1,000 million; *trillion* means 1,000 billion.

The following abbreviations are used:

AIDS	Acquired immune deficiency syndrome
GATT	General Agreement on Tariffs and Trade
GDP	Gross domestic product
GNP	Gross national product
HIPC	Heavily indebted poor country
HIV	Human immunodeficiency virus
NGO	Nongovernmental organization
OECD	Organisation for Economic Co-operation and Development
PPP	Purchasing power parity
SEWA	Self-Employed Women's Association
WTO	World Trade Organization

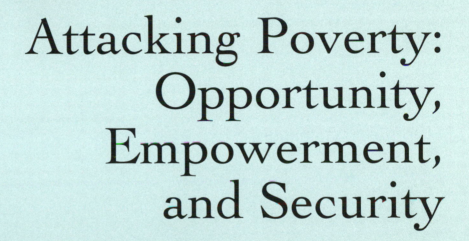

Attacking Poverty: Opportunity, Empowerment, and Security

Poor people live without fundamental freedoms of action and choice that the better-off take for granted.[1] They often lack adequate food and shelter, education and health, deprivations that keep them from leading the kind of life that everyone values. They also face extreme vulnerability to ill health, economic dislocation, and natural disasters. And they are often exposed to ill treatment by institutions of the state and society and are powerless to influence key decisions affecting their lives. These are all dimensions of poverty.

The experience of multiple deprivations is intense and painful. Poor people's description of what living in poverty means bears eloquent testimony to their pain (box 1). For those who live in poverty, escaping it can seem impossible. But it is not impossible. The story of Basrabai—the chair of a local council in an Indian village—illustrates both the many facets of poverty and the potential for action (see page 2).

Basrabai's story serves as a backdrop to the exploration of the nature and causes of poverty and of what can be done. Poverty is the result of economic, political, and social processes that interact with each other and frequently reinforce each other in ways that exacerbate the deprivation in which poor people live. Meager assets, inaccessible markets, and scarce job opportunities lock people in material poverty. That is why promoting opportunity—by stimulating economic growth, making markets work better for poor people, and building up their assets—is key to reducing poverty.

But this is only part of the story. In a world where political power is unequally distributed and often mimics the distribution of economic power, the way state institutions operate may be particularly unfavorable to poor people. For example, poor people frequently do not receive the benefits of public investment in education and health. And they are often the victims of corruption and arbitrariness on the part of the

Basrabai's story

Basrabai lives in Mohadi, a village 500 kilometers from Ahmedabad, in the Indian state of Gujarat, on the shores of the Arabian Sea.[2] She is the first woman to be *sarpanch* of the *panchayat*—chair of the local council—as a result of constitutional amendments that reserve a third of local council seats and a third of headships for women.

Arriving in her village after a long drive, we crossed a small sea inlet on a road impassable at high tide. The first building we saw was a recently built concrete structure—the primary school. In last year's cyclone, the worst in living memory, as the villagers' straw huts were blown away, they took shelter in the only stable structure in the village—the school. When the cyclone relief operation arrived, the villagers asked for more concrete buildings, and the village now has about a dozen of them.

We arrived at Basrabai's one-room concrete house, next to a straw hut. After the usual greetings, talk turned to the school. Since it was a weekday, we wondered if we could sit in on a class. Basrabai informed us that the master (the teacher) was not there and had not been there for a while. In fact, he came only once a month, if that. Protected by the district education officer, he did pretty much what he pleased.

The master came the next day. Word had gotten to him that the village had visitors. He came into Basrabai's house, and we began talking about the school and the children. Believing the educated guests to be kindred spirits, he launched into a litany of his troubles and the difficulties of teaching the children. He referred to them as *junglee*—"from the jungle."

This was too much for Meeraiben, a member of the Self-Employed Women's Association (SEWA), who had arranged our visit. She pointed out that his salary was 6,000 rupees a month (more than six times the Indian poverty line) in a secure job and that his responsibility was at least to show up for work. The parents wanted their children to learn to read and write, even if attending school meant that the boys could not help their fathers with fishing and the girls could not help their mothers fetch water and wood and work in the fields.

Later in the evening Basrabai conducted the village meeting. There were two main topics. The first was compensation for the cyclone: despite the great fanfare with which relief schemes had been announced in the state capital, local delivery left much to be desired and local officials were unresponsive. SEWA organizers took down the names of those who had not yet received the compensation to which they were entitled, and it was agreed that they and Basrabai would meet with local officials the following week.

The second issue was a fishing ban that the government had imposed on coastal waters to protect fish stocks. It was the big trawlers that were responsible for the overfishing, but the small fishers seemed to be paying the price. The big trawlers could continue to fish as long as they paid the right officials.

In the middle of the meeting a commotion occurred at the side. Basrabai's brother had been gored in the face while trying to separate two fighting cows. Without immediate treatment the wound was bound to become infected. But it was late at night, and the nearest doctor was in the next big settlement, 10 kilometers away. Normally, this would have made immediate treatment impossible. As it happened, however, our Jeep was there and could take Basrabai's brother to the doctor.

During our stay we also saw the craft work that the village women have been doing for generations. Demand for their traditional embroidered and tie-dyed products is high, thanks to the international love affair with things Indian and the rediscovery by the growing Indian middle class of its roots. But the traders get away with offering very low prices because of the women's isolation.

The national and state governments have countless schemes to support traditional crafts, none very effective. So SEWA is stepping in to organize the home-based craft workers and to provide direct access to international markets. One piece of embroidery we looked at would fetch 150 rupees in the international market, 60 rupees in government outlets, and 20 rupees from traders.

On the last day of our stay we went to Basrabai's field, an hour's walk from her house. The risks of agriculture were plainly visible. The lack of rain had left the ground hard and dry. If it didn't rain in the next few days, her millet crop would be lost, and with it her outlay to a hired tractor driver to till her field, an investment made possible by the sale of her crafts. When we met her in Ahmedabad days later, it still had not rained.

The interactions with Basrabai and the many thousands of poor people consulted in preparing this report bring to the fore recurrent—and familiar—themes. Poor people mention the lack of income-earning opportunities, the poor links with markets, and the failure of state institutions to respond to their needs. They mention insecurity, such as health risks, the risk of being out of work, and the agricultural risks that make any gains always fragile. Everywhere—from the villages in India to the *favelas* of Rio de Janeiro, the shantytowns outside Johannesburg, and the farms in Uzbekistan—the stories bring forward similar issues.

But talking to Basrabai and other poor people also reveals what is possible. Although local officials and state structures are still not accountable to Basrabai and her village, an explicit affirmative action policy allowed Basrabai's election as *sarpanch,* showing what can be done through state action. And SEWA shows how poor people can make a difference if they organize themselves to defend their rights, take advantage of market opportunities, and protect themselves from risks.

Box 1
The voices of the poor

The *Voices of the Poor* study, based on realities of more than 60,000 poor women and men in 60 countries, was conducted as background for *World Development Report 2000/2001*. It consists of two parts: a review of recent participatory poverty studies in 50 countries involving about 40,000 poor people, and a new comparative study in 1999 in 23 countries engaging about 20,000 poor people. The study shows that poor people are active agents in their lives, but are often powerless to influence the social and economic factors that determine their well-being.

The following quotations are an illustration of what living in poverty means.

Don't ask me what poverty is because you have met it outside my house. Look at the house and count the number of holes. Look at the utensils and the clothes I am wearing. Look at everything and write what you see. What you see is poverty.
—Poor man, Kenya

Certainly our farming is little; all the products, things bought from stores, are expensive; it is hard to live, we work and earn little money, buy few things or products; products are
scarce, there is no money and we feel poor. If there were money . . .
—From a discussion group of poor men and women, Ecuador

We face a calamity when my husband falls ill. Our life comes to a halt until he recovers and goes back to work.
—Poor woman, Zawyet Sultan, Egypt

Poverty is humiliation, the sense of being dependent on them, and of being forced to accept rudeness, insults, and indifference when we seek help.
—Poor woman, Latvia

At first I was afraid of everyone and everything: my husband, the village sarpanch, the police. Today I fear no one. I have my own bank account, I am the leader of my village's savings group . . . I tell my sisters about our movement. And we have a 40,000-strong union in the district.
—From a discussion group of poor men and women, India

Source: Narayan, Chambers, Shah, and Petesch 2000; Narayan, Patel, Schafft, Rademacher, and Koch-Schulte 2000.

state. Poverty outcomes are also greatly affected by social norms, values, and customary practices that, within the family, the community, or the market, lead to exclusion of women, ethnic and racial groups, or the socially disadvantaged. That is why facilitating the empowerment of poor people—by making state and social institutions more responsive to them—is also key to reducing poverty.

Vulnerability to external and largely uncontrollable events—illness, violence, economic shocks, bad weather, natural disasters—reinforces poor people's sense of ill-being, exacerbates their material poverty, and weakens their bargaining position. That is why enhancing security—by reducing the risk of such events as wars, disease, economic crises, and natural disasters—is key to reducing poverty. And so is reducing poor people's vulnerability to risks and putting in place mechanisms to help them cope with adverse shocks.

Poverty in an unequal world

The world has deep poverty amid plenty. Of the world's 6 billion people, 2.8 billion—almost half—live on less than $2 a day, and 1.2 billion—a fifth—live on less than $1 a day, with 44 percent living in South Asia (figure 1). In rich countries fewer than 1 child in 100 does not reach its fifth

birthday, while in the poorest countries as many as a fifth of children do not. And while in rich countries fewer than 5 percent of all children under five are malnourished, in poor countries as many as 50 percent are.

This destitution persists even though human conditions have improved more in the past century than in the rest of history—global wealth, global connections, and technological capabilities have never been greater. But the distribution of these global gains is extraordinarily unequal. The average income in the richest 20 countries is 37 times the average in the poorest 20—a gap that has doubled in the past 40 years. And the experience in different parts of the world has been very diverse (figure 2; see also table 1.1 in chapter 1). In East Asia the number of people living on less than $1 a day fell from around 420 million to around 280 million between 1987 and 1998—even after the setbacks of the financial crisis.[3] Yet in Latin America, South Asia, and Sub-Saharan Africa the numbers of poor people have been rising. And in the countries of Europe and Central Asia in transition to market economies, the number of people living on less than $1 a day rose more than twentyfold.[4]

There have also been major advances and serious setbacks in crucial nonincome measures of poverty. India has seen marked progress in girls attending school, and in the

Figure 1
Where the developing world's poor live

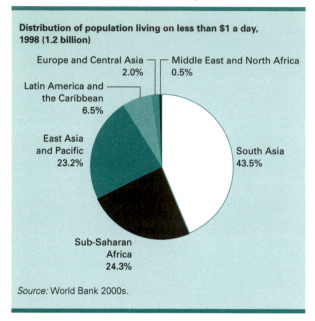

Distribution of population living on less than $1 a day, 1998 (1.2 billion)

Europe and Central Asia 2.0%
Middle East and North Africa 0.5%
Latin America and the Caribbean 6.5%
East Asia and Pacific 23.2%
South Asia 43.5%
Sub-Saharan Africa 24.3%

Source: World Bank 2000s.

Figure 2
Where poverty has fallen, and where it has not

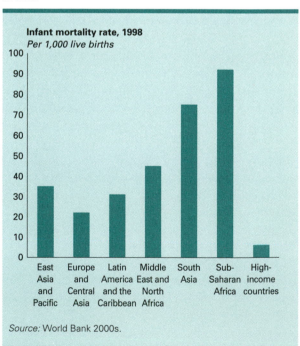

Change in number of people living on less than $1 a day, 1987–98
Millions

Source: World Bank 2000s.

Figure 3
Infant mortality rates vary widely across the world

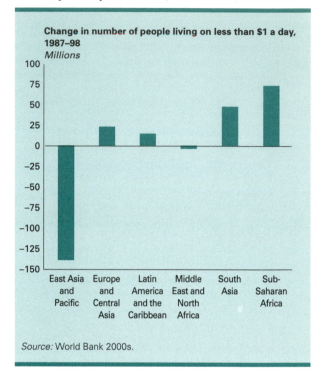

Infant mortality rate, 1998
Per 1,000 live births

Source: World Bank 2000s.

most advanced state, Kerala, life expectancy is greater than in other places with many times the level of income (such as Washington, D.C.). Yet in countries at the center of the HIV/AIDS epidemic in Africa, such as Botswana and Zimbabwe, one in four adults is infected, AIDS orphans are becoming an overwhelming burden on both traditional and formal support mechanisms, and all the gains in life expectancy since the middle of the 20th century will soon be wiped out. The varying infant mortality rates across the world—Sub-Saharan Africa's is 15 times that of high-income countries—give an idea of this widely differing experience (figure 3).

Experiences are also vastly different at subnational levels and for ethnic minorities and women. Different regions in countries benefit to very different extents from growth. In Mexico, for example, total poverty fell—though modestly—in the early 1990s, but rose in the poorer Southeast. Inequalities also exist across different ethnic groups in many countries. In some African countries infant mortality rates are lower among politically powerful ethnic groups, and in Latin American countries indigenous groups often have less than three-quarters the schooling on average of nonindigenous groups. And women continue to be more disadvantaged than men. In South Asia women have only about half as many years of education as men, and female enrollment rates at the secondary level are only two-thirds the male rates.

Box 2
A better world for all: international development goals

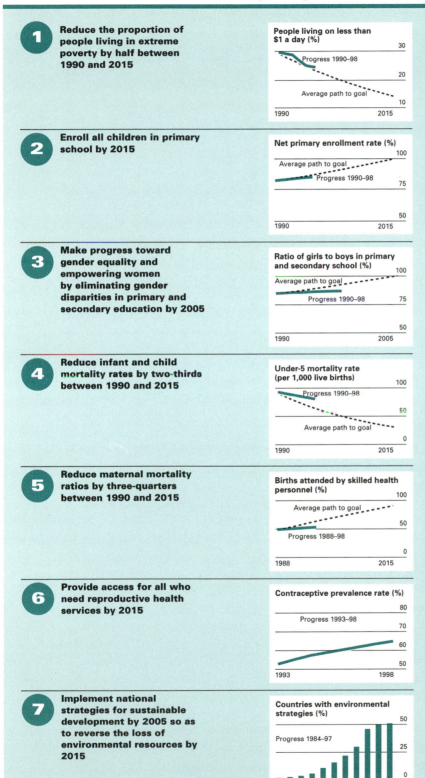

1 Reduce the proportion of people living in extreme poverty by half between 1990 and 2015

People living on less than $1 a day (%)
Progress 1990–98
Average path to goal

2 Enroll all children in primary school by 2015

Net primary enrollment rate (%)
Average path to goal
Progress 1990–98

3 Make progress toward gender equality and empowering women by eliminating gender disparities in primary and secondary education by 2005

Ratio of girls to boys in primary and secondary school (%)
Average path to goal
Progress 1990–98

4 Reduce infant and child mortality rates by two-thirds between 1990 and 2015

Under-5 mortality rate (per 1,000 live births)
Progress 1990–98
Average path to goal

5 Reduce maternal mortality ratios by three-quarters between 1990 and 2015

Births attended by skilled health personnel (%)
Average path to goal
Progress 1988–98

6 Provide access for all who need reproductive health services by 2015

Contraceptive prevalence rate (%)
Progress 1993–98

7 Implement national strategies for sustainable development by 2005 so as to reverse the loss of environmental resources by 2015

Countries with environmental strategies (%)
Progress 1984–97

The goals for international development address that most compelling of human desires—a world free of poverty and free of the misery that poverty breeds.

Each of the seven goals addresses an aspect of poverty. They should be viewed together because they are mutually reinforcing. Higher school enrollments, especially for girls, reduce poverty and mortality. Better basic health care increases enrollment and reduces poverty. Many poor people earn their living from the environment. So progress is needed on each of the seven goals.

In the past decade on average the world has not been on track to achieve the goals. But progress in some countries and regions shows what can be done. China reduced its number in poverty from 360 million in 1990 to about 210 million in 1998. Mauritius cut its military budget and invested heavily in health and education. Today all Mauritians have access to sanitation, 98 percent to safe water, and 97 percent of births are attended by skilled health staff. And many Latin American countries moved much closer to gender equality in education.

The message: if some countries can make great progress toward reducing poverty in its many forms, others can as well. But conflict is reversing gains in social development in many countries in Sub-Saharan Africa. The spread of HIV/AIDS is impoverishing individuals, families, and communities on all continents. And sustained economic growth—that vital component for long-run reductions in poverty—still eludes half the world's countries. For more than 30 of them, real per capita incomes have fallen over the past 35 years. And where there is growth, it needs to be spread more equally.

The goals can be met—with a combination of effective domestic and international actions.

Note: Data are for low- and middle-income countries except for those on environmental strategies, which refer to all countries.
Source: IMF, OECD, United Nations, and World Bank 2000 (www.paris21.org/betterworld/).

Faced with this picture of global poverty and inequality, the international community has set itself several goals for the opening years of the century, based on discussions at various United Nations conferences in the 1990s (box 2). These international development goals, most for 2015, include reducing income poverty and human deprivation in many dimensions (the benchmarks are figures for 1990):

- Reduce by half the proportion of people living in extreme income poverty (living on less than $1 a day).
- Ensure universal primary education.
- Eliminate gender disparity in primary and secondary education (by 2005).
- Reduce infant and child mortality by two-thirds.
- Reduce maternal mortality by three-quarters.
- Ensure universal access to reproductive health services.
- Implement national strategies for sustainable development in every country by 2005, so as to reverse the loss of environmental resources by 2015.

These will have to be achieved in a world whose population will grow by some 2 billion in the next 25 years, with 97 percent of that increase in developing countries. Studies of what must be done to achieve these goals reveal the magnitude of the challenge. For example, cutting income poverty by half between 1990 and 2015 would require a compound rate of decline of 2.7 percent a year over those 25 years. The World Bank's latest estimates indicate a reduction of approximately 1.7 percent a year between 1990 and 1998. Much of the slow progress observed in some regions is due to low or negative growth. In some cases rising inequality compounded this effect; this was particularly so in some countries in the former Soviet Union. The current pace of educational enrollment is unlikely to bring universal primary education, especially in Sub-Saharan Africa. Reducing infant mortality rates by two-thirds between 1990 and 2015 would have required a 30 percent decline between 1990 and 1998, far greater than the 10 percent developing countries experienced. In some parts of Sub-Saharan Africa infant mortality is actually on the rise, partly as a result of the AIDS epidemic. And maternal mortality ratios are declining too slowly to meet the goals.

Attaining the international development goals will require actions to spur economic growth and reduce income inequality, but even equitable growth will not be enough to achieve the goals for health and education. Reducing infant and child mortality rates by two-thirds depends on halting the spread of HIV/AIDS, increasing the capacity of developing countries' health systems to deliver more health services, and ensuring that technological progress in the medical field spills over to benefit the developing world.[5] And meeting the gender equality goals in education will require specific policy measures to address the cultural, social, and economic barriers that prevent girls from attending school.[6] Furthermore, actions to ensure greater environmental sustainability will be crucial in augmenting the assets available to poor people and in reducing the long-term incidence of poverty.[7] These actions will all interact to push toward the achievement of the goals. Hence the need for a broader, more comprehensive strategy to fight poverty.

A strategy for poverty reduction

The approach to reducing poverty has evolved over the past 50 years in response to deepening understanding of the complexity of development. In the 1950s and 1960s many viewed large investments in physical capital and infrastructure as the primary means of development.

In the 1970s awareness grew that physical capital was not enough, and that at least as important were health and education. *World Development Report 1980* articulated this understanding and argued that improvements in health and education were important not only in their own right but also to promote growth in the incomes of poor people.

The 1980s saw another shift of emphasis following the debt crisis and global recession and the contrasting experiences of East Asia and Latin America, South Asia, and Sub-Saharan Africa. Emphasis was placed on improving economic management and allowing greater play for market forces. *World Development Report 1990: Poverty* proposed a two-part strategy: promoting labor-intensive growth through economic openness and investment in infrastructure and providing basic services to poor people in health and education.

In the 1990s governance and institutions moved toward center stage—as did issues of vulnerability at the local and national levels. This report builds on the earlier strategies in the light of the cumulative evidence and experience of the past decade—and in the light of the changed global context. It proposes a strategy for attacking poverty in three ways: promoting opportunity, facilitating empowerment, and enhancing security.

- *Promoting opportunity.* Poor people consistently emphasize the centrality of material opportunities. This means jobs, credit, roads, electricity, markets for their produce, and the schools, water, sanitation, and health services that underpin the health and skills essential for work. Overall economic growth is crucial for generating opportunity. So is the pattern or quality of growth. Market reforms can be central in expanding opportunities for poor people, but reforms need to reflect local institutional and structural conditions. And mechanisms need to be in place to create new opportunities and compensate the potential losers in transitions. In societies with high inequality, greater equity is particularly important for rapid progress in reducing poverty. This requires action by the state to support the buildup of human, land, and infrastructure assets that poor people own or to which they have access.

- *Facilitating empowerment.* The choice and implementation of public actions that are responsive to the needs of poor people depend on the interaction of political, social, and other institutional processes. Access to market opportunities and to public sector services is often strongly influenced by state and social institutions, which must be responsive and accountable to poor people. Achieving access, responsibility, and accountability is intrinsically political and requires active collaboration among poor people, the middle class, and other groups in society. Active collaboration can be greatly facilitated by changes in governance that make public administration, legal institutions, and public service delivery more efficient and accountable to all citizens—and by strengthening the participation of poor people in political processes and local decisionmaking. Also important is removing the social and institutional barriers that result from distinctions of gender, ethnicity, and social status. Sound and responsive institutions are not only important to benefit the poor but are also fundamental to the overall growth process.

- *Enhancing security.* Reducing vulnerability—to economic shocks, natural disasters, ill health, disability, and personal violence—is an intrinsic part of enhancing well-being and encourages investment in human capital and in higher-risk, higher-return activities. This requires effective national action to manage the risk of economywide shocks and effective mechanisms to reduce the risks faced by poor people, including health- and weather-related risks. It also requires building the assets of poor people, diversifying household activities, and providing a range of insurance mechanisms to cope with adverse shocks— from public work to stay-in-school programs and health insurance.

There is no hierarchy of importance. The elements are deeply complementary. Each part of the strategy affects underlying causes of poverty addressed by the other two. For example, promoting opportunity through assets and market access increases the independence of poor people and thus empowers them by strengthening their bargaining position relative to state and society. It also enhances security, since an adequate stock of assets is a buffer against adverse shocks. Similarly, strengthening democratic institutions and empowering women and disadvantaged ethnic and racial groups—say, by eliminating legal discrimination against them—expand the economic opportunities for the poor and socially excluded. Strengthening organizations of poor people can help to ensure service delivery and policy choices responsive to the needs of poor people and can reduce corruption and arbitrariness in state actions as well. And if poor people do more in monitoring and controlling the local delivery of social services, public spending is more likely to help them during crises. Finally, helping poor people cope with shocks and manage risks puts them in a better position to take advantage of emerging market opportunities. That is why this report advocates a comprehensive approach to attacking poverty.

From strategy to action

There is no simple, universal blueprint for implementing this strategy. Developing countries need to prepare their own mix of policies to reduce poverty, reflecting national priorities and local realities. Choices will depend on the economic, sociopolitical, structural, and cultural context of individual countries—indeed, individual communities.

While this report proposes a more comprehensive approach, priorities will have to be set in individual cases based on resources and what is institutionally feasible. Progress in reducing some aspects of deprivation is possible even if other aspects remain unchanged. For example, inexpensive oral rehydration campaigns can significantly reduce infant mortality, even if incomes of poor people do not change.[8] But actions will generally be necessary in all three clusters—opportunity, empowerment, and security— because of the complementarities among the three.

The actions of developed countries and multilateral organizations will be crucial. Many forces affecting poor people's lives are beyond their influence or control. Developing countries cannot on their own produce such things as international financial stability, major advances in health and agricultural research, and international trading opportunities. Actions by the international community and development cooperation will continue to be essential.

Here are the suggested areas for action, first national and then international.

Opportunity

The core policies and institutions for creating more opportunities involve complementary actions to stimulate overall growth, make markets work for poor people, and build their assets—including addressing deep-seated inequalities in the distribution of such endowments as education.

Encouraging effective private investment. Investment and technological innovation are the main drivers of growth in jobs and labor incomes. Fostering private investment requires reducing risk for private investors—through stable fiscal and monetary policy, stable investment regimes, sound financial systems, and a clear and transparent business environment. But it also involves ensuring the rule of law and taking measures to fight corruption—tackling business environments based on kickbacks, subsidies for large investors, special deals, and favored monopolies.

Special measures are frequently essential to ensure that microenterprises and small businesses, which are often particularly vulnerable to bureaucratic harassment and the buying of privilege by the well-connected, can participate effectively in markets. Such measures include ensuring access to credit by promoting financial deepening and reducing the sources of market failure; lowering the transactions costs of reaching export markets by expanding access to Internet technology, organizing export fairs, and providing training in modern business practices; and building feeder roads to reduce physical barriers. Creating a sound business environment for poor households and small firms may also involve deregulation and complementary institutional reform, for example, reducing restrictions on the informal sector, especially those affecting women, and tackling land tenure or registry inadequacies that discourage small investments.

Private investment will have to be complemented by public investment to enhance competitiveness and create new market opportunities. Particularly important is complementary public investment in expanding infrastructure and communications and upgrading the skills of the labor force.

Expanding into international markets. International markets offer a huge opportunity for job and income growth—in agriculture, industry, and services. All countries that have had major reductions in income poverty have made use of international trade. But opening to trade can create losers as well as winners, and it will yield substantial benefits only when countries have the infrastructure and institutions to underpin a strong supply response. Thus the opening needs to be well designed, with special attention to country specifics and to institutional and other bottlenecks. The sequencing of policies should encourage job creation and manage job destruction. A more pro-poor liberalization is not necessarily a slower one; moving fast can create more opportunities for the poor. And explicit policies should offset transitory costs for poor people, as the grants for small Mexican maize producers did in the wake of the North American Free Trade Agreement (NAFTA).

The opening of the capital account has to be managed prudently—in step with domestic financial sector development—to reduce the risk of high volatility in capital flows. Long-term direct investment can bring positive externalities, such as knowledge transfer, but short-term flows can bring negative externalities, particularly volatility. Policies need to address them separately.

Building the assets of poor people. Creating human, physical, natural, and financial assets that poor people own or can use requires actions on three fronts. First, increase the focus of public spending on poor people in particular, expanding the supply of basic social and economic services and relaxing constraints on the demand side (through, for example, scholarships for poor children). Second, ensure good quality service delivery through institutional action involving sound governance and the use of markets and multiple agents. This can imply both reforming public delivery, as in education, or privatizing in a fashion that ensures expansion of services to poor people, as often makes sense in urban water and sanitation. Third, ensure the participation of poor communities and households in choosing and implementing services and monitoring them to keep providers accountable. This has been tried in projects in El Salvador, Tunisia, and Uganda. Programs to build the assets of poor people include broad-based expansion of schooling with parental and community involvement, stay-in-school programs (such as those in Bangladesh, Brazil, Mexico, and Poland), nutrition programs, mother and child health programs, vaccinations and other health interventions, and community-based schemes to protect water resources and other elements of the natural environment.

There are powerful complementarities between actions in different areas. Because of close linkages between human and physical assets, for example, improving poor people's access to energy or transport can increase their access and returns to education. And improving the environment can have significant effects on poverty. This is well documented in terms of the substantial gains in health from reduced air and water pollution—which have a major influence on some of the most important diseases of poor people, including diarrheal problems of children and respiratory infections.

Addressing asset inequalities across gender, ethnic, racial, and social divides. Special action is required in many societies to tackle socially based asset inequalities. Although political and social difficulties often obstruct change, there are many examples of mechanisms that work, using a mix of public spending, institutional change, and participation. One is negotiated land reform, backed by public action to support small farmers, as in Northeast Brazil and the Philippines. Another is getting girls into school, such as by offering cash or food for schooling, as in Bangladesh, Brazil, and Mexico, and hiring more female teachers, as in Pakistan. A third is support for microcredit schemes for poor women.

Getting infrastructure and knowledge to poor areas—rural and urban. Special action is also needed in poor areas, where a combination of asset deprivations—including at the community or regional level—can diminish the material prospects for poor people. Tackling this again requires public support and a range of institutional and participatory approaches. It requires providing social and economic infrastructure in poor, remote areas, including transport, telecommunications, schools, health services, and electricity, as in China's poor areas programs. It also requires broad-based provision of basic urban services in slums, within an overall urban strategy. Also important is expanding access to information for poor villages, to allow them to participate in markets and to monitor local government.

Empowerment

The potential for economic growth and poverty reduction is heavily influenced by state and social institutions. Action to improve the functioning of state and social institutions improves both growth and equity by reducing bureaucratic and social constraints to economic action and upward mobility. However, devising and implementing these changes require strong political will, especially when the changes fundamentally challenge social values or entrenched interests. Governments can do much to influence public debate to increase awareness of the soci-

etal benefits of pro-poor public action and build political support for such action.

Laying the political and legal basis for inclusive development. State institutions need to be open and accountable to all. This means having transparent institutions, with democratic and participatory mechanisms for making decisions and monitoring their implementation, backed up by legal systems that foster economic growth and promote legal equity. Since poor people lack the resources and the information to access the legal system, measures such as legal aid and dissemination of information on legal procedures—for example, by the Ain-O-Salish Kendra (ASK) organization in Bangladesh—are especially powerful instruments for creating more inclusive and accountable legal systems.

Creating public administrations that foster growth and equity. Public administrations that implement policies efficiently and without corruption or harassment improve service delivery by the public sector and facilitate growth of the private sector. Appropriate performance incentives are needed to make public administrations accountable and responsive to users. Access to information such as budgets, participatory budget mechanisms, and performance rating of public services all enhance citizens' capacity to shape and monitor public sector performance while reducing opportunities and scope for corruption. Reforming public administrations and other agencies such as the police to increase their accountability and responsiveness to poor people can have a major impact on their daily lives.

Promoting inclusive decentralization and community development. Decentralization can bring service agencies closer to poor communities and poor people, potentially enhancing people's control of the services to which they are entitled. This will require the strengthening of local capacity and devolution of financial resources. It is also necessary to have measures to avoid capture by local elites. Decentralization needs to be combined with effective mechanisms for popular participation and citizen monitoring of government agencies. Examples include decentralization that fosters community-driven choices for resource use and project implementation. There is also a range of options for involving communities and households in sectoral activities—such as parental involvement in schooling and users associations in water supply and irrigation.

Promoting gender equity. Unequal gender relations are part of the broader issue of social inequities based on societal norms and values. But gender equality is of such pervasive significance that it deserves extra emphasis. While patterns of gender inequity vary greatly across societies, in almost all countries a majority of women and girls are disadvantaged in terms of their relative power and control over material resources (in most countries land titles are vested in men), and they often face more severe insecurities (for example, after the death of their husband). Poor women are thus doubly disadvantaged. Moreover, the lack of autonomy of women has significant negative consequences for the education and health of children.

Greater gender equity is desirable in its own right and for its instrumental social and economic benefits for poverty reduction. There has been progress—for example, in education and health—but much more needs to be done. Experience indicates that a mix of political, legal, and direct public action is required. Thirty-two countries, from Argentina to India, have measures to promote women's representation in local and national assemblies, and this is already transforming women's ability to participate in public life and decisionmaking. Some countries are correcting gender biases in the law, as in the 1994 Colombian Agrarian Law. Use of public resources to subsidize girls' education has been shown to pay off in Bangladesh and Pakistan. A range of measures in productive activities, notably microfinance and farming inputs, have produced documented benefits in terms of increased yields (in Kenya, for example) and increased autonomy for women and better nutritional status of children (in Bangladesh and in virtually every setting where this issue has been examined).

Tackling social barriers. Social structures and institutions form the framework for economic and political relations and shape many of the dynamics that create and sustain poverty—or alleviate it. Social structures that are exclusionary and inequitable, such as class stratification or gender divisions, are major obstacles to the upward mobility of poor people. Governments can help by fostering debate over exclusionary practices or areas of stigma and by supporting the engagement and participation of groups representing the socially excluded. Groups facing active discrimination can be helped by selective affirmative action policies. Social fragmentation can be mitigated by bringing groups together in formal and informal forums and channeling their energies into political processes instead of open conflict. Other actions could include removing ethnic, racial, and gender bias in legislation and the operation of legal systems and encouraging the representation and voice of women and disadvantaged ethnic and racial groups in community and national organizations.

Supporting poor people's social capital. Social norms and networks are a key form of capital that people can use to move out of poverty. Thus it is important to work with and support networks of poor people and to enhance their potential by linking them to intermediary organizations, broader markets, and public institutions. Doing this also requires improving the legal, regulatory, and institutional environments for groups representing poor people. Since poor people usually organize at the local level, actions will also be needed to strengthen their capacity to influence policy at the state and national levels, such as by linking local organizations to wider organizations.

Security

Achieving greater security requires a heightened focus on how insecurity affects the lives and prospects of poor people. It also takes a mix of measures to deal with economywide or regionwide risks and to help poor people cope with individual adverse shocks.

Formulating a modular approach to helping poor people manage risk. Different interventions—at the community, market, and state levels—are needed to address different risks and different segments of the population. A mix of interventions may be needed to support the management of risks for communities and households, depending on the type of risk and the institutional capacity of the country. Microinsurance programs can complement microcredit programs for poor women, built around their organizations, as in the schemes SEWA runs in India for women in the informal sector. Public work schemes can expand in response to local or national shocks. Food transfer programs and social funds to help finance projects identified by communities can also be effective in coping with disaster.

Developing national programs to prevent, prepare for, and respond to macro shocks—financial and natural. Economywide shocks are often the hardest for poor communities and households to cope with, especially when the shocks are repeated, deep, or persistent. To manage the risk of financial and terms of trade shocks, sound macroeconomic policy and robust financial systems are fundamental. But they have to be complemented by prudent management of the opening of the capital account, to reduce the risk of volatile short-run flows. Special measures are also needed to ensure that spending on programs important to poor people—social programs and targeted transfers—does not fall during a recession, especially relative to the rising need. Equally important, countercyclical safety nets should be permanent and ready to be deployed when countries are hit by a shock. These and other actions can also help in coping with natural shocks. "Calamity funds" can finance relief efforts following natural disasters and support new technology and training for better risk assessment. Making investments and insurance arrangements in normal times can reduce personal costs when a disaster occurs.

Designing national systems of social risk management that are also pro-growth. There is demand across the world for national systems of social risk management. The challenge is to design them so that they do not undercut competitiveness and so that poor people benefit. Some examples: systems that both provide insurance for the nonpoor and include social pensions for the poor, as in Chile; health insurance that protects against catastrophic illness that could wipe out a family's assets, as in Costa Rica; and unemployment insurance and assistance that do not compromise the incentive to work. To gain the full benefits of such schemes, however, economies need the institutional capacity to manage them effectively.

Addressing civil conflict. Civil conflict is devastating for poor people: the bulk of conflicts are in poor countries and most are civil wars—more than 85 percent of all conflicts were fought within country borders between 1987 and 1997. In addition to the direct loss of life, they wreak social and economic havoc and create a terrible legacy of psychological and social trauma. Child soldiers are often recruited to fight—as in Sierra Leone—and many more children suffer the loss of family, disruption of schooling, and psychological scars that permanently diminish their prospects.

While it is immensely important to sustain the focus on rebuilding societies after conflict, such as in Cambodia and Rwanda, it is equally urgent to take measures to prevent conflict. There is some evidence that strengthening pluralist institutions—supporting minority rights and providing the institutional basis for peaceful conflict resolution—has a significant influence. Also important for averting conflict are efforts to get different groups to interact through more inclusive and participatory political institutions and through civil institutions. As noted below, international action to reduce access to the resources to finance conflict and to reduce international trade in armaments is also necessary. If countries can get onto a path of inclusive economic development, they have the potential to shift from a vicious to a virtuous cycle. Violent conflict constitutes one of the most urgent and intractable areas for action affecting some of the poorest people in the world.

Tackling the HIV/AIDS epidemic. HIV/AIDS is already one of the most important sources of insecurity in severely afflicted countries in Africa. While the immediate, devastating effects are at the individual and household level, the consequences are much broader, from intolerable strains on traditional child fostering mechanisms to extreme pressures on health systems and loss of productive labor affecting whole communities and nations. More than 34 million people are infected with HIV (90 percent in the developing world), with 5 million more infected each year. More than 18 million people have already died of AIDS-related illness. Action at the international level to develop an AIDS vaccine is crucial for the future, but differing experiences show that what will really make a difference now is effective leadership and societal change to prevent the spread of HIV and care for those already infected. This can involve confronting taboos about sexuality, targeting information and support to high-risk groups such as prostitutes, and providing compassionate care for AIDS sufferers. Brazil, Senegal, Thailand, and Uganda all illustrate what can be done when there is a will to act decisively.

International actions

Action at national and local levels will often not be enough for rapid poverty reduction. There are many areas that require international action—especially by industrial countries—to ensure gains to poor countries and to poor people within the developing world. An increased focus on debt relief and the associated move to make development cooperation through aid more effective are part of the story. Of equal importance are actions in other areas—trade, vaccines, closing of the digital and knowledge divides—that can enhance the opportunity, empowerment, and security of poor people.

Opportunity. Within a rule-based trading system, industrial countries could expand opportunities by opening their markets more completely to imports from poor countries, especially in agriculture, labor-intensive manufactures, and services. It has been estimated that OECD tariffs and subsidies cause annual losses in welfare of almost $20 billion in developing countries, equivalent to about 40 percent of aid in 1998. Many developing countries feel that while they are liberalizing their trade regimes, key dimensions of the trade regimes of rich countries are putting them at a disadvantage. Furthermore, donor countries could strengthen developing countries' ability to pursue poverty reduction, by increasing aid flows to countries with a sound policy environment supportive of poverty reduction and by financing the Enhanced Heavily Indebted Poor Countries Debt Relief Initiative with funds additional to aid budgets.

Empowerment. Global action can empower poor people and poor countries in national and global forums. Aid should be delivered in ways that ensure greater ownership by recipient countries, and it should go increasingly to country-driven, results-oriented poverty reduction programs, developed with the effective engagement of civil society and private sector agents. Poor people and poor countries should have greater voice in international forums, to ensure that international priorities, agreements, and standards—such as in trade and intellectual property rights—reflect their needs and interests.

The international financial institutions and other international organizations should continue their efforts to ensure full transparency in their strategies and actions—and open, regular dialogue with civil society organizations, particularly those representing poor people. International organizations should also support the ongoing global coalitions of poor people so that they may inform global debates. Actions by multinational corporations, such as adhering to ethical investment practices and adopting labor codes, can also empower poor groups.

Security. Actions are also needed to reduce risks from adverse international forces. Jointly with governments and the private sector, the international financial institutions must strengthen the international financial architecture and improve its management to lessen economic volatility, which can be devastating for poor people. Industrial country governments, often in cooperation with the private sector, should also provide more support for international public goods—for developing and distributing vaccines for HIV/AIDS, tuberculosis, and malaria and for producing and disseminating agricultural advances for tropical and semiarid conditions. International action to protect the environment can reduce the harmful effects of environmental degradation, which can be severe in some poor countries. And the international community should seek to stem armed conflict—which affects poor people the most—by taking measures to reduce the international arms trade, promote peace, and support physical and social reconstruction after conflicts end.

Working together to fight poverty

The strategy in this report recognizes that poverty is more than inadequate income or human development—it is also vulnerability and a lack of voice, power, and representation. With this multidimensional view of poverty comes greater complexity in poverty reduction strategies, because more factors—such as social and cultural forces—need to be taken into account.

The way to deal with this complexity is through empowerment and participation—local, national, and international. National governments should be fully accountable to their citizenry for the development path they pursue. Participatory mechanisms can provide voice to women and men, especially those from poor and excluded segments of society. The design of decentralized agencies and services needs to reflect local conditions, social structures, and cultural norms and heritage. And international institutions should listen to—and promote—the interests of poor people. The poor are the main actors in the fight against poverty. And they must be brought center stage in designing, implementing, and monitoring antipoverty strategies.

There is an important role in this for rich countries and international organizations. If a developing country has a coherent and effective homegrown program of poverty reduction, it should receive strong support—to bring health and education to its people, to remove want and vulnerability. At the same time global forces need to be harnessed for poor people and poor countries, so that they are not left behind by scientific and medical advances. Promoting global financial and environmental stability—and lowering market barriers to the products and services of poor countries—should be a core part of the strategy.

A divergent world? Or an inclusive one? A world with poverty? Or a world free of poverty? Simultaneous actions to expand opportunity, empowerment, and security can create a new dynamic for change that will make it possible to tackle human deprivation and create just societies that are also competitive and productive. If the developing world and the international community work together to combine this insight with real resources, both financial and those embodied in people and institutions—their experience, knowledge, and imagination—the 21st century will see rapid progress in the fight to end poverty.

Framework

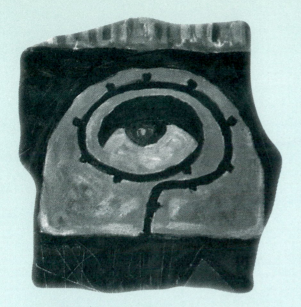

The Nature and Evolution of Poverty

Poverty is pronounced deprivation in well-being. But what precisely is deprivation? The voices of poor people bear eloquent testimony to its meaning (box 1.1). To be poor is to be hungry, to lack shelter and clothing, to be sick and not cared for, to be illiterate and not schooled. But for poor people, living in poverty is more than this. Poor people are particularly vulnerable to adverse events outside their control. They are often treated badly by the institutions of state and society and excluded from voice and power in those institutions.

Poverty's many dimensions

This report accepts the now traditional view of poverty (reflected, for example, in *World Development Report 1990*) as encompassing not only material deprivation (measured by an appropriate concept of income or consumption) but also low achievements in education and health. Low levels of education and health are of concern in their own right, but they merit special attention when they accompany material deprivation. This report also broadens the notion of poverty to include vulnerability and exposure to risk—and voicelessness and powerlessness. All these forms of deprivation severely re-

strict what Amartya Sen calls the "capabilities that a person has, that is, the substantive freedoms he or she enjoys to lead the kind of life he or she values."[1]

This broader approach to deprivation, by giving a better characterization of the experience of poverty, increases our understanding of its causes. This deeper understanding brings to the fore more areas of action and policy on the poverty reduction agenda (chapter 2).

Another important reason for considering a broader range of dimensions—and hence a broader range of policies—is that the different aspects of poverty interact and reinforce one another in important ways (chapter 2). This means that policies do more than simply add up. Improving health outcomes not only improves well-being but also increases income-earning potential. Increasing education not only improves well-being—it also leads to better health outcomes and to higher incomes. Providing protection for poor people (reducing vulnerability in dealing with risk) not only makes them feel less vulnerable—it also allows them to take advantage of higher-risk, higher-return opportunities. Increasing poor people's voice and participation not only addresses their sense of exclusion—it also leads to better targeting of health and education

15

Box 1.1
Poverty in the voices of poor people

Poor people in 60 countries were asked to analyze and share their ideas of well-being (a good experience of life) and "ill-being" (a bad experience of life).

Well-being was variously described as happiness, harmony, peace, freedom from anxiety, and peace of mind. In Russia people say, "Well-being is a life free from daily worries about lack of money." In Bangladesh, "to have a life free from anxiety." In Brazil, "not having to go through so many rough spots."

People describe ill-being as lack of material things, as bad experiences, and as bad feelings about oneself. A group of young men in Jamaica ranks lack of self-confidence as the second biggest impact of poverty: "Poverty means we don't believe in self, we hardly travel out of the community—so frustrated, just locked up in a house all day."

Although the nature of ill-being and poverty varies among locations and people—something that policy responses must take into account—there is a striking commonality across countries. Not surprising, material well-being turns out to be very important. Lack of food, shelter, and clothing is mentioned everywhere as critical. In Kenya a man says: "Don't ask me what poverty is because you have met it outside my house. Look at the house and count the number of holes. Look at my utensils and the clothes I am wearing. Look at everything and write what you see. What you see is poverty."

Alongside the material, physical well-being features prominently in the characterizations of poverty. And the two meld together when lack of food leads to ill health—or when ill health leads to an inability to earn income. People speak about the importance of looking well fed. In Ethiopia poor people say, "We are skinny," "We are deprived and pale," and speak of life that "makes you older than your age."

Security of income is also closely tied to health. But insecurity extends beyond ill health. Crime and violence are often mentioned by poor people. In Ethiopia women say, "We live hour to hour," worrying about whether it will rain. An Argentine says, "You have work, and you are fine. If not, you starve. That's how it is."

Two social aspects of ill-being and poverty also emerged. For many poor people, well-being means the freedom of choice and action and the power to control one's life. A young woman in Jamaica says that poverty is "like living in jail, living in bondage, waiting to be free."

Linked to these feelings are definitions of well-being as social well-being and comments on the stigma of poverty. As an old woman in Bulgaria says, "To be well means to see your grandchildren happy and well dressed and to know that your children have settled down; to be able to give them food and money whenever they come to see you, and not to ask them for help and money." A Somali proverb captures the other side: "Prolonged sickness and persistent poverty cause people to hate you."

Source: Narayan, Chambers, Shah, and Petesch 2000; Narayan, Patel, Schafft, Rademacher, and Koch-Schulte 2000.

services to their needs. Understanding these complementarities is essential for designing and implementing programs and projects that help people escape poverty.

Measuring poverty in its multiple dimensions

Measuring poverty permits an overview of poverty that goes beyond individual experiences. It aids the formulation and testing of hypotheses on the causes of poverty. It presents an aggregate view of poverty over time. And it enables a government, or the international community, to set itself measurable targets for judging actions. In what follows, the chapter discusses the measurement of income poverty and the indicators of education and health—and then turns to vulnerability and voicelessness.

Income poverty

Using monetary income or consumption to identify and measure poverty has a long tradition. Though separated

by a century, Seebohm Rowntree's classic study of poverty in the English city of York in 1899 and the World Bank's current estimates of global income poverty share a common approach and a common method (box 1.2). Based on household income and expenditure surveys, the approach has become the workhorse of quantitative poverty analysis and policy discourse. It has several strengths. Because it is based on nationally representative samples, it allows inferences about the conditions and evolution of poverty at the national level. Moreover, since household surveys collect information beyond monetary income or consumption, the approach makes it possible to obtain a broader picture of well-being and poverty, investigate the relationships among different dimensions of poverty, and test hypotheses on the likely impact of policy interventions.

Poverty measures based on income or consumption are not problem free. Survey design varies between countries and over time, often making comparisons difficult. For example, some countries ask respondents about their food spending over the past month, while others do so

Box 1.2
Measuring income poverty: 1899 and 1998

In a classic study first published in 1901, Seebohm Rowntree calculated that 10 percent of the population of the English city of York in 1899 was living in poverty (below minimum needed expenditures). As we enter the next century, the World Bank calculates that a fourth of the population of the developing world—about 1.2 billion people—is living in poverty (below $1 a day). These two calculations of income poverty are separated by a century and have very different coverage. Nevertheless, the basic concepts and methods they embody have strong similarities.

Rowntree's approach

Rowntree's method was to conduct a survey covering nearly every working-class family in York to collect information on earnings and expenditures. He then defined poverty as a level of total earnings insufficient to obtain the minimum necessities for the maintenance of "merely physical efficiency," including food, rent, and other items. He calculated that for a family of five—a father, mother, and three children—the minimum weekly expenditure to maintain physical efficiency was 21 shillings, 8 pence; he proposed other amounts for families of different size and composition. Comparing these poverty lines with family earnings, he arrived at his poverty estimate.

The World Bank's approach

The World Bank has been estimating global income poverty figures since 1990. The latest round of estimation, in October 1999, used new sample survey data and price information to obtain comparable figures for 1987, 1990, 1993, 1996, and 1998 (the figures for 1998 are preliminary estimates). The method is the same as in past estimates (World Bank 1990, 1996d).

Consumption. Poverty estimates are based on consumption or income data collected through household surveys. Data for 96 countries, from a total of 265 nationally representative surveys, corresponding to 88 percent of the developing world's people, are now available, up from only 22 countries in 1990. Of particular note is the increase in the share of people covered in Africa from 66 to 73 percent, a result of extensive efforts to improve household data in the region.

Consumption is conventionally viewed as the preferred welfare indicator, for practical reasons of reliability and because consumption is thought to better capture long-run welfare levels than current income. Where survey data were available on incomes but not on consumption, consumption was estimated by multiplying all incomes by the share of aggregate private consumption in na-

tional income based on national accounts data. This procedure, unchanged from past exercises, scales back income to obtain consumption but leaves the distribution unchanged.

Prices. To compare consumption levels across countries, estimates of price levels are needed, and the World Bank's purchasing power parity (PPP) estimates for 1993 were used. These estimates are based on new price data generated by the International Comparison Program (ICP), which now covers 110 countries, up from 64 in 1985, and a more comprehensive set of commodities.

Poverty lines. The 1990 calculations of the international poverty lines had to be updated using 1993 price data and the 1993 PPP estimates. In 1990 national poverty lines for 33 countries were converted into 1985 PPP prices, and the most typical line among the low-income countries for which poverty lines were available was selected. In 1999 the same lines were converted into 1993 PPP prices, and the new line was obtained as the median of the 10 lowest poverty lines. That line is equal to $1.08 a day in 1993 PPP terms (referred to as "$1 a day" in the text). This line has a similar purchasing power to the $1 a day line in 1985 PPP prices, in terms of the command over domestic goods. The upper poverty line (referred to as "$2 a day") was calculated by doubling the amount of the lower poverty line, as in 1990, reflecting poverty lines more commonly used in lower-middle-income countries.

Estimates for 1998. To obtain consumption levels for 1998 where survey data were not yet available, estimated growth rates of per capita private consumption from national accounts statistics were used to update consumption data from the latest survey year to 1998. This meant assuming that the distribution of consumption did not change from the time of the last survey to 1998. The per capita private consumption growth rates came from estimates based on the model used for other World Bank forecasts (World Bank 1999j). Surveys were available for 1997 or 1998 only for Belarus, China, India, Jordan, Latvia, Nigeria, Pakistan, Panama, Russia, Thailand, and Yemen. So the 1998 figures should be considered tentative, and trends should be interpreted cautiously, particularly in light of the controversy surrounding Indian data (see box 1.8 later in the chapter).

Country-specific poverty lines. The $1 and $2 a day poverty estimates described here are useful only as indicators of global progress, not to assess progress at the country level or to guide country policy and program formulation. Country-specific poverty lines, reflecting what it means to be poor in each country's situation and not affected by international price comparisons, are used in country-level analysis.

Source: Chen and Ravallion 2000.

for the past week. One-month recall data tend to result in higher poverty estimates than one-week recall data. Converting the information on income or consumption collected in household surveys into measures of well-being requires many assumptions, such as in deciding how to treat measurement errors and how to allow for house-

hold size and composition in converting household data into measures for individuals. Poverty estimates are very sensitive to these assumptions (see, for example, the discussion in box 1.8, later in the chapter).[2]

Moreover, income or consumption data collected at the household level have a basic shortcoming: they cannot reveal inequality within the household, so they can understate overall inequality and poverty. One study that disaggregated household consumption by individual members found that relying only on household information could lead to an understatement of inequality and poverty by more than 25 percent.[3] In particular, the conventional household survey approach does not allow direct measurement of income or consumption poverty among women. That is one reason why data on education and health, which can be collected at the individual level, are so valuable—they allow a gender-disaggregated perspective on key dimensions of poverty.

A key building block in developing income and consumption measures of poverty is the poverty line—the critical cutoff in income or consumption below which an individual or household is determined to be poor. The internationally comparable lines are useful for producing global aggregates of poverty (see box 1.2). In principle, they test for the ability to purchase a basket of commodities that is roughly similar across the world. But such a universal line is generally not suitable for the analysis of poverty within a country. For that purpose, a country-specific poverty line needs to be constructed, reflecting the country's economic and social circumstances. Similarly, the poverty line may need to be adjusted for different areas (such as urban and rural) within the country if prices or access to goods and services differs.[4] The construction of country profiles based on these country-specific poverty lines is now common practice.

Once a poverty line has been specified, it remains to be decided how to assess the extent of poverty in a particular setting. The most straightforward way to measure poverty is to calculate the percentage of the population with income or consumption levels below the poverty line. This "headcount" measure is by far the most commonly calculated measure of poverty. But it has decided disadvantages. It fails to reflect the fact that among poor people there may be wide differences in income levels, with some people located just below the poverty line and others experiencing far greater shortfalls. Policymakers seeking to make the largest possible impact on the headcount measure might be tempted to direct their poverty alleviation resources to those closest to the poverty line (and therefore least poor).

Other poverty measures, which take into account the distance of poor people from the poverty line (the poverty gap) and the degree of income inequality among poor people (the squared poverty gap), can be readily calculated.

In comparing poverty estimates across countries or over time, it is important to check the extent to which conclusions vary with the selection of poverty measure.[5]

Health and education

Measuring deprivation in the dimensions of health and education has a tradition that can be traced back to such classical economists as Malthus, Ricardo, and Marx. Despite Rowntree's primarily income-based approach to measuring poverty, he devoted an entire chapter of his study to the relation of poverty to health and went on to argue that the death rate is the best instrument for measuring the variations in the physical well-being of people.[6] Classifying his sample into three groups ranging from poorest to richest, he found that the mortality rate was more than twice as high among the very poor as among the best paid sections of the working classes. Calculating infant mortality, he found that in the poorest areas one child out of every four born dies before the age of 12 months. According to this argument, mortality could be used as an indicator both of consumption poverty and of ill-being in a broader sense.

The tradition of measuring deprivation in health and education is well reflected in the international development goals (see box 2 in the overview). But data on these nonincome indicators have their own problems. For example, infant and under-five mortality rates derived mostly from census and survey information are available for most countries only at periodic intervals.[7] A complete vital registration system would be the best source for mortality data, but such a system exists in only a few developing countries. For the period between censuses or surveys, estimates of vital rates are derived by interpolation and extrapolation based on observed trends and models, such as life tables that estimate survival from one year to the next. Infant mortality rates are available for most developing countries for only one year since 1990, and the year differs because surveys are conducted at different times. The data situation is even worse for life expectancy, because it is often not measured directly.

Education data are also far from satisfactory. The most commonly available indicator, the gross primary enrollment rate, suffers from serious conceptual shortcomings. The greatest is that school enrollment is only a proxy for actual school attendance. Moreover, the gross primary enrollment rate can rise if grade repetitions increase. The much-preferred net primary enrollment rate (showing the ratio of enrolled primary-school-age children to all primary-school-age children) is available for only around 50 developing countries for 1990–97—not enough to make reliable aggregations by region. A number of ongoing survey initiatives, however, are improving the quantity and quality of data on health and education.

Vulnerability

In the dimensions of income and health, vulnerability is the risk that a household or individual will experience an episode of income or health poverty over time. But vulnerability also means the probability of being exposed to a number of other risks (violence, crime, natural disasters, being pulled out of school).

Measuring vulnerability is especially difficult: since the concept is dynamic, it cannot be measured merely by observing households once. Only with household panel data—that is, household surveys that follow the same households over several years—can the basic information be gathered to capture and quantify the volatility and vulnerability that poor households say is so important. Moreover, people's movements in and out of poverty are informative about vulnerability only after the fact. The challenge is to find indicators of vulnerability that can identify at-risk households and populations beforehand.

Many indicators of vulnerability have been proposed over the years, but there is now a growing consensus that it is neither feasible nor desirable to capture vulnerability in a single indicator. If the government provides an effective workfare program, for example, households may do less than they otherwise would to diversify their income or build up their assets. Similarly, a household that is part of a reliable network of mutual support may see less need for large buffer stocks of food or cattle. So a vulnerability measure based solely on household assets—or on income and its sources—may not reflect the household's true exposure to risk (box 1.3).

Voicelessness and powerlessness

Voicelessness and powerlessness can be measured using a combination of participatory methods (box 1.4), polls, and national surveys on qualitative variables such as the extent of civil and political liberties (box 1.5). However, measuring these dimensions of poverty in an accurate, robust, and consistent way so that comparisons can be made across countries and over time will require considerable additional efforts on both the methodological and data-gathering fronts.

Multidimensionality and measuring progress

Defining poverty as multidimensional raises the question of how to measure overall poverty and how to compare achievements in the different dimensions. One dimension might move in a different direction from another. Health could improve while income worsens. Or an individual might be "income poor" but not "health poor." Or one country might show greater improvement in health than in vulnerability—while another shows the converse.

This brings to the fore the relative value of the different dimensions: how much income are people willing to give up for, say, a unit of improvement in health or in voice? In other words, what weights can be assigned to the different dimensions to allow comparisons across countries, households, or individuals and over time? There are no easy answers.

One approach to addressing comparability is to define a multidimensional welfare function or a composite index. An alternative is to define as poor anybody who is poor in *any one* of the dimensions—without attempting to estimate tradeoffs among the dimensions—or anybody who is poor in *all* dimensions, and to define the intensity of poverty accordingly (box 1.6). This report does not try to define a composite index or to measure tradeoffs among dimensions. Instead, it focuses on deprivation in different dimensions and, in particular, on the multiple deprivations experienced by the income-poor. This is a necessary first step in developing a comprehensive multidimensional framework.

How should indicators be selected to monitor progress? The international development goals are a good starting point. But in practice, these goals will have to be adapted (by lengthening or shortening the time span, for example) and modified (increasing the number of dimensions), depending on context. The specific goals will have to emerge from a participatory process in which governments and civil society agree on priorities. This process is already under way in many countries, and multilateral organizations are helping with resources and technical assistance (box 1.7).[8]

Investing in measurement and monitoring

Measurements of poverty thus must cover many dimensions. So far, the income and consumption dimension has received most attention. Thanks to efforts over the past 20 years by such international agencies as the United Nations, the World Bank, and the regional development

Box 1.3
Measuring vulnerability

Since vulnerability is a dynamic concept, its measurement centers on the variability of income or consumption or on the variability of other dimensions of well-being, such as health or housing. In much of the literature on risk, this variability is measured by the standard deviation or coefficient of variation of income or consumption. From the perspective of poor people, this measure is flawed in several ways:

■ It gives equal weight to upward and downward fluctuations. Yet poor people are concerned primarily with downward fluctuations.

■ It has no time dimension. Given 10 fluctuations, the coefficient of variation is the same whether good and bad years alternate or five bad years are followed by five good ones. Yet bunched downward fluctuations are more difficult for poor people to cope with.

■ A scenario with many small and one large fluctuation may yield the same coefficient of variation as a scenario with equal moderate fluctuations. Yet poor people are likely to be hurt more by the first scenario.

The coefficient of variation is, moreover, a measure after the fact. Needed are indicators that make it possible to assess a household's risk exposure beforehand—information both on the household and on its links to informal networks and formal safety nets:

■ *Physical assets.* A household's physical assets—those that can be sold to compensate for temporary loss of income—are a measure of its capacity to self-insure. What matters is not just the total value of the assets, but also their liquidity. Thus knowledge of the functioning of asset markets is needed to determine the usefulness of the assets as insurance.

■ *Human capital.* Households with limited education tend to be more subject to income fluctuations and less able to manage risk—for example, through access to credit or multiple income sources.

■ *Income diversification.* The extent of diversification of income sources has often been used to assess vulnerability. In rural settings analysts might look at nonfarm income, which tends to fluctuate less than farm income, thus providing a measure of protection against weather-related risks. But income diversification can be a misleading indicator of risk exposure. A single low-risk activity could be preferable to multiple high-risk activities that are strongly covariant. So more diversification is not necessarily less risky. Diversification needs to be evaluated in the context of the household's overall risk strategy.

■ *Links to networks.* Family-based networks, occupation-based groups of mutual help, rotating savings and credit groups, and other groups or associations to which a household belongs—all part of the household's social capital—can be a source of transfers in cash or kind in the event of a calamity. An as-

sessment of vulnerability should be based not only on the observed transfers but also on the household's expectation about the assistance it will receive in a crisis. It is this expectation that determines the household's decisions about engaging in other risk management activities. Unfortunately, household surveys rarely include direct information on networks or on expectations of assistance.

■ *Participation in the formal safety net.* A household's vulnerability is reduced if it is entitled to social assistance, unemployment insurance, pensions, and other publicly provided transfers—and if it can benefit from workfare programs, social funds, and similar mechanisms. So information on such programs and their rules of eligibility is also important in assessing vulnerability and risk exposure.

■ *Access to credit markets.* Similarly, a household's vulnerability is reduced if it has access to credit for consumption smoothing.

Clearly, assessing vulnerability is more complex than measuring poverty at a point in time. The length of time over which vulnerability is to be assessed is of great importance and may well differ across people and circumstances. Conventional annual measures of income or consumption may often be too long. Furthermore, measuring vulnerability requires data on household assets (physical, human, and social capital) in combination with data on formal safety nets, the functioning of markets, and the economic policies that determine a household's opportunity set and the range of activities it can pursue to manage risk. Many of today's household surveys do not provide the needed information.

Cross-sectional surveys need to expand their standard expenditure modules by adding questions on assets, links with networks, perceptions of sources of emergency assistance, and participation in formal safety nets. One World Bank survey has taken a step in this direction: the recent Local-Level Institutions Surveys combine asset data with detailed questions on households' links with local associations. Some Living Standards Measurement Surveys have also begun to incorporate modules on social capital. Ultimately, such enriched cross-sectional surveys need to be combined with panel surveys, monitoring the same households over time, to allow direct observation of how households deal with shocks.

Vulnerability to nonincome risks can be measured by the prevalence of these risks (crime, natural disasters, and so on) in special modules of household surveys. A program sponsored jointly by the Inter-American Development Bank, World Bank, and Economic Commission for Latin America and the Caribbean, the Program for the Improvement of Surveys and the Measurement of Living Conditions (known as Mecovi for its Spanish acronym) is incorporating such modules in specific countries in Latin America (the questionnaire can be found in IDB 2000).

Source: Dercon 1999; Grosh and Glewwe 2000; Holzmann and Jorgensen 1999; IDB 2000; Sinha and Lipton 1999; World Bank 1998t.

Box 1.4
Measuring voice and power using participatory methods

In the *Voices of the Poor* study, in small group discussions, poor people discussed the range of institutions important in their daily lives and then identified the criteria that were important in rating institutions. Once criteria were identified and agreed on, groups rated institutions on these criteria using pebbles, beans, or other local material. Characteristics included trust, participation, accountability, ability to build unity, responsiveness, respect, fairness and caring, and listening and loving. Poor people defined these criteria in clear and simple terms before scoring institutions.

Box 1.5
Measuring governance: participatory methods and cross-country surveys

Can countrywide information on voice and participation be obtained systematically to assess their role in development and to compare countries? A recent study brought together a database covering 178 countries to assess the wider issue of governance, with voice and accountability measured by indicators of civil liberties, political rights, the transparency of the legal system, and the existence of independent media.

The data came from two types of sources: polls of experts on the country or region (including agencies specializing in risk rating, opinion surveys, and political analysis) and cross-country surveys of residents by international organizations and NGOs. Indicators from the two types of data tend to correlate strongly, increasing confidence in the results. The study found a strong positive association between voice and accountability and five other clusters of governance indicators and three development outcomes: per capita income, infant mortality, and adult literacy (Kaufmann, Kraay, and Zoido-Lobaton 1999).

The study also highlighted major weaknesses in existing databases on voice, empowerment, and governance. Margins of error in the results are wide. Significant investment is needed in developing and undertaking surveys, with comparable methods across countries, to collect data on this important dimension of poverty and well-being. National surveys on voice and empowerment would complement participatory assessments. In designing the surveys, care would have to be taken to ensure that they are capable of capturing differences by region, gender, ethnicity, and so on. Such differences are important not just in material poverty but in voice and empowerment as well.

banks, 85 percent of the developing world's population lives in countries with at least two household income or expenditure surveys. These surveys need to be improved greatly and made more accessible to the public. Efforts such as the Living Standards Measurement Surveys at the World Bank and Mecovi[9] in Latin America (see box 1.3)

need to be supported. But the efforts need to go much farther than this, focusing on improving information on education and health indicators. The Demographic and Health Surveys need to be continued and expanded. As important are efforts to expand and improve the very small database on indicators of vulnerability and on voicelessness and powerlessness.

The evolution of poverty

What are the magnitudes and patterns of poverty in the developing world? How has poverty evolved over the past decade? The answers to these questions are important in framing the challenge of attacking poverty.

The rest of this chapter describes global trends in the income (consumption), education, and health dimensions of poverty and shows the large diversity of outcomes—across dimensions, regions, countries, communities, households, and individuals. The differences in performance reflect differences in growth, in the distribution of assets, in the quality and responsiveness of state institutions, in the degree of inclusiveness in societies (lower social barriers for women, ethnic minorities, and the socially disadvantaged more generally), and in how countries and people manage risks.

Highlighting the diversity in outcomes is important for at least two reasons. It allows the identification of successes and failures in poverty reduction and thereby enhances the understanding of what causes poverty and how best to reduce it. And it brings to the fore the fact that aggregate trends can hide significant differences in poverty outcomes—for different ethnic groups, regions, and sectors within a country, for example. Awareness of these differences will help policymakers set priorities, concentrating actions where they are most needed.

Global and regional patterns: income poverty and social indicators

Between 1987 and 1998 the share of the population in developing and transition economies living on less than $1 a day fell from 28 percent to 24 percent (table 1.1). This decline is below the rate needed to meet the international development goal of reducing extreme income poverty by half by 2015 (see box 2 in the overview).

Because of population growth, the number of people in poverty hardly changed. But there are large regional variations in performance. East Asia and the Middle East

Box 1.6
Multidimensionality: dealing with aggregation

There are several possible approaches to aggregating measures of the different dimensions of poverty and well-being.

Welfare function. A welfare function approach includes various dimensions of well-being and defines poor people as all individuals below a specified minimum level of total welfare (Tsui 1995, 1997; Bourguignon and Chakravarty 1998). The welfare function approach allows for tradeoffs, using individuals' own choices for comparing situations and for assessing how much improvement is needed in one dimension to maintain welfare if another dimension worsens. The difficulty is finding a suitable welfare function for comparisons between nonmarket elements of individual welfare. While using a money metric and total expenditure is appropriate for assessing how many additional eggs or apples a person would have to consume to accept less rice, it is less reliable for such important dimensions of welfare as social exclusion and political voicelessness. Moreover, choosing appropriate "weights" to form a single aggregate of these nonmarket elements of individual welfare from existing data has so far proved to be an insurmountable challenge.

Composite index. An alternative to using weights estimated from people's observed choices is to simply impose weights, as a simplistic, special-case application of the welfare function approach. There have been several well-known efforts, such as the physical quality of life index (combining the literacy rate, the infant mortality rate, and life expectancy; Morris 1979) and the human development index (UNDP 1999a). While easy to use, these indexes do not really solve the intractable weighting problem because they assign arbitrary (usually equal) weights to each component (Ravallion 1997b).

Alternative aggregation rules. If the objective is to measure the number of poor people, another possibility is to count as poor everybody who is poor in any one of the dimensions (see all shaded areas in figure). This method adds value because it goes beyond income. But it can be criticized because it would imply, for example, that a person who has very high income but is uneducated is poor. An alternative is to count as poor everybody who is poor in all dimensions (see dark shaded area in figure). In both cases the complications of making comparisons remain when one wants to measure not only the extent but also the intensity of poverty of individuals with multiple deprivations or with deprivations in different dimensions.

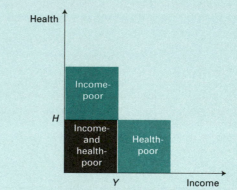

Alternative aggregation rules to measure the multiple dimensions of poverty

Note: H is the threshold defining the health-poor, and *Y* that defining the income-poor.

Box 1.7
Uganda's poverty reduction goals

The recent poverty reduction strategy paper for Uganda presents a clear statement of the poverty reduction goals that the government has set. The goals focus on reducing absolute income poverty to 10 percent by 2017 and achieving universal primary enrollment (along with higher primary completion rates and educational achievement) by 2004–05. The government also set a series of other human development goals for 2004–05:

- Reducing the under-five mortality rate to no more than 103 per 1,000 live births.

- Cutting HIV prevalence by 35 percent.
- Reducing the incidence of stunting to 28 percent.
- Reducing total fertility to 5.4 births per woman.

The poverty reduction strategy paper outlines the government's approach to achieving these goals, with well-developed interventions in four broad areas: creating a framework for economic growth and transformation, ensuring good governance and security, directly increasing the ability of poor people to raise their incomes, and directly improving the quality of life of poor people.

Source: IDA 2000.

and North Africa have reduced their numbers in poverty—East Asia dramatically so. But in all other regions the number of people living on less than $1 a day has risen. In South Asia, for example, the number of poor people rose over the decade, from 474 million to 522 million, even though the share of people in poverty fell from 45 percent to 40 percent. In Latin America and the Caribbean the number of poor people rose by about 20 percent.

Table 1.1
Income poverty by region, selected years, 1987–98

Region	Population covered by at least one survey (percent)	People living on less than $1 a day (millions)				
		1987	1990	1993	1996	1998[a]
East Asia and Pacific	90.8	417.5	452.4	431.9	265.1	278.3
Excluding China	71.1	114.1	92.0	83.5	55.1	65.1
Europe and Central Asia	81.7	1.1	7.1	18.3	23.8	24.0
Latin America and the Caribbean	88.0	63.7	73.8	70.8	76.0	78.2
Middle East and North Africa	52.5	9.3	5.7	5.0	5.0	5.5
South Asia	97.9	474.4	495.1	505.1	531.7	522.0
Sub-Saharan Africa	72.9	217.2	242.3	273.3	289.0	290.9
Total	88.1	1,183.2	1,276.4	1,304.3	1,190.6	1,198.9
Excluding China	84.2	879.8	915.9	955.9	980.5	985.7

Region	Share of population living on less than $1 a day (percent)				
	1987	1990	1993	1996	1998[a]
East Asia and Pacific	26.6	27.6	25.2	14.9	15.3
Excluding China	23.9	18.5	15.9	10.0	11.3
Europe and Central Asia	0.2	1.6	4.0	5.1	5.1
Latin America and the Caribbean	15.3	16.8	15.3	15.6	15.6
Middle East and North Africa	4.3	2.4	1.9	1.8	1.9
South Asia	44.9	44.0	42.4	42.3	40.0
Sub-Saharan Africa	46.6	47.7	49.7	48.5	46.3
Total	28.3	29.0	28.1	24.5	24.0
Excluding China	28.5	28.1	27.7	27.0	26.2

Note: The poverty line is $1.08 a day at 1993 PPP. Poverty estimates are based on income or consumption data from the countries in each region for which at least one survey was available during 1985–98. Where survey years do not coincide with the years in the table, the estimates were adjusted using the closest available survey and applying the consumption growth rate from national accounts. Using the assumption that the sample of countries covered by surveys is representative of the region as a whole, the number of poor people was then estimated by region. This assumption is obviously less robust in the regions with the lowest survey coverage. For further details on data and methodology see Chen and Ravallion (2000).
a. Preliminary.
Source: World Bank 2000s.

Two regions fared particularly badly. In Europe and Central Asia the number in poverty soared from 1.1 million to 24 million. In Sub-Saharan Africa the number of poor people increased from an already high 217 million to 291 million over the same period, leaving almost half the residents of that continent poor.

These variations in regional performance are leading to a shift in the geographical distribution of poverty. In 1998 South Asia and Sub-Saharan Africa accounted for around 70 percent of the population living on less than $1 a day, up 10 percentage points from 1987 (figure 1.1).

While these numbers provide a sense of broad trends, they should be treated with caution in light of the shortcomings of the data mentioned above and the fact that figures for 1998 are tentative because of the limited number of surveys available (see box 1.2).

Relative poverty. The poverty estimates in table 1.1 are based on a poverty line that reflects what it means to be poor in the world's poorest countries (see box 1.2). This definition judges poverty by standards common in South Asia and much of Sub-Saharan Africa, regardless of the region for which poverty is being measured. An alternative definition of poverty—expounded by the British sociologist Peter Townsend, among others—is a lack of the resources required to participate in activities and to enjoy living standards that are customary or widely accepted in the society in which poverty is being measured.[10]

Table 1.2 presents estimates of poverty based on a combination of absolute and relative poverty concepts. The

Figure 1.1
Poverty in the developing world is shifting toward South Asia and Sub-Saharan Africa

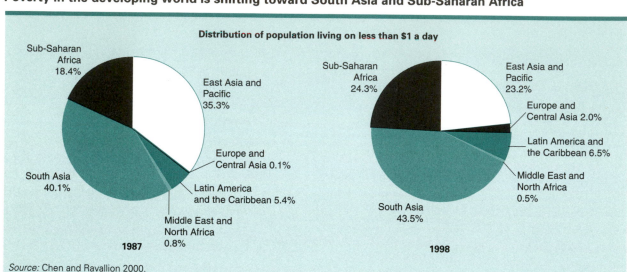

Source: Chen and Ravallion 2000.

poverty estimates are based on the same data and procedures as those in table 1.1, but a different poverty line. A country-specific poverty line was used, equal to one-third of a country's average consumption level in 1993 at 1993 purchasing power parity (PPP), if that figure is higher than the $1 a day poverty line. Otherwise, the $1 a day line was used. The effect of using a relative poverty line—instead of the $1 a day poverty line—is that poverty is now much higher in regions with higher average consumption. It is also higher in regions with greater inequality. In Latin America, for example, where roughly

15 percent of the population was below the $1 a day poverty line, more than 50 percent of the population was under the relative poverty line. Similarly, in the Middle East and North Africa and in Europe and Central Asia poverty estimates are much higher by the relative poverty criterion. But the time trends remain unchanged.[11]

Social indicators. Social indicators in developing countries have improved on average over the past three decades. For example, infant mortality rates fell from 107 per 1,000 live births in 1970 to 59 in 1998. But the decline between 1990 and 1998 was only 10 percent, while

Table 1.2
Relative income poverty by region, selected years, 1987–98

Region	Regional average poverty line (1993 PPP dollars a day)	Share of population living on less than one-third of average national consumption for 1993 (percent)				
		1987	1990	1993	1996	1998[a]
East Asia and Pacific	1.3	33.0	33.7	29.8	19.0	19.6
Excluding China	1.9	45.1	38.7	30.8	23.2	24.6
Europe and Central Asia	2.7	7.5	16.2	25.3	26.1	25.6
Latin America and the Caribbean	3.3	50.2	51.5	51.1	52.0	51.4
Middle East and North Africa	1.8	18.9	14.5	13.6	11.4	10.8
South Asia	1.1	45.2	44.2	42.5	42.5	40.2
Sub-Saharan Africa	1.3	51.1	52.1	54.0	52.8	50.5
Total	1.6	36.3	37.4	36.7	32.8	32.1
Excluding China	1.8	39.3	39.5	39.3	38.1	37.0

Note: See text for a definition of the poverty line.
a. Preliminary.
Source: Chen and Ravallion 2000.

meeting the international development goal would have required 30 percent.

These aggregate figures mask wide regional disparities. Life expectancy in Sub-Saharan Africa in 1997 was still only 52 years—13 years less than the developing world average—and 25 years—a full generation—less than the OECD average. One of the main causes is the still unacceptably high infant mortality rate in Sub-Saharan Africa, 90 per 1,000 live births. The rate is also very high in South Asia (77). Those levels are a far cry from the OECD average of 6 per 1,000. The AIDS crisis has aggravated the situation, leading to rising infant mortality in several African countries. Between 1990 and 1997 the infant mortality rate rose from 62 to 74 in Kenya and from 52 to 69 in Zimbabwe. Maternal mortality also remains exceptionally high in the region: of the 12 countries in the world with rates exceeding 1,000 deaths per 100,000 live births, 10 are in Sub-Saharan Africa.

Regional differences are equally obvious in education indicators. South Asia improved its gross primary enrollment rate from 77 percent to more than 100 percent in 1982–96. But Sub-Saharan Africa's rate remained unchanged at 74 percent (between 1982 and 1993 it actually declined). Other education indicators confirm the importance of regional differences. Almost the entire decline in the illiteracy rate in the developing world has been in East Asia. By contrast, the number of illiterate people increased by 17 million in South Asia and by 3 million in Sub-Saharan Africa.[12] Sub-Saharan Africa also has the lowest net primary enrollment rate.

Variations in poverty across countries

Detailed studies using national income poverty lines and national-level social indicators show equally large variations in poverty performance across countries within each region.

In Europe and Central Asia the proportion of the population living on less than $2 a day (at 1996 PPP) ranges from less than 5 percent in Belarus, Bulgaria, Estonia, Hungary, Lithuania, Poland, and Ukraine to 19 percent in Russia, 49 percent in the Kyrgyz Republic, and 68 percent in Tajikistan.[13] Among seven African countries with data spanning the 1990s, four (Burkina Faso, Nigeria, Zambia, and Zimbabwe) experienced an increase in poverty, matching the regional pattern for the decade, while three (Ghana, Mauritania, and Uganda) had a decline (table 1.3).[14] Available national poverty estimates for Latin America show that between 1989 and 1996 the incidence of poverty fell in Brazil, Chile, the Dominican Republic, and Honduras—and rose in Mexico and República Bolivariana de Venezuela.[15] In another group of countries for which only urban surveys were available, poverty rose in Ecuador, stayed nearly unchanged in Uruguay, and fell in Argentina, Bolivia, Colombia,[16] and Paraguay.

In East Asia poverty trends in the 1990s were influenced by the impact of the recent economic crisis. Indonesia, the Republic of Korea, and Thailand all suffered increases in poverty, though to differing degrees (see chapter 9).[17] In Indonesia one recent study estimated that poverty increased from around 11 percent in February 1996 to 18–20 percent in February 1999. Since then, poverty appears to have declined considerably, though

Table 1.3

Income poverty in seven African countries, various years

Country and period[a]	Area	Share of population below the national poverty line[b] (percent)	
		Year 1	Year 2
Burkina Faso 1994, 1998	Rural	51.1	50.7
	Urban	10.4	15.8
	Total	44.5	45.3
Ghana 1991/92, 1998/99	Rural	45.8	36.2
	Urban	15.3	14.5
	Total	35.7	29.4
Mauritania 1987, 1996	Rural	72.1	58.9
	Urban	43.5	19.0
	Total	59.5	41.3
Nigeria 1992, 1996	Rural	45.1	67.8
	Urban	29.6	57.5
	Total	42.8	65.6
Uganda 1992, 1997	Rural	59.4	48.2
	Urban	29.4	16.3
	Total	55.6	44.0
Zambia 1991, 1996	Rural	79.6	74.9
	Urban	31.0	34.0
	Total	57.0	60.0
Zimbabwe 1991, 1996	Rural	51.5	62.8
	Urban	6.2	14.9
	Total	37.5	47.2

a. The dates in this column correspond to year 1 and year 2.
b. Nutrition-based poverty lines. Comparisons between countries are not valid.
Source: Demery 1999; Ghana Statistical Service 1998.

it is still substantially higher than precrisis levels.[18] Trends in China in 1996–98 are sensitive to the choice of welfare measure. Income poverty measures based on the $1 a day or national poverty line show continued decline. But a consumption-based poverty measure shows a stalling in poverty reduction between 1996 and 1998, suggesting that poor households, especially in rural areas, have been saving an increasingly large share of their incomes.[19] The most recent data for Vietnam show that between 1993 and 1998 the incidence of poverty, based on a national poverty line, fell from 58 percent to 37 percent.[20]

Poverty reduction also varied in South Asia in the 1990s. Bangladesh turned in a good performance despite its worst floods in living memory, with GDP growth of 4.5 percent in 1998–99, thanks to a bumper rice crop after the floods. The concerted relief efforts by the government, NGOs, and donors—and the ongoing food-for-work programs—limited the loss of life and the impact of the floods on poverty. Pakistan and Sri Lanka made little or no progress in poverty reduction in the 1990s.[21] For India, there is an ongoing debate on the accuracy of the statistics. It provides a telling example of how difficult it is to track poverty over time, even within countries (box 1.8).

Variations in poverty within countries

Country aggregates of different dimensions of poverty provide a useful overview of performance. But they hide as much as they reveal. There are distinct patterns of poverty within countries, and different groups within a country can become better or worse off.

Poverty in different areas within a country can—and does—move in different directions. In Burkina Faso and Zambia rural poverty fell and urban poverty rose, but the urban rise dominated and overall poverty rose (see table 1.3).[22] In Mexico, while overall poverty declined—though modestly—between 1989 and 1994, there were large variations across regions within the country.[23] In China rapid income growth has been accompanied by ris-

Box 1.8
Tracking poverty in India during the 1990s

Recent data from India's National Sample Surveys (NSS) suggest that the pace of poverty reduction slowed in the 1990s, particularly in rural areas. This occurred against a backdrop of strong economic growth (GDP growth of 6.1 percent a year during 1990–98), according to the national accounts (NAS). There are signs of rising inequality nationally in the NSS data, due in large part to rising average consumption in urban areas relative to rural areas, though with some signs of higher inequality in urban areas. However, an important factor in the slow rate of poverty reduction was slow growth in average consumption, as measured by the NSS.

Closer examination shows that NSS consumption is an increasingly smaller fraction of private consumption as estimated in the NAS. NSS consumption has declined relative to NAS consumption during the past three decades; the two were much closer in the 1950s and 1960s (Mukherjee and Chatterjee 1974). If the average consumption figures from the NSS are replaced by the average consumption figures from the NAS, and everybody's consumption is adjusted proportionately, poverty would show a downward trend during the 1990s (as found by Bhalla 2000).

But comparing NSS and NAS data is a complex matter, involving differences in coverage, recall biases in the NSS, price imputations (for example, for home-produced consumption and in-kind wages in the NSS and for nonmarketed output in the NAS), and sampling and nonsampling errors in both. Thus, without examining why the differences between the two have widened, adjusting the NSS mean upward to equal the NAS mean would be an arguable procedure. For one thing, it is not clear why the average consumption data from the NSS would be wrong but not the inequality data, the assumption made when everybody's consumption is adjusted proportionately. For example, it cannot be ruled out a priori that nonresponse and nonsampling errors in measuring consumption may differ among income groups. Also, Visaria (2000) finds the differences between the NSS and NAS to be considerably less if one week rather than one month is used in the NSS as the reference period for consumption. Srinivasan (2000) presents a detailed discussion of these issues (Srinivasan and Bardhan 1974 present earlier discussions of these issues.)

There is also evidence that part of the observed trend in rural poverty in the earlier part of the 1990s may result from using inadequate price deflators for rural areas. As a result, "it is likely that the decline in rural poverty rates has been understated in the official poverty counts. Indeed, we are led to suggest as a working hypothesis that, between 1987–88 and 1993–94, there was no great difference in the rate of decline of urban and rural poverty, at least according to the headcount measure" (Deaton and Tarozzi 1999, pp. 34–35).

It is plausible that the NSS-based poverty numbers are underestimating the rate of poverty reduction in India. The issues involved are important not only because of the Indian poverty figures' weight in global poverty trends, but also because similar problems are likely to arise elsewhere. India has a stronger statistical tradition than most poor countries. And it is not simply a matter of getting accurate estimates of poverty. Such surveys are a key resource for identifying the characteristics of poor people and thus are a vital input for focusing policy. Research in this area is a high priority.

ing inequality between urban and rural areas and between provinces.[24]

Poverty tends to be associated with the distance from cities and the coast, as in China, Vietnam, and Latin America.[25] In China many of the poor reside in mountainous counties and townships. In Peru two-thirds of rural households in the poorest quintile are in the mountain region, while fewer than a tenth are in the coastal region.[26] In Thailand the incidence of poverty in the rural northeast was almost twice the national average in 1992, and although only a third of the population lives there, it accounted for 56 percent of all poor.

Differences in health and education between low- and high-income households

Social indicators in many countries remain much worse for the income-poor than for the income-nonpoor—often by huge margins. In Mali the difference in child mortality rates between the richest and poorest households is equal to the average gain in child mortality rates recorded over the past 30 years.[27] In South Africa the under-five mortality rate for the poorest 20 percent is twice as high as the rate for the richest 20 percent, and in Northeast and Southeast Brazil, three times as high.

The picture is the same for malnutrition. A study of 19 countries found that stunting (low height for age—an indicator of long-term malnutrition), wasting (low weight for height—an indicator of short-term malnutrition), and being underweight (low weight for age) are higher among poor people in almost all countries.[28] But the differences between poor and nonpoor tend to be smaller in countries with high average rates of malnutrition.[29]

The incidence of many illnesses, especially communicable diseases, is higher for poor people, while their access to health care is typically less. In India the prevalence of tuberculosis is more than four times as high in the poorest fifth of the population as in the richest, and the prevalence of malaria more than three times as high.[30] In 10 developing countries between 1992 and 1997, only 41 percent of poor people suffering from acute respiratory infections were treated in a health facility, compared with 59 percent of the nonpoor. In the same period only 22 percent of births among the poorest 20 percent of people were attended by medically trained staff, compared with 76 percent among the richest 20 percent.[31] Although HIV/AIDS initially affected the poor and the rich almost equally, recent evidence indicates that new infections occur disproportionately among poor people.

Similar disparities show up in access to schooling and in educational achievement. In some poor countries most children from the poorest households have no schooling at all. A study of Demographic and Health Survey data found 12 countries in which more than half the 15- to 19-year-olds in the poorest 40 percent of households had zero years of schooling: Bangladesh, India, Morocco, Pakistan, and eight countries in Sub-Saharan Africa. In contrast, the median number of years completed by 15- to 19-year-olds in the richest 20 percent of households was 10 in India and 8 in Morocco. In other countries the gap in educational achievement was much smaller: one year in Kenya, two in Ghana and Tanzania, and three in Indonesia and Uganda.[32] In Mexico average schooling was less than 3 years for the poorest 20 percent in rural areas and 12 years for the richest 20 percent in urban areas.

Primary enrollment rates show similar gaps. The enrollment rate for 6- to 14-year-olds is 52 percentage points lower for the poorest households than for the richest households in Senegal, 36 percentage points lower in Zambia, and 19 percentage points lower in Ghana. The gaps are also large in North Africa (63 percentage points in Morocco) and South Asia (49 percentage points in Pakistan).[33]

Within-country differences in social indicators also exist between urban and rural areas, across regions, and across socioeconomic classes. In China there has been a widening rural-urban gap in health status and health care use. While the rural population's use of hospital services declined 10 percent between 1985 and 1993, the urban population's increased by 13 percent.[34] In Russia the increase in mortality during the transition has been concentrated among younger males, and stunting of children, relatively high for an industrialized country, has been most prevalent in rural areas and among poor people.[35]

Gender disparities

One of the key variations within a country is the different achievement of women and men. The allocation of resources within households varies depending on the age and gender of the household member. But estimating the number of poor men and women independently is difficult, if not impossible, because consumption data are collected at the household level.[36] Even so, available health and education data indicate that women are often disadvantaged.

A recent study of 41 countries shows that female disadvantage, defined as the gap between male and female primary enrollment rates, varies enormously. In Benin, Nepal, and Pakistan the male-female gap in the primary enrollment rate is more than 20 percentage points, and in Morocco, 18. But in Brazil, Indonesia, Kenya, Madagascar, the Philippines, and Zambia the enrollment rates of boys and girls are almost the same.[37] The gender gap in education is often lower for the richest housholds and highest for the poorest households. In India the gender gap in enrollment rates is 4.7 percentage points for children from the wealthiest 20 percent of households, compared with 11 percentage points for children from the poorest 20 percent of households.[38]

Disparities by caste, ethnicity, and indigenous status

There may also be groups that face particular social barriers. Disadvantaged in many developing and developed countries and transition economies, ethnic minorities and racial groups often face higher poverty.[39] The indigenous populations have a much higher incidence of income poverty in a sample of Latin American countries for which data are available.[40] Schooling attainments for these disadvantaged groups are also lower than for other groups. The indigenous groups in Guatemala have 1.8 years of schooling, and the nonindigenous 4.9 years.[41] In Peru indigenous people were 40 percent more likely to be poor than nonindigenous groups in 1994 and 50 percent more likely in 1997.[42] In rural Guatemala children of indigenous mothers are more likely than those of nonindigenous mothers to be stunted.[43] In the inner cities of the United States white married couples have an incidence of poverty of 5.3 percent, while black or Hispanic single-mother households have an incidence of more than 45 percent.[44]

Evidence for India shows that scheduled castes and scheduled tribes face a higher risk of poverty.[45] These are among the structural poor who not only lack economic resources but whose poverty is strongly linked to social identity, as determined mainly by caste.[46] They also have worse social indicators. Among rural scheduled caste women in India the literacy rate was 19 percent in 1991, half that for the country, and among scheduled caste men, 46 percent, compared with 64 percent for the country.[47] When several disadvantages are combined—being a woman from a socially excluded group in a backward region—the situation is worse. In Uttar Pradesh, one of India's poorest states, only 8 percent of rural scheduled caste women are literate, a third the rate for rural women in Uttar Pradesh. But new research suggests that literacy rates of rural scheduled caste women are on the rise across India. Although only 31 percent of rural scheduled caste or scheduled tribe girls in the primary school age group were enrolled in school in 1986–87, 53 percent were by 1995–96.[48]

Volatility at the household level

Studies of income poverty changes for the same households over time show significant movement in and out of poverty. While some groups are chronically below the poverty line, other groups face a high risk of falling into poverty some of the time. Studies for China, Ethiopia, Russia, and Zimbabwe find that the "always poor" group is smaller than the "sometimes poor" group.[49] However, these results should be treated with caution because observed changes reflect measurement errors as well as real changes.[50]

One immediate question is whether some types of households are more likely to suffer from chronic (rather than transitory) poverty. The answer differs from country to country, but asset holdings often play a key role. In China a lack of physical capital is a determinant of both chronic and transitory poverty, but household size and education of the head of household determine the likelihood of chronic but not of transitory poverty.[51]

In the transition economies of Europe and Central Asia economic mobility has increased, but chronic poverty is emerging as a key issue.[52] Whether a household joins the ranks of the new poor or the new rich depends very much on its characteristics, especially its links with the labor market. The transition has increased the disadvantage of "old poor" (pensioners, families with large numbers of children, and single-parent families) and given rise to "new poor" (long-term unemployed, agricultural workers, young people in search of their first job, and refugees displaced by civil conflict).[53] In Poland the chronically poor constitute a distinct segment of the population. Larger households, those working on farms, and households dependent on social welfare are most at risk of staying poor.[54] Russia has seen the emergence of new poor during the transition. In the early 1990s new groups of poor formed as a result of the erosion of real wages and pensions and the impact of unemployment,[55] and poverty is becoming longer in term and more resistant to economic recovery.[56]

• • •

This chapter has shown that progress in income poverty reduction and human development varies widely across regions, countries, and areas within countries. It has also shown the existence of significant gaps in performance by gender, ethnicity, race, and social status.

Much of the difference in performance across regions and countries can be attributed to differences in economic growth (chapter 3). The growth collapses in many countries in Africa and the former Soviet Union had a devastating impact on poverty. The economywide crises and natural disasters in East Asia, Latin America, Sub-Saharan Africa, and Europe and Central Asia also led to important setbacks in poverty reduction (chapter 9). By contrast, the spectacular growth performance in China resulted in a sharp drop in income poverty. In the rest of East Asia, despite the financial crisis, steady growth rates also translated into significantly lower poverty over the 1990s.

But the initial inequalities and the pattern of growth also account for the differences in performance in poverty reduction in its multiple dimensions as some geographic areas and social groups are left behind. In some cases initial differences include unequal access to assets, markets, and infrastructure and an uneven distribution of skills (chapters 3, 4, and 5). The differences in health and education among and within countries, for example, also reflect the extent to which state institutions are responsive and accountable to poor people (chapter 6). In other cases social barriers linked with gender, ethnicity, race, and social status help perpetuate income poverty and low levels of health and education among the socially disadvantaged (chapter 7). Policy biases against labor-intensive sectors such as agriculture and light manufacturing at the national (chapter 4) or international (chapter 10) level and skill-biased technological change (chapter 4) can result in lower reductions in income poverty at similar growth rates. This chapter has also noted that there can be large volatility in incomes of households. This brings to the fore the importance of understanding the sources of risk that households face and the mechanisms best suited to managing those risks (chapters 8 and 9).

Finally, this chapter has argued that the experience of poverty goes beyond material deprivation and low levels of health and education. The inability to influence the decisions that affect one's life, ill treatment by state institutions, and the impediments created by social barriers and norms are also dimensions of ill-being. Another is vulnerability to adverse shocks, natural disasters, disease, and personal violence. This broader conception of poverty leads to a deeper understanding of its causes and a broader range of actions for attacking it. These are outlined in chapter 2 and developed in more detail in subsequent chapters.

CHAPTER 2

Causes of Poverty and a Framework for Action

From *World Development Report 1990* . . .
- Labor-intensive growth
- Broad provision of social services

. . . to *World Development Report 2000/2001*
- Opportunity
- Empowerment
- Security

A decade ago *World Development Report 1990* presented a two-part strategy for poverty reduction:

Countries that have been most successful in attacking poverty have encouraged a pattern of growth that makes efficient use of labor and have invested in the human capital of the poor. Both elements are essential. The first provides the poor with opportunities to use their most abundant asset—labor. The second improves their immediate well-being and increases their capacity to take advantage of the newly created possibilities. Together, they can improve the lives of most of the world's poor.

—*World Bank 1990 (p. 51)*

That report also noted that these efforts had to be complemented by safety nets for people exposed to shocks and unable to benefit from the strategy. But safety nets were clearly seen as playing a supporting role for the two main parts of the strategy.

The 1990 report's framework for action was derived from its concept of poverty, its analysis of the causes of poverty, the experience of the 1970s and 1980s, and the state of the world economy at the end of the 1980s. It viewed poverty as low consumption and low achievement in education and health. Economic development—brought about essentially by liberalizing trade and markets, investing in infrastructure, and providing basic social services to poor people, to increase their human capital—was seen as key to reducing poverty.

The experience that defined the 1990 report, from its vantage of 1989, was the contrasting experience in the 1970s and 1980s of East Asia, where poverty had fallen sharply, and of Africa, Latin America, and South Asia, where poverty had declined less or even risen. Why did Indonesia outperform Brazil in the 1970s and 1980s in reducing income and nonincome (education and health) poverty? The answer was labor-intensive growth and broad provision of social services—the report's two-part strategy.

This report uses new evidence and multidisciplinary thinking that together broaden the choices for development action to reduce poverty in its multiple dimensions. The evidence confirms that economywide growth improves the incomes of poor people—and in the longer run reduces nonincome poverty. And expanding the human capabilities of poor people remains central in any poverty reduction strategy, both for the intrinsic value of such capabilities as health and education and for their instrumental contribution to other dimensions of well-being, including income.

But the experiences of the 1990s show that:

■ Growth cannot be switched on or off at will. Market reforms can indeed boost growth and help poor people, but they can also be a source of dislocation. The effects of market reforms are complex, deeply linked to institutions and to political and social structures. The experience of transition, especially in the countries of the former Soviet Union, vividly illustrates that market reforms in the absence of effective domestic institutions can fail to deliver growth and poverty reduction. Furthermore, there is evidence that technological change in the past decade has been increasingly biased toward skills. So in contrast to what was expected and needed, the pattern of growth in developing countries is not necessarily intensive in unskilled labor.

■ The emphasis on social services for building human capital was perhaps too optimistic about the institutional, social, and political realities of public action. Public investment in basic education and health in developing countries has been rising—though in some countries more slowly than GDP, suggesting a possible lack of commitment to expanding social services. In many countries social spending is regressive. Moreover, such investment has been less effective than expected, in part because of serious problems in quality and in responsiveness to poor people's needs—institutional failures highlighted in the *Voices of the Poor* study and other research. But there have been successes even in seemingly difficult conditions of low resources. Experience and research show that effectiveness in service delivery is highly dependent on local institutional capabilities, market structure, and patterns of political influence.

■ There is a powerful case for bringing vulnerability and its management to center stage. Participatory poverty work underlines the importance of vulnerability to economic, health, and personal shocks. So do the financial crises of the 1990s—not least in East Asia, the shining example of success in development and poverty reduction—and the sequence of devastating natural disasters.

BRAZIL

Brazil has made impressive improvements in social indicators. Net enrollment in primary education increased from 88.2 percent in 1992 to 97.1 percent in 1997. Infant mortality fell from 62 per 1,000 live births in the mid-1980s to 38 in the mid-1990s. And much urban infrastructure helps poor people. New programs guarantee minimum per capita spending for basic health care and minimum per student spending in primary schools. Innovative action to get children into school includes the Bolsa Escola, which gives poor families grants if their children go to school.

Despite the advances, the inequalities in health and education remain great, with the poorest fifth of the population having three years of education, and the top fifth more than nine years. The income-poor still leave school with skills inadequate for a middle-income country integrated with the global economy. And reducing income poverty has proved difficult. Indeed, in the unstable macroeconomic environment of the 1980s and early 1990s, poverty rose. Two recent events confirm that the groups most vulnerable to economic insecurity are those with the highest incidence of poverty. Drought in the Northeast hit poor rural workers severely, and the ripple effects of the East Asian crisis, though more benign than expected, reduced the income of workers with the least education.

Some illustrative priorities for action: job growth through productive investment and prudent macroeconomic management is clearly central to increasing income opportunities. But unless structural inequalities are tackled effectively, the gains for poor people will be modest. To reduce structural inequalities, a large land reform program is under way, and there have been promising experiments in negotiated land reform in the Northeast. In the ongoing education effort the next steps will probably require even broader, deeper, and more participatory reforms—many of these are now under discussion. The government is also continuing to ease the constraints of constitutional entitlements, which limit the room for maneuver on public spending. Finally, successful community-driven development approaches—in urban upgrading, small-farm investments, and community health agents—show what is possible when there is an empowering mobilization of citizens.

- Inequality is back on the agenda—in the realm of ideas and experience and in the political discourse of many developing (and developed) countries. New work shows the importance of gender, ethnic, and racial inequality as a dimension—and a cause—of poverty. Social, economic, and ethnic divisions are often sources of weak or failed development. In the extreme, vicious cycles of social division and failed development erupt into internal conflict, as in Bosnia and Herzegovina and Sierra Leone, with devastating consequences for people.

- The global forces of integration, communication, and technological advance have proceeded apace, bringing significant advances to some. But they have passed others by. Private capital flows now dominate official flows in the world, but they reinforce positive economic developments, either neglecting or punishing countries with weak economic conditions.

The new evidence and broader thinking do not negate earlier strategies—such as that of *World Development Report 1990*. But they do show the need to broaden the agenda. Attacking poverty requires actions beyond the economic domain. And public action has to go beyond investing in social services and removing antilabor biases in government interventions in the economy.

Acknowledging the need for a broader agenda, this report proposes a general framework for action in three equally important areas:

- *Promoting opportunity:* expanding economic opportunity for poor people by stimulating overall growth and by building up their assets and increasing the returns on these assets, through a combination of market and nonmarket actions (part II).

- *Facilitating empowerment:* making state institutions more accountable and responsive to poor people, strengthening the participation of poor people in political processes and local decisionmaking, and removing the social barriers that result from distinctions of gender, ethnicity, race, and social status (part III).

- *Enhancing security:* reducing poor people's vulnerability to ill health, economic shocks, policy-induced dislocations, natural disasters, and violence, as well as helping them cope with adverse shocks when they occur (part IV).

Opportunity, empowerment, and security have intrinsic value for poor people. And given the important complementarities among them, an effective poverty reduction strategy will require action on all three fronts, by the full range of agents in society—government, civil society, the private sector, and poor people themselves.

Actions cannot be confined to individual countries in the developing world. Harnessing global forces in favor of poor countries and poor people will be essential. Actions are needed to promote global financial stability—and to ensure that poor countries are not left behind by advances in technology and in scientific and medical research. The markets of rich countries must be opened to the products of poor countries, and aid and debt relief must be increased to help poor people help themselves. And poor countries and poor people need to be given a voice and influence in international forums (part V).

CHINA

China stands out for its extraordinary decline in income poverty and its high levels of education and health. But it has also had significant increases in inequality—between town and country, and between the coastal areas and inland China, with the poor, semi-arid areas of inland China participating little in growth.

Formal structures of security are in transition, and there are deep concerns about the less dynamic parts of urban China, which are experiencing the beginnings of a major shakeout in state enterprise and government employment. Formal provision of security was always weaker in rural areas, but micro evidence suggests that village mechanisms continue to provide high levels of food security through land allocation processes—confirmed as politically popular in villages by democratic votes. Ensuring the voice of the new poor in urban areas and those left behind in inland China will be important in guiding action.

Three areas for action are illustrative. First, maintaining rapid growth through high nonstate investment is crucial if there is to be a smooth process of job destruction in inefficient state activities and smooth reform of the social protection arrangements for state employees. If there is a sustained slowdown, insecurity in areas dependent on now inefficient state production could be acute. Second, the smooth integration of China into the global trading system will be key in locking in reforms and ensuring economic stability and steady job growth. But if new opportunities are not to widen disparities, this will have to be accompanied by greater emphasis on building the assets of people living in the poorer areas. Third, continuing area-based integrated rural development activities in poor areas of inland China and, more generally, balancing investment across geographic areas need to be important parts of any overall strategy.

The causes of poverty

One route for investigating the causes of poverty is to examine the dimensions highlighted by poor people:

- Lack of income and assets to attain basic necessities—food, shelter, clothing, and acceptable levels of health and education.
- Sense of voicelessness and powerlessness in the institutions of state and society.
- Vulnerability to adverse shocks, linked to an inability to cope with them.

To understand the determinants of poverty in all its dimensions, it helps to think in terms of people's assets, the returns to (or productivity of) these assets, and the volatility of returns. These assets are of several kinds:

- *Human* assets, such as the capacity for basic labor, skills, and good health.
- *Natural* assets, such as land.
- *Physical* assets, such as access to infrastructure.
- *Financial* assets, such as savings and access to credit.
- *Social* assets, such as networks of contacts and reciprocal obligations that can be called on in time of need, and political influence over resources.

The returns to these assets depend on access to markets and all the global, national, and local influences on returns in these markets. But returns depend not just on the behavior of markets, but also on the performance of institutions of state and society. Underlying asset ownership and returns to assets are not only economic but also fundamental political and social forces. Access to assets depends on a legal structure that defines and enforces private property rights or on customary norms that define common property resources. Access may also be affected by implicit or explicit discrimination on the basis of gender, ethnicity, race, or social status. And both access to assets and returns to assets are affected by public policy and state interventions, which are shaped by the political influence of different groups.

Also important is the volatility of returns. Volatility results from market fluctuations, weather conditions, and, in some societies, turbulent political conditions. Volatility affects not only returns, but also the value of assets, as shocks undermine health, destroy natural and physical assets, or deplete savings.

Lack of income and assets

If you have a job at all now, you're overworked and underpaid.

—Young woman from Dimitrovgrad, Bulgaria

Some have land, but they can't buy fertilizer; if some work as weavers, they aren't well paid; if some work for daily wages, they aren't paid a just wage.

—Cackchiquel Indian, Guatemala

Poor people consistently emphasize the centrality of work to improving their lives. A country's overall wealth is an important influence on this: as countries grow richer, so on average do poor people in those countries,

INDIA

India suffers severe deprivations in education and health—especially in the North, where caste, class, and gender inequities are particularly strong. In studies in Bihar and Uttar Pradesh poor women and men emphasized their extreme vulnerability and the ineffectiveness of state institutions, from schools to police.

In the past, poverty reduction in India lagged behind that of East Asia because of slower growth and significantly less progress in promoting mass education and basic health. More recently, however, growth has accelerated and poverty has fallen, although the actual impact of growth on poverty reduction remains controversial because of measurement problems (see box 1.8).

There are also marked differences within India—with the South, particularly the state of Kerala, having sharply better education and health. Kerala has life expectancies greater than those in Washington, D.C., despite vastly lower income levels. The effectiveness of public action in Kerala has been attributed to its strong tradition of political and social mobilization.

What are the priorities for action in India? Accelerated poverty reduction will require faster growth, which in turn demands liberalization, especially in agriculture, and better provision of infrastructure, sorely lacking in most of India. In areas with deep deprivation in health and education, the development of social infrastructure is critical. Expanding education and health services will require that state governments reverse the deterioration in their fiscal positions, as subsidies to the loss-making power sector crowd out spending in the social sectors. The higher spending will need to be matched by better service provision. This will require deep improvements in governance, often weakest in India's poorest regions, and in combating teacher absenteeism. Also needed is more equitable service provision, which will require empowering women and members of lower castes.

with the main mechanism being better-paid work. With economic growth, income poverty falls; with economic contraction, income poverty rises (figure 2.1). Some countries in East Asia sustained per capita GDP growth rates of 4–5 percent over four decades, with massive improvements in living standards and in health and education for poor people and for everyone else. Other countries, most in Africa, registered negative growth or no growth at all over the same period, delivering no improvements even in average living standards.

While economic growth is systematically associated with poverty reduction, the rate at which growth translates into lower poverty depends on the initial level of inequality in the distribution of income and how that distribution changes over time. Growth—and its effectiveness in reducing poverty—also depends on sound, stable governance. So confronting socioeconomic inequalities and building sound institutions can be important both for providing a socially sustainable basis for overall growth and for ensuring that poor people gain substantially from that growth.

Voicelessness and powerlessness— the institutional basis of poverty

Those materially deprived feel acutely their lack of voice, power, and independence (see box 1.1 in chapter 1). This helplessness subjects them to rudeness, humiliation, shame, inhumane treatment, and exploitation at the

Figure 2.1
Poverty shows a strong link with economic contractions and expansions

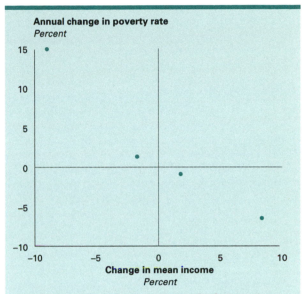

Note: The data refer to 150 country-level spells of poverty change and mean income change from poverty surveys in 1980–98. Each point represents one-fourth of the sample, ordered from strongest contraction to strongest expansion.
Source: World Bank staff estimates based on Chen and Ravallion (2000).

hands of the institutions of state and society (box 2.1). Absence of the rule of law, lack of protection against violence, extortion and intimidation, and lack of civility and predictability in interactions with public officials—all these

JORDAN

Poverty and inequality in Jordan increased at the end of the 1980s as a result of a macroeconomic shock. But between 1992 and 1997 Jordan reduced income poverty, despite lagging—at times even negative— per capita GDP growth rates. The explanation lies in a decline in inequality due in part to the phaseout of regressive food subsidies coupled with expansion of the government safety net (World Bank 1999q). To sustain these gains, it is important to improve growth—to make social spending more affordable and to directly expand opportunities for poor people.

Government assistance is impressive— targeted cash transfers favoring female and elderly heads of household and the disabled, microcredit, and health insurance benefits. But by focusing on the always poor rather than the sometimes poor, government programs fail to address the shallowness of poverty in Jordan. So the vulnerability of the poor and the near-poor to outside shocks is high, though tempered by substantial nongovernmental and religious charitable activity that complements strong family and community networks. That vulnerability can be addressed by community-based public work programs offering low-wage jobs and by unemployment insurance and assistance. The National Aid Fund (in charge of the government safety net) could identify other means of assistance by soliciting ideas from beneficiaries. Its 1998 service delivery survey reflects dissatisfaction among beneficiaries, who complain of procedural difficulties and obstacles, benefits canceled without verification, and inadequate assistance. The fund is acting on some of these findings, moving it closer to true accountability and to empowering poor people.

Jordanians stand to gain much from the long-awaited Arab-Israeli peace dividend. But for the gains to materialize, Jordanians must have the tools that education provides. So continued emphasis on ensuring access for poor people to publicly provided basic education services is critical both for the short and the long run.

Box 2.1
On interacting with state institutions: the voices of the poor

Although there are pockets of excellence, poor people in the *Voices of the Poor* study generally rated state institutions low on fairness, honesty, relevance, effectiveness, responsiveness, and accountability. Nevertheless, they view government agencies as having an important role in their lives, and they have a clear picture of the qualities they would like to see in the institutions with which they interact.

In India the characteristics of credit institutions can deter poor people from seeking loans. Poor people in many regions also report widespread corruption in health care systems. But when facing serious health conditions, they feel they have no choice but to comply with demands for bribes. In Macedonia people conclude, "nobody wants you to come with empty hands."

The behavior of health care providers becomes another deterrent to those needing health services. In Tanzania in many areas, men, women, and youth stated over and over that they are treated like animals, worse than dogs. They report that even before they could explain their symptoms, they would be shouted at, told they smelled bad and were lazy and good-for-nothing.

Poor people in many countries spoke about being kept endlessly waiting while the rich went to the head of the queue.

In Europe and Central Asia pensioners trying to collect their meager pensions experience endless red tape, rude and unresponsive officials, and withholding of information. Poor people in the region criticize mayors and local authorities for their arbitrariness, inefficiency, and often corruption (though there are notable exceptions).

Poor people hunger for institutions that are fair, polite, honest, listening, trustworthy, and neither corrupt nor corrupting. A poor woman in Vila Junqueira, Brazil, summed it all up:

An institution should not discriminate against people because they are not well dressed or because they are black. If you wear a suit you are treated as sir; if you are wearing sandals they send you away.

Source: Narayan, Chambers, Shah, and Petesch 2000; Narayan, Patel, Schafft, Rademacher, and Koch-Schulte 2000.

place a large burden on poor people. They are prevented from taking advantage of new economic opportunities or engaging in activities outside their immediate zone of security. Threats of physical force or arbitrary bureaucratic power make it difficult for them to engage in public affairs, to make their interests known, and to have them taken into account. And unaccountable and unresponsive state institutions are among the causes of relatively slow progress in expanding the human assets of poor people.

In agrarian societies poor people's lack of assets and income-earning opportunities ties them to rich landowners in patron-client relationships. And for women, a lack of savings and assets precludes a more independent role in decisionmaking in the household and the community.

Social norms and barriers can also contribute to voicelessness and powerlessness. While local cultures have intrinsic value, they can sometimes be inimical to reducing human deprivation. Pervasive in almost all societies is inequality between men and women. Poor women are discriminated against in the household and in land, labor, and credit markets. This both causes poverty and undercuts development—for women's agency is a powerful source of human gains, especially for children. Discrimination based on ethnicity, religious beliefs, social status, and race has similar effects.

Vulnerability

Three years ago it was a very bad year. The flood washed away all of our crops, and there was a lot of hunger around here, to the point that many people actually died of hunger. They must have been at least a dozen, mostly children and old people. Nobody could help them. Their relatives in the village had no food either; nobody had enough food for his own children, let alone for the children of his brother or cousin. And few had a richer relative somewhere else who could help.

—*Poor villager, Benin*

Vulnerability is a constant companion of material and human deprivation, given the circumstances of the poor and the near-poor. They live and farm on marginal lands with uncertain rainfall. They live in crowded urban settlements where heavy rains can wipe out their homes. They have precarious employment, in the formal or informal sector. They are at higher risk of diseases such as malaria and tuberculosis. They are at risk of arbitrary arrest and ill treatment at the hands of local authorities. And they—women in particular—are at risk of being socially excluded and victims of violence and crime.

The risks that poor people face as a result of their circumstances are the cause of their vulnerability. But the deeper cause is the inability to reduce or mitigate risk or cope with shocks—a cause that both draws from and feeds into the causes of other dimensions of poverty. Low levels of physical, natural, and financial assets make poor people especially vulnerable to negative shocks—those with more assets can weather these shocks as long as they are temporary. Lack of adequate assets can set up a vicious downward spiral in which actions to cope in the short term worsen deprivation in the long term. Pulling children out of school to earn extra income during an economic crisis. Depleting natural resources beyond the sustainable level. Making quick sales of land or livestock at desperately low prices. Lowering nutritional intake below the levels necessary to sustain health (chapters 8 and 9).

Another underlying cause of vulnerability is the inability of the state or community to develop mechanisms to reduce or mitigate the risks that poor people face. Irrigation, infrastructure, public health interventions, honest police and a fair legal system, public work schemes in times of stress, microcredit to tide people through the aftermath of an adverse shock, social networks of support and insurance, famine relief in extreme circumstances—all reduce vulnerability for poor people. The diverse cross-country experience with each of these mechanisms can help in developing actions to address vulnerability in specific circumstances.

Poor people also are exposed to risks beyond their community—those affecting the economy, the environment, and the society in which they live. Civil conflict and wars, economic crises, and natural disasters affect not only their current living standards but also their ability to escape poverty. And to the extent that global forces—

such as volatile capital flows, global climate change, and arms sales—are the causes of shocks and disruptions in poor countries, the inability or unwillingness of the global community to address them increases the vulnerability of poor people (chapter 10).

A framework for action

What framework for action is needed to effectively reduce poverty in all its dimensions? National economic development is central to success in poverty reduction. But poverty is an outcome of more than economic processes. It is an outcome of economic, social, and political processes that interact with and reinforce each other in ways that can worsen or ease the deprivation poor people face every day. To attack poverty requires promoting opportunity, facilitating empowerment, and enhancing security—with actions at local, national, and global levels. Making progress on all three fronts can generate the dynamics for sustainable poverty reduction.

The areas for action illustrate the complexity of development. How can priorities be decided in practice? Do all actions have to be carried out in all three areas? Both the strategic approach and the areas of suggested action are only a guide. Actual priorities and actions need to be worked out in each country's economic, sociopolitical, structural, and cultural context—indeed, each community's. But even though choices depend on local conditions, it generally is necessary to consider scope for action in all three areas—opportunity, empowerment, and security—because of their crucial complementarities. The country examples in this chapter illustrate how to

RUSSIAN FEDERATION

Like other countries of the former Soviet Union, Russia has had a dramatic rise in both poverty and inequality and a worsening of adult mortality. The Russian people have experienced large increases in insecurity—through macroeconomic volatility, the loss of old job-related forms of security, and the sharp rise in violence—and often acute psychological stress from the rise in poverty. While the electoral process has been important in empowering the citizenry, this has been offset by the profound feelings of disempowerment stemming from the new sources of insecurity and by the problems

of elite capture of the state. As the new oligarchs have also captured privatized assets and resource rents, the rise in inequality is the product not of the market-oriented reforms themselves but of the interactions between the reforms and the political and institutional structures during the transition process.

What are the priorities for action to reduce poverty? Fundamental to improving the overall environment is reducing the elite's capture of the state at the national level, including through further market reforms to deconcentrate economic power.

Today's structural inequality, closely linked to the political structure, runs the risk of becoming deeply embedded, if it has not already become so. Dealing with associated issues of governance is likely to be a prerequisite to reduced macroeconomic volatility and a business environment that fosters the investment needed to counter the extraordinary collapse in formal sector jobs. It is also a prerequisite to pro-poor budget allocations, backed by decentralization and participatory engagement to foster greater accountability and responsiveness in service provision.

identify priorities and areas of action in country-specific poverty reduction strategies.

Opportunity

Growth is essential for expanding economic opportunity for poor people—though this is only the beginning of the story of public action (chapter 3). The question is how to achieve rapid, sustainable, pro-poor growth. A business environment conducive to private investment and technological innovation is necessary, as is political and social stability to underpin public and private investment. And asset and social inequalities directly affect both the pace of growth and the distribution of its benefits. The distribution of growth benefits matters, not least because distributional conflict can undermine the stability needed for overall growth.

Markets are central to the lives of poor people (chapter 4). The evidence shows that on average countries that are open to international trade and have sound monetary and fiscal policy and well-developed financial markets enjoy higher growth. Where market-friendly reforms have been successfully implemented, on average stagnation has ended and growth resumed. But at times reforms to build markets fail entirely. The impact of market reforms on economic performance and inequality depends on institutional and structural conditions, including the comparative advantage of countries and patterns of asset ownership. And the impact of market reforms differs for different groups in an economy—there are winners and losers, and the losers can include poor people. The design and sequencing of such reforms thus need to take account of local conditions and the likely effects on poor people. This does not necessarily mean going slow: rapid reforms can be important to bring gains to poor people and to break down monopoly privileges for the rich. Adverse effects of reforms on poor people can be compensated for by action in other areas, such as safety nets to ease the transition costs.

Relatively neglected is market reform targeted to poor people. Such reforms may have a different focus than other reforms—eliminating or simplifying the regulations affecting microenterprises and small and medium-size firms, strengthening registries to allow small producers to use land as collateral, or developing the policy framework for small-scale insurance.

Key in expanding economic opportunities for poor people is to help build up their assets (chapter 5). Human capabilities such as health and education are of intrinsic value, but also have powerful instrumental effects on material well-being. Also important to the material prospects of poor people is ownership of—or access to—land, infrastructure, and financial services. And social assets, including social networks, often also play an instrumental role.

A range of actions can support poor people in expanding their assets. The state—because of its power to raise revenues and use them as an instrument of redistribution—has a central role, especially in providing basic social services and infrastructure. Where access to land is highly unequal, there is a social and economic case for negotiated land reforms. For many services the state's role in provision can be complemented by market mechanisms, civil society, and the private sector, increasing the benefits to poor people. And for local ser-

SIERRA LEONE

Sierra Leone, by the latest price-adjusted measures, is the poorest country in the world. But this statement fails to convey the true depth of human deprivation in that nation. The people of Sierra Leone remain caught in a tragic conflict—one that has taken a terrible toll through lost lives, rape, mutilation, and the psychological harm to boys abducted into the army and militias.

Work on the sources of conflict in developing countries suggests that material poverty and weak democratic structures interact with ethnic and other social divides to cause internal strife. The effects of conflict—destruction of fragile institutions of governance, flight of skills, personal losses, and social wounds that could take generations to heal—create a vicious cycle of continued poverty and strife.

Sierra Leone has a desperate need for assets—human, physical, and social—and for greater market opportunities. And the personal insecurity is unimaginable. But there can be no progress without mechanisms to resolve the social conflict, deal with citizens' disempowerment by those with guns, and re-create the institutions for mourning and for managing psychological losses.

International action will be important. Once there is a basis for some development, concerted external support will be crucial. The Enhanced Heavily Indebted Poor Countries Debt Relief Initiative provides transitional support to postconflict societies for economic reconstruction. Much more challenging will be the delicate task of social and institutional reconstruction.

vice delivery, engaging poor people and communities can have a powerful impact on effectiveness.

Empowerment

Empowerment means enhancing the capacity of poor people to influence the state institutions that affect their lives, by strengthening their participation in political processes and local decisionmaking. And it means removing the barriers—political, legal, and social—that work against particular groups and building the assets of poor people to enable them to engage effectively in markets.

Expanding economic opportunities for poor people indeed contributes to their empowerment. But efforts are needed to make state and social institutions work in the interests of poor people—to make them pro-poor (chapter 6). Formal democratic processes are part of empowerment. As important are the mechanisms through which everyday state interventions help or hurt poor people. Here, more detailed processes of accountability come into play—mobilizing poor people in their own organizations to hold state institutions accountable and ensuring the rule of law in their daily lives.

Empowering poor people is part of the broader agenda of sound governance and accountability of state institutions to their citizens. National empowerment of citizens can have important indirect effects on poor people, by influencing the quality and pace of economic and social development. But the outcome for poor people depends on the political and social structures within a society. Governments are often more responsive to the concerns of elites than to the needs of poor groups. So the extent to which the concerns of nonpoor and poor groups coincide will frequently determine whether governance is pro-poor.

Improving governance also requires building administrative and regulatory capacity and reducing corruption. The burden of petty corruption falls disproportionately on poor people, who generally have common cause with an anticorruption agenda.

Social interactions between individuals and communities also have an important influence on poverty outcomes. Culture's part in the development process is complex. The beliefs and practices that are part of local culture can be a source of sustainable development. But customary practices and discrimination on the basis of gender, ethnicity, race, religion, or social status can also be a source of inequality in many countries. Removing discrimination and managing these divisions can help reduce poverty. Confronting gender inequities is a fundamental part of this, with direct benefits for women (and men) and instrumental effects on growth and development. Recent evidence shows that greater gender equity is associated with faster growth (chapter 7).

Security

Enhancing security for poor people means reducing their vulnerability to such risks as ill health, economic shocks, and natural disasters and helping them cope with adverse shocks when they do occur (chapters 8 and 9).

Poverty reduction strategies can lessen the vulnerability of poor households through a range of approaches that can reduce volatility, provide the means for poor people to manage risk themselves, and strengthen market or public institutions for risk management. The tasks include preventing or managing shocks at the national and regional level—such as economic downturns and natural disasters—and minimizing the impact on poor people when they do occur.

Supporting the range of assets of poor people—human, natural, physical, financial, and social—can help them

UGANDA

Having emerged from a period of destructive conflict just over a decade ago, Uganda suffers deep poverty in many dimensions. But it also shows what an immensely poor Sub-Saharan African country can achieve.

The first country to receive enhanced debt relief on the basis of its poverty reduction strategy, Uganda stands out for its steady growth in the 1990s. It also stands out for significant reductions in income poverty, impressive efforts toward universal primary education, and a major effort to ensure transparent, poverty-focused budgets, both centrally and locally. One of its main vulnerabilities is health. HIV/AIDS hit Uganda early: a tenth of adults are now infected, and AIDS orphans are straining traditional systems of fostering children.

Three areas are priorities for future action. Consolidating and deepening the accountability and participation in resource allocation and strengthening central and local state institutions, to provide a basis for sound local investment programs in social and physical capital. Tackling the perceived risks in the business environment so that job-creating growth can take off. And furthering current efforts to stop the spread of HIV/AIDS and such diseases as tuberculosis.

manage the risks they face. And supporting the institutions that help poor people manage risk can enable them to pursue the higher-risk, higher-return activities that can lift them out of poverty. Improving risk management institutions should thus be a permanent feature of poverty reduction strategies. A modular approach is needed, with different schemes to cover different types of risk and different groups of the population. The tools include health insurance, old age assistance and pensions, unemployment insurance, workfare programs, social funds, microfinance programs, and cash transfers. Safety nets should be designed to support immediate consumption needs—and to protect the accumulation of human, physical, and social assets by poor people.

In addressing risk and vulnerability, the issue once again is whether public interventions and institutions work well—and in the interests of poor people. Famines are a constant threat in many parts of the world, yet some countries have been able to avoid mass deaths. In the 20th century no democratic country with a free press and a free political opposition ever experienced famine (box 2.2). Access to information and participation can reduce vulnerability.

Interconnections at local and national levels

Just as the dimensions and causes of poverty are interlinked, so the areas for action are interconnected. Action to expand opportunity is itself a potent source of empowerment, in a deep, intrinsic sense with respect to basic human capabilities, but also instrumentally—for as the asset base, incomes, and market opportunities of poor people increase, so will their potential political and social influence. Improving material conditions is also instrumental in enhancing security: adverse shocks have lower costs when a person is above the margin of bare survival, and assets are at the heart of people's risk management strategies. Empowerment is fundamental in determining action in market reforms and the expansion of assets that affect the pattern of material opportunities and in shaping the design of policies and institutions that help poor and non-poor people manage the risks they face. Finally, reducing vulnerability, with all its debilitating consequences, is central to improving material well-being (or preventing reversals) and empowering poor people and communities.

International actions

With global forces having central—and probably rising—importance, actions at the local and national level are not

---

Box 2.2
Preventing famines: the local press matters

Famines are often the result of crises that affect agricultural production—floods or droughts. How quickly governments respond to such crises depends on many factors. A fundamental one is the level of democracy and the extent to which politicians are held accountable for the efficiency of relief programs. A recent study in India shows that the distribution of newspapers can play a big part.

India has a relatively free press, with only 2 percent of newspapers controlled directly by central or state governments. The study looked at the interaction between government responsiveness to floods and droughts (measured in public relief funds) and the circulation of newspapers across Indian states. The hypothesis: an informed population can link inefficiency to a particular politician and therefore elicit a greater response to crises.

The results confirmed the hypothesis: for a given shock (drought or flood), higher newspaper circulation leads to greater public food distribution or relief spending. A 10 percent drop in food production due to a crisis is associated with a 1 percent increase in public food distribution in the states with the median newspaper circulation per capita but a more than 2 percent increase in states in the 75th percentile of newspaper circulation.

Separating newspapers by language yields an interesting result. Among three types of papers—those in Hindi, English, and local languages—only those in local languages seem to enhance government responsiveness to crisis. The state governments' responses to local crises are thus very sensitive to the distribution of local newspapers, typically read by the local electorate.

Source: Besley and Burgess 2000.

---

enough. Global economic advance, access to international markets, global financial stability, and technological advances in health, agriculture, and communications are all crucial determinants of poverty reduction (chapter 10). International cooperation is thus needed to reduce industrial countries' protectionism and avert global financial volatility. And the growing importance of such international public goods as agricultural and medical research calls for a shift in the focus of development cooperation. Furthermore, because of the importance of international actions in poverty reduction, the voices of poor countries and poor people should be strengthened in international forums.

Country-focused aid programs remain essential—to help countries implement poverty reduction strategies that empower poor people, enhance their security, and expand their opportunities (chapter 11). Aid should be

Box 2.3
Attacking poverty in Vietnam

Vietnam has made striking progress against poverty, reducing the share of its population in income poverty from 58 percent to 37 percent in 1993–98. A recent analysis by the Poverty Working Group, with members from government, donors, and NGOs, found that:

- *The main engine of the rapid poverty reduction was reform.* Especially important were the land reforms that Vietnam launched in the mid-1980s, which created enormous opportunities for people to improve their lives and livelihoods.
- *Despite the gains, poor people expressed a sense of voicelessness and powerlessness.* Participatory poverty assessments (done jointly with Oxfam, Actionaid, and Save the Children) found that people were hungry for a two-way flow of information—from the government to them about the nature and timing of public policies and programs affecting their lives and from them to the government to influence those policies and programs.
- *Poverty remains deep and widespread—and the gains fragile.* Millions of people are still vulnerable to poverty. Illness, the death of a family member, and natural disasters (flooding,

drought) remain ever-present threats. Women, ethnic minorities, and unregistered urban migrants remain especially disadvantaged.

The analysis—which involved a wide range of stakeholders—identified three areas of policy action:

- *Launch a new round of reforms* that unleash the dynamism of the private sector and create opportunities for employment and productivity growth, so that incomes rise and poor people are able to escape poverty.
- *Implement the Grassroots Democracy Decree,* which aims to empower people by authorizing their direct participation in local decisionmaking and improving local governance.
- *Strengthen safety nets and targeted programs,* such as the Hunger Eradication and Poverty Reduction Program, to reduce the vulnerability of poor people to risks (illness, poor harvests).

The report on the study has been disseminated widely in Vietnam, including to all 450 members of the National Assembly and to all 61 provinces. The prime minister has asked the Poverty Working Group to translate the findings into a comprehensive poverty reduction strategy for Vietnam before the end of 2000.

Source: World Bank 1999bb.

directed to countries with high levels of poverty. But that should be only part of the criteria for allocating aid. Also essential is having the right policy and institutional framework in place to make poverty reduction a success.

Debt relief for the world's poorest nations, the heavily indebted poor countries, has been the most prominent issue in development cooperation in recent years. This report recognizes that debt reduction must play a central part in an overall strategy for attacking poverty.

The chapters that follow outline different sets of actions to consider in devising a poverty reduction strategy. The priorities cannot be set in the abstract. They must fit the context—and reflect a broad national consensus. Recent experience in Vietnam shows how this process can be set in motion (box 2.3).

• • •

This chapter has presented an overall framework for actions in three areas—opportunity, empowerment, and security—to reduce poverty in its different dimensions. Actions need to be taken by the full range of agents in society—poor people, government, the private sector, and civil society organizations—and at local, national, and global levels. The country examples in this chapter illustrate three fundamental points:

- Actions affecting opportunity, empowerment, and security are interconnected—there is no hierarchy, and advances in one area generally depend on gains in the others.
- In all cases the social, political, and institutional underpinnings for action are of fundamental importance.
- Context matters. While it generally is always desirable to take or sustain action in all three areas, the design of action, and the agents that matter, depend on the economic, social, and political conditions prevailing in the country.

PART II

Opportunity

CHAPTER 3

Growth, Inequality, and Poverty

As countries become richer, on average the incidence of income poverty falls. Other indicators of well-being, such as average levels of education and health, tend to improve as well. For these reasons, economic growth is a powerful force for poverty reduction. This observation is not the end of the story, for it raises the questions of what causes economic growth and why countries with similar rates of economic growth can have very different rates of poverty reduction.

Until the mid-18th century improvements in living standards worldwide were barely perceptible. Most societies were resigned to poverty as an inescapable fact of life.[1] As late as 1820 per capita incomes were quite similar around the world—and very low, ranging from around $500 in China and South Asia to $1,000–1,500 in the richest countries of Europe.[2] Roughly three-quarters of the world's people lived on less than $1 a day.[3]

The onset of modern economic development opened the possibility that growth could significantly improve the living standards of poor people—and everyone else. Over the next two centuries per capita incomes in the richest countries of Europe increased more than tenfold in real terms, in China more than fourfold, and in South Asia threefold. The consequences for poverty have been dramatic. In the rich countries of Europe the fraction of the population living on less than $1 a day has fallen to nil. In China, where growth was slower, less than 20 percent of the population now lives on less than $1 a day. In South Asia, where growth was slower still, around 40 percent of the population does. Today roughly a fifth of the world's people fall below this austere income threshold.

But differences in rates of economic growth, and in the rates at which that growth translates into poverty reduction, are not the consequence of simple choices. Countries do not choose to have slow growth or to undergo painful crises. Nor do they simply choose how equitable growth will be. Instead, the patterns of growth, the changes in the distribution of income and opportunities, and the rates of poverty reduction reflect a complex set of interactions among the policies, institutions, history, and geography of countries. Understanding the forces underlying countries' disparate growth experiences, and the mechanisms through which this growth has reached poor people, is essential for formulating poverty reduction strategies.

This chapter takes up these issues in turn. It first documents the strong links between economic growth and the income and nonincome dimensions of poverty. It next turns to the policies and institutions that underpin growth and provide the basis for poverty reduction. It recognizes that there are substantial deviations from these general relationships reflecting the wide diversity of country experience—and that these deviations reflect a further set of interrelationships between distributional outcomes, policies, and institutions. It therefore discusses how cross-country differences in the poverty-growth nexus are a consequence of initial inequalities in the distribution of income and opportunities —and of changes in the distribution of income that occur with growth. These inequalities themselves reflect an array of factors, which in turn have consequences for economic growth. Last, the chapter explores the interactions between growth and two nonincome dimensions of poverty—health and education.

Economic growth and poverty reduction

Today close to a fifth of the people in the world survive on less than $1 a day. The incidence of this deprivation varies greatly across countries. Not surprising, the richer the country, the higher the average consumption of the poorest fifth of its population—and the smaller on average the fraction living on less than $1 a day (figure 3.1). There are also significant variations around this relationship. Countries with the same average consumption have quite different proportions of the population living on less than $1 a day, reflecting substantial differences in inequality across countries.

Education and health indicators are also better on average for richer countries. In rich countries fewer than 1 child in 100 does not reach its fifth birthday, while in the poorest countries as many as a fifth of children do not (figure 3.2). Similarly, in the poorest countries as many as half of children under five are malnourished —in rich countries fewer than 5 percent. Again, however, there can be striking deviations from the average. For example, the United States is vastly richer than China and India, but the life expectancy of African Americans is about the same as that in China and in some states in India.[4]

Figure 3.1
In general, the wealthier a country, the lower the incidence of poverty

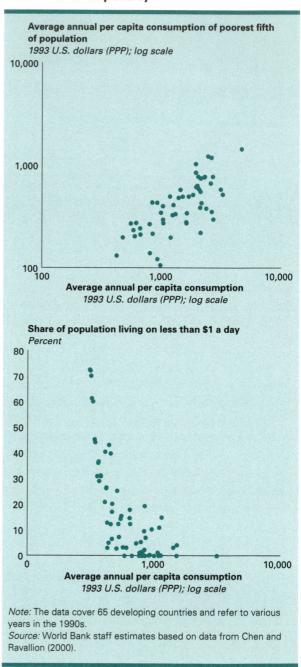

Note: The data cover 65 developing countries and refer to various years in the 1990s.
Source: World Bank staff estimates based on data from Chen and Ravallion (2000).

[Poverty is] . . . low salaries and lack of jobs. And it's also not having medicine, food, and clothes.
—From a discussion group, Brazil

Still, the stark differences in poverty outcomes between rich and poor countries point to the central role of eco-

Figure 3.2
Health indicators improve as incomes rise

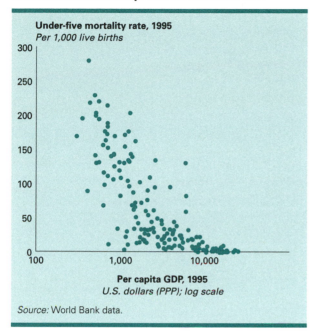

Under-five mortality rate, 1995
Per 1,000 live births

Per capita GDP, 1995
U.S. dollars (PPP); log scale

Source: World Bank data.

Figure 3.3
Poverty trends tracked growth trends in the 1980s and 1990s

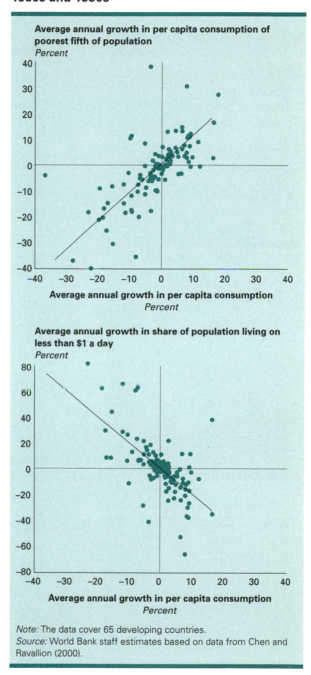

Average annual growth in per capita consumption of poorest fifth of population
Percent

Average annual growth in per capita consumption
Percent

Average annual growth in share of population living on less than $1 a day
Percent

Average annual growth in per capita consumption
Percent

Note: The data cover 65 developing countries.
Source: World Bank staff estimates based on data from Chen and Ravallion (2000).

nomic development in poverty reduction. These differences generally reflect cross-country differences in economic growth over the very long run. But the benefits of growth in reducing income poverty can also be seen over shorter periods. Chapter 1 discusses the highly variable evolution of income poverty across countries in the past two decades. Differences in economic growth across countries account for much of this variation: as in the very long run, growth in the 1980s and 1990s was a powerful force for reducing income poverty. On average, growth in the consumption of the poorest fifth of the population tracked economic growth one-for-one over this period (figure 3.3). In the vast majority of cases growth led to rising consumption in the poorest fifth of the population, while economic decline led to falling consumption.

The pattern is similar for the share of people living on less than $1 a day. On average, every additional percentage point of growth in average household consumption reduces that share by about 2 percent. Although the deviations from this average relationship show that in some countries growth is associated with much more poverty reduction than in others, the relationship highlights the importance of economic growth for improving the incomes of poor people and for moving people out of poverty. Conversely, low or negative growth re-

sulting from the collapse of the state, natural disaster, war, or economic crisis can have a devastating impact on poor people.

As chapter 1 shows, national poverty figures hide much variation in outcomes within countries. But just as cross-country differences in economic growth do much to explain cross-country differences in poverty outcomes, regional and subregional growth does much to explain subnational poverty outcomes. World regions, countries, and provinces within countries have grown at very different rates (figure 3.4). Where growth has occurred, it has been an important source of poverty reduction, and where it has not, poverty has often stagnated. Understanding why countries and regions have had such disparate growth experiences, and how this growth reaches poor people, is essential for formulating poverty reduction strategies.

Figure 3.4

Economic growth was a force for poverty reduction in the 1980s and 1990s . . .

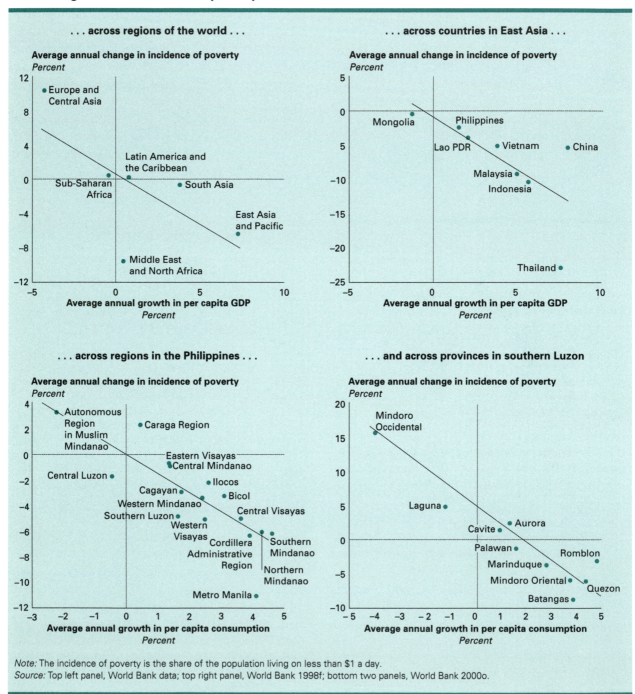

Note: The incidence of poverty is the share of the population living on less than $1 a day.
Source: Top left panel, World Bank data; top right panel, World Bank 1998f; bottom two panels, World Bank 2000o.

What drives economic growth?

Understanding the policies and institutions that lead to sustained and sustainable economic growth is a first step in developing strategies for improving the lot of poor people. Wide divergences in growth reflect the outcome of interactions among countries' initial conditions, their institutions, their policy choices, the external shocks they receive, and no small measure of good luck.

There is evidence that growth depends on education and life expectancy, particularly at lower incomes.[5] For example, it has been shown that female literacy and girls' education are good for overall economic growth.[6] There is also some evidence that rapid population growth is negatively associated with per capita GDP growth and that the changing age structure of the population can also affect growth (box 3.1).[7]

Some economic policies—such as openness to international trade, sound monetary and fiscal policies (reflected in moderate budget deficits and the absence of high inflation), a well-developed financial system, and a moderately sized government—are also strongly conducive to economic growth.[8] Aid can boost growth if such policies are in place, but not if they are absent.[9] Both domestic and external shocks matter as well. Not surprising, wars, civil unrest, and natural disasters all lower growth rates (box 3.2). Less dramatically, so do macroeconomic volatility, adverse terms of trade shocks, and slower growth among trading partners.[10] Poorly sequenced and badly implemented reforms can lead to sudden reversals in capital flows or other macroeconomic disruptions, also slowing growth (chapter 4). These collapses in growth can be particularly devastating for poor people, who have weaker support mechanisms and generally lead a more precarious life than the better-off (chapter 9).

Box 3.1
Population, growth, and poverty

Many studies have documented that as countries become richer, both fertility and mortality decline on average, with reductions in mortality typically preceding reductions in fertility.[1] The interactions between this demographic transition and economic development are complex. They have fueled heated debate at least since 1798, when Thomas Malthus argued that since "food is necessary to the existence of man" and "the passion between the sexes is necessary and will remain nearly in its present state" (1985, p. 70), population growth would inevitably lead to an imbalance between people and available resources.

Malthus's grim prediction on the effects of population growth on economic development failed to materialize—since the turn of the 19th century the world's population has increased more than fivefold, and thanks to improvements in technology of all kinds, per capita incomes have increased by even greater multiples. The links between demographic change and development are more subtle than this. Two issues are noteworthy: the effects of changes in the age structure of the population induced by this demographic transition, and the links between investments in health and education, growth, and demographic outcomes.

First, in many countries sharp declines in fertility have been followed by sharp increases in the working-age share of the population. In some countries, notably in East Asia, the increase in the number of workers per capita was accompanied by faster growth in GDP per capita.[2] These countries' success in tapping the potential of a growing workforce was due to a variety of factors, including strong educational attainment and a supportive policy and institutional environment. In other regions of the world, notably Latin America, a similar change in the composition of the population occurred without a comparable growth benefit. This failure is disappointing since the demographic "bonus" of a larger workforce is temporary and is followed by a period of higher old age dependency rates that place greater demands on the social security institutions that provide support for the elderly.

Second, there is evidence that better education is associated with higher contraceptive use and lower fertility.[3] This evidence may reflect a variety of mechanisms. More education expands economic opportunities for women and so can raise the opportunity cost of having more children (Becker 1960). Infant mortality is often lower in families in which women are better educated, and so fewer births are required to achieve a desired number of children. And better education can improve the effectiveness of contraceptive use. Investments in improving poor people's access to education and health can therefore have a double impact. These investments have been shown to improve growth and reduce poverty directly. To the extent that they are associated with lower fertility and population growth, they can also contribute to a virtuous circle of improved maternal health and better investment in children's health and education, which reinforce these gains.

1. See Livi-Bacci (1997) for a historical survey and Birdsall (forthcoming) for a modern review of the literature on demography and economics.

2. For example, Young (1995) provides a careful assessment of the contribution of a growing labor force and greater participation rates to the rapid growth in per capita GDP observed in four Asian economies.

3. Schultz (1994) provides cross-country evidence on the links between female education and fertility. See Feyisetan and Ainsworth (1996) for microeconomic evidence on education and contraceptive use and Ainsworth, Beegle, and Nyamete (1996) on education and fertility. Pritchett and Summers (1994) provide a more cautious assessment of the magnitude of the effect of contraceptive availability on fertility.

Box 3.2
How war devastates poor people

Wars are devastating wherever they occur. Since they occur disproportionately in poor countries, the devastation falls disproportionately on the world's poor people (see figure). More wars are now civil. During 1987–97 more than 85 percent of conflicts were fought within national borders (14 were in Africa, 14 in Asia, 1 in Europe). Tragically, 90 percent of war deaths are not military (Pottebaum 1999). In Cambodia 1.7 million people died in 20 years of fighting and political mass murder—among them, most of the country's doctors, lawyers, and teachers. Civilian victims are also singled out because of their ethnic identity: as many as 800,000 Tutsis and moderate Hutus were killed by extremist Hutus in Rwanda in 1994.

Nor are children exempt, for they are often recruited to fight. Children lucky enough to survive a conflict bear deep psychological scars. They also pay a heavy price for their abandoned schooling in permanently diminished economic opportunities.

Wars cripple economies by destroying physical, human, and social capital—reducing investment, diverting public spending from productive activities, and driving highly skilled workers to emigrate. In civil war a country's per capita output falls an average of more than 2 percent a year relative to what it would have been without conflict. In more severe and protracted wars, the economic and human costs are even greater (Collier 1999b).

Conflict is overwhelmingly concentrated in poor countries

Share of incidents of civil war and strife, 1990–95
Percent

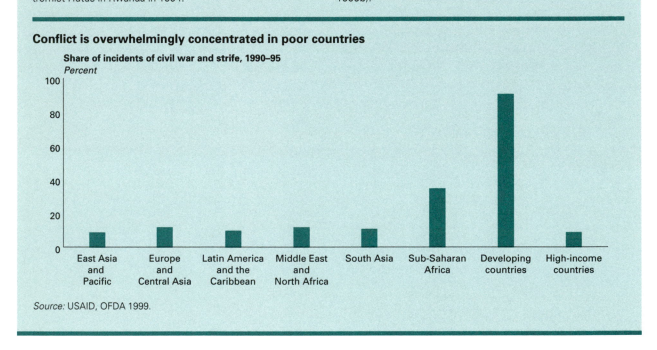

Source: USAID, OFDA 1999.

Institutional factors are also important for growth. For example, there is evidence that strong rule of law and the absence of corruption contribute to growth—by providing a fair, rule-based environment in which firms and households can invest and grow.[11] Strong institutions can also have powerful indirect benefits. For example, adjusting to adverse shocks often requires painful but necessary changes in domestic economic policies. In countries where conflicts between competing interests are pronounced, and the institutions to resolve these conflicts are weak, recovery from shocks is often slower than it is where these institutions are strong.[12]

Similarly, there is growing evidence that ethnic fragmentation has adverse effects on growth. Ethnically fragmented countries and regions within countries tend to provide fewer—and poorer quality—public goods, especially education. Such areas are also more prone to violent ethnic conflict. Institutions that guarantee minority rights and provide opportunities to resolve conflicts have been shown to offset the side effects of polarized societies (chapter 7).[13]

Other exogenous factors, such as geography and initial incomes, matter as well. There is some evidence that geographic characteristics affect growth—for example, a remote or landlocked location acts as a drag on growth.[14] On average, initially poor countries have grown more slowly than rich countries, so that the gap between rich and poor countries has widened (box 3.3). However, there is strong evidence that, controlling for some of the factors mentioned above, growth is faster in

Box 3.3
Divergence and worldwide income inequality

Given the importance of growth for poverty reduction, the failure of growth to take root in some of the poorest countries with the highest incidence of poverty is particularly disappointing. One symptom of this failure is the widening gap in average incomes between the richest and poorest countries. In 1960 per capita GDP in the richest 20 countries was 18 times that in the poorest 20 countries. By 1995 this gap had widened to 37 times, a phenomenon often referred to as *divergence* (see left-hand panel of figure).

Such figures indicate that income inequality between countries has increased sharply over the past 40 years. What has happened to worldwide inequality between individuals? Trends in worldwide inequality between individuals reflect trends in both inequality between countries and inequality between individuals within countries. The contribution of inequality between countries depends on differences in country growth performance and country size: rapid growth in a few large and initially poor countries can offset the disequalizing effect of slow growth in other poor countries. In China, for example, rapid growth from a very low base has helped a fifth of the world's population halve the gap in average per capita incomes with the world as a whole, significantly reducing worldwide inequality between individuals. In contrast, the 20 poorest countries in the world in 1960 accounted for only about 5 percent of the world's population, and so their failure to grow, while

disappointing, contributed less to worldwide inequality between individuals.

Income inequality within countries shows less pronounced trends: in some countries inequality has increased, while in others it has fallen. Recent studies have found that across countries increases and decreases in inequality are roughly equally likely (Deininger and Squire 1996b). Again, however, country size matters: changes in inequality in populous countries such as China, India, or Indonesia will contribute more to changes in worldwide inequality between individuals than will changes occurring in small countries.

Trends in worldwide income inequality between individuals reflect both these factors, with the between-country component typically more important than the within-country component. In light of the difficulties with measuring income described in chapter 1, it is not surprising that estimates of worldwide inequality between individuals are subject to substantial margins of error. But available estimates indicate that there have been some increases in worldwide inequality between individuals in past decades (see right-hand panel of figure). While the size of these increases depends on the methodology used and the period considered, the evidence suggests that the increases in worldwide inequality in recent years are small relative to the much larger increases that occurred during the 19th century.

Widening gaps between rich and poor countries account for much of the increase in worldwide income inequality across individuals over the past 40 years

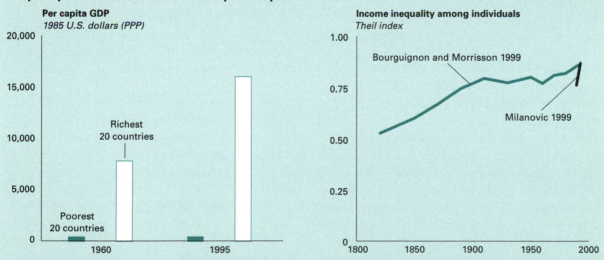

Note: The left panel refers to population-weighted averages of per capita GDP in the indicated groups, based on a sample of 123 countries with complete data on per capita GDP over the period 1960–95. China is excluded from the poorest 20 in 1960. The Theil index is a measure of income inequality; higher values indicate higher inequality.
Source: Summers and Heston 1991; World Bank data; Bourguignon and Morrisson 1999; Milanovic 1999.

countries that are initially poor. This relationship may not be linear, with higher growth kicking in only after countries reach a threshold level of income. This raises the possibility of poverty traps at very low levels of development.[15] Finally, initial inequality can influence later growth, with implications for how growth translates into poverty reduction. This important issue is discussed in the following section.

What determines the sustainability of growth? In addition to the policy, institutional, and geographic factors mentioned above, a further important consideration is whether or not growth is accompanied by environmental degradation, which can in turn undermine growth.[16] Environmental degradation can exact a heavy toll on the economy through poor health and reduced agricultural productivity. For example, heavy reliance on coal without effective controls on particulate, sulfur, and other emissions can cause high rates of lung disease, and sulfur emissions lead to acid rain, which reduces agricultural productivity.[17] In the long run especially, attending to the quality of the environment and the efficiency of resource use is likely to boost investment, accumulation, and growth. Rapid growth and environmental protection can go together—because new additions to industrial capacity can take advantage of cleaner technologies and accelerate the replacement of high-pollution technologies.[18]

Water is life, and because we have no water, life is miserable.

— *From a discussion group, Kenya*

Why are similar rates of growth associated with different rates of poverty reduction?

The general relationship between economic growth and poverty reduction is clear. But there are also significant differences across countries and over time in how much poverty reduction occurs at a given rate of economic growth. The bottom panel of figure 3.3 shows that there can be large variation in poverty reduction for the same growth rate in per capita consumption (though extreme values should be considered outliers). What explains these large differences? For a given rate of growth, the extent of poverty reduction depends on how the distribution of income changes with growth and on initial inequalities in income, assets, and access to opportunities that allow poor people to share in growth.

Changes in the distribution of income

How growth affects poverty depends on how the additional income generated by growth is distributed within a country. If economic growth is accompanied by an increase in the share of income earned by the poorest, incomes of poor people will rise faster than average incomes. Similarly, if economic growth is accompanied by a decline in this share, growth in the incomes of poor people will lag behind growth in average incomes.

The same is true for poverty rates. For a given rate of economic growth, poverty will fall faster in countries where the distribution of income becomes more equal than in countries where it becomes less equal. For example, in Uganda growth with rising equality delivered strong poverty reduction, while in Bangladesh rising inequality tempered the poverty reduction from growth (box 3.4). Another example is Morocco, where the number of poor people increased by more than 50 percent between 1990 and 1998, mainly because of declining real per capita private consumption (–1.4 percent a year). In urban areas the increase in poverty was dampened by a decline in inequality, while in rural areas rising inequality reinforced the increase in poverty.[19]

Does growth itself lead to systematic increases or decreases in income inequality? Do the policies and institutions that contribute to higher growth increase or decrease inequality? Does the regional or sectoral composition of growth affect changes in income inequality? To answer these questions the chapter first looks at the available cross-country evidence—and then turns to more detailed country-specific evidence, which highlights the fact that changes in income inequality are often driven by a complex array of opposing forces.

Many studies show that on average there is no systematic relationship across countries between growth and summary statistics of income inequality such as the Gini coefficient (figure 3.5).[20] While this average relationship is of interest, so are the substantial deviations around it.

The differences in inequality at a given rate of growth could reflect the fact that the combination of policies and institutions that led to this growth differed across countries—and that these differences in policies matter for income distribution. But at the aggregate cross-country level, there is not much evidence that this is the case. A recent study of growth and poverty reduction in a sample of 80 industrial and developing countries found that macroeconomic policies such as a stable monetary

Box 3.4
Inequality trends and poverty reduction

In Uganda growth with rising equality delivered strong poverty reduction . . .

After decades of war and economic collapse, growth recovered in Uganda in the 1990s, averaging more than 5 percent a year. In just six years (1992–98) the share of Ugandans in poverty fell from 56 percent to 44 percent. The benefits of growth were shared by all income groups, by rural and urban households, and by nearly all economic sectors. Real per capita consumption rose for all deciles of the population, implying a reduction in poverty regardless of the poverty line.

Modest reductions in income inequality made growth especially effective in reducing poverty, with the Gini coefficient falling from 0.36 to 0.34 during the five years. Living standards improved more among poorer households. Consumption (per adult equivalent) rose 27 percent for the poorest decile, compared with 15 percent for households in the richest decile. Among cash crop producers—especially coffee farmers, initially as poor as the average Ugandan—poverty fell more than twice as fast as for the country as a whole.

. . . while in Bangladesh rising inequality tempered the poverty reduction from growth

In Bangladesh per capita GDP grew at about 2 percent a year during the 1990s, and poverty declined quite slowly. Between 1983 and 1996 the share of people in extreme poverty fell from 40.9 percent to 35.6 percent—and the share in moderate poverty from 58.5 percent to 53.1 percent. Rural poverty in particular remains very high.

Why the slow decline? Part of the answer lies in rising inequality, in both urban and rural sectors, especially between 1992 and 1996, when the Gini coefficient rose from 0.26 to 0.31. Depending on the poverty measure used, a fifth to a third of the potential poverty reduction from growth may have been lost because of higher inequality. If inequality had not increased, the poverty rate would have been about 7–10 percentage points lower in 1995–96 than it actually was.

The higher inequality in Bangladesh does not imply that growth should not be pursued. To the contrary, faster growth is needed to reduce poverty faster, because growth's net effect on poverty reduction is positive. Also required are efforts to limit rising inequality and to ensure that growth reaches rural areas, where many of the country's poor people live.

Source: Appleton and others 1999; Wodon 1997, 1999, 2000c.

Figure 3.5
Inequality varied widely in the 1980s and 1990s but showed no systematic association with growth

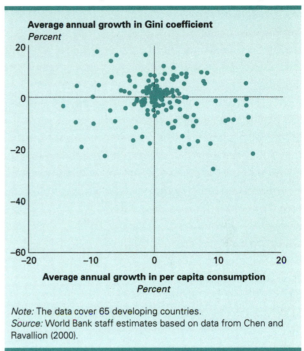

Note: The data cover 65 developing countries.
Source: World Bank staff estimates based on data from Chen and Ravallion (2000).

vors growth and may lower income inequality by improving access to credit.[22]

When I retired, I had 20,000 rubles in my savings account. . . . But what the government did with it—the government we trusted with our money! They re-indexed savings so that inflation ate it! That money is now not enough for bread and water.

—*From a discussion group, Ukraine*

Another possible explanation for the lack of association between growth and inequality is that countries with similar overall growth rates could experience very different changes in income distribution because of differences in the regional and sectoral composition of growth. If growth bypasses poor regions and poor people cannot easily migrate to regions where opportunities are expanding, growth can lead to rising inequality. If growth is concentrated in sectors from which poor people are more likely to derive their income, such as agriculture, growth can be associated with declining income inequality.

In China much of the sharp increase in income inequality between the mid-1980s and mid-1990s reflects the much swifter growth in urban areas relative to rural

policy, openness to international trade, and a moderate-size government raise the incomes of poor people as much as average incomes.[21] In other words, these policies did not systematically affect income distribution.

Other policies, such as stabilization from high inflation, may even disproportionately favor poor people (chapter 9). And greater financial development fa-

areas.[23] India's states tell a similar story of the importance of rural growth in poverty reduction (box 3.5). So does Indonesia.[24] A study of 38 developing countries found that the variation in inequality reflects the abundance of arable land, the prevalence of smallholder farming, and the productivity of agriculture.[25] These findings underscore the importance of removing policy biases against agriculture for generating more equitable growth (chapter 4).

Cross-country evidence can take us only so far in understanding the factors underlying changes in the distribution of income that make growth more or less pro-poor. Careful country-specific analyses paint a more nuanced picture, highlighting a complex set of reinforcing and countervailing forces. These include changes in the distribution of education, changes in the returns to education, labor market choices, and demographic changes (box 3.6). Those changes are the result of:

- Market forces, such as changes in the demand for labor.
- Policies, such as public investment in education.
- Social forces, such as higher participation of women in the labor force or changes in practices discriminating against women and ethnic minorities.
- Institutional forces, such as changes in legal restrictions on the ownership of property by women or ethnic groups.

Not every increase in income inequality should be seen as a negative outcome. As economies develop, income inequality can rise because the labor force shifts from agriculture to more productive activities. For example, if wages are lower in agriculture than in industry and services and the labor force shifts toward those two sectors, many summary statistics, especially those sensitive to changes at the bottom end of the income distribution, will show increases in inequality despite an overall decline in poverty. These trends should not be seen as negative if:

- The incomes at the bottom rise or at least do not fall.
- The development process expands opportunities for all.

Box 3.5
What makes growth pro-poor in India?

Consistent with cross-country evidence for developing countries, consumption poverty in India has fallen with the growth in mean household consumption. Moreover, the regional and sectoral composition of growth affects the national rate of poverty reduction, with far stronger responses to rural economic growth than to urban. And within rural areas growth in agriculture and services has been particularly effective in poverty reduction, while industrial growth has not.

In rural India higher agricultural productivity is crucial for pro-poor economic growth. Data spanning 1958–94 show that higher real wages and higher farm yields raised average living standards and did not affect income distribution. The result: less absolute poverty.

The effectiveness of nonfarm growth in reducing poverty has varied widely across states, reflecting systematic differences in initial conditions. In states with low farm productivity, low rural living standards relative to urban areas, and poor basic education, poor people were less able to participate in the growth of the nonfarm sector. The role of initial literacy is notable: more than half the difference between the elasticity of poverty to nonfarm output for Bihar (the state with the lowest elasticity in India) and that for Kerala (the highest) is attributable to Kerala's substantially higher initial literacy rate. Women's literacy is a slightly more significant predictor of growth's contribution to poverty reduction than men's literacy.

For poor people to participate fully in India's economic growth, agriculture, infrastructure, and social spending (especially in lagging rural areas) need to be higher priorities.

Source: Ravallion and Datt 1996, 1999.

Figure 3.6
Initial inequalities influence the pace of poverty reduction

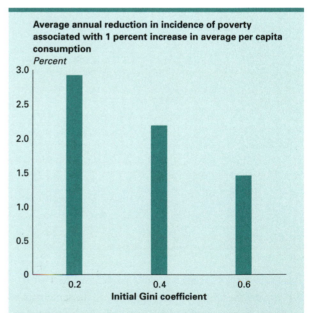

Note: The data cover 65 developing countries in the 1980s and 1990s. The incidence of poverty is the share of the population living on less than $1 a day.
Source: World Bank staff estimates based on the methodology of Ravallion (1997a) and data from Chen and Ravallion (2000).

Box 3.6
Complex patterns of distributional change in three economies

Observed changes in the distribution of income reflect a complex array of factors—among them, changes in the distribution of assets, changes in the returns to these assets, labor market choices, and demographics. Brazil, Mexico, and Taiwan, China, show how these forces can reinforce and offset one another to result in inequality that is respectively lowered, increased, and unchanged .

Brazil—inequality lowered

Income inequality declined in Brazil between 1976 and 1996, with the Gini coefficient falling from 0.62 to 0.59. During the same period the returns to education became more unequal: both wage earners and self-employed workers with more education saw larger increases in earnings than their less-educated counterparts, even after controlling for age and gender. There were no changes in the returns to experience and only small declines in the pay gap between men and women, so overall earnings inequality increased. This disequalizing effect was more than offset by three factors:

■ The distribution of education became more equal.

■ Average educational attainment rose from 3.8 to 5.9 years of schooling, and higher levels of schooling (particularly for women) contributed to a noticeable reduction in family size, with the average household falling from 4.3 to 3.5 members. Since family size fell more for poorer households, inequality fell.

■ Inequality in the returns to characteristics other than education seems to have fallen, suggesting a reduction in labor market segmentation during 1976–96 and a possible decline in regional inequalities.

Mexico—inequality increased

Mexico's Gini coefficient rose sharply between 1984 and 1994, from 0.49 to 0.55. As in the previous two examples, changes in the returns to education were a strongly disequalizing force. But

changes in the distribution of education did not offset this. While educational attainment rose faster for the less educated, the returns to higher education were sufficiently high that the additional earnings due to greater education disproportionately favored the more educated. Superimposed on this were important regional effects, with widening rural-urban real wage differences contributing substantially to inequality, despite some convergence of urban and rural returns to education and experience.

Taiwan, China—inequality unchanged

Noted for its low and stable level of inequality, Taiwan, China, has had a Gini coefficient of about 0.30 for the past 30 years. As in Brazil, this outcome reflects a variety of opposing forces. Despite a rapid increase in their supply, more-educated workers saw larger increases in earnings than less-educated workers. This was more than offset by greater equality in the distribution of education and greater labor market participation by women. The pattern of taxes and transfers was also equalizing, with the effect that the distribution of individual income became more equal. Interestingly, however, income inequality at the household level increased, as many of the new female entrants to the labor force came from initially better-off households.

• • •

These examples show that simple trends in summary measures of income inequality can disguise major structural forces. Some of them, such as changes in the distribution of education, can be influenced by policy—though this takes time. Others, such as changes in the returns to education, reflect primarily market forces and are less amenable to direct policy interventions. And as Taiwan, China, shows, tax and transfer policies can counter increases in primary income inequality.

Source: For Brazil, Ferreira and Paes de Barros (1999b); for Mexico, Legovini, Bouillon, and Lustig (1999); and for Taiwan, China, Bourguignon, Fournier, and Gurgand (1998).

■ The observed trends are not the result of dysfunctional forces such as discrimination.

■ The number of poor people falls.

Initial inequality and poverty reduction

Even when the distribution of income itself does not change with growth, countries with similar rates of growth can have very different poverty outcomes, depending on their initial inequality. Other things being the same, growth leads to less poverty reduction in unequal societies than in egalitarian ones. If poor people get a small share of existing income and if inequality is unchanged, they will also get a small share of the new income generated by growth, muting the effects of growth on poverty. Evidence confirms

this: when initial inequality is low, growth reduces poverty nearly twice as much as when inequality is high (figure 3.6).

Initial inequality in income is not the whole story—for inequality in other dimensions matters too. The sensitivity of poverty to growth depends a great deal on initial inequality in poor people's access to opportunities to share in this growth. If disparities in educational attainment mirror disparities in income, poor people may not have the skills to find employment in dynamic and growing sectors of the economy. This effect is compounded by gender inequality in access to education (chapter 7). In addition, if fixed costs or overt policy barriers hinder movement from remote, rural, and economically depressed regions to more vibrant urban centers, poor people will be less likely to take advantage of opportunities to migrate (box 3.7).

They have always excluded us Mayas, they have discriminated against us. They cut down the tree, but forgot to pull down the roots. That tree is now sprouting.
—*From a discussion group, Guatemala*

If social inequities—such as caste systems or discrimination against indigenous peoples—confine members of disadvantaged groups to employment in stagnant sectors, poor people will benefit less from growth (chapter 7). Or if ethnic discrimination in the marketplace leads to different returns to the same level of education, growth will be less effective in reducing poverty for the group discriminated against. A study in Latin America found that in several countries differences in earnings between indigenous and nonindigenous people cannot be explained by differences in skills or experience, suggesting that discrimination in the labor market may be to blame.[26] These results bring to the fore the importance of eliminating social barriers for women, ethnic minorities, and socially disadvantaged groups in making growth broad based.

Initial inequality and growth

High initial inequality reduces the poverty impact of a given rate of economic growth. It can also undermine poverty reduction by lowering overall economic growth. Early thinking on the effects of inequality on growth suggested that greater inequality might be good for growth—for example, by redistributing income to the rich, who save, from the poor, who do not. This view implied a tradeoff—more growth could be bought for the price of more inequality, with ambiguous effects on poor people.

More recent thinking—and empirical evidence—weaken the case for such a tradeoff: lower inequality can increase efficiency and economic growth through a variety of channels. Unequal societies are more prone to difficulties in collective action, possibly reflected in dysfunctional institutions, political instability, a propensity for populist redistributive policies, or greater volatility in policies—all of which can lower growth. And to the extent that inequality in income or assets coexists with imperfect credit markets, poor people may be unable to invest in their human and physical capital, with adverse consequences for long-run growth.

The effects of inequality on growth have been subjected to considerable empirical scrutiny. Evidence on

Box 3.7
Diversification and migration in rural China

For rural agricultural households in China, opportunities for off-farm employment have been an important source of growth in incomes. These opportunities can be equalizing or disequalizing. To the extent that diversification into nonfarm employment reflects a pull factor—higher returns off the farm—diversification can be disequalizing as richer and better-educated workers take advantage of these opportunities. To the extent that diversification reflects a survival mechanism for the poorest, it can be equalizing.

Evidence from four provinces in China suggests that the pull factor has been more important than the survival mechanism, with access to nonfarm employment accounting for a rising share of income inequality in rural areas between 1985 and 1990. Evidence also suggests that even the modest gap (by international standards) between female and male educational attainment exacerbates these trends, with less-educated women less likely to find off-farm employment. In contrast, migration has had equalizing effects on income. Survey data from the four provinces show that private transfers (largely reflecting migrants' remittances) have been an equalizing force.

Source: World Bank 1997b.

the impact of inequality in assets—and gender inequality—is generally clearest. A recent study of sugar cooperatives in India found that those that are most unequal (in land ownership among cooperative members) are the least productive.[27] Various studies have also found an adverse effect of land inequality on growth.[28] A study in China found that living in a high-inequality area reduced growth rates at the farm household level, controlling for a household's human and physical capital.[29] Other studies have found evidence of a link between education and gender inequality and growth.[30] In contrast, evidence on the effect of initial income inequality on subsequent growth is more mixed. Some studies have found negative effects.[31] Others have found positive effects.[32] Still others have found different effects over different ranges.[33]

These results open the possibility that policies to improve the distribution of income and assets can have a double benefit—by increasing growth and by increasing the share of growth that accrues to poor people. This is not to say that every pro-equity policy will have such desired effects. If the reduction in inequality comes at the expense of the other factors conducive to growth (discussed in the early part of this chapter), the gains from redistribution can vanish. Ex-

Box 3.8
Redistribution can be good for efficiency

Redistribution need not compromise efficiency and growth. In several instances redistributive policies can increase asset accumulation by poor people—while improving efficiency and growth. A few recent studies illustrate the possibilities for win-win outcomes, further strengthening the case for redistribution.

Land reform is a classic example of a redistributive policy. Operation Barga, a tenancy reform in the Indian state of West Bengal in the late 1970s and early 1980s, is one of the few examples of large-scale transfers of property rights not accompanied by major social upheaval. The operation was associated with an 18 percent increase in agricultural output in the state (Banerjee, Gertler, and Ghatak 1998).

Redistribution can also be a source of efficiency gains if transfers to poor people improve their human capital. Public provision of infrastructure targeted to poor people is an important example. Massive primary school construction (61,000 new schools built and staffed in five years) under Indonesia's INPRES (presidential instructions) program, the main mechanism for redistributing the gain from the oil boom in Indonesia, substantially increased education and income. The primary school graduation rate rose 12 percent, and male wages 5 percent (Duflo 2000b).

Universal policies (such as pricing of government services) can have redistributive and efficiency effects as well. Abolishing secondary school fees in Taiwan, China, in 1968 and introducing compulsory education benefited poorer children more than richer children (Spohr 2000). It also substantially increased school attainment (0.4 year for males) and labor force participation, translating into higher earnings (Clark and Hsieh 1999).

Direct income redistribution (through cash transfers) is rare in developing countries. A concern is that cash may not be spent in the most efficiency-enhancing ways. In South Africa at the end of apartheid, the small pension program was dramatically expanded for the black population. In 1993 the pension amounted to twice the median income for blacks in rural areas (Case and Deaton 1998). When the pension was received by the maternal grandmothers of girls, it had large effects on nutrition—halving the gap in height between these girls and those of the same age in the United States (Duflo 2000a). Other studies have shown, however, that the pension, when received by an elderly woman, also led to a reduction in prime-age male labor supply (Bertrand, Miller, and Mullainathan 1999). The results suggest that cash transfers can—but may not—lead to efficiency gains.

---

propriation of assets on a grand scale can lead to political upheaval and violent conflict, undermining growth. And sometimes attempts to redistribute income can reduce incentives to save, invest, and work. But there are a number of win-win possibilities (box 3.8). Policies should focus on building up the human capital and physical assets of poor people by judiciously using the redistributive power of government spending and, for example, market-based and other forms of land reforms (chapter 5; box 5.12).

Economic growth and nonincome poverty

Just as income poverty declines as average incomes increase, so does nonincome poverty, such as in health and education. Just as with income poverty, there are significant deviations around these general relationships: countries and regions with similar per capita incomes can have quite different outcomes in nonincome poverty as well. And just as with income poverty, these deviations reflect a wide array of forces—including initial inequality, the effectiveness of public interventions, and the level of development. Conversely, there is strong evidence that better health and education outcomes contribute to faster economic growth.

Across countries, and across individuals within countries, there are strong correlations between health and education outcomes and incomes. Richer countries and richer individuals within countries have lower rates of mortality and malnutrition.[34] Within and between countries both the quantity and the quality of education improve with income—although quality is difficult to measure.[35] Disparities in educational attainment also decline with income.

These strong correlations reflect reinforcing causal effects from higher income to better health and education outcomes—and from better health and education to higher income. For individuals, this is not surprising. Ill health and malnutrition reduce productivity and time spent working, effects that vary with the level of education. For example, a study of Brazilian men showed that adult height was strongly associated with wages—and that wages increased faster with height among individuals with some (as opposed to no) education.[36] Conversely, individuals with higher incomes can better afford to invest in health and education.[37] Many studies document the positive effects of parental education on children's health and education.

Similar patterns hold for countries, with positive effects of higher per capita income on infant mortality.[38]

Other studies have documented the benefits of lower mortality for faster growth, with most of the growth payoff at low levels of income.[39] And we have already seen the evidence that better education outcomes lead to faster growth.

Moreover, there is some evidence that these relationships are not linear, with stronger increases in health associated with growth in poorer countries and regions. Fairly small differences in economic growth rates can thus have large impacts on human development outcomes in such countries. One study estimated that had growth rates in the developing world (excluding China and India) been as high in the 1980s as they were in the 1960s and 1970s, 656,000 deaths could have been averted during the 1980s among children under five.[40]

These reinforcing effects from human development to economic development and back suggest the possibility of vicious and virtuous circles. Poor countries and poor people can be locked in a vicious circle, as low human development diminishes economic opportunities, making it more difficult to invest in health and education. In contrast, well-targeted public interventions in health and education can contribute to a virtuous circle of greater economic opportunities generating resources for further investments (chapter 5).

The considerable variations in country experience around these general relationships again reflect a combination of factors. One is inequality in income.[41] We have seen that the effects of income on health are most pronounced at low levels of income. This implies that the same rate of economic growth can have very different health and education outcomes, depending on the initial distribution of income and on how that distribution changes with growth. In particular, growth accompanied by a reduction in inequality is more likely to lead to better health outcomes.

Research has found evidence that the correlation across countries between average health indicators and average income vanishes after controlling for differences in the incidence of income poverty and in public spending.[42] The same research has found that cross-country differences in public health spending matter more to the health of the income-poor than to others: the nonpoor are better able to protect their health from lower public spending. These results suggest that growth improves average health attainments through its ability to reduce income poverty and permit more pro-poor social spending.

Figure 3.7

Across countries, the ratio of female to male literacy rises with per capita income

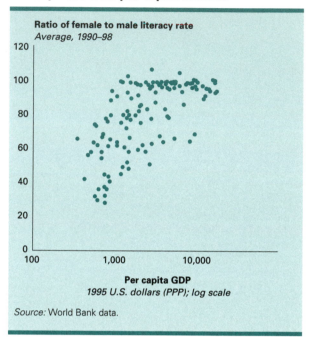

Source: World Bank data.

Nonincome inequalities matter as well. Discrimination by gender and ethnicity—in the allocation of public spending for education and health or in the operation of education and health facilities—can lead to differences in education and health achievements. Gender disparities in educational attainment are especially pronounced in poor countries (figure 3.7). In the Indian state of Kerala—which has a long history of equitable gender relations—education and mortality differ little between men and women. But in such states as Uttar Pradesh—where gender discrimination is high—the female literacy rate is less than half the male rate and the female to male ratio in the population is a disturbing 87.9 to 100.[43] Cross-country studies have also identified geographic factors, ethnic fragmentation, and especially female educational attainment as important in explaining differences in health outcomes at a given income.[44] Finally, the quality and quantity of public spending matter as well, though the size of the impact on poor people depends greatly on supportive policies and institutions (chapter 5).

• • •

This chapter has shown the importance of growth for poverty reduction, particularly for income and human development. It has also shown how low and declining inequality enhances the impact of growth on poverty. Growth can be made more equitable by reducing inequality in access to assets and opportunities. This requires opening market opportunities to poor people and building up their assets. It also requires making state institutions work better for poor people, removing social barriers, and supporting poor people's organizations. These issues are taken up in subsequent chapters.

CHAPTER 4

Making Markets Work Better for Poor People

Markets matter for the poor because poor people rely on formal and informal markets to sell their labor and products, to finance investment, and to insure against risks. Well-functioning markets are important in generating growth and expanding opportunities for poor people. That is why market-friendly reforms have been promoted by international donors and by developing country governments, especially those democratically elected.[1]

But to develop markets and the institutions that support them is difficult and takes time. At times, reforms to build markets fail entirely. When they succeed, they frequently impose costs on specific groups in society. When the losers from reforms include poor people, who are particularly vulnerable to shocks, countries have a special obligation to ease the burden of reform. And even when markets work, societies have to help poor people overcome the obstacles that prevent them from freely and fairly participating in markets.

In the 1950s and 1960s many of those shaping policy believed that economic development and poverty reduction required active participation of the state and protection of local industry. This inward-looking, state-led development path was adopted by a wide array of countries throughout the world, with varying degrees of success. Many countries adopted protectionism, government control of investment, and state monopolies in key sectors. In countries such as India this strategy resulted in persistently slow growth. In other countries, particularly in Latin America, this strategy initially delivered strong growth through the 1960s, but growth eventually faltered as countries were buffeted by oil shocks in the 1970s and the debt crisis of the 1980s. And in China in the late 1970s there was a gradual realization that the economy, especially the agricultural sector, had not realized its full potential under heavy state control.

The increasing disenchantment with inward-looking, state-led development led national governments to implement reforms that replaced state intervention in markets with private incentives, public ownership with private ownership, and protection of domestic industries with competition from foreign producers and investors.[2] Where such market-friendly reforms have been successfully implemented, on average economic stagnation has ended and growth has resumed.

But in some cases reforms were not successfully implemented, often with particularly severe consequences for poor people. The broad diversity of failed reforms does not lend itself to easy generalization.[3] Some reforms proceeded too quickly and failed for want of supporting institutions. Others proceeded too slowly and were captured and undermined by special interests. Yet others were imposed by government elites and foreign donors and foundered for lack of strong domestic leadership and a broad-based commitment to reform.[4]

The debate about reforms is therefore not over a choice between reforms or no reforms: the absence of reforms to develop vibrant, competitive markets and create strong institutions condemns countries to continued stagnation and decline. Nor is the debate over a simplistic dichotomy between gradualism and shock therapy: reforms can proceed either too quickly or too slowly to succeed. Rather, the debate is on how reforms to build markets can be designed and implemented in a way that is measured and tailored to the economic, social, and political circumstances of a country.[5]

Inevitably, market-oriented reforms have different effects on different segments of society. Every reform program has its winners and losers, and poor people may be found in either group. The particular vulnerability of poor people demands a careful assessment of the likely poverty impact and the implementation of appropriate compensating policies.[6] It also calls for careful consideration of the pace of reforms in the light of the likely effects on poor people. Experience shows that direct dialogue with poor people can be particularly effective in informing this process.

Even when markets function, they do not always serve poor people as well as they could. Physical access to markets can be difficult for poor people living in remote areas. Regulatory barriers often stifle economic activity in sectors and regions where poor people are likely to seek jobs. And access to some markets, especially for financial services, can be difficult for poor people since they often engage in small transactions, which traditional market participants find unprofitable or insignificant. Investments in infrastructure, lighter regulatory burdens, and innovative approaches to improving access to financial markets can therefore do much to ensure that the benefits of markets are shared by poor people.

This chapter addresses these issues in turn. It first considers the widely varying experience of countries that implemented market-oriented reforms over the past 20 years, highlighting both success stories and the severe consequences of failed reforms. It then illustrates the complex effects that market reforms have on poor people, with examples from three areas: agriculture, fiscal policy, and trade. Last, it discusses how lightening the regulatory burden, promoting core labor standards, and expanding microfinance can be beneficial in improving the terms on which poor people participate in markets.

Have market reforms delivered growth?

In the 1980s and 1990s much of the developing world moved toward implementing market-friendly reforms. The motivation for reforms and their scope and pace varied widely. In China, for example, the "household responsibility system" replaced communal farming and created new incentives for rural households to produce, invest, and innovate. These reforms were provoked neither by macroeconomic crisis nor by ideological epiphany; rather, they reflected a growing realization that China's agricultural potential was not being fulfilled. These initial agricultural reforms were followed by the introduction of market mechanisms throughout the economy. In other countries macroeconomic crises provided the catalyst for reform: in Mexico, for example, the debt crisis of the 1980s was followed by the introduction of wide-ranging economic reforms. And in the countries of Eastern Europe and the former Soviet Union the political transition precipitated a dramatic progress toward markets that succeeded as spectacularly in some countries as it failed in others.[7]

As a result of this move toward reforms the economic landscape in many developing countries—but not all—has been significantly altered. Government involvement in economic activity has been scaled back. Domestic markets are more open to international trade and capital flows. Revised tax codes are in place. And generally markets, not governments, determine prices, output, and the allocation of resources. Many—but not all—of these reforms reflected the principles of the so-called Washington consensus, which laid out 10 policy priorities that were adopted in different combinations by many countries (box 4.1).

Given the wide diversity of reforms implemented by different countries at different times and under different

Box 4.1
The Washington consensus

The Washington consensus of market-friendly reforms refers to the following 10 objectives of policy:
- Fiscal discipline.
- Redirection of public expenditure toward education, health, and infrastructure investment.
- Tax reform—broadening the tax base and cutting marginal tax rates.
- Interest rates that are market determined and positive (but moderate) in real terms.
- Competitive exchange rates.
- Trade liberalization—replacement of quantitative restrictions with low and uniform tariffs.
- Openness to foreign direct investment.
- Privatization of state enterprises.
- Deregulation—abolishment of regulations that impede entry or restrict competition, except for those justified on safety, environmental, and consumer protection grounds, and prudential oversight of financial institutions.
- Legal security for property rights.

Source: Williamson 1993.

Figure 4.1
Indications of successful policy reforms in the developing world

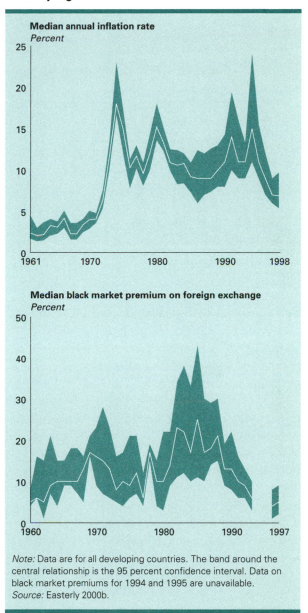

Note: Data are for all developing countries. The band around the central relationship is the 95 percent confidence interval. Data on black market premiums for 1994 and 1995 are unavailable.
Source: Easterly 2000b.

circumstances, summarizing overall progress is difficult. Nevertheless, encouraging indicators are clear (figure 4.1). For example, typical inflation rates in developing countries fell from around 15 percent in the early 1980s to 7 percent in 1997, indicating a broad trend toward more disciplined monetary policy. More important, many countries have escaped the scourge of chronic bouts of high inflation and hyperinflation. The black market premium on foreign exchange—a sure indicator of unrealistic and nonmarket exchange rates—fell from 25 percent for a typical developing country in the mid-1980s to only 5 percent in the late 1990s.

Reducing barriers to international trade and capital movements has been a central part of many reform programs. In Latin America average tariffs were reduced from 50 percent in 1985 to 10 percent in 1996, and maximum tariffs fell from an average of 84 percent to just 41 percent.[8] By 1996 nontariff barriers affected only 6 percent of imports, down from 38 percent before reform.[9] Reforms have also been widespread in other areas, such as liberalizing investment regulations, reducing or eliminating a large assortment of subsidies to bring down fiscal deficits, and privatizing many state enterprises. Only in labor markets have reforms generally been slow.[10]

Have these reforms delivered the expected growth payoff? A large empirical literature has documented that,

on average, countries with market-friendly policies such as openness to international trade, disciplined monetary and fiscal policy, and well-developed financial markets enjoy better long-run growth performance than countries where such policies are absent (chapter 3).

There is also evidence that reforms that move countries closer to such market-friendly policies also contribute to better growth performance in the medium term. Cross-country studies of the impact of reforms typically either

Figure 4.2
Reforms delivered growth in Latin America, although the gains varied

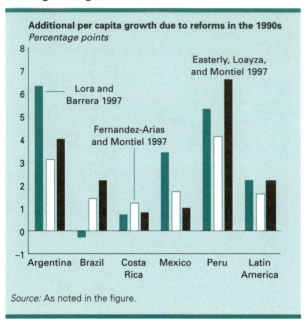

Additional per capita growth due to reforms in the 1990s
Percentage points

Source: As noted in the figure.

compare the performance of countries before and after reforms or else examine whether changes in measures of reforms explain changes in growth rates. Reforms are measured indirectly as changes in such variables as trade volumes, tariff rates, inflation rates, or budget deficits. Such studies often find a strong growth payoff from reforms. Figure 4.2 summarizes the results of three such studies for Latin America, which found a significant growth impact of reforms. Similar studies of the transition economies of Eastern Europe and the former Soviet Union, where success in implementing market reforms has varied widely, found that countries that implemented reforms forcefully and early (and enjoyed favorable initial conditions) achieved stronger growth than reform laggards.[11] A 1999 study of India finds that the states that implemented reforms saw faster growth and stronger improvements in education and primary health care than those that did not.[12]

This does not mean that the developing world as a whole enjoyed rapid growth as a result of reforms in the 1980s and 1990s. Indeed, growth in the developing world has been disappointing, with the typical country registering negligible growth.

A recent study argues that this disappointing growth should not be attributed to the failure of reforms.[13] Despite slow overall growth, the study found that differences in indicators of market-friendly policies continued to

predict cross-country differences in economic performance. But many developing countries were buffeted by large external shocks. World interest rates rose sharply, increasing the burden of debt service obligations. Growth in the industrial countries slowed, lowering growth in their developing country trading partners. In some cases these shocks eroded the benefits of reforms that were being implemented concurrently.

At times, however, reform programs have failed to deliver as much as expected—and at times reforms have failed entirely. Consider what went wrong in East Asia, countries of the former Soviet Union, and Africa (box 4.2). The grim lessons of these failures, and the heavy burdens they placed on poor people, underline the importance of a measured and realistic approach to reforms to ensure that their objectives are attained.[14]

A note of caution on the future of reforms. In many cases the reforms discussed above are straightforward "first-generation" reforms, such as stabilizing from high inflation, moderating chronic budget deficits, and dismantling the most egregious trade barriers. Consolidating the gains from these reforms often requires institution building in much more difficult areas, such as developing an independent judiciary, creating independent and effective regulatory agencies, and instilling professionalism in the public sector. Such "second-generation" reforms are not only much more complex and take much more time—they are also often likely to be opposed by powerful and entrenched interests.[15] This is not to say that such second-generation reforms should be postponed— precisely because they take time to bear fruit, it is important to embark on them as promptly as possible.

In sum, market-oriented reforms have been widespread though uneven throughout the developing world. On average they have delivered lower inflation and higher growth, both powerful forces for reducing income poverty. But reforms can also go awry, with painful consequences for poor people. Lack of supporting institutions, mistakes in sequencing reforms, and the capture of the reform process by powerful individuals or groups lie at the bottom of most failed reforms.

Have market reforms delivered benefits to poor people?

Even when market-friendly reforms have succeeded in delivering growth, the effects on the incomes of poor people have varied. This reflects both initial inequalities in

Box 4.2
Why do reforms sometimes fail?

Reforms can go awry when supportive institutions are absent or powerful individuals or groups manipulate the results.

Incomplete financial sector reforms contributed to the East Asian crisis

During the 1990s several emerging economies in East Asia liberalized their domestic financial markets and lifted capital account restrictions. In the Republic of Korea and Thailand especially, a surge of capital inflows, often through newly formed nonbank financial institutions, placed heavy financial stresses on banks. Prudential regulation of banks and nonbank financial institutions did not keep pace with these developments, and there was rapid growth in often-unhedged short-term foreign currency liabilities. Sudden exchange rate fluctuations in the summer of 1997 wreaked havoc on these foreign currency exposures, contributing to the depth of the ensuing crisis (World Bank 1998f).

This experience matches a broader pattern emerging from cross-country analysis: financial reforms unaccompanied by adequate supervisory institutions are a significant determinant of banking crises worldwide (Demirgüç-Kunt and Detragiache 1998). At the root of the 1995 Mexican peso crisis were inadequacies in the bank privatization process and in financial liberalization (Lustig 1998). These experiences do not invalidate the importance of reforms in developing financial markets. In fact, the effective intermediation of savings to productive investment was a contributing factor in East Asia's remarkable development success, a success that dwarfs the setbacks of the recent crisis. But incautious and excessively rapid reforms can culminate in crises.

Grand corruption subverted reforms in countries of the former Soviet Union

The state steals from us all the time, so deceiving the state is not a sin.
—*From a discussion group, Ukraine*

What kind of government do we have? One hand gives and the other takes away!
—*From a discussion group, Ukraine*

In the countries of the former Soviet Union market reforms and perceptions of corruption are inextricably intertwined (see, for example, Narayan, Patel, Schafft, Rademacher, and Koch-Schulte 2000). This is understandable: most of these countries score very poorly in cross-country comparisons of corruption, and encounters with corruption are dispiritingly frequent for many firms and individuals. Corruption has coincided with worse macroeconomic performance and deeper output declines as these countries have wrestled with the transition to a market economy.

A particularly pernicious form of corruption is "state capture," referring to the ability of firms and powerful individuals to influence the formation of new laws and regulations to their own advantage. This may involve manipulating the judicial, executive, and legislative branches of government to obtain special privileges and mo-nopoly rights and to bias the awarding and pricing of public contracts. State capture runs counter to the premises of a free and fair competitive market economy—and contributes to increasing inequality. State capture is also widespread. In several countries of the former Soviet Union more than 30 percent of firms surveyed in a business environment survey reported that they had suffered as a result of successful state capture by their competitors (Hellman and others 2000).

Market economies cannot function well where the institutional and incentive environment permits such corruption to flourish. Worse, countries may fall into vicious circles, with incomplete reforms creating new incentives for corruption. Fighting the corrosive effects of state capture requires much deeper institutional development—in the organization of the political system, the checks and balances among core state institutions, and the relationships between state and firms and between state and civil society.

Inadequate public investment and excessive bureaucracy have undermined market reforms in Sub-Saharan Africa

Several African countries have failed to grow since the mid-1980s, when, with the support of international financial institutions, they began implementing market reforms, especially in agriculture. The results have been less than spectacular, in part due to inadequate public investment and persistent red tape (World Bank 2000b).

African farmers, like those in other parts of the world, respond vigorously to price and nonprice incentives. But if public infrastructure—such as roads to remote agricultural areas—is undeveloped or underdeveloped, the impact of pricing and marketing reforms on output is muted. Inadequate infrastructure affects other sectors as well. Business surveys carried out in a number of African countries in 1996–97 consistently point to the poor quality of infrastructure services as a critical barrier to expansion into labor-intensive exports in response to trade reform. In Uganda transport and other costs increased the cost of capital goods by almost half. And in Zimbabwe poor transport services mean that delivery of inputs is unreliable, forcing firms to hold large inventories despite high interest rates.

These difficulties have been compounded by a lack of improvement in transparency and accountability. Although legal and regulatory changes are often integral parts of reform packages, their implementation is often flawed or half-hearted. As a result, regulatory barriers to competition remain serious obstacles, and corruption, red tape, and lack of transparency continue to impede trade and investment by raising costs. Business surveys often also identify corruption and bureaucratic red tape as barriers to business expansion and diversification in several African countries. For example, it can take more than a week for intermediate inputs to clear customs on the Ugandan border, and delays of more than a day are routine at customs checkpoints in southern Africa. These obstacles are symptomatic of larger institutional failures that policymakers must address if reforms are to be effective.

income and opportunity, and the effects of reforms on growth and inequality. What has actually happened? And what can be learned from this experience with market-friendly reform?

Cross-country evidence suggests that macroeconomic reforms on average have had little effect on income distribution. For example, recent studies have examined the impact of market-friendly policies—such as openness to international trade, low inflation, a moderate-size government, and strong rule of law—on the incomes of poor people in a large cross-country sample. The findings: these policies on average benefit poor people as much as anyone else.[16] Some policies, notably stabilization from high inflation, may even benefit poor people more than others. This outcome is consistent with survey evidence showing that poor people are more likely to single out high inflation as a pressing concern.

Where reforms have adverse distributional effects, these are generally small compared with the growth benefits that reforms deliver, especially over periods of several years or more.[17] So the macroeconomic evidence does not suggest that the benefits of reform have bypassed poor people—nor even that the benefits only gradually "trickle down" to them. Instead, it suggests a pattern in which all income groups on average benefit equally from reforms. Even among the countries of the former socialist bloc, where reforms have often gone awry, inequality increased least in countries that successfully implemented reforms. It increased most in countries that introduced reforms only partially or not at all.[18]

This kind of cross-country evidence provides only a partial picture of the effects of reforms on poor people. The same reforms may have very different effects in different countries, and so such average results provide only a rough guide to the likely future impact of reforms in a particular country. Furthermore, even when reforms on average have no effect on aggregate income inequality, there will still be winners and losers from reform. And when the main effects of reforms are on the provision of public goods such as health, education, or infrastructure, it may take time before the effects on income distribution and human development outcomes are felt. Detailed case studies of reforms in specific countries shed light on some of the complexities of reform. While it is as difficult to generalize from an individual country's experience as it is to generalize from an average cross-country relationship, both types of evidence provide useful insights into the effects of reforms.

Not surprising, case studies of reform episodes show that market-friendly reforms have uneven costs and benefits—especially in the near term—with the costs concentrated on particular groups and the benefits spread broadly over the economy as a whole. Costs and benefits can also be distributed unevenly over time. For example, trade liberalization can lead quickly to reductions in employment in previously protected sectors, but it may take time for affected workers to develop the skills required to take advantage of growing opportunities in other sectors. In Hungary the average duration of unemployment for those laid off from state enterprises between 1990 and 1992 was more than four years.[19]

Our leaders announced a transition to new market relations and then left us to the mercy of fate. . . .
— *From a discussion group, Georgia*

On the whole these costs do not negate the benefits of the reforms discussed above. But they do point to the importance of social policies to ease the burdens that reforms impose (see chapter 8). This is particularly so for poor people, whose assets, particularly the human capital of their children, can be irreversibly affected by even short-term costs. The costs also remind us that success or failure is not measured only by changes in average incomes. Survey evidence from Latin America indicates that reforms can be unpopular if they are associated with the perception—and often the reality—of greater risk and uncertainty.[20]

Who wins? And who loses? The winners are often those in rural areas, those in countries where the enabling environment for the private sector is strong and private sector capacity to seize new opportunities is good, those with the skills to be absorbed into new activities, and those who are geographically mobile and willing to look for work in new occupations and sectors. The losers have often been in urban areas (where services have been hit), in government jobs, and in jobs where protected insiders once earned more than market wages would support. The losers might also include the unskilled, the immobile, and those without access to the new market opportunities—because they lack human capital, access to land or credit, or infrastructure connecting far-flung areas. The losers may also include otherwise viable firms hit by economic crises not of their own making.

As the state sector contracts, employment opportunities are evaporating.
— *From a discussion group, Ukraine*

Table 4.1
Impact of reforms on agricultural prices, output, and productivity in seven countries
Percentage change, five-year postreform period compared with five-year prereform period

Country	Real agricultural prices	Real exchange rate[a]	Real GDP growth rate (percentage point change)	Agricultural output	Agricultural productivity growth (percentage point change)
Chile	120	105	2.8	40	8.2
Ghana	5	230	3.9	50	12.2
Hungary	−10	−23	..	−15	25.4
Indonesia	20	75	−0.6	42	2.3
Madagascar	11	94	2.0	15	2.9
Mexico	−24	22	−3.7	14	1.3
New Zealand	−31	−2	0.4	5	0.8

.. Not available.
a. An increase indicates depreciation.
Source: Meerman 1997.

Since poor people are represented among both the winners and the losers described here, there can be no general lesson that reforms are good (or bad) for all poor people all the time. But examples of reforms in three areas—agriculture, fiscal policy, and trade—yield important insights into what determines success and failure, how reforms affect poor people, and whether it is possible to mitigate the adverse effects on losers.

Agriculture

Under inward-oriented models of development the structure of tariffs and nontariff barriers and often the exchange rate were biased against agriculture. Market-oriented reforms that reduced this antiagriculture bias—and dismantled various forms of state intervention (price supports, input and credit subsidies, support for marketing products)—have generally increased agricultural growth. Policy reforms such as privatization, reduced regulation, and trade and price liberalization have had a positive impact for many countries.[21] Agricultural output and productivity growth have generally risen in the postreform period, sometimes substantially (table 4.1). Because many poor people are small agricultural producers, they have benefited directly from these reforms. Case studies of Chile, China, Ghana,[22] Uganda, and Vietnam show that reforms have helped raise producer prices for small farmers by eliminating marketing boards, changing real exchange rates through broader economic reforms, lowering tariffs, and eliminating quotas (box 4.3).

As chapter 5 discusses, access to land plays an important part in poverty reduction. Better access to land, accompanied by access to such assets as credit and infrastructure, can improve the productivity of land and labor for poor people. Thus liberalizing land markets has large potential benefits. Evidence from Mexico, for example, indicates that land market reforms expanded small farmers' access to land through the rental market (box 4.4).

Beyond these direct benefits, growth in agricultural incomes appears to have been particularly effective at reducing rural poverty because of demand spillovers to local markets in which the nonfarm rural poor have a large stake. Rural construction, personal services, simple manufacturing, and repair have been major channels through which poor people have shared in agricultural booms, even when they have not been direct beneficiaries of higher crop prices. In Ghana the big beneficiaries of reform—cocoa producers—constitute less than 8 percent of the poor, yet rural poverty fell sharply.

All our problems derive from lack of land. If we have enough land we will be able to produce enough to feed our households, build houses, and train our children.
—Poor man, Nigeria

Another example of the indirect benefits of market reforms comes from cotton smallholders in Zimbabwe.[23] Before the reforms the Cotton Marketing Board used its power as the sole buyer to impose low producer prices on farmers to subsidize the textile industry. Large farmers di-

Box 4.3
Agricultural reforms in Chile and China help small farmers

Chile dramatically illustrates how incomplete reforms can harm agriculture—and how completed reforms can have large benefits. The military government that took power in 1973 implemented a sustained program of policy reform. Agricultural production increased by a quarter in 1974, but then stagnated through 1983, thanks to the uncertainty over future policies and the incompleteness of reforms. In 1978–82 elimination of credit and input subsidies and appreciation in the real exchange rate hit agriculture hard, while delays in implementing reforms in land, labor, and water rights markets prevented an effective response (Valdes 1994).

In 1984 an aggressive devaluation and completion of reforms led to a vigorous recovery. The sector responded strongly. Agricultural labor force participation quickly rose—from a low of 14 percent of the total labor force to more than 19 percent, substantially higher than at any time in the previous decade. Agricultural growth increased from 0.2 percent a year in 1960–74 to 4.9 percent in 1974–90. Greater land productivity was a major factor.

China's agricultural liberalization led to a swift response. Before the reforms in 1979, China had good roads and irrigation infrastructure, excellent technical packages for grains and other crops, and effective application of fertilizer and other inputs. Between the 1940s revolution and the 1970s, irrigation capacity had more than doubled and fertilizer production had increased significantly. But arable land per capita declined from about 0.2 to 0.1 hectare over those 30 years. State-imposed cropping patterns forced most cultivation into rice and other cereals. Collective farms had to fulfill grain quotas for delivery to the cities, and the national grain market was fragmented into 30 self-sufficient regions.

Starting in 1979, family farming through the "household responsibility system" swept the country, replacing communal farming. Although initially farmers were still obliged to deliver grain at low prices, they were otherwise permitted to produce what they wished at mostly market prices. Commerce in rural areas and between farm and city, previously repressed by the state, was allowed to flourish. Rather than have self-sufficient provinces, the state encouraged regional and national markets. Effective demand increased rapidly for high-value products (vegetables, fruits, meat, fish, eggs) that had been repressed by the earlier state-directed policies. China's peasant farmers—skilled, hard working, and strongly motivated—responded to the new opportunities with great vigor and launched five years of the fastest sustained agricultural growth ever recorded anywhere. Between 1978 and 1984 net agricultural output increased 7.7 percent annually and grain output 4.8 percent (Lin 1995). With the vast majority of China's poor people in rural areas, the incidence of poverty fell dramatically.

Source: Meerman 1997.

Box 4.4
Land markets and poor peasants in Mexico

Liberalization of land rental and reorganization of the property rights system in the *ejidos* (communal lands) in 1992 formed the backbone of structural reforms to transform the Mexican economy. Liberalizing land markets and better defining and enforcing land property rights were expected to drastically reduce the costs of transactions in both land and credit markets, improving access to land and credit for poor, small-scale (and perhaps more efficient) producers.

Policies aimed at activating land rental markets would benefit the landless and the land-poor by increasing their access to land through rental and sharecropping transactions. But with both land and credit markets being liberalized, the easing of restrictions on the land rental market could be offset by reduced access to credit for the land-poor, who were less able to use land as collateral. This could have shifted the benefits from smaller to larger holders.

The increased supply of land from large farmers in the rental market allowed the rural poor a small but statistically significant increase in access to land. After controlling for the greater access to credit, it appears that large farmers increased their demand for land rentals. But small farmers appear to have increased their demand for land even more, suggesting that had their access to credit not worsened, land-poor farmers might have benefited even more from land market liberalization.

Source: Olinto, Davis, and Deininger 1999.

versified into unregulated crops, such as horticulture and tobacco. After the reforms cotton prices rose. In absolute terms the gains would be greater for larger farmers, simply because they produce more cotton. But there have been particular gains for smallholders, as newly privatized cotton buyers have chosen to compete with one another in part by providing new extension and input services to smallholders.

We think the earth is generous; but what is the incentive to produce more than the family needs if there are no access roads to get produce to the market?

—From a discussion group, Guatemala

Market-friendly reforms have also sometimes hurt the rural poor. In some countries financial reforms tight-

Box 4.5
Listening to farmers in Zambia

Since 1991 Zambia has radically changed the policy and institutional environment for agriculture. With liberalization and privatization, private suppliers have replaced state agricultural services for credit, inputs, and marketing.

Using participatory rural appraisals and beneficiary assessments, the World Bank–assisted Agricultural Sector Investment Program has established systematic and regular feedback between policymakers, service providers, and those affected by programs. Talking to farmers has helped policymakers understand the farmers' resource constraints, service delivery problems, and strategies for dealing with the vicissitudes of transition.

Participatory assessments also examine local perceptions of the effectiveness of agricultural infrastructure and services. These consultations revealed that agricultural credit and marketing, now handled by the private sector, were uneven and unpredictable—because of poor infrastructure, lack of capacity, and inadequate enforcement mechanisms. Public extension and animal health services, suffering from staff shortages and lack of operating funds, transport, and equipment, were also failing to respond well to farmers' needs.

Farmers want better infrastructure (especially roads and bridges) and more effective regulation of the private sector. They also want more information on markets for agricultural products and easier access to more flexible and responsive credit facilities. And they want advice on subsistence crops and storage methods, which they prefer to get through group extension.

Talking to farmers also identified ways to help those who are economically vulnerable take part in agricultural markets—extending microcredit, promoting local seed production systems, and offering research and extension services for subsistence crops and low-input agriculture. To create the local organizational basis for participatory extension and economically viable joint activities—such as marketing, local financial services, and cattle dipping—support needs to go to producer associations, service-providing NGOs, and other organizations active in communities.

Source: World Bank 1998a.

ened credit and closed rural bank branches, reducing the availability of credit.[24] And in some cases research, data collection, reporting, and quality monitoring disappeared after the abolition of state enterprises and marketing boards. In Cameroon the marketing board had been maintaining rural roads, but the responsibility was not reassigned after the reforms. In Zambia remote farmers had been implicitly subsidized by a uniform pricing policy that did not take into account transport costs, while small farmers without storage facilities were implicitly subsidized by prices held constant across seasons. After the reforms market forces eliminated the implicit subsidies, and transport infrastructure deteriorated significantly, leaving many farmers worse off.

The converse of the gain to small producers from relative price shifts is the cost to poor urban dwellers. Take Ghana. The rural sector gained from higher export prices and greater rural demand as cocoa farmers spent their windfall, but urban residents grew poorer. Living standards in Accra deteriorated in 1988–92, even while conditions were improving elsewhere in the country. Poor and middle-income urban residents suffered from higher food prices. Moreover, the dismantling of the old export marketing system removed an important source of public revenues that was not quickly replaced. This led to higher inflation and public sector retrenchment, with the costs of both felt most by urban residents.

These examples suggest at least two lessons. The first is simple: reforms can benefit poor people but also hurt them. Listening to stakeholders through participatory policymaking can do much to identify and avoid unintended consequences for poor people (box 4.5). Second, when reforms leave an institutional vacuum, performance suffers. As with other reforms, agricultural market liberalization without the proper institutional framework will not deliver the expected results—and could have serious consequences for poor people.

Fiscal policy

In many countries fiscal reforms to strengthen revenue collection capacity and control unsustainable spending have been a central element of broader reform programs. Since raising revenues takes time, fiscal reforms often show up first in spending cuts. When those cuts are felt in social sectors and in subsidies, they can hurt poor people. As chapter 5 discusses, there is evidence that the introduction of user fees in health services hurts the poor more than the rich. In Madagascar the real incomes of poor households in the capital city declined substantially when food prices were decontrolled.[25] But eliminating subsidies does not always hurt the poor. A study in Guinea and Mozambique found that eliminating food subsidies did not hurt poor people because the subsidies had not reached them in the first place.[26] The lesson is clear: lower overall subsidies need not be inconsistent with helping poor people, if the subsidies are better targeted or replaced by other forms of assistance.

In the 1990s governments in Eastern Europe and the former Soviet Union introduced a rapid phaseout of utility subsidies across the board. The urgency was dictated by the need to reduce unsustainable fiscal deficits. This had a huge impact on the welfare of all families, especially poor families. In Ukraine household energy tariffs increased four- to twelvefold (in real terms) between 1992 and 1995, while average household income dropped to less than half its prereform level. To help cushion the impact, a cap of 20 percent of family income was put on what households pay in utility bills and rent. The state budget is supposed to pay any bills in excess of this limit (although arrears in payments continue to be a problem). In Moldova the average winter heating bill would have exceeded 60 percent of the income (cash and in kind) of a typical family of four in the lowest fifth of the income distribution living in a small apartment. Aware that this was unsustainable, the government eventually introduced mechanisms to subsidize families, ranging from tolerating nonpayment to establishing different tariff rates for poor families.[27]

Experience in the countries of the former Soviet Union also shows that fiscal adjustment could have been done in different, and much more pro-poor, ways. For example, before the political transition the ratio of health and education personnel and facilities to the total population was above OECD standards. During the 1990s public revenues and expenditures fell as a share of GDP. And since GDP collapsed as well, government spending in real terms fell dramatically. Rather than downsize personnel, rationalize facilities, and institute some cost-recovery measures, governments allowed real public sector wages to erode, and spending on maintenance and material inputs collapsed. Public sector wages were often in arrears, and public employees responded to their personal financial pressures by demanding under-the-table payments for public services, something poor people could ill afford.[28]

Revenue-raising measures, such as a growing reliance on value added taxes, can also hurt poor people if not implemented carefully. Strong efficiency arguments for value added taxation are being heeded throughout the developing world. But introducing such taxes can have either progressive or regressive effects. If value added taxes replace progressive income taxes or if poor people either avoided or did not qualify for other taxes, such reforms are regressive. Pakistan's introduction of a value added tax

shifted the burden of taxation toward the poor: the tax burden on the richest income group declined 4.3 percentage points, while that on the poorest group rose 10.3 percentage points.[29] In contrast, when tax reforms reduce the reliance on inflationary finance, they can be progressive because of the heavy burden high inflation places on poor people. Moreover, most of the redistributive power of public finance lies on the expenditure side rather than the revenue side. Therefore, even a slightly regressive tax reform can have progressive results if the additional revenue is devoted to expenditures targeted toward poor people.

Trade

Trade reforms—reducing tariffs and nontariff barriers—have had profound effects in many developing countries. As chapter 3 discusses, there is now substantial evidence that open trade regimes support growth and development and that moving toward an open regime and its attendant benefits is the reason for trade reform. But the consequences for poor people depend crucially on how trade liberalization affects the demand for their greatest asset: their (often unskilled) labor. Furthermore, trade reforms in the developing world have not always been matched by complementary reforms by rich countries, where the remaining protection imposes a heavy burden on the developing world (chapter 10).

The initial push for trade liberalization as an instrument for poverty reduction was influenced by a narrow reading of predictions from trade theory: removing trade barriers in developing countries would increase demand for their abundant low-skilled labor and expand unskilled employment and earnings. Not only would trade liberalization raise average incomes—it was also expected to be particularly pro-poor through this effect on unskilled labor. The evidence shows that the actual results in the past 15 years have been mixed. Trade reforms have delivered growth, and thus poverty reduction—but their distributional effects have been more complex. Careful analysis suggests three main factors at work.

First, in some countries trade restrictions had benefited poor people by artificially raising the prices of the goods they produced. In such cases it is not surprising that trade liberalization would hurt poor people. For example, a study of Mexico found that the wages of unskilled labor relative to those of skilled labor declined over 1986–90, and that about a quarter of the decline was from the reduction in tariffs and the elimination of import license requirements (figure 4.3).[30] The authors explain this apparent anomaly by noting that Mexico, despite its comparative advantage in low-skilled industry, had protected labor-intensive sectors—such as textiles and clothing—before adopting trade reforms. Supporting the incomes of the unskilled through trade barriers is very inefficient. Support can often be given in other ways at lower social cost, although designing and implementing such better-targeted programs take time. But it is not surprising in these circumstances that trade liberalization—unaccompanied by compensatory programs—would hurt poor people. In some other countries, however, the pattern was different: urban manufacturing workers protected by trade barriers were more skilled and less likely to be poor.

Second, some countries that liberalized trade were not particularly abundant in unskilled labor. In Africa and Latin America land is relatively abundant, and in Eastern Europe skilled labor is plentiful. Although this does not detract from the efficiency and growth arguments for trade reform, it does call into question the earlier presumption that trade reform might also deliver equalizing effects by raising the demand for unskilled labor. But in countries where unskilled labor is abundant, such as Bangladesh, China, and Vietnam, the gains from integrating into the world economy can be significant for unskilled labor.

Third, trade reforms were often accompanied by other developments that were disequalizing rather than equalizing. In many developing countries that opened to trade, as in many industrial countries, the wages of skilled workers have grown faster than those of unskilled workers. In the United States the wages of unskilled workers have fallen in real terms by 20 percent since the 1970s, despite rapid growth in the overall economy.[31] Studies for countries as diverse as Chile, Colombia, Mexico, Turkey, and Venezuela show a similar phenomenon—premiums paid to skilled workers have increased in all these countries.[32]

Is trade the culprit behind this widening inequality? The balance of evidence suggests that it is not. More important has been technological change favoring workers with better education and skills, sometimes in the form of imported foreign technologies. This can be seen from several pieces of evidence. Even though the relative wages of skilled workers have risen in many countries, there has also been a shift toward greater employment of skilled workers—contrary to what simple trade theory would predict. This shift has been pervasive across industries—again contrary to simple trade models, which would have predicted increases in some sectors and declines in others. And there is evidence that the pattern of shifts toward more

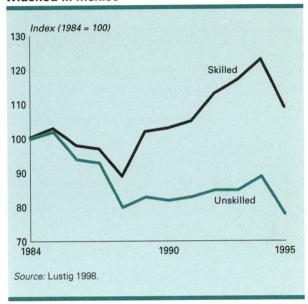

Figure 4.3
The gap between skilled and unskilled wages widened in Mexico

Index (1984 = 100)

Source: Lustig 1998.

skill-intensive employment in the industrial world in the 1970s and 1980s is being matched by a similar, later shift in the developing world.[33]

This is of course not to say that technological change should be avoided because it hurts poor people. On the contrary, technological change is a fundamental determinant of growth and rising living standards, powerful forces for poverty reduction. Instead, the importance of a rising relative demand for skills points to the need to invest in the skills of poor people, to enable them to take advantage of the new opportunities that technological change brings.

Private sector response

These examples of agricultural, fiscal, and trade reforms show that reforms can have complex distributional outcomes. But remember that the objective of market-friendly reforms—a vibrant and dynamic private sector—can be one of the most effective antidotes to the costs of reform. New job creation, technological change that raises labor productivity and wages, and institutions that ensure equal opportunities for gaining access to the new jobs do much to ensure that the benefits from reform are widely shared.

Fortunately, a strong private response appears to be the general experience in developing countries after reform, especially when labor market regulations are not onerous and do not inhibit adjustment.[34] A retrospective study of trade liberalizations found that in 12 of 13 cases where data were available formal manufacturing employment increased within one year after liberalization was completed.[35] The exception was Chile, where increased employment in agriculture offset the decline in manufacturing employment. In Estonia a flexible labor market created many new jobs, leading to minimal unemployment despite the intense job destruction and labor turnover associated with reform.[36] In Panama unemployment fell steeply after liberalization. In South Asia growth in the formal manufacturing sector accelerated from 3.8 percent a year to 9.4 percent after liberalization, as many workers pulled out of informal sector employment.[37] And in Africa the micro and small enterprise sector is the most dynamic in five economies considered in a recent study. Annual employment growth was strong in these enterprises after reform, and new enterprises started up at a high rate.[38]

Making markets do more for poor people

Even where market-friendly reforms have taken hold, there is much that countries can do to improve the benefits that markets offer to the poor. To reach poor people, many reforms need to be accompanied by institutional support, investment in infrastructure, and complementary reforms at the micro level. The incentives for policymakers to undertake such reforms are small because the markets involving poor people are typically small. So the reforms get little attention, even though they can be powerful forces for poverty reduction. But increasing access to productive assets and lightening and improving regulation can do much to involve poor people more directly in markets.[39] New technologies can help as well, especially information technologies that break down some of the barriers of physical remoteness that many poor people face (box 4.6).

The potential of reforms to improve access to markets for poor people can be seen from examples in three areas: lifting the heavy hand of regulation, especially on the small businesses that often provide the poor with employment; promoting core labor standards; and improving access to financial markets for the poor, especially through microfinance.

Lightening the regulatory burden

Compliance with regulations imposes fixed costs that are particularly onerous for small firms. Carefully re-

viewing regulations and exploring possibilities for more flexible requirements can ease the burden. In Chile the government recently simplified the duty-drawback system to reduce the administrative costs for small firms. In Bolivia parts of the tax system were drastically simplified for small firms.[40] In the Philippines there are much lower minimum capital requirements for small thrift and rural banks than for commercial banks.

In contrast, in Indonesia official and unofficial levies are estimated to raise the costs faced by small and medium-size enterprises by as much as 30 percent.[41] In some sectors small enterprises have to secure as many as eight licenses—some of which have identical functions but are issued by different agencies. Obtaining licenses takes so long and procedures are so complicated that some business owners choose to operate illegally.[42] In the Indian state of Gujarat licensing requirements for gum collectors are a barrier that hinder women's collector groups.[43] Reforms to reduce levies and to simplify and shorten licensing and entry procedures for small and medium-size enterprises could ease this burden.

Given the opportunity, small and medium-size enterprises might serve some segments of the markets normally thought of as natural monopolies. In many urban areas in Africa and Latin America small independent water providers bring basic water services at low cost to poor marginal communities. Small enterprises have also been effective in solid waste management.[44] But they often face barriers—such as requirements for experience, complex or expensive procedures for registration and tendering, and noncompetitive behavior in markets. Removing these constraints could allow small and medium-size enterprises to expand their activities in this area, increasing employment opportunities for low-income groups while expanding access to services for poor communities.

Better regulation does not always mean less regulation. Take the privatization of gas, water, electricity, and telecommunications utilities in Argentina in the early 1990s. Privatization improved performance, and poor people, as direct consumers, benefited along with the rest of the economy—and more than proportionately for gas and electricity, major components of their consumption basket. But because privatized utilities are often monopolies, appropriate regulatory institutions were essential to fair pricing. The new regulations to ensure that utility prices yielded only normal rates of return had important indirect benefits for poor people, by encouraging investment

Box 4.6
Attacking poverty with information

Virtual Souk expands market access for artisans in the Middle East and North Africa

Fadma Aoubaida, a Moroccan weaver from Taliouine and a mother of seven—with the money she earned from selling her products on the Virtual Souk—repaired her roof and started building an indoor latrine, one of the few in her village. Ijja Aittalblhsen, another woman artisan in Morocco, spent her profits to buy cement and windows for her house. With future profits, she wants to buy a truck to transport rugs from her village to the market or buy bicycles that women can ride.

—BBC Online News, 14 October 1999

Artisans in the Middle East and North Africa have always crafted high-quality products using traditional techniques and ancestral know-how. But shrinking local markets and difficulties in gaining access to more lucrative national and international markets are leading to a gradual disappearance of culturally rich crafts—and with them an important source of income for poor people.

The Virtual Souk is bucking this trend. Since 1997 this Internet-based marketplace has been providing direct access to international markets for several hundred artisans from Egypt, Lebanon, Morocco, and Tunisia, many of them women. The network is expanding to other countries in the region, and there is demand to adapt the concept to East Asia and Latin America.

Online sales soared tenfold between the first and last quarters of 1999, reaching markets around the world, including countries in Europe and North America and as far as Australia, Japan, and South Africa. Participating artisans receive 65–80 percent of the proceeds, a much larger margin than through traditional channels. And the gains are more than simply financial. Through the Virtual Souk, artisans gain access to opportunities for empowerment, capacity building, income generation—and for the use of their skills with dignity.

Cellular phone technology gives bargaining power to women in Bangladesh

I always sell eggs to middlemen. In the past, whatever prices they offered, I accepted because I had no idea about the going prices of eggs. . . . Last week, the middleman came . . . and desired to pay me 12 taka per hali [four units]. . . . Keeping him waiting, I rushed to check the prices through the Village Phone. The price was 14 taka per hali of eggs in nearby markets. I came back and refused to sell to him at the lower prices. . . . After a brief haggling, we agreed to buy and sell at 13 taka per hali.

—Halima Khatuun, a poor, illiterate woman who sells eggs, Bangladesh

A subsidiary of Grameen Bank, Grameen Telecom operates a village pay phone program that leases cellular telephones to selected bank members, mostly women in rural areas, who use the telephone to provide services and earn money. Today around 2,000 village pay phones are in place. The target is to install 40,000 telephones by 2002, introducing telefax and email services as well.

These phones have helped lower the cost of information gathering. This can be seen in lower prices for poultry feed, more stable diesel prices, and less spoilage of perishable goods due to more precise shipment dates. Women providing the phone services have gained confidence and new status as "phone ladies." Telephone users include both rich and poor, but poor people make more calls for economic reasons.

Source: For the Virtual Souk, see www.peoplink/vsouk/; for the Grameen Telecom cellular phone program, see Burr (2000).

and job creation throughout the economy. One study found that these indirect gains for poor people—reflecting the power of appropriate regulation—were five times as large as the direct gains from lower utility prices and better service.[45]

An appropriate and generally lighter regulatory framework in labor markets could also benefit poor people. In general, excessively burdensome labor market regulations can limit job creation and thus opportunities for poor people to productively employ one of their most important assets—their labor. These constraints are especially important when reforms in other areas create temporary employment dislocations. But the benefits of deregulating labor markets should not be overstated. Often labor market regulations are not well enforced, especially in the informal sector, so relaxing them would have little effect on employment opportunities for poor people.

Promoting core labor standards

Core labor standards have been set out in the Declaration on the Fundamental Principles and Rights at Work adopted by the members of the International Labour Organization in 1998. They include freedom of association and the right to collective bargaining, elimination of forced labor, effective abolition of child labor, and the elimination of discrimination in employment and occupation.[46]

The goals underlying these core labor standards are important, and it is widely agreed that the standards themselves represent worthy targets for economic development. This consensus is especially strong for the most exploitative forms of child labor and forced labor. However, there is no consensus regarding the best way to achieve the labor conditions envisaged by these core standards. How best to implement the objectives set out in these standards is difficult to determine and depends a great deal on the circumstances of individual countries. Some industrial countries take the position that the standards should be enforced through trade agreements or development cooperation. Many developing countries argue—and rightly so—that applying trade sanctions in this way can serve protectionist purposes for industrial countries and that conditioning development cooperation will unfairly hamper development.

It is clear that simply adopting core labor standards will not guarantee their realization. In developing countries problems meeting these standards may be a consequence of poverty.

Consider child labor. Too often children's time spent at work comes at the expense of their formal schooling—with likely adverse long-term consequences. But a child's earnings may make the difference between survival and starvation for the family, or they may help provide the resources for a sibling to stay in school.[47] In these circumstances simple bans on child labor can have adverse consequences for poor families' incomes and can even have the unintended effect of pushing children from work in the formal sector to more exploitative work in firms outside the reach of formal regulations. As a complement to standards against the most exploitative forms of child labor, programs that provide financial incentives that make it affordable to keep children in school can be a very effective strategy.[48]

Implementation of the standards on freedom of association and collective bargaining also raises complex issues for economic development. Enshrining such rights can help eliminate abusive workplace practices and ensure fair compensation, especially for poor people, whose desperate need for employment places them most at risk of unfair and exploitative employers. Unions also are an important dimension of civil society, and consultation with unions can provide a valuable input into policy formulation. However, empirical evidence on the economic benefits of unionization and collective bargaining is generally quite mixed and suggests that both costs and benefits are complex and context specific.[49] Particularly important are the rules that govern collective bargaining and resolution of labor disputes. Some forms of collective bargaining rules may be better at producing efficient and equitable outcomes than others.[50] In any case, the exercise of these rights will best serve development objectives when unions and employers are knowledgeable and independent and bargain in good faith.

The core labor standards, then, set an important target, but a simple strategy of enforcing them through sanc-

tions is unlikely to produce the desired outcomes for workers.[51] Rather, promoting them as part of a broad-based development strategy through information, technical assistance, capacity building, and complementary initiatives is likely to yield the greatest benefits. Using incentives—such as programs to keep children in school—to address the causes of suboptimal labor practices must be a key part of this strategy. Along these lines, and also deserving close attention, are interesting new ideas about complementing public standards with private (market-driven) standards that encourage employers to adopt desirable labor practices.[52]

Improving access to financial markets for poor people

Access to financial markets is important for poor people. Like all economic agents, low-income households and microenterprises can benefit from credit, savings, and insurance services. Such services help to manage risk and to smooth consumption in the face of sharp fluctuations in agricultural yields and prices, economic shocks, and even natural disasters. Savings and credit facilities can help to make larger investments more affordable, and so allow people to take advantage of profitable business opportunities and increase their earnings potential. For economies as a whole, a large literature has documented the importance of well-functioning financial markets for growth.[53]

But financial markets, because of their special features, often serve poor people badly. Asymmetric information between lenders and borrowers creates problems of adverse selection and moral hazard. The traditional solution to these problems is for lenders to demand collateral from borrowers. Since poor people have insufficient traditional forms of collateral (such as physical assets) to offer, they are often excluded from traditional financial markets. In addition, transactions costs are often high relative to the small loans typically demanded by poor people. And in areas where population density is low, physical access to banking services can be very difficult: in the mountains of Nepal people must walk six hours to and from the nearest bank branch at an opportunity cost of a day's wages.[54] Facing such hurdles, poor people are often discouraged and simply do not seek loans since they believe that they will be denied credit or will not be able to fulfill bank requirements. At the same time, conventional banks often find it unprofitable to provide services to poor people using traditional lending practices.

These failures have been used to justify a high level of government intervention in the form of targeted credit, with government-owned financial institutions channeling sizable resources at subsidized interest rates. Often, this approach assumed that poor people required only cheap credit, ignoring their demand for savings instruments.[55] Outcomes were disappointing. The lending institutions were not financially viable, and in countries from Indonesia to Peru government-sponsored rural credit programs collapsed under the weight of their losses. Subsidized interest rates distorted the financial markets. Target groups were not reached.[56]

So many lending institutions have emerged, but their operations are hardly transparent. People do not know how to access them. Those who have tried have been let down by high levels of collateral demanded.
—*From a discussion group, Malawi*

Over the past two decades new approaches known collectively as microfinance have emerged, applying sound economic principles in the provision of financial services to low-income clients and using group as well as individual lending. Pioneers such as Grameen Bank in Bangladesh and the village banks *(unit desas)* of Bank Rakyat Indonesia captured attention worldwide by providing financial products matching the needs of low-income clients, using innovative collective monitoring through group lending to strengthen repayment performance, and charging interest rates that fully cover operational costs.[57] In many cases these innovations led to much higher repayment rates than under previous schemes—and were particularly effective in reaching women.[58]

While such programs have become popular and represent a major step forward from previous public interventions, they are still no panacea for poverty. Not surprising, simply providing access to credit does not create investment opportunities: a study of rural households in Nicaragua and Romania found that removing credit constraints would have only moderate impacts on the number of households making investments and on the amounts invested.[59] In addition, small, locally based microfinance organizations can be particularly vulnerable to shocks such as natural disasters or fluctuations in agricultural yields, which affect a large proportion of their clientele at once. This can raise the riskiness of their loan portfolios and make it more difficult for them to provide more sophisticated financial products. Shar-

ing these risks among microfinance organizations and possibly encouraging a greater role for larger and more geographically diversified and established financial institutions can help in this respect.

Careful measurement of the economic impact of microfinance programs or institutions is fraught with methodological difficulties, and the results of studies are often contradictory.[60] Nevertheless, evidence is gradually emerging. For example, a recent review of 13 microfinance institutions found that borrower households above or on the poverty line experience a higher impact than households below the poverty line, suggesting that while effective, such institutions are not necessarily well targeted toward the poorest households.[61] Another study found that the majority of microfinance programs reviewed still required financial subsidies to be viable.[62] Increasingly, the performance of these institutions is evaluated by two primary criteria: their outreach to target clientele and their dependence on subsidies.[63] Although these criteria do not provide a full assessment of the economic impact of microfinance institutions, they highlight the social cost at which microfinance institutions have reached their objectives.

These results on targeting and the prevalence of subsidy dependence point to the challenges faced by microfinance programs: continuing to move toward financial viability while extending their outreach to their target clientele. Best-practice design features of such institutions as the village banks of Bank Rakyat Indonesia—interest rates that fully cover costs, availability of well-rewarded voluntary savings, performance-based compensation for staff, intensive staff training, innovative low-cost distribution networks, frequent loan collection, products matching the demand of low-income groups, and effective management information systems—are all associated with good financial performance. Stronger capacity building and better dissemination of these best practices can help microfinance institutions wean themselves from subsidies without compromising their ability to provide services to poor people.

Governments can improve financial intermediation for the poor by providing complementary public goods and improved regulation that recognize the special needs of microfinance schemes. For example, better investment in rural infrastructure and literacy promotion can help expand the reach of microfinance organizations, and credit information registries can lower informational costs and allow borrowers to build reputational collateral.

On the regulatory and supervisory fronts outdated usury laws that prevent microfinance institutions from establishing sufficiently high spreads between savings and lending rates to allow them to cover the high transactions costs on small loans should be eliminated. Improving the legal framework for secured transactions, as is being done in Argentina, Mexico, and Romania, can widen credit opportunities for low-income people.

• • •

Well-functioning markets create opportunities for poor people to escape poverty. But establishing such markets where they are absent, making them work better, and ensuring that poor people have free and fair access are difficult and take time. At times, market reforms fail entirely—or have unintended consequences for poor people. The lessons of these failures point to the importance of designing and implementing reforms in a way that is measured and tailored to the economic, social, and political circumstances of a country. Market-friendly re-forms create winners and losers. And when the losers include poor people, societies have an obligation to help them manage the transition.

However, there is no presumption that making reforms pro-poor means making reforms slowly. In some cases poor people will benefit more from rapid market-oriented re-forms, especially in areas that directly affect their economic opportunities or that help break down entrenched mo-nopoly privileges. In view of the urgent need to get coun-tries onto dynamic, job-creating development paths, it is critical that the difficulty of reform and the impossi-bility of compensating every loser not lead to policy paralysis.

Furthermore, to make markets work better for poor people, macro reforms must be complemented by micro reforms and improvements in poor people's access to markets and information—through investment in in-frastructure and modern technologies—as well as sources of credit. Reducing labor market restrictions that limit job creation and stifle competition while promoting core labor standards remains a key challenge.

CHAPTER 5

Expanding Poor People's Assets and Tackling Inequalities

Lacking assets is both a cause and an outcome of poverty. Poor health, deficient skills, scant access to basic services, and the humiliations of social exclusion reflect deprivations in personal, public, and social assets. Human, physical, and natural assets also lie at the core of whether an individual, household, or group lives in poverty—or escapes it. These assets interact with market and social opportunities to generate income, a better quality of life, and a sense of psychological well-being. Assets are also central to coping with shocks and reducing the vulnerability that is a constant feature of poverty.

Assets and their synergies

If we get a road we would get everything else: community center, employment, post office, water, telephone.
—Young woman in a discussion group,
Little Bay, Jamaica

Poor people have few assets in part because they live in poor countries or in poor areas within countries. They also lack assets because of stark inequalities in the distribution of wealth and the benefits of public action. In Bolivia the under-five mortality rate of the poorest 20 percent of the population is more than four times that of the richest 20 percent.[1] In West and Central Africa the rich-poor gap in school enrollment ranges from 19 percentage points in Ghana to almost 52 percentage points in Senegal.[2] And in Ecuador 75 percent of households among the poorest fifth lack piped water, compared with 12 percent among the richest fifth.[3] Poor women and members of disadvantaged ethnic or racial groups may lack assets because of discrimination in the law or customary practices. Low assets and low income are mutually reinforcing: low education translates into low income, which translates into poor health and reduced educational opportunities for the next generation.

There are powerful complementarities across assets—the benefits of one asset can depend crucially on access to another. The synergies between human capital assets—such as a mother's education and her offspring's nutrition levels—are well documented. In Vietnam

Box 5.1
Interactions between human and physical capital

A study of irrigation infrastructure in Vietnam uncovered important complementarities between education and the gains from irrigation. The study tried to explain differences in farm profits as a function of irrigated and nonirrigated land allocations with controls for the observed factors that determined the administrative land allocations to households on decollectivization. Assuming that placement of irrigation is not based on expected rates of return, the results suggest that households with high levels of primary schooling benefit most from irrigation. The figure shows how the marginal benefits from irrigation would vary across per capita consumption expenditures if there were no differences in the education levels of adults across households. The baseline shows the gains at actual levels of education and compares those with the simulated amounts that would result if each head of household had the maximum five years of primary education—or if all adults had the full five years. More education raises the returns to irrigation, and the effect is particularly strong for the poor, who tend to have the least education.

Lack of irrigation infrastructure is only one of the constraints to reducing rural poverty in Vietnam. But the full returns from irrigation investments will not be realized without concomitant investments in education.

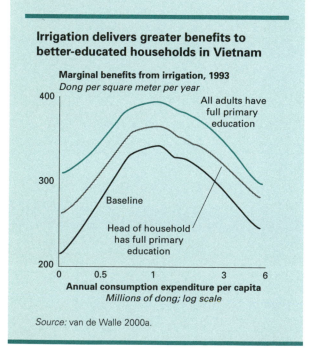

Irrigation delivers greater benefits to better-educated households in Vietnam

Marginal benefits from irrigation, 1993
Dong per square meter per year

Source: van de Walle 2000a.

Box 5.2
Links between the environment and health

There are many critical interactions between the environment and poverty. Among the best documented is the link between the environment and the health of poor people. Pollution—dirty water and air—is a major contributor to diarrhea and respiratory infections, the two most frequent causes of death for poor children.

Research has consistently shown that improving drinking water has less pronounced health benefits than improving sanitation. But the benefits from cleaner water are enhanced when sanitation is improved and water quantity is optimal. When hygiene is also improved, increasing the quantity of water does more to improve health than improving its quality. Education on hygiene is often necessary, though, before communities realize its potential health benefits.

A study of 144 water and sanitation projects found that improved water and sanitation services were associated with a median reduction of 22 percent in the incidence of diarrhea and 65 percent in deaths from diarrhea. But improved excreta disposal and hand washing can reduce under-five mortality rates by 60 percent and cases of schistosomiasis by 77 percent, of intestinal worms by 29 percent, and of trachoma by 27–50 percent. Other work has found significant relationships between air quality and health.

These critical interactions between the environment and health highlight the importance of working across sectors to improve poverty outcomes.

Source: World Bank forthcoming b; Klees, Godinho, and Lawson-Doe 1999.

---

by 15 percent.[5] In Morocco places with better rural roads also have much higher girls' primary school enrollment rates and twice the use of health care facilities.[6]

Another important example of the interactions between assets lies in the influence of the environment on health (box 5.2). Such interactions suggest that poor health indicators in an urban slum, for example, may not be significantly improved by a local health center without the benefits of an effective sewage system. Increasing human well-being is thus likely to require action to simultaneously expand complementary assets.

Public action to facilitate the accumulation of assets

Poor people are central agents in building their assets. Parents nurture, care for, socialize, teach skills to, and help finance the education of their children. Small farmers invest in their land and livestock, while the self-employed

research found that households with higher education levels had higher returns to irrigation, with the largest benefits going to the poor (box 5.1).[4] In rural Philippines electrification was estimated to increase the returns to education

invest in materials, equipment, and market contacts important to their business. Workers migrate to cities and to other countries, and their remittances are often used to invest in household assets. Poor women and men save in housing, in rotating savings and credit societies, and (where available) in local banks and credit associations. Still, the scope for asset accumulation by poor households is severely constrained by inadequacies in the markets they face and by weaknesses in public and private institutions for service delivery. It is also constrained by lack of income, with poor people suffering severe handicaps in financing health, education, and other asset-related investments.

Why does the state have a role in expanding poor people's assets? For two basic reasons. First, markets do not work well for poor people, because of their physical isolation and because of market failures in the financial, health, and insurance sectors, for example. Second, public policy can reduce initial inequalities and increase the opportunities for poor people to benefit from growth.

Equity and efficiency considerations can be largely independent, but they generally overlap. Poor people, faced with a failure of a private market, can be left with only the state to provide services. While both the poor and the nonpoor will seek alternative solutions, the nonpoor have more resources at their disposal and so will clearly have more options. Among the most effective antipoverty policies are those that achieve more equity through redistribution and simultaneously enhance the efficiency of markets used by poor people (box 5.3, see also box 3.8 in chapter 3).

While there is a case for state involvement in expanding poor people's assets, there is no guarantee that the state will be effective. Ineffective state action and unsatisfactory human outcomes partly reflect the fact that government can influence only a few of the multiple sources of well-being. But they also reflect the difficulty many governments have in delivering goods and services. Governments are constrained by the fiscal resources at their disposal and their administrative capacity to deliver services effectively. Also, even if they have the resources and the capacity, state institutions may not be responsive to the needs of poor people.

How can public action enable poor people to expand their assets, and how can it tackle asset inequalities? In three complementary ways. By using the power of the state to redistribute resources, especially in services that create assets, such as education, health, and infrastructure. By implementing policy and institutional reforms to ensure effective delivery of services. And by engaging poor

Box 5.3
Win-win policies in the health sector

The combined objectives of greater equity and efficiency are easier to achieve in some programs than in others, as illustrated in the following two examples from the health sector.

Some health services, such as mosquito and other pest control and health education on basic hygiene and nutrition, are pure public goods. Others, such as combating infectious diseases, have clear positive externalities. Still others, such as curative care for noninfectious conditions, are private goods. Governments are responsible for infectious disease control on efficiency grounds. But such policies have important equity benefits as well. While the poor suffer more from almost all diseases than the nonpoor do, the difference is greatest for infectious diseases. In India the poorest tenth of the population is seven times as likely to suffer from tuberculosis as the richest tenth.

The general inadequacy, if not total absence, of health insurance markets in most developing countries exposes both the poor and the nonpoor to substantial financial risk and insecurity (chapter 8). (The systemic reasons for this failure were originally discussed in detail by Arrow 1963.) While public provision of insurance is one policy option, managing such programs is not easy. A common way of addressing the insurance problem is to subsidize expensive care, usually through public hospitals. But on equity grounds, the value of subsidizing hospitals is not as clear as that of attacking infectious disease. Hospitals are usually in urban areas, and the nonpoor end up benefiting more from the subsidies. Subsidized provision of essential hospital care can enhance equity as well as efficiency. But it will be a win-win policy—enhancing both equity and the efficiency of markets used by poor people—only if poor people can effectively access hospital care, and that poses a significant challenge.

Source: Hammer 1997; Devarajan and Hammer 1998; World Bank 1998t.

households and poor communities in decisions on the choice, operation, monitoring, and evaluation of programs and services that build their assets.

The rest of this chapter focuses on these three principles, with examples from different asset categories. It then discusses the important complementarities in setting priorities across areas of action, using land reform and the provision of urban water and sanitation services as illustrations. (Expanding access to financial assets is dealt with in chapter 4. Mechanisms to improve the accountability and responsiveness of state institutions are the focus of chapter 6. How to build social assets is covered in chapter 7. Using assets and protecting the assets of poor people during adverse shocks are discussed in chapters 8 and 9. And the role of the international community in asset building is covered in chapters 10 and 11.)

Redistributing public spending

The coercive power of the state can be a potent force supporting asset formation by poor people. But there are clear bounds to state action. In today's globally integrated world intrusive state action can undercut the functioning of markets and the incentives for private investment—killing job opportunities, not creating them.

In some instances there are significant tradeoffs between efficiency and equity. States generally mirror the unequal political structure they are founded on, and government action often reflects this. Coercive land reform under highly unequal land ownership, while potentially good for poor people and good for efficiency, rarely has enough political support to be effectively implemented. Nationalizing industrial assets is rarely good for poor people (who do not enjoy the benefits) and can damage efficiency. But there are many other instances in which addressing asset inequality can enhance efficiency and be

good for growth (see box 3.8 in chapter 3). The outcomes of redistributive policies for equity and for efficiency and growth thus need to be carefully evaluated.

The most important domain for state action in building the assets of poor people is the budget. Evidence suggests, for example, that public spending on education and health is not progressive but is frequently regressive (tables 5.1 and 5.2). This is also an area where redistribution is technically feasible and where tradeoffs between redistribution and aggregate growth may be low or negative (indeed, growth can be spurred). But tradeoffs also arise in choosing between competing redistributive actions on which public funds could be spent. The choice has to be guided by an assessment of the relative effectiveness of different instruments in realizing the objectives of redistribution and poverty reduction.

Budgetary action in support of asset redistribution requires two things. The first is a willingness and capacity to raise adequate revenues and devote a significant share of those revenues to development (not to military spending, subsidies to the nonpoor and to loss-making public enterprises, or illicit transfers to foreign bank accounts). The second is

Table 5.1
Public spending on education by income quintile in selected developing countries, various years
Percent

Country	Year	Quintile 1 (poorest)	2	3	4	5 (richest)
Armenia	1996	7	17	22	25	29
Côte d'Ivoire	1995	14	17	17	17	35
Ecuador	1998	11	16	21	27	26
Ghana	1992	16	21	21	21	21
Guinea[a]	1994	9	13	21	30	27
Jamaica	1992	18	19	20	21	22
Kazakhstan	1996	8	16	23	27	26
Kenya	1992/93	17	20	21	22	21
Kyrgyz Republic	1993	14	17	18	24	27
Madagascar	1993/94	8	15	14	21	41
Malawi	1994/95	16	19	20	20	25
Morocco	1998/99	12	17	23	24	24
Nepal	1996	11	12	14	18	46
Nicaragua	1993	9	12	16	24	40
Pakistan	1991	14	17	19	21	29
Panama	1997	20	19	20	24	18
Peru	1994	15	19	22	23	22
Romania	1994	24	22	21	19	15
South Africa	1993	21	19	17	20	23
Tanzania	1993	13	16	16	16	38
Vietnam	1993	12	16	17	19	35

a. Includes only primary and secondary education.
Source: Li, Steel, and Glewwe 1999; World Bank 1997i (for Romania), 2000f (for Ecuador).

Table 5.2

Public spending on health by income quintile in selected developing countries, various years

Percent

Country	Year	Quintile 1 (poorest)	2	3	4	Quintile 5 (richest)
Argentina	1991	33		60 [a]		6
Brazil	1990	8	18	30	25	20
Bulgaria	1995	13	16	21	26	25
Chile	1982	22		66 [a]		11
Ghana	1994	12	15	19	21	33
Indonesia	1987	12	14	19	27	29
Kenya	1992	14	17	22	22	24
Malaysia	1989	29		60 [a]		11
Mongolia	1995	18	20	19	19	24
South Africa	1993	16		66 [a]		17
Uruguay[b]	1989	37	21	17	14	11
Vietnam	1993	12	16	21	22	29

a. Distribution across these quintiles not distinguished in original source.
b. Quintiles defined by households rather than individuals.
Source: Filmer and Pritchett 1999b.

the allocation and management of development spending to support asset formation for poor people—especially human and infrastructure assets. Increasing transparency in budgets at both the national and the local level can reveal the extent to which public resources are used in a pro-poor manner and can improve local accountability (chapter 6).

Public financing of services is a core element of poverty reduction policy and practice. Experience suggests two lessons. First, higher public spending on social services and infrastructure may not translate into more or better services for poor people because programs for poor people are too often of low quality and unresponsive to their needs, and because the incidence of public expenditures is often regressive. However, subsidies to the nonpoor cannot be fully avoided because gaining political support for quality programs may sometimes require providing services to a broader segment of the population than just the poor alone. Second, it is important to use public resources to relax demand-side constraints. Even when health, education, and infrastructure services are publicly financed, poor people face constraints that limit their ability to benefit from them (for example, complementary costs, such as transportation to medical care).

Raising resources and making public spending pro-poor

As just noted, effective public redistribution requires a willingness and capacity to raise revenues, especially from the

nonpoor. In middle-income developing countries with high inequality, the nonpoor are often reluctant to contribute their fair share. Unblocking this resistance requires actions to build pro-poor coalitions (chapter 6). Low-income countries have the added problem of low public revenues: in 1997 government revenues in these countries averaged about 17.5 percent of GDP (excluding China and India).[7] Compare that with around 29.6 percent for high-income countries.

One reason for the disparity is the high cost of raising revenues in poor countries, costs that sometimes outweigh the benefits of public spending.[8] This in turn is explained by a combination of factors: a narrow tax base, high (and distorting) tax rates, weak tax administration, and poor public sector governance. So the payoff from tax reforms that seek to broaden the base, lower rates, and strengthen revenue collection (often by contracting it out to the private sector) can be substantial, making additional resources available for effective redistribution. In unequal societies, making tax collection as progressive as possible without seriously compromising efficiency is also desirable. For example, inheritance and real estate taxes could be very progressive.

Often, however, the real problem is that the limited public resources are not spent on activities—such as education, health, slum upgrading, and rural development—that help poor people accumulate assets. Part of the reason is that many low-income countries are simply spending too much on other areas, such as debt service, subsidies to the nonpoor, loss-making or inefficient public enterprises, and the military. In the heavily indebted poor countries more than a fifth of public funds goes to debt repayments.[9] Six heavily indebted poor countries in Africa spend more than a third of their national budgets on debt service and less than a tenth on basic social services.[10] Niger spends more than twice as much servicing debt as it does providing primary health care. For several other low-income countries, debt service is not the constraint because they are not meeting their debt obligations. Still, debt levels and debt service obligations are unsustainable for several countries and incompatible with helping poor people accumulate assets.

Military spending in developing countries fell from 4.9 percent of GDP in 1990 to 2.4 percent in 1995.[11] In several countries this lower military spending permitted greater spending on health and higher education.[12] But in other countries—especially those experiencing armed conflicts or facing unresolved tensions with neighbors—military spending continues to cut into pro-poor spending. Many such countries have some of the worst health and education indicators in the world but spend more than twice as much on the military as on education and health combined. High military spending also has significant costs in lost opportunities for asset building. Beyond this crowding-out effect, the destruction of physical and social infrastructure and the slowdown in growth often associated with military conflicts further limit asset accumulation and poverty reduction (see box 3.2 in chapter 3).

Spending on the military and on broader security nevertheless has a role in development. The challenge is to inform budget allocation by making an intelligent assessment of the threats that a country faces. Better governance and transparency in managing military spending can help keep it in check.[13] So can the peaceful resolution of ongoing or potential conflicts.

Between the mid-1980s and mid-1990s public spending on education and health increased in a large number of low-income countries, though slowly. For 118 developing and transition economies, real per capita spending increased on average by 0.7 percent a year for education and 1.3 percent a year for health. Such spending also rose as a share of total spending and national income.[14] But allocating more funds to these sectors is not enough. To support asset accumulation by poor people, the distribution within sectors must favor basic services

used more by the poor and with the greatest market failures—typically not the case. For example, education and health resources go disproportionately to tertiary education and to hospital and curative care, used more by better-off groups.[15]

Several studies confirm that public resources favor the better-off. In Nepal the richest quintile receives four times as much public education spending as the poorest quintile (see table 5.1). In Ghana the richest quintile receives nearly three times the public health spending received by the poorest quintile (see table 5.2).[16] Infrastructure spending also tends to disproportionately benefit wealthier groups.[17] Subsidizing electricity in Croatia and water in Russia helps the rich much more than the poor.[18] In Bangladesh infrastructure subsidies for the better-off are about six times those for the poor.[19]

Governments face important political issues in redistributing public spending to support asset accumulation by poor people. With finer targeting, public funds may in principle reach more poor people. But such targeting may lack political support from powerful groups that may lose out. Hence the importance of building pro-poor coalitions (chapter 6). This may require allocating some of the resources to actions and programs that also benefit the nonpoor.

Making public spending more pro-poor will involve reducing military spending and subsidies to the nonpoor. Privatizing loss-making or inefficient public enterprises releases resources that can potentially be used to address poor people's needs. Simplifying bureaucratic procedures reduces not only wasteful spending but the opportunities for corruption and diversion of resources to illicit activities as well. Prudent macroeconomic management can lower debt payments and make space for pro-poor spending. Periodic reviews of overall public expenditure outcomes can shed light on how efficiently public resources are used and how well they benefit poor people (see box 9.2 in chapter 9).

For the poorest countries, domestic actions will not suffice. These actions will have to be complemented by efforts from the international community to bring about debt relief and expand government resource bases through development cooperation (chapter 11).

Providing services and targeting subsidies

Public spending can provide services directly to poor people—through the construction of roads, schools, health clinics, or water supply schemes. But redistribution can also be achieved by relaxing demand-side constraints for poor people by subsidizing the consumption of privately provided services and covering complementary and opportunity costs. The *Voices of the Poor* study shows how the cost of services can prevent poor households from obtaining them (box 5.4).

Case studies confirm the cost constraints that poor people face in accumulating a wide range of assets. In rural areas in the Kyrgyz Republic 45 percent of patients sold assets (produce or livestock) to pay for hospital care.[20] Indirect costs to households in forgone income from child labor or in household chores no longer performed by children who are in school can also be significant.[21] In rural Madagascar, where access to water is poor, the high opportunity cost of girls' school attendance in time spent fetching water significantly reduces girls' education.[22] In Uganda primary enrollment nearly doubled in the 1997/98 school year when the requirement that parents pay half the cost of school fees was lifted and parent-teacher association levies were banned.[23]

Poor people often pay enormous amounts for infrastructure services. In Nouakchott, Mauritania, most low-income households spend 14–20 percent of their budgets on water—costs reflecting the minimal water infrastructure and the higher cost of the small quantities poor people buy.[24] A cubic meter of water from private water vendors in Port-au-Prince, Haiti, costs 6–10 times as much as a cubic meter from the public water service.[25] Similarly, high connection costs prevent poor households from enjoying energy services.[26] In rural areas, connecting to an electricity grid can cost $20–1,000.[27] In too many cases poor people simply do not have the choice of consuming cheaper water and energy from a commercial network.[28]

Redistribution, by providing services for free or subsidizing their demand, can help poor people expand their assets. Free primary education for poor people is critical for expanding their human assets, especially for girls. Similarly, subsidizing prevention of infectious diseases and helping poor households finance the costs of catastrophic health episodes need to be key elements in strengthening poor people's health assets and reducing their vulnerability to health shocks (see box 5.3; chapter 8).

In both education and health services—even when they are provided for free—demand-side subsidies can help

Box 5.4
Locked out by health and education fees

Whether to seek medical treatment or education for their children presents agonizing choices for poor people. Among participants in the *Voices of the Poor* study, illness was the most frequent trigger of a slide into deeper poverty. Nha, a 26-year-old father in Vietnam, reported that he had had to sell four buffalo, a horse, and two pigs to pay for his daughter's operation. The operation failed to cure her, and the need for further treatment transformed his family from one of the most prosperous in the community to one of the poorest.

In Pakistan many households reported that they had borrowed large sums of money, sold assets, or removed a child from school at least once to cover medical costs. Said an old woman from Ghana, "If you don't have money today, your disease will take you to your grave."

Although the greatest fear for poor people is the risk of large hospital fees, illegal payments for primary care can also be painful. Corruption in health care is widely reported. Poor women from Madaripur, Bangladesh, said that the doctor in the government health care center ignored them, giving preferential treatment to patients wearing good clothes and to those who could afford side payments referred to as "visit fees." A study participant from Vares, Bosnia and Herzegovina, exclaimed, "Before, everyone could get health care. But now everyone just prays to God that they don't get sick because everywhere they just ask for money."

Difficulties with paying school fees and other costs associated with sending children to school are also widely reported. A mother from Millbank, Jamaica, explained that she could not send her six-year-old daughter to school because she could not afford the uniform and other costs. Another daughter had to drop out of school because the family could not afford the $500 for school fees. The woman said, "My son will be ready for school in September but I can't see how I'll be able to send all three of them to school."

In some countries children are pulled out of school because fees are due when families can least afford them. In Ethiopia payments are due at the start of the school year in September, a time of two important festivals and the harvest. Amadi, a 14-year-old boy in Nigeria, said that he had been in and out of school because his parents could not pay his school fees regularly and promptly. He missed his promotion exams several times and remains in primary school while others his age have gone on to secondary school.

In formerly centrally planned economies the cost of schooling is a serious concern for poor families because education was free in the past. People also reported problems with teachers soliciting bribes and special "tutoring fees" in exchange for passing grades and diplomas.

Source: Narayan, Chambers, Shah, and Petesch 2000; Narayan, Patel, Schafft, Rademacher, and Koch-Schulte 2000.

poor families invest further in the human capital of their children (to cover transport costs, for example). To increase access to education for girls or minority, indigenous, or poor children, public funds—in vouchers, stipends, scholarships, grants, and so on—are paid directly to individuals, institutions, and communities. In Bangladesh the government pays stipends covering 30–54 percent of direct school expenses for girls in grades 6–10. In Colombia in the past poor children received public vouchers to attend the secondary school of their choice. In Balochistan, Pakistan, community grants are provided for girls to attend community schools. These programs raise the demand for education among poor households. Mexico's Progresa,[29] for example, has boosted enrollments among beneficiaries compared with similar families not in the program (box 5.5).

An alternative to transfers is subsidies on the price of services. Few developing countries, however, have successfully implemented price discrimination in health services through sliding scale fees.[30] In most African countries such exemptions tend to benefit wealthier groups (such as civil servants).[31] In Ghana's Volta Region in 1995 less than 1 percent of patients were exempt from health user fees, and 71 percent of exemptions went to health service staff.[32] In Indonesia and Vietnam poor people can have user fees waived through an affidavit of indigence, but few people seem to take advantage of this—partly perhaps be-

cause of social stigma attached to declaring oneself indigent.[33] Sometimes private and nongovernmental providers are in a better position to implement sliding scales, since they frequently know their patients' background and have an incentive to charge what the market will bear.[34]

For water and energy many developing countries use increasing block tariffs, charging a low tariff (often below cost) for the first block of consumption and rising tariffs for additional blocks. In Asia 20 of 32 urban water utilities use this tariff structure.[35] Such tariffs appear to be more equitable (since they force firms and wealthier consumers to subsidize consumption by poor households). They also discourage waste. But there are problems. In many developing countries few poor households are served by network utilities, and governments choose large initial consumption blocks, putting most of the financial benefit in the hands of middle- and upper-income consumers. Ironically, increasing block tariffs discriminate against poor households that share a water connection with several other households, because even if the consumption of each household is low, total consumption is high. In addition, tariffs charged to industries have often been so high that they choose to self-provide, undermining the financial viability of service providers.[36]

Still, in countries where network access is high, a well-designed increasing block tariff can outperform cash transfers administered by poorly funded social protection offices, as in some countries in Eastern Europe and the former Soviet Union.[37] But in countries where poor households have limited access, the subsidy of choice should be support for a connection, not for consumption. One way to mitigate high connection costs is to extend credit to poor users.[38] Another is to subsidize all or part of the connection fee. Infrastructure subsidies can also be made more pro-poor if financed through the general budget or through industry levies in ways that are not discriminatory.[39] This approach, compatible with free entry, provides strong incentives to serve the poorest if the subsidy is paid to the provider only after service has been delivered.

How redistribution is best achieved through transfers and price subsidies varies with a government's ability to identify the poor and administer subsidies. If it is possible to identify poor people individually, any number of policies can help in redistribution. Direct cash payments, or the subsidy of any good at all, are fine if the benefits can be restricted to poor people alone. But it usually is not possible to tell precisely who is eligible, necessitating more indirect means (box 5.6).

Box 5.5
Mexico's Progresa: paying parents to send children to school

Mexico's Progresa, an integrated poverty reduction program initiated in 1997, subsidizes education, health care, and nutrition for poor rural households. It aims to reduce current poverty and increase investment in human capital, breaking intergenerational poverty. Progresa covers 2.6 million families—about 80 percent of the population in extreme poverty in rural areas.

Progresa provides grants to poor families for each child under 18 enrolled between the third grade of primary and the third grade of secondary school. The grants increase for higher grades and are slightly higher for girls than boys. For a child in the third year of secondary school, grants are equal to 46 percent of the average earnings of an agricultural worker. Families of children who miss more than 15 percent of the school days in a month do not receive the grant that month.

Progresa has pushed up enrollments at all levels, with the largest effect (17 percent) on the transition from sixth grade to the first year of secondary school (traditionally when many children drop out).

Source: IDB 2000.

Box 5.6
Some general principles on how to design subsidies

Even when poor people cannot be identified individually by administrative means, subsidies can be designed to reach the poor.

- *Self-targeting.* Programs can be designed to ensure "self-selection"—say, by paying wages below prevailing market rates. The Maharashtra Employment Guarantee Scheme in India relies on providing work that only poor people would find attractive (Ravallion 1999a; see box 8.9 in chapter 8).
- *Geographic targeting.* Subsidies can go to specific locations, so that rural and remote areas receive most of the benefits. This works best if the correlation between poverty and location is high—less well if poor and nonpoor live close together. It also works best if the subsidy is attached to goods that are hard to transport, such as direct services in education and health.
- *Commodity targeting.* Subsidies should go to commodities that poor people consume proportionately more of than other people, ensuring that they will receive most of the subsidy. Food and primary education usually rank high on this criterion.

Pooling risk through insurance is another way to address cost constraints on demand for health care. Several middle-income countries are pursuing universal health insurance (chapter 8). Chile managed to reach the 15 percent of its population not covered by social insurance by creating a national health fund (Fonasa) that collects both payroll deductions for social insurance and a general revenue subsidy for health care. Still, public resources may be better spent and poor people may benefit more if governments focus on insuring against catastrophic health incidents—which most poor households are less able to finance.[40] Social insurance schemes, even when intended to be universal, frequently serve the better-off first, with poor people receiving coverage late. Indeed, before coverage becomes universal poor people may suffer—since the demand and prices for private care can increase as a result of the insurance program, as was the case in the Philippines.[41]

Institutional reforms for effective delivery: governance, markets, and competition

I heard rumors about assistance for the poor, but no one seems to know where it is.

—From a discussion group,
Tanjugrejo, Indonesia

Once countries have settled the political problem of how much should be redistributed and the more technical question of what is to be redistributed, the next step is to make sure that services do in fact reach the poor. How can poor people get effective delivery of the services they need to form assets? The old model of universal state provision too often fails because of lack of financial and administrative resources or the failure to respond to poor people's needs.

Part of the problem may be technical and logistical. Poor people often live in remote, low-density rural areas that are expensive and difficult to serve. Resources for poverty reduction may simply not stretch far enough in these environments.

But the problem is quite frequently management and motivation, with inadequate incentives for conscientious service delivery (chapter 6). For services that require the presence of an educated professional—education, health care, judicial services—it is often difficult to induce skilled civil servants to live in remote or rural areas.[42] With children of their own, they often resist living where the educational and cultural opportunities are limited. Besides geography there is another kind of "distance" between providers of services and the poor. Since doctors, teachers, and judges are highly educated, they are often from very different social classes than the communities they serve, making interaction difficult and strained. If pay is determined by civil service rules and differentials for difficult postings do not fully compensate for living conditions, it is very difficult for the public sector to serve poor people.[43]

Public provision is generally only part of the picture for services supplied to poor people, however, and other actors can often overcome the limitations on state provision. Religious groups often do much in providing education. NGOs are also a major force in many countries: in Bangladesh such agencies as the Bangladesh Rural Advancement Committee play a substantial role in delivery, with better results than the government's. And the private sector has always delivered services. More than half the health services in developing countries are private. In Bolivia almost three-quarters of visits to health clinics for treatment of diarrhea or acute respiratory infections are to private facilities.[44] The private sector also began playing a bigger role in infrastructure provision in the 1990s.

Sound governance, competition, and markets—and free entry for multiple agents, whether government, nongovernment, or private—are essential for effective service delivery, especially to poor people. (Indeed, nonpoor communities and people are more likely to make effective use of state systems.) This is not an issue of the state versus the market, but of the use of different agents and mechanisms depending on the type of activity. In education the national curriculum and exams are a public function, but multiple agents can provide schooling and communities can hold teachers accountable.

The mix of state and market—and the mix of agents—depends on the nature of the service and the institutional context.[45] Where governments are weak, there might be a stronger case for open entry and reliance on private and nongovernment agents. But this, too, may require more monitoring and regulatory capacity than the government can muster. The importance of institutional reforms, good governance, and markets in providing quality services to poor people is illustrated here with examples from health and telecommunications.

Improving the delivery of health services

Sometimes I stay for long hours until I can see one of the doctors, then afterwards the nurse comes and tells me that he is not coming or he came but he will not be able to see me.

—*Poor woman, El Mataria, Egypt*

Despite impressive advances in health in recent decades, and despite the potential effectiveness of policies and programs, health services often fail to reach poor people. A fundamental problem: it is difficult to maintain staff in rural areas and to ensure conscientious care by those who do show up. In countries as diverse as Brazil, India, Indonesia, and Zambia, staff vacancies in health posts are much more numerous and last longer in poor and rural areas than in richer and urban ones.

Improving health services in poor communities might involve changing the incentive structure for public providers, switching from public provision to public financing of private or NGO providers, or changing the type of services the government is committed to offer, favoring those whose delivery is easier to manage.

Changing incentives in the public sector is often difficult, with civil service rules often tightly constraining hiring, firing, promotion, and pay (chapter 6). Different methods, all with their own risks, have been used, such as allowing private practice to supplement incomes, making education subsidies contingent on public service, or

paying extra allowances for hardship posts. None of them is problem free.

In recent years there have been more attempts to decentralize health services to subnational levels of government. This also changes the incentives for providers because they have to satisfy a different set of employers. Local governments may be more responsive to feedback from clients. But the jury is still out on the benefits of decentralization in health. Sometimes decentralization has simply shed responsibilities from the central government—not an example of good decentralization. Successful decentralization relies on increased participation of people as monitors of quality (see next section on participation).

Rather than provide services directly, governments can make better use of the private sector and NGOs. In many countries even very poor people prefer to spend money on services from the private sector (or from NGOs) if they perceive the quality to be higher than that of public services.[46] This preference can be exploited by changing the role of government from provider to financier.

Effective partnerships draw on the strengths of each sector—public, private, nonprofit—in improving provision of health services to poor people. The World Health Organization's immunization program has been a remarkable success (box 5.7). In Brazil, by having NGOs compete for funding, the government has harnessed the private sector's energy and expertise in the battle against AIDS and other sexually transmitted diseases. NGOs can often reach segments of society that shy away from official contact yet run the highest risk of HIV infection. By the end of 1994 NGOs financed under this system had distributed an estimated 2.6 million condoms and taken 11,000 calls to hotlines. Stringent government supervision has also been important in ensuring that all but 4 of the 191 NGO-run projects financed have gone forward without a hitch.[47]

Governments might rethink the types of services they choose to offer, based simply on what they can credibly promise. Maintaining permanent staff in rural primary health care clinics may be too difficult for some governments to manage. Changing the mode of delivery or the types of services may be called for. India recently introduced a campaign to combat polio, reducing reliance on permanent clinics with short trips by medical personnel to rural areas—with good results.[48] Similarly, rather than relying on permanent health staff who are

Box 5.7
Effective public-private partnership in immunization

In 1974 the World Health Organization (WHO) launched the Expanded Immunization Program, aiming for 80 percent coverage of children under five by 1990. Although the program started as a WHO initiative, it soon included many multinational organizations, and volunteers, private entrepreneurs, and government workers did the actual work within countries. The Rotarians, for example, raised more than $240 million to provide polio vaccine to some 500 million children in 103 countries. Private manufacturers also took part, providing large volumes of vaccine at a low price to the United Nations Children's Fund's global distribution network and still making a profit.

The results have been spectacular. By 1990 the program had achieved its goal of immunizing 80 percent of children against the most common childhood diseases. The initiative succeeded because it combined public, private, and multinational efforts, with each organization using its comparative strength to fit each country's circumstances.

Source: van der Gaag 1995.

difficult to monitor and motivate, governments might find infrastructure projects providing clean water and sanitation both easier to manage and more likely to improve health conditions.[49] And rather than fighting doctors' preference to work in hospitals, governments might choose to focus more on gaining access to hospital services for poor people.[50]

Providing telecommunications services to poor people

Given the right policies and regulations, the private sector is well positioned to provide telecommunications services to poor people. Better communications, bringing new influences and broader views of the world, can raise the earnings of poor people.[51] In Sri Lanka telephone service in rural areas increased farmers' share of the price received for crops sold in the capital city from 50–60 percent to 80–90 percent.[52]

Since the mid-1980s developing countries have been opening telecommunications to private participation and competition.[53] The arrangements range from private investment in publicly owned companies (China) to complete privatization and widespread competition, leaving the state to focus on regulation (Chile). Private participation has generally resulted in rapid growth in access, lower prices, and better service. In Peru five years after

reform, the number of fixed lines had increased more than 165 percent, the number of mobile lines had risen from 20,000 to nearly 500,000, and the number of locales with access to telephones had more than doubled. Between 1995 and 1996 the share of households in the poorest quintile with telephones increased from 1 percent to 7 percent.[54]

Large and small providers can offer services side-by-side, facilitated by a wide range of innovative technologies. When local entrepreneurs were allowed to offer telecommunications services in Senegal, costs dropped and access more than doubled (box 5.8).[55] Provision of pay phones can greatly enhance poor people's access to telecommunications services, particularly in countries where telephone call rates are low but connection charges are high.[56] Advances in cellular technology have also dramatically increased access to telecommunications in countries where laws and regulations encourage geographically widespread coverage. Grameen Telecom, a nonprofit in Bangladesh, uses cellular technology, combined with the entrepreneurial talents of rural women, to provide services to villages (see box 4.6 in chapter 4). India, Peru, South Africa, and Thailand have seen dramatic growth in privately owned and operated telecenters, providing rural inhabitants with new sources of information and new opportunities.[57]

Because private providers focus on the most profitable market segments, some pockets of the population—particularly poorer groups—may not receive access because of the high cost and low revenue potential of extending

Box 5.8
Local entrepreneurs increase access to telecommunications services

Allowing local entrepreneurs to offer telecommunications services is an important first step in lowering the costs of public access. Pay phones in particular benefit those who cannot afford a household connection. In 1995 Senegal had more than 2,000 private telecenters, each with a telephone and many with a fax machine—four times the number just two years before. By 1998 it had 6,000. Sonatel (the Senegalese public telecommunications company) franchises phone service to the telecenter owner, who may charge a tariff up to 140 percent above the Sonatel price per call unit. On average, telecenters have paid $3,960 to Sonatel and kept $1,584 each year. The result: public access to telephones has more than doubled.

Source: Ernberg 1998; CSIR 1998.

service to them. To avoid leaving out poor people, innovative public-private partnerships and well-targeted government subsidies may be needed.[58] Chile used government resources to improve access for low-income households, people with disabilities, and public schools, health centers, and libraries and auctioned subsidies to private providers to pay for rural telecommunications rollout. In about half the chosen locations, bids to provide service did not require subsidies as initially expected; the demand analysis done by the privatization group persuaded private investors of the profitability of providing services in these areas. Within two years 90 percent of rollout objectives had been achieved for about half the initial budget.[59]

Despite successes in extending telecommunications services to poor people, privatization is unlikely to significantly increase access in the absence of greater competition and more effective regulation to prevent abuse of market power. To make private participation propoor in telecommunications—and in infrastructure more broadly—policymakers may need to refocus regulations and transaction processes. A study of telecommunications provision in 30 African and Latin American countries found that strong competition is correlated with per capita increases in mainlines, pay phones, and connection capacity—and with decreases in the price of local calls. It also found that well-designed regulation was important in improving connection capacity.[60] A study on infrastructure reform in Argentina suggests that public-private partnerships can, with the right policies and regulations, also improve access to infrastructure for poor people.[61]

Participation: choice, monitoring, and accountability

The third principle for public action to promote asset accumulation involves engaging poor communities and poor people. Participation has three main objectives:

- To ensure that the preferences and values of communities are reflected in the choice and design of interventions.
- To use community and participant monitoring to improve implementation, transparency, and accountability.
- To give poor people more influence over their lives.

Participation, while potent, is no panacea. Depending on local organizations and power structures, shifting influence to local communities can lead to greater cap-

ture of benefits by local elites (chapter 6). In Bangladesh the extent to which food-for-education transfers go to poor or nonpoor households depends on the relative strength of organizations for the poor and the nonpoor.[62] Similarly, some local values may be inimical to some groups of poor people—as with biases against women in many parts of the world, against lower castes in India, or against other disadvantaged ethnic or social groups. Shame, denial, and stigma over HIV/AIDS are in some countries reasons for local inaction.

The complexities of participation imply that it needs to be fostered by actions that strengthen the voice of poor groups in confronting social stratification or stigma. This implies that participation needs to be shaped in a broader institutional context. Local government is in the middle of the picture, with core interactions between municipalities and communities—as in the design of the Decentralization and Popular Participation Laws in Bolivia in the past decade. But local governments often need to be strengthened and made accountable: too often disempowered in the past, they face difficulties of weak capacity and local capture. Civil society organizations can also increase the influence of poor people and poor communities. These broader issues are taken up in chapters 6 and 7; here the importance of participation in enabling poor people to expand their assets is illustrated with examples from education, local infrastructure, and forest management.

Increasing local participation and accountability in education

Parents and local communities are demanding more of a say in children's education. As education systems have expanded in many developing countries, concerns have mounted about the quality of instruction. Central structures are weak in dealing with daily administrative tasks and too distant to take effective action against teachers who do not perform.

Community participation in primary education frequently focuses on monitoring teacher performance and ensuring the availability of school supplies. In the functions most suitable for local management—in-service training and pedagogical supervision—teachers unions can complement local parent-teacher associations. But teachers unions often fiercely oppose devolving control of hiring and firing to local levels, because that has often resulted in delayed salary payments and at times abuse by local officials, inciting teacher strikes in Nigeria and

Zimbabwe.[63] Ongoing reform efforts in Nicaragua are seeking to overcome such problems (box 5.9).

The overall trend in education is to decentralize. In 1993 Sri Lanka established school development boards to promote community participation in school management. In Bangladesh school management committees have been reactivated by the Social Mobilization Campaign, to involve communities in education. El Salvador started involving rural communities in school management in 1995.[64] In several communities in developing countries parent groups have responsibility for hiring and firing teachers and for supplying and maintaining equipment, under contract from education ministries. So far, however, there has been little experience with full-scale decentralization of teacher management to schools.

One of the few available quantitative impact evaluations, for the Primary Education Project in Mexico, shows that educational achievement improved significantly during decentralization and that the lower the initial achievement level, the greater the scope for

improvement.[65] There is also evidence that supervision incentives are the most cost-effective input for rural and indigenous schools. Nicaragua's experience with school autonomy reform indicates that a higher level of decisionmaking by schools is associated with higher student test scores, particularly in schools exerting greater autonomy in teacher staffing, monitoring, and evaluation.[66] In Nigeria teachers have shown up on time since local supervision was introduced.[67] And social assessments of Brazil's Minas Gerais program and El Salvador's Community Participation in Education program (Educación con participación de la comunidad, or Educo) indicate that as a result of the programs, teachers meet more often with parents and are regarded more highly by them. Their attendance is also better, which lowers student absences.[68]

Other evidence suggests that community management of education can increase efficiency. Preliminary results for the Philippines show that primary schools that rely more on local support have lower costs, holding quality and enrollments constant.[69] In Mauritius parent-teacher associations have been so successful that government funds are being used to further stimulate this partnership.[70]

Effective community management in education may, however, be hard to achieve. Finding qualified people to manage schools can be difficult, and the results are uneven. Botswana has had trouble attracting talented people to school boards.[71] In the Zambezia province of Mozambique parent management committees have led to beneficial partnerships between communities and schools in some villages, but in others they barely function. Many villagers are afraid to openly criticize school staff, and committees have been co-opted by corrupt officials.[72] There is also evidence that community involvement may have little impact where adults are barely literate.[73] Despite Educo's success in expanding access in El Salvador, it has not delivered higher achievement scores than traditional schools in the poor rural communities that were the top priorities.[74]

Overall, experience suggests that a strong regulatory framework is needed and that training parents is vital to make local monitoring of schools effective. Many other concerns about greater household involvement in education can be addressed through public funding.[75] Continued monitoring and evaluation of local participation in education can tell much about what works and what does not.

Box 5.9
Local participation in Nicaragua's decentralized education system

Since 1993 Nicaragua's Ministry of Education has been decentralizing public primary and secondary education to local management boards, based on the following model:

- Legal responsibility for public education rests with the ministry, but some teacher management is delegated to other levels of the system.
- The center controls teacher preparation, establishes staffing levels, funds teacher salaries, and sets standards for teacher qualifications and pedagogical performance. It also drafts regulations and financial controls.
- The departmental level is responsible for supervisory functions, providing pedagogical support to teachers, and monitoring compliance with standards.
- Municipal education councils composed of local representatives discharge the administrative functions delegated to the local level. These councils pay teacher salaries (with central funds) and approve teacher appointments, transfers, leaves of absence, and dismissals in accord with central laws and regulations. They also oversee teacher incentives and issue incentive payments to eligible teachers.
- Teachers are accountable for what happens in their classroom. Parents monitor their attendance and report to the municipal education councils, which inform teachers weekly of their status in relation to incentives.

Source: Gaynor 1998.

Fostering ownership through participation and choice in local infrastructure

The policy of the party is that the people know, the people discuss, the people do, but here people only implement the last part, which is the people do.
— *From a discussion group, Ha Tinh, Vietnam*

Community involvement in planning and managing local infrastructure services can greatly increase ownership and sustainability—if communities make informed choices. While local infrastructure is scarce in most developing countries, the infrastructure that exists is often poorly conceived and maintained. Why?

Past efforts to provide local infrastructure have often failed to involve communities in key decisions, with central ministries deciding on what local communities needed and communities learning of a project only when the bulldozer showed up. Another problem has been a lack of choice. Faced with take-it-or-leave-it, few communities turn down a free or heavily subsidized investment.[76] This can kill local ownership, and upkeep of the investment becomes somebody else's responsibility. The incentive structures for agency staff can also compromise community participation—when the preference is speed in implementation. True community participation processes take time—it took years for the Orangi community in Pakistan to agree on the sewers it wanted to install[77]—but they generate ownership and sustainability.

Involving beneficiaries in decisionmaking is the starting point in creating local ownership of infrastructure assets, ownership that is important in three key dimensions. First, it helps in choosing priorities, particularly in areas difficult to tackle through economic analysis, such as the relative value of social and productive investment, the complementarity between investments, and targeting within communities.[78] Second, it is essential for good operation and maintenance, because governments can rarely be relied on to perform timely upkeep of local infrastructure. Third, given the precarious budget situation of most developing country governments and the vast infrastructure needs (and total costs), local ownership is required for community cost sharing in investments and operation.

For the participatory process to generate ownership, all groups in the community—men and women, those well represented in the community and those in the minority—must be able to voice their demands. Local communities reflect existing social, ethnic, gender, and economic divisions, and unless the question of who constitutes the community is understood and addressed up front, men and local elites may dominate decisionmaking and capture project benefits. In rural Sub-Saharan Africa men often identify roads as high-priority interventions, while women, when consulted, prefer to improve the footbridges and paths that make up the local transport system on which they rely.[79] In a village water supply project in rural India, water supply points were placed near influential households.[80] And in Honduras beneficiary assessments showed that in places where the social fund had financed piped sewerage, the choice of better-off households with water connections, most community members had wanted roads and bridges.[81] Provider agencies—local governments, NGOs, project facilitators—can reduce the risk of capture by elites, but these agencies sometimes also try to capture benefits.

Requiring beneficiaries to share in the cost of investment can also improve ownership.[82] Contributions usually come more readily when the communities and local governments responsible for operation and maintenance are given a voice in design and implementation. Local contributions vary. In Ghana communities contribute 5 percent of the cost for improved water systems and 50 percent for sanitation systems. Cost sharing in menu-driven or social fund–type projects is typically between 5 and 20 percent of project costs.[83] Significant financial contributions—between 20 and 55 percent of project costs—have been suggested as important for sustainability in a study of rural water projects.[84] There is also compelling evidence that ownership is a function of the institutional relationship between communities and service providers (chapter 6).[85]

There is a trend toward providing local infrastructure through community-based multisectoral approaches.[86] By giving greater choice, such approaches have the potential to respond better to the priorities of each community, contributing to ownership and sustainability.[87] But it may not be desirable to offer open menus in every project. If there is a critical need for institutional or policy reform in water or transport, for example, multisectoral approaches are unlikely to address it (box 5.10). Similarly, some types of infrastructure involving more than one community, such as roads linking many communities, will rarely be demanded by individual communities even if they are needed. Such infrastructure is thus best supplied

Box 5.10
Single-sector and multisector arrangements for improving rural roads in Zambia

In Zambia in 1997 there was a critical need to clarify the institutional arrangements for managing and financing rural roads. Many communities had constructed roads without the involvement of the local council, motivated by food aid from NGOs or by free-standing projects. But these communities, which had been fully compensated for their work, were unwilling to carry out maintenance on a voluntary basis. Local councils, strapped for resources, were unable to assume responsibility for the roads. As a result, scarce infrastructure assets were going back to bush, leaving communities in isolation.

To improve rural accessibility, the government of Zambia included district and community roads as part of a road sector investment project (Roadsip) in 1998. Recognizing the importance of local ownership in infrastructure, Roadsip addresses the institutional arrangements for the entire road sector—from the main highways to the community roads—and the government is exploring ways to put community ownership of roads into law.

Experience shows that efforts for sustainable improvements in rural accessibility at the community level also have to address sector policy and institutional reform and must involve the future owners of each road. Improving the roads owned by different levels of government took a vertical single-sector approach working through local governments and the Ministries of Transport and Communications, Public Works, and Local Government and Housing. The approach for the community roads was a horizontal multisectoral approach working with the Zambian social fund.

Only by working through the social fund, which has a well-established system for facilitating community participation, could Roadsip ensure that communities would choose their priority investment. When communities request improvements to roads, footbridges, or paths, they pay 25 percent of project costs and the social fund and Roadsip pay 75 percent. On completion of a road project, the community forms a road owners association and applies to the national road board for grant support for maintenance (75 percent community, 25 percent road fund). Providing cost-sharing grants to communities for maintaining their roads does not have to cost much. At $300 a kilometer, the cost of supporting the maintenance of 5,000 kilometers of community roads would be less than 2 percent of annual road fund revenues.

Source: World Bank 1998u, 1999ee.

and managed by local governments, although in consultation with communities,[88] using a unified investment planning process. Such a process can be followed by multisector or single-sector projects.

Among the attempts to introduce participatory processes that allow choice, social funds have been the most widely studied. Social funds aim to empower communities by promoting their participation in the selection, implementation, and operation and maintenance of their development projects, usually for local infrastructure.[89] But merely making financing available for investments in a variety of sectors is not enough to ensure that beneficiaries exercise their choice.[90] In many social fund projects community members are unaware of the full range of options eligible for financing. In Peru only 16 percent of beneficiaries could cite more than 5 of 19 eligible project types.[91] Furthermore, the mere fact that communities have a choice does not necessarily mean that it will be an informed one.

For local infrastructure investments to be effective and sustainable, the demand-based approach generally has to be complemented by supply-side inputs (capacity building, information, outreach). Balancing a bottom-up identification of investments with carefully selected supply-side inputs will enhance the prospects for equitable and sustainable infrastructure services for poor people.[92]

Promoting local management of forests

Common property resources, because they possess characteristics of both public and private goods, are subject to free-rider problems that may lead to degradation or depletion in a free market. Poor people suffer the most from these problems when they depend heavily on natural resource assets.[93] The common response has been state management, with regulations to induce user behavior consistent with resource conservation. But the deplorable environmental outcomes under state-led programs, dwindling public resources, and the general shift from top-down to bottom-up partnership approaches have recently increased the emphasis on community-based natural resource management. This approach recognizes and reinforces the role of communities living in and around vulnerable natural resources, tapping their ideas, experience, values, and capabilities for preserving their natural resources.[94]

Communities often manage natural resources in cooperation with—and with support from—other communities and higher (or external) entities, such as local or district governments, government agencies, or NGOs.[95]

Often, such arrangements apply to forests. At the center of joint forest management is an agreement between governments and communities on the distribution of use rights and the sharing of benefits,[96] usually with communities getting a larger share of forest assets if they achieve agreed conservation and sustainability objectives.[97] The state, through the forest department, is often the owner of the forest and also regulates the system.[98] The approach has been widely applied in South Asia—for example, in the Indian state of Andhra Pradesh (box 5.11). In Africa community participation has helped restore forest resources in The Gambia and led to broader participation in rural development in Zimbabwe.

But the mixed record in other cases signals the challenges in making joint management an effective tool for promoting poor people's access to key natural assets. Overly centralized administrative structures have been one reason for failure. The experience of many countries confirms that powerful resistance at the national level to devolving rights to forest users can blunt effective community participation. And forest users or communities, often unorganized and with diverging interests, may lack the capacity, interest, and incentives to manage large forest areas.[99] The applicability and success of joint management will in each case be determined by the institutional context—including private interests, local norms, and traditions—and by the quality of state and local organizations and institutions. Part of the challenge of joint management is identifying the sociogeographic units that can work together to manage and conserve natural resources.[100]

Several approaches have been used to overcome these obstacles. Providing incentives for stakeholder participation is essential: granting secure tenure and rights to forest users,[101] more fully transferring management authority over forests (rather than user rights alone) to communities, sharing benefits, and using socially acceptable technologies that provide adequate revenue.[102] Effective mechanisms for resolving conflicts are also critical, especially where resource users' livelihoods compete with other objectives, such as biodiversity protection or sustainable forestry.[103] Contracts between the government, villages, and fuelwood collectors in Burkina Faso and Madagascar specify which subgroups of users manage options in watershed and protected areas. Effective enforcement of these contracts is essential. In the Czech Republic, Ecuador, the Slovak Republic, and Ukraine sites outside protected areas are rezoned to accommodate

Box 5.11
Rejuvenating India's forests through joint action

The state government of Andhra Pradesh has introduced joint forest management on a massive scale. People on the fringes of forests are forming village organizations to protect forests—*vana samrakashna samithi* (VSSs). The organizations work with the state forest department, sharing the responsibilities and benefits of forest restoration, protection, and management.

The forest department is responsible for organizing and providing technical and administrative support to the VSSs. Villages and VSSs are selected carefully, but people from scheduled castes and tribes are automatically eligible for membership. The VSSs protect the forest from encroachment, grazing, theft, and fire, improving it according to a joint forest management plan. As compensation, the VSSs are entitled to all the forest's products (nontimber products as well as all the income from the harvest of timber and bamboo) as long as they set aside half the income for the future development of the forest.

The program got off to a slow start in 1992 because villagers were hesitant to assume responsibility for forest management. In addition, forest department staff had reservations about joint forest management. But in 1999 more than 5,000 VSSs were managing more than 1.2 million hectares of degraded forests in the state.

Results are impressive, and the program is expanding rapidly. The degraded forests have sprung back to life, timber smuggling has almost stopped, and cattle grazing is under control. There has been no further encroachment by agriculture on lands managed by the VSSs. Many villagers now work in the forests, and outmigration has declined. Soil conservation has resulted in higher water tables in many areas, increasing agricultural production. And local plants and animals are flourishing.

Source: Venkataraman and Falconer 1999.

multiple land uses.[104] Where local capabilities to control and manage resource use have been eroded or have broken down, external assistance can help strengthen and monitor resource sharing and management.[105]

As in other examples of local participation, social inequalities can reinforce the influence of politically powerful and better-off groups, further reducing access for other groups.[106] In particular, women and poor people who depend on communal assets for their livelihoods can be pushed into deeper poverty if they are excluded.[107] While the forest management groups in Andhra Pradesh successfully involved women, a few programs in other Indian states still allow only one household member to participate—effectively excluding women. In several Indian villages women were barred from collecting any forest products on protected lands.[108]

Even when women are not excluded, their numbers and their influence in management committees are low.[109] A policy and legal framework that promotes participation by poor users in the management of natural resources can help change this.[110] Greater inclusion of women will also require awareness-raising activities to break through societal norms that keep women from playing an equal role with men.

Complementarities in public action

Recall the three principles for building assets for poor people—redistribution by the state, effective governance and use of markets, and participation. Effective action generally involves applying all three principles in a particular area or sector. The extent to which each principle is applied depends on the structural conditions, the type of action, the state of governance, and the extent of participatory involvement and social inequality. Take education. There is a case for public redistribution that seeks to ensure free or subsidized basic education for all. Effective delivery often involves multiple agents providing schooling—public, private, and civil society. And in poor areas participation of parents is important for increasing coverage, quality, and accountability.

In this section the mix of actions is illustrated for a natural asset (land) and for two physical assets (urban water and sanitation). The complementarities imply that action is needed on several fronts. But the priorities should depend on what poor people lack most relative to their potential opportunities. In poor rural areas this may be basic economic infrastructure, land-enhancing investment, water and sanitation services, and basic education and health care. In urban slums it may be infrastructure. And secure property rights on land are important for both.

Enabling good governance, active markets, and broad participation in land reform

Land reform has returned to the policy agenda in the past decade, as many developing countries move beyond implementing macroeconomic reforms to addressing the often weak micro-level supply responses in agriculture.[111] It is easy to see why farmland is a key asset for the rural poor. But secure access to land and for whom and under what conditions remains a thorny issue.[112] Poor people, especially poor women, often lack land rights. Land ownership remains concentrated, and efforts to increase land equality have often generated conflict.[113] New approaches to land reform stress the importance of bringing together various stakeholders—the landless and their associations, the private sector (landowners), and government institutions at the local and national levels.

There are many ways to gain secure access to land—some informal and others formal, some spontaneous and others requiring extensive government intervention.[114] In general, secure access to land can be gained through ownership, tenure, or customary use rights.[115] Ownership rights are the most secure but also the least likely to be enjoyed by the poor and other socially excluded groups. Poor people often gain access to land through the rental market and customary use rights.[116] In India, of the estimated 19 percent of rural households that lease land, more than 90 percent are landless or own very little land.[117] When land is relatively abundant or poor people are well organized and influential, they can have secure land access without formal property rights and registration.[118] This is still the case in many parts of Sub-Saharan Africa, though in recent decades population growth and market integration have accelerated the shift to individual land rights.[119]

Public action is critical to ensuring secure access to land for poor people. Land reform that enhances equity and productivity through government-supported programs is usually what first comes to mind (see box 3.8 in chapter 3). But many other actions can improve access to land. Policies and laws that clearly define land rights and protect poor people against land grabbing can greatly enhance their ability to use land as collateral and invest in land they already "own." Well-functioning rental markets can raise the efficiency of land use and help the landless climb the "agricultural ladder" to ownership.[120] Providing legal assistance to poor people enables them to press their legal claim to a plot of land. Similarly, public support to institutions that protect women's rights can be instrumental where deep-seated social norms and customs inhibit women from exercising effective control over land even when there are legal provisions for them to do so (chapter 7).[121]

Attempts at land reform often fail because they rely on government alone. New approaches emphasize continuous mechanisms of adjustment in land access, greater reliance on traditional forms of access, and greater use of land markets.[122] Brazil, Colombia, the Philippines, and South Africa are experimenting with decentralized, community-based, demand-driven negotiations between stakeholders to find less antagonistic ways to improve access to land.

Such negotiated land reform relies to a great extent on experience gained in past attempts at land reform and on the successful aspects of demand-driven social funds. It addresses both supply and demand. Landlords are paid in cash rather than with highly discounted government bonds, as in the past. Beneficiaries receive grants for productivity-enhancing investments, because experience shows that unless those who receive land can make productive use of it, reforms will be undermined.[123]

The negotiated approach has several innovative components, including strong involvement of local governments and communities in organizing land transfers and assisting the beneficiaries—and a high degree of transparency (box 5.12). In Colombia municipalities must develop a comprehensive plan to identify potential sellers and beneficiaries, and the plan is widely circulated to avoid corruption. Potential beneficiaries are offered training in farm management and assistance in developing land use plans. These plans must then be approved in public meetings of municipal councils.[124] Beneficiaries are supported by national, regional, or state councils that provide technical guidance and resolve administrative obstacles.

The results on the ground from the community-based approach are encouraging. Yet it is still too early to fully evaluate this new generation of reforms. While the negotiated land reform has been criticized for, among other things, burdening beneficiaries with loans they cannot repay and trying to replace expropriative land reform, revisions to the approach have sought to address these and other concerns. Another issue is costs. Although in Brazil and elsewhere this approach has achieved savings of as much as 40 percent relative to expropriative reforms, it still requires significant public outlays.[125] Its effectiveness needs to be assessed relative to other instruments for reducing poverty.[126]

Providing water and sanitation services to the urban poor

The sewage runs right in your front door, and when it rains, the water floods into the house and you need to lift things . . . the waste brings some bugs. Here we have rats, cockroaches, spiders, and even snakes and scorpions.

—From a discussion group, Nova California, Brazil

To improve water and sanitation services to urban residents, governments and municipalities the world over are

Box 5.12
A new approach to land reform in Brazil

Brazil has been expropriating and redistributing land since the mid-1960s, reaching an impressive number of beneficiaries, but with high costs and uneven quality.

To increase quality, lower costs, and speed reform, five state governments in the Northeast started a pilot program of negotiated, decentralized, community-driven land reform in 1997. The program provides loans for land purchases to landless rural dwellers (sharecroppers, renters, landless workers, labor tenants) or to smallholders who organize themselves in beneficiary associations. The associations have to identify landlords interested in selling them land, an approach that fosters direct negotiations between owners and the associations and reduces government intervention.

The pilot program also provides grants for productivity-enhancing community projects identified by the beneficiary associations, drawing on well-established poverty alleviation projects in the five states. The philosophy of the projects is that beneficiary associations are best placed to identify, rank, and implement investments, drawing on technical assistance as necessary. The same participatory philosophy has been adopted in the land reform pilots.

The program has three grant elements constituting about 50 percent of the cost of the land: an inherent subsidy in the interest rate, a grant for the complementary infrastructure investment, and an installation grant. A credit with a maximum term of 20 years is provided for the land. The land guarantees the loan and has to meet a number of requirements, including a price comparable to what prevails in the local market. Since there is a maximum grant per beneficiary family and the infrastructure investment grant is a residual, there is an incentive for the association to buy the land at the lowest possible cost.

Although the number of beneficiary families is still modest (about 10,000 in 330 projects), the pilot program has picked up momentum, and its success has prompted the central government to expand the program nationwide. Complementing the larger, expropriative program, the new program focuses on purchasing properties that cannot be legally expropriated.

Source: Deininger forthcoming.

exploring alternative approaches involving the private sector and local neighborhood and civil society groups. Working together, these actors seek to provide quality services to poor consumers while ensuring financial sustainability.

Water and sanitation services have traditionally been provided by public agencies. While there are exceptions, few developing countries have elicited strong, sustained performance from public water and wastewater utilities. Weak performance incentives and difficulties in sheltering management decisions from political interference have locked many utilities into a cycle of poor service, low user willingness to pay, and insufficient maintenance. The inability of supply to keep pace with increasing demand from growing urban populations has forced poor households to find their own solutions. In many countries small informal water vendors and sanitation providers reach poor urban areas unserved by government utilities. In West African cities independent entrepreneurs supply most poor households (box 5.13). Similarly, in Guatemala City and Lima, Peru, which both have major utility companies, most families depend on private informal providers.[127] Although local suppliers can be more expensive than public providers, households would be worse off without them.

Since the early 1990s there has been a marked increase in large-scale private participation in water and sanitation in developing countries, reflecting a desire to deliver better services at lower cost—including services to poor urban neighborhoods.[128] Private participation can boost service coverage and make utility operations more effi-

cient, and the early results are encouraging. Coverage has increased rapidly, and in some cases tariffs have fallen (as in Manila, Philippines). The water supply system in Côte d'Ivoire, which introduced the first private concession in Sub-Saharan Africa, performs better than other urban water systems in West Africa.[129]

But large-scale private participation in water and sanitation does not automatically mean better services for poor people. Unless carefully crafted, contracts may preclude the extension of services to low-income areas and create local monopolies. Contracts often mandate tariff structures and set connection fees that do not vary with the true cost of connection. These features discourage concessionaires from delivering service to low-income areas.[130] In Guayaquil, Ecuador, residential water tariffs did not cover collection costs. Every new connection, even if fully grant financed, was a net revenue drain on the utility.[131] To serve low-income households better, concessions in Buenos Aires, Argentina, and La Paz-El Alto, Bolivia, have been restructured based on negotiations between governments and private providers and input from local stakeholders.

Good pricing policy is a key element of pro-poor policy.[132] Whether water and sanitation utilities are publicly or privately managed, those most successful in expanding these services charge tariffs that cover costs. Such tariffs can increase access for low-income households by attracting private investment to expand supply and enhance quality. They can also end general government subsidies that go mostly to the nonpoor, releasing public resources for more targeted assistance to poor people. Notwithstanding the overall trend in water and sanitation toward greater cost recovery, governments can ensure greater access for poor people by subsidizing connections or, where network access is high, using well-designed block tariffs.[133]

Additional measures to benefit poor households and attract private investors to water and sanitation include simplifying contracts, contracting out some regulatory functions, and increasing the predictability of regulatory discretion.[134] The design of regulation—particularly to reduce monopoly power—is also critical for pro-poor outcomes.[135] Regulation can enhance competition by permitting greater entry, including by nonconventional suppliers, and by changing service standards to fit local needs—for example, focusing on the potability of water rather than on technical construction standards set at industrial country levels.[136]

Also important is involving users and local institutions in designing private sector options with user preferences in

Box 5.13
West African businesses pioneer water and sanitation services for the urban poor

Africa's independent water and sanitation providers suggest that the market has found solutions that benefit everyone: providers, utilities, and, above all, low-income customers. Recent studies in seven West African cities show that half the residents rely on private independent providers for their water and at least three-quarters rely on independent operators for sanitation. Depending on the city, independent providers cover up to 85 percent of marginal and low-income neighborhoods, and they serve many better-off families as well.

Independent sanitation providers, working without an official mandate or arrangement with local governments, include small informal operators as well as a few that have grown and become "legitimate." Providers rely on good client relations, since their operations are completely demand driven. Consumer ability to pay and competition among providers determine prices.

Independent sanitation providers charge higher prices than subsidized public companies, but public companies rarely recoup their operating costs—let alone the costs of installing sewer networks. And the independent providers are generally reliable and responsive to their customers. They extend credit (for a few days at least) and spread collections over days and weeks, far easier for poor clients to fathom than the three-month bills from public companies.

Source: Solo 1999.

mind—and fully leveraging the presence of alternative service providers. This is the approach of the Water and Sanitation Program—a partnership of donors, governments, and NGOs that focuses on poor rural and periurban areas. In each context this demand-responsive approach must be tailored to local conditions. Brazil's Prosanear (Water and Sanitation Program for Low-Income Urban Populations) follows six principles to provide sustainable water and sanitation services to poor households (box 5.14).

A similar approach aims to cover 35 towns in an urban water and sanitation project in the Philippines. Communities decide to participate (borrowing money from the Development Bank of the Philippines) after extensive consultations involving consumers, the mayor, and the town council. Service charges are used to repay the loan and cover operation and maintenance. The involvement of users, together with local government decisionmaking on participation, appears to ensure the ownership needed to enhance prospects for long-term sustainability.[137]

•   •   •

The assets that poor people possess—or have access to—directly contribute to their well-being and have a potent effect on their prospects for escaping poverty. Human, physical, natural, financial, and social assets can enable poor people to take advantage of opportunities for economic and social development (just as their lack can prevent this). Expanding the assets of poor people can strengthen their economic, political, and social position and their control over their lives. Assets empower the poor. And assets help people manage risks (chapters 8 and 9).

Box 5.14
Sustainable water and sanitation for Brazil's urban poor

The first phase of Prosanear (1992–97) was a period of learning that led to six guiding principles for sustainable provision of water and sanitation in poor urban neighborhoods in Brazil:
- Start community participation at the very beginning of project preparation.
- Ensure that cost-recovery and subsidy rules are clear and transparent.
- Make formal, long-term arrangements for operating and maintaining systems an integral part of the design.
- Discuss all feasible technical options and their costs with communities.
- Coordinate projects with the local government's urban development plan from the outset of preparation.
- Confirm that the local government has a strong commitment to the project and to poverty reduction.

Source: Katakura and Bakalian 1998.

But because there is a two-way causal relationship between political and social structures and the assets of poor people, it may be necessary to tackle exclusionary or weak social structures in order to form assets (chapter 7).

Public action is essential to expand poor people's assets and to tackle asset inequalities—particularly in the distribution of human assets. Effectively using the redistributive power of the state and involving multiple agents (civil society, markets, and the state) and stakeholders in the provision of services are crucial to this end. Expanding poor people's assets is at the core of getting the benefits of growth to reach poor people faster. And it can be pro-growth (chapter 3).

PART III

Empowerment

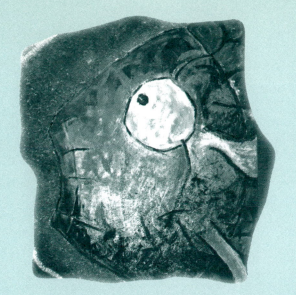

CHAPTER 6

Making State Institutions More Responsive to Poor People

Poverty is an outcome not only of economic processes—it is an outcome of interacting economic, social, and political forces. In particular, it is an outcome of the accountability and responsiveness of state institutions.[1]

As this chapter discusses, the state will deliver more effectively to all its citizens, but to poor people in particular, if:

- Public administrations implement policies efficiently and are accountable and responsive to users, corruption and harassment are curbed, and the power of the state is used to redistribute resources for actions benefiting poor people (chapter 5).
- Legal systems promote legal equity and are accessible to poor people.
- Central and local governments create decentralized mechanisms for broad participation in the delivery of public services and minimize the scope for capture by local elites.
- Governments generate political support for public action against poverty by creating a climate favor-

able to pro-poor actions and coalitions, facilitating the growth of poor people's associations, and increasing the political capacity of poor people.
- Political regimes honor the rule of law, allow the expression of political voice, and encourage the participation of poor people in political processes.

Public administration and poverty reduction

It is hard to get to the right person in the municipality, and when you do he says, "I'm sorry, I am not able to help you."
—*From a discussion group, Zenica, Bosnia and Herzegovina*

In most developing countries poor people have trouble getting prompt, efficient service from the public administration (box 6.1). To change this, the first step is building the capacity of public administration. Officials also need tractable regulatory frameworks, with proper performance incentives and mechanisms to ensure ac-

Box 6.1
Poor people are often harassed by public officials

Poor women and men in the *Voices of the Poor* study stressed that officials are often unresponsive to them. They shared countless examples of criminality, abuse, and corruption in their encounters with public institutions and said they have little recourse to justice. In describing their encounters with institutions, poor people also drew attention to the shame and indignity of being treated with arrogance, rudeness, and disdain.

When they assist you they treat you like a beggar . . . but we aren't . . . we pay taxes. . . . There must be transparency in government actions, tax money has to be well employed. . . . They invent these useless constructions and grab our money . . .
—*Poor man, Vila Junqueira, Brazil*

Some receive us, others don't. It's awful. . . . They are abusive . . . They treat one almost like a dog. . . . The municipality only serves the high-society ones. . . .
—*From a discussion group, Esmeraldas, Ecuador*

The officials of the social assistance department are impolite and even crude with ordinary people from the village. I go there for my social benefit for my children. I have to wait for two hours; they treat me very badly. If I cry and shout that my child is ill, they'll give me something. But it happens seldom.
—*Woman, Novy Gorodok, Russian Federation*

We in the country get up at 6 a.m. to take the collective bus. We arrive. We go to the doctor at the hospital. You arrive at 8 a.m. or sometimes not until 1 p.m. You are stuck there until the afternoon, without eating, without being able to drink . . . you spend hours and hours hungry. You have to go back before the doctor has seen you. You miss the bus. You have to go however you can . . .
—*Twenty-five-year-old mother, Los Juries, Argentina*

We would rather treat ourselves than go to the hospital, where the angry nurse might inject us with the wrong drug.
—*Poor youth from Kitui, Tanzania*

Source: Narayan, Chambers, Shah, and Petesch 2000; Narayan, Patel, Schafft, Rademacher, and Koch-Schulte 2000.

countability and responsiveness to clients, including poor people.[2] Poor organizational design engenders inefficiency and corruption, typically hurting poor people the most.

Focusing public action on social priorities

In nearly every country the public sector often pursues activities that are not socially justified and, in some cases, that generate rents for the elite. During the past two decades, as societies and their governments have become aware of this problem, they have launched public sector reforms to focus public action and programs on social priorities and increase the capacity of the state to reduce poverty.

Public sector reform and modernization have great potential to reduce poverty, if they are at the core of a development strategy that establishes clear priorities for public action. The functional and organizational structure of the public sector needs to be rationalized to improve resource allocation for programs that are social priorities and have greater capacity to reduce poverty. Most important is to streamline and "rightsize" public administrative entities and privatize public enterprises and other operational public programs.

Beyond rationalizing the structure of the public sector there is a need to improve public management systems to make public programs more efficient and accountable. Involving civil society in planning, monitoring, and evaluating public programs and policies is also crucial to ensure steady progress toward a fully responsive and accountable state.

Enabling and motivating public administrations

Having the right performance incentives smooths the delivery of public services. Key incentives include merit-based recruitment, clear specification of tasks, rewards for good performance, and insulation from excessive political pressure.[3] Together with skilled technocrats and close collaboration with the business community, these make up what has been termed "the developmental state."[4]

Merit-based recruitment goes a long way toward improving administrative performance. When nepotism or cronyism exists, it is difficult to motivate staff to perform well.[5] Cross-country analyses indicate that merit-based recruitment is associated with less corruption and fewer delays (figure 6.1). Merit-based promotion is also essential for motivating staff. If there are few opportunities for promotion, or if promotion is unrelated to performance, staff have much less incentive to perform. What is important is to promote an evaluation culture, for staff and for agencies. Also important to good performance are clearly specified and tractable tasks and competitive salaries. Compensation of public servants that is severely out of line with that in the private sector affects performance incentives and encourages corruption.[6]

Figure 6.1
Merit-based recruitment in government is associated with less corruption and bureaucratic delay

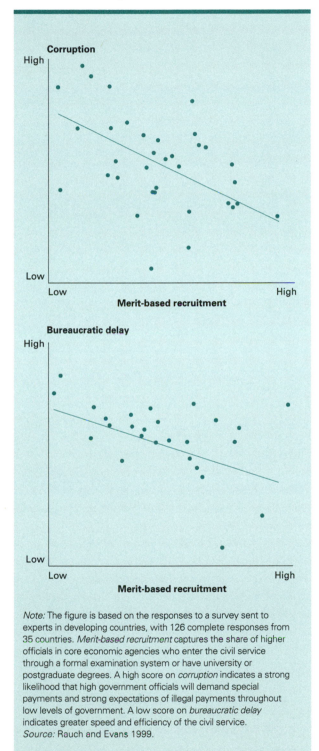

Note: The figure is based on the responses to a survey sent to experts in developing countries, with 126 complete responses from 35 countries. *Merit-based recruitment* captures the share of higher officials in core economic agencies who enter the civil service through a formal examination system or have university or postgraduate degrees. A high score on *corruption* indicates a strong likelihood that high government officials will demand special payments and strong expectations of illegal payments throughout low levels of government. A low score on *bureaucratic delay* indicates greater speed and efficiency of the civil service.
Source: Rauch and Evans 1999.

Legislative oversight of the executive, carried out according to transparent procedures, is an important part of monitoring and improving performance. Public administrations also need to be supported and actively monitored by political leaders. Surveys in several developing countries show that public officials' performance improves when they know that elected representatives are overseeing their work. But sometimes this process becomes subject to the personal goals or whims of elected representatives, resulting in excessive political interference. The quality of public service is reduced when public officials are held accountable more to their hierarchical superiors than to the people they serve.[7]

Making the public sector more responsive to client needs

Many different kinds of measures help improve public sector service delivery. One important measure is simplifying procedures and making them transparent to clients. In the Philippines several public agencies have streamlined procedures to curb corruption. At the outset of a transaction clients receive a list of required documents along with a timetable showing how long the process will take and a schedule of fees.[8] More generally, simplifying and improving regulatory and tax systems and privatizing state-owned enterprises can reduce the opportunities and scope for corruption.

Another important measure is disseminating information to allow people to monitor public services. Using newspapers and other popular information sources to disseminate information on budget allocations and spending enables people to hold civil servants accountable, reducing inefficiency and corruption. In Uganda, when primary enrollments did not improve despite substantial increases in budget allocations, a survey of schools examined public spending on primary education. The study found that budget allocations may not matter when institutions or their popular control is weak: in 1991–95 on average less than 30 percent of the intended nonsalary public spending on primary education reached schools. The government has since improved performance by increasing the flow of information within the system. A major breakthrough was achieved by making regular announcements in local newspapers and on the radio of the public funds transferred to districts and posting information on transfers at each school. A follow-up survey in 1999 showed dramatic improvements since 1995, with schools receiving close to 100 percent of the nonwage public funding.[9]

Fostering communication between civil servants and their clients is also important. Many developing country administrations have poor mechanisms for learning about and responding to users' demands. In India the "report card" on Bangalore's public services shows how a public feedback mechanism can make public agencies more accountable to their clients. Launched in 1993 by a group of committed citizens, the report card provided citizens' views of public service delivery in the city. Respondents focused on agencies they dealt with to redress a problem or to get a service—ranking their satisfaction and indicating the time spent. The findings were disseminated to public agencies, the media, and NGOs, triggering some service providers to become more efficient and accountable. The Bangalore City Corporation helped set up an informal network of city officials and nongovernmental groups to meet periodically and work out answers to priority problems.[10]

Curbing corruption

Corruption takes a toll on economic performance, undermines employment opportunities, and clouds prospects for poverty reduction. Even petty corruption dramatically raises the cost of engaging in productive activities. In West Africa bribes in the transport industry are crippling. The estimated cost of transporting goods from Côte d'Ivoire to Niger includes bribes to customs, police, and transport officials that represent three-quarters of payments to the administration.[11] Similarly, a transport trip in Benin encountered 25 roadblocks over 753 kilometers—roadblocks staffed by state agents who demanded bribes that added up to 87 percent of the cost of the trip.[12]

The burden of petty corruption falls disproportionately on poor people (figure 6.2). For those without money and connections, petty corruption in public health or police services can have debilitating consequences. Corruption affects the lives of poor people through many other channels as well.[13] It biases government spending away from socially valuable goods, such as education. It diverts public resources from infrastructure investments that could benefit poor people, such as health clinics, and tends to increase public spending on capital-intensive investments that offer more opportunities for kickbacks, such as defense contracts.[14] It lowers the quality of infrastructure, since kickbacks are more lucrative on equipment purchases. Corruption also undermines public service delivery.

Streamlining bureaucratic procedures, simplifying tax systems, eliminating excessive regulations, and motivating

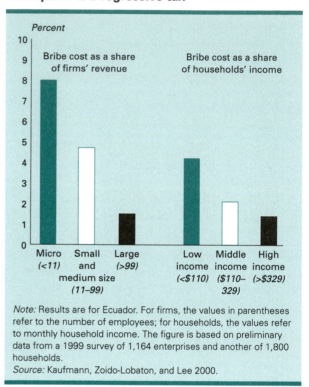

Figure 6.2
Corruption is a regressive tax

Percent

Bribe cost as a share of firms' revenue

Bribe cost as a share of households' income

Micro (<11)
Small and medium size (11–99)
Large (>99)
Low income (<$110)
Middle income ($110–329)
High income (>$329)

Note: Results are for Ecuador. For firms, the values in parentheses refer to the number of employees; for households, the values refer to monthly household income. The figure is based on preliminary data from a 1999 survey of 1,164 enterprises and another of 1,800 households.
Source: Kaufmann, Zoido-Lobaton, and Lee 2000.

public servants can help reduce the opportunities for corruption. And community participation and monitoring can keep it in check.

Poor people and the rule of law

There are four dragons: law court, prosecutor's office, khokimiat, and head of police. Nobody can get anything until they are satiated.

—From a discussion group, Oitamgali, Uzbekistan

The rule of law means that a country's formal rules are made publicly known and enforced in a predictable way through transparent mechanisms. Two conditions are essential: the rules apply equally to all citizens, and the state is subject to the rules. How state institutions comply with the rule of law greatly affects the daily lives of poor people, who are very vulnerable to abuses of their rights.

The rule of law is upheld through many channels, the most formal being the legal and judicial system. The legal and judicial system constrains and channels government action—and maintains clear rules and procedures for upholding an individual's constitutional rights. This system is essential for guarding against abuse of power by the state or other actors, and it requires that the judiciary be independent of the executive and legislative branches. The rule of law protects life and personal security and guards against human rights abuses. Thus defined, the rule of law is tremendously important for all citizens—but especially for poor people, who have few private means of protecting their rights (box 6.2).

The rule of law is associated with better overall economic performance (figure 6.3), and in this sense it also promotes poverty reduction. It does this by creating a predictable and secure environment for economic agents to engage in production, trade, and investment, thereby expanding poor people's employment opportunities and incomes.[15] Market mechanisms depend on credible threats of punishment for breaking contractual obligations, backed by prompt methods for resolving disputes and enforcing contracts. Without these deterrents, the transactions costs of doing business can be very high.

Although the rule of law benefits poor people in many ways, laws and statutes are not necessarily geared to protecting their interests. Legal systems, the product of power relations between different groups in society, typically focus on protecting the interests of those with political strength and representation. Making laws and their interpretation more sensitive to the needs of the disadvantaged requires building coalitions to this end. This is the goal, for example, of efforts to make laws more equitable in their treatment of women and minorities (chapter 7).

Legal obstacles leave poor people vulnerable to exploitation by local bosses and the police, and arbitrary harassment, lawlessness, and violence are constants in their lives. For poor people, a crucial aspect of the rule of law is the ability to live without fear of lawlessness and harassment. An effective modern police force is needed to maintain order by enforcing the law, dealing with potentially disorderly situations, and attending to citizens in distress.

Making the legal system more responsive to poor people

Even when the legal system is well run, poor people face constraints in using it.[16] Poor people typically have lit-

Box 6.2
Lawlessness contributes to poverty

At a hospital in Babati district in Tanzania a new delivery of essential medical supplies purchased with foreign currency disappears from the public dispensary within hours but is available for purchase at the doctor's home that evening. The poor do not receive the free medical care promised by the government, but those with the right connections and the ability to pay can secure pharmaceuticals in abundance.

In Johannesburg, South Africa, rates of theft and violent crime are among the highest in the world. Wealthy residents can afford sophisticated alarms, security guards, and other forms of private policing to protect their property and persons. Poor people are stuck in poorly built homes, sometimes without even simple locks, and are vulnerable to theft, assault, murder, and other violent crimes.

In Pakistan a man too old to work is left without assets or income after his son is murdered. To gain access to his son's estate, he needs a succession certificate from the civil court in Lahore—more than 160 kilometers away. The train ticket and the bribe demanded by the clerk of the court send the man deeper into debt, yet after five trips to the court in as many months, he still has not received the stamped piece of paper to which he is legally entitled. The clerk refuses to produce the certificate, while the authorities in the man's home village refuse to give him access to his son's assets until the certificate is produced.

Source: Michael Anderson 1999.

Figure 6.3
Better rule of law is associated with higher per capita income

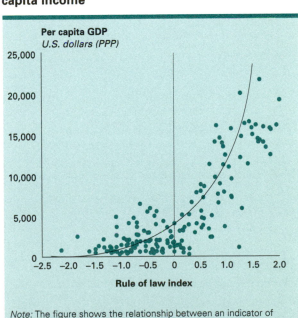

Note: The figure shows the relationship between an indicator of rule of law and per capita GDP for 166 countries in 1997–98.
Source: Kaufmann, Kraay, and Zoido-Lobaton 1999.

tle knowledge of their rights and may be deliberately misinformed. Contemporary legal systems are written and are conducted on the basis of written documents—making access inherently difficult for poor people, who usually have little formal education. Language, ethnic, caste, and gender barriers and other exclusionary practices add to these problems.

The intrinsic complexity of legal systems is exacerbated in many developing countries by the superimposition of new laws and constitutional rights over colonial legislation and customary law.[17] The resulting confusion makes it difficult to know one's rights, introduces arbitrariness in law enforcement, and enables the powerful to choose which legal system to apply.[18] This reduces poor people's confidence in the legal system. It also gives enormous discretion to authorities, often making connections and bribes central to negotiating the legal system. Making the rules simpler and clearer is especially important in the areas of greatest concern to poor people, such as labor disputes, land titling, human rights abuses, and police violence.

Although poor people need to access the legal system for registration and other administrative purposes, they use the judicial system much less frequently than the nonpoor. Court systems in many developing countries are poorly funded and equipped, and mechanisms for enforcing judgments often weak. These add to the other problems poor people face in using the judicial system, such as financial costs. Waiving court fees for people with low incomes could provide some relief. Ecuador and Peru provide exemptions for court fees in certain cases. To assist poor people, legal aid is provided in many developing countries, but often more in principle than in practice. To be effective, such aid must be delivered promptly: in Trinidad and Tobago it takes the legal office about three months to process applications for legal assistance, in effect denying access to those unable to wait that long.[19]

In addition to government-provided services, legal aid can be provided through alternative sources. Many countries require law school graduates to provide legal aid before becoming attorneys—others require practical training of law students. In Chile and Peru lawyers must complete a specified amount of practical training after law school, often in legal aid offices, thereby providing important resources for poor people.[20]

Streamlining the operation of the judicial system to reduce costs and delays will address some of the problems poor people face in the courts.[21] Reforming court procedures helps—simplifying rules (while respecting due

process), shortening proceedings, allowing parties to represent themselves. Broader reforms, such as changing the structure of the courts, also help increase poor people's access to justice. Small claims courts and other informal proceedings can reduce the backlog and widen access.[22] And the teaching and practice of law can be amended to sensitize the legal profession to the needs of poor people and to the use of the law to further the public interest.

Alternative dispute resolution mechanisms hold considerable potential for reducing the delays and corruption that characterize much dispute settlement. In El Salvador mediation provides parties a means to settle disputes without a lawyer and within two months.[23] In Sri Lanka the Asia Foundation has assisted the Ministry of Justice since 1990 in establishing a national network of community-based mediation boards. In 1998, 100,000 cases were referred to the mediation boards, with two-thirds of cases resolved to both parties' satisfaction. An independent evaluation found that the boards enjoyed an outstanding reputation and successfully provided low-cost, accessible justice to poor people in rural areas.[24] In Bangladesh some NGOs have adopted the *shalish* (an indigenous practice that uses outside parties to help resolve disputes) to aid women and other disadvantaged groups, such as low-income farmers with land-related disputes. A 1999 study in Dhaka shows that women who have been through NGO-initiated mediation expressed satisfaction with the results by a four-to-one margin.[25] That the NGOs can back up the mediation process with litigation is a factor in that success.

These alternative mechanisms may provide more predictable outcomes than the formal system, because community mediators are typically more familiar with the details of cases than are judges.[26] The risk of such mechanisms is that they can give undue power to conservative forces in a community (which might, for example, be biased against gender equity) and be subverted to serve the interests of local elites. To minimize these risks, alternative dispute resolution mechanisms need to be carefully regulated and supervised by more formal legal structures. They can also be introduced gradually—for example, through pilot programs sponsored and supervised by regular courts.

Promoting legal service organizations

Civil society organizations such as legal service organizations seek to help poor people gain access to the benefits and protection of the legal system inside and outside the court system (box 6.3). Protecting individuals against unlawful discrimination at work and eviction from their homes, such organizations help people collect their entitlements, obtain basic services, and get court orders to protect women from domestic violence. They can also protect communities from being dispossessed.

Legal service organizations can help poor people by taking legal action on behalf of a group of plaintiffs. Often, large numbers of poor people suffer from similar injuries, so seeking redress as a group provides poor people with otherwise inaccessible judicial protection. Legal advocacy organizations in Bangladesh helped avert the eviction of urban slum dwellers. Evicted residents became petitioners in litigation, where the basic argument rested on fundamental constitutional guarantees: demolishing their home deprives the poor of a livelihood, in violation of the constitution.[27] Public interest litigation can also benefit poor people. In India it has improved the delivery of some public services and reduced environmental contamination.[28]

The most effective legal service organizations work outside the judicial system, protecting rights without resorting to lawsuits—important, because the costs of lawsuits can sometimes outweigh any resulting gains.

This goes far beyond the conventional idea of offering free legal representation to poor individuals and helping people or communities assert their rights through the courts.

More generally, the work of legal service organizations helps create a culture of rights that changes the way people think about themselves relative to those who have power over their lives—spouses, landlords, employers, government agencies. This encourages poor people to avail themselves of the protection that the formal legal system offers. These organizations also generate pressure for changing the way the rules are applied by judges, bureaucrats, and the police. Legal literacy and legal aid have the maximum benefit if they help create a process of self-empowerment and social empowerment that moves citizens to activate their rights and to redefine and reshape inequitable laws and practices.

Legal service organizations help change the rules that affect poor people, whether in constitutions, statutes, regulations, municipal ordinances, or myriad other codes. In Thailand the Women and the Constitution Network was very active in constitutional reform that led to

---

Box 6.3
Legal service organizations help poor people gain access to the protections of the legal system

Almost any form of legal assistance is of value. But comprehensive services from independent legal service organizations are especially valuable to poor people, and the demand for such services is high. Standards should be developed to make them even more effective. Legal service organizations also need financial support from donors and civil society, but they have to be allowed to function autonomously, taking direction from poor people themselves.

Bangladesh
The Ain-O-Salish Kendra (ASK), established in 1986, seeks to reform the law through its representation of poor women and children, organized groups of workers, the rural poor, and slum dwellers. It provides legal aid primarily on family matters, including violence against women. Litigation on behalf of victims is undertaken in criminal cases and when basic legal rights are violated. ASK investigates and monitors violations of law and human rights, including police torture, murder, rape, and deaths in garment factories. It also monitors police stations to collect information on violence against women and children and to track cases reported at the stations. The work by ASK is significant because of the substance of what it does—work on basic issues for disenfranchised people—and because of the way it does it—through mediation, discussion groups, legal awareness training, individual court cases, administrative and legal lobbying, group representation, and public interest litigation.

Cambodia
Legal aid organizations in Cambodia are struggling to create a justice system—from almost nothing. The Cambodia Defenders Project, established in 1994, focuses on criminal defense and community legal education. It collaborates with NGOs to provide services and represent women in court, especially in domestic violence cases. The organization's lawyers run training programs, comment on draft laws, and work with civil society groups to explore legal tools for influencing government. The Legal Aid Society of Cambodia works to increase public understanding of and respect for the law, while providing free legal services in criminal and civil cases. It is especially active in defending farmers being dislodged from their land by powerful business interests.

South Africa
The Legal Resources Center, a national organization founded in 1979 to serve poor people, initially used legal advocacy to exploit contradictions in the apartheid legal system. Since the end of apartheid the center has used legal advocacy to address land and housing issues. It successfully represented the Makuleke community in its restitution claim to land in Kruger National Park. Other activities have included cases to restore water service terminated because residents were too poor to pay and to protect the land rights of an aboriginal community in the privatization of a diamond mine.

Source: Manning 1999.

amendments recognizing equal rights for women. The network followed up this success by launching a mass campaign to educate Thai citizens—women and men—about the new constitution and its implications.[29]

How can decentralization be made pro-poor?

State institutions are often accused of being too remote from the daily realities of poor people's lives, and decentralization is often recommended as a solution. Decentralization can be powerful for achieving development goals in ways that respond to the needs of local communities, by assigning control rights to people who have the information and incentives to make decisions best suited to those needs, and who have the responsibility for the political and economic consequences of their decisions.[30] It is not in itself a goal of development, but a means of improving public sector efficiency. And there are important caveats. The most important is that decentralization can bolster the power of elites in settings with highly unequal power structures.[31] To benefit poor people, it must have adequate support and safeguards from the center and effective mechanisms of participation.

Decentralization can mean different things. Here it refers to the formal devolution of power to local decisionmakers. Less extensive forms of decentralization include deconcentration (the central government posts employees at the local level) and delegation (powers are delegated to the local level).[32] The size of decentralized units of government can vary enormously: decentralization to the state or province in Brazil, China, and India merely breaks government into units the size of many countries. Decentralization to smaller units increases the scope for interaction with the citizenry served.

Decentralization can make state institutions more responsive to poor people, but only if it allows poor people to hold public servants accountable and ensures their participation in the development process. The pace and design of decentralization affect its impact on efficiency, accountability, participation, and ultimately poverty reduction. But only general principles from successful models can be transferred from one setting to another.[33]

Moving programs closer to users
Local information has many advantages. It can help identify more cost-efficient ways of building infrastructure, pro-

viding public services, and organizing their operation and maintenance. A study in South Africa found that community involvement reduced the cost of creating jobs and improved the cost-effectiveness of transferring resources to poor people (figure 6.4). Moreover, knowing what local needs are most pressing can help the disadvantaged. In Indonesia greater local control over funds led to more spending on health and education in priority areas for poor people—and to more spending on small infrastructure, boosting nonfarm employment and incomes.[34]

Local monitoring and supervision for many types of projects and programs are more effective and less expensive because of proximity to the point of provision and better interactions at the local level (box 6.4). In Nicaragua students attending schools that were "autonomous"—as measured by the share of decisions on teacher staffing made by the school—achieved better test scores than students in schools with limited or no local autonomy.[35]

What is required to reach poor people?
Decentralization can greatly enhance the state's capacity to accelerate local development and reduce poverty, but only if it is effectively designed. Local authorities and agen-

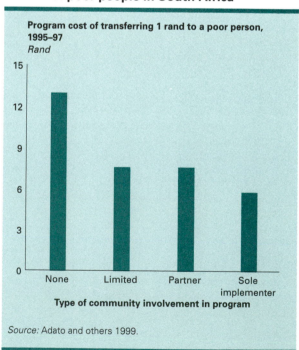

Figure 6.4
Decentralization lowers the cost of raising the income of poor people in South Africa

Program cost of transferring 1 rand to a poor person, 1995–97
Rand

Type of community involvement in program

Source: Adato and others 1999.

cies need considerable autonomy, including on fiscal
matters, as well as considerable support and safeguards
from the center. Moreover, decentralized government
needs mechanisms to ensure high levels of participation
in the design and monitoring of programs and policies
by all sections of the population to be served.

Autonomy and fiscal decentralization. Local authorities
need to have enough fiscal control to plan their activities.
But locally raised revenues are often only a small part of the
budget of decentralized units, weakening ownership of locally designed policies and threatening their sustainability.
While decentralized units need an adequate budget base,
enforcing hard budget constraints is also essential, to make
them accountable. If ad hoc funds from outside units are
available to meet budget shortfalls, local bodies can lose their
incentive to function efficiently. Moreover, such funding
erodes the real power of the local body and its ability to effect change, as attention goes to extracting these benefits.[36]

While a certain degree of fiscal devolution is needed for
effective decentralization, it carries the risk of exacerbating
inequalities between regions.[37] In China, where provinces
and local bodies are expected to be self-financing, social services are greatly underfunded in poorer provinces.[38] Mechanisms for redistribution from the central budget can
mitigate these inequalities, but this is politically contentious.
The problem needs to be addressed through consensus
building and tax sharing so that the central government has
resources to make transfers where necessary.

Support and safeguards from the center. Central support
is required to ensure that national policies are adhered to
and to coordinate the interregional interests of different
administrative units—as with highway charges and access to common water resources. Common macroeconomic and redistributive goals also need to be supported.
The danger of decentralization without safeguards is illustrated by the situation of Brazil in January 1999,
when one state's action threatened the macroeconomic
stability of the entire country.[39]

Support for training is also required. Studies of successful
decentralization indicate the importance of creating administrative capacity.[40] Many local governments lack the
administrative capacity for large-scale decentralization
and need training in accounting, public administration,
financial management, public communications, and community relations. If subnational governments have strong
administrative capacity and accountability mechanisms,
decentralization can reduce the scope for corruption. If
they do not, it can increase corruption and reduce access
to basic social services,[41] as in Central Asia, the South Cau-
casus, and the Baltics.[42]

Safeguards are also needed to monitor financial pro-
bity and discourage the capture of local bodies by powerful elites. One of the most serious pitfalls of
decentralization occurs when power imbalances are
large at the local level. In such a situation higher levels of government, less subject to local political pressures, may be more motivated than local bosses to help
the disadvantaged. For example, the U.S. federal government has a long history of doing more to protect
minority civil rights than state governments, which
have greater representation of those interested in sub-
verting those rights.[43] Studies of Argentina indicate that
subnational governments can sometimes be less effective than central governments at targeting poor areas.[44]
Similar problems are noted elsewhere in Latin America and South Asia.[45]

Participation. Widespread popular participation is vital to successful decentralization—without it, the potential benefits of local information cannot be realized. Moreover, participation creates a virtuous circle. Participating in local government helps build civil society and ensure that majority needs are heard and goals are achieved. It also helps increase the voice of poor people in local affairs.

One direct way of ensuring participation is to hold regular elections for local government. Electoral rules can also foster broad participation by reserving seats for marginal groups. In India a third of *panchayat* (local council) presidents, vice presidents, and elected members must be women. In addition, certain other disadvantaged groups must be allotted memberships and executive positions proportional to their number in the area. Such measures can transform power relations over time.[46]

Participation on a more frequent basis than just at election time also needs to be fostered. In Bolivia, Brazil, and the Philippines decentralization laws require local governments to incorporate or formally associate grassroots organizations with their deliberative procedures and to give such organizations a role in administering services and projects.[47] Successful participatory budgetmaking in Porto Alegre, Brazil, shows that having local communities decide on the use of municipal resources can be very effective for local development.[48] Good information channels between governments and communities are also necessary for good results. In Chile, where calls for community fund proposals are publicly broadcast and formats for project presentation are distributed through municipalities, a survey of beneficiaries found that fund disbursements were biased toward neighborhoods and social organizations well connected with municipal and regional governments. Those with weaker connections received fewer funds.[49]

Decentralizing powers and resources to the submunicipal level—such as neighborhoods or villages—requires special effort, but the benefits can be considerable.[50] In South Africa partnerships between communities and local governments sharply increase the probability of long-term returns to the community.[51] In Guinea a pilot project showed that communities are adept at designing and managing such projects as building and maintaining new infrastructure. Communities mobilized local resources, used grant funds equitably and efficiently, and targeted funds to help vulnerable women and children.[52]

The politics of poverty reduction: pro-poor coalitions

If we aren't organized and we don't unite, we can't ask for anything.

—*Poor woman, Florencio Varela, Argentina*

Pro-poor coalitions that link the interests of the poor and the nonpoor are important for poverty reduction. Improving the capacity of poor people to participate productively in economic activity also helps lay the foundation for faster growth. The state can support the growth of pro-poor coalitions by:

- Fostering a political climate favorable to pro-poor actions and coalitions.
- Removing legal barriers to pro-poor associations and offering them technical and other support to scale up their activities.
- Fostering state-community synergies and increasing the capacity of poor people to participate in development and local governance.

Such transformations are essentially political and have to be effected through political processes involving changes in political configurations and power balances.[53]

Creating political support for pro-poor actions and coalitions

The interests of the poor and the nonpoor are intertwined in many ways, making it beneficial for the nonpoor to take an interest in redistributive measures and pro-poor actions. This interest can be motivated by a recognition that efforts to reduce poverty can promote social and economic development for the whole nation, thereby also raising the living standards of the nonpoor. The industrializing economies of East Asia, where the creation of a skilled, healthy workforce was crucial to success, show that investing in mass education and human capital formation provides a significant boost to national economic growth.

Control of communicable diseases is another case in which all citizens benefit from programs focused on the poor, as it is almost impossible for any group to avoid these diseases unless the sources of contagion are eradicated. Poor people, undernourished and living in environments with greater exposure to disease, are especially vulnerable to infection. They are also less likely to receive adequate preventive and curative health services. Thus poor people tend to form pockets of contagion from which diseases can spread to other groups. This was one of the main driving forces behind the public health movements in the West at the turn of the 20th century (box 6.5). The spread of disease is intensified today by the vastly increased volume of travel: if health services are of poor quality or unaffordable for poor people in one country, drug-resistant strains of malaria and tuberculosis can spread around the globe. So both national and global efforts are needed to address some of the health problems of poor people (chapter 10).

Another motivation for the nonpoor to support pro-poor action is the specter of mass migration to urban areas, with attendant problems of growing slums and rising demands on already overburdened urban services. China and India have reduced incentives for urban migration by providing infrastructure and other services in rural areas—not just supplying schools, health services, electricity, and other basic amenities, but also ensuring that employment creation is geographically dispersed and that transport networks allow people to commute to work from their villages.

To build political support for public action against poverty, governments have to enhance the perception of common interests between the poor and the nonpoor.[54] Key to this is systematically introducing into the public debate the notion that poverty reduction is a public good and can further the well-being of the nonpoor. How these issues are framed in the public debate can greatly influence the outcome. Poverty's character, causes, and solutions are malleable concepts, which can be reinterpreted and represented in a variety of ways, many of them conducive to public action against poverty. In the early 20th century state governments in the United States were persuaded, mainly by national middle-class women's organizations, to spend public money to support poor families—on the grounds that this was the only way to protect the moral and physical integrity of the nation.[55]

Understanding the benefits of helping the less fortunate can thus be a powerful stimulus for public action. Without such understanding, the living conditions of the disadvantaged are sometimes used to justify their further exclusion. Latin American elites have sometimes viewed poor people as a danger to public well-being. This mindset makes it more difficult to eradicate poverty and mitigate its negative impact on the economy and society.

Facilitating the growth of poor people's associations

The state's most important task in fostering poor people's organizations is to remove legal and other barriers to

Box 6.5
National coalitions against communicable diseases in the West

Sanitary neglect is mistaken parsimony: the physical strength of a nation is among the chief factors of national prosperity.
—John Simon (1858) as cited in Rosen (1993)

The public health movement in Europe and the United States brought rapid improvements in the health conditions of poor and rich alike in the late 19th and early 20th centuries, long before the discovery of antibiotics. The politics of public responsibility for reducing communicable diseases were motivated by a blend of economic, political, and humanitarian interests. Industrialists were concerned with reducing the drain on labor force productivity. States were concerned with having enough fit young men to serve in the army and expand spheres of influence. Elites felt that their environment was detrimentally affected by the ill health of poor people—and that the dangers for the population as a whole needed to be reduced. Intellectuals pointed out the connections between ill health and poverty, demanding radical change as a solution to the problems of endemic and epidemic diseases.

To reduce everyone's exposure to communicable diseases, strenuous efforts had to be made to improve the health of poor people. Measures included control of food and drugs, smallpox vaccinations, and quarantine. Central to the endeavor was securing a pure water supply, effective waste disposal, clean streets, and reduced pollution. Housing regulations were enforced to ensure adequate ventilation, toilet facilities, drainage, and sewerage in homes. Restrictions on private behavior included forbidding spitting and urinating in public spaces and banning livestock from domestic premises. Massive health education campaigns used extensive outreach to change personal health behavior and increase people's understanding of how to avoid ill health and care for the sick. These state interventions, combined with rising living standards, dramatically improved health and life expectancy between 1880 and 1920.

Paradoxically, improvements in curative technologies in recent decades may have led to less vigilance against communicable diseases in some developing countries. These powerful curative technologies need to be combined with strong public health policies aimed at improving environmental sanitation and encouraging healthy lifestyles. This will help increase economic growth and reduce poverty, averting negative consequences for national and global health as drug-resistant strains of diseases multiply.

Source: Rosen 1993; Preston and Haines 1991; Schofield, Reher, and Bideau 1991; Caldwell and others 1990.

forming associations and to provide an administrative and judicial framework supportive of such associations.[56] Without this, it is very difficult for poor people's associations to flourish and to influence public policy. Poor people face enormous constraints in forming associations to increase their voice and improve their circumstances. They usually take little part in politics because participation seems irrelevant to their primary concerns, futile, or both. They often have low expectations of their government—and may even fear reprisals from state or local authorities if they organize. Even for matters where the government is viewed as relevant, poor people see individual and collective efforts to exert influence as having little effect. When poor people do participate, their class identity is not the only influence on their decision to do so. As with other citizens, the forces that move them to action are often tangible, short term, and local.

Reducing asymmetries in information can do much to change poor people's hesitance to participate—and to empower them. Formal education enables people to gain access to better economic opportunities (chapter 5) and gives them the means to articulate their needs and demands in public forums and in political processes. All this is enhanced by widespread dissemination of information. Today's information technology and lower information costs, combined with rising demand for greater access to public documents, can have powerful benefits for the poor.

Major impediments to organization by poor people are lack of time, resources, information, and access to outside sources of help. Added to that are physical constraints on collaboration, such as geographic dispersion and poor transport and communications infrastructure. Ethnic and other social divisions are another impediment (chapter 7).[57] Despite these difficulties, many countries have seen an explosion of community-based, participatory grassroots organizations in the past few decades. Throughout Latin America popular and indigenous organizations, sometimes based on traditional forms of association, now give voice to the underprivileged and deal with immediate needs in health, schooling, and public infrastructure.

Such grassroots organizations require many forms of support from the state and from civil society. They often need technical assistance and skill building to become sustainable and effective. They also need help in scaling up their membership, range of functions, and political engagement.[58] Many grassroots initiatives are limited in scope and depth and never reach the national political arena. Studies in Latin America have found that some organizations are effective in addressing some of the immediate concerns of poor people, but their sustainability is constrained by difficulties in linking up with external

agencies.[59] To counter these problems, some peasant organizations in Bolivia and Ecuador have worked through NGOs to link up with national agricultural agencies, enormously expanding their range and effectiveness.[60]

In most developing countries NGOs are central actors in antipoverty policies and programs.[61] The social and educational background of many NGO staff enables them to interact easily with the staff of national institutions, and they can help create bridges between these institutions, outside agencies, and grassroots organizations. NGOs can also be very effective in delivering technical assistance to poor people,[62] as Mopawi has been in Honduras (box 6.6).

In Bolivia a Dutch NGO helped a *campesino* federation link with research institutions involved in the national

Box 6.6
NGOs can help mobilize and empower communities

Since 1985 the NGO Mopawi (Moskitia Pawisa, or Development of La Mosquitia) has been working alongside the indigenous communities of La Mosquitia, a remote area of western Honduras and one of the last remaining areas of tropical forest in Central America. Over the years Mopawi has developed a large and complex development program. It has worked to change government policy for the region through continuous lobbying and advocacy, helping to form links between government, international NGOs, research organizations, and indigenous organizations to raise awareness and inspire action. It has worked with local communities to find ways of improving livelihoods without harming the environment. Mopawi has also addressed deforestation in La Mosquitia, combining advocacy with practical prevention. Most of its staff are from La Mosquitia, which has proved to be a major strength.

The organization has helped improve people's livelihoods by identifying alternative models of resource use and involving local communities in decisionmaking and management. For example, small businesses have been set up, and experiments conducted with agriculture and agroforestry. An agroforestry and pasture project being conducted with settlers and indigenous communities includes experiments with sustainable management of the forest and restoration of degraded areas. And efforts targeting women are aimed at cultivating vegetable plots to improve health and nutrition.

To strengthen local organizations, Mopawi has worked with Masta (Mosquitia Alsa Tanka), the federation of representative indigenous organizations in La Mosquitia. With Mopawi's help, local organizations have taken on legalization of land ownership and use rights and developed their capacity for advocacy.

Source: Brehm 2000.

potato program by contracting with an international expert to work with the federation at the onset of the project. The consultant had no difficulty establishing high-level contacts with research institutions, and on the basis of these meetings the federation established strong links with the national potato program. The result was higher crop incomes for federation members.[63]

Sometimes NGOs reflect the political system in which they thrive, or local interest groups, and thus may not serve the interests of poor people as well as they might.[64] NGOs are no panacea—it is important that they be accountable for their actions, especially to the poor groups that they seek to represent.

Fostering state-community synergies in growth and poverty reduction

The state can facilitate interactions between local administrations and communities to engender development and reduce poverty.[65] There are two main aspects to this role: reducing obstacles to collective action in communities and encouraging greater collaboration between communities and local governments. To forge ties within communities and facilitate local collective action, the state can initiate programs that build up the assets of poor people and make public services more accessible. Such programs reduce the perception among poor people that their survival depends on avoiding risks and keeping their patrons happy—releasing their energies to pursue actions for upward mobility and to collaborate with others on a more equal footing.

The combination of a more egalitarian social organization at the community level and better local administration enables the creation of powerful coalitions for rapid development. Strong links between local administrations and communities improve service delivery and reduce the potential for local capture of development programs. This arrangement has been used successfully in very different political and administrative settings: Brazil in the 1980s, the Republic of Korea in the 1960s and 1970s, and Taiwan, China, in the 1950s.[66]

The example of Brazil shows that institutional change is considerably more difficult in highly unequal settings. Lacking the prior extensive land reform of East Asian countries, the state in its efforts to reform local government had to tackle problems of landlord interests and political connections with local government. This created problems, because large landowners, private contractors, and relief suppliers were accustomed to cornering resources. In the 1987 drought the state used agricultural extension workers to break the grip of patronage in the distribution of drought relief. But sustaining such successes requires much continuing effort.

The Brazilian experience also shows that many of these obstacles can be overcome by bringing grassroots electoral pressure to bear on local governments. Political interference has been kept at bay by the state governments' insistence that municipal councils for disbursing development funds have at least 80 percent representation from end-user communities. Moreover, if communities feel they are treated unfairly by the municipal councils, they can apply for funds directly from the state government.[67]

The state can undertake several key actions to foster developmental synergies between communities and local governments (figure 6.5):

- Generating community demand for better public administration and service delivery, through intensive dissemination of information.
- Forming dense networks between the state and communities and making available to communities the information and technical, marketing, credit, and other support they need to implement programs.
- Changing local agencies' mode of operation by putting pressure on them from above and below. In Brazil the state used official job recognition to motivate staff.
- Motivating grassroots workers and leaders through positive and negative sanctions, including respect from peers. Where the workers are also community members, as in the Republic of Korea, the potential sanctions are especially strong.
- Adjusting the roles of higher levels of government, training and motivating their staff to focus on managing overall strategy, and providing technical support, regulations, and facilitation.

These initiatives yield substantial political payoffs for the governments in legitimacy and in popular support. In a municipal election in Brazil candidates said that if they wanted to get elected, they had to support the new arrangements for increasing public accountability of local government and improving public service delivery.[68] This helped to strengthen potentially weak governments and motivate them to engage in these difficult tasks. At the same time the conditions for a plural polity were strengthened.

Collaboration between communities and local governments can also promote many different forms of development. In addition to local improvements in

Figure 6.5
State-community coalitions can foster rapid development and better service delivery

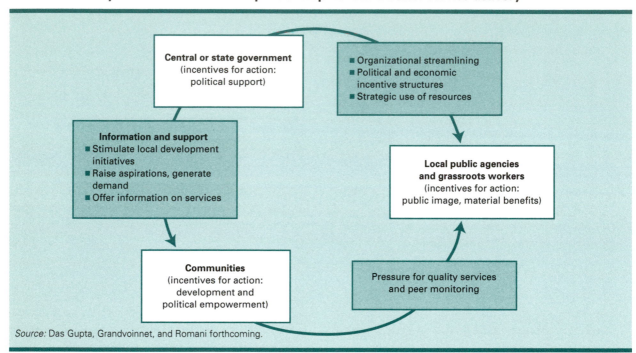

Source: Das Gupta, Grandvoinnet, and Romani forthcoming.

infrastructure and living conditions, such collaborative efforts have delivered health and drought relief in Brazil and supported industrial production for export markets in Taiwan, China.

Changes are incremental and can often take time, but as success stories accumulate in a given setting, they create a demonstration effect for others. The examples suggest that it is possible, in the space of decades, to reengineer state institutions to quicken the pace of development, growth, and poverty reduction. They also show that with creative political thinking these changes are possible even in relatively weak institutional settings.

Political regimes and poverty

Voicelessness and powerlessness are key dimensions of poverty, and an important aspect of voice relates to political rights and civil liberties.[69] Democracy is intrinsically valuable for human well-being as a manifestation of human freedom. Political freedoms have enormous impact on the lives and capabilities of citizens.[70]

Participatory political processes can also help build a good institutional base for the polity, society, and economy, enabling all voices to be heard and to interact in determining outcomes (figure 6.6).[71] Civil and political

Figure 6.6
Good political and administrative institutions go hand in hand with economic growth

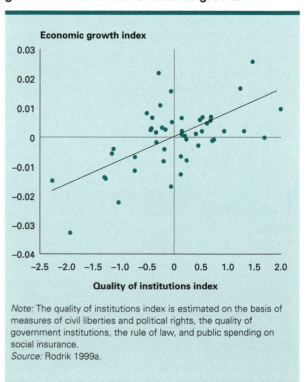

Note: The quality of institutions index is estimated on the basis of measures of civil liberties and political rights, the quality of government institutions, the rule of law, and public spending on social insurance.
Source: Rodrik 1999a.

liberties, along with competitive elections, are powerful instruments for holding governments accountable for their actions. To translate this potential into reality, many institutions need to be in place to ensure that democratic processes function as they should—among them, independent media to monitor electoral and administrative processes, an independent judiciary to uphold the constitution and rule of law, and strong parliamentary institutions with the capacity to monitor the executive through such mechanisms as public accounts committees. Building these institutions takes time, and constant vigilance is required to ensure that democratic processes function as they should. But it is worth the effort, for these processes offer the most effective means of guaranteeing voice and participation.

Promoting democratic politics to foster stable environments for growth

Evidence on the relationship between the type of political regime and the rate of economic growth is mixed.[72] In part this reflects measurement problems,[73] and in part, the experiences of growth with significant poverty reduction in a few notably development-oriented countries, such as the Republic of Korea, before they became pluralist democracies. These countries developed the preconditions for a developmental state—notably, political elites committed to development and supported by an efficient public administration that was insulated from political pressures and had close links to the business community.[74]

Another major factor in the success of these economies was their early emphasis on equity—especially extensive land reform and universal education, which laid the foundation for rapid and equitable growth.[75] These efforts were facilitated in some cases by the devastation caused by war and the attendant disempowerment of entrenched elites. These circumstances lowered the resistance of politically powerful vested interests to drastic land reform.

In most nondemocratic settings, however, lack of institutionalized accountability has resulted in poor performance in growth and poverty reduction. Even successful developmental states point to an important lesson: undemocratic regimes face serious abuses of state power, and they are prone to rapid policy reversals that can make their development gains fragile. These states are moving to resolve some of these problems by changing their political institutions to increase official accountability.

The checks and balances of participatory democratic regimes—and the procedures for consensus building—limit the scope for rent seeking and drastic policy reversals, offering a much more reliable and sustainable path to development.[76] Participatory political regimes are associated with more stable growth[77]—very important for poverty reduction, given the highly adverse effects that shocks have on poor people (chapters 8 and 9). There are several reasons for this association.

First, participatory political processes encourage the use of voice rather than violence to negotiate conflict. Combined with guaranteed political rights, these processes reduce the potential for ethnic and other intergroup conflict, averting major sources of social and economic vulnerability for poor people.[78] For example, India's strong democratic political institutions help mediate the potentially conflicting demands of its highly heterogeneous population.

Second, political and civil rights and a free press allow people to draw attention to their needs and demand appropriate public action.[79] This is especially important for averting or responding quickly to major disasters. And third, democratic elections confer legitimacy on governments, fostering sociopolitical and economic stability.

How can democracy deliver more effectively for poor people?

Democracy—both representative and participatory—is a good in itself. But democratic political processes alone are not enough to ensure that poverty reduction is taken as a key priority in society's efforts. Political and social ideologies shape the extent to which democratic systems actually reduce poverty. Different philosophies underlying welfare policies in OECD countries produce very different outcomes in poverty reduction—despite the fact that all these countries have a long history of democratic political institutions and high per capita income (box 6.7).

Representative politics allow all citizens' interests to be expressed, but the outcomes depend on how different group interests play out.[80] Groups that are politically connected or better educated have a natural advantage over others in influencing public policy. This is reflected in the United States in the large discrepancies between affluent and poor communities in funding appropriations for law enforcement and public schools. In developing countries, where the distribution of education and po-

Box 6.7
Politics and poverty in OECD countries

Poverty is not restricted to developing countries. There are significant pockets of poverty in some OECD countries. Although these countries are all affluent market economies with democratic systems, ideological differences and corresponding differences in popular support for poverty reduction programs result in very different levels of poverty for their citizens.

A comparative study of poverty trends in Germany, the Netherlands, and the United States examined the incidence of poverty and how it was affected over a 10-year period by government programs. The study found wide differences in poverty incidence among the three countries, differences that were widened by government programs. Levels of "pregovernment" poverty (based on earned and unearned personal income excluding taxes and transfers from government) vary, largely a result of marked differences in labor laws and other market factors. Pension payments reduce poverty in all three countries, but the design and impact of other public transfers and taxes aimed at reducing poverty differ.

Especially striking are the low levels of poverty in the Netherlands, a result of universal benefits. Although the transfers have large targeting errors—they go to the non-poor as well as the poor—they do not appear to have resulted in slower economic growth compared with the other countries.

Government programs widen differences in poverty among OECD countries

Share of population under age 60 living in poverty, 1985–94

Note: Policy steps: 0 = "pregovernment" poverty rate, 1 = social insurance pensions, 2 = 1 + other public transfers, 3 = 2 + taxes. Poverty is defined as having less than half the median disposable household income of the country. Incomes (net of inflation) were cumulated for the 10-year period. *Source:* Goodin and others 1999.

litical know-how is far more skewed than in the United States, large segments of the population remain underserved.[81] In Côte d'Ivoire 35 percent of public education spending goes to the richest 20 percent of the population (see table 5.1 in chapter 5), and 55 percent of tertiary students come from this group.[82] Democratic politics are also subject to manipulation by political leaders. Leaders may favor spending resources on immediate consumption rather than investment, on populist rather than productive measures.[83] In addition, interest groups can be bought off or co-opted with favors from politicians.[84]

There are three main ways to strengthen the institutional environments of democratic regimes to make them more effective at reducing poverty. First, democratic processes must permeate all major levels of decisionmaking. Some regimes are more democratic in principle than in practice. Others, like India, are genuinely democratic at most levels but have historically found it difficult to ensure that political accountability reaches all levels of decisionmaking, particularly for the poor. India's ongoing *panchayati raj* drive toward decentralization and community empowerment is an effort to correct this by increasing the powers of local elected councils.

Second, citizens must be given systematic access to information so that they can hold their civil servants and politicians accountable. If information on budgets and on the use of funds—from the federal to the local level—is made available in newspapers and other information sources, people can hold their leaders accountable for results. Such public accountability can help to reduce inefficiency and corruption. This dissemination of information needs to be legally mandated to ensure that it does not stop with a change of government. Progress in information technology and increasing exposure to global currents help to create a new environment of public awareness that reinforces democratic politics.

Third, strong civil society organizations can promote the political empowerment of poor people, pressuring the state to better serve their interests and increasing the effectiveness of antipoverty programs.[85] Case studies in the Indian state of Kerala and elsewhere show that a highly engaged civil society contributes to better outcomes in health and education.[86] What is needed is an enabling institutional environment for civil society to develop and thicken (box 6.8).[87]

Box 6.8
The evolution of civil society and state reform in Mexico

Traditionally, Mexico has had well-institutionalized systems for channeling and controlling political activities—and using state resources to cement political support for the regime. These systems were more concerned with controlling society's demands than responding to them. The state had developed a highly effective and sophisticated machinery for co-opting and managing demands and dissent. Although the capacity of civil society to demand responsiveness was limited, the state was sensitive to the ongoing need to cement loyalties, garner support, and resolve conflict.

In the 1980s these relatively strong political capacities came under siege: responsiveness, representation, and participation became issues of great contention. Day-to-day management of political and economic conflict became an increasingly difficult task for public officials. Financial resources reached historically low levels, and government legitimacy plummeted. While civil society demanded that the basic social contract between state and society be renegotiated, political leaders and parties attempted to respond in ways that would give them the leverage to determine the scope and nature of that contract. This conflict remained unresolved in the early 1990s, with the potential to develop a more open political system depending on the capacity of civil society to force change.

In recent years prospects of real change have emerged in Mexico. A much more open and democratic political process has developed, and an independent electoral commission and civil society organizations widely encouraged citizens to vote according to their conscience, free of coercion and inducements, in the July 2000 election. While much remains to be done to open the door further to civil society participation and the expression of citizen demands, this is a cautious, lurching, but in the end irreversible, first step.

Source: Grindle 1996.

* * *

Respect for the rule of law, an efficient public administration, and high-quality political systems facilitate the emergence of state institutions inclusive of poor people. But the impact of these factors on poverty depends on how effectively they are translated into empowerment at the community level. Even in states with extensive political and civil liberties and with governments that are neither captured by elites nor corrupt, poor people are often voiceless—and their interests figure little in public policy. Poor people need direct voice in the interventions that affect their daily lives, as well as the ability to organize and vote. Actions are needed to bring down barriers—legal, political, administrative, social—that work against particular groups and to build up the assets of poor people to prevent their exclusion from the market. Some major social barriers to poverty reduction are discussed in the following chapter.

CHAPTER 7

Removing Social Barriers and Building Social Institutions

Social institutions—kinship systems, community organizations, and informal networks—greatly affect poverty outcomes. They do so by affecting the productivity of economic assets, the strategies for coping with risk, the capacity to pursue new opportunities, and the extent to which particular voices are heard when important decisions are made. Social institutions can help poor people get by and get ahead.[1] But they can also place barriers between poor people or the socially disadvantaged and the opportunity and resources they need to advance their interests. Discrimination on the basis of gender, ethnicity, race, religion, or social status can lead to social exclusion and lock people in long-term poverty traps.

Values, norms, and social institutions may reinforce persistent inequalities between groups in society—as with gender-based prejudice throughout much of the world, the caste system in India, and race relations in South Africa and the United States.[2] In the extreme, these social divisions can become the basis of severe deprivation and conflict. Legal and other measures to overcome these inequalities must be accompanied by efforts to raise awareness about culturally based attitudes such as those toward women and people of different races, religions, or ethnic origin. Otherwise these measures will be unable to produce real change. Social barriers can take many forms. Here the focus is on key barriers arising from gender inequality, social stratification, and social fragmentation.[3]

Gender discrimination and poverty

Until we became organized as a SEWA cooperative, the middlemen could cheat us. But now I can negotiate with them as the representative of our cooperative and as an elected member of our local council. One day near the bus stop, I heard a couple of men saying, "There's the woman who is giving us all this trouble. Shall we beat her up?" I told them, "Go ahead and just try it. I have 40,000 women behind me."

—Woman laborer, speaking at World Summit for Social Development and Beyond, Geneva, June 2000

The extent and manifestations of gender inequality vary among societies, shaped to a considerable degree by kinship rules.[4] Rules of inheritance determine ownership of productive resources. Rules of marriage determine women's domestic autonomy: if these rules require that women join their husband's family, women have far less autonomy than if they are able to form a new household or live with their own family (which is uncommon). The most pervasive forms of gender inequality appear where both inheritance and marriage rules are heavily weighted in favor of men. By contrast, where such rules are more gender balanced, women have greater voice in the household and in public spaces and face fewer constraints on becoming independent economic and social actors.[5]

Norms for gender roles and rights form part of the moral order of a community and permeate other institutions, including those of the state. This further reinforces gender inequities, unless conscious efforts are made to avoid it. Legal systems play a key part, either reinforcing customary gender rights and roles—or deliberately seeking to alter them. Also important is the provision of public goods and services, which often bypass women unless specific efforts are made to reach them.

Inequalities in voice and access to resources

Customary gender norms and values can lead to political, legal, economic, and educational inequalities that perpetuate women's lack of access to resources, control over decisionmaking, and participation in public life. Greater political representation could help change this—in no country do women hold more than a very small share of the seats in parliament.[6]

Legal systems can constrain women from becoming independent economic actors. In many countries family laws are heavily stacked against women, restricting their rights in divorce and in inheritance of land and other productive resources. In most developing countries titles to land are normally vested in men.[7] Since the great majority of the world's poor people live in agrarian settings, this is a fundamental source of vulnerability for poor women.

Some countries use the legal system to formalize customary rules that explicitly limit women's rights. In the Republic of Korea, for example, customary laws restricting women's rights were formalized in the Civil Code of 1962, and women's legal rights have been very slow to improve. After decades of struggle by women's organizations, key amendments in 1990 gave women the right to inherit their parents' and husband's property.[8] Di-

vorce laws were changed to allow women equal rights to property acquired during marriage, and child custody is no longer granted automatically to the father. But the law continues to insist on male household headship, which women's organizations see as the main source of gender inequality in the family and in other social institutions. So while women in Korea have become educated and participate actively in the labor force, their unequal status serves to maximize their economic contribution while minimizing advances in gender equity.[9]

In many countries women continue to be denied even basic legal rights. In Botswana, Lesotho, Namibia, and Swaziland married women, according to both customary and common law, are under the permanent guardianship of their husband and have no independent right to manage property (except under prenuptial contract).[10] In Guatemala men can restrict the kind of employment their wife can accept outside the home. In some countries women need their husband's permission to obtain a passport and move about freely.[11]

Poor women face a double disadvantage in access to resources and voice—they are poor, and they are women. Poor people have much less access to education and health care than the nonpoor, and the gender gap in these services is larger among poor people.[12] The same is true for credit and agricultural extension services: unless strong countervailing measures are taken, the poor receive less than the nonpoor, and women receive the least. Studies from many countries show that agricultural extension agents focus on male farmers, even though women are often the primary cultivator because husbands work off the farm.[13] So women face disadvantages not only in land ownership, but in gaining access to the resources and information that would improve yields.

The toll of gender inequality on society

If the rights of men and women are flagrantly unequal, it is very difficult to establish a democratic and participatory sociopolitical order and an environment of equal opportunity. Moreover, the more extreme manifestations of power inequality between men and women constitute gross violations of human rights. Domestic violence has been shown to be startlingly prevalent around the world—among people at all income levels (see box 8.1 in chapter 8).

In some societies the lower value assigned to women and girls translates into excess mortality. Estimates based on official national censuses find that as a result of excess female mortality, about 7 percent of girls under age five are "missing" in China and Korea and more than 4 percent in India and other parts of South Asia.[14] Without such discrimination there would be an estimated 60–100 million more women in the world.[15]

Gender inequality also has strong repercussions for human capital in the next generation, because the burden of bearing and rearing children falls largely on women. Women deprived of education and decision-making power in the home face serious constraints in rearing healthy, productive children. They also tend to have more children than they wish, compounding the pressures on themselves and their family. Better-educated women are able to communicate better with their spouse about family size decisions, use contraception more effectively, and have higher aspirations for their children.[16]

Low autonomy for women takes an independent toll. Studies in China and India find that even controlling for education, household income, and other socioeconomic characteristics, low domestic autonomy is associated with higher infant and child mortality rates.[17] Studies consistently show that women's education improves child survival.[18] And longitudinal studies in the United Kingdom and the United States find that, controlling for other household-level factors, mother's education is associated with better child cognitive development.[19]

Among children of women who have greater financial autonomy, either because they earn cash incomes of their own or have a greater role in domestic decisionmaking, nutrition and education are higher. Studies in Brazil show that more income in the hands of mothers is associated with better nutritional outcomes and physical development.[20] Microcredit programs in Bangladesh find that giving income-generating loans to women improves the nutritional status of their children, a result that does not hold for men.[21]

Education and autonomy reinforce each other. Women with more education and greater domestic autonomy are better able to nurture and protect their children.[22] Low education and low autonomy make it more difficult for women to obtain medical care, comply with instructions, and follow up with the health care provider if the instructions seem ineffective. They also make it more difficult for women to obtain healthcare information, prevent illness, and care for the sick.

More equitable distribution of opportunities and resources between men and women also leads more directly to higher economic growth and productivity.[23] Cross-

Figure 7.1

Closing the gender gap in schooling more rapidly would boost economic growth

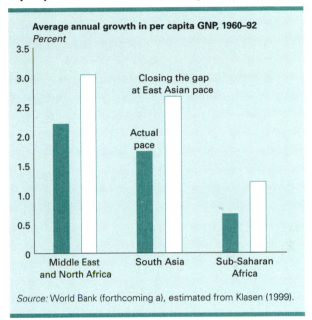

Source: World Bank (forthcoming a), estimated from Klasen (1999).

country analysis indicates that countries that invest in girls' education have higher rates of economic growth (figure 7.1).[24] Country studies show the benefits of increasing women farmers' access to agricultural extension, credit services, and other productive inputs.[25] Raising their education increases their efficiency as producers, by increasing their adoption of new technologies and their efficiency in using resources. Analysis from Kenya suggests that giving women farmers the same education and inputs as men increases yields by as much as 22 percent.[26] For Burkina Faso analysis of household panel data suggests that farm output could be increased 6–20 percent through a more equitable allocation of productive resources between male and female farmers.[27] Further analysis is needed to determine the impact of such a reallocation on overall household income and nutritional well-being.

Scope for change

While political and legal equality between men and women have increased in most regions, it takes effort and perseverance to change people's gender values and beliefs.[28] But much can be done—and much has been done—to improve women's voice and access to resources by increasing their political representation, their legal rights, and their command over physical, financial, and human capital (figure 7.2). Efforts are

Figure 7.2

Trends in female education and life expectancy reflect increasing equality between women and men

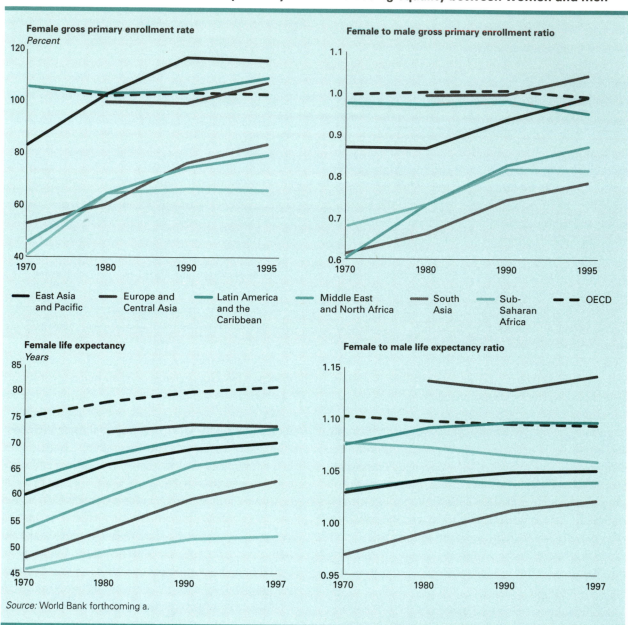

Source: World Bank forthcoming a.

under way in at least 32 countries to increase women's political representation by reserving seats for them in local and national assemblies.[29] In India two amendments to the constitution reserve a third of local council seats for women, giving rise to a new class of women (some 600,000 strong) with political influence; similar reservation is under consideration for higher political levels.[30] In Argentina at least a third of the candidates on national election lists must be women.[31]

Women's legal rights have been broadened considerably in many countries. In a growing number of countries daughters and sons now have equal legal rights to inherit from their parents. The existence of such legal rights does not mean that deeply rooted cultural norms immediately change, however. Moreover, the legal system often gives people scope for implementing their own norms. For example, the option of writing a will allows people to maintain cultural norms on inheritance favoring sons.[32] When

Box 7.1
Making land titling less gender biased in Latin America

The land titling process, rife with inequities, has often reduced women's access to land. Statutory law in several Latin American countries required that the beneficiaries of earlier land reform programs be heads of household. Since custom dictated that men were the head of the household, it was difficult for women to benefit from such programs. During the 1980s and 1990s, however, reform measures changed, and the more progressive agrarian codes of the 1990s gave special attention to this problem.

A study based on gender-disaggregated data for six countries (Chile, Colombia, Ecuador, Honduras, Mexico, and Peru) shows that women make up a larger share of beneficiaries under current land titling programs than under past agrarian reforms. Still, several obstacles to improving women's formal rights to land remain:

- Women often are unaware of their rights or of the land titling program.
- Land titling projects are often arbitrary. The problem usually starts with lack of clarity about the bundle of property rights to land within one household: those of the wife, those of the husband, and those to jointly acquired property. At the enforcement stage, this confusion often works to women's disadvantage.
- Some legal dispositions are gender biased. Procedures ceding rights to land often aim at individualizing land rights—one person per household. To work in favor of women, land titling programs need to give female heads of household priority, as in Chile.

Two sets of measures are particularly important for preventing gender bias in land titling and promoting the rights of women:

- Making joint titling of land to couples mandatory. Joint titling guarantees married women property rights to land that has been jointly acquired. In Colombia land titled jointly to couples accounted for 60 percent of land adjudications in 1996, up from 18 percent in 1995. Land titled exclusively to men declined from 63 percent to 24 percent over the same period.
- Fostering partnerships between government departments and NGOs that defend the rights of women—to increase women's awareness of their rights and support them in claiming title to land in the face of a possibly hostile bureaucracy or family. In Bolivia and Ecuador, where women's land rights featured little in the negotiations leading to new agrarian codes and where there was no movement toward joint titling or special rights for women, the reforms did not improve women's land rights.

Source: World Bank forthcoming a (based on Deere and Leon 1997, 1999); Deere and Leon forthcoming.

legislation conflicts too sharply with customary law, problems can surface.[33] Still, even if laws are not self-enforcing, they are a necessary first step toward gender equity.

More direct efforts to ensure women's access to productive resources include recent land titling programs to grant land rights to women. The 1994 Colombian Agrarian Law gave top priority to redistributing land to households headed by women and to women who lacked protection or had been displaced by war (including single and childless women).[34] The scheme—"a parcel of one's own"—was the only guarantee of secure livelihood for women and their children upon separation or divorce. Several other Latin American countries have been working on this issue, with varying success (box 7.1).

Women also need more equitable access to credit and associated productivity-enhancing services. Studies of the effect of networking schemes, such as group-based microcredit, suggest that these schemes have enormous potential for reducing poverty. Some of these credit programs, such as Grameen Bank in Bangladesh, are targeted more to women than to men.[35] Using peer pressure and group obligations rather than legal contracts, group-based schemes rely on social collateral rather than traditional financial assets as security.[36] The schemes have helped women acquire nonland assets and have also been associated with positive effects on girls' schooling.[37]

Critical to these programs are services that complement credit and savings facilities, such as training in entrepreneurial skills—especially for women, who are typically cut off from the normal paths for acquiring such skills. Given the opportunity, women can become successful entrepreneurs. In southern Africa women own an impressive share of small, informal sector businesses: 67 percent in Zimbabwe, 73 percent in Lesotho, and 84 percent in Swaziland.[38] The next step is to ensure greater access for women to business opportunities in the formal sector.

Recognizing the constraints women face in gaining access to public services and other opportunities makes antipoverty interventions more effective. In education, female teachers and separate sanitary facilities—or even single-sex schools—can boost girls' enrollments in some regions.[39] Demand-side interventions can also be effective (box 7.2). In agricultural extension, efforts to hire and train female extension agents—and to focus extension efforts on women farmers—help make new agricultural methods and technologies more accessible to them and increase productivity.

Box 7.2
Using subsidies to close gender gaps in education

Evaluations of recent initiatives that subsidize the costs of schooling indicate that demand-side interventions can increase girls' enrollments and close gender gaps in education. A school stipend program established in Bangladesh in 1982 subsidizes various school expenses for girls who enroll in secondary school. In the first program evaluation girls' enrollment rate in the pilot areas rose from 27 percent, similar to the national average, to 44 percent over five years, more than twice the national average (Bellew and King 1993). After girls' tuition was eliminated nationwide in 1992 and the stipend program was expanded to all rural areas, girls' enrollment rate climbed to 48 percent at the national level. There have also been gains in the number of girls appearing for exams and in women's enrollments at intermediate colleges (Liang 1996). While boys' enrollment rates also rose during this period, they did not rise as quickly as girls'.

Two recent programs in Balochistan, Pakistan, illustrate the potential benefits of reducing costs and improving physical access. Before the projects there were questions about whether girls' low enrollments were due to cultural barriers that cause parents to hold their daughters out of school or to inadequate supply of appropriate schools. Program evaluations suggest that improved physical access, subsidized costs, and culturally appropriate design can sharply increase girls' enrollments.

The first program, in Quetta, the capital of Balochistan, uses a subsidy tied to girls' enrollment to support the creation of schools in poor urban neighborhoods by local NGOs. The schools admit boys as long as they make up less than half of total enrollments. In rural Balochistan the second program has been expanding the supply of local, single-sex primary schools for girls by encouraging parental involvement in establishing the schools and by subsidizing the recruitment of female teachers from the local community. The results: girls' enrollments rose 33 percent in Quetta and 22 percent in rural areas. Interestingly, both programs appear to have also expanded boys' enrollments, suggesting that increasing girls' educational opportunities may have spillover benefits for boys.

Source: World Bank forthcoming a; Kim, Alderman, and Orazem 1998.

Box 7.3
Toward stronger female voice in policymaking: women's budget initiatives in southern Africa

The South African Women's Budget Initiative began as an innovative "joint venture" between several NGOs and new parliamentarians in the first post-apartheid government. The parliamentarians were members of the Gender and Economic Policy Group of the Joint Standing Committee on Finance, while many of the NGO representatives were involved in budget-related and more general policy research. The purpose of the initiative has been to highlight the gender dimensions of the government's budget—including in taxation, expenditure, and the budget process itself—and to ensure that gender equity is better served by the budget process and allocations.

The initiative has undertaken four rounds of budget analysis on a range of sectors. While the early rounds focused largely on the national budget process, the fourth has begun to focus on local government and on dissemination of findings and messages to a broader constituency of South Africans—to better equip ordinary citizens to engage in policy discussions.

The South African initiative has inspired several others. A three-year gender budget initiative was started in Uganda in 1997, led by the Parliamentary Women's Caucus in cooperation with the Forum for Women in Democracy, an NGO. Like the South African program, the Ugandan initiative involves the coordinated efforts of parliamentarians and NGO researchers. Already a powerful force in Uganda, the Women's Caucus has pushed through several legislative changes, including the clause in the local government law requiring that women constitute at least a third of executive committee members at the parish and village levels. The gender budget initiative has focused on macroeconomic policy and gender, including the effects of structural adjustment on poor women.

In Tanzania another three-year initiative, also started in 1997, is spearheaded by a coalition of NGOs led by the Tanzania Gender Networking Program. It focuses on understanding the budget processes of the National Planning Commission and the Ministry of Finance, how those processes affect government spending on basic services, and how government spending decisions affect women's and men's access to health and education services. The initiative has begun disseminating key findings in simple language to make them broadly accessible.

Source: World Bank forthcoming a; Budlender 1999; TGNP 1999.

Increasing gender equity has enormous benefits in establishing a culture of human rights as well as more immediate material benefits through its effects on productivity and the human capital of the next generation. Paths to gender equity include giving men and women equal rights under the law, equal access to education and health care, and equal access to services related to income generation. Gender budgeting and publication of gender-disaggregated development indicators can help generate public support for such efforts (box 7.3). All these interventions need to be backed by efforts to increase the political participation of women, so that they can contribute more fully to society.

Antidiscriminatory legal, institutional, and policy reforms for increasing gender equality have both instrumental value for development and poverty reduction and intrinsic value for furthering human rights and well-being. More equitable access to material resources and to needed services increases economic productivity and growth. More generally, increasing gender equity is an important component of efforts to encourage greater citizen participation in public life and in monitoring state institutions.

Social stratification and poverty

Because we had no schooling we are almost illiterate. Sometimes we cannot even speak Spanish; we can't add. Store-owners cheat us, because we don't know how to count or anything else. They buy at the prices they want and pay less. They cheat us because we are not educated.
—*Indigenous woman in Asociación de 10 Agosto, Ecuador*

Economic inequalities reinforced by social barriers make it especially difficult for poor people to move out of poverty. When social distinctions between groups are used to perpetuate inequalities in access to material resources, they generate rigid sociopolitical hierarchies, which constitute powerful social barriers explicitly aimed at preserving the status of the better-off. They place crippling constraints on individuals. For poor people, naturally risk averse because they live close to the margin of survival, the prospect of incurring the wrath of powerful elites by challenging these barriers is intimidating. Rigid stratification also creates obstacles to collective action: if the distribution of power in a community is too skewed, prospects for trust and cooperation are low.

Social inequality in villages undermines efforts to manage collective goods such as water.[40] In the hands of village elites, control of these resources can be used to further discriminate against poor people. One of the most glaring manifestations of inequality is in access to land. In most developing countries large inequalities in land ownership make it virtually impossible for poor people to rise from the bottom of the agrarian hierarchy. But land reform and broader efforts to diversify economic opportunities can break some of these barriers and reduce rural poverty (chapter 5; box 7.4).

In many settings discrimination and social inequality are the outcome of entire social groups having little political voice. These groups are discriminated against or neglected in the distribution of public goods, which translates into lower access to education and health—and lower income. Most damaging are the poverty traps that arise from

Box 7.4
Using development programs to break the power of agrarian elites: a case study from eastern Uttar Pradesh, India

The socioeconomic hierarchy in the village is apparent: there is one large white-washed brick mansion standing out among a sea of mud huts. The mansion is the home of the *talukdar*, the large landowner whose duty it was to collect land revenues for the colonial power. The *talukdar*'s family lost some of its holdings when land ceilings were imposed in the 1950s, although it held onto much of its land through fictitious division.

For the next couple of decades the *talukdar*'s family consolidated its relationships with the new power structures of the state. In a typical pattern of diversifying family networks, the father arranged for one son to be in the police service, while another managed the land. They continued to be the main source of credit and employment for the villagers, who acknowledged their social superiority by prefacing every interaction with the greeting "Touching your feet, Lord."

For this family, well educated and well connected, it was easy to divert development funds for its own benefit. The other villagers generally never knew about the entitlements they were being deprived of. Even if they did know, they could hardly protest, because the *talukdar*'s family had guns and was known to rape and maim at will.

Around 1970 agricultural extension agencies brought information on tubewells to the village. Some middle-level peasants pooled their resources to sink a tubewell to irrigate their contiguous plots. Eager to maximize their profits, they began to sow cash crops and raised the wages they offered agricultural laborers. The *talukdar*'s son responded by striding around at the weekly market with a gun slung over his shoulder, threatening to shoot anyone who offered laborers more than the going rate. That temporarily thwarted the peasants' efforts.

But new opportunities offered by tubewells and the opening of a government milk collection center in the village made it more difficult for the *talukdar*'s family to retain its position. Over time the middle-level peasants increased their incomes and offered new sources of employment and credit for poor people. The village shifted away from a bipolar polity toward a broader distribution of power.

A study of another Uttar Pradesh village noted similar tensions. There the *talukdar*'s family had tried such methods as arson and election rigging to maintain its power, but the middle-level peasants' determined use of new agrarian opportunities eventually weakened that power. By the 1990s the middle-level peasants had become prosperous and educated and formed a serious political challenge to the *talukdar*'s family, defeating them in local elections. The hegemony of the old colonial landowning elite has been effectively challenged through continuing development programs and participatory political institutions.

Source: Das Gupta, Grandvoinnet, and Romani forthcoming; Drèze, Lanjouw, and Sharma 1998.

Figure 7.3
Minority groups in Vietnam have less access to services than nonminorities

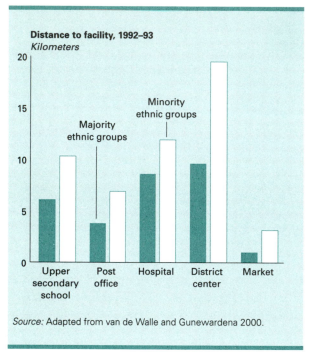

Distance to facility, 1992–93
Kilometers

Majority ethnic groups

Minority ethnic groups

Upper secondary school · Post office · Hospital · District center · Market

Source: Adapted from van de Walle and Gunewardena 2000.

active discrimination, which can inflict psychological damage on those discriminated against.

Some poverty traps are created in part by geographic isolation. Differential outcomes based on geographic isolation are a form of stratification, even if not consciously designed. For example, the disproportionately high poverty among indigenous groups in Latin America partly reflects their greater distance than others from markets, schools, hospitals, and post offices. Similar constraints are documented for minority ethnic groups in Vietnam (figure 7.3). Indigenous groups in Latin America also receive less education on average than nonindigenous groups. Ethnic discrimination exacerbates the effects: returns to schooling are lower among indigenous groups. Indigenous people are more likely than others to be sick and less likely to seek medical treatment, which may also help account for the difference in earnings.[41] This is a vicious circle, as low income reduces the probability of improving one's health.

Isolation and lack of education can create poverty traps that persist over generations, as children living in different locations experience different types of human capital accumulation. Even the neighborhood in which one lives can have a powerful influence on income and

human capital.[42] Living in a better-off neighborhood exposes individuals to social and cultural factors that increase their productivity.[43] Neighborhood effects can also reduce economic mobility and widen income disparities across communities, as in Ethiopia.[44] Similar results have been reported in industrial countries, where the rich often live apart from the rest of the population.

Other poverty traps result directly from prolonged discrimination against minority groups, as in the United States, or even against majority groups, as during the apartheid regime in South Africa.[45] In these countries, as in Latin America, blacks have lower education and income than whites. But their disadvantages run even deeper: their life expectancy at birth is also lower, a gap not explained by socioeconomic disparities alone.[46]

The cumulative effects of discrimination in education, employment opportunities, and information weaken the opportunities for members of these groups to find good jobs.[47] This dynamic is powerfully boosted by the psychological damage from discrimination—and the psychological obstacles to upward mobility add to the physical and financial obstacles to obtaining qualifications. People cease to believe in their abilities and stop aspiring to join the economic and social mainstream. This social dynamic emerges forcefully in the context of race relations in the United States (box 7.5).

Mitigating the impact of social stratification requires multifaceted approaches. Ensuring that public agencies and other state institutions serve all sectors of the population equally can make a big difference. This practice can be furthered by mobilizing excluded groups to be more assertive of their needs and rights. In situations of active discrimination, carefully designed affirmative action policies can help equalize access to opportunities.

Reforming institutions

In societies not deeply stratified, reform of state institutions can increase social equity. A fairly simple reform is to ensure that delivery of public services does not neglect disadvantaged groups. Broader reforms involve making legal systems equitable and ensuring that administrative and political institutions are accessible and responsive to all. Rather than create barriers, these systems should facilitate the full participation of the entire population. Citizenship laws may also need reform—to reduce social tensions and enable disadvantaged groups to participate in political life, which is important to their ability to organize on their own behalf.[48] In some countries, having

Box 7.5
Discrimination is psychologically devastating

In an analysis of social exclusion and the need for affirmative action in the United States, Glenn Loury draws attention to the psychological havoc that long-standing discrimination can wreak on black ghetto dwellers:

Here is a youngster to whom one says, "Why don't you marry the girl you got pregnant? Instead of standing on the street corner hustling, why don't you go to the community college and learn how to run one of these machines in the hospital? You could learn that with a couple of years at the community college instead of being a misfit," and the answer is not, "I have done my sums and the course you suggest simply does not pay." Instead, his answer is, *"Who, me?"* He cannot see himself thus.

Black ghetto dwellers in the United States are a people apart, susceptible to stereotyping, ridiculed for their cultural styles, isolated socially, experiencing an internalized sense of helplessness and despair, with limited access to communal networks of mutual assistance. In the face of their despair, violence, and self-destructive behavior, it is morally obtuse and scientifically naive to argue that if "those people" would just get their acts together we would not have such a horrific problem. Social processes encourage the development of self-destructive behavior. This is not to say that individuals have no responsibility for the wrong choices they may make. Instead, it is to recognize a deep dilemma, one that does not leave us with any good choices.

Because the creation of a skilled workforce is a social process, the meritocratic ideal—that in a free society individuals should be allowed to rise to the level of their competence—should be tempered with an understanding that no one travels that road alone. "Merit" is produced through social processes. For this reason, there should be a collective public effort to mitigate the economic marginality of those blacks who languish in the ghettos of America. Public goals ought not to be formulated in race-neutral terms, even if the instruments adopted for the pursuit of those goals are, in themselves, color-blind.

Source: Passages excerpted from various sections of Loury (2000).

crease their access to health, education, and other public services, improving their living conditions and raising their incomes. Early results from innovative "ethno-development" programs in Ecuador show the importance of cultivating genuine demand, enhancing self-management, and building local capacity—instructive lessons for development practitioners and policymakers.[49]

Taking affirmative action

In deeply stratified societies these efforts need to be supplemented by affirmative action programs—to counter the disabilities from long-standing discrimination. To compete in economic and political arenas, those discriminated against need special assistance in acquiring education, information, and self-confidence. Affirmative action begins with legislation against discrimination in access to public and private goods and services, such as housing, credit, transport, public places, and public office.

Prominent in affirmative action are efforts to reduce the cumulative disadvantages of low access to education and employment. This typically involves helping members of discriminated-against groups acquire skills and access to opportunities through financial support for education, preferential admission to higher education, and job quotas.[50] These policies, of two main types, make a big difference in outcomes:[51]

- *Developmental policies* seek to enhance the performance of members of disadvantaged groups. Examples are financial and other inputs to improve educational qualifications, and management assistance for those establishing their own business.
- *Preferential policies* seek to reduce cumulative disadvantages more rapidly by giving members of disadvantaged groups opportunities even when they may be less qualified than others. Although the quickest way to social and economic mobility, these policies can backfire by reinforcing negative stereotypes about the lower abilities of the disadvantaged.[52] Even qualified members of disadvantaged groups cannot escape this shadow.

A crucial role for affirmative action policies is to create role models who can alter the deep-rooted beliefs about different worth and abilities that permeate segregated societies (box 7.6). Such beliefs, psychologically devastating for the disadvantaged, are also shared by those who offer jobs and promotions, reducing the likelihood that they will give equal consideration to minority candidates, even when they have the necessary qualifications.

accountable judicial institutions would also help protect disadvantaged groups from discrimination.

Poor, marginalized communities can be mobilized to help reduce their poverty by drawing on and strengthening their social institutions. Groups with a strong collective identity—and a willingness to collaborate with outside agents to forge new solutions—can work to in-

Box 7.6
Using affirmative action against caste-based discrimination in India

The caste system in India separated people into economic and social strata by birth, reinforcing these divisions through differences in ritual status. This rigid hierarchy remained largely in place for many centuries, despite periodic challenges from social and religious reform movements. But in 1950 the newly independent government of India set out to transform the system. The constitution abolished untouchability in private or public behavior and empowered the government to take corrective action by reducing the social and educational disadvantages faced by lower-caste people and introducing affirmative action in employment. Seats in the national parliament and state assemblies were reserved for members of scheduled (lower) castes and tribes, and an act was adopted making the practice of untouchability a criminal offense.

The process of change has been fraught with difficulties. Legal challenges have been mounted against the policies on grounds also reflected in the public debate—that lower-caste people have no monopoly on poverty and that the gains of affirmative action have been cornered by a subgroup of the lower castes. And political resistance arose when the scope of preferential policies was expanded in recent decades to reserve larger shares of government sector jobs for lower-caste people. By contrast, the developmental policies aimed at helping lower-caste people gain access to education for upward mobility have been effective and less contentious.

Despite these difficulties, the affirmative action programs have done much to lower the barriers faced by lower castes. Lower-caste people now occupy positions in the highest walks of life, serving as role models for others. Still, a great deal remains to be done, as economic and educational inequalities persist. A survey in 1992–93 found that 57 percent of heads of household were illiterate in scheduled castes, compared with 35 percent in other castes. And special efforts are needed in the few remaining regions where the police are still dominated by upper-caste interests. Nevertheless, the experience of affirmative action in India illustrates how, with political will, the effects of long-standing patterns of discrimination can be overcome.

Source: Deshpande 2000; Dushkin 1972; Galanter 1972; Srinivas 1987; Tummala 1999.

Affirmative action seeks to alter these perceptions of different worth by bringing some members of discriminated-against groups into the mainstream economy and society. This has an important demonstration effect: having black or low-caste doctors, for example, shows everyone, including their own group, that members of this group can be good doctors.

Do affirmative action programs reduce efficiency or engender political strife? Evidence shows that these negative effects are largely associated with preferential policies and can be averted through greater use of developmental policies. In the United States affirmative action has redistributed income to women and minorities, with minimal loss of efficiency.[53] Preferential policies may be costly in the long term. Job quotas for minorities may distort the allocation of labor, impede efficiency, and create tensions between the "favored" and the others.[54] Preferential policies can also have negative political repercussions. Political elites, seeking to benefit from political clientelism, can manipulate policies aimed at reducing segregation or reserving employment for particular groups. Developmental policies, less likely to elicit resentment from other groups, are politically less challenging than preferential policies, and have enormous potential for reducing the cumulative disadvantages of longstanding discrimination.

Social fragmentation and conflict

Group differentiation by such characteristics as ethnicity, race, religion, and language can sometimes result in social fragmentation, with groups perceiving themselves as having distinct interests even though they may have similar socioeconomic status. Ethnicity—a multidimensional phenomenon and a controversial notion—is based on perceived cultural differences between groups in a society, differences that form a powerful source of identity and a base for political mobilization.[55] Some scholars have treated ethnicity as a form of capital—a resource or asset on which members of a particular ethnic community call in their business and political dealings.[56] Common ethnic affiliations can be a basis for bonding social capital (see next section), providing community members with a range of benefits (credit, employment, marital partners) while imposing significant obligations and commitments (financial support, conformity). Membership in an ethnic community can also generate negative externalities, as with conflict between ethnic groups (box 7.7).[57] Such divisions can be obstacles to collective action: in the United States greater ethnic fragmentation is associated with lower participation in civic activities.[58]

Ethnicity can become a basis for competition for political power and for access to material resources.[59] Unless institutions of the state and civil society offer forums for mediating intergroup rivalries and forging crosscutting ties among diverse ethnic groups, these ethnic cleavages can lead to conflicts, tearing a society and economy apart, leaving everyone vulnerable to poverty.

The extent to which social fragmentation leads to conflict depends largely on administrative and political institutions. To create a functioning society, a whole range of social and political institutions must work together. By contrast, breakdowns in governance and in the delivery of public goods and related social services create conditions for social unrest and conflict—as do breakdowns in the institutions of conflict mediation, such as representative politics and the rule of law.

Ethnic cleavages can affect development outcomes in many ways. They can influence the internal organization of government and the allocation of public spending, leading to unequal distribution of public goods and services. They can encourage rent seeking, reducing the efficiency of public spending.[60] Further economic distortions enter when powerful ethnic groups use their political power to increase their incomes relative to those of others. Recent studies in Ghana show that locally dominant groups receive a 25 percent premium over the wages of other groups in the public sector—a discrepancy that leads to

unrest and poor performance in the sector.[61] Such distortions in the distribution of resources and the efficiency of their use show up in development outcomes. In several African countries, for example, child survival is higher in dominant ethnic groups.[62]

Building political alliances

Countries with high ethnic diversity need to build the political conditions for integrating diverse groups so that they can function collectively.[63] With well-functioning administrative and political institutions, multiethnic societies can be effectively shaped into an "imagined community" of nation and state.[64] Knitting diverse communities together through a multiplicity of civil and state channels—to avert conflict—was a major goal of the early designers of European unity.[65] The communist regimes of the Soviet Union and Yugoslavia, despite their economic and political failures, not only reduced economic inequalities but also managed ethnic conflict. With their collapse, violent ethnic conflicts broke out because no alternative ideological and institutional framework had evolved to mediate them.

In Sub-Saharan Africa nation-states were fashioned out of arbitrary divisions of territory by colonial powers—divisions often based on convenient geographic markers such as lines of latitude and longitude, with no consideration of the social units of local populations. With disparate groups and few supraethnic institutions to mediate among them, the creation of nation and state has been fraught with problems. Colonial rulers and local politicians have often manipulated ethnic tensions for private gain, sometimes leading to gruesome civil wars.[66] Inflaming ethnic tensions and civil unrest is a frequent strategy for gaining and keeping power in these circumstances, since it justifies expanding brutal military forces while undermining the capacity of opposition groups demanding reform. Over time ethnic minorities, especially those facing discrimination, inequality, or conflict, can become ethno-classes,[67] groups whose ethnicity-based sensibilities and demands become independent causes of conflict.[68]

Building good institutions

Constructing high-quality public institutions is essential for ensuring that diverse identities become a developmental asset, not a source of political division and violence (figure 7.4).[69] This is especially important in countries with abundant natural resources, such as oil, diamonds, and minerals.[70] In environments with little institutional

Box 7.7
Ethnic divisions and civil conflict

Ethnic fragmentation, in its most extreme form and under conditions of economic deprivation and nondemocratic government, can descend into civil conflict. Ethnic conflict intensified in the second half of the 20th century, as the pattern of conflict shifted from wars between nations to conflicts within states. Civil conflict is both a cause and a consequence of poor economic performance. Research has shown that during civil wars per capita output falls by more than 2 percent a year on average.

The most important cost of civil conflict is loss of life—a humanitarian tragedy and an obstacle to reconstruction. Other costs include destruction of physical, human, and social capital; lower investment in physical and human capital; disruption of markets and other forms of economic and social order; diversion of human resources and public expenditure away from productive or productivity-enhancing activities; migration of highly skilled workers; and transfers of financial assets abroad. These costs can trap countries in poverty—and in conflict.

Civil conflict can also accelerate the collapse of the state, disproportionately hurting poor people. And the problems of civil conflict spill across borders, increasing the burdens of neighboring countries. In 1998 there were an estimated 12.4 million international refugees and 18 million internally displaced people, almost half of them in Africa.

Source: Collier and Hoeffler 1998; Austin 1999; Stewart, Humphreys, and Lea 1997; Collier 1999c; Luckham 1999.

Figure 7.4
Ethnic diversity is associated with violence where institutional quality is low

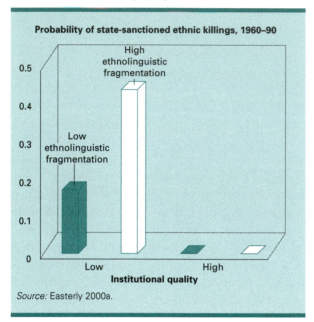

Source: Easterly 2000a.

accountability and transparency, the exorbitant rents from these resources become a primary source of competition among ruling factions.

Civil society organizations and the state can do much to lay the institutional foundation for groups to cooperate for the common good. Institutions need to be participatory, credible, and accountable, so that people can see the benefits of cooperation. Underpinning these institutions need to be constitutional and legal systems and representative political systems, which allow groups to work out their interests through mechanisms other than violence. Some social integration can be achieved by encouraging people to learn each other's languages. Another important requirement for effectively helping excluded groups is to collect accurate data on them.[71]

Building social institutions and social capital

Whenever there is a funeral, we work together . . . women draw water, collect firewood, and collect maize flour from well-wishers . . . while the men dig the grave and bury the dead. . . . We work together on community projects like molding bricks for a school. . . . Women also work together when cleaning around the boreholes.

—*From a discussion group, Mbwadzulu, Malawi*

In addition to removing social barriers, effective efforts to reduce poverty require complementary initiatives to build up and extend the social institutions of the poor. Social institutions refer to the kinship systems, local organizations, and networks of the poor and can be usefully discussed as different forms or dimensions of social capital.

Bonding, bridging, and linking social capital

Distinguishing among different dimensions of social capital within and between communities is useful for understanding the problems faced by poor people (box 7.8).

- The strong ties connecting family members, neighbors, close friends, and business associates can be called *bonding social capital.* These ties connect people who share similar demographic characteristics.
- The weak ties connecting individuals from different ethnic and occupational backgrounds can be referred to as *bridging social capital.*[72] Bridging social capital implies horizontal connections to people with broadly comparable economic status and political power. A theory of social capital that focuses only on relations within and between communities, however, opens itself to the criticism that it ignores power.[73]
- A third dimension, *linking social capital,* consists of the vertical ties between poor people and people in positions of influence in formal organizations (banks, agricultural extension offices, the police).[74] This dimension captures a vitally important additional feature of life in poor communities: that their members are usually excluded—by overt discrimination or lack of resources—from the places where major decisions relating to their welfare are made.

Research on the roles of different types of social networks in poor communities confirms their importance. An analysis of poor villages in rural North India, for example, shows that social groups play an important role in protecting the basic needs of poor people and mediating against risk (chapter 8). In contrast, the more extensive, leveraged networks of the nonpoor are used for strategic advantage, such as procuring better jobs and higher wages and seizing new economic opportunities (in some cases by directly mobilizing to secure a disproportionate share of public resources and services).[75]

Strikingly similar results emerge from work on the relationship between enterprise performance and the structure of business networks in Africa. Poor entrepreneurs operating small local firms in traditional industries form "solidarity networks," sharing personal information about members' conduct and intentions in order to reduce risk and uncertainty. In contrast, larger regional firms form "innovation networks," which share knowledge about technology and global markets in order to increase productivity, profits, and market share.[76] Studies of agricultural traders in Madagascar show that social relationships are more important to traders than input prices. Close relationships with other traders are used to lower the transactions costs of exchange, while ties to creditors and others who can help out during times of financial hardship are vital sources of security and insurance.[77] In Bolivia, Burkina Faso, and Indonesia field surveys attempting to measure

household social capital have found a positive association with household consumption, asset accumulation, and access to credit.[78]

Researchers and practitioners have long recognized that the bonding and bridging social capital in local organizations is necessary but insufficient for long-term development. In Kenya a participatory poverty assessment found more than 200,000 community groups in rural areas, but most were unconnected to outside resources and unable to help poor people rise out of poverty.[79] The creation of linking social capital is essential, and external support has often been important in its emergence.[80] External support—from NGOs and religious organizations, for example—can help create social capital that increases the voice and economic op-

Box 7.8
How does social capital affect development?

There are at least four views on the relationship between social capital and development (Serageldin and Grootaert 2000; Woolcock and Narayan 2000). The narrowest holds social capital to be the social skills of individuals—one's propensity for cooperative behavior, conflict resolution, tolerance, and the like (Glaeser, Laibson, and Sacerdote 2000).

A more expansive meso view associates social capital with families and local community associations and the underlying norms (trust, reciprocity) that facilitate coordination and cooperation for mutual benefit. This view highlights the positive aspects of social capital for members of these associations but remains largely silent on the possibility that social capital may not impart benefits to society at large and that group membership itself may entail significant costs.

A more nuanced meso view of social capital recognizes that group membership can have both positive and negative effects (Coleman 1990; Burt 1992; Portes 1995; Massey and Espinoza 1997). This approach broadens the concept of social capital to include associations in which relationships among members may be hierarchical and power sharing unequal. These forms of associations and networks address a wider range of objectives: some of them serve only the private interests of members, while others are motivated by a commitment to serve broader public objectives. This view emphasizes that groups, in addition to providing benefits to members, can make significant noneconomic claims on them.

A macro view of social capital focuses on the social and political environment that shapes social structures and enables norms to develop. This environment includes formalized institutional relationships and structures, such as government, political regime, rule of law, the court system, and civil and political liberties. Institutions have an important effect on the rate and pattern of economic development (North 1990; Fukuyama 1995; Olson 1982).

An integrating view of social capital recognizes that micro, meso, and macro institutions coexist and have the potential to complement one another. Macro institutions can provide an enabling environment in which micro institutions develop and flourish. In turn, local associations help sustain regional and national institutions by giving them a measure of stability and legitimacy—and by holding them accountable for their actions (Evans 1996; Woolcock 1998; Narayan 1999; Serageldin and Grootaert 2000; Putnam 1993).

While the mechanisms by which social capital operate are generally well understood, there is less consensus on whether they qualify social capital as "capital." In many cases norms and institutions have the durability and lasting effects associated with capital (Collier 1998; Narayan and Pritchett 1999). Some argue, however, that the sacrifice of a present for a future benefit, typical of traditional forms of capital, is not present in social networks—to the extent that these networks are built for reasons other than their economic value to participants (Arrow 2000). Even so, social networks and organizations are clearly key assets in the portfolio of resources drawn on by poor people to manage risk and opportunity. They are also key assets for the rich, who advance their interests through such organizations as country clubs and professional associations, but their relative importance is greater for poor people.

Social capital has its dark side, however. Where groups or networks are isolated, parochial, or working at cross-purposes to society's collective interests (gangs, drug cartels), the social capital within them serves perverse rather than productive purposes, undermining development (Rubio 1997; Levy 1996; Portes and Landolt 1996). Organized crime syndicates, such as those in Latin America and Russia, generate large negative externalities for the rest of society—lost lives, wasted resources, pervasive uncertainty (Rose 1999). And in India, for example, obligations to family members and pressures to fulfill community expectations lead many young girls to drop out of school (Drèze and Sen 1995; PROBE Team 1999).

Box 7.9
The federation of *comedores* in Peru:
the creation of linking social capital

The *comedores* (community kitchens) movement, one of the most dynamic women's groups in Peru, emerged in the mid-1980s. Participants sought to move beyond their traditional survival strategy and make demands on the political system. Federations were formed at the neighborhood level, then at the district level, and finally at the metropolitan and national levels. Centralization of the movement lowered the cost of inputs, such as food and kitchen equipment, and increased the availability of educational workshops.

The highest-level organization, the CNC (National Commission of Comedores), became the officially recognized representative of the *comedores*. One of its central demands was to include all poor women in welfare programs, not just those with connections to the ruling party. Besides influencing policymaking, the *comedores* have had a significant impact on local power relations in the shantytowns and, by extension, on the structure of the political system.

Although the movement's actions have been limited by the structure of the Peruvian state (with few formal channels for political action), the network of *comedores* represents a form of social capital that has enhanced poor women's value as an electoral constituency. The *comedores* have also increased women's negotiating power in their families.

Source: Houtzager and Pattenden 1999.

portunities of poor people (box 7.9). This support is most effective when it is sustained over time, emphasizes capacity building, and is based on a sensitive understanding of the local conditions and a relationship of trust and partnership.

This approach characterizes the work of Myrada, an Indian NGO delivering microfinance services. Myrada acts as a medium-term intermediary between poor people and commercial banks.[81] Its initial task is to mobilize the bonding social capital within village communities to form credit management groups and then over time to form regional federations made up of representatives from each credit group (thereby enhancing each group's bridging social capital). From the outset credit management groups hold accounts with commercial banks, progressively gaining the confidence and skills they need to participate independently in formal institutions (linking social capital). After five years of training and hard-won experience, group members are able to manage these accounts—and even arrange for annual external audits—without the involvement of Myrada staff, who move on to start the process afresh.

Using social capital to improve program effectiveness

The state plays a vital role in shaping the context and climate in which civil society organizations operate (chapter 6).[82] In some cases the state can also create social capital. In 1987 the Department of Health of the state of Ceara, Brazil, launched a rural health program—since then expanded to most of the country—that increased vaccination rates significantly and reduced infant mortality. The success of the program has been attributed largely to the building of trust between government workers and poor people. The program made building trust an explicit part of the health workers' mandate by adopting a client-centered, problem-solving approach to service delivery. Workers were helped by government media campaigns that publicized the program regularly and gave them a sense of calling. The result was a total reversal of attitude: mothers who once hid their children from government workers saw the agents as true friends of the community.[83]

Many case studies show that social capital can improve project design and sustainability (box 7.10). Recent evaluations of World Bank rural development projects show that outcomes turn heavily on the nature of the power relations between key stakeholder groups and on the fit between external interventions and local capacities. How relations between stakeholders evolve over time has an important bearing on the generation of trust. Project and community leaders who create confidence and goodwill are crucial, suggesting that high turnover among field staff can undermine project effectiveness. The Gal Oya irrigation project in Sri Lanka has succeeded in a destitute region with high levels of ethnic violence because of the patience and long-standing commitment of field staff (aptly called institutional organizers). The project's key contribution has been integrating local knowledge with external expertise and forging cooperation between NGOs and government officials.[84] In Africa recent innovations in community-driven development programs have shifted responsibility for maintaining hand pumps and latrines directly to communities.[85] Where previously such items broke down quickly and took months to repair, they are now in good condition.

A key lesson for practitioners and policymakers is the importance of using existing forms of bridging social capital in poor communities as a basis for scaling up the efforts of local community-based organizations.[86] Creating more accessible formal institutions helps poor people articulate their interests to those in power more clearly, confidently, and persuasively.

Box 7.10
Mobilizing and creating social capital in development projects

Development programs have relied on local groups of project beneficiaries or local associations to improve the success of development projects for more than two decades.[1] What is new is the umbrella label *social capital* to refer to the underlying social force or energy.

In Bangladesh Grameen Bank relies on groups of poor women to implement programs, and the Bangladesh Rural Advancement Committee on groups of village workers with little or no land. In Pakistan the Aga Khan Rural Support Program gives assistance to village organizations to supplement their self-help efforts. The Kenya Tea Development Authority worked with grower committees to promote production, obtaining a one-third share of the country's tea exports within 15 years. The 6-S movement in nine West African countries organized peasant federations in more than 2,000 communities to help farmers overcome the hardships of the dry season. The Center for Social and Economic Development in Bolivia has supported more than 250 peasant organizations that promote programs in agriculture, livestock, forestry, artisan production, and community infrastructure (Uphoff 1993; Krishna, Uphoff, and Esman 1997).

Local groups have also been used frequently in irrigation, water supply, and sanitation programs. The Orangi Pilot Project in Pakistan provided low-cost self-help sewerage facilities and other services to poor settlements and helped autonomous local institutions implement projects. In Côte d'Ivoire rural water supply improved significantly when responsibility for maintenance was shifted from the national water distribution company to community water groups. Breakdown rates were reduced from 50 percent to 11 percent, while costs fell nearly 70 percent. These results were sustained, however, only in villages in which well-functioning community organizations existed and demand for water was high (Hino 1993).

In many cases, challenging existing norms and practices increases the social capital of previously excluded groups while decreasing the power of local elites, helping reduce obstacles to poverty reduction. Development programs such as women's microfinance in Bangladesh change the social relationships in a village—indeed, their success depends on it. Breaking the grip of moneylenders, overcoming the resistance of certain religious leaders, and giving women more decisionmaking power within their household all require a fundamental realignment of traditional social relationships. Many development programs are inherently political (Fox and Gershman 1999), and powerful vested interests can be expected to mobilize against reforms that seek to erode their position in the name of poor people. Development researchers, policymakers, and practitioners must recognize these tensions and respond appropriately.

1. Among the first systematic evaluations of community participation was Esman and Uphoff (1984).

• • •

Many aspects of social norms and practices help generate and perpetuate poverty. Discriminatory practices associated with gender, ethnicity, race, religion, or social status result in the social, political, and economic exclusion of people. This creates barriers to upward mobility, constraining people's ability to participate in economic opportunities and to benefit from and contribute to economic growth. It also constrains their effective participation in political processes and civil action to ensure that state institutions are accountable to citizens and responsive to their needs.

Policies and programs for mitigating social exclusion depend on the nature of the exclusion. In some cases exclusion can be addressed simply by improving the outreach of public services to neglected areas. Where more active discrimination is involved, it is important to ensure equity in the law and in the functioning of state institutions. In addition, affirmative action policies may be needed to reduce the cumulative disadvantages of discriminatory practices and create visible role models for others to follow. Where there is considerable ethnic heterogeneity and social fragmentation, conflict can be averted through efforts to increase the civic interaction of different groups and engage them in resolving potential conflicts through political processes. Gender-based discrimination is qualitatively different from these other forms of discrimination because it involves intrahousehold distinctions in assigning value to people and allocating resources accordingly. Reducing gender-based social barriers requires changing deep-rooted beliefs about appropriate gender roles, as well as taking action to ensure greater gender equity in the functioning of formal public institutions.

Increasing the participation of the poor in development and reducing social barriers are important complements to creating an environment in which they have greater opportunity and security. This empowerment is enhanced by scaling up social institutions, increasing the capacity of poor people and the socially disadvantaged to engage society's power structure and articulate their interests and aspirations.

PART IV

Security

CHAPTER 8

Helping Poor People Manage Risk

To be well is to know what will happen with me tomorrow.

—*Middle-aged man, Razgrad, Bulgaria*

Poverty means more than inadequate consumption, education, and health. As the voices of the poor cry out, it also means dreading the future—knowing that a crisis may descend at any time, not knowing whether one will cope. Living with such risk is part of life for poor people, and today's changes in trade, technology, and climate may well be increasing the riskiness of everyday life. Poor people are often among the most vulnerable in society because they are the most exposed to a wide array of risks. Their low income means they are less able to save and accumulate assets. That in turn restricts their ability to deal with a crisis when it strikes.

Economic growth is one way of reducing the vulnerability of poor people. As their incomes rise, they are better able to manage risks. However, at any point in time those who are poor will see their vulnerability lessened if mechanisms to reduce, mitigate, and cope with risks are available to them.

Poor people have developed elaborate mechanisms for dealing with risk. But the mechanisms are far from capable of eliminating vulnerability. Many of the mechanisms offer short-term protection at long-term cost, preventing any escape from poverty.

The policy response to vulnerability must be aimed at helping poor people manage risk better by reducing and mitigating risk and lessening the impact of shocks. Such policies address the immediate problems of shocks and the inability to cope with them. But they also lay the foundations for investment by poor people that can take them out of poverty. This report advocates a modular approach to risk management that adapts safety nets to the specific pattern of risk in each country and complements existing risk management arrangements. This chapter briefly reviews experience with seven tools especially relevant for poor people: health insurance, old age assistance and pensions, unemployment insurance and assistance, workfare programs, social funds, microfinance programs, and cash transfers.

135

Table 8.1
Main sources of risk

Type of risk	Idiosyncratic — Risks affecting an individual or household (micro)	Covariant — Risks affecting groups of households or communities (meso)	Covariant — Risks affecting regions or nations (macro)
Natural		Rainfall Landslide Volcanic eruption	Earthquake Flood Drought High winds
Health	Illness Injury Disability Old age Death	Epidemic	
Social	Crime Domestic violence	Terrorism Gang activity	Civil strife War Social upheaval
Economic		Unemployment Resettlement Harvest failure	Changes in food prices Growth collapse Hyperinflation Balance of payments, financial, or currency crisis Technology shock Terms of trade shock Transition costs of economic reforms
Political		Riots	Political default on social programs Coup d'état
Environmental		Pollution Deforestation Nuclear disaster	

Source: Adapted from Sinha and Lipton (1999) and World Bank (2000q).

A typology of risks

One way to understand risks better and design appropriate policy responses is through a typology of risks and shocks to which people are vulnerable (table 8.1). Risks can be classified by the level at which they occur (micro, meso, and macro) and by the nature of the event (natural, economic, political, and so on). Micro shocks, often referred to as idiosyncratic, affect specific individuals or households. Meso shocks strike groups of households or an entire community or village. These shocks are common (or covariant) to all households in the group. Shocks can also occur at the national or international level.

This distinction by level of risk is critical. A risk that affects an entire village, for example, cannot be insured solely within the village. It requires pooling with areas not subject to the risk. In practice, many shocks have both idiosyncratic and covariant parts, though most empirical studies find that the idiosyncratic part of income risk is large.[1] This chapter focuses on risks that usually have large idiosyncratic components: illness and injury, old age, violence, harvest failure, unemployment, and food price risk (box 8.1). Covariant risks are discussed in chapter 3 (box 3.2) and chapter 7 (war and civil strife) and chapter 9 (macroeconomic shocks and natural disasters).

The extent to which a risk is covariant or idiosyncratic depends considerably on the underlying causes. For

Box 8.1
Poor people's exposure to risk

Poor people are exposed to a wide range of risks.

Illness and injury

Poor people often live and work in environments that expose them to greater risk of illness or injury, and they have less access to health care (Prasad, Belli, and Das Gupta 1999). Their health risks are strongly connected to the availability of food, which is affected by almost all the risks the poor face (natural disasters, wars, harvest failures, and food price fluctuations; de Waal 1991). Communicable diseases are concentrated among the poor, with respiratory infections the leading cause of death (Gwatkin, Guillot, and Heuveline 2000). A recent study of poverty in India found that the poor are 4.5 times as likely to contract tuberculosis as the rich and twice as likely to lose a child before the age of two (World Bank 1998t).

Illness and injury in the household have both direct costs (for prevention, care, and cure) and opportunity costs (lost income or schooling while ill; Sinha and Lipton 1999). The timing, duration, and frequency of illness also affect its impact. A study of South India found that households can compensate for an illness during the slack agricultural season, but illness during the peak season leads to a heavy loss of income, especially on small farms, usually necessitating costly informal borrowing (Kochar 1995).

Old age

Many risks are associated with aging: illness, social isolation, inability to continue working, and uncertainty about whether transfers will provide an adequate living. The incidence of poverty among the elderly varies significantly. In most Latin American countries the proportion of people in poverty is lower for the elderly than for the population at large (IDB 2000). In contrast, in many countries of the former Soviet Union the incidence of poverty is above average among the elderly, particularly among people 75 and older (Grootaert and Braithwaite 1998; World Bank 2000l). Women, because of their longer life expectancy, constitute the majority of the elderly, and they tend to be more prone to poverty in old age than men (World Bank forthcoming a). The number of elderly people in the developing world will increase significantly in coming decades with the rapid demographic transition.

Consultations with poor people show that income security is a prime concern of the elderly, followed closely by access to health services, suitable housing, and the quality of family and community life. Isolation, loneliness, and fear all too often mark old people's lives (Narayan and others 1999). As an elderly woman in Ukraine put it, "If I lay down and died, it wouldn't matter, because nobody needs me. The feeling of being unnecessary, of being unprotected, is, for me, the worst of all."

Crime and domestic violence

Crime and domestic violence reduce earnings and make it harder to escape poverty. While the rich can hire private security guards and fortify their homes, the poor have few means to protect themselves against crime. In São Paulo, Brazil, in 1992 the mur-

der rate for adolescent males in poor neighborhoods was 11 times that in wealthier ones (Sinha and Lipton 1999). Poor people frequently voice their fear of violence and the resulting powerlessness, "I do not know whom to trust, the police or the criminals."

Crime also hurts poor people indirectly. Children exposed to violence may perform worse in school (Morrison and Orlando 1999). A study of urban communities in Ecuador, Hungary, the Philippines, and Zambia showed that difficult economic conditions lead to destruction of social capital as involvement in community organizations declines, informal ties among residents weaken, and gang violence, vandalism, and crime increase (Moser 1998). Violence and crime may thus deprive poor people of two of their best means of reducing vulnerability: human and social capital.

Rich and poor women alike are victims of domestic violence, but the incidence is often higher in poor households. In Santiago, Chile, 46 percent of poor women and 29 percent of wealthy women suffer from domestic violence; in Managua, Nicaragua, 54 percent and 45 percent (Morrison and Orlando 1999).

Unemployment and other labor market risks

Labor market risks include unemployment, falling wages, and having to take up precarious and low-quality jobs in the informal sector as a result of macroeconomic crises or policy reform. The first workers to be laid off during cutbacks in public sector jobs are usually those with low skills, who then join the ranks of the urban poor, a pattern observed in Africa and Latin America during the structural adjustment reforms of the 1980s and early 1990s (ECLAC 1991; Sinha and Lipton 1999). The East Asian crisis also had pronounced effects on labor markets, with real wages and nonagricultural employment falling in all affected countries (World Bank 1999j). As state enterprises in Eastern Europe and the countries of the former Soviet Union were privatized, poverty increased among displaced workers with low education and obsolete skills, not qualified to work in emerging industries. Wage arrears in Russia intensified the problem (Grootaert and Braithwaite 1998).

Fluctuations in demand for labor often disproportionately affect women and young workers. Most public sector retrenchment programs have affected women's employment more than men's (World Bank forthcoming a), and women are more likely than men to work for small firms, which tend to be more sensitive to demand fluctuations (Horton and Mazumdar 1999). As incomes fall, poor households try to increase their labor market participation, especially for women and children. This response has been documented in many countries (Horton and Mazumdar 1999; Grootaert and Patrinos 1999).

Harvest failure and food price fluctuations

Weather-related uncertainties (mainly rainfall), plant disease, and pests create harvest risk for all farmers, but technologies for reducing such risks (irrigation, pesticides, disease-resistant

(box continues on next page)

Box 8.1
Poor people's exposure to risk (continued)

varieties) are less available in poor areas. In 1994–96 less than 20 percent of all cropland was irrigated in low- and middle-income countries (only 4 percent in Sub-Saharan Africa).

Fluctuations in food prices are a related risk. Since poor households spend a large part of their income on food, even small price increases can severely affect food intake. Households that meet their food needs through subsistence agriculture are less vulnerable than households that have to buy all their food.

Liberalization of markets often boosts the price of staples—a benefit to small farmers if they are net sellers of food. Hurt are the urban poor and the landless rural poor, as net food buyers, and farmers who engage in seasonal switching, selling food after the harvest when food is plentiful and cheap and buying it when it is scarce and expensive (Sinha and Lipton 1999). Where transport facilities are good, traders can step in and equalize prices

over the year through arbitrage, but such infrastructure is lacking in many areas. In Madagascar the mean price of rice, the main staple, rose 42 percent and the variance increased 52 percent after the price liberalization of the 1980s. Two-thirds of rice farmers were hurt because they consumed more rice than they produced, and poverty deepened (Barrett 1996, 1998a).

For the rural poor, crop diversification and income diversification into nonfarm activities hold the greatest promise for reducing food price and harvest risks. Reducing consumption as food prices rise can have major and lasting adverse health effects, especially for children. Successive harvest failures because of insufficient monsoons in Sri Lanka in 1995 and 1996 led to increased indebtedness in 80 percent of households in eight villages, and 30 percent of households reported increased incidence of illness (Sinha and Lipton 1999).

example, job loss can be an individual risk, or it can be common to most workers in a country if it is the result of a macroeconomic crisis. The risk of becoming ill can be idiosyncratic, or it can have a large common component if there is an epidemic. The HIV/AIDS pandemic is a health risk at the global level, with devastating effects on poor people and poor countries (box 8.2).

Knowing the source of shocks is important for preventing them, but identifying the source is not always straightforward. Many exogenous events can have similar effects on household income. A macroeconomic shock, a hurricane, or a civil war can all lead to severe decline in income and deplete a household's assets. But how a shock is transmitted to households is greatly affected by a country's institutions. Not every drought causes famine, illness, and death. The effect of a disaster depends on how well the government functions, whether there is peace or civil strife, how well the safety net and other institutions include the poor, and so on.

The typology can be refined by distinguishing the severity and frequency of shocks. Consumption smoothing is more difficult with repeated shocks, because households may have depleted their assets in coping with the initial shock, leaving them unable to absorb subsequent shocks.[2] And one shock might lead to another. A natural disaster could wipe out poor people's food supply, leaving them weak and susceptible to illness. Severity can range from catastrophic (a natural disaster, death of the breadwinner) to minor (a slight illness, a few days without work for casual laborers).

The nature and magnitude of vulnerability

Vulnerability affects everyone (box 8.3). Even well-paid civil servants are vulnerable to losing their jobs and sliding into poverty. For the poor, and for people just above the poverty line, vulnerability is a graver concern because any drop in income can push them into destitution. As a result, poor people are highly risk averse and reluctant to engage in the high-risk, high-return activities that could lift them out of poverty. One slip could send them deeper into poverty.

Large fluctuations in income are common for poor people.[3] For South Indian villages estimates of the coefficient of variation of annual income from the main crops range between 0.37 and 1.01[4] and are as high as 1.27 for total farm profits.[5] In rural Ethiopia three of four households suffered a harvest failure over a 20-year period, resulting in significant fluctuations in farm income.[6]

Furthermore, because poor people have fewer assets and less diversified sources of income, these fluctuations affect them more than other groups. In South Indian villages an increase in risk (from the monsoon arriving too soon or too late) reduced farm profits for the poorest quarter of households by 35 percent but left the wealthiest farmers nearly unaffected.[7] In Vietnam participants in the *Voices of the Poor* study said of harvest losses due to floods:

The wealthy can recover losses in one year, but poor people, who have no money, will never recover.

Box 8.2
AIDS and poverty

More than 34 million people worldwide are infected with HIV, and more than 18 million people have died of AIDS. More than 90 percent of people infected with HIV/AIDS are in the developing world. Cross-country evidence indicates that both low income and unequal distribution of income are strongly associated with HIV infection rates. Countries with high gender inequality also have higher infection rates. Sub-Saharan Africa has more cases of existing and new infections than the rest of the world combined, though the rate of increase is now steepest in Asia and in the countries of the former Soviet Union.

All 20 countries with the highest HIV prevalence are in Sub-Saharan Africa. In Botswana and Zimbabwe 1 in 4 adults is infected. In 10 other African countries more than 1 in 10 adults are infected. The effect on life expectancy will be devastating. Had AIDS not affected these countries, life expectancy would have reached 64 years by 2010–15. Instead, it will have regressed to 47 years, reversing the gains of the past 30 years. The impact on child mortality is also enormous. In Zambia and Zimbabwe 25 percent more infants are dying than would have without HIV.

Despite the strong correlation at the country level between poverty and AIDS, the evidence for individuals does not suggest that poor people are most likely to be infected. Indeed, early on, the disease struck mainly the better-off groups. Evidence for the 1980s and the first half of the 1990s indicates a positive correlation between HIV infection and education, income, and socioeconomic status, probably because wealthier and better-educated people were more likely to have multiple sexual partners. Nonsexual modes of transmission—intravenous drug use and mother-to-child transmission—are associated more with poverty. In recent years the profile of HIV-infected people has been changing rapidly, and AIDS is becoming a disease of poor people.

With the more educated responding to the information available on AIDS and adopting protective sexual practices (condoms), the share of new infections is rising among low-income and less educated people.

With 5 million people becoming infected annually, urgent action is needed to stop the spread of HIV/AIDS. Successful intervention programs require strong government commitment and partnerships with the private sector, NGOs, and community leaders. Interventions shown to be effective include conducting public information campaigns to change individual behavior and social norms for sexual contact; making condoms more available and affordable; providing voluntary counseling, testing, and treatment of sexually transmitted diseases; ensuring a safe blood supply; and taking measures to reduce mother-to-child transmission. In addition, care activities need to be scaled up to support the vast numbers of people infected and affected.

AIDS has a devastating impact on poor people. During the illness it leads to loss of labor and causes poor households to dispose of productive assets to pay for treatment. The impact of an adult death from AIDS is more severe in poor households. The recommended policy approach is to concentrate on poor households most in need of survivor assistance, focusing on the period immediately after a death, when food consumption has fallen but there has not yet been a permanently damaging impact.

The view that HIV/AIDS is a central development issue is embodied in the International Partnership against HIV/AIDS in Africa, launched in 1999 by the cosponsors of the Joint United Nations Programme on HIV/AIDS (UNAIDS), including the World Bank. In collaboration with African governments, the program aims to increase resources and technical support, establish targeted prevention and treatment efforts, and expand the knowledge base to assist countries.

Source: Ainsworth and Semali 1998; Basu 1995; Over 1998; Rugalema 1999; UNAIDS 2000; World Bank 1997d, 1999m.

Box 8.3
Some key terms: risk, risk exposure, and vulnerability

As traditionally defined and measured, poverty is a static concept—a snapshot in time. But insecurity and vulnerability are dynamic—they describe the response to changes over time. Insecurity is exposure to risk; vulnerability, the resulting possibility of a decline in well-being. The event triggering the decline is often referred to as a shock, which can affect an individual (illness, death), a community, a region, or even a nation (natural disaster, macroeconomic crisis).

Risk, risk exposure, and vulnerability are related but not synonymous. Risk refers to uncertain events that can damage well-being—the risk of becoming ill, or the risk that a drought will occur. The uncertainty can pertain to the timing or the magnitude of the event. For example, the seasonal fluctuation of farm income is an event known in advance, but the severity is not always predictable. Risk exposure measures the probability that a certain risk will occur. Vulnerability measures the resilience against a shock—the likelihood that a shock will result in a decline in well-being. As this chapter explores, vulnerability is primarily a function of a household's asset endowment and insurance mechanisms—and of the characteristics (severity, frequency) of the shock.

In China 40 percent of an income decline is passed on as lower consumption for the poorest tenth of households, but only 10 percent for the richest third of households, because they have better access to insurance.[8]

One measure of the vulnerability of the poor and near-poor is how often a household falls below the poverty line. A study of seven countries for which panel surveys are available found that in six of them the "sometimes poor" group was significantly larger than the "always poor" group.[9] A nine-year panel survey of households in South Indian villages found that 20 percent of households were poor in each of the nine years and that only 12 percent were never poor, with movement in and out of poverty the norm for the vast majority of households.[10] These findings show both the high vulnerability and the strong resilience of poor households—the ability to escape poverty again after suffering an income shock. Relative income mobility can be quite large. In South Africa 29 percent of households in the poorest quintile moved up two or more quintiles from 1993 to 1998, while in Peru 37 percent of households did so between 1985 and 1990.[11]

Another approach is to define long-term poverty as average long-term consumption below the poverty line and then to ask how much of measured poverty is transitory. This approach implicitly considers the duration and depth of transitions into and out of poverty. By this method about half the estimated poverty in South Indian villages[12] and about half the severe poverty in China are transitory.[13]

Both methods suggest that transitory poverty is a large part of total poverty in many settings. Generally, households with the fewest assets are most likely to be chronically poor. Education almost always reduces chronic poverty, but its effects on transitory poverty differ. Better educated households in Côte d'Ivoire and Hungary were found to recover better from downward income fluctuations, but in China education is not correlated with transitory poverty.[14] The duration of transitory poverty also depends on the frequency of shocks: households are more likely to bounce back from a single shock than from repeated income shocks.[15]

Vulnerability is multidimensional, and poor households face manifold risks, so variations in income and consumption can occur for a variety of reasons. Rural households in Ethiopia, for example, face natural shocks such as harvest failure, health-related shocks such as illness or disability, and macro-level shocks such as the effects of

Table 8.2
Shocks faced by rural households in Ethiopia

Event	Percentage of households reporting a hardship episode in past 20 years
Harvest failure (drought, flooding)	78
Policy shock (taxation, forced labor)	42
Labor problems (illness, death)	40
Oxen problems (illness, death)	39
Other livestock problems (illness, death)	35
Land problems (land expropriation, reform)	17
Asset losses	16
War	7
Crime (theft, violence)	3

Source: Dercon 1999.

taxation, land expropriation, and war (table 8.2). Rainfall-induced income shocks have idiosyncratic components of 23 percent, but crop damage from other sources (pests, animals, weeds) have idiosyncratic components of 65–87 percent. Income shocks from illnesses have an even larger idiosyncratic component.[16] The cumulation of different shocks is a source of significant stress for households:

As if land shortage is not bad enough, we live a life of tension worrying about the rain: will it rain or not? We live hour to hour.

—*Woman, Kajima, Ethiopia*

Responses to risk by households and communities

For poor people, dealing successfully with the range of risks they are exposed to is often a matter of life or death. To manage risks, households and communities rely on both formal and informal strategies (table 8.3). Informal strategies include arrangements that involve individuals or households or such groups as communities or villages. Formal arrangements include market-based activities and publicly provided mechanisms. Informal and formal strategies are not independent: public policies and the availability of formal mechanisms heavily influence how extensively informal arrangements are used and which kinds are used.

Table 8.3
Mechanisms for managing risk

Objective	Informal mechanisms		Formal mechanisms	
	Individual and household	**Group based**	**Market based**	**Publicly provided**
Reducing risk	■ Preventive health practices ■ Migration ■ More secure income sources	■ Collective action for infrastructure, dikes, terraces ■ Common property resource management		■ Sound macroeconomic policy ■ Environmental policy ■ Education and training policy ■ Public health policy ■ Infrastructure (dams, roads) ■ Active labor market policies
Mitigating risk *Diversification*	■ Crop and plot diversification ■ Income source diversification ■ Investment in physical and human capital	■ Occupational associations ■ Rotating savings and credit associations	■ Savings accounts in financial institutions ■ Microfinance	■ Agricultural extension ■ Liberalized trade ■ Protection of property rights
Insurance	■ Marriage and extended family ■ Sharecropper tenancy ■ Buffer stocks	■ Investment in social capital (networks, associations, rituals, reciprocal gift giving)	■ Old age annuities ■ Accident, disability, and other insurance	■ Pension systems ■ Mandated insurance for unemployment, illness, disability, and other risks
Coping with shocks[a]	■ Sale of assets ■ Loans from money-lenders ■ Child labor ■ Reduced food consumption ■ Seasonal or temporary migration	■ Transfers from networks of mutual support	■ Sale of financial assets ■ Loans from financial institutions	■ Social assistance ■ Workfare ■ Subsidies ■ Social funds ■ Cash transfers

Note: The white shaded area shows household and community responses through informal mechanisms to improve risk mitigation and coping. The dark shaded area shows the publicly provided mechanisms for insuring against risk and coping with shocks—the social safety net.
a. Publicly provided coping mechanisms can also serve risk mitigating purposes if they are in place on a permanent basis.
Source: Adapted from Holzmann and Jorgensen (2000).

Risk management strategies can be further classified as risk reduction and mitigation measures (actions in anticipation of a shock) and coping measures (actions in response to a shock).[17] Risk reduction aims at reducing the probability of a shock or negative fluctuation. Individuals or households can sometimes take such action themselves (digging wells, getting vaccinated). But to reduce most risks effectively, action is also needed at the meso or macro level. The risk of flooding can be reduced if the community builds a dike or the government builds a dam. Sound economic and environmental policies, education and training, and other measures can also reduce a wide variety of risks (and are discussed elsewhere in the report).

Risk mitigation aims at reducing the impact of shocks. Households mitigate risk through diversification (acquiring assets whose returns are not perfectly correlated) and insurance. Common diversification strategies are planting different crops and plots, combining farm and nonfarm income in rural areas, and combining wage income and income from household enterprises in urban areas. Households can take most of these actions on their own—though group or government action (agricultural extension, infrastructure) can sometimes facilitate diversification. Households also mitigate risk through insurance, including self-insurance, informal insurance, and formal insurance—though market-based formal insurance plays a minor role for poor people.

Coping strategies aim to relieve the impact of a shock after it occurs. Actions by individuals include drawing down savings or selling assets, borrowing, and calling on support networks. Actions by government include activating the transfers or workfare mechanisms that constitute the social safety net. If these measures prove insufficient, households may need to reduce consumption or increase labor supply. Many of these coping responses force a high long-term cost on households for a short-term benefit.

This chapter focuses primarily on how to improve risk mitigation and coping by poor people. It examines households' and communities' own responses through informal mechanisms. The chapter then explores the conditions for public action to supplement poor people's own risk management efforts—and the forms this intervention can take. In particular, it discusses the range of safety nets that can be used for risk mitigation and coping (see table 8.3).

Mitigating risk through diversification

Many studies document how households throughout the developing world diversify their income sources to smooth the flow of income over time.[18] A review of 25 studies in Africa shows that rural households receive an average of 45 percent of income from nonfarm activities, with the share ranging from 15 to 93 percent.[19] Farmers also diversify across crops and plots and by working for other farmers.

Evidence suggests, however, that the net effect of these efforts is limited and that the variability of farmers' income remains high. The income options typically open to farmers tend to move together during crises. Drought, for example, reduces nonfarm income as well as harvest income because crop failure leads to a generalized drop in income that reduces demand for nonfarm services.[20]

The range of income options available to farming households is often quite restricted. Evidence from Burkina Faso, Ethiopia, India, Kenya, and Tanzania shows entry constraints—including lack of working capital, skills, and inputs—for many activities that could allow farmers to diversify their incomes. Startup costs for setting up a shop or providing services are often 10–20 times the cost of other activities that poor people typically undertake, such as charcoal making, dung cake collection, or simple food processing, activities that provide only weak income diversification.[21] As a result, poor farmers in Africa tend to be less effectively diversified than rich farmers (table 8.4).[22] Poor farmers in other parts of the world have had more success in diversifying income sources. In Pakistan 55 percent of farmers' income in 1986–89 came from nonfarm sources, and this share was three times as high for poor as for rich farmers.[23] In Egypt as well, poor farmers were found to be more diversified than rich farmers.[24]

Where the possibilities for effective diversification are limited, poor farmers will specialize in low-risk, low-return activities, making it hard to escape poverty. Poor

Table 8.4
Income diversification among African farmers

Country	Period	Average share of nonfarm income in total income (percent)	Ratio of rich farmers' nonfarm share to poor farmers'
Botswana	1985–86	77	2.5
Burkina Faso	1981–84	37	2.5
Ethiopia	1989–90	36	1.2
Gambia	1985–86	23	1.3
Malawi	1990–91	34	1.0
Mozambique	1991	15	2.5
Niger	1989–90	52	2.0
Rwanda	1990	30	5.0
Senegal			
North	1988–89	60	2.0
Central	1988–90	24	1.0
South	1988–90	41	2.6
Sudan	1988	38	1.0
Zimbabwe	1988–89	42	1.0

Source: Reardon 1997.

Indian farmers devote a larger share of land to traditional varieties of rice and castor than to high-return varieties.[25] Tanzanian farmers without livestock grow more sweet potatoes, a low-risk, low-return crop, than do farmers who own livestock. As a result, returns to farming per adult household member are 25 percent higher for the wealthiest group than for the poorest.[26] Poor farmers are at a further disadvantage because harvest shocks are typically covariant over a fairly large area. This limits the usefulness of group-based strategies and networks of mutual support, because all or most group members are likely to be affected simultaneously.[27]

Mitigating risk through insurance

In principle, any shock with a probability that can be calculated from historical records is insurable. In practice, there are almost no insurance markets in developing countries because of problems of contract enforcement and asymmetric information. People, especially poor people, have to rely largely on self-insurance and informal insurance instead. These problems have been overcome in developed countries through strong legal and other institutions.

Self-insurance. Households insure themselves by accumulating assets in good times and drawing on them in bad. The strategy is effective if assets are safe and have a positive rate of return, especially if the rate of return exceeds the rate of time preference (of present consumption over future consumption). In practice, returns to assets may be negative, and many poor households have very high rates of time preference (they are "impatient," often out of necessity), which impedes asset accumulation.[28]

Another problem is that asset values and income are often covariant following a macro shock, so that the value of assets is lowest just when they are needed most. A drought that destroys a harvest may also weaken and kill cattle, which farmers in many poor countries use as a buffer stock. The terms of trade of assets relative to consumption goods may also deteriorate as a result of the shock, as everyone tries to sell assets and buy staples at the same time. Both supply and demand factors push down asset prices: the income shock induces everyone to sell assets, and the decline in purchasing power reduces demand (unless buyers from outside the shock zone show up). In good times the process works in reverse: everyone wants to buy the buffer asset, pushing up its price and making the strategy very costly.[29]

Simulations with household risk models suggest that self-insurance quickly loses effectiveness when the correlation between income and the terms of trade of assets exceeds 0.5. Households then have to curtail the sale of assets during crises because they gain so little extra consumption in return. During the 1984–85 famine in Ethiopia asset terms of trade collapsed, and households cut their consumption drastically rather than sell assets.[30] During the 1981–85 drought in Burkina Faso livestock sales compensated for only 15–30 percent of the shortfall in crop income.[31]

Buying and selling cattle, though a common strategy for coping with income fluctuations, is not a feasible one for many poor households. Buying a cow requires a large, one-time outlay (and significant prior saving). In western Tanzania a cow costs about a fifth of mean annual crop income, explaining why only half of households own cattle.[32] Where possible, poor households use smaller animals (goats, sheep) or more divisible items as buffer stocks. In three South Indian villages farmers held buffer stocks of grains and currency as their main risk management strategy.[33] In rural China, by contrast, households increased their holdings of unproductive liquid assets only slightly in response to income risk.[34]

Because the indivisibility and riskiness of many assets (price risk, survival risk for cattle) limit asset-based risk management strategies, poor people need a wider range of assets and greater stability of asset values. This would allow them to take better advantage of opportunities for income growth (described in part II of this report). Savings accounts hold great promise as a divisible asset with a fixed value and positive return. Given some assurances about the safety of the financial institution holding the accounts, the main risk would be inflation. Several recent experiences have underscored the great demand by poor households for safe savings accounts. Bank Rakyat Indonesia has more than 16 million low-income depositors. SafeSave, an NGO in Dhaka, Bangladesh, has adapted the principles of a traditional rotating savings and credit association; its agents collect small sums of money daily for deposit in members' accounts.[35]

Informal insurance. Households also use group-based mechanisms of informal risk sharing that rely on the social capital of groups of households. Typically, informal insurance involves a mutual support network of members of a community or extended household, often within ethnic groups; among members of the same occupation; or between migrants and their households of origin.

Like consumption smoothing, which aims to equalize marginal utilities over time, group-based insurance aims to equalize marginal utilities across members of the group.[36] When one member's consumption falls, the others transfer resources to rebalance marginal utilities. These networks are effective only against shocks common to some members but not all. So the wider the group, the less likely a shock is to affect all members, and the more effective they all are at risk pooling.[37]

A network operates through transfers, gifts, or loans between members, typically with expectations of reciprocity. Transfers respond to an emergency befalling a member of the network, thus serving risk management purposes, but they also fulfill a social function in forging community cohesion.[38] The importance of gifts and transfers varies greatly. In Bulgaria fewer than a fifth of households receive transfers; in Jamaica more than half do (table 8.5). In most countries the bulk of transfers goes to the poorest households, often representing a large share of income. Private transfers increase the poorest quintile's share of aggregate income by about 50 percent in Jamaica and Nepal and by almost 70 percent in Russia (figure 8.1).

The occurrence of transfers is not always a sign of adequate protection against crises. The key feature of informal insurance is reciprocity, self-enforced by the group. In situations of high economic stress, norms and social pressure may not be enough to ensure that members of the group do in fact transfer resources to other members. Informal insurance works best where people value future protection highly (rates of time preference are low) and fear of future exclusion from the insurance scheme keeps compliance high. But this works against poor people, who tend to value current consumption highly relative to future consumption (usually out of necessity). For this reason, poor people, even though they need insurance most, are more likely to drop out of informal arrangements. Informal insurance also works better when the rate of transfers is high (because frequent interactions create trust in future compliance) and shocks are idiosyncratic (because covariant shocks can wipe out the entire network's resources).[39]

To determine the need for a formal safety net, researchers have tried to measure how well informal insurance works, but measurement has proved difficult. It is hard to distinguish between the effects of informal insurance and those of self-insurance. And because measurement requires information about consumption and trends for all members (or a statistically valid sample of them), it is especially difficult when a network extends past

Table 8.5
Private cash and in-kind transfers for poor households
Percent

Country (year)	Share of households giving transfers	Share receiving transfers All households	Share receiving transfers Poor households[a]
Jamaica (1997)	13.1	53.0	65.0
Nepal (1996)	17.4	44.7	55.3
Peru (1994)	14.3	37.3	46.7
Panama (1997)	15.5	37.8	40.9
Kazakhstan (1996)	20.2	27.5	33.8
Kyrgyz Republic (1996)	15.7	35.5	31.7
Russian Federation (1997)	23.7	25.2	31.5
Bulgaria (1995)	15.0	17.0	21.4

a. Households in the lowest quintile of the per capita income distribution.
Source: Cox, Galasso, and Jimenez 2000.

Figure 8.1
Private transfers represent a large share of the income of the poor

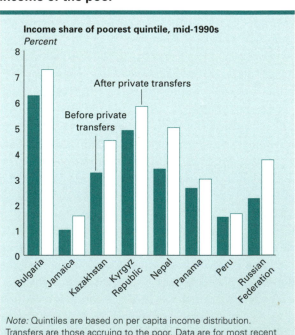

Note: Quintiles are based on per capita income distribution. Transfers are those accruing to the poor. Data are for most recent year available.
Source: Cox, Galasso, and Jimenez 2000.

the boundaries of a village or other geographical entity. Evidence from Côte d'Ivoire, India, Thailand, and Uganda suggests that informal insurance exists, but is far from perfect.[40] Evidence from China and India indicates that the poor and the landless are much less protected from income fluctuations than the rich and the large landholders.[41]

Coping with shocks

When a shock hits, people cope by cashing in their insurance: selling livestock or other assets, or calling on support networks for transfers or loans. If these mechanisms fail or fall short, households may increase their labor supply, working more hours, involving more household members (women or children), or migrating to unaffected areas. If all else fails, households reduce consumption and go hungry.[42]

The poor have fewer options than the wealthy for coping with shocks. Because they own fewer physical assets, poor people are more likely to increase their labor supply. If the shock is covariant and the local labor market has collapsed, migration is the only answer. And if the men in the household migrate, women and children may need to pick up the slack locally.[43]

Coping with shocks often requires more than these economic responses. During a prolonged crisis people may delay marriage and childbearing, families may move in together (especially in urban areas), and people may resort to illegal activities (theft, robbery, prostitution). Ultimately, the social mechanisms meant to help households cope with shocks may come undone under the continuing pressure of a prolonged shock.

Effects within households

So far, the discussion of risk management has viewed the household as the unit of impact and decision. Yet risk sharing within the household may not be equal, and the burden of the household's response may fall disproportionately on the weakest members, especially women and children. Two situations are possible. A shock affecting the household as a whole may have different effects on different household members. Or an individual shock (illness, loss of job) may have different effects on consumption depending on whether the affected person is a man or a woman. There is more evidence on the first situation than the second.[44]

Because poor households tend to have many children, children are more exposed to poverty and vulnerability than other groups. Children in poor households are especially vulnerable to fluctuations in household income and consumption. They are more likely than other children to be underweight, so that further declines in food consumption can cause irreversible harm. In Bangladesh children's growth suffered during major floods.[45] In rural India child mortality rates increased in times of drought, especially in landless households.[46]

The evidence on gender bias in the responses to such shocks is mixed. No such bias was found following floods in Bangladesh.[47] Studies in India, however, found that girls' nutrition suffered more than boys' during periods of low consumption in the slack agricultural season.[48] Price changes also were found to affect girls' consumption more than boys'.[49] For children under the age of two, rainfall shortages were associated with more deaths for girls than for boys.[50]

Some studies have found that women suffer more than men from adverse shocks. Rising food prices led to larger reductions in nutrient intake for women than for men in Ethiopia and India.[51] Cultural and traditional factors can increase women's exposure to risk. Divorced and widowed women in South Asia often face higher health risks and are more likely than married women to be poor because they lose access to their husband's property.[52] In some African countries women may lose access to household land when their husband dies.[53] There is also evidence of a pro-male bias in household health and nutrition expenditures, but it is not clear whether the bias affects poor households more than others. A recent study in Pakistan found limited evidence that gender bias in health expenditures decreases with rising income.[54]

On balance, the evidence points to important differences in intrahousehold effects from shocks. But the evidence comes mainly from South Asia. Whether similar effects occur elsewhere is still unknown.

The poverty trap and the long-term consequences of inadequate risk management

As households move closer to extreme poverty and destitution, they become very risk averse: any drop in income could push them below the survival point. The poorest households try to avoid this even if it means forgoing a large future gain in income. Despite facing the highest risk, they have the fewest resources for dealing with that risk. And forced onto the most marginal lands (floodplains, hillsides) and into areas with poor infrastructure, they are most at risk from natural disasters and usually far from health facilities.

Extreme poverty deprives people of almost all means of managing risk by themselves. With few or no assets, self-insurance is impossible. With poor health and bad nutrition, working more or sending more household members to work is difficult. And with high default risks, group insurance mechanisms are often closed off.

The poorest households thus face extremely unfavorable tradeoffs. When a shock occurs, they must obtain immediate increases in income or cut spending, but in so doing they incur a high long-term cost by jeopardizing their economic and human development prospects. These are the situations that lead to child labor and malnourishment, with lasting damage to children, and the breakdown of families.

In Côte d'Ivoire severe economic recession caused households, especially the poorest, to sharply increase the labor supply of children.[55] In rural India child labor was found to play a significant role in households' response to seasonal variations in household income.[56] In every part of the world participants in the *Voices of the Poor* study mentioned child labor as an undesirable coping mechanism. In Egypt children were sent to work in a storehouse packing vegetables. During periods of drought in Ethiopia children were taken out of school and sent to towns to be employed as servants, with their earnings sent back to their families. In the lean season in Bangladesh children work on farms, tend cattle, or carry out household tasks in exchange for food. Parents are often aggrieved by the undue physical labor of their children and worry especially about the vulnerability of girls to beatings and sexual assaults.[57]

Inadequate risk management can also compromise nutrition in poor households. After the devastating floods of 1988 in Bangladesh, many households took out loans to meet consumption needs, but landless households were less able to do so and their children suffered more severe malnutrition.[58] A study of rural Zimbabwe found that the 1994–95 drought caused a 1.5–2-centimeter decline in annual growth among children one to two years old. Although this study found the reduction to be permanent, other studies have found evidence of catch-up during subsequent good periods.[59]

What do households suffering these unfavorable long-term effects on the education and nutrition of their children have in common? Low asset endowments (physical, human, social) and little or no access to credit and insurance markets—a chronic trap for poor people, unable to accumulate enough assets to escape poverty. When households do not have some threshold of assets, they are

forced to engage in defensive actions to protect the assets they do have. One study estimated that poor households engaging in this strategy could have boosted their incomes by 18 percent with a more entrepreneurial management strategy (but one that requires access to credit).[60]

Dysfunctional factor markets can also create or aggravate poverty traps. Take child labor. When a crisis strikes and households cannot borrow or when adult unemployment is high or wages low, children are pulled out of school and sent to work. The lost schooling leads to a lifelong loss in earning ability for these children. Failures in the credit or labor markets thus transmit poverty and vulnerability across generations.[61]

Policy responses for improving risk management

Since poor people cannot fully manage risk on their own, any poverty reduction strategy needs to improve risk management for the poor—reducing and mitigating risk and coping with shocks. The strategy should include formal and informal mechanisms, provided by both the public and the private sector.

In principle and excluding cost considerations, the best approach is to reduce the risk of harmful shocks.[62] Next would be risk mitigation to reduce the possible impact of a shock. Coping would be a residual approach to address the failures of the first two.[63] In practice, different direct and opportunity costs may well change the ranking of options. Some risk reduction and mitigation strategies are prohibitively expensive, especially those for dealing with infrequent but catastrophic shocks.

Comparative cost data and cost-benefit analyses are generally not available to help policymakers choose from different types of risk management interventions. Furthermore, the distributional implications of different strategies need to be considered. A comparative study in India found that, at the margin, public work programs benefit the poorest quintile the most, while credit programs benefit the second and third poorest quintiles the most.[64]

Most developing countries pay too little attention to risk reduction and mitigation and rely too much on interventions after disaster strikes. Efforts to cope with the Mexican peso crisis of 1995 and the East Asian financial crisis of 1997 have shown how difficult it is to put effective safety nets in place after the fact (chapter 9).

The balance needs to shift from policies for coping to those for reducing and mitigating risk. That means ensuring that social safety nets such as workfare programs, targeted human development programs, and social funds are in place on a permanent basis and can be scaled up when a shock occurs (see table 8.3). Interventions following the 1998 floods in Bangladesh were effective because of the existing network of NGOs and other mechanisms ready to be activated to help poor people.[65] It also means providing better access to credit and financial assets, facilitating income diversification, managing labor market risk better (especially child labor), and providing health insurance. Such actions would allow poor people to pursue higher-risk, higher-return activities that could pull them out of poverty.[66] Social safety nets can also serve as an automatic compensatory mechanism for the unwanted distributional effects of policy reforms (chapter 4). By doing so, they will help make reform socially and politically feasible. While a new balance is needed, coping mechanisms will remain vital for dealing with unforeseen and infrequent shocks where it is prohibitively expensive to put mechanisms in place ahead of time.

Not every country needs to set up a comprehensive social safety net. But each does need to construct a modular system of programs based on its own patterns of risk and to cultivate a suitable mix of providers (public and private) and administrative arrangements (box 8.4). The first step in selecting and designing programs is to understand the general principles of how safety nets complement existing risk management arrangements. The next is to identify specific types of risk (illness, old age, unemployment) and the mechanisms for dealing with them.

General principles of safety nets and risk management

Reducing risk is possible for some categories of risk but not all. For example, building a dam can reduce the risk of flooding. Immunizations and other public health campaigns can reduce the risk of illness. Policies undertaken primarily for other purposes can also contribute to risk reduction. Good education policies, including scholarships for poor families, can reduce child labor. Environmental policies can limit deforestation, reducing damage from hurricanes and deaths from mudslides. Sound macroeconomic policies can reduce the risks of high inflation and unemployment.

But the focus in this chapter is primarily on mitigating risk (diversification and insurance) and on coping. Making a wider variety of crops and extension services

---

Box 8.4
Managing risk: the modular approach to social safety nets

Constructing a social safety net is far from an exact science, and the process will vary from country to country depending on the context, data availability, and political urgency. But the process should have certain analytic elements, including establishing the country context, constraints, and challenges; identifying sources of risk, vulnerable groups, and potential interventions; and identifying the optimal mix of programs. Malawi illustrates the mix of preferred programs that can result, depending on prevailing conditions.

Malawi is a low-income country, with more than half its population in severe poverty. The vast majority of the population depends on subsistence agriculture. There is little government revenue surplus to redistribute and limited administrative capacity to manage complex programs. There is no formal social safety net.

Identifying sources of risk and vulnerable groups
Vulnerable groups in Malawi were identified on the basis of a poverty analysis conducted in the early 1990s. Four groups were found to be most at risk: rural households with small landholdings, female-headed households, AIDS orphans and their relatives, and those who could not care for themselves. In addition, four major risks were identified: seasonal price increases and food shortages, periodic drought, large periodic macroeconomic shocks, and the threat of HIV/AIDS. Potential interventions to address these risks were developed.

Identifying the optimal mix of risk management interventions
A cost-effectiveness analysis of existing programs was conducted before potential new interventions were ranked by priority. The results, together with consideration of the vulnerable groups, the risks, and the need to focus on productivity-enhancing interventions, led to the following modular system of programs:
- Public work (risk mitigation and coping).
- Transfers for orphans in poor communities (risk mitigation and coping).
- Nationwide nutrition program (risk reduction and coping).
- Targeted cash transfers to the needy (coping).

Source: World Bank forthcoming b.

---

available to farmers can help rural residents to diversify. Opening trading opportunities through investments in infrastructure and other means can also stimulate diversification. But liberalizing markets (say, by privatizing state commodity boards) can have mixed effects and will not always benefit poor people. Sometimes dealers step in between farmers and export traders and capture most of the gains from open trade.

Policies should also make it easier for poor people to build up assets while reducing the covariance between asset values and income. Covariance is a big problem in rural areas, where asset values (livestock) often move in tandem with farm income. This could be addressed through better integration of asset markets with the wider economy—by investing in transport infrastructure, disseminating price information, and removing structural and institutional market barriers. Macroeconomic stability promotes more stable asset prices, reducing inflation-driven deterioration in the terms of trade of assets relative to consumption goods. And easier access to credit would facilitate the acquisition of costly indivisible assets, such as cattle.[67]

Another critical intervention is the provision of insurance, especially for covariant risk. Self-insurance has limits, mainly because poor people cannot accumulate enough assets, especially after successive shocks. And informal insurance, which relies on risk sharing across a community or network, is ineffective for covariant shocks.

The first question with insurance is whether market or government provision is more cost-effective than informal mechanisms. Can the state provide less costly insurance for risks that are self-insured by poor people or insured through group-based risk sharing? Because the public sector can pool risks over a larger area, the possibility exists for providing insurance at a lower cost than informal agents can (assuming that information problems can be dealt with; see below). Publicly provided insurance could thus yield a net gain to society—if the state is perceived as credible and the insurance scheme is fiscally sustainable.

But if trust in the state is low, few people will put their faith in the government system and give up their personal or group insurance. And even if credibility is not an issue, fiscal constraints may prevent the state from making payments during a crisis. People who had given up their informal insurance mechanisms would then be left worse off than before the state offered insurance. Relative cost-effectiveness, trust, and sustainability thus all need to be considered in deciding on government intervention.

Government spending on social safety nets varies considerably. Figure 8.2 illustrates this with one component: spending on social security by the central government. But costs are only part of the picture. These expenditures are also investments in human capital formation. By providing poor people access to basic services and allowing them to undertake higher-risk, higher-return activities, the investments can have positive effects on poverty and economic development. Costs are still likely to be an issue,

Figure 8.2

Central government spending on social security varied greatly in 1995

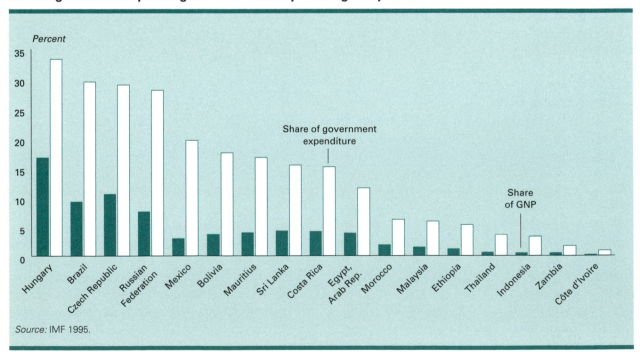

Source: IMF 1995.

but they can often be reduced by more explicitly considering the role of private providers.[68]

Concerns that formal safety nets will displace self-insurance or group-based mechanisms also need to be considered. Empirical estimates of this effect vary, so the country context is important. A study of the urban Philippines estimated that government-provided unemployment insurance would displace 91 percent of private transfers to the unemployed.[69] Another study estimated that providing a basic pension benefit to black South Africans displaced only 20–40 percent of private transfers to the elderly.[70] Studies of other countries also found displacement rates on the order of 20–40 percent.[71]

Displacements of private transfers need not imply a social loss. If poverty reduction objectives are considered along with insurance objectives, there may well be a net social gain, despite the displacements.[72] In South Africa many of the displaced transfers were from young to old households, both of them poor. The new pension program left more money in the pockets of poor young households and also covered many elderly residents who had not been receiving private transfers. Overall, then, the pension scheme significantly strengthened South Africa's social safety net.[73]

When should the state step in and provide a social safety net for poor people—and how? The general answer is that it depends on the types of shocks likely to occur and the kinds of private insurance arrangements in place.

■ If informal arrangements insure adequately against idiosyncratic risk, the state should step in to insure against covariant risk. In most circumstances providing this coverage will improve overall risk management and increase welfare, without crowding out informal insurance.[74] But since households' overall risk exposure will have declined, self-insurance (precautionary savings or other asset buildups) may decline.[75]

■ Where informal insurance is ineffective—because of enforcement problems or because shocks are too frequent or too large—household welfare could be increased if the social safety net insured against both idiosyncratic and covariant risks. Whether coverage should come from the state or private insurers depends largely on the type of risk. The state is often best able to cover covariant risks, but most idiosyncratic risks may be better handled by private providers (communities, insurance firms). The government's role should then be to facilitate and, if necessary, regulate private provision.[76]

■ Where group-based informal insurance works well, the state should avoid safety net programs targeted to individuals or households. Most safety nets target specific types of people or households: the ill, the elderly, the women heading households with many children, and the like. The danger is that improving the risk position of one person belonging to a group-based insurance scheme creates an incentive to drop out of the group. If this leads to the collapse of the group scheme, members not covered by the safety net could end up worse off. The solution is to target broad groups (say, a credit program for the entire community or specific groups within it), although doing so can be difficult because insurance groups do not always coincide with communities or other easily identifiable target groups. Of course, if the safety net protects almost everyone, the disappearance of informal insurance arrangements may not matter, at least if the formal safety net is more cost-effective and sustainable.[77]

In the end, decisions on safety nets need to weigh the negative effects of displacement against the positive effects of long-term improvements in the welfare of poor households. Safety nets are not the only way to improve poor households' ability to manage risk and to engage in higher-risk, higher-return activities. Stable macroeconomic policies may do more to reduce employment risk than public work programs. But sound economic policies may increase the risk for some categories of households. Trade liberalization may lower the cost of imported clothes and utensils, reducing demand for weaving and handicrafts—two activities with low entry costs frequently used by poor people to diversify income.[78] So the decision about providing safety nets needs to be viewed in the full context of economic and social policies and of the impacts on household risk.

Where there is a strong concern for the poor, especially the very poor, the formal-informal, public-private balance generally shifts in favor of public provision of insurance.[79] Concerns for sustainability and other incentives in group-based insurance and credit schemes generally work against inclusion of the poorest, who have a higher perceived risk of default.[80] Similar concerns tend to exclude poor people from market-based insurance. Thus public insurance provision is not likely to undercut any informal arrangements involving the poorest households.

Further strengthening the case for public intervention is the ineffectiveness of the insurance mechanisms used by poor people against repeated shocks—mechanisms that also tend to be costly.[81] A study of six South Indian villages found that farmers sacrifice as much as 25 percent of average income to reduce exposure to harvest risk.[82]

Several practical issues have to be considered in setting up state insurance programs. These include obtaining information about the people to be insured and dealing with the political economy issues in providing insurance.

Obtaining information about people to be insured is costly. That is why so many traditional credit and insurance institutions are local. Moneylenders or members of a rotating savings and credit association have a better chance of knowing who is a bad risk than would an outside insurance program.[83] Asymmetric information creates problems of moral hazard and adverse selection, leading to the underprovision of insurance (relative to the social optimum) by private providers.[84] Because information problems are especially acute for poor people, the social gains from government provision of insurance may be large.

Because the government has no comparative advantage in obtaining local information on who should be in-

sured, coproduction is frequently recommended: the government provides the financial and technical means, and local institutions or peer groups take care of implementation and monitoring. Or the government provides funds to communities, which are responsible for identifying poor beneficiaries (box 8.5).

The political economy may strengthen or weaken the case for publicly provided risk mitigation. The state may well be the best agent to provide insurance, but lack the necessary institutional strength, financial resources, or management capacity. Capacity building may then be required inside the government. The political support to allocate resources may also be lacking, since it requires getting the rich to support a program that does not benefit them. If the insurance program is not self-supporting, it may have to be funded out of general tax revenue, at the expense of other programs that benefit the rich. (Chapter 6 discusses the political economy of poverty reduction further.)

Box 8.5
Is targeting by the community a good idea?

In most social safety net programs the central government provides funds and sets the eligibility criteria, ostensibly guaranteeing equal treatment across the country. But local needs may vary across the country, and benefits may leak to ineligible households in varying degrees. In an effort to improve targeting, an increasing number of programs rely on communities to determine eligibility rules and identify beneficiaries. The success of this approach depends in part on the degree of social cohesion in the community and whether the community can be effectively mobilized in a consultative process to allocate benefits.

Targeting efficiency also depends on the entity charged with allocating benefits. In Uzbekistan quasi-religious community groups known as *mahallas* target child benefits and other types of social assistance to low-income families. They have considerable discretion over amounts and criteria for assistance. An external review concluded that benefits were targeted fairly well. In Armenia subsidies for

school textbooks are allocated locally by parent-teacher associations or the school principal. The program has not been formally evaluated, but informal appraisals suggest that the system has been well accepted by parents, and it may be expanded to other types of aid.

The Kecamatan Development Project in Indonesia provides block grants to 10,000 villages. Each community decides on the use of the funds through an extensive process of information dissemination, community facilitation, and proposal preparation and selection. Field assessments indicate that the process works best when both traditional and official community leaders are on board from the start (KDP Secretariat 1999).

In Albania the Economic Support Program helps poor rural households and people who lose their jobs in the transition. Local governments receive block grants to allocate within their communes. Local targeting compares favorably with that of safety net programs in other countries.

Advantages and disadvantages of allowing communities to allocate benefits

Advantages	Disadvantages
Better information is available on needy households	Program may be used to serve interests of the elite
Allocation criteria are adapted to local needs	Participation of community leaders may have opportunity cost
Decentralized administration is more efficient	
Community mobilization may build social capital	Allocation rules may cause increased divisiveness in the community
	Externalities across communities may not be taken into account

Source: Conning and Kevane 1999.

Box 8.6
Insurance options for the informal sector

The simple expansion of statutory coverage of formal sector social insurance programs (pensions, unemployment insurance, disability insurance) to small enterprises will not meet the risk management needs of the informal sector. Schemes need to accommodate the lower contributory capacity and greater earnings volatility of self-employed and informal workers.

Lines may need to be blurred between strict contributory self-financed insurance schemes and assistance paid out of general tax resources. Also called for are flexible partnerships between different providers: the state, private insurance companies, communities, NGOs, and organizations representing the informal sector workers.

Many contributory, and often self-managed, schemes for informal sector workers have emerged in recent years. They are either adapted from formal systems or based on cooperatives and mutual benefit societies. In some cases they complement indigenous risk management arrangements, such as burial and rotating savings and credit societies.

In the Indian state of Andhra Pradesh pension coverage has been given to about 425,000 home-based workers in the *beedi* (leaf-rolled cigarettes) industry, under the Employees' Provident Fund Act. A simple procedural mechanism—issuing identity cards—was crucial to success. In addition, a welfare fund for *beedi* workers was set up by the central government, funded through an earmarked tax collected from employers and manufacturers in the *beedi* industry. This delinks the collection of contributions and the delivery of welfare services from individual employee-employer relationships, removing a major bottleneck to including informal sector workers in contributory schemes.

Several Indian states recently tried a more experimental group insurance scheme. In Gujarat about 20,000 landless agricultural laborers received life and accident insurance coverage. Most group insurance schemes are not fully self-financed and require state government contributions.

In surveys informal sector workers regularly single out health insurance as their greatest insurance need. In China rural health insurance covers hospital and primary health care costs through private and public contributions. Premiums paid by beneficiaries are supplemented through a village public welfare fund and government subsidies.

In Tanzania a pilot project in Dar es Salaam provides health insurance through five mutual associations of informal sector workers. In Igunga, a town in the northwest, a community health fund covering primary health care services has achieved 50 percent participation. Since the scheme relies on matching funds, sustainability remains an issue.

Key to the success of contributory insurance schemes for the informal sector are their organization around an association based on trust and mutual support (professional group, village) and the administrative capacity to collect contributions and provide benefits. Administrative capacity can be fortified by an umbrella organization that joins local groups and provides them with technical support.

Source: van Ginneken 1999.

Public risk mitigation may also reduce profit opportunities for the rich (from money lending) or undercut patron-client relationships between rich and poor by making the poor more independent.[85] Allowing the rich (or at least the middle class) to participate in some insurance programs and showing that insurance is less costly than other poverty reduction efforts can boost political support for publicly funded insurance. Above all, as chapters 5 and 6 argue, public risk mitigation will succeed only if poor people have a channel for dialogue with government on issues of risk and vulnerability.

Special considerations stem from the large (and growing) informal sectors in many developing countries (box 8.6). Employment in the informal sector in 12 Latin American countries rose from 50 percent of the economically active population to 54 percent between 1990 and 1997.[86] A large "gray" economy has sprung up during the economic transition in Eastern Europe and the former Soviet Union. Unemployment insurance will not reach workers in the informal sector, but social assistance programs can. Community-based and integrated provision of insurance are two innovative approaches showing promise. Such programs recognize the strong links between labor market risks and other risks in the informal economy.[87] Packages that combine different types of insurance or assistance for the self-employed may be particularly attractive. In Chile many self-employed people participate in the pension system to get health insurance.[88]

Specific instruments and the lessons of experience

While the general principles discussed here are useful in framing choices for policymakers, it is their application to specific cases and the lessons of experience that really matter. Many tools are available for public interventions to improve the ability of households to manage risk. The rest of this chapter covers seven tools especially relevant for poor people: health insurance, old age assistance and pensions, unemployment insurance and assistance, workfare programs, social funds, microfinance programs, and cash transfers. Some of these instruments address primarily one type of risk—others are useful for a wide range of risks.

Health insurance. Several studies have shown that many households in developing countries cannot insure against major illness or disability. Significant economic costs are associated with these conditions, both in income losses and in medical expenses. The policy response should be to provide health insurance and to direct public health spending to facilities serving primarily poor people (or poor areas).[89]

Some middle-income countries have set up universal health insurance, as Costa Rica and the Republic of Korea did in the 1980s. But most low-income countries can offer only limited health insurance, usually providing minimum benefits for all illnesses ("first dollar coverage") rather than full insurance for infrequent but very costly illnesses.[90] This choice may look pro-poor (benefits are provided regardless of income and there is no deductible or copayment), but the evidence suggests that catastrophic illnesses and disabling injuries create much greater problems for poor people than frequent, minor illnesses. Households in Indonesia were able to smooth more than 70 percent of consumption fluctuations caused by moderate health shocks, but only 40 percent of those caused by large health shocks.[91] An average hospital stay in Indonesia costs 131 percent of the annual income of the poorest quintile of households, but only 24 percent of the income of the richest quintile.[92] In China households could smooth only 6 percent of consumption fluctuations caused by overall medical care costs, but 100 percent of fluctuations involving health care expenses of less than 50 yuan.[93]

Public provision of insurance against catastrophic health risks could thus significantly improve the welfare of poor people where households are unable to insure against these risks themselves. The evidence further suggests that premiums can be quite low (because major illness is rare) and well below households' willingness to pay.[94] Countries as diverse as Costa Rica and Singapore have implemented health insurance schemes with near universal coverage (box 8.7). Where administrative capacity or other constraints make catastrophic health insurance infeasible for poor people, subsidies for hospital care can be used instead. For this to be pro-poor, however, there must be equity in referrals and access to hospitals.[95] In both approaches the objective is to avoid a need for poor people to pay for medical emergencies through debt, distress sales of assets, or cuts in consumption.

Injuries and chronic illnesses that result in long-term disability affect an estimated 5–10 percent of people in developing countries.[96] Disability is associated with low education, poor nutrition, high unemployment and underemployment, and low occupational mobility—all factors that increase the likelihood of being poor. And being poor adds to the risk of becoming disabled. Much disability in developing countries is caused by injuries or by communicable, maternal, and prenatal diseases, some of them preventable. Medical prevention of disease becomes easier with rising incomes, of course.

In the long run policy efforts need to focus on prevention, especially on maternal and child health care. Programs to eradicate measles, to fight onchocerciasis (river blindness), and to reduce micronutrient deficiencies have already greatly reduced disabilities.[97] Preventive programs that keep simple diseases from becoming chronic disabilities are especially important for children.[98] War and civil conflict have also caused many disabilities. Land mine accidents have increased sharply over the past 15 years: a study of four war-affected countries found that 6 percent of households had a member who had been killed or permanently disabled by land mines.[99]

People with disabilities incur extra medical costs and are often excluded from services and community activities.[100] Most people with disabilities depend on their families for support and cannot increase their labor supply in response to income crises. One study found that 61–87 percent of land mine victims went into debt to pay their medical bills, and 12–60 percent had to sell assets.[101] Prevention and better health care hold the key to reducing disabilities in the future. Those who are already disabled need community-based rehabilitation programs and public transfers to the families that provide care.[102]

Old age assistance and pensions. The risks associated with old age have social as well as economic dimensions, and policies need to address both. To reduce the social isolation of many of the elderly, social policies should facilitate access to community groups or associations that cater to the elderly. Proximity to health facilities is also a major concern, since elderly people have difficulty reaching faraway clinics.

On the economic side, many elderly are poor because they have been poor all their lives.[103] Poverty reduction policies that increase people's income during their working lives will also make them better off during retirement. Well-functioning financial markets that facilitate saving and investment will help workers accumulate financial as-

Box 8.7
Two universal health insurance systems: Costa Rica and Singapore

Costa Rica and Singapore have vastly different income levels and administrative capacity, but each has succeeded in establishing universal health care coverage. They also have some common characteristics that are helpful in targeting fee waivers to poor people, such as almost universal literacy and a system of formal documentation of vital events (births, marriages) and transactions (employment contracts, utility bills).

Costa Rica

In Costa Rica the public sector designs and carries out health care policies. The role of the private sector in health care is very limited: barely 2 percent of hospital beds in the country are in private facilities. The Costa Rican Social Security Fund was created in 1943, and coverage for health services was extended to the entire population in 1971. About 85 percent of the population actually participates. Funding comes through payroll deductions and voluntary, income-based contributions of the self-employed. Public spending on health care has remained high, ranging from 4.7 to 6.8 percent of GDP during 1975–93. Universal health insurance went hand in hand with health care strategies aimed at preventing disease, addressing specific risk factors, and extending service coverage to rural and urban areas. Health indicators responded. Between 1975 and 1990 infant mortality declined from 37.9 to 15.3 per 1,000 live births, and medically assisted births rose from 82.5 percent to 95.2 percent.

The 15 percent of the population not covered by the national health insurance program is concentrated at the lowest end of the income distribution. A free health insurance program covers more than three-fourths of this group. Eligibility is verified through systematic evaluations by social workers, based on documentation provided by applicants on household composition, earnings, and housing conditions. The administrative reviews of applicants are methodical and effective: 55 percent of program benefits go to the poorest quintile.

Equity concerns are further addressed in the primary health care reform started in 1995. The country has 800 health zones, each served by a comprehensive health care team that ensures universal access to primary care and suitable referral to higher-level facili-

ties. Each health care team is supported by a health committee set up by the community.

Still, all is not well in Costa Rican health care. Waiting times are long, and there have been complaints of improper treatment of users. As a result, many people entitled to public services go to private providers for low-cost procedures. And because eligibility is not linked to a specific number of premiums, some people pay premiums only when they need costly treatment. This violates the solidarity principle of an insurance system. Costa Rica has introduced reforms to deal with these problems.

Singapore

Between 1984 and 1993 Singapore set up a three-tiered system of health insurance: Medisave, Medishield, and Medifund. The program insures against intermediate-level health risks through individual or household Medisave accounts. These mandatory savings accounts, part of Singapore's compulsory social security system, are funded by a 40 percent payroll tax (shared equally by employers and employees). Of this contribution, 6–8 percent is allocated to Medisave accounts, which can be used to pay hospitalization expenses of up to about $170 a day. Individuals are expected to cover minor health costs out of pocket or through private insurance.

Catastrophic health risks are covered through Medishield, optional backup insurance for expenses exceeding the maximum coverage provided by Medisave. Eighty-eight percent of Medisave account holders have opted for Medishield coverage. The coinsurance rate is 20 percent, and the deductible amount varies with the comfort class of the medical facility.

Equity backup is provided through subsidies from Medifund, to remedy the nonprogressive nature of Medisave accounts and Medishield. A catastrophic health shock would cost 55 percent of annual per capita expenditures for the poorest quintile of households, and just 21 percent for the richest quintile. The Medifund subsidies are differentiated by class of facility and thus are self-targeted to poorer users. As a last resort, patients who are unable to pay all their medical bills can apply for a means-tested grant from their hospital Medifund committee, financed from the government's budget surplus.

Source: Grosh 1994; Prescott and Pradhan 1999; Sauma 1997.

sets over their lifetime. This is especially important for informal sector workers and the self-employed, who rarely participate in pension plans. Higher incomes and better risk management for today's prime-age workers will also help them support their parents financially.

Formal pension systems are limited in most developing countries, covering only 16 percent of the labor force in the developing world.[104] In the poorest countries in South Asia and Sub-Saharan Africa pensions cover less than 10 percent of the labor force.[105] Coverage can be increased through suitable reform, but this takes time: coverage rates above 50

percent of the labor force are usually seen only in countries with annual per capita income exceeding $5,000.[106]

The general recommendation for pension reform is to establish a multipillar system: combining a publicly managed defined-benefit plan with a privately managed defined-contribution plan, supplemented by voluntary retirement savings. The publicly managed plan, funded from general tax revenues, can address poverty and equity concerns. The privately managed plan, fully funded by participant contributions, serves as wage replacement after retirement.[107] Several countries, mainly in Latin

America and Eastern Europe, have multipillar pension systems. But successful management of such systems requires considerable administrative capacity.

Even a well-structured pension system will not initially reach the poor. Coverage in formal pension systems tends to be much greater for high-income workers: in Chile more than 40 percent of workers in the poorest income decile do not participate in the pension system, compared with fewer than 20 percent of workers in the richest decile.[108] In general, coverage is lowest among the poor, the uneducated, the self-employed, and women who have worked in the household rather than in the labor market for most of their lives.

Contributing to this lower coverage are market and institutional failures and incentives that discourage individuals from seeking coverage. The profile of risks that poor households face may mean that illness or harvest failure are of much more concern to them than old age income security. In a credit-constrained environment mandatory contributions to a pension system may be difficult for poor or self-employed households to meet. If in addition the public pension system lacks credibility, many households will continue to rely for old age income security on traditional informal arrangements, often based in the household, extended family, or tribe.[109]

Addressing the needs of the elderly poor thus requires more than pensions. Preventive measures include facilitating saving and investment and providing poverty reduction programs during people's working lives. Different forms of direct and indirect support are needed for today's elderly. Programs can provide assistance to families that care for live-in elderly.[110] Retraining and workfare programs adapted to older workers can make it easier for them to continue working.[111] And social assistance or social pensions should cover the poorest and the very old (categories that frequently overlap) and those without family support (box 8.8). Widows will often make up a large part of this group.[112]

Unemployment insurance and assistance. Labor market risk can be reduced significantly by improving the functioning of labor markets and by adopting sound macroeconomic policies. Many labor markets in developing countries are segmented (effectively barring entry to some groups) and excessively regulated. Reform of labor laws and regulations needs to balance greater efficiency in the labor market with promotion and enforcement of core labor standards to protect vulnerable workers (chapter 4). Eliminating the most exploitative forms of child labor

---

Box 8.8
Social pensions in Chile and Namibia

Countries as different as Chile and Namibia have established social pension schemes to cover the most vulnerable elderly. Chile has a multipillar pension system, with pensions that depend on years of employment and contributions. Gender differences in earnings and in years in the labor market lead to wide differences in pension payments. Take a woman with an incomplete primary education and with average tenure in the labor market who retires at her statutory retirement age of 60: she would receive only 29 percent of the pension of an equally qualified man who retires at his statutory retirement age of 65.

In addition to this formal pension system, the government finances a social assistance pension intended for poor women and men over 65 not covered by the formal system. Because the program is means tested rather than employment based, benefit amounts are not differentiated by gender. Since elderly women are generally poorer than elderly men, the program benefits women proportionately more than men, especially in rural areas.

Namibia administers a social pension program for individuals over age 60. Unlike Chile's program, Namibia's is universal, not means tested. In practice, 88 percent of eligible pensioners receive the pension. The social pension contributes significantly to poverty reduction. It is the main source of income for 14 percent of rural households and 7 percent of urban households.

The social pension program also indirectly helps children, because many elderly people in Namibia look after grandchildren and pay their school fees when the parents are away working or looking for work or because the children are AIDS orphans or disabled.

Source: Cox Edwards 2000; Subbarao 1998; World Bank forthcoming a.

---

should be a primary objective.[113] In the informal sector, where laws and regulations are seldom applied, public action can complement customary informal arrangements to improve the environment in which workers operate.

Reform and enforcement need to be combined with programs of skill enhancement, job search assistance, and microenterprise development. Since experience with government-run training programs is mixed, partnerships with the private sector need to be explored.[114] Labor markets can also be made more effective by improving relationships among labor market partners (employers organizations, trade unions, and government) and by strengthening collective bargaining and contracting.[115]

Even a well-functioning labor market will not fully eliminate the risk of unemployment or underemployment, however. Displaced workers will need unemployment benefits to protect them from large income losses and poverty. In some countries the link between unemployment and poverty is very strong. A study of poverty in countries of Eastern Europe and the former Soviet Union found a 40–80 percent higher incidence of poverty among households that had one unemployed member than among households that had no unemployed member. Households with several unemployed members had poverty rates twice the national average or more in some countries.[116] Typical unemployment programs in the region include retraining, wage subsidies, job counseling and referral services, public work and community employment, and small business creation programs.[117]

Unemployment insurance, the traditional means of mitigating the risk of job loss, is not appropriate for most developing countries because of their low administrative capacity and large informal sectors. The irregular and unpredictable earnings typical of the informal sector make it hard for workers to participate in a contributory insurance program.[118] Many of the market and institutional failures discussed under pension systems apply also to unemployment insurance. Better options for assisting the unemployed are means-tested social assistance and public work programs (workfare).[119] Means testing has proved difficult in most settings, but promising approaches that use easily observable indicators for targeting are being pilot tested.[120]

Workfare programs. Public work programs are a useful countercyclical instrument for reaching poor unemployed workers. They can easily be self-targeting by paying wages below market rates. A well-designed and well-funded workfare program is a mix of risk mitigation and coping. To mitigate risk, the program must inspire confidence that it will continue to be available after a crisis. Only if the government is perceived as credible will such programs induce households to give up costly self-insurance or group insurance, freeing resources for other productive purposes.[121] The program functions as a coping mechanism by providing jobs when a crisis strikes. Providing households with income following a crisis helps them avoid costly and damaging strategies (selling assets, reducing food intake). Some workfare programs—such as Trabajar in Argentina, the Temporary Employment Program in Mexico,[122] and the Maharashtra Employment Guarantee Scheme in India—have succeeded in creating employment for poor people (box 8.9). Other programs not originally designed as workfare programs may actually perform very similar functions. This is the case for Mexico's self-targeted Probecat, which provides training to the urban unemployed.[123]

Workfare programs are not necessarily an inexpensive way of delivering benefits to poor people. Their cost-effectiveness needs to be compared with that of alternative transfer programs. The cost per person-day of employment created varies greatly across countries, ranging from as low as $1–2 in several South Asian programs to $8 in Bolivia. The cost depends on the wage rate, type of projects undertaken, costs of local private contractors, and administrative effectiveness. Wages typically represent 30–60 percent of total costs.[124]

Social funds. Social funds help finance small projects identified and implemented by poor communities, which usually provide cofinancing. Almost 50 countries, most in Latin America and Sub-Saharan Africa, operate social funds or similar entities. The world's largest is in Egypt. Recently, Eastern European and Central Asian countries have begun to set up social funds, with 10 already in operation or under preparation.

The first social fund was set up by the Bolivian government in 1987 as an emergency response to a general economic downturn. Generally, however, social funds are not coping instruments. Instead, they address a wide range of objectives, including infrastructure, community development, social services, and support for decentralization.[125] But some have been used to respond to emergencies—Hurricane Mitch in Central America (chapter 9), civil war in Cambodia, an earthquake in Armenia, drought in Zambia. Social funds have also gradually assumed a greater role in risk mitigation—supporting income generation projects, stimulating school enrollment and health center use, and strengthening the social capital of communities. They have proved to be flexible, quick to respond, and cost-effective. But the record is mixed when it comes to sustainability and poverty reduction.[126]

Social funds use three targeting devices to reach poor people: investment selection (mainly basic services), project screening (to ensure that most beneficiaries are poor), and geographical targeting (of poor areas). The poverty targeting strategy and the demand-driven approach of social funds are sometimes in conflict. To enhance their effectiveness, many funds initially financed projects in better-off communities with good organizational skills. The poorest communities, which often have difficulties putting investment proposals together, received fewer benefits.

To address this problem, some social funds (Argentina, Chile, Mali, Romania) have supported capacity building in poor communities. Others have temporarily assumed some implementation responsi-

Box 8.9
Principles of successful workfare programs

In many programs for the poor a large share of benefits go to the nonpoor. This problem has stimulated interest in self-targeting schemes, such as public work programs (workfare), which have been especially effective. Two successful workfare programs are the Maharashtra Employment Guarantee Scheme in India and Trabajar in Argentina.

Launched during the severe drought of 1970–73, the Maharashtra scheme expanded rapidly to reach some 500,000 workers monthly. In a typical year the scheme provides 100 million person-days of employment. Argentina set up Trabajar II in the mid-1990s (as an expanded and reformed version of an earlier program) to cope with sharply rising unemployment, which reached 18 percent in 1996–97 and was concentrated among poor people.

Project selection
Both programs concentrate on infrastructure projects (roads, irrigation schemes, embankments). Local authorities, in collaboration with communities and NGOs, propose projects, which must use labor-intensive technologies, benefit the local community, and target poor areas.

Wage rate and self-targeting
To ensure that most participants are poor and to maintain incentives for workers to move on to regular work when it becomes available, programs should pay no more than the average wage for unskilled labor. Trabajar set the wage rate at about 75 percent of average monthly earnings from the main job of the poorest 10 percent of households in Greater Buenos Aires. The Maharashtra scheme uses the average wage rate of rural unskilled labor. Both programs have been highly successful in reaching the poorest of the poor. About 9 of 10 Maharashtra scheme participants were living below the local poverty line; 4 of 5 Trabajar participants were poor by Argentine standards. For the poorest 5 percent of participants, program benefits were 74 percent of their pre-program income.

Benefits to the poor
Since poor people can rarely afford to be totally idle, they often give up some form of income to join a workfare scheme. Estimates suggest that forgone income could represent as much as 50 percent of the wages paid by workfare schemes. But because the employment is guaranteed, it provides major insurance benefits to poor people. Incomes in villages where the Maharashtra scheme operates have just half the variability of incomes in villages without the scheme. Poor people also derive indirect gains from a workfare program if the infrastructure created by the program benefits them. Experience is mixed. In some cases better-off households have appropriated the assets created (not an unqualified liability, since it may increase the political acceptance of the scheme by the rich, apparently the case in Maharashtra).

Principles of success
Workfare programs can improve their effectiveness by adhering to several principles.
- The wage rate should be determined by the local market wage for unskilled labor, not by the program's budget. If resources are insufficient to meet demand, the program should target areas with a high concentration of poor people. Using additional eligibility criteria should be avoided.
- Wage schedules should be gender neutral. Women can be encouraged to participate through suitable project selection, decentralized work sites, and the provision of child care.
- Labor intensity should be higher than the local norm for similar projects.
- Communities should be involved in project selection to maximize the capture by the poor of indirect benefits of the infrastructure created.
- To get the most risk mitigation, the program should be available at all times, expanding automatically during crises as demand increases.

Source: Jalan and Ravallion 1999c; Lipton 1998; Ravallion 1991, 1999a.

bilities while communities increased their capacity (box 8.10). Several funds are improving their poverty targeting. In Malawi and Zambia social funds are introducing poverty mapping to identify pockets of poverty.[127] Beneficiary assessments have identified community orientation (responsiveness to community priorities, helpfulness in promoting social cohesion) as one of the strengths of social funds.[128]

Microfinance (credit, savings, and insurance). Microfinance programs can help poor households smooth consumption during an adverse shock. Access to credit may help them avoid distress sales of assets and replace productive assets destroyed in a natural disaster. But microfinance programs do more than help households cope with shocks—they can also provide capital to create or expand microenterprises. Microfinance thus helps households diversify their sources of income and reduces their vulnerability to income shocks. Microfinance programs have been especially important for women and households headed by women, who often have difficulty getting credit. However, microfinance institutions, depending on their size and diversification, are unlikely to be effective against large covariant shocks (chapter 4).

Microfinance programs have been more successful in reaching moderately poor and vulnerable (not necessarily poor) households than extremely poor households. Most programs reach clients just above or just below the poverty line. Efforts to direct microcredit programs explicitly to poor households often fail, although there is evidence that some programs successfully use geographic targeting to reach poor people.[129] Having appropriate local groups identify beneficiaries or targeting beneficiaries by size of landholdings (as in the 0.5-acre limit used by Grameen Bank) has proved more successful.[130]

Empirical studies find that clients often use loans to reduce risk rather than to cope with shocks, meaning that loans are not usually "diverted" to consumption. Poor and nonpoor clients alike use loans to smooth consumption by smoothing income flows, mainly by increasing diversification. Loans help households accumulate a variety of assets: physical and productive (vehicles, equipment, housing, livestock), financial (savings accounts), human (education, health care), and social (contributions to funerals and weddings or to networks of mutual support).[131]

As a risk management tool, the key strength of microfinance programs is the knowledge that loans will be available in time of need, making it possible for households to dispense with less effective and less desirable strategies (child labor, money under the mattress). There is a parallel here with employment guarantee schemes: the confidence in future availability is the key to the success of microfinance programs as a risk management tool.

The availability of microfinance services enables poor households to move from reactive to proactive approaches: they can plan to mitigate risk. Most clients, well aware of this benefit, go to great lengths to repay their loans so that they do not lose access to future loans. Clients continued to repay loans even during and after the floods in Bangladesh.[132] Evidence suggests that microcredit has especially improved the lives of poor women, by strengthening their bargaining position with their husbands, boosting their self-confidence, and increasing their participation in public life.[133]

The success of microfinance in reducing vulnerability through income diversification and asset accumulation suggests that these programs should be a priority for government and donor support.[134] But expanding the client base to poorer households remains a challenge. To some degree, microfinance products could be redesigned to reach poorer households. Loan size and repayments could be made more flexible to better match the income flows and repayment capacity of borrowers.[135] There probably is a practical limit to this accommodation, since at some point the increasing costs of making such loans will undermine the sustainability of microfinance institutions. The very poorest may well be more effectively helped with targeted cash transfers.

Program effectiveness would be increased by combining microcredit with savings and insurance products so that clients would not have to take out loans to cope with illness or death (box 8.11). Bank Rakyat Indonesia and SafeSave in Bangladesh demonstrate the potential of combining

---

Box 8.10
The Eritrean Community Development Fund

After the war of independence, the government of Eritrea promised to provide each province with basic economic and social infrastructure. But many poor communities lacked the capacity to implement the projects themselves. Eritrea's innovative solution was to combine social fund and public work mechanisms in the Eritrean Community Development Fund. The fund combines the bottom-up selection of projects with the top-down selection of intervention areas. Contracting procedures are kept flexible to reach even communities without implementation capacity. If a community cannot form a project committee to supervise a project, the fund takes over procurement, contracting, and technical supervision. If necessary, the fund even manages the community's contribution. This flexible approach is combined with an ambitious capacity-building program, which trains community and local government staff in project design, maintenance, and operation.

Source: Frigenti, Harth, and Huque 1998.

Box 8.11
The Self-Employed Women's Association of India

Established in 1972, the Self-Employed Women's Association (SEWA) is a registered trade union for women in India's informal sector. SEWA's 220,000 members are hawkers, vendors, home-based workers, and laborers. In addition to its conventional labor union functions (ensuring minimum wages and work security), SEWA provides legal aid and operates a bank and a social security scheme. The bank offers savings accounts and loans to members. The social security scheme, which insures about 14 percent of SEWA members, covers health, life, and asset insurance. Slightly more than half the cost of the insurance program is covered by premiums. The rest is financed by SEWA and a public subsidy. SEWA views this arrangement as a first step toward increased contributions by members and self-sustainability. The combination of banking, insurance, and union services has helped increase SEWA's membership and raise the incomes of its members. SEWA now plans to expand health benefits and add a pension component.

Source: Lund and Srinivas 1999b; Mirai Chatterjee, general secretary, SEWA, email communication, 3 May 2000.

microcredit with savings. Other microfinance programs have successfully introduced life insurance, at low rates and with limited benefits (burial costs and repayment of debts).[136]

Cash transfers. Cash transfers (excluding transfers through such contributory systems as regular pensions and unemployment insurance) include social assistance payments for the elderly, child allowances, targeted human development programs, and fee waivers for basic services. In countries with large informal sectors, where formal unemployment insurance is not feasible, means-tested social assistance is an important way of assisting the unemployed and underemployed.

The role of cash transfers in a social risk management strategy depends on a country's income. In high-income countries cash transfers are part of social insurance, offering a broad guarantee of minimum income. In transition economies family assistance payments represented 0.4–5.1 percent of GDP in 1992–93. Cash social assistance programs operate in only a few Asian countries, where they account for less than 1 percent of GDP, and are negligible in Africa and Latin America.

Cross-country experience suggests that family assistance and targeted social assistance are effective for reducing poverty in the short term, especially in countries with relatively little poverty. The difficulty is finding an appropriate targeting mechanism compatible with the country's administrative capacity. Decentralized solutions may be preferable if communities have better information on who is needy (see box 8.5).[137]

Targeted human development programs for poor households with children transfer income in cash or in kind on the basis of such observable criteria as children's age, attendance in school, or participation in a health care program. They thus serve the dual objectives of poverty reduction and human development. When effective, they prevent the long-term damage to children that occurs when households, unable to adequately manage risk, respond to shocks by underfeeding their children or pulling them out of school to work.

In the Bangladesh Food-for-Education program the transfer to a household of 100 kilograms of rice increased the probability of boys' schooling by 17 percent and girls' schooling by 160 percent.[138] The Brazilian Bolsa Escola program targets scholarships to regions and communities where child labor is greatest, seeking to keep children in school by compensating parents for the income children would have earned. The Mexican scheme Progresa provides health and education benefits for 2.6 million households in 2000. Evaluation results suggest that the program is able to target benefits to the poorest households and that it has raised the enrollments of children in beneficiary households (see box 5.5 in chapter 5).[139]

Fee waivers can be effective in counteracting falling school enrollment in the aftermath of a crisis or shock. Following the crisis in Indonesia, primary school enrollment of boys in the poorer areas of Jakarta fell 8.3 percent and junior secondary enrollment fell countrywide, with the greatest drops in poorer areas. In 1998 the Indonesian government abolished entrance fees for public schools and lowered monthly fees and exam fees at the primary level, providing relief for many parents who had fallen behind on fee payments as a result of the crisis. An individual scholarship program and block grants to schools, both targeted to poorer areas, supplemented the fee waivers to restore school enrollment rates.[140]

• • •

Poor people are exposed to a wide array of risks that make them vulnerable to income shocks and losses of well-being. This chapter argues that helping poor people manage risk is thus an essential part of poverty reduction programs—and should complement efforts to increase average income and improve the distribution of income, which are discussed elsewhere in this report. The focus has been on risks occurring primarily at the individual, household, and community (micro and meso) levels, such as illness and injury, crime and domestic violence, old age, harvest failure, and fluctuations in food prices and demand for labor. (Chapter 9 discusses macro-level risks such as macroeconomic crises and natural disasters.)

Poor people respond to their risk exposure through diversification of assets and sources of income and various types of self-insurance (buffer stocks, savings) and informal insurance (networks of mutual support)—all means to reduce the risk or soften its impact. Where these preemptive mechanisms prove inadequate, households cope with shock by increasing or diversifying labor supply (child labor, migration), selling assets, or reducing consumption.

These mechanisms work, but not well enough. Volatility in household income remains high in many areas, and many households suffer episodic declines in well-being. Some recover, but not all do. Shocks common to a large area, which can wipe out an entire network's resources, are most likely to overwhelm the risk management tools of poor households. And because shocks do not affect all members of poor households equally, with women and children frequently the most at risk, inadequate risk management can cause long-term harm to children through malnourishment, child labor, and loss of schooling.

In most developing countries today, risk management emphasizes interventions after a disaster strikes. The balance needs to shift to favor policies to reduce and mitigate risk. Health, environmental, labor market, and macroeconomic policies can all reduce risk. And safety nets put in place before adverse shocks hit can serve both risk mitigation and coping purposes.

To counter the incentive and information problems that exclude poor people from many market-based insurance mechanisms, the state has a special role in providing or regulating insurance and setting up safety nets. This report advocates a modular approach that adapts the safety net to the specific pattern of risk in each country or area and complements existing risk management arrangements. Many solutions will involve partnerships among poor communities, the private sector, and the state.

CHAPTER 9

Managing Economic Crises and Natural Disasters

There is nowhere to work. We get sick and we don't have the money to get cured, we don't have medicines because they are expensive. The government makes everything expensive. . . . We don't have money to buy fertilizers, seeds, everything is in dollars. We don't have anything to eat. Everything is so expensive.

> —From a discussion group of adult women at the time of a banking crisis, Juncal, Ecuador

[Security is] . . . the ability of persons to cope with disasters.

> —From a discussion group, Little Bay, Jamaica

Economic crises and natural disasters can bring deep and sudden collapses in national output—and sharp increases in income poverty. Together with violent conflicts (see box 3.2 in chapter 3), they are great sources of vulnerability and insecurity. Worse, because of the collateral damage they cause, such as irreversible loss of human capital, they affect not only the current living standards of poor people but their ability to escape from poverty as well.

Malnutrition and dropout rates among poor chil-

dren may rise during economic crises and natural disasters. Poor households are often forced to sell their meager assets at depressed prices. These responses perpetuate chronic poverty, possibly reducing future economic growth because of the irreversible losses in human and physical capital. That is why preventing economic crises and natural disasters is so crucial. And that is why, when they occur, among the top priorities should be to protect poor people. Required for that protection are not only resources but also the instruments (safety net programs) to channel those resources to poor households. While developing countries and transition economies in general are vulnerable to crises and natural disasters, small states are especially vulnerable to adverse external events because of their remoteness and isolation, high degree of openness, susceptibility to natural disasters, and limited diversification.[1]

Preventing and coping with economic crises

Even our limited access to schools and health is now beginning to disappear. We fear for our children's

future. . . . What is the justice in sending our children to the garbage site every day to support the family?
    —*Mother and father commenting on need to pull their children from school in the wake of economic crisis, Thailand*

Economywide crises entail sharply falling output, declining incomes, and rising unemployment. Pervasive in the 1990s, they came in different forms: fiscal crises, balance of payments crises, terms of trade shocks, currency crises, banking crises, hyperinflation. The economic crises in Mexico in 1995, in East Asia in 1997, and in Brazil and Russia in 1998 received wide media coverage. But they were not the only episodes of economic distress.[2] Most crises have been brought on by varying combinations of policy mismanagement and such external factors as terms of trade shocks, volatile capital flows, and contagion in international capital markets.

Economic crises hurt both the poor and the nonpoor, but they are far more devastating for those already in poverty or nearly poor, even if they are not hurt disproportionately. The welfare losses are larger for poor households and those who fall into poverty than for the rest of the population. Poor people are unlikely to have enough savings or self-insurance to see them through bad times, and they have little or no access to insurance schemes, whether social or market based (chapter 8).

An economic crisis affects the living standards of poor people and those living close to poverty through different channels:

- Typically, real wages fall and unemployment rises, driving down labor earnings.
- Nonlabor incomes fall as economic activity slows, and the prices of the goods and services produced by poor people may fall relative to other prices.
- Private transfers, particularly from family members, are likely to shrink as living standards fall across the nation.
- The meager assets of poor people are exposed to inflation or a collapse in prices.
- Macroeconomic crises slow the accumulation of human, financial, and physical capital, weakening the ability of poor people to escape poverty.

Is the observed fall in incomes during crises made worse by the policies to respond to the crises? The debate on this is long-standing. That rising poverty coincides with the policy responses does not mean that the policies caused the rise. Crises can occur because of past unsustainable macroeconomic policies or inability to adjust to

external shocks (terms of trade shocks, higher international interest rates, sudden movements in capital flows as a result of contagion). In such circumstances restrictive fiscal and monetary policies are inevitable and less costly than the alternative of delaying such measures, which could lead to a larger crash.

Once adjustment policies are accepted as inevitable, the way governments introduce fiscal austerity can worsen the adverse effects on the living standards of the poor and near-poor. For example, removing food or fuel subsidies would exacerbate the effects on poor people—unless compensatory measures are taken (chapter 4). So would increasing the rates and sometimes the coverage of indirect taxes on food and other products that figure large in the consumption basket of poor people. Net government transfers may decline as governments cut social assistance as part of a fiscal austerity program. Reducing the quantity and quality of public services used by the poor and near-poor would also worsen their situation.

But government actions can also mitigate the impact of crises on poor people. The task of the policymaker is to implement the combination of macroeconomic measures that results in the lowest cost in forgone output and affords the greatest protection to the living standards of poor people. A key element of a poverty-sensitive response is the right composition of revenue-raising measures and fiscal cuts. A poverty-sensitive response should also allow for the expansion of safety nets targeted to poor people (the "social insurance" component of social spending) during periods of macroeconomic adjustment.

Social impact of crises

There is a strong link between macroeconomic downturns and rising income poverty (table 9.1; see also figure 2.1).[3] During crises many people become temporarily poor, and social indicators tend to worsen or to improve more slowly. Data suggest that the human capital of poor people, particularly poor children, can deteriorate. The damage can be irreversible, affecting the ability of these children to escape poverty when they reach adulthood.

In most countries in East Asia poverty rose as a result of the financial crises of the late 1990s: it is estimated that it rose almost 50 percent in Indonesia and that urban poverty doubled in the Republic of Korea.[4] In both

Table 9.1
Effect of economic crises on incidence of poverty in selected countries
Percent

Country and type of crisis	Before crisis	Year of crisis	After crisis
Argentina, hyperinflation and currency	25.2	47.3	33.7
	(1987)	(1989)	(1990)
Argentina, contagion	16.8	24.8	26.0
	(1993)	(1995)	(1997)
Indonesia, contagion and financial	11.3	18.9	11.7
	(1996)	(1998)	(1999)
Jordan, currency and terms of trade	3.0	..	14.9
	(1986–87)	(1989)	(1992)
Mexico, currency and financial	36.0	..	43.0
	(1994)	(1995)	(1996)
Russian Federation, financial	21.9	32.7	..
	(1996)	(1998)	
Thailand, currency and financial	11.4	12.9 [a]	..
	(1996)	(1998)	

.. Not available.
Note: Based on national poverty lines and per capita household income except for Indonesia (per capita expenditure), Mexico (household income), and Russia (household expenditure per equivalent adult). Data for Argentina refer to Greater Buenos Aires. For Indonesia poverty estimates before and during the crisis are based on the full SUSENAS (the national socioeconomic survey) conducted in February 1996 and 1999; estimates after the crisis are based on a smaller sample. Figures are not comparable across countries because poverty lines differ.
a. Based on the socioeconomic survey conducted between February 1998 and January 1999, which does not fully reflect the impact of the crisis. Estimates from a smaller survey conducted during June–September 1999 put the poverty incidence at 15.9 percent.
Source: Ministerio de Economía de Argentina 1998; World Bank 1994c, 1999dd; ECLAC 1999b; Lokshin and Ravallion 2000b.

countries, however, poverty fell as the economies recovered. In Russia the incidence of poverty rose from 21.9 percent to 32.7 percent between 1996 and 1998. In every crisis in Latin America and the Caribbean the incidence of poverty increased and several years later remained higher than it had been before the crisis.

Inequality may rise, fall, or remain unchanged during a crisis. In Latin America inequality (as measured by the Gini coefficient) rose in 15 of 20 crisis episodes for which there are data. In East Asia during the recent crisis, however, inequality remained practically unchanged, and in Mexico following the peso crisis in 1995 it fell. When crises are accompanied by increases in inequality, economic contractions can more than reverse previous gains in poverty reduction. In Latin America the poverty reduction from a 3.7 percent increase in per capita income for urban areas and a 2 percent increase for rural areas in the 1970s was reversed by just a 1 percent decline in per capita income in the 1980s.[5] Even if inequality increases, the poorest fifth of the population is not always hurt disproportionately. In Latin America the income share of the middle fifths of the population often fell most during the 1980s debt crisis, but the share of the top tenth always rose, sometimes substantially.[6]

The impact of economic crises on living standards is not fully captured by measures of inequality and income poverty. Economic crises are characterized by extensive mobility: previously nonpoor people may fall into poverty, and previously poor people may escape it. Evidence of sharp downward and upward mobility was found after the 1998 crisis in Russia, for example.[7] Mean expenditures of people classified as poor in 1996 actually rose, and 42 percent of them escaped poverty after the crisis. By contrast, 61 percent of those who were poor after the crisis had not been poor in 1996. Put another way, 20 percent of the population fell into poverty as a result of the economic downturn. Even though overall inequality fell and a large share of the poor escaped poverty after the crisis, there was substantial downward mobility for many who were not previously poor and for some who were already poor. Those who become poor during economic crises often have different characteristics than the chronically poor. For example, they may be better educated. A study in the Philippines found that households with more education are more vulnerable to wage and employment shocks.[8]

Table 9.2
Social impacts of economic crises in selected countries

	Main crisis indicators	Health indicators	Education indicators
Argentina 1995	■ Per capita GDP fell 4.1%. ■ Per capita private consumption fell 5.6%.	■ Per capita daily protein intake fell 3.8% in 1995, but increased 1.9% in 1996.	■ Growth in gross primary enrollment declined from 2.2% in 1993 to 0.8% in 1996.
Mexico 1995	■ Per capita GDP fell 7.8%. ■ Per capita private consumption fell 11.1%.	■ Among children under age 1, mortality from anemia increased from 6.3 deaths per 100,000 live births in 1993 to 7.9 in 1995. ■ Among children ages 1–4, the mortality rate from anemia rose from 1.7 to 2.2 per 100,000.	■ Gross primary enrollment increased 0.44% in 1994, but fell 0.09% in 1995.
Indonesia 1998	■ Per capita GDP fell 14.6%. ■ Per capita private consumption fell 5.1%.	■ The share of women whose body mass index is below the level at which risks of illness and death increase rose 25%. ■ Most indicators of child nutritional status remained stable. The exception may be the weight (conditional on height) of children under age 3, suggesting that families may be investing in some members at the expense of others.	■ The dropout rate for children in the poorest fourth of the population rose from 1.3% in 1997 to 7.5% in 1998 for those ages 7–12 and from 14.2% to 25.5% for those ages 13–19. In both cohorts the poorest fifth experienced the largest increase. ■ The share of children in the poorest fourth of the population not enrolled in school rose from 4.9% in 1997 to 10.7% in 1998 for those ages 7–12 and from 42.5% to 58.4% for those ages 13–19. In both cohorts the poorest fourth had the largest increase.

Note: Gross enrollment ratios are used because net ratios were not available. These data should be used with caution.
Source: World Bank 1999cc; IDB Statistical and Social Database; PAHO 1998; Thomas 1999; Frankenberg, Thomas, and Beegle 1999.

Most social indicators either deteriorate or improve at a slower pace during a macroeconomic crisis (table 9.2). Social indicators such as infant mortality rates continued to improve in Latin America in the 1980s, though more slowly than in the previous decade. But health indicators more sensitive to consumption or income downturns worsened. In Chile the share of low-birthweight infants and undernourished children rose as the economy declined. In Mexico infant and preschool mortality caused by nutritional deficiency rose in the 1980s, reversing the trend of the previous decade, and rose again with the economic crisis of 1995. In Argentina and Venezuela the daily per capita intake of protein declined as per capita GDP fell. In Indonesia the share of women whose body mass index is below the level at which risks of illness and death

increase rose by a quarter in 1998, and the average weight of children under age three declined.

School attendance and literacy also take hits during crises. In the Philippines secondary school enrollments increased only 0.9 percent between the 1997/98 and 1998/99 academic years, after growing at an average annual rate of 2.6 percent in the previous five years. In Mexico the proportion of each graduating class that enrolled in the next education level declined during the 1980s debt crisis, particularly among high school and university students. The percentage of age-appropriate children entering primary school also declined. In rural areas the dropout rate rose by 40 percent. In Argentina and Mexico growth in gross primary enrollment slowed in 1995. A study for South India found that children are often taken out of school in response to adverse shocks.[9]

There is no question that economic crises increase transitory poverty.[10] They can also increase persistent or chronic poverty because of hard-to-reverse effects on the human capital of poor people. While the trends cited for malnutrition, infant mortality, and enrollment are national averages, they most likely reflect a deterioration in these indicators among poor people. For Indonesia, information by income group shows that the dropout rate in the lowest fourth of the income distribution rose from 1.3 percent in 1997 to 7.5 percent in 1998 among children ages 7–12 and from 14.2 percent to 25.5 percent among those ages 13–19. The proportion of poor children not enrolled in school increased from 4.9 percent to 10.7 percent.

Recent research shows a link between macroeconomic downturns and education indicators. The average annual increase in years of schooling in 18 Latin American countries fell from 1.9 years in the 1950s and 1960s to 1.2 in the 1970s and 1980s. Worsening macroeconomic conditions (short-term GDP shocks, volatility, and adverse trade shocks) explain 80 percent of the decline, according to one study.[11] As evidence from Mexico shows, the negative "income effect" of falling income tends to outweigh the positive "price effect" of the lower opportunity cost of attending school.[12] Simulation results suggest that the gross secondary enrollment rate in Mexico would have been 11 percentage points higher in 1991 if the economy had grown during the 1980s at half the rate of the 1970s.

Avoiding crises

Clearly, avoiding crises should be a top priority in any antipoverty strategy. There is wide agreement on the kind of macroeconomic and financial policies governments need to reduce vulnerability to policy-induced crises or adverse external shocks.[13] They should avoid profligate fiscal and monetary policies, overvalued exchange rates, and unsustainable current account deficits—all problems in the 1970s and 1980s.

Many parts of the world have made great progress in steering away from irresponsible fiscal policy. Leading examples are the large economies in Latin America and some of the transition economies, where the ensuing fall in inflation rates has helped build investor confidence and reduced, if not eliminated, the potential long-term effects of inflation on efficiency and growth.[14] Lower inflation has also helped reduce poverty, since high inflation often hurts the poor more than the nonpoor. In Argentina, for example, ending hyperinflation brought about a significant one-time drop in the incidence of poverty: in Greater Buenos Aires the incidence of poverty dropped from 34.6 percent in 1989 to 22.6 percent in 1991.[15]

The 1990s saw various types of crises, triggered by weak banking systems and weak financial regulation in a world of large and volatile international capital flows. Liberalizing the financial sector was expected to put economies on a more stable footing. But the transition from more repressed to more open financial systems in the developing world has been difficult to manage. Banking crises have been more numerous in the past two decades, when stroke-of-the-pen financial liberalization became popular.[16]

Some of the reforms introduced in the financial sector backfired because the institutional rules allowed excessively risky behavior while the costs of that behavior had to be paid by society as a whole. A vivid example is the Mexican financial crisis of 1995.[17] At the root of the crisis was a weak banking system, its fragility traced to the privatization process used for the banks, some aspects of the financial liberalization program, and weak regulatory institutions. Rescuing the banking sector will cost Mexican taxpayers an amount equal to about 20 percent of GDP (in present value terms).

To prevent financial crises, governments need to improve the prudential regulation and supervision of financial intermediaries, introduce new standards for data dissemination, and implement corporate bankruptcy reform.[18] These measures are already under way in many developing countries, but there is still a long way to go. At the same time, a cautious approach should be taken to capital account liberalization. Controls on capital inflows—such as those Chile used until recently—can be an appropriate instrument for tempering the volatility of capital flows. There is evidence that capital controls can shift the composition of capital flows toward longer-maturing investments.[19]

Other initiatives and measures are also important for avoiding crises, such as mechanisms to diversify and insure against risk. Some governments, such as Chile, self-insure using fiscal stabilization funds. Others, such as Argentina, negotiate contingent credit lines between the central bank and private international financial institutions to ensure access to foreign currency in the event of a sudden slowdown in capital inflows.[20]

However, actions at the national level may not be enough to prevent economywide crises. Domestic actions will have to be complemented by actions at the international level to foster global financial stability (chapter 10) and help countries, particularly the poorest and the smallest, manage commodity price shocks.

Formulating a crisis response that protects poor people

No matter how skillful the economic management, crises are likely to affect the developing world and transition economies for some time to come. That is why articulating a response to crises must take into consideration its impact on poor people. A poverty-sensitive response to crisis should steer toward:

- Helping poor households maintain their consumption.
- Ensuring that poor people do not lose whatever access they have to basic social services.
- Preventing permanent reversals in the accumulation of human and physical capital.
- Averting self-defeating behavior, such as criminal activity, prostitution, and exploitative forms of child labor.

A poverty-sensitive response should also provide mechanisms for those at risk of becoming poor as a result of the crisis.

What does it take to protect those who are already poor and those at risk of becoming so from sharp declines in short-term income? Appropriate macroeconomic responses and well-functioning safety nets can enhance equity and result in better growth outcomes. Some of the recommendations here are already being incorporated in the standard approach for dealing with crises. The Republic of Korea, for example, introduced or expanded safety nets relatively quickly in the wake of the 1997 financial crisis (box 9.1). But in general the response continues to be ad hoc—with measures thrown together in the heat of a crisis.

Adopting the right macroeconomic policy mix. Responding with the right macroeconomic policy mix after an adverse shock is one of the biggest challenges policymakers face. Driven by political considerations, policymakers may postpone needed adjustment and stabilization measures because they are painful—making the situation far worse. Peru was an extreme case in the 1980s. The government refused to implement an adjustment program and in July 1985 announced a cap on external debt payments (a de facto unilateral moratorium) equal to 10 percent of exports. Peru did well for a while, but the disequilibria continued to mount and in 1988 the econ-

omy crashed, with per capita GNP falling by 13.4 percent and real wages by 40.6 percent. Altogether, real wages fell by 67 percent between 1988 and 1990.[21]

The 1997 crisis in Thailand shows what happens when there are no corrective measures to address the buildup of vulnerability.[22] True, the financial panic of domestic and international investors suddenly concerned about the fate of their portfolios lit the fuse for the explosion. But the buildup of structural vulnerabilities provided the dynamite—sharply rising short-term debt that far exceeded international reserves, a financial sector that had done a poor job of intermediating capital inflows and found itself saddled with hugely mismatched assets and liabilities, and corporations that were massively overleveraged and exposed to interest and exchange rate fluctuations.

Not all problems arise from a failure to adjust to an adverse shock or from unsound macroeconomic policies. In some cases the policy response errs in the direction of too much adjustment, with fiscal and monetary policy more restrictive than necessary to restore equilibrium in the currency market, the current account, or the capital account. Overreaction can cause more pain than necessary and in some circumstances can be self-defeating. An initial overreaction on the fiscal front can lead to a higher fiscal deficit down the road because the larger-than-expected recession lowers government revenues, defeating the purpose of the initial austerity measures. The reason for overshooting often is that cautious policymakers prefer to err on the side of excessive adjustment, since timid adjustment can be far more devastating.

Although it may be hard to tell whether a policy package is excessively restrictive, there are some indications that those in place in East Asia during the recent crisis were just that. In Thailand the tax increase in September 1997 made the ensuing recession worse. In Korea the restrictive fiscal policy initially made room for the expected costs of bank restructuring. But the fiscal target was subsequently relaxed as both the authorities and the international financial institutions recognized that it was unrealistic in light of the larger-than-expected slowdown in growth. Aiming toward the original target in the face of worsening economic conditions would have been self-defeating. And for Malaysia and the Philippines the trend of cyclically adjusted deficits (for both revenues and expenditures) suggests that they did not relax their fiscal policy, even though the actual deficit made it look as though they had.

Even if excessively restrictive policies are later corrected, the short-term costs can be significant, particu-

Box 9.1
Providing social protection in response to crisis in the Republic of Korea

The Republic of Korea was making sustained progress in reducing poverty in the 1990s: the urban poverty rate fell an average 20 percent a year during 1990–97, and there were no increases in inequality. But then economic crisis struck, sharply increasing unemployment and poverty. The incidence of poverty in urban areas doubled from 9 percent in 1997 to 19.2 percent in 1998.[1] Unemployment rose from 2.6 percent in the second quarter of 1997 to a peak of 8.7 percent in early 1999. Real wages declined 20.7 percent. Most of the newly unemployed were low-paid workers: in December 1998 three-quarters were temporary, daily, self-employed, or unpaid family workers, and about 20 percent were the head of a household with no other income earners.

Expansionary fiscal policies in 1998 and 1999 were critical in stemming the economic downturn. Social protection spending was increased threefold—from 0.6 percent in 1997 to 2.0 percent in 1999. The government used three main instruments of social protection to help the unemployed, the poor, and the elderly:

- *Unemployment insurance.* Korea expanded its nascent unemployment insurance program—the only such program among the East Asian crisis countries—from firms with more than 30 employees to all firms. It also included temporary and daily workers, shortened the contribution period required for eligibility, and extended the duration of unemployment benefits. This expanded the eligible workforce from 5.7 million workers at the beginning of 1998 to 8.7 million at the end of the year. Beneficiaries increased tenfold—from around 18,000

in January 1998 to 174,000 in March 1999, still only 10 percent of the unemployed workforce.

- *Public work.* Since most of Korea's jobless did not benefit from the expansion of unemployment insurance, the government introduced a temporary public work program in May 1998, enrolling 76,000 workers. By January 1999 the program was providing 437,000 jobs, though the number of applicants was higher still, at 650,000. By the first quarter of 1999 the public work program was benefiting around 2.5 times as many people as the unemployment insurance program.

- *Livelihood protection.* In May 1998 the government introduced a temporary livelihood protection program, with funding to cover 750,000 beneficiaries. It also introduced a means-tested noncontributory social pension for 600,000 elderly people.

Although the government's social protection response was quite exemplary, public spending on health and education did not increase in line with the overall budget, and real spending either fell or remained constant. But even within the smaller envelope for health, spending on primary care was protected.

The government is now focusing on consolidating social safety nets, reducing income disparities, and creating the basis for a competitive and knowledge-based economy. Policies to achieve these objectives include a law guaranteeing a minimum standard of living, to take effect in October 2000. The law will entitle all Koreans living under the poverty line to receive income support for living, education, and housing expenses. Nearly 2 million poor people are expected to benefit, four times the current number.

1. The poverty rates were calculated using seasonally adjusted expenditure data and a national poverty line equivalent to about $8 a day (in 1993 PPP dollars).
Source: World Bank 1999w, 2000d.

larly for poor people. If there are vicious cycles of poverty, low education, and poor health, a recession can cause permanent damage for the poor.

Do the macroeconomic responses to crises that are best for the overall output levels of the economy differ from those that would be best for the incomes of poor people? Perhaps. Different policy combinations imply different costs for the poor than for the nonpoor because of the way the reduction in per capita output is distributed.[23] But even if distributive outcomes were the same, the poor and the nonpoor could well prefer different policy packages.[24]

Poor people are more likely to prefer an adjustment that leads to the smallest drop in GDP at any point in time even if it implies a slower recovery. Nonpoor people are more likely to prefer a program that reduces income more severely in the short run but yields higher growth in the medium run. This difference results simply from the fact that the welfare losses from an economic downturn are

higher for poor people. Moreover, because poor people live close to the subsistence level, their preference may reflect application of the safety principle (minimizing the probability that their income will fall below a certain level). Or the poor and nonpoor may discount future consumption differently, with the poor putting a larger premium on present consumption than the nonpoor.

The distributive and intertemporal implications of alternative adjustment policies are important, but policymakers rarely have the luxury of choosing among different adjustment paths. In general, the optimal combination of policies—to achieve the necessary balance of payments adjustment with the smallest decline in output—depends on initial conditions.[25] When a currency is under speculative attack, a spike in interest rates will in most cases be needed to stop the attack. But when a country introduces adjustment measures early on, the government may have more freedom to choose among different policy combinations and thus be more likely to manage a soft landing. Unfortunately, macroeconomic analysis in its current state can offer little guidance in assessing the distributive and intertemporal implications of alternative policy packages, clearly an area in need of far more analytical and applied research.

Protecting spending that benefits poor people. How governments raise revenues and cut public (nondebt) spending has important policy implications for who bears the burden of adjustment and whether poor people are protected.[26] To design a poverty-sensitive fiscal adjustment to avoid or respond to a crisis, policymakers need to assess the distributional effects of spending programs. A useful tool for this is the public expenditure review (box 9.2).

As a general rule, areas important for poor people—basic education, preventive health care, water and sanitation, rural infrastructure—should be protected from budget cuts to ensure that services are adequate. That means ensuring that schools and health posts in poor areas have at least the basic minimum of supplies. General subsidies on food staples might need to be maintained in the short run—even if the benefits leak to the nonpoor—unless they can be effectively replaced by targeted programs. Safety nets and social assistance programs targeted to poor people should be protected if not expanded.

It may seem obvious that governments should protect spending that benefits poor people and expand the safety net programs targeted to them. But this does not necessarily happen in practice. Recent research in some countries in Latin America has found that a 1 percent decline in per capita GDP leads to an estimated 2–3 percent decline in targeted public spending per poor person.[27] And a study on the Argentine employment program Trabajar found that its performance in reaching poor people deteriorated sharply with cuts to its budget.[28]

There may be several reasons for such "antipoor" patterns in fiscal adjustment. Without budgetary guidelines to direct fiscal austerity, governments may go for proportional cuts to minimize bureaucratic infighting and ease acceptance by the legislature. Another reason may be that governments lack the instruments to target resources to the poor—instruments that are difficult to put in place in the heat of a crisis. Even if the instruments exist, political forces may be such that the resources going to poor people are cut more than proportionately. In some countries information can be the major constraint: governments may lack reliable records of their budget or programs.

What can be done to counter these factors? One way to protect spending that benefits poor households is for the government and legislature to rank current programs by their importance as part of the budget approval process. When spending cuts are needed, the order of the cuts would be determined by the priority assigned to each program. Government agencies could be required to evaluate social programs to help policymakers identify those that are most cost-effective in reducing poverty and therefore should be protected during a crisis.

Peru has introduced guidelines for protecting programs that benefit poor people as part of its public finance reform law (box 9.3). The guidelines combine fiscal rules with measures to increase fiscal transparency and accountability. The program creates a stabilization fund with the proviso that programs benefiting poor people should be protected. Although such budget protocols may not be classified as antipoverty programs, they can have an important effect on poverty by protecting pro-poor spending during fiscal retrenchment.

If benefits targeted to poor people are cut for political economy reasons, a third party—such as the multilateral lending organizations—could advocate for the poor and help governments implementing austerity measures design a viable way to protect programs and spend-

Box 9.2
Public expenditure reviews to assess the impact of fiscal retrenchment on poor people

Public expenditure reviews—assessments of public sector issues that focus on the efficiency and rationale of the public budget—could be useful tools for evaluating the impact of fiscal adjustment programs and public sector reforms on social programs and safety nets. In economywide crises that lead to spending cuts, these reviews could help establish a transparent budget mechanism for rationalizing, allocating, executing, and managing public spending to protect poor people and ensure private sector efficiency.

Public expenditure reviews typically analyze and project public revenues and determine the level and composition of public spending, assessing the allocation of resources among and within sectors. When planning fiscal retrenchment, a short review should be done, focusing on the sectors that account for the bulk of the public budget (agriculture, education, health, infrastructure). The review should rank expenditures on social programs, considering the tradeoff between these programs and other nonessential spending (such as military spending) that could be minimized during a crisis. This type of adjustment is clearly more efficient in protecting vulnerable groups and maintaining private sector efficiency than the typical uniform spending cut.

Source: World Bank 1999v.

ing that benefit the poor. This happened to some degree in several countries in the 1990s.

Changes in the incentive system embedded in targeted programs could also facilitate cuts for nonpoor beneficiaries during periods of austerity. The argument is this: it is often said that for political economy reasons some of the benefits of targeted programs have to go to the nonpoor—through "leakage"—to ensure continuing support for programs. The same forces will presumably act to limit the welfare losses to the nonpoor from cuts.

Box 9.3
Protecting poor people during fiscal adjustment: Peru's Fiscal Prudence and Transparency Law

Peru's Fiscal Prudence and Transparency Law, overwhelmingly approved by the national congress in 1999, does much to ensure that social protection is maintained during a fiscal adjustment.

First, the law established fiscal rules on the maximum annual deficit of the consolidated public sector, capping it at 2 percent of GDP in 2000, 1.5 percent in 2001, and 1 percent thereafter. (The consolidated public sector includes the central and regional governments, decentralized agencies, and national public enterprises; it excludes local governments and their agencies and enterprises.) In the event of a national emergency, international crisis, or fall in GDP, the fiscal deficit can increase to 2 percent of GDP. The law also set limits on increases in public spending and debt. The maximum annual growth of nonfinancial public spending is equivalent to the inflation rate plus 2 percentage points, implying a future reduction in the relative size of the public sector.

Second, the law created a fiscal stabilization fund, to be funded from three sources: the revenues above the average collected during the previous three years, three-fourths of future privatization proceeds, and half of all revenues from future concessions. (Savings accumulated in the fund in excess of 3 percent of GDP will be transferred to the public pension fund or used to reduce public debt.) Up to 40 percent of the fund's resources can be used in a given year if current revenues fall below the average collected over the previous three years. Fund resources can also be used in emergencies, such as an economic crisis or a natural disaster.

Third, the law mandates that the fund's spending on targeted poverty reduction programs be given priority over spending on other programs.

To enhance fiscal transparency, the law introduced a three-year fiscal framework to be developed, approved, and published by the government. And to improve fiscal accountability, it requires that the finance minister submit to congress and publish annual reports assessing the execution of the fiscal goals in the multiyear framework.

Source: Ruprah 1999.

One way to avoid this political economy constraint is to design programs with low marginal benefits or high marginal costs for the nonpoor.[29]

Evaluating different types of spending can be difficult when data are poor, the case in most developing countries. Efficiency indicators are almost nonexistent, and data on actual spending, as opposed to budgeted amounts, are available only after long lags. Usually an evaluation should take the available intermediate information and complement it to determine whether public resources reach the intended beneficiaries effectively. A social monitoring and early response unit, such as the one set up in Indonesia during its recent crisis, can help ensure quick and reliable information for evaluating spending in specific social programs.[30] Where field surveys are infeasible (because of budget or time constraints), recent household surveys can be used to try to determine an efficient and rational allocation of government resources among social programs and safety nets.

Putting safety nets in place before a crisis. If the problem is a lack of instruments for protecting poor people, the solution is to introduce, during normal times, safety net programs that can operate as insurance in times of economic distress. Safety nets are important for several reasons. They can play a crucial role in mitigating the effects of crises on the poor and protecting the near-poor from falling into poverty. A study estimated that if the targeted program Progresa (see box 5.5 in chapter 5) had existed when the 1995 crisis hit Mexico, the poverty gap index in rural areas and the squared poverty gap index (which gives greater weight to the poverty of the poorest)[31] would have declined by 17 percent and 23 percent in the year after the crisis.[32] Safety nets can also help prevent irreversible damage to the human capital of poor people. And they can aid political acceptance of stabilization and reforms, preventing conflicts over resource distribution that can create stalemates, deepen economic crises, even cause governments to fall. Recent work has shown that institutional weaknesses, including lack of safety nets, have been responsible for many crises over the past 25 years.[33]

Most developing countries lack effective safety nets that protect poor people from the output, employment, and price risks associated with systemic adverse shocks. When these mechanisms are not in place before a crisis occurs, policymakers are often forced to improvise or to use programs designed for other purposes and other beneficiaries. Emergency responses to emergency situations are often prepared without technical analysis to identify the groups most vulnerable to the shocks and to evaluate the cost-effectiveness of different social protection options. Programs put in place and operating—even on a small scale—before crises hit do better at protecting poor people than ad hoc emergency measures.

To be effective, safety nets should include a wide range of programs—public work programs, scholarships for poor children, cash transfers, food-related transfers, food subsidies, social funds, and fee waivers for essential services (chapter 8). Social programs that focus on long-term development (for example, such targeted human development programs as Mexico's Progresa) can also perform a safety net function during economic downturns. The appropriate mix of safety net programs will depend on the characteristics of the poor and vulnerable, the type of crisis, and the government's institutional and administrative capacity.

The international community can play an important part by providing policy advice, contributing financial support, and helping policymakers design and fund safety nets. International financial institutions can help countries design pro-poor fiscal adjustment programs and safety nets and, for countries too poor to fund a safety net during a crisis, can provide financing.[34]

Reducing vulnerability to natural disasters

The biggest shock we ever had was Hurricane Gilbert; . . . all what we found after Gilbert was one wooden chair.
—*Woman, Millbank, Jamaica*

Economic development is repeatedly interrupted by natural disasters—by earthquakes, droughts, floods, landslides, volcanic eruptions, windstorms, forest fires. Like economic crises, natural disasters can cause sharp increases in poverty and slow the pace of human development. And like economic crises, they hurt poor people in the short run and diminish their chances of escaping poverty in the longer run.

The damage to agriculture and infrastructure varies by type and intensity of natural disasters, as do the implications for their indirect and secondary impacts. Droughts, for example, can result in heavy crop and livestock losses while leaving infrastructure and productive capacity largely unaffected.

Between 1988 and 1997 natural disasters claimed an estimated 50,000 lives a year and caused damage valued at more than $60 billion a year.[35] Dramatic as these fig-

ures are, the full human and economic costs are even greater. Human costs include injuries and temporary and permanent disabilities, temporary and permanent displacement of people, the breakup of families and social networks, increased poverty and disease, and psychological scars. Economic costs, based largely on direct physical impacts or losses of fixed capital and inventory, are also underestimated. Many indirect and secondary effects on economic activity—such as changes in fiscal policies, the long-term consequences of the reallocation of investment resources, or the losses in human capital—go unrecorded.

Over the past 10 years the incidence of natural disasters has increased.[36] This could be due in part to social factors, as settlements have sprung up in hazardous areas. The urban poor in megacities—for example, in Rio de Janeiro and its *favelas*—are often forced to build on steep, marginal land prone to landslides that kill or leave homeless thousands of people every year. But there are also natural factors. The El Niño events, associated with anomalous floods, droughts, and storms, are getting larger and more frequent.[37] And warming of the surface of the Atlantic is increasing the frequency and severity of hurricanes.[38] Still, it is often asked whether it would be more correct to label many of these disasters as "human-made" rather than "natural." They are probably both.

Impact of natural disasters on poor countries and poor people

Unfortunately for me, the land on which I made my farm was a swampy area and when it rained the whole farm submerged with water and was destroyed.
—*Elderly man, Atonsu Bokro, Ghana*

Developing countries, especially their most densely populated regions, suffer the brunt of natural disasters. Between 1990 and 1998, 94 percent of the world's 568 major natural disasters and more than 97 percent of all natural disaster–related deaths were in developing countries (figure 9.1). In Bangladesh alone three storms, four floods, one tsunami, and two cyclones killed more than 400,000 people and affected another 42 million. In southern Africa in 1991–92, Malawi, South Africa, Zambia, and Zimbabwe experienced severe droughts.[39] In Latin America and the Caribbean major natural disasters associated with El Niño, Hurricane Mitch, Hurricane Georges, and the Quindio earthquake in Colombia claimed thousands of lives and caused billions of dollars of damage between

Figure 9.1
Developing countries bore the brunt of natural disasters in 1990–98

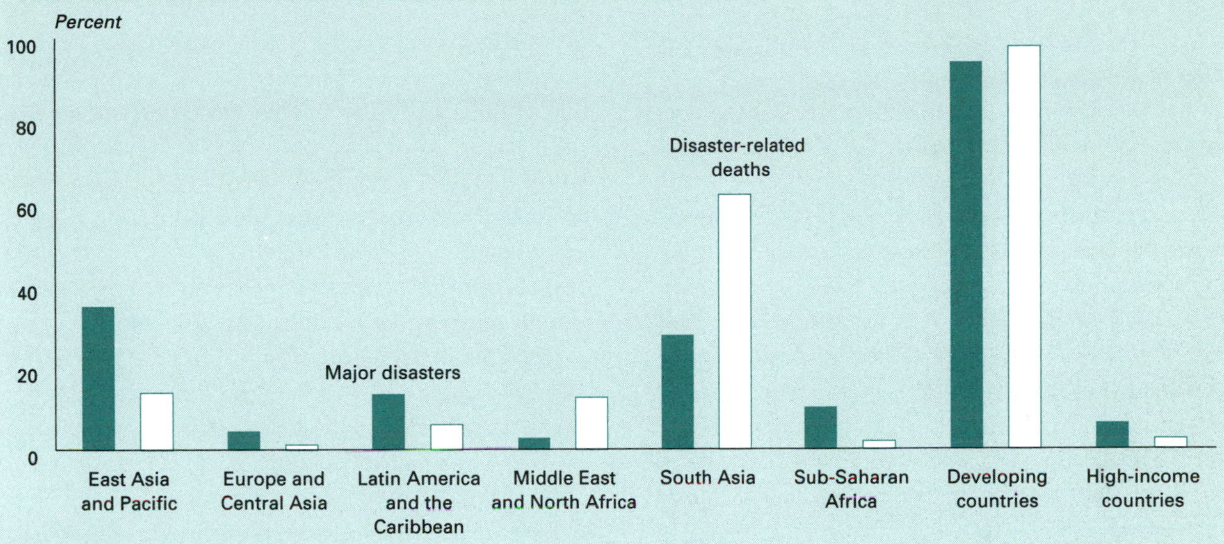

Note: A disaster is classified as major if it caused more than 50 deaths or affected more than 100,000 people.
Source: USAID, OFDA 1999.

1995 and 1998.[40] In 1998 severe flooding of the Yangtze River caused devastation in China, and a large earthquake occurred in Armenia. Another long series of disasters struck in 1999—a major earthquake in Turkey, a cyclone in Orissa, India, floods in central Vietnam, torrential rains and catastrophic mudslides in parts of Venezuela, floods in Mozambique. The list goes on.

Poverty and lagging development amplify the adverse effects of natural disasters. Developing countries are particularly vulnerable, because they have limited capacity to prevent and absorb these effects. People in low-income countries are four times as likely as people in high-income countries to die in a natural disaster.[41] Despite similar patterns of natural disasters in Peru and Japan, fatalities average 2,900 a year in Peru but just 63 in Japan.[42] Average costs as a proportion of GDP are 20 percent higher in developing countries than in industrial economies.[43]

Poor people and poor communities are frequently the primary victims of natural disasters, in part because they are priced out of the more disaster-proof areas and live in crowded, makeshift houses.[44] The incidence of disasters tends to be higher in poor communities, which are more likely to be in areas vulnerable to bad weather or seismic activity. And there is evidence that the low qual-

ity of infrastructure in poor communities increases their vulnerability.

While natural disasters hurt everyone affected by them, poor families are hit particularly hard because injury, disability, and loss of life directly affect their main asset, their labor. Disasters also destroy poor households' natural, physical, and social assets, and disrupt social assistance programs.[45] Long-term disabilities and the destruction of assets can trap families in chronic poverty. Malnutrition impairs children's ability to learn.

The few studies that have analyzed the impact of natural disasters on poverty show that the harm to current and future living standards can be significant. In Ecuador El Niño may have increased the incidence of poverty in affected areas by more than 10 percentage points.[46] In Honduras Hurricane Mitch caused an estimated 7 percent decline in agricultural output in 1998.[47] Loss of crops was extensive, affecting a quarter to a half of households. Rural households, most dependent on agriculture, lost the most.[48]

In the 1984 drought in Burkina Faso the income of the poorest third of the rural population fell 50 percent in the Sahelian zone, the poorest agroclimate, and 7 percent in the Sudanian zone.[49] There was also evidence that poor people sold livestock out of desperation. Because they had very small stocks of animals to begin with, these distress sales may have dangerously depleted their buffer stocks, leaving them extremely vulnerable to future drought and other shocks and possibly trapping them permanently in dire poverty.[50]

Studies of the impact of the 1994–95 drought in Zimbabwe found that women and young children were the most affected. For women, the drought's effect on health (as measured by body mass) was temporary. With good rains the following year, they regained much of the lost body mass. But for children ages 12–24 months the drought will probably have a permanent effect. These young children lost an average 1.5–2.0 centimeters of linear growth in the aftermath of the drought. The impact was most severe among children in households with little livestock, the principal asset of these households for smoothing consumption.[51] The drought had no impact on men's health.

On balance, female-headed households fare worse than male-headed households following a natural disaster, in part because of their smaller average resource base.[52] Customary or formal laws can make this worse. Among the Tonga of Zambia, for example, a widow has no entitlement to any of the household's possessions.[53]

The effect of a natural disaster on poverty can go well beyond the households directly affected. Research on Sub-Saharan Africa suggests that both agricultural and overall GDP are sensitive to downward fluctuations in rainfall. The 1991–92 drought in southern Africa slowed growth in agricultural and total output in Malawi, South Africa, Zambia, and Zimbabwe.[54] The impact of drought shocks on GDP and the recovery time depend in part on the economic importance of the agricultural sector and its integration and links with industry. The second-round and subsequent effects are more pronounced in more integrated economies. In Senegal and Zimbabwe the effect of droughts spilled over from agriculture to manufacturing.[55] The value of Zimbabwe's manufacturing output declined 9.5 percent in 1992, largely as a result of the 1991–92 drought, and export receipts from manufactures declined 6 percent.[56]

The destruction of infrastructure by catastrophic natural disasters also has both immediate implications and longer-term, second-round poverty effects. In Asia, for example, where 70 percent of the world's floods occur, the average annual cost of floods over the past decade was estimated at $15 billion, with infrastructure losses accounting for 65 percent.[57]

The need to replace damaged infrastructure in disaster-stricken countries diverts government resources from longer-term development objectives and consumes a significant share of multinational lending resources. In Mexico as much as 30 percent of the funds approved by the World Bank for improving rural water supply over the past decade have been diverted to postdisaster rehabilitation.[58]

Risk reduction and mitigation: lessening vulnerability to disasters

Cumulative experience with natural disasters points to an urgent need to move from fatalism to prevention, from response to preparation, from mobilizing resources after the fact to reducing and transferring risk before the fact. There is a distinct difference in approach to emergency management between many developing and developed countries. Developing countries emphasize preparedness and response—making sure that the resources to respond to emergencies are available and ready for dispatch and then that they are dispatched quickly and used efficiently after an emergency has occurred. Developed countries increasingly emphasize reducing or mitigating the impacts of disasters (box 9.4).

Disaster reduction and mitigation can lessen the disruption caused by natural disasters, save lives, and protect property. From a purely economic point of view, investing in risk reduction pays off. For example, a cost-benefit analysis for eight cities in the Argentina Flood Rehabilitation Project found an internal economic rate of return of 35 percent. The estimated $187 million (1993 dollars) in avoided damages from the 1997 flood more than covered the $153 million in investment. By installing flood control dams and improving drainage, the Rio Flood Reconstruction and Prevention Project reduced total floodable areas by 40 percent, achieving an estimated 6.5 benefit-cost ratio for seven subbasins of the Iguaçu and Sarapui Rivers.[59] Comprehensive disaster risk management can be integrated into development investment decisions. In Turkey international lenders and donors worked with the government to develop a new disaster management framework in the aftermath of the 1999 earthquakes (box 9.5).

Resettlement—tailored to the needs of poor people—is often the appropriate risk reduction strategy in flood-prone or volcanic areas. Where resettlement is not feasible or desirable, neighborhood improvement programs are an

Box 9.4
Mitigation is the cornerstone of emergency management in the United States

Mitigation—the ongoing effort to lessen the impact disasters have on people and property—is the cornerstone of emergency management in the United States. It involves keeping homes away from floodplains, engineering bridges to withstand earthquakes, creating and enforcing effective building codes to protect property from hurricanes, and more.

Over the past 10 years the U.S. Federal Emergency Management Agency (FEMA) has spent $25 billion to help people repair and rebuild communities after natural disasters. Other government agencies and insurance companies have responded with billions of dollars more. Beyond this, the costs of emergencies also include lost lives, jobs, and business opportunities. A big emergency can reduce local GDP by as much as 10 percent.

In 1995 the high and escalating costs of emergencies led FEMA to adopt a national mitigation strategy, with two goals: to protect people and structures from disasters and to minimize the costs of disaster response and recovery. FEMA estimates that every dollar spent on mitigation saves two in response and recovery.

The strategy promotes a community-based approach to reducing vulnerability to natural hazards:
- Altering the hazard (seeding clouds during a drought).
- Averting the hazard (building dams to control floodwaters).
- Avoiding the hazard (moving parts of communities out of floodplains).
- Adapting to the hazard (constructing earthquake-proof buildings).

In February 2000 FEMA announced Project Impact: Building Disaster-Resistant Communities, a project to provide expertise and technical assistance to about 200 communities striving to become disaster resistant. Three principles drive the project: Preventive actions must be decided at the local level. Private sector participation is vital. Long-term efforts and investments in prevention are essential.

Source: Olsson 2000.

Box 9.5
Mitigating the risks of natural catastrophes: lessons from the 1999 earthquakes in Turkey

A powerful earthquake shook northwestern Turkey in the summer of 1999, killing more than 17,000 people, injuring tens of thousands, and razing several population centers. Three months later a second quake hit, raising the number of victims and the social and economic losses. Industry and businesses in the areas hit by the quakes had contributed more than 35 percent of the country's GDP. Their destruction is likely to affect growth in Turkey for many years to come.

The international community assisted Turkey in relief and immediate recovery efforts. In partnership with the Turkish government, the European Investment Bank, the Council of Europe's Social Development Fund, and other donors, the World Bank coordinated the preparation of a framework for a $1.7 billion reconstruction program. A crucial part of the framework is a disaster management and response system to prevent similar losses in the future.

Disaster and land development laws will be reviewed and modified, and the capacity of municipalities to regulate, plan, and implement disaster-resistant development will be strengthened. Pilot projects in selected municipalities will help planning and building departments develop risk-based municipal master plans, means for effective implementation of building codes, municipal regulations to ensure that builders follow appropriate licensing procedures, and programs for evaluating existing buildings.

The government's earthquake insurance program will expand its catastrophic risk management and risk transfer capabilities. The program will create an insurance mechanism to make funds readily available to owners (those paying real estate taxes) who need to repair or replace a dwelling destroyed or damaged by an earthquake. It will also ensure the financial solvency of the insurance pool after all but the most catastrophic events and reduce the government's financial dependence on donors following major earthquakes.

Source: Kreimer 1999.

---

alternative. In these programs residents of low-income urban areas improve their houses themselves or with community help. The programs reduce building code violations by training informal sector construction workers in mitigation techniques and by providing finance for low-cost improvements that bring housing to stipulated standards. International assistance, channeled through local NGOs, has often helped turn housing reconstruction efforts into low-cost opportunities for mitigating risks in future disasters (box 9.6). Other important neighborhood upgrading activities include constructing drainage works and reducing the risk of flooding and mudslides.

Low-cost local initiatives can also reduce the vulnerability of communities' income to natural disasters. In rural areas such initiatives might focus on environmental conservation and reforestation. For places prone to droughts and floods, community food banks can help. In Burkina Faso local cereal banks were introduced to improve storage, lower food prices, and stabilize them over the year, including during the drought season.[60] Community agricultural cooperatives can help small farmers obtain credit or crop insurance. And various strategies can help diversify the economic activities within a community.

Box 9.6
Turning reconstruction into risk mitigation with the help of a local NGO

In a poor area of Peru partly destroyed by an earthquake in 1990, Caritas, a local NGO, initiated a reconstruction program that was also designed to mitigate earthquake-related risks. After consulting with the community, Caritas decided to construct housing from *quincha*, a local material capable of withstanding earthquakes. To directly assist the neediest families, such as households headed by women, Caritas provided materials in exchange for participation in communal work. An earthquake in 1991 showed the advantage of using *quincha*: most houses resisted the earthquake, which registered 6.2 on the Richter scale.

Source: Schilderman 1993.

Box 9.7
Mitigating risk with catastrophe bonds

Catastrophe bonds—or cat bonds—offer an alternative to insurance in countries lacking active private insurance markets. A before-the-fact risk transfer mechanism, cat bonds provide financial protection against disaster losses.

Consider a government that wants protection against the risk of flood damage to one of its water treatment plants in the next year. Experts estimate the chance of a flood at 1 in 100, a risk low enough to induce an institutional investor to purchase a cat bond whose payoff is tied to flood damage to the treatment plant. The investor buys the bond at the beginning of the risk period at par. At the end of the risk period the investor loses the entire principal if the water treatment plant is damaged. But if no damage occurs, the investor recovers the principal plus interest, normally above the market rate to reflect the risk of losing the principal.

The government invests the funds, which will be used only if a catastrophe occurs, in risk-free securities. The cost to the government is equal to the difference between the interest rate it receives from the risk-free securities and the interest rate it pays the bondholder—a cost analogous to paying an insurance premium. The value of the bond—and the government's interest payments—would be lower if the government flood-proofs the treatment plant. So, besides performing an insurance function, the cat bond gives the government an incentive to invest in mitigation efforts.

A potential problem with catastrophe bonds is the difficulty of verifying damage. The public agency operating the water treatment plant might exaggerate damage to ensure that the bondholder pays. One way to deal with this moral hazard is to tie payouts to an objective index (such as flood height) rather than to actual damage.

Source: Kunreuther 1999.

Reducing economic vulnerability also involves encouraging—or mandating—the purchase of private insurance for those who can afford it and identifying mechanisms for transferring risk, such as catastrophic reinsurance and catastrophe bonds (box 9.7). While risk transfer mechanisms can efficiently cover much of the cost of repairing and rebuilding infrastructure, freeing up scarce government resources, they may not be easy to apply in poor countries. For one thing, they require systems for verifying damage that cannot be easily manipulated by those (governments, for example) who would collect the insurance benefits. To deal with this problem in floods, for example, a country could establish a high-quality measuring and reporting system. This would facilitate insurance contracts that link payment schedules to a rainfall index.[61]

Coping with natural disasters

In the emergency phase following a disaster, efforts should focus on providing food, water, shelter, and medicine. That makes temporary repair of such infrastructure as roads and water supply critical. Priorities need to be based on the magnitude of damages and level of vulnerability. The most vulnerable groups—women, children, and the elderly—need special attention. Involving women in the management of shelters, establishing workfare programs adapted to women's needs, and ensuring gender neutrality in housing acquisition can improve recovery for women and households headed by women. Expanding early childhood development programs, particularly mother and child feeding programs, is also important. Rebuilding schools should be a top priority—to avoid loss of human capital and perhaps to provide shelter for displaced people. Cash transfers to poor families reduce the likelihood that they will need to pull their children out of school. Where children need to participate in recovery efforts, schools can adopt flexible schedules.

Following a widespread natural disaster, national and local governments need to establish a macroeconomic management scheme to tackle fiscal and current account effects—lower tax revenues and higher public spending, lower exports and higher imports. A calamity fund like that in Mexico can improve governments' ability to cover the costs of coping with natural disasters (box 9.8). Calamity funds should focus on absorbing the catastrophic risks that cannot be absorbed by third parties, such as disaster-related damage affecting farmers and urban dwellers unable to afford private

Box 9.8
Sharing the costs of catastrophes: the Mexican fund for natural disasters

With tremendous diversity in geography and climate, Mexico is susceptible to a wide range of natural disasters—floods, droughts, earthquakes, wildfires, tropical cyclones, volcanic eruptions. Since 1980 direct damage from natural disasters has totaled some $6.5 billion, and about 7,000 people have lost their lives.

In 1996, to help reduce the country's vulnerability to natural disasters, the government established Fonden (Fondo para desastres naturales, or Fund for Natural Disasters). This federal fund was to be financier of last resort for emergency response equipment, disaster relief activities, and reconstruction of public infrastructure and protected areas.

In 1998, following a period of particularly heavy losses from natural disasters, the government decided to use Fonden more strategically, to provide incentives for insurance use and disaster mitigation. After broad consultation with stakeholders, in March 1999 the government changed Fonden's operating guidelines to:

■ Increase clarity and transparency in the decision rules for granting access to the fund and in loss assessment processes.

■ Limit moral hazard by encouraging greater use of private insurance by Fonden's beneficiaries and establishing clear cost-sharing formulas for financing disaster losses falling under the responsibility of state and municipal governments.

■ Encourage mitigation in the reconstruction programs financed by Fonden and in beneficiaries' regular investment programs.

■ Refinance disaster response activities initially financed through emergency liquidity facilities to speed disaster recovery.

These changes are being formalized through voluntary agreements between the federal government and the state governments that set out the parties' rights and responsibilities, Fonden's rules, and agreed cost-sharing formulas for disaster relief and reconstruction activities. The agreements will also lead to the establishment of trusts between the federal government and each state. Under the terms of each trust, spending decisions and contracting of eligible emergency activities will be carried out by a technical committee consisting of state and municipal representatives, acting on advice from federal entities.

If successful, these measures will increase transparency, accountability, and efficiency in the use of Fonden's resources and redistribute the costs of natural disasters between government and the private sector. Over time they will also reduce the share of costs borne by the federal government for mitigating and coping with disasters.

Source: Barham 2000.

insurance, and providing social assistance to poor disaster victims.

In the aftermath of a natural disaster targeted international assistance can help maintain macroeconomic stability, accelerate recovery, and protect poor people. But to enable countries to accept financial assistance, international financial institutions may have to relax some adjustment targets during crises. In Zambia in 1992–93 the tight public spending policy being implemented as part of adjustment restricted the government's ability to raise external financing because of the lack of counterpart resources in the local currency. As a result, international funds for drought relief were not fully used.[62]

The reconstruction period provides an opportunity to reduce vulnerability to natural events (see box 9.6). Targeted assistance locally for the most affected populations (with the poor the top priority) and consultation with affected communities and households should be a key strategy. Including local people in reconstruction activities can foster leadership and promote solidarity, helping reduce the psychological trauma caused by natural disasters (box 9.9).[63]

Countries that have social or rural infrastructure investment funds can use them to channel resources efficiently.[64] Given their experience in building infrastructure and providing social services to communities, these funds can quickly identify local spending priorities and help minimize corruption. The Honduras Social Investment Fund performed this role in the aftermath of Hurricane Mitch. It financed the opening of several important secondary roads, began the rehabilitation of some water systems in secondary towns, and undertook cleanup activities. The fund rapidly put in place a decentralized operating structure and responded to the pressing needs of local municipalities and communities. Procedures established by the fund immediately after the disaster simplified project preparation and authorization and expedited contracting and disbursement of funds. Close monitoring by local residents of private contractor equipment and employment of local residents in cleanup activities helped ensure that funds were well accounted for.[65]

The experience produced valuable lessons on how to improve the capacity of such funds to cope with disaster: providing adequate financial resources to meet postdisaster needs, ensuring that investment projects go beyond rehabilitation and cleanup to include expansion of existing facilities and new construction, and expanding the fund's mandate to allow direct social assistance to vulnerable people.[66]

Box 9.9
Involving communities in postdisaster reconstruction: lessons from the Maharashtra Emergency Earthquake Rehabilitation Program

On 30 September 1993 an earthquake struck the Indian state of Maharashtra, killing some 8,000 people and damaging 230,000 houses in Latur, Osmanabad, and 11 other districts. With the help of the World Bank, the government of Maharashtra created the Maharashtra Emergency Earthquake Rehabilitation Program. The program institutionalized community participation and formal consultation with beneficiaries at all stages.

The program divided communities into two categories: those that needed to be relocated—the 52 villages that sustained the worst damage—and those that needed to be reconstructed, repaired, or strengthened. The Tata Institute of Social Sciences worked in the 52 relocation villages, which had some 28,000 families. The Society for Promotion of Area Resource Centers organized community participation in the 1,500 villages—with some 190,000 families—in which rebuilding or repair was to take place.

Over time the program became a people's project. As results materialized, community participation received greater acceptance. Initially skeptical, officials in the project management unit later came to acknowledge community participation as an effective tool for dealing with problems that arise during implementation.

Participation also had a positive psychological effect on communities. Involving local people in the reconstruction helped them overcome the trauma caused by the earthquake. Recognizing this, the government began reconstruction in small villages even before the rehabilitation program began, appealing to donors, corporations, NGOs, and religious organizations to "adopt" villages for reconstruction. Some organizations also worked on social issues, such as schooling for children.

Information on the program, its processes, and the mechanisms for redress was accessible—and awareness was high. The participatory process opened many informal channels of communication between the people and the government, helping to narrow the gap between them. Beneficiaries learned of their entitlements and worked hard to secure them. People who felt that their grievances were not addressed appropriately in the village or *taluka* (an administrative unit that includes several villages) could take them to the district authorities and the government in Mumbai.

Source: Vatsa 1999.

Workfare programs can usefully be introduced or expanded in disaster areas in conjunction with reconstruction operations, providing a livelihood to people who can no longer support themselves (chapter 8). They can also help people affected by the less visible impacts of a disaster, such as the poor fishers in Ecuador and Peru who fell deeper into poverty as fish fled the waters warmed by El Niño. In Northeast Brazil the program Frente de Trabalho (Work Front) provided similar employment opportunities in periods of drought. During the 1979–84 drought it employed up to 3 million workers in construction and drought-related jobs.[67] Public work programs that build social or community infrastructure or help in cleanup and reconstruction can also be a good option.

• • •

Large adverse shocks—economic crises and natural disasters—cause poor people to suffer not only in the short run. They undercut the ability of the poor to move out of poverty in the long run as well, by depleting their human and physical assets. Particularly harmful are the effects on poor children, who may suffer irreversible damage if a crisis or natural disaster increases malnutrition or forces them to drop out of school. Integral to any poverty reduction strategy should thus be measures to prevent and manage economic crises and natural disasters—and to establish safety nets, with ensured financing, to help poor people cope when these adverse shocks do occur.

PART V

International Actions

CHAPTER 10

Harnessing Global Forces for Poor People

Throughout this report we have seen that policies and institutions at the country and local level are the keys to enhancing the opportunity, empowerment, and security of poor people. But the lives of poor people are also affected by forces originating outside their countries' borders—global trade, capital flows, official development assistance, technological advance, diseases, and conflicts, to name just a few. Actions at the global level are therefore crucial complements to country-level actions. They can accelerate poverty reduction and help narrow the gaps—in income, health, and other dimensions—between rich countries and poor.

This chapter discusses four key areas of international action for poverty reduction:

- Expanding market access in rich countries for developing countries' goods and services.
- Reducing the risk of economic crises.
- Encouraging the production of international public goods that benefit poor people.
- Ensuring a voice for poor countries and poor people in global forums.

Also important for poverty reduction is development cooperation—foreign aid and debt relief—discussed in chapter 11. Other global forces that affect the poor include international labor migration, commodity price volatility, global warming and environmental degradation, promotion of political and human rights, and the international arms sales and trade in illicit gems that spur or prolong conflict in countries. Several of these were discussed in last year's *World Development Report*.

Expanding market access in high-income countries

At first glance, it seems that rich countries benefit more from the opportunities of the global economy. After all, they have averaged faster growth than poor countries over the past 40 years. But it is also true that poor countries that are more integrated with international markets have grown as fast as or faster than rich countries.[1] As chapter 3 detailed, trade can provide a powerful engine for growth and poverty reduction. It has also been argued that trade with richer countries can speed the process of "catch-up."[2]

Expanding access to rich country markets can thus do much to help poor countries grow faster and to

Figure 10.1
High-income countries protect manufacturing and agriculture

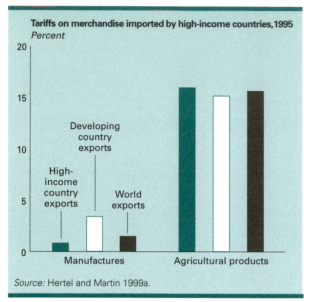

Tariffs on merchandise imported by high-income countries, 1995
Percent

Source: Hertel and Martin 1999a.

reduce poverty in the developing world. This is particularly so for agricultural products, since more than two-thirds of the developing world's poor people live in rural areas. Not only do foreign markets represent important sources of demand for developing countries' agricultural goods—because the demand for basic food products is inelastic—but exporting can expand nonfarm employment and stimulate the entire rural economy. Agricultural exports have been shown to be a strong determinant of overall agricultural growth.[3] So it is disturbing that while world trade in manufactured products expanded at 5.8 percent a year from 1985 to 1994, agricultural trade grew at only 1.8 percent.

One reason for this slow growth is the continuing protection of agricultural products by developed countries—protection not only through tariffs and quotas but also through export subsidies.[4] The tariffs that high-income countries impose on agricultural goods from developing countries, especially such staples as meat, sugar, and dairy products, are almost five times those on manufactures (figure 10.1). The European Union's tariffs on meat products peak at 826 percent.[5] These barriers are huge obstacles for developing countries striving to break into export markets. High-income countries' agricultural tariffs and other distortions, such as subsidies, have been estimated to cause annual welfare losses of $19.8 billion for developing countries—equivalent to about 40 per-

cent of the official development assistance given to developing countries in 1998.[6] This is a serious setback to development efforts in poor countries.

In general, trade reforms in poor countries have failed to deliver their full benefits because they have not been matched by reforms in rich countries. For manufactured goods (including food products), which now account for almost three-quarters of developing country exports, tariffs facing developing country exports to high-income countries are, on average, four times those facing industrial country exports to the same market.

High-income countries' tariffs are not only higher for manufactures from developing countries, they also escalate with the level of processing. For example, in Japan and the European Union fully processed food products face tariffs twice as high as those on products in the first stage of processing. In Canada the ratio is even higher, with tariffs on fully processed food products 12 times those on products in the first stage. This escalation can discourage industrialization efforts in developing countries.

Developed countries' trade barriers can place significant constraints on poor countries' efforts to grow. Finding ways to unblock the political obstacles to removing such barriers would do much to aid poverty reduction in the developing world. By some estimates the welfare losses for high-income countries from their own distortionary trade policies are large—$63 billion a year for agricultural distortions alone.[7] It should be feasible to put in place compensatory mechanisms for the relatively small—but politically powerful—groups of producers as part of an agreement to lower trade barriers. But more than anything, reducing trade barriers will require real political will on the part of the leaders of developed countries. Special priority should go to reducing the scope and scale of protection on agricultural goods, labor-intensive manufactures, and services.

Reducing the risk of economic crises

As chapter 9 details, economic crises in developing countries can be devastating for poor people. So creating the conditions for macroeconomic stability is essential for enhancing the security of the poor and avoiding reversals in poverty reduction.

Countries can take measures on their own to reduce the risk of macroeconomic crises (chapter 9). Among the most important are sound macroeconomic policies and adequate prudential regulation and supervision of financial institutions. But even if a country follows such policies, it can still be hit by contagion and by waves of panic or herd behavior in world capital markets. A premium must therefore be placed on ensuring stability in the international economy, particularly in the financial sector.

International efforts to achieve stability, intense during the Asian crisis, have tapered off as the crisis eased. One focus has been to create and enforce international standards for financial data dissemination and financial practices. The goal is to ensure that financial markets and the public have timely and reliable data for making decisions—and to ensure that financial institutions run effectively. Toward this end, the International Monetary Fund (IMF) has developed standards on financial data dissemination, financial sector soundness, and fiscal, monetary, and financial transparency. Other standard-setting bodies are working on bankruptcy, corporate governance, securities market regulation, and accounting and auditing.

But efforts have stalled in other areas. For example, there has been little progress in setting up early warning devices that could alert the international community to danger.[8] Efforts have been similarly unproductive in designing clear guidelines for private sector involvement in crisis prevention and resolution, which can limit moral hazard, strengthen market discipline by fostering better risk assessment, and improve the prospects for both debtors and creditors in debt workouts. There is a risk that an apparent lack of urgency in the aftermath of the Asian recovery could lead to inaction—but history teaches that more crises are a real possibility.

Recognizing this, developing countries may wish to implement short-term safeguards to limit their exposure.[9] These safeguards are of two types: controls on capital flows and measures to enhance liquidity. Controls on capital—including Chilean-type taxes on inflows, quantitative controls on the banking sector's international short-term liabilities, and restrictions on capital outflows—have their problems, ranging from evasion to implementation difficulties and opportunistic imposition. They can also restrict a country's access to much-needed capital. But each type of control can be effective in some situations in dampening the volatility of capital flows, thus helping to prevent crises.

One way of enhancing a country's liquidity is to maintain higher reserves. But besides being expensive for the government and perhaps creating a significant fiscal burden, even large reserves are likely to be inadequate in some situations. An alternative is to impose higher liquidity requirements on the banking sector, effectively shifting the burden of holding reserves to the private sector (and possibly making banks safer, with beneficial long-term effects). Another is to contract with an institution for a contingent credit line. Both private banks and the IMF offer such arrangements, which provide varying degrees of automatic access to credit at predetermined interest rates.

Even if these short-term safeguards are put in place countries will often be unable to withstand serious international volatility. That is why priority must be placed on increasing the momentum for international systemic financial reforms that promote stability and ensure the availability of liquidity for countries facing severe adverse shocks or hit by economywide crises.

Producing pro-poor international public goods

Many of the challenges facing poor countries have solutions that involve the production of international public goods. One important characteristic of public goods is the difficulty of restricting people from consuming them without paying—free riding—once they are produced. This characteristic means that if production of public goods were left to the market, there would be an undersupply unless the government stepped in to produce the goods or to provide incentives (such as subsidies) for their production. Governments have long intervened in this way, providing such national public goods as defense, infrastructure, law and order, and rules and standards.

The problem is more complex for international public goods, such as control of communicable diseases or research to raise yields in agriculture. Just as for national public goods, the incentives—for countries or for the private sector—to produce international public goods are weak or absent. But there is no world government to help spur the production of these goods—countries must decide to cooperate to produce them. Today, as international problems grow more pressing, attention is focusing on how this cooperation can be achieved.[10]

Indeed, international cooperation has had some remarkable successes in producing and spreading public goods. The green revolution—one of the 20th century's most important development advances—was an outcome of international research on high-yielding plant

Box 10.1
A success story: the fight against river blindness in Africa

The international effort to control river blindness (oncho-cerciasis) is one of the most successful programs in the history of development cooperation. A painful and debilitating disease caused by a parasitic worm, river blindness has been virtually eliminated in the 11 West African countries included in the Onchocerciasis Control Program. Before the program began in 1974, more than a million people were infected with the disease, suffering from itching, disfigurement, eye lesions, and, for 100,000 of them, blindness. When the program winds down in 2002, after a 28-year effort to eliminate the black flies that carry the parasite, 34 million people will be protected, 600,000 cases of blindness will have been prevented, and 5 million years of productive labor will have been saved.

Partners in the program have included African governments, local communities, international organizations, bilateral donors, corporations, foundations, and NGOs. A key contributor has been the Merck Corporation, which has distributed the drug ivermectin free of charge.

While the program has been highly successful, onchocerciasis remains a problem in countries outside the program area. So in 1996 the African Program for Onchocerciasis Control was created, extending the effort to control river blindness to the 19 remaining African countries where it is endemic. Seventy development partners participate in this project.

Source: World Bank (www.worldbank.org/gper).

Figure 10.2
The burden of HIV/AIDS is heavily concentrated in Sub-Saharan Africa

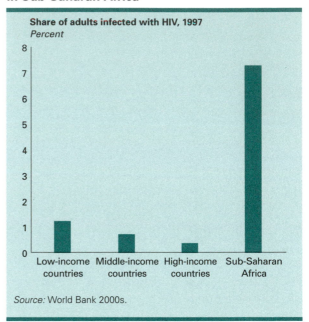

Share of adults infected with HIV, 1997
Percent

Source: World Bank 2000s.

Controlling infectious diseases

The potential benefits of international cooperation to control infectious diseases are exemplified in the AIDS pandemic. More than 34 million people worldwide are infected with HIV, and more than 18 million have died of AIDS.[13] The epidemic continues largely unabated: 5.4 million people were infected with HIV in 1999, and some 15,000 are infected every day. AIDS has no cure—nor is there yet a preventive vaccine. More than 90 percent of the infections are in the developing world, nearly 70 percent in Sub-Saharan Africa (figure 10.2). Despite its concentration in developing countries, AIDS poses a risk to all countries—not only through its health effects but also through its destabilizing economic and social effects.[14] The United States this year classified AIDS as a national security risk.

While preventive behavior is the key to controlling the epidemic, an effective vaccine could help dramatically.[15] But progress in developing a vaccine has been slow. More than 25 candidate vaccines have been tested, but only one is in large-scale efficacy trials in humans. There are two main reasons for the slow progress. The first is scientific: the correlates of HIV immunity are unknown, and many different approaches will probably have to be tested in parallel, with little certainty about their effectiveness. This raises the up-front costs and risks for investors in AIDS vaccine de-

varieties at institutes established around the world expressly to develop technologies to relieve the world's food problem. More recently, international cooperation in the campaign against river blindness in Africa brought tremendous benefits to 11 poor countries (box 10.1). Another success story is the Montreal Protocol on ozone depletion: 165 parties to the protocol agreed to full phaseout of 94 ozone-depleting substances.

Still, international public goods have received relatively little attention in international cooperation.[11] And there have been failures—the Kyoto Protocol on greenhouse gases that contribute to global warming, for example, has languished.[12] Given the potential that some public goods hold for poverty reduction, more attention to ensuring their provision is warranted. The benefits of such goods, and the difficulty of creating the right incentives for their production, are well illustrated by the attempts to control infectious diseases and boost agricultural yields—two international public goods that would do much to help poor people. There are many others, as well.

velopment. The second reason is economic: investors would likely take the risks associated with research if demand were sufficient, but there are too few market incentives to invest in an AIDS vaccine that would be effective and affordable in developing countries. Africa, for example, accounts for only 1 percent of world drug sales.

The result is that international investment in research and development for an AIDS vaccine is quite low—$300–350 million a year.[16] Of this, $50–120 million is estimated to come from the private sector, which has a crucial role in converting research to product development and distribution. And most of the research focuses on a vaccine that could be marketed in North America and Western Europe. Only about $10–25 million is spent annually on development of a vaccine for the virus subtypes and health systems of developing countries.[17] In contrast, more than $2 billion is spent each year on research and development for AIDS treatment, much of it in the private sector, driven primarily by the market represented by the 3 million people with HIV/AIDS in industrial countries.

What is true for AIDS is true for other diseases as well. The World Health Organization estimates that only 10 percent of the $50–60 billion in health research worldwide each year goes for the diseases that afflict 90 percent of the world's people.[18] Developing countries account for only about 8 percent of world spending on research and development, mainly because they lack resources.[19] Of the 1,233 new medicines patented between 1975 and 1997, only 13 (1 percent) were for tropical diseases. The effect of the research and spending gaps is devastating: malaria, tuberculosis, and AIDS cause 5 million deaths a year—about 9 percent of all deaths in the world—most of them in developing countries. Even when medical remedies exist, countries may not be able to afford them. Despite an effective vaccine, hepatitis B still kills some 92,000 people a year, and chronic hepatitis B contributes to another 700,000 deaths through cirrhosis and liver cancer.[20] About 350 million people are chronically infected hepatitis-B carriers, able to transmit the disease for many years.

The international community could accelerate progress on vaccines in two ways. First, international organizations and national governments could "push" research and development by subsidizing or reducing the costs of vaccine development and strengthening the capacity of developing countries with a strong scientific base to be partners in vaccine research. For example, in 1996 the Rockefeller Foundation launched the International AIDS Vaccine Initiative, an international nonprofit that stimulates investment in and demand for AIDS vaccines for global use. The initiative works with the public and private sectors on targeted support to research and development for novel vaccine approaches and on measures to reduce obstacles to private investment. Donor governments, for their part, could provide tax breaks or subsidies for product development relevant to poor countries.

Second, the international community could demonstrate or ensure a substantial future market in developing countries for vaccines. It could pledge to fully implement programs for the childhood vaccines already on the market (immunization rates in many countries have slipped in the past decade). To ensure a large market for vaccines in poor countries, it could create a fund or other credible precommitment mechanism for purchasing, for the poorest countries, many doses of vaccines shown to be both effective and affordable.[21] Prices should cover not just production costs but some of the research costs as well. Multilateral development banks might also issue contingent loans for vaccine purchase to developing countries, to be released once a vaccine is developed. Similar arrangements could be put in place for other medical advances.

Boosting agricultural yields

Like advances in medical research, advances in agricultural technology can have profound effects on the lives of poor people (box 10.2). The green revolution is among the most famous examples of an international public good used for development. The revolution began when foundations, governments, and NGOs took the lead in trying to transfer to farmers in developing countries what scientists already knew about plant genetics and new high-yielding varieties of grains. Private companies had shown little interest because of the difficulty of making an adequate return on investments in new varieties—farmers could simply collect seeds from the original plants. Complementary public efforts at the national level were essential. Many developing countries (such as Brazil and India) established national agricultural research organizations to develop second-generation modern varieties better suited to local conditions. They also set up agricultural extension services to disseminate the knowledge to farmers and get feedback on the new varieties and cultivation techniques.

These efforts had a dramatic effect on the lives of the rural poor. In Africa the adoption of improved maize raised yields an estimated 12–14 percent, with gains as high as

Box 10.2
Research, maize, and pigs in rural Guizhou

Anyone who doubts the impact of agricultural research on farm income and household food security (and thus poverty) should visit rural areas in Guizhou, the poorest province of China. In remote villages, on small farms set in the mountainous countryside, there has been an almost miraculous turnaround in the lives of poor people thanks to the introduction of quality protein maize.

Until recently annual incomes were less than $50 per capita, and for up to three months a year families had virtually no food. Then hybrids were introduced in Guizhou in 1994. Quality protein maize is higher yielding than conventional varieties, but more important, it has higher levels of two essential amino acids vital for the growth of children. Today the local people are better fed, and surplus maize has been used to produce pork, increasing food security and disposable incomes. The extra income has been used for yield-enhancing investments such as irrigation.

Having transformed the lives of 25,000 families in Guizhou, cultivation of the hybrid variety of maize is being adapted to neighboring provinces.

Source: Bale 1999.

40 percent reported in areas with favorable conditions.[22] A survey in southern India concluded that the average real income of small farmers rose 90 percent in 1973–94 and that of the landless—among the poorest in farming communities—125 percent.[23] Higher productivity also brought lower prices. It has been estimated that wheat prices would have risen 34 percent more in 1970–95 without the international agricultural research efforts—rice prices, 41 percent more. And because of the lower prices, 1.5–2 percent fewer children in developing countries are malnourished.[24]

Despite these advances, the growth rate of cereal yields in developing countries has been declining steadily, from 2.9 percent a year in 1967–82 to 1.8 percent in 1982–94. With demand for foodgrains in developing countries predicted to increase 59 percent in the next 25 years, the challenge for agriculture remains significant, particularly if yield growth is to be environmentally sustainable.[25]

One type of technology that might make a significant difference is biotechnology—using living organisms to make or modify products to improve plants and animals. With far greater speed and accuracy than conventional technology, biotechnology can identify desirable traits and introduce them into plant and animal strains

(an example of such traits is increased nutritional quality, as in vitamin A rice). More research is needed on the potential benefits and risks of specific uses of biotechnology in developing countries. But it is likely that biotechnology, if steered by the right policies, including biosafety measures, could be a key part of the solution to the problems of food security and poverty.[26]

So far, however, biotechnology has had little impact in most developing countries. Unlike the advances of the green revolution, much of the progress in biotechnology has been concentrated in the private sector. Government funding of agricultural research, so crucial in the green revolution, has stagnated or even declined, a casualty of general fiscal restraint and a more skeptical view of the social benefits of investing in science (despite the high returns on agricultural research).[27] Private institutions now hold a majority of the patents in biotechnology research, which makes the research excludable (box 10.3). Because the knowledge is private, the cost of acquiring it is much greater. Figuring out how to allow developing countries to capitalize on advances in biotechnology research remains a key challenge for policymakers concerned with food security and poverty. Part of the answer may lie in how intellectual property rights are used.

Safeguarding the interests of poor people in the intellectual property rights regime

Intellectual property rights are important for encouraging innovation, particularly in such areas as medicine and agriculture. When creators of knowledge do not retain exclusive rights of ownership for a period of time, there is far less incentive to produce new knowledge. This was one of the arguments for laying down standards under the Agreement on Trade-Related Aspects of Intellectual Property Rights (TRIPS), negotiated in the Uruguay Round of trade negotiations in 1986–94. But intellectual property rights can sometimes prevent the distribution of potential international public goods helpful to poor countries, which can seldom afford the prices charged by patent owners.[28]

Three trends in intellectual property rights are particularly worrying to developing countries. The first is that basic research and knowledge are increasingly being generated by private companies alone. The second is that industrial countries continue to account for the vast majority of patents worldwide—97 percent.[29] Only 31 of the 26,088 applications for patents filed in 1997 under the auspices of the African Intellectual Property Organization

Box 10.3
Most biotechnology patents are private

The public sector is often instrumental in pioneering biotechnology research, later transferring it to private firms. That pattern is evident in the utility and plant patents directly involving insect toxicity of the *Bacillus thuringiensis* (Bt) microorganism. Until 1987 the public sector held the majority of the patents. Since then the ownership of patents in force (whose overall number has increased) has shifted dramatically toward the private sector (see figure). Patents are now particularly concentrated in the "big 6," the six large corporations actively consolidating their global positions in agricultural biotechnology research, intellectual property, and markets (Dow, Novartis, Aventis, Monsanto, AstraZeneca, and DuPont).

Holdings of biotechnology patents have shifted sharply toward the private sector

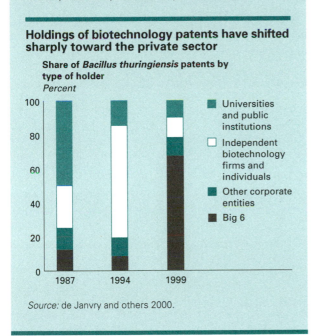

Share of *Bacillus thuringiensis* patents by type of holder
Percent

Legend:
- Universities and public institutions
- Independent biotechnology firms and individuals
- Other corporate entities
- Big 6

Source: de Janvry and others 2000.

Developing countries have responded to these trends by proposing safeguards for the intellectual property rights regime. Among them:

- Recognizing the rights of farmers cultivating traditional varieties.
- Prohibiting the patenting of life forms or biological processes.
- Reconciling World Trade Organization (WTO) provisions on intellectual property rights with the International Convention on Biodiversity and the International Undertaking on Plant Genetic Resources.
- Ensuring access to essential medicines at reasonable cost.

Negotiating a new intellectual property rights regime that encourages private innovation while safeguarding the interests of poor countries and poor people in the benefits of that innovation will take time and much debate. Like the production of all international public goods, it will require creating incentives for participation by all those with an interest in the outcome, including the private sector.

Ensuring a voice for poor people in global forums

Actions with a global reach are generally discussed in global and international forums, such as nation groups, international organizations, and United Nations conferences and other gatherings. Ensuring that poor countries, and especially poor people in these countries, have a strong voice in these forums will help ensure that these institutions respond to the needs of poor people. Productive partnerships—whether to agree on standards, produce public goods, or work toward other common goals—require that all partners have an effective voice.

Strengthening the capacity of poor countries to represent their interests

Not all partnerships should be global—because not all international problems are global. Solutions to an international problem—such as river blindness or pollution in a lake bordering two countries—should be guided primarily by the countries affected.[32] If those countries need assistance, financial or otherwise, the assistance should go to the smallest relevant group—for example, the Economic Community of West African States for cross-border problems involving only its member states. This principle of subsidiarity can be applied all the way up the geographic scale of international public goods, but

were from residents of Africa. And only 7 of 25,731 applications registered that year by the African Regional Industrial Property Organization were filed by residents.[30]

The third trend is that genetic science—enabling companies to patent such innovations as recombinant DNA techniques, monoclonal antibodies, and new cell and tissue technologies—is gaining primacy. This raises a concern that a system of property rights designed to protect industrial machinery may not be able to cope fairly and effectively with the complexities of genetically manipulated organisms.[31] In some cases breeders of plant varieties protected by patents can prevent farmers from reusing harvested seed. And if broadly written, patents on biotechnology processes such as research tools can deter invention in other fields using the same processes.

it must also be reconciled with economies of scale and scope.[33]

Subsidiarity implies that regional institutions should be significantly strengthened to handle cross-border problems. Given the importance of ownership, such institutions would in many cases be a better choice for solving local problems than such global institutions as the World Bank and the United Nations. And because most regional institutions lack wide-ranging expertise, sector-specific organizations should also be strengthened to assist when needed.

But many problems are global, and participation by developing countries in finding solutions is just as important as for regional problems. Since international institutions will generally facilitate the discussions of global problems, these institutions need to take the lead in making information available, ensuring all parties a seat at the table, and strengthening countries' capacity to analyze issues and effectively communicate their interests.

Because knowledge is essential to decisionmaking, international organizations must place a premium on transparency in information and in their operations. In addition to publishing as much information as possible, they need to ensure independent evaluation of their actions—to make themselves more accountable and more effective. This is the direction in which international organizations have been moving in the past few years.

Even with all the right information, developing countries cannot represent their interests without a seat at the table. Many global decisions continue to be made mainly by the group of seven largest industrial democracies (the G-7). Mechanisms are needed to ensure that developing countries contribute effectively to those decisions.[34] Better progress has been made in discussions about the international financial architecture. In 1999 the Group of 20 was established to conduct ongoing discussions on preventing and managing systemic financial crises. Seven developing countries (Argentina, Brazil, China, India, the Republic of Korea, Mexico, and South Africa) are part of this group. Still, the arrangement lacks formal provisions for including any of the poorest or smallest countries, which, though not yet integrated enough into the global economy to present a risk of starting systemic crises, can certainly be affected by them. A better model for integrating developing countries into global problem solving is the Global Environment Facility, which works to foster international cooperation to protect the environment. Half the representatives on its council are from developing countries (box 10.4).

In addition to participating in discussions and solutions, developing countries must be able to represent their own interests well—and this requires capacity building. For example, poor countries are at a significant disadvantage in WTO negotiations on such issues as labor, the environment, and intellectual property rights. Why? Negotiating in the WTO is a continuous process, involving as many as 45 meetings or more a week by one estimate. Yet only two-thirds of developing countries even have offices in Geneva, including only 12 of the 29 least developed WTO members, and these offices frequently must represent the country at other international organizations as well. Moreover, developing country officials often lack the expertise to participate in the increasingly technical trade debates. It has been estimated that almost 60 percent of the developing country members of the WTO are handicapped in their participation.[35]

One attempt to address such problems is the Integrated Framework for Trade-Related Assistance to Least Developed Countries, which seeks to enhance the trade-related assistance provided by the six participating international agencies and other development partners.[36] Despite "needs assessments" submitted by 40 poor countries, progress has been slow, with new donor projects in just one country (Uganda). Developing countries have expressed disappointment with the limited financial pledges.[37] At the request of donors, an independent review is being conducted with the hope that the program's weaknesses can be corrected. If the problems can be resolved, the program could be a model for capacity building in other areas to help developing countries represent their interests.

Building global networks of poor people's organizations

At last those above will hear us. Before now, no one ever asked us what we think.

—Poor man, Guatemala

Like the voices of poor countries, the voices of organizations of poor people are essential in ensuring that global actions are targeted toward poverty reduction. Such organizations, particularly when linked up in global coalitions amassing strength and capacity, can have a

Box 10.4
The Global Environment Facility: a model for developing country participation

The Global Environment Facility (GEF) is a financial mechanism for fostering international cooperation and action to protect the global environment. Through grants and concessional financing, it funds the additional costs incurred when a national, regional, or global development project also addresses environmental concerns related to biological diversity, climate change, international waters, and depletion of the earth's ozone layer. Efforts to stem land degradation are also eligible for funding.

The GEF was started in 1991, and after a trial period was capitalized by 34 nations (including 13 developing countries) at $2 billion for four years. In 1998, 36 countries donated a total of $2.75 billion to keep the facility running until 2002. Its governing structure ensures representation by all stakeholders. The GEF assembly, with representatives from all 165 participating countries, meets every three years to review general policies. The GEF council, with representatives from 32 countries (16 developing, 14 developed, and 2 transition economies), meets every six months on operational policies and programs. The GEF Secretariat translates the decisions of the assembly and council into action.

The GEF's three implementing agencies—the United Nations Development Programme, the United Nations Environment Programme, and the World Bank—develop projects for GEF funding

and implement them through executing agencies. They partner with a wide variety of organizations to execute the projects, including government agencies, other international organizations, private institutions, and international, national, and local nongovernmental and civil society organizations.

Each participating country has a political focal point—the contact point with the GEF Secretariat and other participating countries—and an operational focal point, which identifies project ideas that meet country priorities and ensures that GEF proposals are consistent with them. These organizations help to ensure country ownership, as do the 16 regional NGOs that disseminate information and provide coordination between national and local NGOs and the GEF.

A recent independent evaluation of the GEF found that in a short time and with few resources, it had performed effectively in creating new institutional arrangements and approaches and in leveraging cofinancing for GEF projects. It has also had a positive impact on policies and programs in recipient countries. Although there is room for improvement, particularly in efforts to mainstream attention to the environment, the evaluators concluded that the GEF had potential for much greater success and that donors should strengthen it.

Source: Porter and others 1998.

---

major influence on international debates. For example, a coalition of the Jubilee 2000 movement and other groups concerned with debt reduction worked closely with international financial institutions and industrial country governments to forge a consensus for deeper, faster, and broader debt relief for heavily indebted poor countries (chapter 11).

Innovative solutions are needed to increase poor people's connections to each other and to global decisionmakers. The most important shift needed is in the mind-set of global actors—to be directly informed by the experiences of poor men and women who will be affected by or are expected to benefit from global actions. Also critical is information technology, which can help build networks to channel the voices of the poor to global decisionmakers. With the right tools and organization, these networks can be powerful in spurring the integration of poor people's priorities and analyses into global discussions.

One such global network of poor people is HomeNet. It was created in the mid-1990s by unions, grassroots organizations, and NGOs working with home-based workers and street vendors in developing and developed

countries and concerned about the adverse impact of globalization on the livelihoods of poor women in the informal economy. HomeNet's objective was international recognition of the rights of home-based workers, embodied in an International Labour Organization (ILO) convention. That convention was ratified by the ILO in 1996, thanks in part to an alliance of researchers at Harvard University and the United Nations Development Fund for Women (UNIFEM), who compiled statistics for HomeNet to make the informal economy visible. In 1997 the alliance of grassroots organizations, researchers, and international organizations gave birth to WIEGO (Women in Informal Employment: Globalizing and Organizing), a global network to promote better statistics, research, and policy in support of poor women in the informal economy. HomeNet, with active member organizations in more than 25 countries, publishes a newsletter that reaches organizations in more than 130 countries.

Strengthening such networks will fortify a much-needed voice in international cooperation: the voice of the poor themselves. Just as for national policies, their voice is essential in ensuring that global policies meet their needs.

• • •

The four areas of action highlighted in this chapter illustrate the importance of international cooperation in the fight against poverty. Many of the most pressing problems in developing countries—from trade barriers to financial crises to infectious diseases—can be solved only with cooperation from high-income countries. Yet in the past, international cooperation has consisted primarily of financial transfers from rich countries to poor countries, notably aid. But aid is not enough—prospects for poverty reduction depend on policy changes in high-income countries and cooperative actions at the global level. These include lowering trade barriers, increasing financial stability, producing international public goods that particularly benefit poor people, and ensuring a voice for poor countries and poor people in global forums.

The need for these international actions should redefine the role of international cooperation in poverty reduction. Even with more effective aid, the subject of the next chapter, progress against poverty will be slower without the international actions recommended here.

CHAPTER 11

Reforming Development Cooperation to Attack Poverty

Development cooperation is being reformed. From the relationship between donor and recipient to the way in which aid is delivered and the framework for debt relief for the poorest countries, many of the old ways of assisting development are beginning to be replaced by new forms.

Much of this is due to a reaffirmed commitment by the international community to fight poverty. The World Summit for Social Development in Copenhagen in 1995 set forth the goal of eradicating poverty in the world through decisive national actions and international cooperation. Donors have included halving poverty between 1990 and 2015 and other targets among their international development goals (see box 2 in the overview).[1] In the 12th replenishment of the International Development Association (IDA) in 1998, donors reaffirmed their mission to support programs to reduce poverty and improve the quality of life in IDA's poorest member countries.[2] The Jubilee 2000 movement helped put deeper debt relief at the heart of development cooperation strategies for poverty re-

duction. And donors are working to resolve differences in approaches to poverty reduction through the OECD's Development Assistance Committee (DAC), which expects by mid-2001 to agree on guidelines for poverty reduction to help donor agencies make their programs more effective.[3]

But while the international community's commitment to attack poverty was strengthened in the 1990s, official development assistance shrank. This, despite the optimism at the start of the 1990s that development cooperation would reap a post–cold war "peace dividend" from cutbacks in military spending.[4] Indeed, after peaking in 1992 (in real terms), official development assistance fell consistently over the decade—despite the robust economic growth of DAC countries—rebounding only slightly in 1998 during the global financial crisis (figure 11.1). Sixteen of the 21 DAC countries spent a smaller share of their GNP on development assistance in 1997–98 than in 1988–92.[5] The regional distribution of this aid remained roughly constant between 1987 and

Figure 11.1
While donor countries' economies grew after 1992, their development assistance shrank

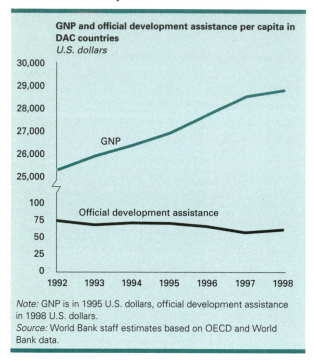

GNP and official development assistance per capita in DAC countries
U.S. dollars

Note: GNP is in 1995 U.S. dollars, official development assistance in 1998 U.S. dollars.
Source: World Bank staff estimates based on OECD and World Bank data.

Figure 11.2
With the exception of Europe and Central Asia, the regional distribution of official development assistance remained roughly constant . . .

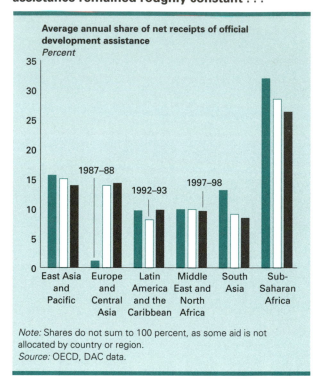

Average annual share of net receipts of official development assistance
Percent

Note: Shares do not sum to 100 percent, as some aid is not allocated by country or region.
Source: OECD, DAC data.

1998, apart from an increase in the share going to Europe and Central Asia (figure 11.2). But total development assistance fell in every region except Latin America and the Caribbean after 1992–93 (figure 11.3). Preliminary estimates show that official development assistance rose again in 1999, by about 5 percent, though it is too soon to know whether this reflects more than the response to the Asian crisis and indicates a much-needed real and sustained reversal of the downward trend in the 1990s.

The decline has been costly for many countries. Although it has coincided with massive inflows of private capital to developing countries, very little of that capital goes to the poorest countries. Net private capital flows to low- and middle-income countries reached $268 billion in 1998 and now dwarf aid flows in some countries. Overall, private flows to developing countries surged during the 1990s, from 43 percent of total resource flows in 1990 to 88 percent in 1997, just before the East Asian financial crisis. However, inflows of private capital have been concentrated in relatively few countries; a large number of countries receive little or nothing. In 1997, before the financial crisis, the top 15 developing country recipients received 83 percent of

private capital flows to developing countries, leaving some 140 developing countries and territories (with about 1.7 billion people) to share the remainder. Almost entirely left out were the 61 low-income countries besides China and India.[6] For example, all of Sub-Saharan Africa received only 1.2 percent of flows to developing countries in 1998. These are the countries that need aid most, and they are hit hard by its decline.

There is no single reason for the decline. Donors initially cited their fiscal deficits as a large part of the problem. Yet even as these deficits declined (from 4.3 percent of GDP in 1993 to 1.3 percent in 1997), official development assistance continued to shrink, dropping 14 percent from 1996 to 1997.[7] A more likely explanation is that donors continue to view development cooperation through a strategic lens rather than a poverty lens, seeing other uses for their money as strategically more important. Historically, aid flows have been determined more by political and strategic interests than by poverty reduction goals.[8]

Perhaps more noteworthy is the decline in support from the traditional proponents of official development

Figure 11.3

. . . while receipts fell after 1992–93 in all regions but Latin America and the Caribbean

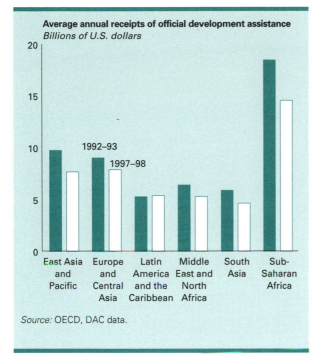

Average annual receipts of official development assistance
Billions of U.S. dollars

1992–93
1997–98

East Asia and Pacific · Europe and Central Asia · Latin America and the Caribbean · Middle East and North Africa · South Asia · Sub-Saharan Africa

Source: OECD, DAC data.

assistance. The preeminence of geopolitical interests is not new.[9] But what is new is the falloff in countervailing support from advocates for development assistance on humanitarian grounds. Many fell victim to "aid fatigue" and were far less vocal supporters in the 1990s than before.

Not every country was affected by aid fatigue—indeed, aid flows increased from some countries—but its symptoms were clearly evident. For example, in the United States a comprehensive poll found that an overwhelming majority of the population favored foreign aid in principle—and that only 35 percent thought it should be cut from current levels.[10] Yet more than 80 percent of respondents believed that waste and corruption kept foreign aid from reaching the people who need it. This kind of public disillusionment may have made it harder for donor governments to maintain foreign aid, let alone increase it. If aid is not working, the sentiment goes, the money could be better spent elsewhere.

In contrast to the rise in aid fatigue in some places was a major upsurge in support and activism around debt reduction, most notably under the auspices of the Jubilee 2000 movement of religious organizations and other civil society groups. They rallied around the cause of

cutting debt for poor countries to support poverty reduction and human development. So there is clearly continuing support for the principle of providing resources for improving the lives of poor people in the developing world, but widespread questioning of the traditional mechanisms for providing such resources.

Is aid working? Can it work better? What is the role of debt reduction in concessional support? Developing countries themselves will largely determine through their own policies whether they achieve the international development goals. But aid and debt relief can provide crucial support. So finding out how to make these more effective—and then doing what it takes—remains vital.

In answering these questions, this chapter outlines a vision for a better system of development cooperation, one based on new thinking and new practices. This vision includes a reformed framework for country-focused aid and debt relief for the poorest countries—underpinned by a renewed emphasis on the policy and institutional environment and the fundamental priority of poverty reduction. Donors would work in partnership with countries, directing aid and debt relief along the lines of a broad-based poverty reduction framework (as advanced by many donors and laid out in this report), supporting countries that can put these resources to good use for poor people.

Supporting good policies and institutions is important, but it is not enough. We learned in the 1990s that process is as important as policy in foreign aid and the management of unsustainable debt burdens. The way donors and recipients interact strongly influences the effectiveness of development cooperation. Relationships have tended to follow the preferences of donor countries, leaving recipient countries with little sense of ownership of the aid-financed activities. Along with advancing a broad-based poverty reduction framework, this report emphasizes how much local realities matter in development. That aid relationships have too often failed to take local realities into account, undermining ownership, is an important flaw.

If development cooperation is to attack poverty effectively and efficiently, donors will need to:

- Pay more attention to local conditions and country ownership.
- Deliver aid in ways that intrude less on government functions, including greater use of sectorwide approaches and a movement away from old forms of aid conditionality.

■ Provide sustained support for policy and institutional environments that are strongly conducive to poverty reduction, in preference to ones that are not.

The chapter begins by exploring how these new approaches can make aid more effective. It then examines the issues associated with relieving the debt problem of poor countries.

Making aid more effective in reducing poverty

Recent studies confirm what anecdotal evidence has long hinted: the experience of aid has been mixed.[11] Early predictions that aid would close the financing gap that prevented developing countries from moving ahead have not come to pass. If all the aid that went to Zambia between 1961 and 1994 had gone into productive investment, and if investment had been as important to growth as initially predicted, the country's per capita income would have been more than $20,000 in 1994, not $600.[12]

And yet there have been many aid successes. The Onchocerciasis Control Program is but one example (see box 10.1). Aid was important, in different periods, in East Asia's extraordinary success in poverty reduction over the past few decades. The rapid progress in Vietnam in the 1990s is another example. So aid can work. The challenge for the international community is to understand how to make it work consistently—and then to do what it takes.

The key problems with aid

Aid's difficulties in reducing poverty go deeper than the sway of geopolitical interests over development interests, which has often directed aid to countries whose policies were not focused on reducing poverty. Aid has been hindered by the frequent differences in donors' perspectives on development policies, even though the past 50 years have been punctuated by times of relatively wide consensus on the best way to pursue development.[13] Donor differences have played a key role in preventing aid from achieving full effectiveness. Donors have often failed to coordinate their efforts, countries have not taken ownership, and there has been heavy use of conditionality both at the project level and economywide.

In the first two decades after World War II state-led industrialization was generally seen as the best way to pursue development, a consensus undone in the 1970s by world events, including the demise of the fixed exchange rate system and two oil shocks, which had devastating im-

pacts on developing countries. It was widely believed that government interference in the economy had prevented developing countries from adjusting to these shocks. Subsequently, a new consensus began to form, eventually to be known as the "Washington consensus" (see box 4.1 in chapter 4).[14] To many, including staff at the World Bank and other multilateral financial institutions, fiscal prudence, free markets, and outward orientation had clearly demonstrated their superiority as the most efficient way for countries to grow and develop.[15]

But it has become clear that simple strategies for development and poverty reduction are elusive. While markets are a powerful force for poverty reduction, institutions that ensure that they operate smoothly and that their benefits reach poor people are important as well. As the 21st century begins, donors are coalescing around a development strategy that includes investing in people through health and education services, promoting inclusive and equitable growth, supporting good governance, and protecting the environment.[16] This strategy also recognizes the centrality of local conditions: that the most effective development policies will vary by situation.

Despite this growing consensus on the broad development framework, agreement on the right policies in particular conditions has tended to elude donors and recipients. Donors come to development problems with their own mandates, histories, ideologies, and political realities and often do not see situations in the same way as other donors or the recipient countries. Even in health and education, which all donors agree are essential, the right reforms are open to debate. As an analyst commented, there is "a bewildering multitude of national systems and experiences, with varied (and hotly debated) advantages and disadvantages associated with each."[17] So while the days of adhering strictly to either state-led or market-led solutions are over, between these extremes lie a host of options, and the debate on them is far from over.

The lack of consensus on the broad outlines and the details of national and local policies and projects has reduced the effectiveness of development assistance.[18] This effect is especially evident in problems of ownership, donor coordination, fungibility, and conditionality—the four main issues affecting aid in the 1990s.

Ownership. Because donors and recipients often disagree, donors have looked for ways to ensure that their money is spent as they intend. They have run their own projects, required detailed reports from countries on projects, and attached conditions—usually policy oriented—

to the use of funds. A major study on relations between donors and African recipients found that "in spite of some improvements, donors still tend to dominate the project cycle and pay inadequate attention to the preferences of the government or project beneficiaries."[19] These efforts to ensure that aid is spent effectively, evidence now shows, have often had the opposite effect by diminishing ownership by the recipient country.

Analyses show that ownership is a key ingredient of aid effectiveness.[20] How strongly a country believes that a project or reform will bring benefits affects the effort put into the activity, the domestic resources contributed, and the commitment to the activity after the donor has left—all substantial determinants of success. To succeed, reforms and projects must foster ownership by the people for whom the policy or project is ostensibly being implemented.

Donor coordination. When different donor priorities and project-related conditions (including donor-specific reporting and procurement requirements) are multiplied many times over, they can create an unworkable environment for a recipient government. Just the sheer number of donors and donor projects can be challenging. At one point there were 405 donor-funded projects in the Mozambican Ministry of Health alone. In the early 1990s in Tanzania there were 40 donors and more than 2,000 projects. In Ghana during the same period 64 different government or quasi-government institutions were receiving aid.[21] Coordinating these efforts to support a coherent development strategy—even at the sector level—is nearly impossible.

Fungibility. Studies show that aid funds allocated to a particular sector tend to free up for other purposes money that the government would otherwise have spent in that sector.[22] This means that in funding specific projects or sectors, donors may actually be helping to increase spending on sectors they do not want to finance, such as the military. This has profound implications for development cooperation. Project-level evaluations will not reflect the true impact of aid, since aid is likely to be freeing up resources for other activities.[23]

Even where resources are fungible, donor support can still have some impact, from the design of certain policies to institutional development. Moreover, in countries highly dependent on aid, donors as a group could lead to shifts in government resource allocations, because of the sheer size of flows. A potentially important part of this is the preference of donors to support development budgets, which can lead to a net shift in resources out of the recurrent budget—not always a good thing for develop-

ment because of the importance of recurrent spending in maintaining basic social and economic services.[24]

Conditionality. Donors know that even properly implemented projects will have limited impact in poor policy environments.[25] A well-built school will be useful only if money is budgeted annually for teachers, books, and supplies—and if the economic environment enables children to go to school. The role of good policies and institutions in ensuring sustainable results suggests that aid should flow more to countries with a good overall policy environment and good policies for poverty reduction. But the relationship between good policies and aid flows has not been strong.[26]

This finding would be understandable if aid were spurring policy reform by influencing countries to change their policies or by helping them do so. This has been the intention of many donors, and it is one reason (fungibility is another) that many of them have reduced the share of their portfolio allocated to projects and increased the share allocated to program and policy-based aid.[27] Most program and policy-based aid has been tied to the enactment of certain policy reforms. But studies in the 1990s showed little systematic relationship between conditionality and policy changes, though case studies do find positive effects under some conditions, especially where conditionality supports the hand of reforming groups.[28]

The dynamics between aid donors and recipients explain why conditionality fails. Recipients do not see the conditions as binding, and most donors are reluctant to stop giving aid when conditions are not met.[29] As a result, compliance with conditions tends to be low, while the release rate of loan tranches remains high.[30] Thus aid has often continued to flow despite the continuation of bad policies.

In addition to performing poorly in influencing policy reform, policy-related conditions, often combined with project-related conditions, severely burden developing country administrators—a problem that has become more pronounced as conditionality has expanded. Conditions on World Bank adjustment loans, having mushroomed in the 1980s, continued to grow in the 1990s along with the expanding development agenda.[31] As one recent assessment put it: "Although much has been added to the conditionality menu since 1981, nothing has been taken off."[32] The time government officials spent negotiating and monitoring these conditions is time they could better have spent analyzing development problems and designing development strategies. Ownership has been shown to be central to the sustainability of both projects and policy reform, and the fact that the delivery of aid weakens it is a fundamental flaw of current development cooperation mechanisms.

Solutions that accommodate different perspectives

While the dominant forms of donor-recipient relations have allowed donors to pursue their own priorities, the result has generally been a fragmented system that undermines their efforts. The challenge in reforming international development cooperation is to accommodate different perspectives on development without overburdening the recipient or undermining ownership.

Achieving global uniformity in development strategies might be one solution, but history shows that uniformity is undesirable. Development is determined to a great extent by local conditions, including social institutions, social capability, ethnic fragmentation, inequality, and geography.[33] In studies these variables significantly explain the variation in growth rates over the past 30 years.[34] Studies also show that external shocks—and the ability to respond to them—can have as much effect on growth as policies do.[35] The approach to designing development strategies should therefore be flexible enough to adjust to both internal and external conditions.

This perspective began to take hold in the development community in the late 1990s. Combined with new thinking on aid effectiveness, it has prompted proposals to address the problems of aid. Three prominent themes are ownership and partnership, less intrusive aid delivery mechanisms that focus on the overall policy and expenditure framework, and selectivity. Together, they form the agenda for the international community to improve development cooperation in the coming decade.

Ownership and partnership. Recognizing the importance of ownership and the problem of donor coordination, most donors have embraced partnership as a guiding principle in interactions among donors, governments, and citizens in developing countries.[36] Most partnership frameworks have two parts. The first is a partnership between the recipient government and its citizens, who share responsibility for developing their national development strategy. This strategy can take shape through a consultation process involving government, civil society, and the private sector. The second is a partnership between the government and donors, with donors designing their assistance strategies to support the government's strategy. In the new thinking the focus is on how to shape this external part-

nership, or contract, in a way that provides the incentives for country-driven, long-term poverty reduction strategies while also strengthening the internal partnerships necessary for social stability and economic development.

Consultations between governments and civil society and between governments and donors have been carried out in a number of countries piloting the World Bank's Comprehensive Development Framework, the European Union's partnership approach, and other such approaches. The consultations under the Comprehensive Development Framework have proved fruitful in several countries —such as Bolivia, the Dominican Republic, and Ghana— but have also highlighted the need for government commitment and for capacity as key ingredients of successful consultations (box 11.1).

This emerging approach to development cooperation has been incorporated into the new initiative by the World Bank and International Monetary Fund (IMF) to link their support of low-income countries to nationally designed poverty reduction strategies, working within the principles of the Comprehensive Development Framework (box 11.2). Concessional funds and debt relief from the World Bank and IMF will be linked to the goals of poverty reduction strategies prepared by governments in consultation with civil society organizations, the private sector, and donors. Based on a good understanding of the poverty situation in the country, the strategies will identify actions with the greatest expected impact and set up monitoring and evaluation processes. The goal is for these strategies, described in poverty reduction strategy papers, to form the basis for assistance not only from the World Bank and IMF, but from other assistance agencies as well.[37] Similar initiatives are under way in the regional development banks.

Less intrusive aid delivery mechanisms focusing on the overall policy and expenditure environment. Donors have used many means to influence recipient country policies. Old forms of policy conditionality have often had disappointing results, depending on country circumstances and how the conditionality was used. Policy review processes also have had limited success. Public expenditure reviews, for example, have evaluated the level and composition of countries' expenditures and identified ways to improve expenditure policy and use donor funds more efficiently (see box 9.2 in chapter 9). But several studies have found this type of intervention to be ineffective in many cases, largely because recipient countries have not been closely involved in the reviews—and so have felt little inclination to comply with the findings.[38]

Box 11.1
Learning about the consultative process through the Comprehensive Development Framework

In 1999 the World Bank announced its Comprehensive Development Framework, a tool for improving country ownership and donor coordination in development cooperation. The framework is based on four principles: country ownership of the policy agenda, partnership with all stakeholders, attention to social and structural concerns as well as macroeconomic and financial issues, and a long-term, holistic approach built on national consultations.

The country develops its national strategy in consultation with civil society and the private sector—and then, with donors, designs a matrix linking development goals and development actors. The activities of actors in support of each goal are listed in the matrix, revealing any gaps or overlaps.

The framework is being implemented in 13 countries, encouraging wide consultation between governments and their citizens and enhancing partnerships with donors in the design of comprehensive national development strategies. But progress has been varied, reflecting different starting dates and country circumstances.

Bolivia is an early case. In late 1997 the new government embarked on an analysis of the country's development challenges and the preparation of a national action plan to address them. A key part was a national consultation with a wide range of representatives of civil society—NGOs, unions, religious organizations, opposition parties, and academics—and the private sector to discuss development constraints and propose solutions. The results of this national dialogue were presented to the government as input to the national action plan.

All discussions with donors now take place in the context of the national action plan. At a consultative group meeting in April 1998 donors pledged 45 percent more than they had in 1997. Donors have also been encouraged to formulate their strategies in support of the national action plan. The World Bank recently redesigned its country assistance strategy to align it with the plan, choosing to support three of the plan's four pillars. The government continues to lead donor coordination, chairing the consultative group meeting in Paris in 1999, where it presented its version of the Comprehensive Development Framework. It has also agreed with donors on intermediate indicators for monitoring outcomes.

Other countries have not progressed as far. The difficulties of some highlight potential problem areas. For example, it is clear that country ownership depends largely on national capacity. The country must be able to hold broad consultations with all elements of society and to conduct the complex analysis necessary to design national strategies that balance macroeconomic and financial issues with social, structural, and institutional concerns. And, of course, the country must be able to implement the strategy.

Without this ownership—and the country leadership from it—donor coordination will remain difficult. While there is some evidence that some donor countries are gradually aligning their strategies with those of recipient countries, stronger leadership by the recipient government will be required to accelerate progress.

Source: Wolfensohn 1999; World Bank 1999d, 1999u.

Box 11.2
The new poverty reduction strategy initiative

The poverty reduction strategy initiative of the World Bank and International Monetary Fund seeks to link external support to domestically developed, results-based poverty strategies. It is also intended to improve the effectiveness of World Bank and IMF relations (and those of other donors as well) with recipient countries. As important as the recipient country strategy is the process leading up to it. A broad, participatory dialogue with representatives of civil society and the private sector is expected to:

- Help national authorities develop a better understanding of the obstacles to poverty reduction and growth—and devise good indicators of progress in poverty reduction.
- Deepen a shared vision of desired poverty reduction goals across society.
- Lead to formulation of priorities for public actions to achieve the desired poverty reduction outcomes.
- Encourage the development of participatory processes for setting poverty reduction goals and monitoring implementation and progress.

The results will be periodically reported in poverty reduction strategy papers expected to reflect a broadly owned development strategy. The strategies will generally focus on three-year cycles, with annual progress reports in the intervening years, all embedded in a long-term framework for poverty reduction. While the actual form of the strategy will be decided by the country—there is no single blueprint—most strategies would likely include:

- Long-term goals for key poverty reduction targets, and the macroeconomic, structural, and institutional framework for achieving them (see, for example, Uganda's goals in box 1.7).
- Mechanisms for monitoring and evaluating progress toward the poverty reduction targets, linked to public actions.
- A consistent policy and institutional framework that includes the underpinnings for rapid, sustained growth and poverty reduction (including macroeconomic policies, institutional reforms, sector strategies, and associated domestic and external financing needs).

Donors can help by providing technical assistance in some areas. Initial experience in Africa and Latin America indicates that countries are strong in laying out a poverty profile and a general poverty reduction strategy but weaker in preparing quantified targets, costing the strategy, and evaluating tradeoffs under limited resources. As in other aspects of development cooperation, the country should determine its own need for assistance—to maintain ownership of this important process.

Source: IMF and IDA 1999; World Bank and IMF 2000a.

Perhaps more surprising, donor compliance has been weak as well. A recent evaluation found public expenditure reviews to have had little effect on either recipient country policies or donor lending practices.[39] So donors are searching for new mechanisms for strengthening policy environments that encourage country ownership rather than undermine it. They have begun, for example, to encourage countries to participate fully in the public expenditure review process, and they are experimenting with new instruments.

One new instrument that has received much attention is the sectorwide approach: the government designs an overall sector strategy, and donors sign on to fund the sector, not individual projects. This resolves the problem of donor coordination by eliminating the need for it: all activity in the sector is conducted by the recipient country, using its own funds in addition to those of donors. This instrument responds to a broader policy environment while also ensuring ownership. Although the approach is too new to have a track record, some early experiences are promising (box 11.3).

Some proponents have suggested applying the principles of the sectorwide approach to all development cooperation (box 11.4). Others consider project-based lending to be desirable and consistent with the new thinking on development cooperation for poverty reduction. Project support can be effective for results-based sector development—if it falls within a sector framework that systematically links investments and policy and institutional development to poverty outcomes (and to intermediate indicators for tracking and interpreting progress). The choice of instrument will depend on the policy and institutional conditions of particular countries (or sectors within countries) and the preferences of individual donors. But a premium should be placed on putting the country in charge and ensuring that the mechanisms of aid delivery do not compromise its ownership.

Selectivity. For aid to be most effective at reducing poverty, it must be well targeted. If all aid money were allocated on the basis of high poverty rates and reasonably effective policies and institutions, a recent study estimates, even today's small aid flows could lift 19 million people out of poverty each year—almost twice the estimated 10 million now being helped.[40]

Currently, about a third of aid goes to middle-income countries, whose average GNP per capita is roughly six times that of low-income countries (figure 11.4). While only a few major donors target more of their aid to mid-

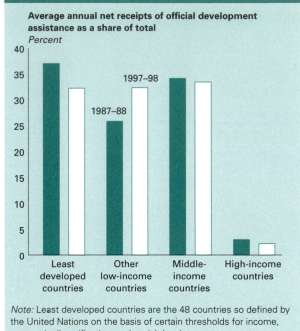

Figure 11.4
Aid does not go only to poor countries

Average annual net receipts of official development assistance as a share of total
Percent

Note: Least developed countries are the 48 countries so defined by the United Nations on the basis of certain thresholds for income, economic diversification, and social development.
Source: OECD, DAC 2000.

dle-income countries (most donors target aid to the poorer countries), that still means that global aid is not heavily targeted to areas where the incidence of poverty is greatest. Aid, and especially nonconcessional development flows, still has a role in reducing poverty in middle-income countries, when the policy environment is sound and the resources are well targeted.

In addition to targeting poverty, donors should allocate aid on the basis of the policy environment. Aid has been shown to be effective in promoting growth and poverty reduction in poor countries with sound economic policies and sound institutions—ineffective where these are lacking.[41] Aid driven by political and strategic interests rather than by the recipient country's development policy environment is largely wasted from a poverty reduction perspective. Several instruments have been developed to assess the policy and institutional environment in recipient countries, generally covering macroeconomic management, structural policies, policies for social inclusion (poverty, gender), and public sector management (box 11.5).

Factoring in the level of poverty and the quality of policies should make aid much more efficient in reducing poverty, and there is evidence that donors began to do this in the 1990s.[42] In replenishing IDA in 1998, for

Box 11.3
Sectorwide development cooperation

To address problems of ownership, donor coordination, and fungibility, donors are experimenting with pooling their resources to support sectorwide strategies designed and implemented by the recipient government. The country, in consultation with key stakeholders, designs a sector strategy and a budget framework extending several years forward, and donors put their money into the central expenditure pool for the sector. The approach encourages country ownership of sector strategies and programs. It also links sector expenditure with the overall macroeconomic framework. And it ensures coordination of donor and recipient activities.

Some benefits of a sectorwide program are evident in the Zambian health sector. In 1994 the government presented its national health policy and strategy to donors and—to ensure equitable distribution of services and coherent implementation of the strategy—asked them not to fund specific provinces or projects but to fund the Ministry of Health centrally. Hesitant at first, donors began to comply. An independent evaluation in 1997 found that "health workers are better motivated; clinics are functioning; funds are flowing to the districts; some modicum of decentralization is in place; [and] an important part of the private sector has become formally involved."

The approach ensures full ownership by the country and eliminates problems of donor coordination. With the country having more ownership and control over what happens, the use of resources can be much more efficient. But it also means great changes in donor-recipient relations and perhaps greater difficulties in implementation. Several sectorwide programs have stumbled because of the recipient country's inadequate institutional capacity. Lack of consistency with the macroeconomic program has been another problem. And donors often have too many requirements and thus too much of a problem (or too little interest) in harmonizing them (Harrold and associates 1995). Furthermore, these arrangements greatly diminish donor control and monitoring of exactly how money is spent.

The changes required imply that gaining support for the approach will be difficult. The recipient government has to be very confident, because strict adherence to a sectorwide approach means donors that do not participate in common implementation arrangements are not allowed to act in the sector (that is, they do not have their own projects). The result may be less donor funding for a sector. Governments might therefore opt for less strict sectorwide programs, choosing instead to allow donors to implement projects as long as they fit into the overall sector strategy.

Box 11.4
The common pool for development cooperation

Seeing the potential of the sectorwide approach, some propose extending the idea to the country level (Kanbur, Sandler, and Morrison 1999). Donors would cede complete control to the recipient country government—advancing their own perspective on development strategy through dialogue with the country and with one another rather than through specific programs and projects. Rather than fund their own projects, donors would give central budget support to countries with good development strategies (and the capacity to implement them).

A country would first develop its own strategy, programs, and projects in consultation with its people and with donors. It would then present its plans to donors, which would put unrestricted financing into a common pool of development assistance, to be used along with the government's own resources to finance the development strategy. Earmarking would disappear. Donor monitoring and control of specific projects and programs would not be permitted. And no conditions would be placed on donor aid.

How much donors give would depend on their assessments of the country's policy environment, including how the country came to agreement on the strategy and how capable it is of implementing the strategy and monitoring progress. In this way the common pool approach would be a more rigorous form of conditionality, because donors would need to evaluate the overall policy environment, direction, and capacity of countries. These assessments would be made known to the country and to other donors during the dialogue leading up to the financing decision.

This approach would entail many of the same challenges facing the sectorwide approach, including the need for recipient countries to have both the capacity to implement their strategy and the confidence to follow through even if donors do not support it. In addition, donors might resist common pools at the national level because they would likely mean a reduction in donor staff, since donor agencies would no longer be developing and monitoring projects or negotiating and monitoring conditions.

However, like the sectorwide approach, the common pool approach would ensure full ownership by the country and eliminate donor coordination problems. It would also preserve two important benefits of the current development cooperation approach:

- The knowledge transferred in donor-implemented projects, an important side effect of aid. A road building project, for example, might transfer knowledge of engineering or even project accounting to local workers. This transfer would not be lost in a common pool arrangement. Recipient countries could still ensure knowledge transfer through their choice of companies and the terms of contracts.
- The support that conditionality gives to reform factions in governments. Support for reform elements in a country is perhaps the only effective part of the present system of conditionality. Donor-imposed conditions can strengthen the position of reformers in national debates or serve as a "self-imposed" constraint on government officials. The approach to conditionality in a common pool arrangement would be far different, but it would not sacrifice this benefit. Donors could strengthen the hand of reformers by publicizing the criteria used to assess country strategies and adjusting the volume of their assistance. This would form the basis for a more open and honest relationship between donors and recipients and preserve the benefits of the current conditionality while eliminating its problems.

Box 11.5
Assessing country policies and institutions

The World Bank has designed a measure of policy and institutional soundness—the Country Policy and Institutional Assessment, which gives equal weight to 20 components that have evolved as the measure has been refined. Each component is rated by country specialists on a scale of 1–6 using standard criteria. Although care is taken to ensure that the ratings are comparable within and between regions, the scores include an irreducible element of judgment. But when the measure has been included in regression analyses of growth along with other commonly used policy variables, it has had statistical significance, while other policy measures have not. It thus appears to be a good summary indicator of the overall policy environment for economic development. The 20 components:

Economic management
Management of inflation and the current account
Fiscal policy
Management of external debt
Management and sustainability of the development program

Structural policies
Trade policy and foreign exchange regime
Financial stability and depth
Banking sector efficiency and resource mobilization

Competitive environment for the private sector
Factor and product markets
Policies and institutions for environmental sustainability

Policies for social inclusion and equity
Equality of economic opportunity
Equity of public resource use
Building of human resources
Safety nets
Poverty monitoring and analysis

Public sector management and institutions
Property rights and rule-based governance
Quality of budgetary and financial management
Efficiency of revenue mobilization
Efficiency of public expenditures
Transparency, accountability, and corruption in public services

Developing a consistent basis for rating economic and structural policies has been relatively straightforward, but doing so for social inclusion and public sector management has proved more challenging. Work to refine the indicators and reference points continues.

Source: Collier and Dollar 2000; World Bank 1999h.

---

example, donors called for allocating funds on the basis of each country's policy performance.[43]

How selectivity is applied will likely evolve as the international community continues to learn about the environments in which aid is most effective.[44] Some analysts stress that the level of poverty in a country is more important to aid effectiveness than the policy environment, though both are crucial.[45] Others show that external shocks—such as declining terms of trade, volatility in export prices, and even climate change—can impede countries' efforts in growth and poverty reduction (chapter 9).[46] It has been argued that aid can make a larger difference in these countries (and therefore be more effective) than in countries not experiencing shocks.[47] Refining the criteria for selectivity should continue. Adhering to the basic principle that aid should go where it is most effective in reducing poverty will be key if the international community is to achieve the international development goals.

Implementation difficulties and practical steps

These three components—ownership and partnership, aid delivery mechanisms that are less intrusive, and selectivity—provide the framework for substantially improved international development cooperation. But progress toward that vision will not be easy. Each component of improved development cooperation brings great challenges in implementation.

For example, while almost everyone agrees that partnership is a good idea, there is no consensus on how to implement it.[48] Some analysts note that ownership is relative and that reaching consensus on strategies is essentially a political process, involving the same power relations that exclude poor people from discussions or discriminate against them (as seen in chapter 6).[49] Others voice doubts that donors will really come to terms with the implications of ownership and partnership for their actions: that donors should interfere less in recipient country policymaking.[50] Many donor practices—such as maintaining control over resource monitoring and tying aid to specific procurement requirements—run contrary to the idea of partnership.[51] The recipient country's capacity to design and implement development strategies and its ability (and willingness) to hold broad consultations with all elements of society also pose significant challenges.

The combination of greater selectivity and a broader, less intrusive approach to delivering development assistance presents its own challenges. Determining how much support to give to a sector or national budget is difficult—and likely to prove contentious. Some country expenditures may not seem to fit into a "best" poverty reduction strategy, but donors will have to evaluate the poverty reduction impact of the overall program, not the individual expenditures.

A more fundamental problem arises when a country does not have an overall policy environment worth supporting, so that aid is largely ineffective. How should donors proceed?

Most important, they must understand that policies are driven primarily by the domestic political economy—and that donors are simply not very effective in influencing them.[52] But donors can have some influence by tailoring their involvement to a country's commitment to reform. Until a country commits seriously to reform, the best that donors can do is to provide technical assistance and policy dialogue, without large budget or balance of payments support (box 11.6). If donors pour large amounts of aid into poor policy environments, they are likely to sustain poor policies longer. When the country finally commits to reform, evidence shows that finance should be increased as policies improve.[53]

In addition to this more nuanced approach to influencing policy reform, donors can address the challenges of the new development cooperation framework by taking several other steps:

- *Move the donor-recipient dialogue to the country and turn its leadership over as well.* Donor-recipient consultations—consultative groups or roundtables—have traditionally taken place in donor countries, chaired by the World Bank, the United Nations Development Programme, or another donor institution. Meetings are now beginning to be held in recipient countries and chaired by their governments, to foster ownership.

- *Continue to experiment with sectorwide approaches.* National capacity—and donor-recipient partnerships—can be built up sector by sector. While many countries will for some time not have the overall technical capacity, accountability, and transparency to monitor funds to the satisfaction of donors, these may be more advanced in some sectors than in others. The advanced sectors could be funded through the sectorwide approach as soon as possible, taking into account the lessons from experience with this approach.[54] And donors should continue to improve their

Box 11.6
How aid can help in countries with a weak policy environment

When a country has poor policies and no coherent political movement to change the situation, aid can have a limited but effective role, as Ghana, Uganda, and Vietnam all illustrate. In their prereform periods (before 1983 for Ghana, 1986 for Uganda, and 1991 for Vietnam), these countries received very little aid, probably reflecting their governments' political estrangement from the West. But the aid was instrumental in laying the foundation for policy reform.

For example, when Ghana was dealing with a macroeconomic crisis in the early 1980s, its well-trained economists found the policy dialogue with international financial institutions to be helpful in working out plans. A few years later, when Uganda's leaders were trying to design new policies, donors financed helpful study tours to Ghana. In 1991 the United Nations Development Programme and World Bank organized a meeting for Vietnamese leaders with economic ministers from Indonesia, the Republic of Korea, and Malaysia, who laid out some key policies that had worked for them and also some of the detailed issues in stabilization, trade liberalization, foreign investment, and other economic policies.

In successful cases political leaders learn from other countries and from their own mistakes. Low-key assistance can help with this policy learning, which generally has to take place at a country's own pace. Even in countries that do not reform for a long time, technical assistance can lay the foundation for policy learning. In Kenya, for example, donors are supporting the Institute of Policy Analysis and Research to help develop local capacity in research and policy analysis. This kind of capacity building is not going to have large benefits as long as vested interests resist serious reform. But it is an essential foundation if a political movement for change develops.

Source: Devarajan, Dollar, and Holmgren 2000; World Bank 1998b.

own practices—for example, by harmonizing procedures and reporting requirements among themselves—so that they can contribute effectively to these new aid relationships.

- *Strengthen monitoring and evaluation practices.* Donors' systems of monitoring and assessing the impacts of their own projects have failed to focus on how poor people benefit.[55] But doing this will be even more important (and challenging) when looking at a sectorwide or nationwide program. Donors should encourage local monitoring by participants, to ensure ownership of the results. Furthermore, donors tend to be weak in disseminating information and incorporating knowledge from evaluations.[56] Feedback and learning are essential to successful aid practices, and donors must ensure that they happen effectively. As part of this, donors and recipients should continue to strengthen their efforts against corruption, a major obstacle to economic performance that occasionally also affects donor agencies.

■ *End tied aid.* In 1998 almost a quarter of official development assistance was tied, meaning that the procurement contracts were limited to the donor country or a group of countries. Driven by domestic political interests, this practice goes against the very free-market principles that most donors are trying to encourage in developing countries and results in inefficient use of aid. It has been estimated that tying aid reduces its value by 15–30 percent.[57] The practice should be ended as quickly as possible, and contracts should go to the best bids.[58]

■ *Make technical assistance demand driven.* Turning more responsibility over to recipient countries for designing national development strategies and leading consultation meetings will require rapid capacity development. Recipient countries will also need strong auditing and accounting skills if donors are to relinquish monitoring and control of projects. But technical assistance, the obvious choice for building capacity, has a spotty record at best, particularly in countries where capacity is already weak. The main reason is that it has often not been demand driven—it has often been tied aid and designed to develop capacity only in donor-supported activities.[59] Instead, technical assistance should be incorporated into a national strategy and expenditure plan, with the recipient government deciding what assistance it needs and who should provide it. This is likely to require initial support to countries on how to use the market for technical assistance.

■ *Continue to learn about how to work effectively with NGOs.* Relationships between donors and NGOs are complex, with much room for improvement.[60] Good data on the extent and effectiveness of donor-NGO relationships are scarce, but an estimated $5 billion in aid is now channeled through NGOs, either in subsidies to their activities or in contracts to implement donor activities (figure 11.5). NGOs appear to be an effective channel for aid when they are involved early in projects (at the design phase), when they are chosen for their proven capacity and experience, and when they are treated as partners rather than contractors.[61] The long-term impact of NGO projects remains unknown, perhaps because so little money has

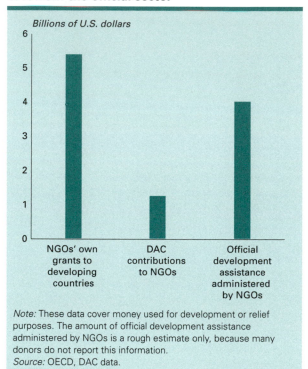

Figure 11.5
NGOs channeled some $10 billion to developing countries in 1998, about half of it from the official sector

Billions of U.S. dollars

Note: These data cover money used for development or relief purposes. The amount of official development assistance administered by NGOs is a rough estimate only, because many donors do not report this information.
Source: OECD, DAC data.

gone into funding their evaluation and monitoring efforts.[62] Even with better monitoring, though, NGO projects face the same problems of fungibility as donor projects, and policy environments strongly influence their effectiveness. Donors and NGOs should continue to improve their working relationships, sharing best practices for making aid more effective in the long term.

■ *Relieve more debt.* Debt relief for the poorest countries is essential for effective aid. Heavy debt burdens reduce incentives for policy reform, while debt negotiations and the constant circulation of new aid money to service old debt distract government officials from the needs of their citizens. The next section turns to this issue.

Relieving the debt burden of poor countries

The most prominent issue in development cooperation at the end of the 20th century and the beginning of the 21st has been debt relief for the poorest countries. There has been a steady increase over two decades in the indebtedness of a group of poor countries now referred to as the heavily

Figure 11.6

As per capita income in the heavily indebted poor countries has gone down, debt has gone up—and vice versa

Note: The observed association between declining income and rising debt should not be viewed as implying that debt reduction will automatically result in higher incomes. Government policies are the key to growth and poverty reduction, and bad policies can lead to both higher debt and lower incomes.
Source: Easterly 1999c.

indebted poor countries (figure 11.6). Public attention has been drawn to their plight in large part through the tireless efforts of NGOs in developed and developing countries, whose campaign for debt cancellation by 2000 has captured the world's interest.[63] At the 1999 annual meetings of the World Bank and IMF, member countries agreed on an enhanced plan for debt relief, an acknowledgment of the detrimental effects of debt on country policy environments and overall expenditure frameworks (box 11.7).

The effects of heavy debt burdens

Many heavily indebted poor countries spent as much as a fifth of their annual budgets on debt service in the 1990s, and some spent much more.[64] Because this is often more than the amount spent on social programs, debt servicing is viewed by many as a severe impediment to improving the lives of the world's poor.

It has been argued, however, that debt servicing is not really a problem because heavily indebted poor countries receive more money from donor countries than they pay back. Actual debt service payments are

Box 11.7

The Enhanced Heavily Indebted Poor Countries Debt Relief Initiative

The Heavily Indebted Poor Countries (HIPC) Debt Relief Initiative was announced in late 1996. Realizing that the initiative did not go far enough, leaders of the Group of Seven (G-7) countries endorsed an Enhanced HIPC Initiative at a summit in Cologne, Germany, in July 1999. The enhanced initiative was approved by the full membership of the World Bank and International Monetary Fund in September 1999 as an integral part of the new poverty reduction strategy initiative (see box 11.2). The Enhanced HIPC Initiative changed the eligibility requirements for debt relief and the timing of relief.

Eligibility

To be eligible, a country must be very poor, have an unsustainable debt burden, and pursue good policies.

- *Poor* is defined as both eligible for support under the IMF's Poverty Reduction and Growth Facility (the reformed and renamed Enhanced Structural Adjustment Facility, or ESAF) and eligible only for concessional financing from the World Bank, through the International Development Association.
- An *unsustainable debt burden* is defined as a stock of debt that is more than 150 percent of exports in present value terms after the full use of traditional debt relief mechanisms or (for countries with certain structural characteristics) a ratio of debt to government revenue of more than 250 percent.
- *Good policies* are interpreted to mean macroeconomic, structural, and social policies consistent with poverty reduction and sustained growth.

These new eligibility criteria increase from 26 to 33 the number of countries likely to qualify for relief.

Timing of relief

The Enhanced HIPC Initiative provides for the possibility of interim relief for countries after they pass the decision point, when the World Bank and IMF determine a country's eligibility. A reduction in debt service payments is therefore possible even before a country reaches the completion point, when the stock of debt is reduced. Under the earlier HIPC agreement the debt stock was reduced only after completion of two full ESAF programs—a minimum of six years. Now the completion point can be moved up if the country's performance is particularly good. Relief is intended to be frontloaded as much as possible.

Combined with traditional debt relief arrangements, the Enhanced HIPC Initiative is likely to cut by half the net present value of public debt for the 33 countries likely to qualify. As many as 20 countries may reach a decision point on debt relief by the end of 2000, depending on progress in developing their poverty reduction strategies and on how much financing is available from donors.

Source: World Bank (www.worldbank.org/hipc).

Figure 11.7

Concessional transfers largely compensate for negative net transfers of nonconcessional resources

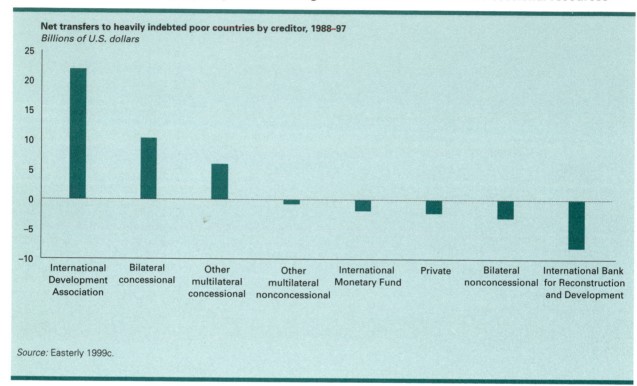

Net transfers to heavily indebted poor countries by creditor, 1988–97
Billions of U.S. dollars

Source: Easterly 1999c.

almost always far less than scheduled payments, because the countries cannot make the full payments. The debts are serviced by rescheduling some loans and financing the rest through a combination of new loans and grants.[65] Overall, while net transfers of nonconcessional resources tend to be negative because new nonconcessional borrowing is strongly discouraged, transfers of concessional resources tend to more than compensate (figure 11.7).

However, heavy debt burdens bring additional problems that can affect a country's growth performance and ability to focus government action on social priorities. Debt service is financed largely by scarce domestic budgetary resources and thus competes with domestic recurrent spending, while concessional assistance goes to new investment projects. This mix can mean resources for new health centers and roads but not for nurses or maintenance. In addition, many grants go to donor-managed activities that are not included in the budget. These are subject to all the problems of ownership and donor coordination discussed above and can contribute to the further institutional weakening of an already weakened, insolvent state.[66] And debt negotiations and mon-

itoring take up much of the already stretched time and capacity of government officials.

These resource inflows can also be unstable, making it difficult for governments to manage their spending and maintain sound fiscal policies.[67] Furthermore, if resource flows are positive because countries have to rely on continuous recheduling and on grants and concessional lending, their access to private capital flows will remain very low. And where debts are not serviced in full, countries' debt stocks continue to grow, creating a potential disincentive to investment, since investors may fear that future profits will be affected by debt-related macroeconomic problems or higher taxes to service debt.[68]

Debt is therefore as much a problem of how gross flows and debt management affect ownership, policy, and capacity as it is a problem of net flows. In this, it shares many of the problems that have diminished the effectiveness of aid. Debt relief can play an important role here by reducing the burden on recurrent budgets and allowing government officials to focus on sound spending strategies rather than continual renegotiation of debt. And it can be particularly crucial for countries emerging from civil conflict and war.

There is also some evidence that high debt service obligations (including those to international financial institutions) tend to weaken the link between concessional flows and the quality of the policy and institutional framework—and so the effectiveness in reducing poverty. This could be because donors try to avoid defaults on loans, and as countries become more indebted, donors give new loans to cover the old ones. (Between 1989 and 1997 debt relief for the 41 heavily indebted poor countries totaled $33 billion and new borrowing $41 billion.)[69] Not only does this compromise the ability of donors to target aid to where it will be most effective, but it may also deter reform in countries with poor policies, because they have less incentive to reform if they can expect relief and resources anyway.[70]

Debt relief can ease all these problems by reducing the gross flows and, if structured correctly, encouraging a structure of new inflows that is more effective for poverty reduction.

An improved initiative for debt relief

To be effective, debt relief needs to be delivered in ways that encourage country ownership, using instruments that provide incentives to use the resources for poverty reduction. This is the same issue as for traditional aid flows, but in the context of a one-time decision to reduce debt. How much impact debt relief has on net transfers to a country depends, of course, on what happens to gross aid flows—on whether the resources for debt relief are additional or not. But even if the resources are not entirely additional, debt relief can ease policy and budgetary constraints for the recipient country, since it frees up resources from the recurrent budget. What will guarantee that these resources are used for poverty reduction? There are two related challenges:

- Linking resources from debt relief to results in poverty reduction.
- Strengthening accountability in the use of public resources, to minimize diversion to other uses (especially through corruption).

The lessons from the past—including those from the experience with aid outlined above—indicate that both are best tackled through their links to the overall policy and institutional environment, especially for public resource use. Experience also shows that debt relief alone will not improve policies. Twenty years of gradually increasing debt relief have not improved policies in heav-

ily indebted poor countries.[71] That is why the principle is to grant debt relief on the basis of reputation—an established track record in using resources effectively for poverty reduction.

The design of the Enhanced Heavily Indebted Poor Countries (HIPC) Debt Relief Initiative incorporates these lessons. Debt relief will be granted to eligible countries with a viable and comprehensive poverty reduction strategy and a framework for linking public actions to monitorable results in poverty reduction. The strategy is to be defined through a participatory process involving government, the private sector, and civil society. The participatory process is important for the design of the strategy—and to help ensure good use of external (and internal) resources. Debt relief will be integrated with other sources of external finance in the country's overall budgetary framework for poverty reduction, rather than being earmarked for certain expenditures. The goal of the Enhanced HIPC Initiative is to contribute directly to poverty reduction and to ensure that countries that receive debt relief do not have policies that will lead them deeply into debt again.

In May 2000 Uganda became the first country to receive debt relief under the Enhanced HIPC Initiative (box 11.8). The relief was based on several years of progress in the participatory formulation of its poverty reduction strategy, results in key areas (getting children into school, reducing income poverty through agricultural and aggregate growth), and mechanisms to help increase accountability for public funds and reduce leakages.

The cost of the Enhanced HIPC Initiative is estimated at $28 billion. If the debt relief is to be additional, financing must come from outside the normal aid and concessional lending budgets of donor institutions. Under current plans the cost will be financed roughly equally by bilateral and multilateral creditors. Although many donors have endorsed the Enhanced HIPC Initiative and made political commitments for funding, the mobilization of resources has been slow, and some donors have not yet committed to the initiative. Because a key principle underlying the initiative is that debt relief should be coordinated among all creditors, with broad and equitable participation, this lagging of resources and commitments seriously endangers the initiative. Donors need to give high priority to securing sufficient funding for the Enhanced HIPC Initiative.

Box 11.8
How debt relief fits into a poverty reduction strategy: Uganda's Poverty Action Fund

Fundamental in the fight against poverty is improving the overall allocation of resources, including those from debt relief, through more poverty-oriented and transparent budgets. There are many ways of achieving this end, and in Uganda a special fund to use the savings from debt relief is proving useful.

The government chose to create the Poverty Action Fund as a conduit for the savings from debt relief under the HIPC Initiative (about $37 million a year; the Enhanced HIPC Initiative is expected to double this amount). The fund has been earmarked for priorities of the poverty eradication action plan adopted in 1997 to address poverty and social conditions. The plan emphasizes maintaining macroeconomic stability while increasing the incomes and the quality of life of poor people by developing rural infrastructure, promoting small businesses and microenterprises, creating jobs, and improving health services and education. The Poverty Action Fund focuses on schools, rural feeder roads, agricultural extension,

and district-level water and sanitation. Specific outcome targets have been identified, such as the construction of 1,000 additional classrooms to support the primary education program.

Two crucial features of the Poverty Action Fund are its integration into the overall budget and the Ugandan government's effort to create a transparent and accountable structure of management. Reports on financial allocations are released at quarterly meetings attended by donors and NGOs. The Inspector General's office monitors the use of funds at the district and national levels. This self-imposed conditionality reflects the government's strong commitment to tackling corruption. But it is also an attempt to address creditor concerns about the capacity of a debtor country to link debt relief to poverty reduction. Several measures have been proposed for improving monitoring, ranging from including district-level officials in the quarterly meetings to having local NGOs do community-based monitoring of the poverty fund's spending.

Source: UNICEF and Oxfam International 1999.

• • •

Many questions remain about the implementation of debt relief and of the new development cooperation framework advanced in this chapter. Despite the financing difficulties of the Enhanced HIPC Initiative, some observers call for even deeper and faster debt relief, arguing that the debt deemed "sustainable" under the Enhanced HIPC Initiative is still too burdensome.[72] How to move quickly to relieve debt while still allowing enough time to build country ownership of the poverty reduction strategy is another concern. Some countries wonder about their capacity to prepare their own poverty assessments and poverty reduction strategies. Others question whether donors can support the formulation and implementation of poverty reduction strategies without undermining country ownership. Questions also remain about the participatory process—how best to consult with poor people, how to fit consultative processes into the context of national political processes, and how to develop effective feedback and monitoring systems. And countries wonder how well donors will be able to realign

their procedures and interventions along the lines laid out in their poverty reduction strategies.[73] All these issues reflect the state of international development cooperation at the turn of the 21st century. There is profound, ongoing change in the way developing and developed countries work together to fight poverty.

While many issues remain, the right direction for the international community is clear. Country-focused assistance should incorporate a greater emphasis on partnership between donors and developing countries. It should apply less intrusive mechanisms of aid delivery that focus on the overall policy and expenditure environment. And it should exercise greater selectivity in allocating aid where it will be most effective. More aid and debt relief need to be available to countries with effective poverty reduction programs. Donor evaluations of these programs must be informed by an awareness of the conditions each country faces and by the new approach to poverty reduction presented in this report. And to relieve the burden of the heavily indebted poor countries, donor countries should finance the Enhanced HIPC Initiative with money *additional* to their aid budgets.

Bibliographic Note

This report draws on a wide range of World Bank documents and on numerous outside sources. Background papers and notes were prepared by Daron Acemoglu, Michelle Adato, Mary B. Anderson, Michael R. Anderson, Simon Appleton, Gareth Austin, Michael Banton, Pranab Bardhan, Paolo Belli, Timothy Besley, Pilwha Chang, Monique Cohen, Michelle Connolly, Richard C. Crook, Robert A. Dahl, Partha Dasgupta, Shelton Davis, Alain de Janvry, Stefan Dercon, Ann Elwan, Gary S. Fields, Gary Gereffi, Gregory Graff, George Gray-Molina, Lawrence Haddad, John Harriss, Ronald J. Herring, John Hoddinott, Naomi Hossain, Peter P. Houtzager, Rajshri Jayaraman, Noushin Kalati, Marcus Kurtz, Edward E. Leamer, Jennifer Leavy, David Lindauer, Michael Lipton, Frances Lund, Daniel S. Manning, James Manor, Martha Argelia Martinez, Jacob Meerman, Mick Moore, Samuel A. Morley, Kimberly J. Niles, Anthony Oliver-Smith, Jonathan Pattenden, Anan Pawasuthipaisit, Louis Pouliquen, Kameshwar Prasad, James Putzel, Danny Quah, Elisa Reis, James A. Robinson, Francisco Rodriguez, Elisabeth Sadoulet, Sombat Sakuntasathien, Peter K. Schott, Jennefer Sebstad, Saurabh Sinha, Lina Song, Smita Srinivas, Alan Sturla Sverrisson, Robert M. Townsend, Ben Turok, Ashutosh Varshney, Howard White, Laurence Whitehead, L. Alan Winters, Quentin Wodon, Shahin Yaqub, and David Zilberman.

Background papers for the report are available either on the World Wide Web (www.worldbank.org/poverty/wdrpoverty) or through the World Development Report office. The views expressed in these papers are not necessarily those of the World Bank or of this report.

Many people, both inside and outside the World Bank, gave advice and guidance to the team. Valuable comments and contributions were provided by Taoufik Ben Abdallah, Richard Adams, Nisha Agrawal, Sadiq Ahmed, Martha Ainsworth, George Akerlof, Harold Alderman, Titus Alexander, Jock Anderson, Hutton Archer, Anthony Atkinson, Gareth Austin, Robert Ayres, Malcolm Bale, Namrata Bali, Andrew Balls, Abhijit Banerjee, Pranab Bardhan, Christopher Barham, Douglas Barnes, Tamsyn Barton, Ananya Basu, Kaushik Basu, Amie Batson, Anthony Bebbington, Alan Berg, Timothy Besley, Gordon Betcherman, Andre Beteille, Surjit Bhalla, Vinay Bhargava, Ela Bhatt, Mihir R. Bhatt, Hans Binswanger, Nancy Birdsall, Yonas Biryu, Mark Blackden, Rebecca Blank, David Bloom, Želco Bogetić, Jan Bojo, Rene Bonnel, Ed Bos, César Bouillón, François Bourguignon, Samuel Bowles, Carlos A.

Primo Braga, John Briscoe, Penelope Brooks, Stephen Brushett, Robin Burgess, Sara Calvo, Sarah Cambridge, Roy Canagarajah, Gerard Caprio, Teresa Carbo, Guy Carrin, Soniya Carvalho, Robert Chambers, Jacques Charmes, Celine Charveriat, Mirai Chatterjee, Mrinal Datta Chaudhuri, Rodrigo Chaves, Sandeep Chawla, Shaohua Chen, Susan Chen, Kenneth Chomitz, Alberto Chong, Ralph Christy, Mariam Claeson, John Clark, Monique Cohen, Paul Collier, Tim Conway, Giovanni Andrea Cornia, Uri Dadush, Dana Dalrymple, Amit Dar, Koen M. Davidse, Adrian Davis, Gloria Davis, Alain de Janvry, Samantha De Silva, Naa dei Nikoi, Angus Deaton, Klaus Deininger, Lionel Demery, Stephen Denning, Stefan Dercon, Mahendra Dev, Shantayanan Devarajan, Ishac Diwan, David Dollar, Philippe Dongier, Donna Dowsett-Coirolo, Jean Drèze, Jean-Luc Dubois, Steven Durlauf, Chris Dye, Tim Dyson, William Easterly, Judith Edstrom, Dag Ehrenpreis, Lars Ekengren, Ibrahim Elbadawi, David P. Ellerman, Diane Elson, Gunnar Eskeland, Wolfgang Fengler, Marco Ferroni, Deon Filmer, Ben Fine, Ariel Fiszbein, Ann Florini, Emmanuel Forestier, Justin Forsyth, Paul Freeman, Jose Furtado, Andreas Galanakis, Emanuela Galasso, Joaquin Garcia, Michel Garenne, Roberta Gatti, Guido Geissler, Alan Gelb, Paul J. Gertler, Coralie Gevers, Ashraf Ghani, Maitreesh Ghatak, Alan Gilbert, Michael Goldberg, Jeff Goldstein, Fr. Xabier Gorostiaga (and his colleagues from Asociación de Universidades Confiadas a la Compañía de Jesus en America Latina), Vincent Gouarne, Heather Grady, Peter Grant, Stefanie Grant, Cheryl Gray, Duncan Green, Margaret Grosh, Sumit Guha, Patrick Guillaumont, Sanjeew Gupta, Davidson R. Gwatkin, Lawrence Haddad, Peter Hakim, Gillette Hall, Kristin Hallberg, Jeffrey Hammer, Lucia Hanmer, Nancy Happe, Caroline Harper, Ricardo Hausmann, Yujiro Hayami, John Healey, Gerry Helleiner, Jesko Hentschel, Alicia Herbert, Norman L. Hicks, John Hoddinott, Robert Holzmann, Peter P. Houtzager, Albert D. Howlett, Chia-Hsin Hu, Gregory Ingram, Keiko Itoh, Vijay Jagannathan, Selim Jahan, K. Jankovsky, Mahieu Jarret, Renana Jhabvala, Emmanuel Jimenez, Ian Johnson, Gerd Johnsson, Ben Jones, Christine Jones, Steen Jorgensen, Sonia Kapoor, Dani Kaufmann, Masahiro Kawai, Allen Kelley, Charles Kenny, Michel Kerf, Christine Kessides, Roger V. Key, Anupam Khanna, Stuti Khemani, Tony Killick, Ronald Kim, Elizabeth King, Stephan Klasen, Jeni G. Klugman, Steve Knack, Grzegorz Kolodko, Valerie Kozel, Annette Krauss, Alcira Kreimer, Jean-Louis Lamboray, Jack Langenbrunner, Patricia Laverley, Richard Leete, Arianna Legovini, Danny Leipziger, Brian Levy, Maureen Lewis, Michael Lipton, Jennie Litvack, Laszlo Lovei, James Christopher Lovelace, Landis Mackellar, François Régis Mahieu, Nick Manning, Tamar Manuelyan Atinc, Timothy Marchant, Rachel Marcus, Tiffany Marlowe, Ricardo Martin, Will Martin, Antonio Martin del Campo, Keith Maskus, Andrew Mason, Simon Maxwell, Bill Mayville, Elizabeth McAllister, Milla McLachlan, John Mellor, Jean-Roger Mercier, Tom Merrick, Rick Messick, Dilip Mookherjee, William Moomaw, Michael Moore, Mick Moore, Jonathan Morduch, Daniel Morrow, Robert Moulie, Peter Mousley, Ranjana Mukherjee, Joseph Mullen, Rinku Murgai, Edmundo Murrugara, Philip Musgrove, David Nabarro, Mustapha Nabli, Reena Nanavaty, Deepa Narayan, Richard Newfarmer, Juan Pablo Nicolini, Michel Noel, Barbara Nunberg, Veronic Nyhan, Abena D. Oduro, Marcelo Olarreaga, Jonathan Olsson, Azedine Ouerghi, Mead Over, Margaret Owen, Howard Pack, Truman Packard, Sheila Page, Robert Palacios, Ok Pannenborg, Sulekha Patel, Harry Anthony Patrinos, Guillermo Perry, Jean Pesme, Patti Petesch, Guy Pfeffermann, Claire Pierangelo, Jean-Philippe Platteau, Boris Pleskovic, Louis Pouliquen, Alexander Preker, Giovanna Prennushi, William C. Prince, Lant Pritchett, Felicity Proctor, James Putzel, Dagmar Raczynski, Atiqur Rahman, Mamphela Ramphele, James Rauch, Martin Ravallion, Susan Razzaz, Thomas Reardon, Ritva Reinikka, Ana L. Revenga, Carolyn Reynolds, Helena Ribe, Michelle Riboud, Peter Roberts, Richard D. Robinson, Alberto Rodriguez, John Roemer, Halsey Rogers, Andrew Rogerson, Jaime Ros, Jaime Saavedra, Elisabeth Sadoulet, David E. Sahn, Joanne Salop, Susana Sanchez, Todd Sandler, Sven Sandstrom, Filomeno Santa Ana, Justine Sass, David Satterthwaite, Dieter Schelling, Anita Schwarz, Christopher Scott, Jennefer Sebstad, Marcelo Selowsky, Amartya Sen, Elena Serrano, Nemat Shafik, Shekhar Shah, Jim Shea, Geoffrey Shepherd, Lynne D. Sherburne-Benz, John D. Shilling, Paul Bennett Siegel, Hilary Silver, William Silverman, Marcia Simoes, John Sinclair, Saurabh Sinha, Richard Skolnick, Tova Maria Solo, Paul Spray, Lyn Squire, T. N. Srinivasan, Nicholas Stern, David Stiedl, David Stifel, Joseph E. Stiglitz, Kalanidhi Subbarao, Parita Videt Suebsaeng, Eric Valdeman Swanson, Vinaya Swaroop, Simon Szreter, Cecilia Tacoli, Kazuo Takahashi, Vito Tanzi (and the team at the Fiscal Affairs Department of the International Monetary Fund), David Tarr, Judith Tendler, Sumeet Thakur, Duncan Thomas, Kirsten Thompson, Robert Thompson, Erik Thorbecke, Mariano Tommasi, Lee Travers, Kerstin Trone, Carrie Tudor, Wendy Tyndale, Zafiris Tzannatos, Christopher Udry, Alberto Valdes, Dominique van de Walle, Julie van Domelen, M. Willem van Eeghen, Wouter van Ginneken, Warren Van Wicklin, Jan Vandemoortele, Krishna Vatsa, Anthony Venables, Mathew A. Verghis, Louis-Charles Viossat, Tara Vishwanath, Milan Vodopivec, Joachim von Amsberg, Jayshree Vyas, Robert Wade, Mike Waghorne, Adam Wagstaff, Michael Walton, Kevin Watkins (and an Oxfam team), Catherine Watt, Richard Webb, L. Alan Winters, Quentin Wodon, Adrian Wood, John Worley, Gustavo Yamada, Jacob Yaron, Shahid Yusuf, Roberto Zagha, and Elaine Zuckerman.

The team was assisted by students from the Internship Program of the Washington Center: Anju Aggarwal, Waldo Aleriano, Juan Carlos Arandia, Hector Cabrera, Mario de la Cruz, Celeste de la Huerta, Joaquin de la Torre, Alison Drury, Nilima Gulrajani, Tomoko Hagimoto, Daniel Hernandez Ruiz, Virginia Iglesias, Mika Iwasaki, Alejandra Lua, Felix Marklein, Nadia Montiel, Mark Schlueter, and Neil Thompson.

Despite efforts to be as comprehensive as possible in compiling the list above, some who contributed may have been inadvertently omitted. The team apologizes to any who were and reiterates its gratefulness to all who contributed.

Endnotes

Overview

Unless otherwise noted, all quotations in the overview are drawn from *Voices of the Poor* (Narayan, Chambers, Shah, and Petesch 2000; Narayan, Patel, Schafft, Rademacher, and Koch-Schulte 2000).

1. Sen 1999.
2. This account is of a visit by Ravi Kanbur, director of the report until May 2000.
3. Note that 1998 is the most recent year for which data are available. However, figures for 1998 are preliminary.
4. While these numbers provide a sense of broad trends, they should be treated with caution in light of the data shortcomings mentioned in chapter 1 and the fact that figures for 1998 are tentative because of the limited number of surveys available (see box 1.2).
5. Hanmer and Naschold 1999.
6. Hanmer and Naschold 1999; McGee 1999.
7. For a discussion of the relationship between environment and growth, see chapter 4 of World Bank (2000p).
8. For further information see the UNICEF statistical database at www.unicef.org/statis.

Chapter 1

Unless otherwise noted, all quotations in the chapter are drawn from *Voices of the Poor* (Narayan, Chambers, Shah, and Petesch 2000; Narayan, Patel, Schafft, Rademacher, and Koch-Schulte 2000).

1. Sen 1999, p. 87.
2. Szekély and others forthcoming.
3. Haddad and Kanbur 1990.
4. Ravallion and van de Walle 1991.
5. The poverty gap index is the sum of the income shortfalls of all poor people—the amount by which their incomes fall short of the poverty line—divided by the total population. The squared poverty gap index is the sum of the squared shortfalls. The poverty gap index is

$$\frac{1}{N}\sum_{i=1}^{Q}\left(\bar{y}-y_i\right)^{\alpha},$$

where N = the total population, $\bar{y}$ = the poverty line, y_i = income of individual i, Q = the total population below the poverty line, and α = 1. For the squared poverty gap index, α = 2. When α = 0, the measure is the well-known headcount ratio. See Foster, Greer, and Thorbecke (1984) and Foster and Shorrocks (1988).

6. Rowntree 1901.
7. World Bank 1999j.
8. For more details see the information on poverty reduction strategy papers at www.worldbank.org/poverty/strategies/index.htm.
9. Mecovi is Programa para el Mejoramiento de las Encuestas y la Medición de las Condiciones de Vida en America Latina y el Caribe (Program for the Improvement of Surveys and the Measurement of Living Conditions in Latin America and the Caribbean). See www.iadb.org/sds/pov.
10. Townsend 1985.
11. Atkinson and Bourguignon forthcoming; Chen and Ravallion 2000.
12. World Bank 1999t.
13. World Bank 2000l.
14. Demery 1999.
15. Wodon, Ayres, Barenstein, Lee, Peeters, Siaens, and Yitzhaki 2000.
16. The incidence of urban poverty in Colombia has increased steadily since 1996, however.
17. World Bank 2000e.
18. Suryahadi and others 1999. Poverty appears to have fallen from February 1996 to around the third quarter of 1997. There are several alternative estimates of Indonesian poverty, discussed in detail in Suryahadi and others (1999), but they tell a reasonably consistent story. The increase in the poverty rate from the lowest point (August–October 1997) to the highest (September–December 1998) is around 164 percent, which can be regarded as the maximum impact of the crisis on poverty. The poverty rate peaked around the middle of the second half of 1998, following the large surge in the price of rice and before the beginning of the stabilization of general inflation.
19. Data on the distribution of consumption are not available for both 1996 and 1998. Thus an estimate of consumption was

obtained by multiplying all incomes by the share of aggregate private consumption in national income based on national accounts data. Actual consumption data, available for 1998, suggest that the estimation procedures yield broadly accurate headcount ratios.

20. World Bank 1999bb.

21. World Bank 1999t.

22. Demery 1999.

23. Lustig 1998.

24. Yao 1999.

25. Minot 1998; Jalan and Ravallion 1999b.

26. Lopez and della Maggiora forthcoming.

27. Bonilla-Chacin and Hammer 1999.

28. Wagstaff forthcoming b.

29. Wagstaff forthcoming b.

30. World Bank 1998t.

31. World Bank 1999t.

32. Filmer and Pritchett 1998.

33. Filmer 1999b; Ghana Statistical Service 1999.

34. Liu, Hsiao, and Eggleston 1999.

35. Vella 1997.

36. World Bank forthcoming a.

37. Filmer 1999b.

38. World Bank 1998t.

39. In China ethnic minority groups make up less than 9 percent of the population, but are believed to account for about 40 percent of the remaining absolute poor (World Bank 2000e).

40. Psacharopoulos and Patrinos 1994.

41. Psacharopoulos and Patrinos 1994.

42. World Bank 1999s.

43. Gragnolati 1999.

44. U.S. Census Bureau 1999.

45. World Bank 1997g. A 1994 survey by the National Council of Applied Economic Research shows that in rural India roughly half the members of scheduled castes and scheduled tribes lived below the poverty line, and that while these groups represent about a third of the population, they make up 43 percent of poor people.

46. Kozel and Parker 2000; PROBE Team 1999; World Bank 1998t, table 2; World Bank 1999z, subnational database of India.

47. Drèze and Sen 1995.

48. Deaton 2000.

49. Baulch and Hoddinott forthcoming.

50. In addition, one caveat in interpreting these results is that the people who move frequently in and out of poverty may be primarily those whose income is permanently close to the poverty line. If that is the case, many who are considered transitorily poor could actually be chronically poor.

51. Jalan and Ravallion 1998b, 1999b.

52. Fields 1999.

53. Falkingham 1999.

54. Okrasa 1999.

55. Braithwaite 1997.

56. Klugman and Braithwaite 1998.

Chapter 2

Unless otherwise noted, all quotations in the chapter are drawn from *Voices of the Poor* (Narayan, Chambers, Shah, and Petesch 2000;

Narayan, Patel, Schafft, Rademacher, and Koch-Schulte 2000).

Reference material for this chapter is cited in the relevant chapters of the report rather than repeating it here.

Chapter 3

Unless otherwise noted, all quotations in the chapter are drawn from *Voices of the Poor* (Narayan, Chambers, Shah, and Petesch 2000; Narayan, Patel, Schafft, Rademacher, and Koch-Schulte 2000).

1. Lipton and Ravallion 1995.

2. Figures are in constant 1990 U.S. dollars adjusted for differences in purchasing power parity, as reported in Maddison (1995).

3. Bourguignon and Morrisson 1999.

4. Sen 1999.

5. On the effects of human capital on growth, see Barro (1997) and Bhargava and others (2000).

6. Summers 1993. There is debate on this. See Benhabib and Spiegel (1994), who find no effect of human capital growth on output growth, and Krueger and Lindahl (1999), who argue that the lack of association is due to measurement error.

7. See, for example, Mankiw, Romer, and Weil (1992), who find a consistently negative and sometimes significant effect of population growth on output growth consistent with the predictions of the Solow model. Levine and Renelt (1992) find more mixed evidence of the robustness of this result, while Kelley and Schmidt (1994) argue more strongly for a negative effect. Young (1995) and Bloom and Williamson (1997) provide evidence on the importance of demographic change for growth in East Asia.

8. On openness and growth, see Sachs and Warner (1995) and Frankel and Romer (1999). A critical review of the evidence is provided by Rodriguez and Rodrik (1999), and a rebuttal of this review can be found in Bhagwati and Srinivasan (1999). On fiscal policy and growth, see Easterly and Rebelo (1993). On inflation and growth, see Bruno and Easterly (1998) and Barro (1997). And on financial development and growth, see Levine (1997).

9. See Burnside and Dollar (forthcoming).

10. On civil unrest, terms of trade shocks, and growth, see Easterly and others (1993). On volatility and growth, see Ramey and Ramey (1995). And on slow trading partner growth, see Easterly (2000b).

11. On corruption and growth, see Mauro (1995). On rule of law and growth, see Kaufmann, Kraay, and Zoido-Lobaton (1999).

12. Rodrik 1998.

13. On ethnic fragmentation and growth, see Easterly and Levine (1997). On the role of institutions, see Easterly (2000a).

14. See Gallup, Sachs, and Mellinger (1999).

15. Ros 2000.

16. World Bank 2000p.

17. World Bank 1997c.

18. World Bank 1997a.

19. Royaume du Maroc, Ministère de la Prévision Economique et du Plan, Direction de la Statistique 1999; World Bank 2000j.

20. Bruno, Ravallion, and Squire 1998; Deininger and Squire 1996b; Ravallion and Chen 1997; Dollar and Kraay 2000.

21. Dollar and Kraay 2000.

22. Li, Squire, and Zou 1998.

23. World Bank 1997b.

24. Thorbecke and Jung 1996.

25. Bourguignon and Morrisson 1998.

26. Psacharopoulos and Patrinos 1994.

27. Banerjee and others 2000.

28. Birdsall and Londoño 1997; Deininger 1999a.

29. Ravallion 1998.

30. Thomas and Wang 1998; Klasen 1999; Dollar and Gatti 1999.

31. Alesina and Rodrik 1994; Persson and Tabellini 1994; Perotti 1996a; Clarke 1995; Deininger and Squire 1998 (with land inequality). Rodriguez (1999) provides a survey of the cross-country evidence.

32. Li and Zou 1998; Forbes forthcoming.

33. Banerjee and Duflo 2000.

34. World Bank 1993a; Pritchett and Summers 1996; Filmer and Pritchett 1999a; WHO 1999b; van Doorslaer and Wagstaff 1997; Gwatkin and others 2000; Schalick and others 2000; Wagstaff 2000; Wagstaff and Watanabe 2000; Kakwani 1993; Jamison and others 1996; Kim and Moody 1992; Anand and Ravallion 1993.

35. Behrman and Knowles 1997; Oxfam International 1999; Filmer and Pritchett 1999a; Behrman 1987; Hanushek and Kimko forthcoming; PROBE Team 1999.

36. Strauss and Thomas 1998.

37. Lavy and others 1996; Thomas, Lavy, and Strauss 1996.

38. Pritchett and Summers 1996.

39. Barro 1997; Bhargava and others 2000; Hamoudi and Sachs 1999.

40. Pritchett and Summers 1996.

41. On income inequality and average health, see Rodgers (1979), Flegg (1982), Waldmann (1992), and Filmer and Pritchett (1999a).

42. Anand and Ravallion 1993; Bidani and Ravallion 1996.

43. Drèze and Sen 1995.

44. Filmer and Prichett 1999a.

Chapter 4

Unless otherwise noted, all quotations in the chapter are drawn from *Voices of the Poor* (Narayan, Chambers, Shah, and Petesch 2000; Narayan, Patel, Schafft, Rademacher, and Koch-Schulte 2000).

1. Rodrik (2000) presents evidence that democratically elected governments are more likely to undertake reforms.

2. See Collier, Dollar, and Stern (2000) for a discussion of these shifting perspectives.

3. Eichengreen (1999), IDB (1997), and Tommasi and Velasco (1996) all provide careful discussions of the experience with reforms.

4. Tommasi and Velasco 1996.

5. Kornai (2000, p. 24–25) emphasizes this point and cautions against evaluations based on short-term results. "The transformation of society is not a horse race. The main indicator of success is not who passes the winning post first. Excessive emphasis on speed leads

to impatience, aggressiveness, and arrogance. . . . The transition from socialism to capitalism . . . is a trial and error process. . . . Each element in the process might be very rapid, fairly rapid or slow. Each has its own appropriate speed."

6. This point is emphasized in World Bank and IMF (2000b).

7. For Mexico, see Lustig (1998); for transition economies, see EDRB (1999).

8. Birdsall, Graham, and Sabot 1998.

9. IDB 1997.

10. Lindauer 1999.

11. World Bank 1996f.

12. Bajpai and Sachs 1999.

13. Easterly 2000b.

14. Berg and Taylor 2000.

15. Tommasi and Velasco (1996) suggest this classification of reforms and provide a thorough review of the political economy of reform.

16. Dollar and Kraay 2000; Gallup, Radelet, and Warner 1998. There is some debate, however, over the cross-country evidence on the distributional impact of trade liberalization. See, for example, Lundberg and Squire (2000).

17. See, for example, Morley (1999) and Dollar and Kraay (2000).

18. World Bank 2000l.

19. Haltiwanger and Singh 1999.

20. de Ferranti and others 2000.

21. This discussion draws heavily from Meerman (1997).

22. Sarris 1994; Alderman 1994.

23. Winters 1999.

24. This discussion draws heavily on Akiyama and others (forthcoming).

25. Sahn, Dorosh, and Younger 1997.

26. Sahn, Dorosh, and Younger 1997.

27. World Bank 2000l.

28. World Bank 2000l.

29. Kemal 1994.

30. Hanson and Harrison 1999.

31. Freeman 1995.

32. The country studies are Vélez, Kugler, and Bouillón (1999) for Colombia; Contreras and others (2000) and Legovini, Bouillón, and Lustig (1999) for Mexico; and Ruprah and Marcano (1999) for Venezuela. Also see Revenga (1997).

33. Berman and Machin 2000.

34. Pessino (1997) provides evidence on how labor market regulations hindered labor market adjustment in Argentina in the 1990s.

35. Papageorgiou, Choksi, and Michaely 1995.

36. Haltiwanger and Vodopivec 1999.

37. CUTS 1999.

38. Parker, Riopelle, and Steel 1995.

39. Birdsall and de la Torre (2000) provide a valuable discussion of regulatory burdens in Latin America.

40. Hallberg 1999.

41. Hallberg 1999.

42. Asia Foundation and AKATIGA 1999.

43. SEWA 1997.

44. Haan, Coad, and Lardinois 1998.

45. Chisari, Estache, and Romero 1999.

46. ILO 2000.

47. Basu 1999a.

48. Examples of such programs include Progresa (Programa de Educación, Salud y Alimentación, or Program of Education, Health, and Nutrition) in Mexico and Bolsa Escola in Brazil. Tzannatos (1998) shows that different incentives may be required to keep children of different ages in school.

49. Martin and Maskus (2000) review the economic arguments for core labor standards with an emphasis on implications for trade. Aidt, Schlemmer-Schulte, and Tzannatos (2000) provide a lengthy review of the empirical evidence on the benefits of the right to unionize and bargain collectively.

50. Pencavel (1997) reviews arguments that the gains won by unionized workers come at the expense of nonunionized workers rather than from profits.

51. It is increasingly clear that it is counterproductive to use trade sanctions as an international enforcement mechanism for core labor standards, as the costs of such sanctions are too often borne by the poor. See Marcus (2000) for a review of arguments.

52. Sable, O'Rourke, and Fung 2000.

53. Levine 1997.

54. Bennett, Goldberg, and Hunte 1996.

55. Adams 1984; Paxton and Cuevas 1996.

56. See von Pischke, Adams, and Donald 1984; Yaron, Benjamin, and Piprek (1997); Braverman and Guasch (1993).

57. See Chaves and Gonzalez-Vega (1996) and Yaron (1992), for example.

58. Morduch 1999c.

59. Chaves and Sánchez 2000; Sánchez 2000.

60. See, for example, Khandker (1998) and Morduch (1999b).

61. Hulme and Mosley 1996.

62. Morduch 1999c.

63. For example, the subsidy dependence index, developed in Yaron (1992), measures the extent to which the lending interest rate would have to be raised to cover all operating costs in the absence of subsidies.

Chapter 5

Unless otherwise noted, all quotations in the chapter are drawn from *Voices of the Poor* (Narayan, Chambers, Shah, and Petesch 2000; Narayan, Patel, Schafft, Rademacher, and Koch-Schulte 2000).

1. Wagstaff 2000.

2. Ghana Statistical Service 1999; Filmer 1999b.

3. Instituto Nacional de Estadística y Censos 1998.

4. van de Walle 2000a.

5. Barnes, van der Plas, and Floor 1997.

6. Levy 1996. Strong associations are often found between roads and social indicators, though the direction of causality is unclear (van de Walle 2000b).

7. China raised about 5.8 percent of GDP in central government revenues, while India raised 12.2 percent (World Bank 2000s).

8. Ahmad and Stern (1987) calculated the additional cost of raising a rupee through the sales tax in India as 60 paise. Devarajan,

Suthiwart-Narueput, and Thierfelder (2000) calculated the cost of raising Cameroon's export tax as 1.7 times the revenue raised.

9. The debt levels of the 41 heavily indebted poor countries on average far exceed their GDP and are about twice the levels considered to be sustainable (van Trotsenburg and MacArthur 1999).

10. UNICEF and Oxfam International 1999.

11. Gupta, Schiff, and Clements 1996.

12. On average in 18 heavily indebted poor countries the share of military spending in GDP fell by the same amount (0.6 percent) as the increase in the share of education and health spending (IMF 1999).

13. Costa Rica shows that low military spending need not compromise external or internal security.

14. Experience varied across regions, however. There were large increases in real per capita spending on education and health in Asia and Latin America and the Caribbean. In Sub-Saharan Africa per capita spending fell in education and rose only moderately in health. In transition economies both education and health spending declined sharply (Gupta, Clements, and Tiongson 1998).

15. Patrinos and Ariasingam 1997.

16. Benefit incidence analysis is a well-established tool for understanding who benefits from public spending, but it has limitations. Average benefits, even when correctly measured, may not be a reliable guide to the change in aggregate spending on a given program or to the distributional impact of a reallocation between programs. Program participation may be nonhomogeneous, causing the marginal impacts of program expansion or contraction to differ greatly from the average impacts (Lanjouw and Ravallion 1999).

17. van de Walle 1996.

18. In Croatia in 1998 more than 90 percent of the energy subsidy went to nonpoor households. In Russia in 1997 about 74 percent of the water subsidy went to middle- and high-income consumers. In both cases subsidies increased rather than reduced inequality (Lovei and others 2000).

19. World Bank 1994e.

20. Lewis 2000.

21. In some cases child labor may be a consequence rather than a cause of children being out of school (Oxfam International 1999).

22. Bredie and Beehary 1998.

23. Oxfam International 1999.

24. Azandossessi 2000; Pouliquen 1999b.

25. Constance 1999.

26. Barnes and Halpern 2000.

27. Barnes, van der Plas, and Floor 1997.

28. In energy, for example, the prospects of better services for many poor people in the foreseeable future will depend on finding cheaper off-grid sources (Villagran 2000).

29. Programa de Educación, Salud y Alimentación, or Program of Education, Health, and Nutrition.

30. Nolan and Turbut 1995.

31. Gilson 1998.

32. Nyonator and Kutzin 1999.

33. Gertler and Hammer 1997.

34. World Bank 1996a.

35. Boland and Whittington 2000.

36. This is the case for water supply in Jakarta, Indonesia (Boland and Whittington 2000).

37. Lovei and others 2000.

38. Barnes, van der Plas, and Floor 1997.

39. Irwin 1997.

40. World Bank 1998t.

41. Gertler and Solon 1998.

42. Filmer, Hammer, and Pritchett 1998.

43. Chomitz and others (1998) show that the pay differential needed to get medical personnel to outer areas in Indonesia is several times any realistic amount.

44. See www.worldbank.org/html/extdr/hnp/health/ppi/contents.htm.

45. Girishankar 1999a.

46. World Bank 1998t; Filmer, Hammer, and Pritchett 1998.

47. van der Gaag 1995.

48. World Bank 1998t.

49. World Bank 1998t; Bonilla-Chacin and Hammer 1999.

50. Filmer, Hammer, and Pritchett 1998.

51. Better communications also have a positive impact on social capital (Pouliquen 1999a).

52. World Bank 1998aa.

53. Izaguirre 1999. More than 90 developing countries opened their telecommunications sector to private participation in 1990–98.

54. Osiptel 1996.

55. For more on telecenters in Senegal, see www.idrc.ca/acacia/engine/eng_6.htm and www.sonatel.sn/c-telece.htm.

56. World Bank 1994e.

57. Ernberg 1998.

58. Subsidies may be required in telecommunications and such sectors as water and energy (Wellenius 1997; Barnes and Halpern 2000).

59. Wellenius 1997.

60. Wallsten 1999.

61. Chisari, Estache, and Romero 1999.

62. Ravallion and Wodon forthcoming.

63. Gaynor 1996.

64. World Bank 1995b.

65. Gaynor 1998.

66. King and Özler 1998.

67. Gaynor 1996.

68. Gaynor 1998.

69. Jimenez and Paqueo 1996.

70. World Bank 1995b.

71. World Bank 1995b.

72. Oxfam International 1999.

73. Jimenez and Sawada 1998.

74. Educo's failure to raise standardized test scores in mathematics and languages may reflect the absence of direct incentives for teachers, parents, and parent-teacher associations to do so (Jimenez and Sawada 1998).

75. These concerns include increased difficulties in implementing systemwide education policies, enforcing broader national objectives, avoiding social segregation, and promoting equity if schools accept students based on ability to pay (World Bank 1995b).

76. Pouliquen 1999b.

77. The Orangi project was founded in 1980 by the commu-

nity organizer Akhter Hameed Khan (World Bank 1992b). Knowing the tradeoff between ownership and speed of implementation, he allowed the participatory decisionmaking processes to take all the time needed.

78. Pouliquen 1999a.

79. Barwell 1996.

80. White 1997.

81. Walker and others 1999.

82. Pouliquen 1999a.

83. Rawlings, Sherburne-Benz, and van Domelen forthcoming.

84. Sara and Katz 1997.

85. Tendler and Freedheim 1994.

86. Since 1987 the World Bank has approved funding for about 100 multisectoral social fund–type projects worth a total of $3.4 billion in more than 60 countries (Parker and Serrano forthcoming). Many other donors are also supporting social funds.

87. While choice among investments can help ensure sustainability, unrestricted choice is rare in multisectoral projects. Yet a truly demand-driven approach requires an open menu of investments.

88. Community ownership is difficult to instill for infrastructure that serves many communities. Such infrastructure is usually better managed by local or higher-level government (Malmberg Calvo 1998).

89. Social funds are cross-sectoral financing mechanisms that focus on poor communities but also channel grants to local governments and NGOs. Originally emergency financing mechanisms, they have evolved into long-term mechanisms for development financing (chapter 8). A common pitfall is to assume that social fund projects provide open choice. Some studies of social funds indicate that the menus of eligible projects may not be inclusive enough and that projects may be too narrowly defined (Owen and van Domelen 1998; Walker and others 1999).

90. Pouliquen 1999a.

91. Owen and van Domelen 1998.

92. Carvalho 1999a.

93. In Zimbabwe a study showed that roughly 35 percent of income in rural households comes from freely provided environmental goods and that the share increases as income declines (Cavendish 1999).

94. Uphoff 1998.

95. In 1990 the government of India issued a circular to state governments recommending the adoption of joint forest management on areas of state forestland. By 1995, 15 states had adopted such programs, involving local communities in managing and protecting forestlands in return for rights to use specified forest products (Arnold forthcoming).

96. For example, allowing village communities to own neighborhood forests and grasslands while the government owns far-off forestlands (Murty 1994).

97. Arnold forthcoming.

98. Arnold forthcoming.

99. In addition, very high population growth rates may so reduce the benefits to members that their incentive to participate is eroded.

100. Uphoff 1998.

101. A forestry project in Nepal allowed user communities to take over forest management, following approval of forest man-

agement plans, and issued certificates ensuring long-term rights to forest benefits (World Bank 1989).

102. Experience also shows that community participation is higher when appropriate technologies allow for an adequate return from activities. For example, fuelwood plantations that use closely spaced planting, which results in poor survival rates for trees, elicit low levels of community involvement. By contrast, community participation is high when trees are planted farther apart and the plantations allow for an annual income flow from nontimber products (agricultural intercrops, fodder or thatch grass, commercially valuable seeds or leaves; Banarjee and others 1997).

103. Devising effective, autonomous, and honest court systems is as important as designing appropriate property rights systems (Ostrom forthcoming).

104. Banarjee and others 1997.

105. Carney 1998.

106. Banarjee and others 1997.

107. Women and children are often the primary collectors of fuel and fodder for home consumption and sale to urban markets and so act as de facto managers of forests. Forest products are especially important where women and children are unable to obtain sufficient income from agriculture or wage employment and few other options exist (Arnold forthcoming). In such cases forest-related activities are likely to be labor intensive and household based (Arnold 1998).

108. Agarwal 1997.

109. Agarwal 1997.

110. Carney 1998.

111. de Janvry, Gordillo, Platteau, and Sadoulet forthcoming.

112. de Janvry, Gordillo, Platteau, and Sadoulet forthcoming. A secure land title facilitates access to credit and induces more environment-friendly farming practices, particularly in forest areas. It also provides an incentive to invest in productivity-enhancing techniques and improve local infrastructure (Hoff, Braverman, and Stiglitz 1993; Schneider 1995).

113. Deininger and Binswanger 1999. Secure property rights are also a major issue for the urban poor.

114. de Janvry, Platteau, Gordillo, and Sadoulet forthcoming.

115. Mearns (1999) distinguishes individuals' rights, claims, or interests in land according to whether they may be legally upheld under prevailing law (strict legality), are socially perceived to be legitimate regardless of their strict legality (social legitimacy), or are exercised in practice and therefore translate into effective control over land (effective control).

116. Mearns 1999. Sharma and Drèze (1996), however, found that in Palanpur, India, tenancy has lost much of its equalizing influence. As agriculture has become more capital intensive, there has been growing equality between landlords and tenants, in part reflecting the exclusion of the landless from tenancy contracts and the increased leasing-in by large landowners.

117. Parthasarthy as cited in Mearns (1999).

118. de Janvry, Gordillo, Platteau, and Sadoulet forthcoming.

119. Platteau and Baland forthcoming.

120. Sadoulet, Murgai, and de Janvry forthcoming. See box 4.4 in chapter 4.

121. Mearns 1999.

122. de Janvry, Gordillo, Platteau, and Sadoulet forthcoming.

123. Deininger 1999b.

124. de Janvry, Gordillo, Platteau, and Sadoulet forthcoming.

125. Deininger forthcoming.

126. de Janvry, Gordillo, Platteau, and Sadoulet forthcoming.

127. Many local suppliers have network services that undersell even subsidized public companies (Solo 1998a).

128. The number of large-scale water and sanitation management contracts, leases, concessions, and divestitures in developing countries increased from 4 in 1993 to 29 in 2000. Private investment in the sector peaked in 1997 at $8.4 billion (Roger 1999).

129. The main reason for this performance is the good fit between the institutional endowment, with the long-standing acceptance of private participation, and the guarantees it provides to investors (Menard and Clarke 2000).

130. Brook Cowen and Tynan 1999.

131. The system sought to cover costs through industrial cross-subsidies, but the resulting tariffs were so high that most industries opted out. While service declined to all users, poor households—both served and unserved—suffered the most (Yepes 1999).

132. Price reforms should be implemented before switching to private providers or introducing programs to increase public utility efficiency (World Bank forthcoming b).

133. If needed in countries where connections are few, subsidies should be used for new connections, not for consumption. Where connections are widespread, such as in many countries in Eastern Europe and the former Soviet Union, well-designed block tariffs can be more pro-poor (Lovei and others 2000).

134. Brook Cowen 1997. Regulatory structures need to be both sufficiently rigid to provide investors and managers with the certainty they need to judge long-term profitability and sufficiently flexible to adjust to changing conditions (Savedoff and Spiller 1999).

135. While much effort has gone into regulation to stop utilities from abusing their monopoly power, relatively little has been done to reduce that monopoly power (Webb and Ehrhardt 1998).

136. Brook Cowen and Tynan 1999.

137. World Bank 1998o.

Chapter 6

Unless otherwise noted, all quotations in the chapter are drawn from *Voices of the Poor* (Narayan, Chambers, Shah, and Petesch 2000; Narayan, Patel, Schafft, Rademacher, and Koch-Schulte 2000).

1. Skocpol 1992; Bates 1989; North 1990.

2. World Bank 1997l.

3. Evans and Rauch 1999.

4. Woo-Cumings 1999; Evans 1999; Cheng, Haggard, and Kang 1999.

5. Collier forthcoming.

6. van Rijckeghem and Weder 1997; Adams 1998.

7. Wade 1985.

8. Grandvoinnet and Tamesis 2000.

9. Ablo and Reinikka 1998.

10. Paul 1998.

11. *Marchés Tropicaux et Méditerranéens* 1995.

12. IRIS-USAID 1996.

13. Wei 1999a, 1999b.

14. Tanzi and Davoodi 1997; Gupta, Davoodi, and Alonso-Terme 1998; Gray and Kaufmann 1998.

15. Norton 1998.

16. Grandvoinnet 2000.

17. Berkovitz, Pistor, and Rischard 1999; Posner 1997.

18. Bouderbala and Pascon 1970.

19. Dakolias 1996.

20. Dakolias 1996.

21. Garro 1999.

22. World Bank 1999a.

23. Dakolias 1996.

24. Asia Foundation [www.asiafoundation.org].

25. Mc Clymont and Golub 2000.

26. Dakolias 1996.

27. Manning 1999.

28. Michael Anderson 1999; Manning 1999.

29. Yost 1999.

30. Bardhan 1997b.

31. Bardhan 1997b; R. Adams 1986.

32. Ranis and Stewart 1994.

33. Tommasi and Weischelbaum 1999.

34. Ranis and Stewart 1994.

35. King and Ozler 1998.

36. Bardhan 1997b.

37. Brown and Oates 1987.

38. Hsiao 1995.

39. EIU 1999a.

40. Crook and Sverisson 1999.

41. Fisman and Gatti 1999; Treisman 1998.

42. World Bank 2000l.

43. Foner 1989.

44. Ravallion 1999b, forthcoming; Litvack and Rondinelli 1999.

45. Bardhan 1997b; Bardhan and Mookherjee 1999; Harriss 1999; Drèze and Sen 1995; Burki, Perry, and Dillinger 1999.

46. Blair 2000.

47. Manor 1999.

48. World Bank 1996b.

49. Owen and van Domelen 1998.

50. Fox 1995.

51. Adato and others 1999.

52. World Bank 1999b.

53. Bhatt 2000.

54. Moore and Putzel 1999.

55. Skocpol 1992.

56. Moore and Putzel 1999.

57. Huntington and Nelson 1976.

58. Uvin 1995.

59. Paerregaard 1998.

60. Bebbington 1996.

61. Riddell and Robinson 1995.

62. Brown and Ashman 1996.

63. Bebbington 1996.

64. van de Walle forthcoming; Narayan, Chambers, Shah, and Petesch 1999; Narayan, Patel, Schafft, Rademacher, and Koch-Schulte 2000.

65. Das Gupta, Grandvoinnet, and Romani forthcoming.

66. For Brazil, see Tendler (1997); for Korea, Whang (1981); and for Taiwan, China, Fei, Ranis, and Kuo (1979).

67. Coirolo 2000.

68. Coirolo 2000.

69. Sen 1997b.

70. Sen 1999.

71. The empirical result shown in figure 6.6, however, has to be taken with caution. It could also be the case that higher growth leads to institutions of better quality. Nevertheless, historical analysis reveals that the creation of some foundational institutions (property rights, for example) was key in the process of development.

72. For example, Sah (1991), Bardhan (1997b), Harriss (1999), Varshney (1999a), Niles (1999), and Moore and Putzel (1999).

73. Alesina and Rodrik 1994; Barro 1996b; Brunetti 1997; Campos 1994; Bardhan 1999a.

74. Johnson 1982; Wade 1991; H. Stein 1999; Woo-Cumings 1999.

75. Acemoglu and Robinson 1999.

76. Dethier 1999.

77. Rodrik 1999a.

78. Collier 1999c; Collier and Gunning 1999.

79. Sen 1997b; Besley and Burgess 2000.

80. Diamond, Linz, and Lipset 1988; Joseph 1999.

81. Bardhan and Mookherjee 1999.

82. Li, Steele, and Glewwe 1999. See also Castro-Leal and others (1999).

83. Przeworski and Limongi 1993; Bratton and van de Walle 1997; Sah 1991; Varshney 1999a.

84. Burki and Perry 1998.

85. de Waal 1999.

86. Drèze and Sen 1995.

87. Joshi and Moore forthcoming.

Chapter 7

Unless otherwise noted, all quotations in the chapter are drawn from *Voices of the Poor* (Narayan, Chambers, Shah, and Petesch 2000; Narayan, Patel, Schafft, Rademacher, and Koch-Schulte 2000).

1. Briggs 1998; Hirschman 1984.

2. Banton 1999.

3. World Faiths Development Dialogue 2000.

4. This section draws heavily on World Bank (forthcoming a) for examples and other materials.

5. Das Gupta 1995, 1999; Goody 1976, 1990.

6. World Bank forthcoming a.

7. Gray and Kevane 1996; Deere and Leon 1997; Agarwal 1994; Saito, Mekonen, and Spurling 1994.

8. KIHASA and UNDP 1998; Kim 1991.

9. Das Gupta and others 2000.

10. World Bank forthcoming a.

11. UNDP 1995.

12. Filmer 1999b.

13. Quisumbing 1994; Chi and others 1998; Saito and Spurling 1992.

14. Sen and Drèze 1989; Coale 1991; Klasen 1994.

15. Das Gupta and others 1997; Zeng and others 1993.

16. Jejeebhoy 1995.

17. Ren 1996; Das Gupta 1995.

18. Hobcraft 1993; Hill and King 1995; Klasen 1999.

19. Joshi and others 1999.

20. Thomas 1990, 1997.

21. Khandker 1998.

22. Jejeebhoy 1995.

23. Dollar and Gatti 1999.

24. Klasen 1999.

25. Saito, Mekonen, and Spurling 1994; Quisumbing 1994; Due and Gladwin 1991.

26. Quisumbing 1996.

27. Udry and others 1995; Udry 1996.

28. Gopal 1999.

29. World Bank forthcoming a.

30. Sen 1999; Singh 1999.

31. Jones 1998.

32. Das Gupta and others 2000; Agarwal 1994.

33. Agarwal 1994; Andors 1983; Das Gupta and others 2000; Davin 1976, 1995; Uberoi 1999; Wolf 1985.

34. Deere and Leon 1999.

35. Pitt and Khandker 1998.

36. Besley and Coate 1995.

37. Khandker, Khalily, and Khan 1996.

38. Rhyne and Holt 1994.

39. See World Bank (forthcoming a).

40. Wade 1987.

41. Psacharopoulos and Patrinos 1994.

42. However, spatial poverty traps can (and do) emerge purely out of the interaction of factor market imperfections with externalities. See Jalan and Ravallion (1999a).

43. Borjas 1992.

44. Jones 1998.

45. Borjas 1997; Borjas and Sueyoshi 1997; Turok 1999.

46. Davey Smith and others 1998; Lowell and Wood 1998; Meerman 1999.

47. The strongest empirical evidence for this comes from poor urban communities in the United States. See, among others, Wilson (1996) and Sampson, Morenhoff, and Earls (1999).

48. Herbst 1999.

49. van Nieuwkoop and Uquillas 2000.

50. Bardhan 1997a; Coate and Loury 1993.

51. The distinction between the two types of affirmative action policies is made powerfully by Loury (2000).

52. Coate and Loury 1993; Steele 1999.

53. Holzer and Neumark 1999.

54. Bardhan 1997a.

55. Horowitz 1999.

56. Borjas 1997; Casella and Rauch 1997.

57. Bates 1999.

58. Alesina and La Ferrara 1999.

59. Turton 1997.

60. See Alesina, Baqir, and Easterly (1998) on U.S. cities.

61. Collier and Garg 1999.

62. Brockerhoff and Hewett 1998.

63. Varshney 1999b.

64. Anderson 1983.

65. Monnet 1988.

66. Austin 1999; Reno 1998.

67. Gurr and others 1993.

68. See Chua (1998) on "ethno-nationalism" in Kazakhstan, the Philippines, South Africa, Thailand, and Vietnam.

69. Easterly 2000a.

70. Collier and Hoeffler 2000; Woolcock, Pritchett, and Isham 1999.

71. IDB 2000, p. 27. Of 26 countries in the region, only four have adequate data on Afro-Latin populations: Bolivia, Brazil, Guatemala, and Peru.

72. Gittell and Vidal 1998; Narayan 1999.

73. Fine 1999.

74. Woolcock 2000.

75. Kozel and Parker 2000.

76. Barr 1998, 1999. See also van Dijk and Rabellotti (1997).

77. Fafchamps and Minten 1999.

78. Grootaert 1999b; Grootaert and Narayan 2000; Grootaert, Oh, and Swamy 1999. For an overview of these studies, see Grootaert (1999a).

79. Narayan and Nyamwaya 1996.

80. Bebbington and Carroll 2000.

81. Fernandez 1994.

82. Singerman 1995.

83. Tendler 1997.

84. Uphoff 1992.

85. World Bank forthcoming c.

86. Fox 1992; Bebbington 1999.

Chapter 8

Unless otherwise noted, all quotations in the chapter are drawn from *Voices of the Poor* (Narayan, Chambers, Shah, and Petesch 2000; Narayan, Patel, Schafft, Rademacher, and Koch-Schulte 2000).

1. Deaton 1997; Townsend 1995; Udry 1991.

2. The recurring nature of shocks is also referred to as the degree of autocorrelation. Deaton (1991) develops a theoretical model showing the effect of repeated shocks on buffer stock behavior.

3. Some downward income fluctuations are predictable, such as preharvest food shortages in rural areas. While this food shortfall is strictly speaking not a risk (although its magnitude may be uncertain), households will still try to smooth consumption, and this carries costs. They may need to borrow, to build and fill a grain store, or to call on a social network for support, activities that may be harder for the poor (Sinha and Lipton 1999). Poor farmers may be forced to "presell" their crops to wealthier farmers or middlemen at below-market prices (Search 1999). Similarly, income declines associated with old age are often predictable, but their magnitude may not be because of uncertainties of health and life expectancy. The chapter's discussion of risk management includes management of predictable fluctuations because many of the tools available for dealing with risk also help households smooth predictable fluctuations.

4. Townsend 1994.

5. Rosenzweig and Binswanger 1993.

6. Dercon 1999; Kinsey, Burger, and Gunning 1998.

7. Rosenzweig and Binswanger 1993.

8. Jalan and Ravallion 1997a.

9. Baulch and Hoddinott forthcoming.

10. Gaiha and Deolalikar 1993.

11. Maluccio, Haddad, and May 1999; Glewwe and Hall 1998.

12. Ravallion 1988.

13. Severe poverty was measured by the squared poverty gap index (Jalan and Ravallion 1997a).

14. Grootaert, Kanbur, and Oh 1997; Jalan and Ravallion 1999c; Lokshin and Ravallion 2000a.

15. Lokshin and Ravallion 2000a.

16. Dercon and Krishnan 2000a.

17. The three-tiered framework of risk reduction, risk mitigation, and coping is developed in Holzmann and Jorgensen (2000) and World Bank (2000q). Some of the literature on risk uses a different classification that labels only ex ante strategies as "risk management" and ex post strategies as "coping." Risk management is seen as all efforts at reducing income variability (diversification, migration). Coping consists of consumption smoothing, either across time (borrowing, self-insurance, saving) or across households (risk sharing, through formal or informal insurance). See Alderman and Paxson (1992).

18. Households diversify their income sources not only to deal with risk but also to increase income. Through such activities as intercropping and seasonally varying their labor supply, households increase their mean income and in some cases may reduce their risk as well (Dercon 1999).

19. Reardon 1997.

20. Fafchamps, Udry, and Czukas 1998.

21. Dercon 1999.

22. Reardon 1997; Dercon and Krishnan 1996.

23. Adams 1995.

24. Adams 1999.

25. Morduch 1990.

26. Dercon 1996.

27. Sinha and Lipton 1999.

28. The theoretical model of precautionary saving and asset building is discussed in Deaton (1991) and Dercon (1999).

29. The covariance between asset values and income is not just a problem for the poor. As the recent East Asian experience has shown, an economic crisis usually coincides with a collapse of the securities market, undercutting the use of financial assets for precautionary purposes.

30. Dercon 1999.

31. Fafchamps, Udry, and Czukas 1998.

32. Dercon 1998.

33. Lim and Townsend 1998.

34. Jalan and Ravallion 1998a.

35. Morduch 1999a.

36. Dercon 1999. The extent to which marginal utilities are equalized depends on the internal homogeneity of the network.

37. Wider networks may find it more difficult to enforce the reciprocal obligations among members, however.

38. Morduch 1999a.

39. Dercon 1999; Coate and Ravallion 1993.

40. Ravallion and Chaudhuri 1997; Deaton 1997; Townsend 1995; McDonald, Schiller, and Ueda 1999.

41. Jalan and Ravallion 1997a; Townsend 1994.

42. See, for example, Kochar (1999) and Jacoby and Skoufias (1997) for India, Moser (1998) for Ecuador and Zambia, and Dercon (1999) for Ethiopia.

43. Migration is a coping strategy but also serves insurance and income diversification purposes. Of course, much migration takes place for reasons other than risk management. A detailed discussion of the role of migration (domestic and international) is beyond the scope of this chapter.

44. Udry 1999.

45. Foster 1995.

46. E. Rose 1999.

47. Foster 1995.

48. Behrman 1988.

49. Behrman and Deolalikar 1990.

50. E. Rose 1999.

51. Dercon and Krishnan 2000b; Behrman and Deolalikar 1990.

52. Sinha and Lipton 1999; Lanjouw and Stern 1991.

53. FAO 1995. The effects of AIDS may change the customary treatment of widows. In a Tanzanian village AIDS widows are no longer dispossessed, so that they can take care of the many AIDS orphans and compensate for the reduction in the male labor supply (Rugalema 1999).

54. Alderman and Gertler 1997.

55. Grootaert 1998.

56. Jacoby and Skoufias 1997.

57. Narayan, Chambers, Shah, and Petesch 2000.

58. Foster 1995.

59. Hoddinott and Kinsey 1998.

60. Zimmerman and Carter 1999.

61. Barrett and Carter 1999; Grootaert and Kanbur 1995a.

62. This priority ranking reflects a concern for preventing the hardship and deprivation that frequently result from shocks, especially for the poor. It does not imply that all risk should be eliminated, because this would have strong, undesirable incentive effects. In the extreme, the absence of all income risk would lead to an incentive to undertake no activity at all—the essence of the moral hazard problem (Devarajan and Hammer 1997).

63. This three-pronged policy response to risk is elaborated further in Holzmann and Jorgensen (2000).

64. World Bank 1998t.

65. Zaman 1999.

66. World Bank 2000q.

67. Dercon 1999.

68. Holzmann and Jorgensen 2000.

69. Cox and Jimenez 1998.

70. Jensen 1998.

71. Cox and Jimenez 1998.

72. Morduch 1999a.

73. Morduch 1999a; Jensen 1998.

74. Dercon 1999.

75. Deaton 1991.

76. Morduch 1999a; Baulch and Hoddinott forthcoming.

77. Dercon 1999.

78. Dercon 1999.

79. Sinha and Lipton 1999.

80. Besley 1995a; Sebstad and Cohen 1999.

81. Sinha and Lipton 1999.

82. Walker and Ryan 1990.

83. Sinha and Lipton 1999.

84. Moral hazard, in this context, means the possibility that people will engage in riskier behavior once they know the risk is insured. Adverse selection refers to the tendency of people most exposed to a certain risk to apply for insurance.

85. Sinha and Lipton 1999.

86. Holzmann, Packard, and Cuesta 1999.

87. Lund and Srinivas 1999b.

88. Holzmann, Packard, and Cuesta 1999.

89. Birdsall and Hecht 1995.

90. Gertler 2000.

91. Gertler and Gruber 1997.

92. Prescott and Pradhan 1999.

93. Gertler 2000.

94. Gertler 2000.

95. World Bank 1998t.

96. Part of the difficulty in measuring the incidence of disability stems from definitional confusion. The World Health Organization (WHO 1980) defines disability as any restriction or lack (resulting from an impairment) of the ability to perform an activity considered normal for a human being. What constitutes "normal" activity is clearly open to debate. In addition, many surveys measure impairment rather than disability. And there is a long-standing debate on whether a corrected impairment constitutes a disability. See the discussion in Elwan (1999).

97. Elwan 1999.

98. Khan and Durkin 1995.

99. Andersson, Palha da Sousa, and Paredes 1995.

100. Abu-Habib 1997; Harris-White 1996.

101. Andersson, Palha da Sousa, and Paredes 1995.

102. Elwan 1999.

103. Flanagan 1999.

104. By comparison, in OECD countries pension coverage is 85 percent of the labor force (Palacios and Pallares-Miralles 1999).

105. Palacios and Pallares-Miralles 1999.

106. Holzmann, Packard, and Cuesta 1999.

107. World Bank 1994b. In some circumstances the defined-contribution pillar could also be managed publicly.

108. Holzmann, Packard, and Cuesta 1999.

109. Holzmann, Packard, and Cuesta 1999; James 2000.

110. James 2000.

111. Flanagan 1999.

112. Flanagan 1999; Grootaert and Braithwaite 1998; World Bank forthcoming a.

113. Extensive discussions of child labor issues and policies can be found in Grootaert and Kanbur (1995a), Grootaert and Patrinos (1999), and Fallon and Tzannatos (1998). Also see chapter 4.

114. World Bank 1995c, 2000q; Dar and Tzannatos 1999.

115. World Bank 1995c.

116. Grootaert and Braithwaite 1998.

117. World Bank 2000q.

118. van Ginneken 1999.

119. World Bank 2000q.

120. Grootaert and Braithwaite 1998.

121. Ravallion 1991; Baulch and Hoddinott forthcoming.

122. Wodon 2000b.

123. Wodon and Minowa 2000.

124. Subbarao 1997.

125. This diversity of objectives means that social funds can be a delivery vehicle for a wide range of programs. In that sense they differ from specific interventions, such as pensions or health insurance, discussed elsewhere in the chapter.

126. Jorgensen and van Domelen 1999; Frigenti, Harth, and Huque 1998; Bigio 1998.

127. Jorgensen and van Domelen 1999; Frigenti, Harth, and Huque 1998.

128. van Domelen and Owen 1998.

129. Ravallion and Wodon forthcoming.

130. Sebstad and Cohen 1999; Lipton 1998.

131. Sebstad and Cohen (1999) provide many sources documenting these different uses of loans.

132. Zaman 1999.

133. Sebstad and Cohen 1999.

134. The specific roles government, donors, and NGOs should play in the delivery of microfinance remains an open question. Experiences across countries vary widely. But programs operated directly by governments tend to have higher default rates (Morduch 1999a).

135. Sebstad and Cohen 1999.

136. Morduch 1999a, 1999c; Zeller 1999.

137. Subbarao and others 1997.

138. World Bank 1999n.

139. IDB 2000. Progresa is Programa de Educación, Salud y Alimentación, or Program of Education, Health, and Nutrition.

140. Filmer and others 1998.

Chapter 9

Unless otherwise noted, all quotations in the chapter are drawn from *Voices of the Poor* (Narayan, Chambers, Shah, and Petesch 2000; Narayan, Patel, Schafft, Rademacher, and Koch-Schulte 2000).

1. Joint Commonwealth Secretariat–World Bank Task Force on the Small States 2000.

2. World Bank 2000l.

3. See, for example, Lustig (forthcoming), World Bank (1999j), Poppele, Sumarto, and Pritchett (1999), Reyes and Mandap (1999), and Lokshin and Ravallion (2000b).

4. The estimates for Indonesia should be treated cautiously, as the large devaluations of the rupiah made it difficult to estimate price levels, particularly in rural areas.

5. de Janvry and Sadoulet 2000a.

6. See Lustig (1995).

7. Lokshin and Ravallion 2000b.

8. Datt and Hoogeveen 2000.

9. Jacoby and Skoufias 1997.

10. See, for example, Jalan and Ravallion (1997a) for China and Gaiha and Deolalikar (1993) for India.

11. Behrman, Duryea, and Székely 1999.

12. Binder 1999.

13. See Eichengreen (1999) and IDB (1995).

14. Tommasi 1999.

15. Morley 1994. These numbers differ from those in table 9.1 because they are from a different source.

16. Caprio and Klingebiel 1996.

17. Lustig 1998.

18. These are not matters for emerging markets only. Banks and other financial actors in developed countries have acted irresponsibly. In 1998 the U.S. Federal Reserve was forced to orchestrate a bailout of Long-Term Capital Management, a hedge fund based in Connecticut.

19. De Gregorio, Edwards, and Valdés forthcoming.

20. Kiguel 1999.

21. Dornbusch and Edwards 1991.

22. World Bank 1998f, 2000e.

23. See, for example, Bourguignon and Morrisson (1992), World Bank (1991b), Thorbecke (1991), de Janvry, Fargeix, and Sadoulet (1991), and Bruno, Ravallion, and Squire (1998).

24. See the example in Lustig (2000).

25. See, for example, the discussion by Perry and Lederman (1999).

26. Gupta and others 1998.

27. Wodon, Hicks, Ryan, and Gonzalez 2000; Hicks and Wodon 2000.

28. Ravallion 1999c.

29. Ravallion 1999b, pp. 13–14.

30. Social Monitoring and Early Response Unit (www.smeru.or.id/about.htm).

31. See note 5 for chapter 1.

32. Davis, Handa, and Soto 1999.

33. Rodrik 1998.

34. See, for example, World Bank (forthcoming b).

35. International Federation of Red Cross and Red Crescent Societies 1999, tables 5 and 12.

36. Freeman 1999.

37. Patterns vary greatly, however, even within regions. The Sahel, for example, has experienced a significant decline in average rainfall between 1960 and 1990 compared with the previous three decades. In contrast, southeastern Africa has experienced an 18- to 20-year cycle of relatively drier and wetter periods, and East Africa has not shown a change in trends or any cyclical patterns (Benson and Clay 1998).

38. Gray and others 1999.

39. Benson and Clay 1998.

40. USAID, OFDA 1999. The database maintained by USAID's Office of U.S. Foreign Disaster Assistance includes all natural hazards declared a disaster by the U.S. government as well as major undeclared disasters causing a substantial number of deaths and injuries and substantial damage to infrastructure, agricultural production, and housing.

41. International Federation of Red Cross and Red Crescent Societies 1993, p. 34.

42. Anderson and Woodrow 1989.

43. Funaro-Curtis 1982.

44. Bhatt 1999b.

45. Benson 1997a, 1997b, 1997c.

46. Vos, Velasco, and de Labastida 1999.

47. IDB 2000.

48. Morris and others 2000.

49. Reardon and Taylor 1996.

50. Asset reduction was also the coping strategy of many households in Zimbabwe in the aftermath of the 1991–92 drought. Households were forced to sell their goats—a form of savings used to pay for secondary education—to sustain short-term consumption (Hicks 1993).

51. Hoddinott and Kinsey 1998, 2000; Owens 2000.

52. Bonitatibus and Cook 1996.

53. Ainsworth and Over 1994.

54. Benson and Clay 1998.

55. Benson and Clay 1998.

56. Robinson 1993.

57. Freeman and MacKellar 1999b. Major destruction of infrastructure can have an asymmetric effect on output: the loss of output caused by the destruction of infrastructure can exceed the increase in output caused by the eventual expansion of infrastructure (World Bank 1994e).

58. Kreimer 1999.

59. World Bank 1999c, 1999e.

60. Anderson and Woodrow 1989.

61. The government of Nicaragua, for example, is considering establishing such a system (World Bank 2000m).

62. Benson and Clay 1998.

63. Levav 1999.

64. For a discussion on social funds, see chapter 8.

65. Davis and Oliver-Smith 1999.

66. Davis and Oliver-Smith 1999.

67. Magalhaes and Glantz 1992.

Chapter 10

Unless otherwise noted, all quotations in the chapter are drawn from *Voices of the Poor* (Narayan, Chambers, Shah, and Petesch 2000; Narayan, Patel, Schafft, Rademacher, and Koch-Schulte 2000).

1. Ades and Glaeser 1999.

2. Quah 1999.

3. Scandizzo 1998.

4. Another reason is that developing countries may not respond to trade opportunities. This underlines the importance of policy and institutional reforms in developing countries to create a more favorable incentive framework.

5. World Bank and IMF 2000b.

6. Anderson, Hoekman, and Strutt 1999.

7. Anderson, Hoekman, and Strutt 1999.

8. Goldstein, Kaminsky, and Reinhart 2000.

9. World Bank 2000g.

10. Kaul, Grunberg, and Stern 1999a; Kanbur, Sandler, and Morrison 1999.

11. Cook and Sachs (1999) estimate that less than 10 percent of aid has gone to international public goods. Although it is difficult to disaggregate aid flows in this way, the 10 percent figure is calculated on the basis of how much aid goes to regional rather than national projects.

12. See World Bank (1999dd) for a comparison and analysis of the Kyoto and Montreal Protocols.

13. UNAIDS 2000.

14. National Intelligence Council 2000.

15. Pilot prevention projects and national programs in Brazil, India, Senegal, and Thailand show that greater condom use and safer injecting and sexual behavior can have substantial impact.

16. World Bank 2000a.

17. Estimate by the International AIDS Vaccine Initiative.

18. WHO 1999b.

19. These expenditures include but are not limited to health research.

20. WHO 1999a.

21. For a discussion of how such a fund might operate, see Sachs, Kremer, and Hamoudi (1999).

22. Byerlee and Heisey 1996; Smale and Heisey 1994.

23. Rosenzweig 1998.

24. Evenson 2000.

25. Pinstrup-Andersen, Pandya-Lorch, and Rosengrant 1997; de Janvry and others 2000.

26. Persley and Doyle 1999.

27. Alston, Pardey, and Smith 1998.

28. However, intellectual property rights can also facilitate the diffusion of knowledge, because patent claims are published and sometimes contain valuable information for other potential inventors (David 1993). Furthermore, patents play a role in the creation of markets for information and knowledge by providing more information to buyers and sellers of technology (Primo Braga, Fink, and Sepulveda 2000).

29. UNDP 1999a.

30. World Bank 2000s.

31. UNDP 1999a.

32. Breton 1965; Olson 1969.

33. Kanbur, Sandler, and Morrison 1999.

34. See Woods (1999) and Helleiner (2000a).

35. Blackhurst 1997a; Ohiorhenuan 1998; Michalopoulos 1999.

36. This initiative was instituted by the High-Level Meeting on Integrated Initiatives for LDCs' Trade Development in October 1997. The participating agencies are the International Monetary Fund, International Trade Center, United Nations Conference on Trade and Development, United Nations Development Programme, World Bank, and World Trade Organization.

37. World Bank and IMF 2000b.

Chapter 11

1. OECD, DAC 1996.

2. IDA 1998.

3. Ehrenpreis 1999.

4. World Bank 1990, p. 4.

5. OECD, DAC 2000.

6. Countries classified by the World Bank as low income in 1997 were those with a GNP per capita of $785 or less.

7. German and Randel 1998.

8. Alesina and Dollar 1998; Alesina and Weder 1999.

9. See, for example, Schraeder, Hook, and Taylor (1998) and Maizels and Nissanke (1984).

10. Kull, Destler, and Ramsay 1997.

11. See Boone (1994) and World Bank (1998b).

12. Easterly 1999a.

13. For a discussion of the changing consensus on development strategies over time, see Thorbecke (2000).

14. Williamson 1990.

15. While much structural adjustment lending, especially in the 1980s, emphasized these principles, most aid, including most World Bank lending, continued to be in traditional projects, especially in infrastructure, rural development, and, increasingly, the social sectors and the environment.

16. See, for example, IDA (1998).

17. Nelson 1999, p. 22. Also see Colclough (1996).

18. Kanbur, Sandler, and Morrison 1999.

19. van de Walle and Johnston 1996, p. 55.

20. van de Walle and Johnston 1996. See also Collier (1997).

21. Wuyts 1996; van de Walle and Johnston 1996; Aryeetey 1996.

22. Feyzioglu, Swaroop, and Zhu 1998.

23. Devarajan, Squire, and Suthiwart-Narueput 1997.

24. Devarajan and Swaroop 1998.

25. World Bank 1992a; Isham and Kaufmann 1999.

26. Burnside and Dollar forthcoming; Devarajan, Dollar, and Holmgren 2000.

27. Mosley and Eeckhout 2000.

28. Alesina and Dollar 1998. Although no systematic relationship can be found between conditionality and reform, a recent 10-country case study found that conditionality can be useful at the beginning of reform processes if the government is fully behind the reforms (Devarajan, Dollar, and Holmgren 2000). In these cases the government uses the conditions as a kind of "self-restraint" mechanism. The problem, however, is that donors have not adapted conditionality to different scenarios. This is likely to be the reason that no systematic relationship appears between conditionality and reform.

29. See Mosley, Harrigan, and Toye (1995) and Collier (1997).

30. See World Bank (1992a) and Mosley, Harrigan, and Toye (1995).

31. Killick, Gunatilaka, and Marr 1998.

32. Mosley and Eeckhout 2000.

33. On social institutions, see Collier and Gunning (1999). On social capability, see Temple and Johnson (1998). On ethnic fragmentation, see Easterly and Levine (1997). On inequality, see Bénabou (1996) and Perotti (1996a). And on geography, see Bloom and Sachs (1998).

34. Temple 1999. These factors are also likely to have had an effect on aid effectiveness (see Hansen and Tarp 2000).

35. Easterly and others 1993; Rodrik 1998.

36. See, for example, OECD, DAC (1996), United Kingdom, Secretary of State for International Development (1997), World Bank Partnerships Group (1998b), and UNDP (1999b).

37. IMF and IDA 1999.

38. Berg 2000. Also see World Bank (1994a) and Datta-Mitra (1997).

39. World Bank 1998k.

40. Collier and Dollar 2000.

41. World Bank 1998b.

42. Dollar 2000.

43. IDA 1998. IDA funds are allocated using a country performance rating that combines the Country Policy and Institutional Assessment (CPIA—given a weight of 80 percent in the rating) with a measure of the IDA project portfolio performance (weighted at 20 percent). In cases of severely weak governance a downward adjustment may be made to the rating to adjust for the fact that governance criteria make up only a fourth of the CPIA (World Bank 1999h).

44. For example, Llavador and Roemer (2000) have proposed a new analytical framework for the allocation of aid, based on the notion of equalizing opportunities among recipient countries for achieving growth.

45. Benyon 1999.

46. See, for example, Guillaumont, Guillaumont Jeanneney, and Brun (1999), Rodrik (1998), and Collier and Gunning (1997).

47. Guillaumont and Chauvet 1999.

48. OECD 1999.

49. See, for example, Seymour and others (2000) and Buse (1999).

50. Helleiner 2000b; World Bank Partnerships Group 1998a.

51. Sweden, Ministry for Foreign Affairs 1999.

52. Killick 1997.

53. Devarajan, Dollar, and Holmgren 2000.

54. Many such lessons are outlined in Walt and others (1999) and Foster (1999).

55. OECD 1999.

56. OECD 1999.

57. Jepma 1991.

58. Chinnock and Collinson 1999.

59. Berg 1993; World Bank 1996e.

60. van Rooy 1998.

61. Gibbs, Fumo, and Kuby 1999. Also see Kruse and others (1997).

62. See Denmark, Ministry of Foreign Affairs (2000).

63. Jubilee 2000 Coalition (www.jubilee2000uk.org).

64. Oxfam International 1999; Sachs and others 1999.

65. Killick, Gunatilaka, and Marr 1998.

66. Sachs and others 1999.

67. See, for example, Claessens, Oks, and Wijnbergen (1993).

68. Claessens and others 1997.

69. Easterly 1999c. New borrowing does not include rescheduling.

70. Bruno and Easterly 1996.

71. Easterly 1999c.

72. Sachs 2000.

73. The issues in this paragraph were all raised in wide-ranging consultations held by the World Bank and International Monetary Fund to inform and consult with partners about the poverty reduction strategy initiative. See World Bank and IMF (2000a).

Background papers and notes

Acemoglu, Daron, and James A. Robinson. "On the Political Economy of Institutions and Development."

Adato, Michelle, Timothy Besley, Lawrence Haddad, and John Hoddinott. "Participation and Poverty Reduction: Issues, Theory and New Evidence from South Africa."

Anderson, Mary B. "The Impacts of Natural Disasters on the Poor: A Background Note."

Anderson, Michael R. "Access to Justice and Legal Process: Making Legal Institutions Responsive to Poor People in LDCs."

Appleton, Simon, and Lina Song. "Income and Human Development at the Household Level: Evidence from Six Countries."

Austin, Gareth. "Background Note on Civil Strife and Poverty in Sub-Saharan Africa."

Banton, Michael. "Discrimination and Poverty."

Bardhan, Pranab. "Political Economy, Governance, and Poverty Reduction."

Centre L.-J. Lebret. "Attacking Poverty."

Chang, Pilwha. "Gender and Violence."

Connolly, Michelle. "The Impact of Removing Licenses and Restrictions to Import Technology on Technological Change."

Crook, Richard C., and Alan Sturla Sverrisson. "To What Extent Can Decentralized Forms of Government Enhance the Development of Pro-poor Policies and Improve Poverty-Alleviation Outcomes?"

Dahl, Robert A. "A Note on Politics, Institutions, Democracy and Equality."

Dasgupta, Partha. "Valuation and Evaluation: Measuring the Quality of Life and Evaluating Policy."

Davis, Shelton, and Anthony Oliver-Smith. "Post–Hurricane Mitch Rehabilitation and Reconstruction Mission."

de Janvry, Alain, Gregory Graff, Elisabeth Sadoulet, and David Zilberman. "Technological Change in Agriculture and Poverty Reduction."

Dercon, Stefan. "Income Risk, Coping Strategies, and Safety Nets."

Elwan, Ann. "Poverty and Disability."

Fields, Gary S. "Distribution and Development: A Summary of the Evidence for the Developing World."

Gereffi, Gary, and Martha Argelia Martinez. "Blue Jeans and Local Linkages: The Blue Jeans Boom in Torreon, Mexico."

Harriss, John. "How Much Difference Does Politics Make? Regime Differences across Indian States and Rural Poverty Reduction."

Herring, Ronald J. "Political Conditions for Agrarian Reform and Poverty Alleviation."

Hossain, Naomi, and Mick Moore, with Noushin Kalati, James Manor, and Elisa Reis. "Elites, Poverty and Development."

Houtzager, Peter P., and Jonathan Pattenden. "Finding the Shape of the Mountain: When 'the Poor' Set the Agenda."

INADES Formation Tchad. "Synthèse de la consultation de la Banque mondiale sur la pauvreté au Tchad."

Jayaraman, Rajshri. "Kerala and Uttar Pradesh: A Case Study."

Kurtz, Marcus. "The Political Economy of Pro-poor Policies in Chile and Mexico."

Leamer, Edward E., and Peter K. Schott. "Natural Resources as a Source of Latin American Income Inequality."

Lindauer, David. "Labor Market Reform and the Poor."

Lund, Frances, and Smita Srinivas. "Learning from Experience: A Framework for Social Protection for Workers in the Informal Economy."

Lustig, Nora. "Crises and the Poor: Socially Responsible Macroeconomics."

Manning, Daniel S. "The Role of Legal Services Organizations in Attacking Poverty."

Meerman, Jacob. "Slow Roads to Equality: A Study of Four Hard-Core Minorities—Issues from the Literature Review."

Moore, Mick, and James Putzel. "Politics and Poverty."

Moore, Mick, Jennifer Leavy, Peter P. Houtzager, and Howard White. "Polity Qualities: How Governance Affects Poverty."

Morley, Samuel A. "The Impact of Reforms on Equity in Latin America."

Niles, Kimberly J. "Economic Adjustment and Targeted Social Spending: The Role of Political Institutions (Indonesia, Mexico, and Ghana)."

Pawasuthipaisit, Anan, Sombat Sakuntasathien, and Robert M. Townsend. "Report to the Ford Foundation: Impact of the Thai Crisis."

Pouliquen, Louis. "Infrastructure and Poverty."

Prasad, Kameshwar, Paolo Belli, and Monica Das Gupta. "Links between Poverty, Exclusion, and Health."

Quah, Danny. "6 x 10^9: Some Dynamics of Global Inequality and Growth."

Rodriguez, Francisco. "Inequality, Economic Growth and Economic Performance."

Sebstad, Jennefer, and Monique Cohen. "Microfinance, Risk Management and Poverty."

Sinha, Saurabh, and Michael Lipton. "Damaging Fluctuations, Risk and Poverty: A Review."

Turok, Ben. "South Africa: From Exclusion to Integration."

Varshney, Ashutosh. "Democracy and Poverty."

Whitehead, Laurence, and George Gray-Molina. "The Long-Term Politics of Pro-poor Policies."

Winters, L. Alan. "Trade, Trade Policy and Poverty: What Are the Links?"

Wodon, Quentin. "Extreme Poverty and Human Rights: Essays on Joseph Wresinski."

Yaqub, Shahin. "How Equitable Is Public Spending on Health and Education?"

Bibliography

Ablo, Emmanuel, and Ritva Reinikka. 1998. "Do Budgets Really Matter?" Policy Research Working Paper 1926. World Bank, Washington, D.C.

Abu-Habib, Lina. 1997. *Gender and Disability: Women's Experiences in the Middle East.* Oxford: Oxfam International.

Acemoglu, Daron, and James A. Robinson. 1999. "On the Political Economy of Institutions and Development." Background paper for *World Development Report 2000/2001.* Massachusetts Institute of Technology, Cambridge, Mass.; University of California at Berkeley; and World Bank, Washington, D.C.

Adams, Dale. 1984. "Mobilizing Household Savings through Rural Financial Markets." In J.D. von Pischke, Dale W. Adams, and Gordon Donald, eds., *Rural Financial Markets in Developing Countries: Their Use and Abuse.* Baltimore, Md.: Johns Hopkins University Press.

Adams, Dale W., Douglas Graham, and J.D. von Pischke. 1992. "Microenterprise Credit Programmes: Déjà Vu." *World Development* 20(10): 1463–70.

————, eds. 1983. *Limitations of Cheap Credit in Promoting Rural Development.* Economic Development Institute. Washington, D.C.: World Bank.

Adams, Richard. 1986. "Bureaucrats, Peasants, and the Dominant Coalition: An Egyptian Case Study." *Journal of Development Studies* 22: 336–54.

————. 1995. "Sources of Income Inequality and Poverty in Rural Pakistan." Research Report 102. International Food Policy Research Institute, Washington, D.C.

————. 1998. "The Political Economy of the Food Subsidy System in Bangladesh." *Journal of Development Studies* 35(10): 66–88.

————. 1999. "Nonfarm Income, Inequality, and Land in Rural Egypt." Policy Research Working Paper 2178. World Bank, Washington, D.C.

Adato, Michelle, Timothy Besley, Lawrence Haddad, and John Hoddinott. 1999. "Participation and Poverty Reduction: Issues, Theory and New Evidence from South Africa." Background paper for *World Development Report 2000/2001.* International Food Policy Research Institute and World Bank, Washington, D.C.

Ades, Alberto, and Edward Glaeser. 1999. "Evidence on Growth, Increasing Returns and the Size of the Market." *Quarterly Journal of Economics* 114(3): 1025–46.

Agarwal, Bina. 1994. "Gender and Legal Rights in Agricultural Land in India." *Economic and Political Weekly* 30: A39–56.

————. 1997. "Environmental Action, Gender Equity and Women's Participation." *Development and Change* 28(1): 1–44.

Aghion, Philippe, Eve Caroli, and Cecilia Garcia-Peñalosa. 1999. "Inequality and Income Growth: The Perspective of New Growth Theories." *Journal of Economic Literature* 27: 1615–60.

Ahmad, Ehtisham, and Nicholas Stern. 1987. "Alternative Sources of Government Revenue: Illustrations from India, 1979–80." In David Newbery and Nicholas Stern, eds., *The Theory of Taxation for Developing Countries.* New York: Oxford University Press.

Aho, Gilbert Sylvain Lariviere, and Frederic Martin, eds. 1997. *Manuel d'analyse de la pauvreté: Applications au Bénin.* Quebec City: Université Laval, Université Nationale du Bénin, and United Nations Development Programme.

Aidt, Toke, Sabine Schlemmer-Schulte, and Zafiris Tzannatos. 2000. "Core Labor Standards and the Freedom of Association." World Bank, Washington, D.C.

Ainsworth, Martha, and Mead Over. 1994. "AIDS and African Development." *World Bank Research Observer* 9(2): 203–40.

Ainsworth, Martha, and Innocent Semali. 1998. "Who Is Most Likely to Die of AIDS? Socioeconomic Correlates of Adult Deaths in Kigera Region, Tanzania." In Martha Ainsworth, Lieve Fransen, and Mead Over, eds., *Confronting AIDS: Evidence from the Developing World.* Luxembourg: European Commission.

Ainsworth, Martha, Kathleen Beegle, and Andrew Nyamete. 1996. "The Impact of Women's Schooling on Fertility and Contraceptive Use: A Study of Fourteen Sub-Saharan African Countries." *World Bank Economic Review* 10: 85–122.

Akin, John, David K. Guilkey, and Hazel E. Denton. 1995. "Quality of Services and Demand for Health Care in Nigeria: A Multinomial Probit Estimation." *Social Science and Medicine* 40(11): 1527–37.

Akiyama, Takamasa, John Baffes, Jonathan Coulter, Donald F. Larson, and Panos Varangis. Forthcoming. "Commodity Market Reform in Africa: Why, How and What." World Bank and Natural Resource Institute, Washington, D.C.

Alderman, Harold. 1994. "Ghana: Adjustment's Star Pupil?" In David Sahn, ed., *Adjusting to Policy Failure in African Economies.* Ithaca, N.Y.: Cornell University Press.

Alderman, Harold, and Paul Gertler. 1997. "Family Resources and Gender Differences in Human Capital Investments: The Demand for Children's Medical Care in Pakistan." In Lawrence Haddad, John Hoddinott, and Harold Alderman, eds., *Intrahousehold Resource Allocation in Developing Countries: Methods, Models, and Policy.* Baltimore, Md.: Johns Hopkins University Press.

Alderman, Harold, and Victor Lavy. 1996. "Household Responses to Public Health Services: Cost and Quality Tradeoffs." *World Bank Research Observer* 11(2): 3–22.

Alderman, Harold, and Christina Paxson. 1992. "Do the Poor Insure? A Synthesis of the Literature on Risk and Consumption in Developing Countries." Policy Research Working Paper 1008. World Bank, Washington, D.C.

Alderman, Harold, Peter Orazem, and Elizabeth M. Paterno. 1996. "School Quality, School Cost, and the Public/Private School Choices of Low-Income Households in Pakistan." Impact Evaluation of Education Reforms Paper 2. World Bank, Washington, D.C.

Alderman, Harold, Simon Appleton, Lawrence Haddad, Lina Song, and Yisehac Yohannes. 2000. *Reducing Child Malnutrition: How Far Does Income Growth Take Us?* Washington, D.C.: World Bank.

Alesina, Alberto, and David Dollar. 1998. "Who Gives Foreign

Aid to Whom and Why?" NBER Working Paper 6612. National Bureau of Economic Research, Cambridge, Mass.

Alesina, Alberto, and Eliana La Ferrara. 1999. "Participation in Heterogeneous Communities." NBER Working Paper 7155. National Bureau of Economic Research, Cambridge, Mass.

Alesina, Alberto, and Dani Rodrik. 1994. "Distributive Politics and Economic Growth." *Quarterly Journal of Economics* 109: 465–90.

Alesina, Alberto, and Beatrice Weder. 1999. "Do Corrupt Governments Receive Less Foreign Aid?" NBER Working Paper 7108. National Bureau of Economic Research, Cambridge, Mass.

Alesina, Alberto, Reza Baqir, and William Easterly. 1998. "Public Goods and Ethnic Divisions." Policy Research Working Paper 2108. World Bank, Washington, D.C.

Alston, Julian M., Philip G. Pardey, and Vincent H. Smith. 1998. "Financing Agricultural R&D in Rich Countries: What's Happening and Why." *Australian Journal of Agricultural and Resource Economics* 42(1): 51–82.

Alston, Lee J., Gary D. Libecap, and Robert Schneider. 1996. "The Determinants and Impact of Property Rights: Land Titles on the Brazilian Frontier." NBER Working Paper 5405. National Bureau of Economic Research, Cambridge, Mass.

Altieri, Miguel A., and Peter Rosett. 1999. "Ten Reasons Why Biotechnology Will Not Ensure Food Security, Protect the Environment and Reduce Poverty in the Developing World." Paper presented at International Conference on Ensuring Food Security, Protecting the Environment, and Reducing Poverty in Developing Countries: Can Biotechnology Help? Consultative Group on International Agricultural Research and U.S. Academy of Sciences, October, Washington, D.C.

Altimir, Oscar, and Luis Becaria. 1998. "Política macroeconómica y pobreza en América Latina y el Caribe." In Enrique Ganuza, Lance Taylor, and Samuel A. Morley, eds., *Efectos de los cambios macroeconomicos y de las reformas sobre la pobreza urbana en la Argentina.* Mexico City: Mundi-Prensa.

Amis, Philip. 1994. "Indian Urban Poverty: Labor Markets, Gender, and Shocks." *Journal of International Development* 6(5): 635–43.

Anand, Sudhir, and Ravi Kanbur. 1993. "Inequality and Development: A Critique." *Journal of Development Economics* 41: 19–43.

Anand, Sudhir, and Martin Ravallion. 1993. "Human Development in Poor Countries: On the Role of Private Incomes and Public Services." *Journal of Economic Perspectives* 7: 133–50.

Anderson, Benedict. 1983. *Imagined Communities: Reflections on the Origin and Spread of Nationalism.* London: Verso.

Anderson, Jock R. 1998. "Selected Policy Issues in International Agricultural Research: On Striving for International Public Goods in an Era of Donor Fatigue." *World Development* 26(6): 1149–62.

Anderson, Jock R., and Dana G. Dalrymple. 1999. "World Bank, the Grant Program, and the CGIAR: A Retrospective Review." OED Working Paper Series, no. 1. World Bank, Washington, D.C.

Anderson, Kym. 1999. "Agriculture, Developing Countries, and the WTO Millennium Round." Centre for International Economic Studies Discussion Paper 99/28. University of Adelaide, Australia.

Anderson, Kym, Bernard Hoekman, and Anna Strutt. 1999. "Agriculture and the WTO: Next Steps." Paper presented at Second Annual Conference on Global Economic Analysis, Avernaes Conference Centre, 20–22 June, Helnaes, Denmark.

Anderson, Mary B. 1999. "The Impacts of Natural Disaster on the Poor: A Background Note." Background paper for *World Development Report 2000/2001.* Cornell University, Ithaca, N.Y.; and World Bank, Washington, D.C.

Anderson, Mary B., and Peter Woodrow. 1989. *Rising from the Ashes: Development Strategies in Times of Disaster.* Boulder, Colo.: Westview.

Anderson, Michael R. 1999. "Access to Justice and Legal Process: Making Legal Institutions Responsive to Poor People in LDCs." Background paper for *World Development Report 2000/2001.* World Bank, Washington, D.C.

Andersson, Neil, Cesar Palha da Sousa, and Sergio Paredes. 1995. "Social Cost of Land Mines in Four Countries: Afghanistan, Bosnia, Cambodia, and Mozambique." *British Medical Journal* 311: 718–21.

Andors, Phyllis. 1983. *The Unfinished Liberation of Chinese Women, 1949–1980.* Bloomington: Indiana University Press.

Aoyama, Atsuko. 1999. *Toward a Virtuous Circle: A Nutrition Review of the Middle East and North Africa.* Washington, D.C.: World Bank.

Appleton, Simon, and Lina Song. 1999. "Income and Human Development at the Household Level: Evidence from Six Countries." Background paper for *World Development Report 2000/2001.* University of Bath, Department of Economics and International Development; and World Bank, Washington, D.C.

Appleton, Simon, with Tom Emwanu, Johnson Kagugube, and James Muwonge. 1999. "Changes in Poverty in Uganda, 1992–1997." Working Paper 99.22. Oxford University, Centre for the Study of African Economies.

Aristy, Jaime, and Andres Dauhajre. 1998. "Efectos de las politicas macroeconomicas y sociales sobre la pobreza en la República Dominicana." Inter-American Development Bank, Sustainable Development Department, Washington, D.C.

Arnold, Michael J.E. 1998. "Forestry and Sustainable Rural Livelihoods." In Diana Carney, ed., *Sustainable Rural Livelihoods: What Contribution Can We Make? Implementing the Sustainable Rural Livelihoods Approach.* London. U.K. Department for International Development.

————. Forthcoming. "Devolution of Control of Common-Pool Resources to Local Communities: Experiences in Forestry." In Alain de Janvry, Gustavo Gordillo, Jean-Philippe Platteau, and Elisabeth Sadoulet, eds., *Access to Land, Rural Poverty and Public Action.* New York: Oxford University Press.

Arrow, Kenneth. 1963. "Uncertainty and the Welfare Economics of Medical Care." *American Economic Review* 53: 941–73.

————. 2000. "Observations on Social Capital." In Partha Dasgupta and Ismail Serageldin, eds., *Social Capital: A Multifaceted Perspective.* Washington, D.C.: World Bank.

Arulpragasam, Jehan, and Carlo del Ninno. 1996. "Do Cheap Imports Harm the Poor? Rural-Urban Tradeoffs in Guinea." In

David E. Sahn, ed., *Economic Reform and the Poor in Africa.* Oxford: Clarendon.

Aryeetey, Ernest. 1996. "Aid Effectiveness in Ghana." Overseas Development Institute, London.

Asia Foundation and AKATIGA. 1999. *The Impact of Economic Crisis on Indonesian Small and Medium Enterprises.* Jakarta: Asia Foundation.

Asiimwe, Delius. 1997. "Informal Health Markets and Formal Health Financing Policy in Uganda." London School of Hygiene, London; and Makerere Institute of Social Research, Kampala.

Atkinson, Anthony Barnes. 1981. "On Intergenerational Income Mobility in Britain." *Journal of Post-Keynesian Economics* 3: 194–218.

———. 1998. "Equity Issues in a Globalizing World: The Experience of OECD Countries." Paper presented at conference on economic policy and equity, International Monetary Fund, June, Washington, D.C.

Atkinson, Anthony Barnes, and François Bourguignon. Forthcoming. "Poverty and Inclusion from a World Perspective." In Pierre-Alain Muet and Joseph E. Stiglitz, eds., *Global Governance, Markets and Equity.* New York: Oxford University Press.

Austin, Gareth. 1999. "Background Note on Civil Strife and Poverty in Sub-Saharan Africa." Background paper for *World Development Report 2000/2001.* London School of Economics and Political Science; and World Bank, Washington, D.C.

Azandossessi, Arsène. 2000. "The Struggle for Water in Urban Areas of Nouakchott, Mauritania." *WATERfront* 13. United Nations Children's Fund, New York.

Bajpai, Nirupam, and Jeffrey Sachs. 1999. "The Progress of Policy Reform and Variations in Performance at the Sub-National Level in India." Development Discussion Paper 730. Harvard Institute for International Development, Cambridge, Mass.

Bale, Malcolm. 1999. "The Rural Poor: A Thematic Approach." World Bank, East Asia and Pacific Region, Washington, D.C.

Bale, Malcolm, and Tony Dale. 1998. "Public Sector Reform in New Zealand and Its Relevance to Developing Countries." *World Bank Research Observer* 13(1): 103–21.

Banarjee, Ajit, Gabriel Campbell, Maria Concepcion J. Cruz, Shelton H. Davis, and Augusta Molnar. 1997. "Participation in Forest Management and Conservation." Environment Department Paper 49. World Bank, Washington, D.C.

Banerjee, Abhijit V., and Esther Duflo. 2000. "Inequality and Growth: What Can the Data Say?" Massachusetts Institute of Technology, Department of Economics, Cambridge, Mass.

Banerjee, Abhijit V., Paul Gertler, and Maireesh Ghatak. 1998. "Empowerment and Efficiency: The Economics of Agrarian Reform." Massachusetts Institute of Technology Working Paper 98-22. Department of Economics, Cambridge, Mass.

Banerjee, Abhijit V., Dilip Mookherjee, Kaivan Munshi, and Debraj Ray. 2000. "Inequality, Control Rights and Rent Seeking: Sugar Cooperatives in Maharashtra." Boston University; Massachusetts Institute of Technology, Cambridge, Mass.; and Instituto de Análisis Económico, Barcelona.

Banerji, Arup, and Hafez Ghanem. 1997. "Does the Type of Political Regime Matter for Trade and Labor Market Policies?" *Economic Review* 11(1): 171–94.

Banton, Michael. 1999. "Discrimination and Poverty." Background paper for *World Development Report 2000/2001.* Cambridge University; and World Bank, Washington, D.C.

Bardhan, Pranab. 1997a. "Method in the Madness? A Political-Economy Analysis of the Ethnic Conflicts in Less Developed Countries." *World Development* 25(9): 1381–98.

———. 1997b. *The Role of Governance in Economic Development: A Political Economy Approach.* OECD Development Centre Study. Washington, D.C.: Washington Center Press.

———. 1999a. "Democracy and Development: A Complex Relationship." In Ian Shapiro and Casiano Hacker-Cordón, eds., *Democracy's Values.* New York: Cambridge University Press.

———. 1999b. "Political Economy, Governance and Poverty Reduction." Background paper for *World Development Report 2000/2001.* University of California at Berkeley, Institute of International Studies; and World Bank, Washington, D.C.

Bardhan, Pranab, and Dilip Mookherjee. 1999. "Capture and Governance at Local and National Levels." University of California at Berkeley, Institute of International Studies; and Boston University, Department of Economics.

Bardhan, Pranab, and Christopher Udry. 1999. *Development Microeconomics.* New York: Oxford University Press.

Barham, Christopher. 2000. "The Mexican Fund for Natural Disasters (Fonden)." Box for *World Development Report 2000/2001.* World Bank, Washington, D.C.

Barnes, Douglas F., and Jonathan Halpern. 2000. "The Role of Energy Subsidies." In Energy Sector Management Assistance Programme, *Energy and Development Report 2000: Energy Services for the World's Poor.* Washington, D.C.: World Bank.

Barnes, Douglas F., Robert van der Plas, and Willem Floor. 1997. "Tackling the Rural Energy Problem in Developing Countries." *Finance and Development* 34: 11–15.

Barr, Abigail. 1998. "Enterprise Performance and the Functional Diversity of Social Capital." Working Paper Series, no. 98-1. Oxford University, Institute of Economics and Statistics.

———. 1999. "Collective Action and Bilateral Interaction in Ghanaian Entrepreneurial Networks." Oxford University, Centre for the Study of African Economies.

Barraclough, Solon, and Daniel Moss. 1999. *Toward Greater Food Security in Central America following Hurricane Mitch.* Boston: Oxfam America.

Barrett, Christopher. 1996. "On Price Risk and the Inverse Farm-Size Productivity Relationship." *Journal of Development Economics* 51(2): 193–215.

———. 1998a. "Food Aid: Is It Development Assistance, Trade Promotion, Both or Neither?" *American Journal of Agricultural Economics* 80(3): 566–71.

———. 1998b. "Immiserized Growth in Liberalized Agriculture." *World Development* 26: 743–53.

———. 1999. "On Vulnerability, Asset Poverty and Subsidiarity." Comments to Ford–Rockefeller Foundation Seminar Series Session, Managing Vulnerability and Shocks within the Agro-Food System, 20 May, New York.

Barrett, Christopher, and Michael Carter. 1999. "Can't Get Ahead for Falling Behind: New Directions for Development

Policy to Escape Poverty and Relief Traps." U.S. Agency for International Development, Washington, D.C.

Barrett, Christopher, and Paul Dorosh. 1996. "Farmers' Welfare and Changing Food Prices: Nonparametric Evidence from Rice in Madagascar." *American Journal of Agricultural Economics* 78: 656–69.

Barrett, Scott. 1999. "Montreal versus Kyoto: International Cooperation and the Global Environment." In Inge Kaul, Isabelle Grunberg, and Marc Stern, eds., *Global Public Goods: International Cooperation in the 21st Century.* New York: Oxford University Press.

———. Forthcoming. "A Theory of Full International Cooperation." *Journal of Theoretical Politics.*

Barro, Robert J. 1996a. *Health and Economic Growth.* Washington, D.C.: Pan American Health Organization.

———. 1996b. "Institutions and Growth: An Introductory Essay." *Journal of Economic Growth* 1(1): 145–48.

———. 1997. *Determinants of Economic Growth: A Cross-Country Empirical Study.* Cambridge, Mass.: MIT Press.

———. 1999. "Inequality, Growth, and Investment." Harvard University, Department of Economics, Cambridge, Mass.

Barro, Robert J., and Xavier Sala-i-Martin. 1995. *Economic Growth.* New York: McGraw-Hill.

Barros, Ricardo, Rosane Mendonca, and Sonia Rocha. 1995. "Brazil: Welfare, Inequality, Poverty, Social Indicators, and Social Programs in the 1980's." In Nora Lustig, ed., *Coping with Austerity.* Washington, D.C.: Brookings Institution.

Barwell, Ian. 1996. "Transport and the Village: Findings from African Village-Level Travel and Transport Surveys and Related Studies." Africa Region Series Discussion Paper 344. World Bank, Washington, D.C.

Basta, Samir S., Alan Berg, and Susan Brems. 1986. *Guidelines for Work in Nutrition.* Population, Health, and Nutrition Department. Washington, D.C.: World Bank.

Basu, Alaka Malwade. 1995. "Poverty and AIDS: The Vicious Circle." Division of Nutritional Sciences Working Paper 95.02. Cornell University, Ithaca, N.Y.

Basu, Kaushik. 1998. "Child Labor: Cause, Consequence, and Cure, with Remarks on International Labor Standards." Policy Research Working Paper 2027. World Bank, Washington, D.C.

———. 1999a. "Child Labor: Cause, Consequence, and Cure, with Remarks on International Labor Standards." *Journal of Economic Literature* 38: 1083–119.

———. 1999b. "International Labor Standards and Child Labor." *Challenge* 42(5): 80–93.

Basu, Kaushik, and Pham Hoang Van. 1998. "The Economics of Child Labor." *American Economic Review* 88: 412–27.

Bates, Robert H. 1989. *Beyond the Miracle of the Market: The Political Economy of Agrarian Development in Kenya.* New York: Cambridge University Press.

———. 1997. "Political Institutions and Economic Growth in Africa." Development Discussion Paper 583. Harvard Institute for International Development, Cambridge, Mass.

———. 1999. "Ethnicity, Capital Formation and Conflict." Center for International Development Working Paper 27. Harvard University, Cambridge, Mass.

Batson, Amie, and Piers Whitehead. 1999. "HIV/AIDS Vaccines: What Motivates Private Investment in R&D?" AIDS Vaccine Task Force Commissioned Paper. Mercer Management and World Bank, Washington, D.C.

Baudot Sundberg, Barbara, and William Moomaw, eds. 1999. *People and Their Planet.* New York: St. Martin's.

Baulch, Bob, and John Hoddinott. Forthcoming. "Economic Mobility and Poverty Dynamics in Developing Countries." *Journal of Development Studies.*

Baum, Warren. 1986. *Partners against Hunger.* Washington, D.C.: World Bank.

Bebbington, Anthony. 1996. "Organizations and Intensification: Campesino Federations, Rural Livelihoods and Agricultural Technology in the Andes and Amazonia." *World Development* 24(7): 1161–78.

———. 1997. "Social Capital and Rural Intensification: Local Organizations and Islands of Sustainability in the Rural Andes." *Geographical Journal* 163(2): 189–97.

———. 1999. "Capitals and Capabilities: A Framework for Analyzing Peasant Viability, Rural Livelihoods and Poverty." *World Development* 27(12): 2021–44.

Bebbington, Anthony, and Thomas Carroll. 2000. "Induced Social Capital and Federations of the Rural Poor." Social Capital Initiative Working Paper 19. World Bank, Social Development Department, Washington, D.C.

Bebbington, Anthony, and Thomas Perreault. 1999. "Social Capital, Development and Access to Resources in Highland Ecuador." *Economic Geography* 75(4): 395–418.

Becker, Gary. 1960. "An Economic Analysis of Fertility." In Universities-National Bureau Committee for Economic Research, *Demographic and Economic Change in Developed Countries.* National Bureau of Economic Research Conference Series, no. 11. Princeton, N.J.: Princeton University Press.

Behrman, Jere R. 1987. "Schooling in Developing Countries: Which Countries Are the Over- and Underachievers and What Is the Schooling Impact?" *Economics of Education Review* 6(2): 111–27.

———. 1988. "Intra-Household Allocation of Nutrients in Rural India: Are Boys Favored? Do Parents Exhibit Inequality Aversion?" *Oxford Economic Papers* 40(1): 32–54.

———. 1996. "The Impact of Health and Nutrition on Education." *World Bank Research Observer* 11(1): 23–37.

Behrman, Jere R., and Anil Deolalikar. 1990. "The Intra-Household Demand for Nutrients in Rural South India: Individual Estimates, Fixed Effects and Permanent Income." *Journal of Human Resources* 24(4): 655–96.

Behrman, Jere R., and James C. Knowles. 1997. "How Strongly Is Child Schooling Associated with Household Income?" University of Pennsylvania, Philadelphia; and Abt Associates, Cambridge, Mass.

Behrman, Jere R., Suzanne Duryea, and Miguel Székely. 1999. "Aging and Economic Options: Latin America in a World Perspective." Inter-American Development Bank, Office of the Chief Economist, Washington, D.C.

Bellew, Rosemary T., and Elizabeth M. King. 1993. "Educating Women: Lessons from Experience." In Elizabeth M. King and Anne M. Hill, eds., *Barriers, Benefits, and Policies*. Baltimore, Md.: Johns Hopkins University Press.

Bénabou, Roland. 1996. "Inequality and Growth." In Ben Bernanke and Julio Rotemberg, eds., *National Bureau of Economic Research Macroeconomics Annual*. Cambridge, Mass.: MIT Press.

Benhabib, Jess, and Mark M. Spiegel. 1994. "The Role of Human Capital in Economic Development: Evidence from Aggregate Cross-Country Data." *Journal of Monetary Economics* 34(2): 143–73.

Bennett, Lynn, Mike Goldberg, and Pamela Hunte. 1996. "Ownership and Sustainability: Lessons on Group-Based Financial Services from South Asia." *Journal of International Development* 8(2): 271–88.

Benson, Charlotte. 1997a. "The Economic Impact of Natural Disasters in Fiji." Working Paper 97. Overseas Development Institute, London.

———. 1997b. "The Economic Impact of Natural Disasters in the Philippines." Working Paper 99. Overseas Development Institute, London.

———. 1997c. "The Economic Impact of Natural Disasters in Vietnam." Working Paper 98. Overseas Development Institute, London.

Benson, Charlotte, and Edward Clay. 1998. *The Impact of Drought on Sub-Saharan African Economies: A Preliminary Examination*. World Bank Technical Paper 401. Washington, D.C.

Benyon, Jonathan. 1999. "*Assessing Aid* and the Collier/Dollar Poverty Efficient Aid Allocations: A Critique." U.K. Department for International Development, London.

Berg, Elliott J. 1993. *Rethinking Technical Cooperation: Reforms for Capacity Building in Africa*. New York: United Nations Development Programme.

———. 2000. "Aid and Failed Reforms: The Case of Public Sector Management." In Finn Tarp, ed., *Foreign Aid and Development: Lessons Learnt and Directions for the Future*. London: Routledge.

Berg, Janine, and Lance Taylor. 2000. "External Liberalization, Economic Performance, and Social Policy." Center for Economic Policy Analysis Working Paper Series I, Working Paper 12. New School University, New York.

Berkovitz, Daniel, Katherina Pistor, and Jean-François Rischard. 1999. "Economic Development, Legality and the Transplant Effect." University of Pittsburgh; and Max Planck Institute, Rostock, Germany.

Berman, Eli, and Stephen Machin. 2000. "Skilled-Biased Technology Transfer: Evidence of Factor-Biased Technological Change in Developing Countries." Boston University, Department of Economics.

Berry, Sara. 1989. "Social Institutions and Access to Resources." *Africa* 59(1): 41–55.

Bertrand, Marianne, Douglas Miller, and Sendhil Mullainathan. 1999. "Public Policy and Extended Families: Evidence from South Africa." Princeton University, Princeton, N.J.

Besley, Timothy. 1995a. "Property Rights and Investment Incentives: Theory and Evidence from Ghana." *Journal of Political Economy* 103(5): 903–37.

———. 1995b. "Savings, Credit and Insurance." In Jere R.

Behrman and T.N. Srinivasan, eds., *Handbook of Development Economics*. Amsterdam: Elsevier Science.

Besley, Timothy, and Robin Burgess. 1998. "Land Reform, Poverty Reduction and Growth: Evidence from India." New Series, DERP-13. London School of Economics and Political Science.

———. 2000. "Does Media Make Government More Responsive? Theory and Evidence from Indian Famine Relief Policy." Suntory and Toyota International Centres for Economics and Related Disciplines (STICERD), London School of Economics and Political Science.

Besley, Timothy, and Stephen Coate. 1995. "Group Lending, Repayment Incentives and Social Collateral." *Journal of Development Economics* 46: 1–18.

Bhagwati, Jagdish, and T.N. Srinivasan. 1999. "Outward Orientation and Development: Are the Revisionists Right?" Paper contributed to festschrift in honor of Anne Krueger. [www.columbia.edu/cu/economics/].

Bhalla, Surjit. 2000. "Growth and Poverty in India: Myth and Reality." Oxus Research and Investments, New Delhi.

Bhargava, Alok. 1997. "A Longitudinal Analysis of Infant and Child Mortality Rates in Developing Countries." *Indian Economic Review* 32: 141–53.

Bhargava, Alok, Dean Jamison, Lawrence Lau, and Christopher Murray. 2000. "Modelling the Effects of Health on Economic Growth." World Health Organization, Geneva.

Bhatt, Ela. 1989. "Toward Empowerment." *World Development* 17(7): 1059–65.

———. 2000. "Notes on the Politics of Poverty Reduction." In Gudrun Kochendörfer-Lucius and Boris Pleskovic, eds., *Inclusion, Justice, and Poverty Reduction*. Berlin: German Foundation for International Development.

Bhatt, Mihir. 1999a. "Natural Disaster as National Shocks to Poor and Development." Paper presented at *World Development Report 2000/2001* Summer Workshop, World Bank, July, Washington, D.C.

———. 1999b. "Vulnerability Matters." Paper presented at International Decade for Natural Disaster Reduction Programme Forum, United Nations Development Programme, July, Geneva.

Bidani, Benu, and Hyeok Jong. 1999. "Explaining the Dynamics of Inequality in Thailand: 1981–1996." World Bank, East Asia and Pacific Region, Washington, D.C.

Bidani, Benu, and Martin Ravallion. 1996. "Decomposing Social Indicators Using Distributional Data." *Journal of Econometrics* 77(1): 125–40.

Bigio, Anthony, ed. 1998. *Social Funds and Reaching the Poor: Experiences and Future Directions*. Washington, D.C.: World Bank, Economic Development Institute.

Binder, Melissa. 1999. "Schooling Indicators during Mexico's Lost Decade." *Economics of Education Review* 18(2): 183–99.

Binswanger, Hans, and Shahidur Khandker. 1995. "The Impact of Formal Finance on the Rural Economy of India." *Journal of Development Studies* 32(2): 234–62.

Biodiversity Support Program. 1993. *African Biodiversity: Foundation for the Future*. Washington, D.C.

Birdsall, Nancy. Forthcoming. "New Findings in Economics and

Demography: Policy Implications." In Nancy Birdsall, Allen C. Kelley, and Steven Sinding, eds., *Population Does Matter: Demography, Growth, and Poverty in the Developing World.* New York: Oxford University Press.

Birdsall, Nancy, and Augusto de la Torre. 2000. "Economic Reform in Unequal Latin American Societies." Carnegie Endowment for International Peace and Inter-American Dialogue, Washington, D.C.

Birdsall, Nancy, and Robert Hecht. 1995. "Swimming against the Tide: Strategies for Improving Equity in Health." Human Resources Development and Operations Policy Working Paper 55. World Bank, Washington, D.C.

Birdsall, Nancy, and Robert Z. Lawrence. 1999. "Deep Integration and Trade Agreements: Good for Developing Countries?" In Inge Kaul, Isabelle Grunberg, and Marc Stern, eds., *Global Public Goods: International Cooperation in the 21st Century.* New York: Oxford University Press.

Birdsall, Nancy, and Juan Luis Londoño. 1997. "Asset Inequality Matters: An Assessment of the World Bank's Approach to Poverty Reduction." *American Economic Review* 87(2): 32–37.

Birdsall, Nancy, Carol Graham, and Richard H. Sabot. 1998. *Beyond Tradeoffs: Market Reform and Equitable Growth in Latin America.* Washington, D.C.: Inter-American Development Bank and Brookings Institution.

Birdsall, Nancy, Allen C. Kelley, and Steven Sinding, eds. Forthcoming. *Population Does Matter: Demography, Growth, and Poverty in the Developing World.* New York: Oxford University Press.

Bisat, Amer, R. Barry Johnston, and Vasudevan Sundararajan. 1999. "Sequencing Financial Reform and Liberalization in Five Developing Countries." In Barry R. Johnston and Vasudevan Sundararajan, eds., *Sequencing Financial Sector Reforms: Country Experiences and Issues.* Washington, D.C.: International Monetary Fund.

Blackden, Mark, and Chitra Bhanu. 1999. *Gender, Growth and Poverty Reduction: Special Program of Assistance for Africa.* World Bank Technical Paper 428. Washington, D.C.

Blackhurst, Richard. 1997a. "The Capacity of the WTO to Fill Its Mandate." In Anne Krueger, ed., *The WTO as an International Organization.* Chicago: University of Chicago Press.

———. 1997b. "The WTO and the Global Economy." *World Economy* 20: 527–44.

Blair, Harry. 2000. "Participation and Accountability at the Periphery: Democratic Local Governance in Six Countries." *World Development* 28(1): 21–39.

Blair, Harry, and Gary Hansen. 1994. "Weighing in on the Scales of Justice: Strategic Approaches for Donor-Supported Rule of Law Programs." Assessment Report 7. U.S. Agency for International Development, Program and Operations, Washington, D.C.

Blanchard, Olivier, and Andrei Shleifer. 2000. "Federalism with and without Political Centralization: China versus Russia." NBER Working Paper 7616. National Bureau of Economic Research, Cambridge, Mass.

Bloom, David E., and Jeffrey D. Sachs. 1998. "Geography, Demography, and Economic Growth in Africa." *Brookings Papers on Economic Activity* 2: 207–95.

Bloom, David E., and Jeffrey G. Williamson. 1997. "Demographic Transitions and Economic Miracles in Emerging Asia." NBER Working Paper 6268. National Bureau of Economic Research, Cambridge, Mass.

Bodart, Claude, and Jennie L. Litvack. 1993. "User Fees Plus Quality Equals Improved Access to Health Care: Results of a Field Experiment in Cameroon." *Social Science and Medicine* 37(3): 369–83.

Boland, John, and Dale Whittington. 2000. "Water Tariff Design in Developing Countries: Disadvantages of Increasing Block Tariffs (IBTs) and Advantages of Uniform Price with Rebate (UPR) Designs." World Bank, Development Research Group, Washington, D.C.

Bonilla-Chacin, Maria, and Jeffrey S. Hammer. 1999. "Life and Death among the Poorest." World Bank, Development Research Group, Washington, D.C.

Bonitatibus, Ester, and Jonathan Cook. 1996. "Incorporating Gender in Food Security Policies: A Handbook for Policymakers in Commonwealth Africa." Commonwealth Secretariat, London.

Boone, Peter. 1994. "The Impact of Foreign Aid on Savings and Growth." London School of Economics and Political Science.

Booth, David, John Milimo, Ginny Bond, and Silverio Chimuka. 1995. "Coping with Cost Recovery: A Study of the Social Impact and Responses to Cost Recovery in Basic Services (Health and Education) in Poor Communities in Zambia." Task Force on Poverty Reduction Working Paper 3. Swedish International Development Cooperation Agency, Stockholm.

Borjas, George J. 1992. "Ethnic Capital and Intergenerational Mobility." *Quarterly Journal of Economics* 107(1): 123–50.

———. 1997. "To Ghetto or Not to Ghetto: Ethnicity and Residential Segregation." NBER Working Paper 6176. National Bureau of Economic Research, Cambridge, Mass.

Borjas, George J., and Glenn T. Sueyoshi. 1997. "Ethnicity and the Intergenerational Transmission of Welfare Dependency." NBER Working Paper 6175. National Bureau of Economic Research, Cambridge, Mass.

Bouderbala, Negib, and Paul Pascon. 1970. "Le droit et le fait dans la société composite." Essai d'introduction au système juridique marocain BESM 117. Rabat.

Bourguignon, François. 1999. "Inclusion, Structural Inequality and Poverty: Interplay of Economic and Social Forces." World Bank, Research Advisory Staff, Washington, D.C.; and Delta, Paris.

Bourguignon, François, and Satya Chakravarty. 1998. "Multidimensional Measures of Poverty." Delta Working Paper 98-12. Paris.

Bourguignon, François, and Pierre-Andre Chiappori. 1992. "Collective Models of Household Behavior." *European Economic Review* 36(2–3): 355–64.

Bourguignon, François, and Christian Morrisson, eds. 1992. *Adjustment and Equity in Developing Countries: A New Approach.* Paris: Organisation for Economic Co-operation and Development.

———. 1998. "Inequality and Development: The Role of Dualism." *Journal of Development Economics* 57: 233–57.

———. 1999. "The Size Distribution of Income among World

Citizens." Delta and University of Paris, Département et laboratoire d'économie théorique et appliquée, Paris.

Bourguignon, François, Albert Berry, and Christian Morrisson. 1981. *The World Distribution of Incomes between 1950 and 1977.* Paris: Ecole Normale Supérieure.

Bourguignon, François, Francisco Ferreira, and Nora Lustig. 1997. "The Microeconomics of Income Distribution Dynamics in East Asia and Latin America." Research proposal. Inter-American Development Bank and World Bank, Washington, D.C.

Bourguignon, François, Myra Fournier, and Marc Gurgand. 1998. "Distribution, Development and Education: Taiwan, 1979–1994." World Bank, Research Advisory Staff, Washington, D.C..

Bourguignon, François, Sylvie Lambert, and Akiko Suwa-Eisenmann. 1996. "Distribution of Export Price Risk in a Developing Country." CEPR Discussion Paper 1482. Centre for Economic Policy Research, London.

Boyce, James K. 1987. *Agrarian Impasse in Bengal: Agricultural Growth in Bangladesh and West Bengal 1949–1980.* Oxford: Oxford University Press.

Braithwaite, Jeanine D. 1997. "The Old and New Poor in Russia." In Jeni Klugman, ed., *Poverty in Russia: Public Policy and Private Responses.* Economic Development Institute. Washington, D.C.: World Bank.

Brandsma, Judith, and Rafika Chaouali. 1998. "Making Microfinance Work in the Middle East and North Africa." World Bank, Private Sector Development and Finance Group, Washington, D.C.

Bratton, Michael, and Nicolas van de Walle. 1997. *Democratic Experiments in Africa: Regime Transitions in Comparative Perspective.* New York: Cambridge University Press.

Brautigam, Deborah. 1997. "Substituting for the State: Institutions and Industrial Development in Eastern Nigeria." *World Development* 25(7): 1063–80.

Braverman, Avishay, and José-Luis Guasch. 1993. "Administrative Failures in Government Credit Programs." In Karla Hoff, Avishay Braverman, and Joseph E. Stiglitz, eds., *The Economics of Rural Organization: Theory, Practice, and Policy.* New York: Oxford University Press.

Bredie, Joseph W.B., and Girindre K. Beehary. 1998. *School Enrollment Decline in Sub-Saharan Africa.* World Bank Discussion Paper 395. Washington, D.C.

Brehm, Vicky Mancuso. 2000. "Environment, Advocacy, and Community Participation: MOPAWI in Honduras." *Development in Practice* 10(1): 94–98.

Breton, Albert. 1965. "A Theory of Government Grants." *Canadian Journal of Economics and Political Science* 31: 147–57.

Briggs, Xavier. 1998. "Brown Kids in White Suburbs: Housing Mobility and the Multiple Faces of Social Capital." *Housing Policy Debate* 9(1): 177–221.

Brockerhoff, Martin, and Ellen Brennan. 1998. "The Poverty of Cities in Developing Regions." *Population and Development* 24(1): 75–114.

Brockerhoff, Martin, and Paul Hewett. 1998. "Ethnicity and Child Mortality in Sub-Saharan Africa." Population Council Working Paper 107. New York.

Brook Cowen, Penelope. 1997. "Getting the Private Sector Involved in Water: What to Do in the Poorest of Countries." Viewpoint 103. World Bank, Finance, Private Sector, and Infrastructure Network, Washington, D.C.

Brook Cowen, Penelope, and Nicola Tynan. 1999. "Reaching the Urban Poor with Private Infrastructure." Viewpoint 188. World Bank, Finance, Private Sector, and Infrastructure Network, Washington, D.C.

Brown, Charles, and Wallace Oates. 1987. "Assistance to the Poor in a Federal System." *Journal of Public Economics* 32: 307–30.

Brown, David, and Darcy Ashman. 1996. "Participation, Social Capital, and Intersectoral Problem Solving: African and Asian Cases." *World Development* 24(9): 1467–79.

Brunetti, Aymo. 1997. "Political Variables in Cross-Country Analysis." *Journal of Economic Surveys* 11(2): 163–90.

Bruno, Michael, and William Easterly. 1996. "Inflation's Children: Tales of Crises That Beget Reforms." NBER Working Paper 5452. National Bureau of Economic Research, Cambridge, Mass.

———. 1998. "Inflation Crises and Long-Run Growth." *Journal of Monetary Economics* 41: 3–26.

Bruno, Michael, Martin Ravallion, and Lyn Squire. 1998. "Equity and Growth in Developing Countries: Old and New Perspectives on the Policy Issues." In Vito Tanzi and Ke-young Chu, eds., *Income Distribution and High-Quality Growth.* Cambridge, Mass.: MIT Press.

Budlender, Debbie. 1999. "The South African Women's Budget Initiative." Paper presented at workshop on pro-poor, gender-, and environment-sensitive budgets, United Nations Development Programme in partnership with United Nations Development Fund for Women, Community Agency for Social Enquiry, 28–30 June, New York.

Bunce, Valerie. 1999. "The Political Economy of Post-Socialism." *Slavic Review* 58(4): 756–93.

Burki, Shahid Javed, and Guillermo Perry. 1998. *Beyond the Washington Consensus: Institutions Matter.* Washington, D.C.: World Bank.

Burki, Shahid Javed, Guillermo Perry, and William Dillinger. 1999. *Beyond the Center: Decentralizing the State.* Washington, D.C.: World Bank.

Burnside, Craig, and David Dollar. Forthcoming. "Aid, Policies, and Growth." *American Economic Review.*

Burr, Chandler. 2000. "Grameen Village Phone: Its Current Status and Future Prospects." International Labour Organization, Geneva. [www.ilo.org/public/english/employment/ent/papers/grameen.htm].

Burt, Ronald. 1992. *Structural Holes: The Social Structure of Competition.* Cambridge, Mass.: Harvard University Press.

Buse, Kent. 1999. "Keeping a Tight Grip on the Reins: Donor Control over Aid Coordination and Management in Bangladesh." *Health Policy and Planning* 14(3): 219–28.

Byerlee, Derek, and Paul Heisey. 1996. "Past and Potential Impacts of Maize Research in Sub-Saharan Africa: A Critical Assessment." *Food Policy* 21(3): 255–77.

Caldwell, John. 1986. "Routes to Law Morality in Poor Countries." *Population and Development Review* 12: 171–220.

Caldwell, John, Sally Findley, Pat Caldwell, Gigi Santow, Wendy Cosford, Jennifer Braid, and Daphne Broers-Freeman, eds. 1990. "What We Know about Health Transition: The Cultural, Social and Behavioural Determinants of Health." *Health Transition Series* 2(1). Australian National University, National Centre for Epidemiology and Population Health, Canberra.

Campos, Jose Edgardo. 1996. *The Key to the Asian Miracle: Making Shared Growth Credible.* Washington, D.C.: Brookings Institution.

Campos, Nauro. 1994. "Why Does Democracy Foster Economic Development? An Assessment of the Empirical Literature." University of Southern California, Los Angeles.

Cao, Yuanzheng, Yingyi Qian, and Barry Weingast. 1998. "From Federalism, Chinese Style, to Privatization, Chinese Style." CEPR Discussion Paper 1838. Centre for Economic Policy Research, London.

Caprio, Gerard, and Daniela Klingebiel. 1996. "Bank Insolvencies: Cross-Country Experience." Policy Research Working Paper 1620. World Bank, Washington, D.C.

Carbonnier, Gilles. 1998. *Conflict, Postwar Rebuilding and the Economy: A Critical Review of the Literature.* War-Torn Societies Project Occasional Paper 2. Geneva: United Nations Research Institute for Social Development.

Cardoso, Eliana. 1992. "Inflation and Poverty." NBER Working Paper 4006. National Bureau of Economic Research, Cambridge, Mass.

Carney, Diana, ed. 1998. *Sustainable Rural Livelihoods: What Contribution Can We Make? Implementing the Sustainable Rural Livelihoods Approach.* London: U.K. Department for International Development.

Carter, Michael R., and Rene Salgado. Forthcoming. "Land Market Liberalization and the Agrarian Question in Latin America." In Alain de Janvry, Gustavo Gordillo, Jean-Philippe Platteau, and Elisabeth Sadoulet, eds., *Access to Land, Rural Poverty and Public Action.* New York: Oxford University Press.

Carvalho, Soniya. 1999a. "Social Funds." Paper presented at Center for Urban Development Studies, Harvard University, 12 October, Cambridge, Mass.

———. 1999b. "What Are Social Funds Really Telling Us?" Paper presented at International Conference on Poverty Reduction and Evaluation, World Bank, 5–7 June, Washington, D.C.

Case, Anne, and Angus Deaton. 1998. "Large Cash Transfers to the Elderly in South Africa." *Economic Journal* 108(450): 1330–61.

Casella, Alessandra, and James E. Rauch. 1997. "Anonymous Market and Group Ties in International Trade." NBER Working Paper 6186. National Bureau of Economic Research, Cambridge, Mass.

Castro-Leal, Florencia, Julia Dayton, Lionel Demery, and Kalpana Mehra. 1999. "Public Social Spending in Africa: Do the Poor Benefit?" *World Bank Research Observer* 14(1): 49–72.

Cavendish, William. 1999. "Empirical Regularities in the Poverty-Environment Relationship of African Rural Households." Working Paper Series, no. WPS/99.21. Oxford University, Centre for the Study of African Economies.

Centre L-J. Lebret. 1999. "Attacking Poverty." Background paper for *World Development Report 2000/2001.* World Bank, Washington, D.C.

CGIAR (Consultative Group on International Agricultural Research), System Review Secretariat. 1998. "The International Research Partnership for Food Security and Sustainable Agriculture." Third System Review of the Consultative Group on International Agricultural Research. Washington, D.C.

Chambers, Robert. 1983. *Rural Development: Putting the Last First.* Essex: Longman Scientific and Technical.

———. 1995. "Poverty and Livelihoods: Whose Reality Counts?" Institute for Development Studies Discussion Paper 347. Sussex University, Brighton.

Chang, Pilwha. 1999a. "Gender and Violence." Background paper for *World Development Report 2000/2001.* Asian Center for Women's Studies, Seoul; and World Bank, Washington, D.C.

———. 1999b. "Impact of Economic and Financial Crisis on Women in South Korea." Asian Center for Women's Studies, Seoul.

Chaves, Rodrigo, and Claudio Gonzalez-Vega. 1996. "The Design of Successful Rural Financial Intermediaries: Evidence from Indonesia." *World Development* 24(1): 65–78.

Chaves, Rodrigo, and Susana Sánchez. 2000. "Romania: Financial Markets, Credit Constraints, and Investment in Rural Areas." Report 19412-RO. World Bank, Romania Country Unit, Washington, D.C.

Chen, Shaohua, and Martin Ravallion. 2000. "How Did the World's Poorest Fare in the 1990s?" Policy Research Working Paper. World Bank, Washington, D.C.

Cheng, Tun-Jeng, Stephan Haggard, and David Kang. 1999. "Institutions and Growth in Korea and Taiwan: The Bureaucracy." In Yilmaz Akyuz, ed., *East Asian Development: New Perspectives.* London: Frank Cass.

Chi, Truong, Thi Ngoc, Lisa Leimar Price, and Mahabub M. Hossain. 1998. "Impact of IPM Training on the Male and Female Farmers' Knowledge and Pest Control Behavior: A Case Study of Vietnam." Working Paper. International Rice Research Institute, Manila.

Chin, Christine B.N. 1997. "Walls of Silence and Late Twentieth-Century Representations of the Foreign Female Domestic Worker: The Case of Filipina and Indonesian Female Servants in Malaysia." *International Migration Review* 31: 353–85.

Ching, Panfila. 1996. "User Fees, Demand for Children's Health Care and Access across Income Groups: The Philippine Case." *Social Science and Medicine* 41(1): 37–46.

Chinnock, Jeffrey, and Sarah Collinson. 1999. *Purchasing Power: Aid Untying, Targeted Procurement and Poverty Reduction.* London: ActionAid. [www.actionaid.org].

Chisari, Omar, Antonio Estache, and Carlos Romero. 1999. "Winners and Losers from the Privatization and Regulation of Utilities: Lessons from a General Equilibrium Model of Argentina." *World Bank Economic Review* 13: 357–78.

Chomitz, Kenneth. 1999. "Environment-Poverty Connections in Tropical Deforestation." Paper presented at *World Development Report 2000/2001* Summer Workshop, World Bank, July, Washington, D.C.

Chomitz, Kenneth, and David Gray. 1996. "Roads, Land Use, and Deforestation: A Spatial Model Applied to Belize." *World Bank Economic Review* 10(3): 487–512.

Chomitz, Kenneth, with Gunawan Setiadi, Azrul Azwar, Nusye Ismail, and Wadiyarti. 1998. "What Do Doctors Want? Developing Incentives for Doctors to Serve in Indonesia's Rural and Remote Areas." Policy Research Working Paper 1888. World Bank, Washington, D.C.

Chong, Alberto, and Jesko Hentschel. 1999. "The Benefits of Bundling." World Bank, Poverty Division, Washington, D.C.

Chua, Amy L. 1998. "Markets, Democracy and Ethnicity: Toward a New Paradigm for Law and Development." *Yale Law Journal* 108(1): 1–107.

Claessens, Stijn, Daniel Oks, and Sweder van Wijnbergen. 1993. "Interest Rates, Growth, and External Debt: The Macroeconomic Impact of Mexico's Brady Deal." Policy Research Working Paper 1147. World Bank, Washington, D.C.

Claessens, Stijn, Enrica Detragiache, Ravi Kanbur, and Peter Wickham. 1997. "Highly Indebted Poor Countries' Debt: A Review of the Issues." *Journal of African Economies* 6(2): 231–54.

Clark, Diana, and Chang-Tai Hsieh. 1999. "Schooling and Labor Market Impact of the 1968 Nine-Year Education Program in Taiwan." University of California at Berkeley.

Clarke, George R.G. 1995. "More Evidence on Income Distribution and Growth." *Journal of Development Economics* 47: 403–27.

Coale, Ansley. 1991. "Excess Female Mortality and the Balance of the Sexes: An Estimate of the Number of 'Missing Females'." *Population and Development Review* 17: 517–23.

Coate, Stephen, and Glenn Loury. 1993. "Will Affirmative Action Policies Eliminate Negative Stereotypes?" *American Economic Review* 83: 1220–40.

Coate, Stephen, and Martin Ravallion. 1993. "Reciprocity without Commitment: Characterization and Performance of Informal Insurance Arrangements." *Journal of Development Economics* 40: 1–24.

Cohen, John M. 1995. "Ethnicity, Foreign Aid and Economic Growth in Sub-Saharan Africa: The Case of Kenya." Discussion Paper 520. Harvard Institute for International Development, Cambridge, Mass.

Coirolo, Luis. 2000. Personal communication. World Bank, Latin America and the Caribbean Region, Washington, D.C.

Colclough, Christopher. 1996. "Education and the Market: Which Parts of the Neoliberal Solution Are Correct?" *World Development* 24(4): 589–610.

Coleman, Brett E. 1999. "The Impact of Group Lending in Northeast Thailand." *Journal of Development Economics* 60: 105–41.

Coleman, James. 1988. "Social Capital in the Creation of Human Capital." *American Journal of Sociology* 94: S95–120.

———. 1990. *Foundations of Social Theory*. Cambridge, Mass.: Harvard University Press.

Colletta, Nat, Markus Kostner, and Ingo Wiederhofer. 1996a. *Case Studies in War-to-Peace Transition: The Demobilization and Reintegration of Ex-Combatants in Ethiopia, Namibia, and Uganda*. World Bank Discussion Paper 331. Africa Technical Department Series. Washington, D.C.

———. 1996b. *The Transition from War to Peace in Sub-Saharan Africa*. Washington, D.C.: World Bank.

Collier, Paul. 1997. "The Failure of Conditionality." In Catherine Gwin and Joan Nelson, eds., *Perspectives on Aid and Development*. Policy Essay 22. Washington, D.C.: Overseas Development Council.

———. 1998. "Social Capital and Poverty." Social Capital Initiative Working Paper 4. World Bank, Social Development Department, Washington, D.C.

———. 1999a. "Ethnicity, Politics, and Economic Performance." World Bank, Development Research Group, Washington, D.C.

———. 1999b. "On the Economic Consequences of Civil War." *Oxford Economic Papers* 51(1): 168–83.

———. 1999c. "The Political Economy of Ethnicity." In Boris Pleskovic and Joseph E. Stiglitz, eds., *Annual World Bank Conference on Development Economics 1998*. Washington, D.C.: World Bank.

———. 2000. "Implications of Ethnic Diversity." World Bank, Development Research Group, Washington, D.C.

———. Forthcoming. "Consensus-Building, Knowledge, and Conditionality." In Boris Pleskovic and Joseph E. Stiglitz, eds., *Annual World Bank Conference on Development Economics 2000*. Washington, D.C.: World Bank.

Collier, Paul, and David Dollar. 1999. "Can the World Cut Poverty in Half? How Policy Reform and Effective Aid Can Meet the DAC Targets." World Bank, Development Research Group, Washington, D.C.

———. 2000. "Aid Allocation and Poverty Reduction." World Bank, Development Research Group, Washington, D.C.

Collier, Paul, and Ashish Garg. 1999. "On Kin Groups and Wages in the Ghanaian Labour Market." *Oxford Bulletin of Economics and Statistics* 61: 133–52.

Collier, Paul, and Jan Willem Gunning. 1997. *Trade Shocks in Developing Countries: Theory and Evidence*. Oxford: Clarendon.

———. 1999. "Explaining African Economic Performance." *Journal of Economic Literature* 37: 64–111.

Collier, Paul, and Anke Hoeffler. 1998. "On the Economic Causes of Civil War." *Oxford Economic Papers* 50: 563–73.

———. 2000. "Greed and Grievance in Civil War." Policy Research Working Paper 2355. World Bank, Washington, D.C.

Collier, Paul, David Dollar, and Nicholas Stern. 2000. "Fifty Years of Development." Paper presented at Annual World Bank Conference on Development Economics in Europe, World Bank, 26–28 June, Paris.

Colson, Elizabeth. 1999. "Gendering Those Uprooted by Development." In Doreen Marie Indra, ed., *Engendering Forced Migration: Theory and Practice*. Oxford: Berghahn Books.

Conning, Jonathan, and Michael Kevane. 1999. "Community-Based Targeting Mechanisms for Social Safety Nets." Williams College, Department of Economics, Williamstown, Mass.

Connolly, Michelle. 1999. "The Impact of Removing Licenses and Restrictions to Import Technology on Technological Change." Background paper for *World Development Report 2000/2001*. World Bank, Washington, D.C.

Constance, Paul. 1999. "What Price Water?" *IDB America* (July–August): 3–5.

Contreras, Dante, David Bravo, Tomás Rau, and Sergio Urzúa. 2000. "Income Distribution in Chile, 1990–1998: Learning from Microeconomic Simulations." Universidad de Chile, Department of Economics, Santiago.

Cook, Lisa D., and Jeffrey Sachs. 1999. "Regional Public Goods in International Assistance." In Inge Kaul, Isabelle Grunberg, and Marc Stern, eds., *Global Public Goods: International Co-operation in the 21st Century*. New York: Oxford University Press.

Coppin, Addington, and Reed Neil Olsen. 1998. "Earnings and Ethnicity in Trinidad and Tobago." *Journal of Development Studies* 34(3): 116–34.

Cornia, Giovanni Andrea. 1999. "Liberalization, Globalization and Income Distribution." WIDER Working Paper 157. United Nations University, Helsinki.

Cornia, Giovanni Andrea, Richard Jolly, and Frances Stewart. 1987. *Adjustment with a Human Face*. New York: Oxford University Press.

Cowell, Frank. 1995. *Measuring Inequality*. New York: Prentice Hall/Harvester Wheatsheaf.

Cox, Donald, and Emmanuel Jimenez. 1998. "Risk Sharing and Private Transfers: What about Urban Households?" *Economic Development and Cultural Change* 46(3): 621–37.

Cox, Donald, Emanuela Galasso, and Emmanuel Jimenez. 2000. "Inter-Country Comparisons of Private Transfers." World Bank, Development Research Group, Washington, D.C.

Cox Edwards, Alejandra. 2000. "Pension Projections for Chilean Men and Women: Estimates from Social Security Contributions." Background paper for forthcoming World Bank Policy Research Report *EnGendering Development*. World Bank, Washington, D.C.

Crook, Richard C., and Alan Sturla Sverrisson. 1999. "To What Extent Can Decentralized Forms of Government Enhance the Development of Pro-poor Policies and Improve Poverty-Alleviation Outcomes?" Background paper for *World Development Report 2000/2001*. U.K. Department for International Development, London; and World Bank, Washington, D.C.

CSIR (Council of Scientific and Industrial Research). 1998. "Knowledge in Development: Multi-Media, Multi-Purpose Community Information Centers as Catalysts for Building Innovative Knowledge-Based Societies." Background paper for *World Development Report 1998*. World Bank, Washington, D.C.

Currie, Janet, and Ann Harrison. 1997. "Sharing the Costs: The Impact of Trade Reform on Capital and Labor in Morocco." *Journal of Labor Economics* 15: 44–71.

CUTS (Consumer Unity and Trust Society). 1999. "Conditions Necessary for the Liberalization of Trade and Investment to Reduce Poverty." Final report to U.K. Department for International Development, London.

Dahl, Robert A. 1999. "A Note on Politics, Institutions, Democracy and Equality." Background paper for *World Development Report 2000/2001*. World Bank, Washington, D.C.

Dakolias, Maria. 1996. *The Judicial Sector in Latin America and the Caribbean: Elements of Reform*. World Bank Technical Paper 319. Washington, D.C.

Daly, Mary, Greg Duncan, George Kaplan, and John Lynch. 1998. "Macro-to-Micro Links in the Relation between Income Inequality and Mortality." *Milbank Quarterly* 76(3): 315–39.

Dar, Amit, and Zafiris Tzannatos. 1999. "Active Labor Market Policies." Social Protection Discussion Paper 9901. World Bank, Human Development Network, Washington, D.C.

Das Gupta, Monica. 1995. "Lifecourse Perspectives on Women's Autonomy and Health Outcomes." *American Anthropologist* 97(3): 481–91.

———. 1999. "Lifeboat versus Corporate Ethic: Social and Demographic Implications of Stem and Joint Families." *Social Science and Medicine* 49(2): 173–84.

———. 2000. "Social Exclusion and Poverty: Preliminary Thoughts for *World Development Report 2001*." In Gudrun Kochendörfer-Lucius and Boris Pleskovic, eds., *Inclusion, Justice, and Poverty Reduction*. Berlin: German Foundation for International Development.

Das Gupta, Monica, and Li Shuzhuo. 1999. "Gender Bias and the Marriage Squeeze in China, South Korea and India, 1920–1990: The Effects of War, Famine and Fertility Decline." *Development and Change* 30(3): 619–52.

Das Gupta, Monica, Helene Grandvoinnet, and Mattia Romani. Forthcoming. "State-Community Synergies in Development: Laying the Basis for Collective Action." Policy Research Working Paper. World Bank, Washington, D.C.

Das Gupta, Monica, Jiang Zhenghua, Xie Zhenming, and Li Bohua. 1997. "The Status of Girls in China." Proceedings of the Symposium of Chinese Scholars on the Demography of China. International Union for the Scientific Study of Population, October, Beijing.

Das Gupta, Monica, Sunhwa Lee, Patricia Uberoi, Danning Wang, Lihong Wang, and Xiaodan Zhang. 2000. "State Policy and Women's Autonomy in China, South Korea and India, 1950–2000: Lessons from Contrasting Experience." Background paper for forthcoming World Bank Policy Research Report *EnGendering Development*. Also presented at Population Association of America annual meeting, March, Los Angeles.

Dasgupta, Partha. 1999. "Valuation and Evaluation: Measuring the Quality of Life and Evaluating Policy." Background paper for *World Development Report 2000/2001*. Cambridge University; and World Bank, Washington, D.C.

Datt, Gaurav. 1998. "Poverty in India and Indian States: An Update." Discussion Paper 47. International Food Policy Research Institute, Food Consumption and Nutrition Division, Washington, D.C.

———. 1999. "Has Poverty in India Declined since the Economic Reforms?" *Economic and Political Weekly* 34(50).

Datt, Gaurav, and Hans Hoogeveen. 2000. "El Niño or El Peso? Crisis, Poverty and Income Distribution in the Philippines." World Bank, East Asia and Pacific Region, Washington, D.C.

Datt, Gaurav, and Martin Ravallion. 1998. "Farm Productivity and Rural Poverty in India." *Journal of Development Studies* 34: 62–85.

Datta-Mitra, Jayati. 1997. *Fiscal Management in Adjustment Lending*. Washington, D.C.: World Bank.

Davey Smith, George, James D. Neaton, Deborah Wentworth,

Rose Stamler, and Jeremiah Stamler. 1998. "Mortality Differences between Black and White Men in the USA: Contribution of Income and Other Risk Factors among Men Screened for the MRFIT." *Lancet* 351(9107): 934–36.

David, Paul. 1993. "Intellectual Property Institutions and the Panda's Thumb: Patents, Copyrights, and Trade Secrets in Economic Theory and History." In Mitchel B. Wallerstein, Roberta A. Schoen, and Mary E. Mogee, eds., *Global Dimensions of Intellectual Property Rights in Science and Technology.* Washington, D.C.: National Academy Press.

Davin, Delia. 1976. *Womenwork: Women and the Party in Revolutionary China.* Oxford: Clarendon.

———. 1995. "Women, Work and Property in the Chinese Peasant Household of the 1980s." In Diane Elson, ed., *Male Bias in the Development Process.* New York: Manchester University Press.

Davis, Benjamin, Sudhanshu Handa, and Humberto Soto. 1999. "Crisis, Poverty, and Long-Term Development: Examining the Mexican Case." International Food Policy Research Institute, Washington, D.C.

Davis, Shelton, and Anthony Oliver-Smith. 1999. "Post–Hurricane Mitch Rehabilitation and Reconstruction Mission." Background note for *World Development Report 2000/2001.* World Bank, Washington, D.C.

de Ferranti, David, Guillermo Perry, Indermit Gill, and Luis Servén. 2000. *Securing Our Future in a Global Economy.* Latin American and Caribbean Studies Series. Washington, D.C.: World Bank.

De Gregorio, José, Sebastian Edwards, and Rodrigo Valdés. Forthcoming. "Controls on Capital Inflows: Do They Work?" *Journal of Development Economics.*

de Haan, Arjan. 1997. "Poverty and Social Exclusion: A Comparison of Debates on Deprivation." Poverty Research Unit Working Paper 2. Sussex University, Brighton.

de Janvry, Alain, and Elisabeth Sadoulet. 1999a. "Asset Positions and Income Strategies among Rural Households in Mexico: The Role of Off-farm Activities in Poverty Reduction." University of California at Berkeley, Department of Agricultural and Resource Economics; and World Bank, Development Research Group, Washington, D.C.

———. 1999b. "Growth, Poverty and Inequality in Latin America: A Causal Analysis, 1970–94." Paper presented at conference on social protection and poverty, Inter-American Development Bank, February, Washington, D.C.

———. 1999c. "Rural Poverty and the Design of Effective Rural Development Strategies." University of California at Berkeley, Department of Agricultural and Resource Economics; and World Bank, Development Research Group, Washington, D.C.

———. 2000a. "Growth, Poverty and Inequality in Latin America: A Causal Analysis, 1970–1994." In Nora Lustig, ed., *Shielding the Poor: Social Protection in the Developing World.* Washington, D.C.: Brookings Institution.

———. 2000b. "Making Investment in the Rural Poor into Good Business: New Perspectives for Rural Development in Latin America." Paper presented at Social Equity Forum, annual meeting of boards of governors of Inter-American Development Bank and Inter-American Investment Corporation, 24–25 March, New Orleans.

de Janvry, Alain, Andre Fargeix, and Elisabeth Sadoulet. 1991. "Political Economy of Stabilization Programs: Feasibility, Growth and Welfare." *Journal of Policy Modeling* 13: 317–45.

de Janvry, Alain, Gustavo Gordillo, Jean-Philippe Platteau, and Elisabeth Sadoulet, eds. Forthcoming. *Access to Land, Rural Poverty and Public Action.* New York: Oxford University Press.

de Janvry, Alain, Gregory Graff, Elisabeth Sadoulet, and David Zilberman. 2000. "Technological Change in Agriculture and Poverty Reduction." Background paper for *World Development Report 2000/2001.* University of California at Berkeley, Department of Agricultural and Resource Economics; and World Bank, Development Research Group, Washington, D.C.

de Janvry, Alain, Jean-Philippe Platteau, Gustavo Gordillo, and Elisabeth Sadoulet. Forthcoming. "Access to Land and Land Policy Reforms." In Alain de Janvry, Gustavo Gordillo, Jean-Philippe Platteau, and Elisabeth Sadoulet, eds., *Access to Land, Rural Poverty and Public Action.* New York: Oxford University Press.

de Janvry, Alain, Elisabeth Sadoulet, Benjamin Davis, and Gustavo Gordillo de Anda. 1996. "*Ejido* Sector Reforms: From Land Reform to Rural Development." In Laura Randall, ed., *Reforming Mexico's Agrarian Reform.* Armonk, N.Y.: M.E. Sharpe.

de la Rocha, Mercedes. 1995. "The Urban Family and Poverty in Latin America." *Latin American Perspectives* 22(2): 12–31.

De Silva, Samantha. 1999. "Community Contracting in Bank-Funded Projects: A Review of Stakeholder Experience." World Bank, Human Development Network, Washington, D.C.

De Soto, Hernando. 1989. *The Other Path: The Invisible Revolution in the Third World.* New York: Harper and Row.

———. Forthcoming. *The Mystery of Capital.*

de Waal, Alex. 1991. "Emergency Food Security in Western Sudan: What Is It For?" In S. Maxwell, ed., *To Cure All Hunger: Food Policy and Food Security in Sudan.* London: Intermediate Technology Development Group.

———. 1999. "Democratic Political Processes and the Fight against Famine." University of London, School of Oriental and African Studies, International Africa Institute.

Deaton, Angus. 1991. "Savings and Liquidity Constraints." *Econometrica* 59(5): 1221–48.

———. 1997. *The Analysis of Household Surveys: A Microeconomic Approach.* Baltimore, Md.: Johns Hopkins University Press.

———. 2000. "Enrollment of Children in School in the 42nd (1986–87) and 52nd (1995–96) Rounds of the NSS." World Bank, Washington, D.C.

Deaton, Angus, and Alessandro Tarozzi. 1999. "Prices and Poverty in India." Princeton University, Princeton, N.J.

Deere, Carmen Diana, and Magdalena Leon. 1997. "Women and Land Rights in the Latin American Neoliberal Counter Reforms." Women in International Development Working Paper 264. Michigan State University, East Lansing.

———. 1999. "Institutional Reform of Agriculture under Neoliberalism: The Impact of the Women's and Indigenous Movements." Keynote address at the conference Land in Latin America: New Context, New Claims, New Concepts, Centre for Latin American Research and Documentation, Centre for Resource Studies, and Wageningen Agricultural University, 26–27 May, Amsterdam.

———. Forthcoming. *Gender, Property and Empowerment: Land, State and Market in Latin America.* Pittsburgh: University of Pittsburgh Press.

Deininger, Klaus. 1999a. "Asset Distribution, Inequality, and Growth." World Bank, Development Research Group, Washington, D.C.

———. 1999b. "Making Negotiated Land Reform Work: Initial Experiences from Brazil, Colombia, and South Africa." Policy Research Working Paper 2040. World Bank, Washington, D.C.

———. 1999c. "Negotiated Land Reform: Brazil, Colombia, South Africa." Draft. World Bank, Development Research Group, Washington, D.C.

———. Forthcoming. "Negotiated Land Reform as One Way of Land Access: Initial Experiences from Colombia, Brazil and South Africa." In Alain de Janvry, Gustavo Gordillo, Jean-Philippe Platteau, and Elisabeth Sadoulet, eds., *Access to Land, Rural Poverty and Public Action.* New York: Oxford University Press.

Deininger, Klaus, and Hans Binswanger. 1999. "The Evolution of the World Bank's Land Policy." *World Bank Research Observer* 14(2): 247–76.

Deininger, Klaus, and Gershon Feder. 1998. "Land Institutions and Land Markets." Policy Research Working Paper 2014. World Bank, Washington, D.C.

Deininger, Klaus, and Bart Minten. 1996. "Poverty, Policies and Deforestation: The Case of Mexico." *Economic Development and Cultural Change* 47: 313–44.

Deininger, Klaus, and Pedro Olinto. 2000. "Asset Distribution, Inequality, and Growth." Policy Research Working Paper 2375. World Bank, Washington, D.C.

Deininger, Klaus, and Lyn Squire. 1996a. "Measuring Income Inequality: A New Database." Development Discussion Paper 537. Harvard Institute for International Development, Cambridge, Mass.

———. 1996b. "A New Data Set Measuring Income Inequality." *World Bank Economic Review* 10(3): 565–91.

———. 1998. "New Ways of Looking at Old Issues: Inequality and Growth." *Journal of Development Economics* 57: 259–87.

Delion, Jean. 1999. "Producer Organizations: Donor Partnerships in Project Implementation." World Bank, Africa Region, Washington, D.C.

Demery, Lionel. 1999. "Poverty Dynamics in Africa: An Update." World Bank, Africa Region, Poverty Reduction and Social Development Unit, Washington, D.C.

Demery, Lionel, and Lyn Squire. 1996. "Macroeconomic Adjustment and Poverty in Africa: An Emerging Picture." *World Bank Research Observer* 11: 39–59.

Demirgüç-Kunt, Asli, and Enrica Detragiache. 1998. "Financial Liberalization and Financial Fragility." Policy Research Working Paper 1917. World Bank, Washington, D.C.

Denmark, Ministry of Foreign Affairs. 2000. *Impact Study of Danish NGOs.* Copenhagen.

Dercon, Stefan. 1996. "Risk, Crop Choice and Savings: Evidence from Tanzania." *Economic Development and Cultural Change* 44(3): 485–514.

———. 1998. "Wealth, Risk, and Activity Choice: Cattle in Western Tanzania." *Journal of Development Economics* 55: 1–42.

———. 1999. "Income Risk, Coping Strategies and Safety Nets." Background paper for *World Development Report 2000/2001.* Katholieke Universiteit Leuven; Oxford University, Centre for the Study of African Economies; and World Bank, Washington, D.C.

Dercon, Stefan, and Pramila Krishnan. 1996. "Income Portfolios in Rural Ethiopia and Tanzania: Choices and Constraints." *Journal of Development Studies* 32(6): 850–75.

———. 1998. "The Urban Labour Market during Structural Adjustment: Ethiopia 1990–1997." Centre for the Study of African Economies Working Paper Series, no. 98-9. Oxford University.

———. 1999. "Vulnerability, Seasonality and Poverty in Ethiopia." Oxford University, Centre for the Study of African Economies.

———. 2000a. "In Sickness and in Health: Risk Sharing within Households in Rural Ethiopia." *Journal of Political Economy* 108(4).

———. 2000b. "Vulnerability, Seasonality and Poverty in Ethiopia." *Journal of Development Studies.*

Dervis, Kemal, Jaime de Melo, and Sherman Robinson. 1982. *General Equilibrium Models for Development Policy.* New York: Cambridge University Press.

Desai, Meghnad. 1991. "Human Development: Concepts and Measurement." *European Economic Review* 35: 350–57.

Deshpande, Ashwini. 2000. "Does Caste Still Define Disparity? A Look at Inequality in Kerala, India." *American Economic Review* 90: 322–25.

Dethier, Jean-Jacques. 1999. "Governance and Economic Performance: A Survey." Discussion Paper on Development Policy 5. Universität Bonn, Zentrum für Entwicklungsforschung.

Devarajan, Shantayanan, and Jeffrey Hammer. 1997. "Public Expenditures and Risk Reduction." World Bank, Development Research Group, Washington, D.C.

———. 1998. "Risk Reduction and Public Spending." Policy Research Working Paper 1869. World Bank, Development Research Group, Washington, D.C.

Devarajan, Shantayanan, and Vinaya Swaroop. 1998. "The Implications of Foreign Aid Fungibility for Development Assistance." Policy Research Working Paper 2022. World Bank, Washington, D.C.

Devarajan, Shantayanan, David Dollar, and Torgny E. Holmgren, eds. 2000. *Aid and Reform in Africa.* Washington, D.C.: World Bank.

Devarajan, Shantayanan, Lyn Squire, and Sethaput Suthiwart-Narueput. 1997. "Beyond Rate of Return: Reorienting Project Analysis." *World Bank Research Observer* 12(1): 35–46.

Devarajan, Shantayanan, Sethaput Suthiwart-Narueput, and Karen Thierfelder. 2000. "The Marginal Cost of Taxation in Developing Countries." World Bank, Development Research Group, Washington, D.C.

Devarajan, Shantayanan, Danyang Xie, and Heng-fu Zou. 1998.

"Should Public Capital Be Subsidized or Provided?" *Journal of Monetary Economics* 41(2): 319–31.

DFID (U.K. Department for International Development). 1999. *Sustainable Livelihoods Guidance Sheets.* London.

Diamond, Larry. 1996. "Is the Third Wave Over?" *Journal of Democracy* 7(3).

Diamond, Larry, Juan J. Linz, and Seymour Martin Lipset, eds. 1988. *Democracy in Developing Countries.* London: Adamantine.

Diop, François, Abdo Yazbeck, and Ricardo Bitran. 1995. "The Impact of Alternative Cost Recovery Schemes on Access and Equity in Niger." *Health Policy and Planning* 10(3): 223–40.

Dollar, David. 2000. "Has Aid Efficiency Improved in the 1990s?" World Bank, Development Research Group, Washington, D.C.

Dollar, David, and Roberta Gatti. 1999. "Gender Inequality, Income and Growth: Are Good Times Good for Women?" Policy Research Report on Gender and Development Working Paper Series, no. 1. World Bank, Washington, D.C.

Dollar, David, and Aart Kraay. 2000. "Growth Is Good for the Poor." World Bank, Development Research Group, Washington, D.C.

Dollar, David, Raymond Fisman, and Roberta Gatti. 1999. "Are Women Really the 'Fairer' Sex? Corruption and Women in Government." Policy Research Report on Gender and Development Working Paper Series, no. 4. World Bank, Washington, D.C.

Dornbusch, Rudiger, and Sebastian Edwards. 1991. *Macroeconomics of Populism.* Chicago: University of Chicago Press.

Dow, William, Paul Gertler, Robert Shoeni, John Strauss, and Duncan Thomas. 1997. "Health Care Prices, Health and Labor Outcomes: Experimental Evidence." Rand, Santa Monica, Calif.

Downing, Thomas. 1996. "Mitigating Social Impoverishment When People Are Involuntarily Displaced." In Christopher McDowell, ed., *Understanding Impoverishment: The Consequences of Development-Induced Displacement.* Oxford: Berghahn Books.

Drèze, Jean. 1999. "Militarism, Development and Democracy." Lecture given at Maharaja Sayajirao University of Baroda, October, Baroda, India.

Drèze, Jean, and Bhatia Bela. 1998. "For Democracy and Development." Delhi School of Economics, Center of Development Economics; and Cambridge University, Centre of South Asian Studies.

Drèze, Jean, and Haris Gazdar. 1997. "Uttar Pradesh: The Burden of Inertia." In Jean Drèze and Amartya Sen, eds., *Indian Development: Selected Regional Perspectives.* Oxford: Oxford University Press.

Drèze, Jean, and Amartya Sen. 1995. *India: Economic Development and Social Opportunity.* New Delhi: Oxford University Press.

———. 1999. "Public Action and Social Security: Foundations and Strategy." In Ehtisham Ahmad, Jean Drèze, John Hills, and Amartya Sen, eds., *Social Security in Developing Countries.* New York: Oxford University Press.

Drèze, Jean, Peter Lanjouw, and Naresh Sharma. 1998. "Economic Development in Palanpur, 1957–93." In Peter Lanjouw and Nicholas Stern, eds., *Economic Development in Palanpur over Five Decades.* Oxford: Clarendon.

Dube, Shyama Charan. 1997. "Ethnicity: Myth, History and Politics." In Arvind M. Shah, Baburao S. Baviskar, and E.A. Ramaswamy, eds., *Social Structure and Change.* Vol. 4. New Delhi: Sage.

Due, Jean, and Christina Gladwin. 1991. "Impacts of Structural Adjustment Programs on African Women Farmers and Female-Headed Households." *American Journal of Agricultural Economics* 73(5): 1431–39.

Duflo, Esther. 2000a. "Child Health and Household Resources in South Africa: Evidence from the Old Age Pension Program." *American Economic Review* 90(2).

———. 2000b. "Schooling and Labor Market Consequences of School Construction in Indonesia: Evidence from an Unusual Policy Experiment." Massachusetts Institute of Technology, Department of Economics, Cambridge, Mass.

Durlauf, Steven. 1996. "A Theory of Persistent Income Inequality." *Journal of Economic Growth* 1(1): 75–93.

Duryea, Suzanne. 1998. "Children's Advancement through School in Brazil: The Role of Transitory Shocks to Household Income." Inter-American Development Bank, Research Department, Washington, D.C.

Dushkin, Lelah. 1972. "Scheduled Caste Politics." In Michael Mahar, ed., *The Untouchables in Contemporary India.* Tucson: University of Arizona Press.

Dyson, Tim. 1996. *Population and Food: Global Trends and Future Prospects.* New York: Routledge.

Easterly, William. 1999a. "The Ghost of the Financing Gap: Testing the Growth Model used in the International Financial Institutions." *Journal of Development Economics* 60(2): 423–38.

———. 1999b. "Happy Societies: The Middle-Class Consensus and Economic Development." Policy Research Working Paper 2346. World Bank, Washington, D.C.

———. 1999c. "How Did Highly Indebted Poor Countries Become Highly Indebted? Reviewing Two Decades of Debt Relief." Policy Research Working Paper 2225. World Bank, Washington, D.C.

———. 2000a. "Can Institutions Resolve Ethnic Conflict?" World Bank, Development Research Group, Washington, D.C.

———. 2000b. "The Lost Decades . . . and the Coming Boom? Policies, Shocks, and Developing Countries' Stagnation, 1980–98." World Bank, Development Research Group, Washington, D.C.

Easterly, William, and Stanley Fischer. 1999. "Inflation and the Poor." Paper presented at Annual World Bank Conference on Development Economics, 28–30 April, Washington, D.C.

———. 2000. "Inflation and the Poor." Policy Research Working Paper 2335. World Bank, Washington, D.C.

Easterly, William, and Aart Kraay. 1999. "Small States, Small Problems?" Policy Research Working Paper 2139. World Bank, Washington, D.C.

Easterly, William, and Ross Levine. 1997. "Africa's Growth Tragedy: Policies and Ethnic Divisions." *Quarterly Journal of Economics* 62(11): 1203–50.

———. 2000. "It's Not Factor Accumulation: Stylized Facts and Growth Models." World Bank, Development Research Group, Washington, D.C.

Easterly, William, and Sergio Rebelo. 1993. "Fiscal Policy and Economic Growth: An Empirical Investigation." *Journal of Monetary Economics* 32: 417–58.

Easterly, William, Roumeen Islam, and Joseph E. Stiglitz. 1999. "Shaken and Stirred: Explaining Growth Volatility." World Bank, Development Research Group, Washington, D.C.

Easterly, William, Norman Loayza, and Peter Montiel. 1997. "Has Latin America's Post-Reform Growth Been Disappointing?" *Journal of International Economics* 43: 287–311.

Easterly, William, Carlos A. Rodríguez, and Klaus Schmidt-Hebbel. 1994. *Public Sector Deficits and Macroeconomic Performance.* New York: Oxford University Press.

Easterly, William, Michael Kremer, Lant Pritchett, and Lawrence Summers. 1993. "Good Policy or Good Luck? Country Growth Performance and Temporary Shocks." *Journal of Monetary Economics* 32: 459–83.

Eastwood, Robert, and Michael Lipton. 1998. "Demographic Transition and Poverty: Effects via Economic Growth, Distribution, Conversion." Sussex University, Department of Economics, Brighton.

———. 1999. "The Impacts of Changes in Human Fertility on Poverty." *Journal of Development Studies* 36(1): 1–30.

EBRD (European Bank for Reconstruction and Development). 1998. *Transition Report 1998: The Financial Sector in Transition.* London.

———. 1999. *Transition Report 1999: Ten Years of Transition.* London.

Eccles, Stephen, and Catherine Gwin. 1999. *Supporting Effective Aid: A Framework for Future Concessional Funding of Multilateral Development Banks.* Policy Essay 23. Washington, D.C.: Overseas Development Council.

Echeverri-Gent, John. 1988. "Guaranteed Employment in an Indian State: The Maharashtra Experience." *Asian Survey* (28): 1294–310.

ECLAC (Economic Commission for Latin America and the Caribbean). 1989. "Antecedentes estadisticos de la distribucion del ingreso en el Peru, 1961–1982." Serie distribucion del ingreso 8. Santiago.

———. 1991. "El perfil de la probeza en América Latina a comienzos de los años 90." Santiago, Chile.

———. 1993. "Antecedentes estadisticos de la distribucion de ingreso en los años 80." Serie distribucion del ingreso 13. Santiago.

———. 1995. *Human Settlements: The Shelter of Development.* Santiago.

———. 1997a. *Social Panorama of Latin America 1996.* Santiago.

———. 1997b. *Statistical Yearbook for Latin America and the Caribbean.* Santiago.

———. 1999a. *Economic Indicators.* Santiago.

———. 1999b. *Social Panorama of Latin America 1998.* Santiago.

Economic and Political Weekly Research Foundation. 1998. "Marathwada Earthquake: Efforts at Participatory Rehabilitation and the Role of Community Participation Consultants." Mumbai.

Edwards, Sebastian. 1994. "Trade and Industrial Policy Reform in Latin America." NBER Working Paper 4772. National Bureau of Economic Research, Cambridge, Mass.

———. 1999. "How Effective Are Capital Controls?" NBER Working Paper 7413. National Bureau of Economic Research, Cambridge, Mass.

Ehrenpreis, Dag. 1999. "Development Cooperation in Support of Poverty Reduction." Paper presented at research workshop on poverty, World Bank, 6–8 July, Washington, D.C.

Eichengreen, Barry. 1999. *Toward a New International Financial Architecture: A Practical Post-Asia Agenda.* Washington, D.C.: Institute for International Economics.

EIU (Economist Intelligence Unit). 1999a. *Business Latin America.* London.

———. 1999b. *Country Report on Indonesia.* London.

Ekbom, Anders, and Jan Bojo. 1999. "Poverty and Environment: Evidence of Links and Integration into the Country Assistance Strategy Process." Environment Group Discussion Paper 4. World Bank, Africa Region, Washington, D.C.

Ellis, Frank. 1999. "Rural Livelihood Diversity in Developing Countries: Analysis, Policy, Methods." U.K. Department for International Development, London.

Elwan, Ann. 1999. "Poverty and Disability." Background paper for *World Development Report 2000/2001.* World Bank, Washington, D.C.

English, Philip. 1998. "Mauritius: Reigniting the Engines of Growth—A Teaching Case Study." World Bank, Economic Development Institute, Washington, D.C.

Ernberg, Johan. 1998. "Universal Access for Rural Development: From Action to Strategies." Paper presented at International Telecommunication Union Seminar on Multipurpose Community Telecentres, 7–9 December, Budapest.

Escobal, Javier, Jaime Saavedra, and Maximo Torero. 1998. "Los activos de los pobres en el Peru." Documento de trabajo 26. Grupo de Analisis para el Desarrollo, Lima.

Esman, Milton, and Norman Uphoff. 1984. *Local Organizations: Intermediaries in Rural Development.* Ithaca, N.Y.: Cornell University Press.

Esteban, Joan-Maria, and Debraj Ray. 1994. "On the Measurement of Polarization." *Econometrica* 62(4): 819–51.

Estes, Richard. 1988. *Trends in World Social Development: The Social Progress of Nations, 1970–1987.* New York: Praeger.

———. 1996. "Social Development Trends in Asia, 1970–1994: The Challenge of a New Century." *Social Indicators Research* 37(2).

———. 1998. "Trends in World Social Development, 1970–1995: Development Challenges for a New Century." *Journal of Developing Societies* 14(1).

Evans, Peter. 1996. "Government Action, Social Capital and Development: Reviewing the Evidence on Synergy." *World Development* 24(6): 1119–32.

———. 1999. "Transferable Lessons? Reexamining the Institutional Prerequisites of East Asian Economic Policies." In Yilmaz Akyuz, ed., *East Asian Development: New Perspectives.* London: Frank Cass.

Evans, Peter, and James Rauch. 1999. "Bureaucracy and Growth: A Cross-National Analysis of the Effects of 'Weberian' State

Structures on Economic Growth." *American Sociological Review* 64(5): 748–65.

Evenson, Robert. 2000. "Crop Genetic Improvement and Agricultural Development." Consultative Group on International Agricultural Research, Washington, D.C.

Fafchamps, Marcel, and Bart Minten. 1999. "Social Capital and the Firm: Evidence from Agricultural Trade." Social Capital Initiative Working Paper 17. World Bank, Social Development Department, Washington, D.C.

Fafchamps, Marcel, Christopher Udry, and Katherine Czukas. 1998. "Drought and Saving in West Africa: Are Livestock a Buffer Stock?" *Journal of Development Economics* 55: 273–305.

Fajnzylber, Pablo, and Daniel Lederman. 1999. "Economic Reforms and Total Factor Productivity Growth in Latin America and the Caribbean (1950–1995): An Empirical Note." Policy Research Working Paper 2114. World Bank, Washington, D.C.

Fajnzylber, Pablo, Daniel Lederman, and Norman Loayza. 1998. *Determinants of Crime Rates in Latin America and the World: An Empirical Assessment.* Washington, D.C.: World Bank.

———. 1999. *Income Inequality and Violent Crime.* Washington, D.C.: World Bank.

Falkingham, Jane. 1999. "Welfare in Transition: Trends in Poverty and Well-Being in Central Asia." Centre for the Analysis of Social Exclusion Paper 20. London School of Economics and Political Science.

Fallon, Peter, and Zafiris Tzannatos. 1998. *Child Labor: Issues and Directions for the World Bank.* Washington, D.C.: World Bank.

FAO (Food and Agriculture Organization of the United Nations). 1995. *The Effects of HIV/AIDS on Farming Systems in Eastern Africa.* Rome.

Feder, Gershon, Tongroj Onchan, Yangyuth Chalamwong, and Chira Hongladarom. 1988. *Land Policies and Farm Productivity in Thailand.* Baltimore, Md.: Johns Hopkins University Press.

Fei, John C.H., Gustav Ranis, and Shirley W.Y. Kuo. 1979. *Growth with Equity: The Taiwan Case.* New York: Oxford University Press.

Fernandez, Aloysius. 1994. *The Myrada Experience: Alternative Management Systems for Savings and Credit for the Rural Poor.* Bangalore: Myrada.

Fernández-Arias, Eduardo, and Peter Montiel. 1997. *Reform and Growth in Latin America: All Pain, No Gain?* Washington, D.C.: Inter-American Development Bank.

Ferreira, Francisco, and Julia A. Litchfield. 1998. "Education or Inflation? The Roles of Structural Factors and Macroeconomic Instability in Explaining Brazilian Inequality in the 1980s." STICERD Discussion Paper 41. London School of Economics and Political Science, Suntory and Toyota International Centres for Economics and Related Disciplines.

Ferreira, Francisco, and Ricardo Paes de Barros. 1999a. "Climbing a Moving Mountain: Explaining the Declining Income Inequality in Brazil from 1976 to 1996." Inter-American Development Bank, Washington, D.C.

———. 1999b. "The Slippery Slope: Explaining the Increase in Extreme Poverty in Urban Brazil, 1976–96." Policy Research Working Paper 2210. World Bank, Washington, D.C.

Ferreira, Francisco, Peter Lanjouw, and Marcelo Neri. 2000. "A New Poverty Profile for Brazil Using PPV, PNAD and Census Data." Texto para discussão 418. Pontifícia Universidade Católica do Rio de Janeiro, Departamento de Economia.

Feyisetan, Bamikale, and Martha Ainsworth. 1996. "Contraceptive Use and the Quality, Price, and Availability of Family Planning in Nigeria." *World Bank Economic Review* 10: 159–87.

Feyzioglu, Tarhan, Vinaya Swaroop, and Min Zhu. 1998. "A Panel Data Analysis of the Fungibility of Foreign Aid." *World Bank Economic Review* 12(1): 29–58.

Fields, Gary S. 1987. "Measuring Inequality Change in an Economy with Income Growth." *Journal of Development Economics* 26: 357–74.

———. 1991. "Growth and Income Distribution." In George Psacharopoulos, ed., *Essays on Poverty, Equity, and Growth.* New York: Pergamon.

———. 1999. "Distribution and Development: A Summary of the Evidence for the Developing World." Background paper for *World Development Report 2000/2001.* Cornell University, Ithaca, N.Y.; and World Bank, Washington, D.C.

Filmer, Deon. 1999a. *Educational Attainment and Enrollment Profiles: A Resource Book Based on an Analysis of Demographic and Health Surveys Data.* Washington, D.C.: World Bank.

———. 1999b. "The Structure of Social Disadvantage in Education: Gender and Wealth." Policy Research Report on Gender and Development Working Paper Series, no. 5. World Bank, Washington, D.C.

Filmer, Deon, and Lant Pritchett. 1998. *Educational Enrollment and Attainment in India: Household Wealth, Gender, Village and State Effects.* Washington, D.C.: World Bank.

———. 1999a. "The Effect of Household Wealth on Educational Attainment: Evidence from 35 Countries." *Population and Development Review* 25(1): 85–120.

———. 1999b. "The Impact of Public Spending on Health: Does Money Matter?" *Social Science and Medicine* 49: 1309–23.

Filmer, Deon, Jeffery Hammer, and Lant Pritchett. 1998. "Health Policy in Poor Countries: Weak Links in the Chain." Policy Research Working Paper 1874. World Bank, Washington, D.C.

Filmer, Deon, Elizabeth King, and Lant Pritchett. 1999. *Gender Disparity in South Asia: Comparisons between and within Countries.* Washington, D.C.: World Bank.

Filmer, Deon, Haneen Sayed, Boediono, Jiyono, Nanik Suwaryani, and Bambang Indriyanto. 1998. "The Impact of Indonesia's Economic Crisis on Basic Education: Findings from a Survey of Schools." World Bank, Development Research Group, Washington, D.C.

Fine, Ben. 1999. "The Developmental State Is Dead: Long Live Social Capital?" *Development and Change* 30: 1–19.

Fiscella, Kevin, and Peter Franks. 1997. "Poverty or Income Inequality as Predictor of Mortality: Longitudinal Cohort Study." *British Medical Journal* 314(7096): 1724–27.

Fisman, Raymond, and Roberta Gatti. 1999. "Decentralization and Corruption: Cross-Country and Cross-State Evidence." World Bank, Development Research Group, Washington, D.C.; and Columbia Business School, New York.

Fiszbein, Ariel, George Psacharopoulos, Samuel Morley, Haeduck Lee, and Bill Wood. 1993. "La pobreza y la distribucion de los ingresos en America Latina: Historia del decenio de 1980." Latin America and the Caribbean Technical Department Report 27. World Bank, Washington, D.C.

Flanagan, Kerry. 1999. "Aging and Poverty: A Policy for the Elderly Poor." World Bank, Social Protection Department, Washington, D.C.

Flegg, A. 1982. "Inequality of Income, Illiteracy, and Medical Care as Determinants of Infant Mortality in Developing Countries." *Population Studies* 36(3): 441–58.

Foley, Gerald. 1997. "Rural Electrification in Costa Rica: A Case Study." Joint United Nations Development Programme and World Bank Energy Sector Management Assistance Programme, Washington, D.C.

Foley, Michael, and Bob Edwards. 1999. "Is It Time to Disinvest in Social Capital?" *Journal of Public Policy* 19: 141–73.

Foner, Eric. 1989. *Reconstruction: America's Unfinished Revolution, 1863–1877.* New York: Harper and Row.

Forbes, Kristin. Forthcoming. "A Reassessment of the Relationship between Inequality and Growth." *American Economic Review.*

Foster, Andrew. 1995. "Prices, Credit Markets and Child Growth in Low-Income Rural Areas." *Economic Journal* 105: 551–70.

Foster, Andrew, and Mark Rosenzweig. 1995. "Learning by Doing and Learning from Others: Human Capital and Technical Change in Agriculture." *Journal of Political Economy* 103(6): 1176–209.

Foster, James E., and Anthony Shorrocks. 1988. "Poverty Orderings." *Econometrica* 56(1): 173–77.

Foster, James E., Joel Greer, and Erik Thorbecke. 1984. "A Class of Decomposable Poverty Measures." *Econometrica* 52(3): 761–66.

Foster, Mick. 1999. *Lessons of Experience from Sector-Wide Approaches in Health.* Geneva: World Health Organization.

Fox, Jonathan. 1992. "Democratic Rural Development: Leadership Accountability in Regional Peasant Organizations." *Development and Change* 23(2): 1–36.

———. 1995. "Governance and Rural Development in Mexico: State Intervention and Public Accountability." *Journal of Development Studies* 32: 1–30.

———. 1996. "How Does Civil Society Thicken? The Political Construction of Social Capital in Rural Mexico." *World Development* 24(6): 1089–103.

Fox, Jonathan, and John Gershman. 1999. "Investing in Social Capital? Comparative Lessons from Ten World Bank Rural Development Projects in Mexico and the Philippines." University of California at Santa Cruz, Department of Latin American and Latino Studies.

Frankel, Jeffrey, and David Romer. 1999. "Does Trade Cause Growth?" *American Economic Review* 89: 379–99.

Frankenberg, Elizabeth, Duncan Thomas, and Kathleen Beegle. 1999. "The Real Costs of Indonesia's Economic Crisis: Preliminary Findings from the Indonesia Family Life Surveys." Labor and Population Working Paper Series, no. 99-04. Rand, Santa Monica, Calif.

Freeman, Paul. 1999. "The Indivisible Face of Disaster." In World Bank, *Investing in Prevention: A Special Report on Disaster Risk Management.* Washington, D.C.

Freeman, Paul, and Landis MacKellar. 1999a. "Economic Impacts of Natural Disasters." Box for *World Development Report 2000/2001.* World Bank, Washington, D.C.

———. 1999b. "Impact of Natural Disasters on Infrastructure." Box for *World Development Report 2000/2001.* World Bank, Washington, D.C.

Freeman, Richard. 1995. "Are Your Wages Set in Beijing?" *Journal of Economic Perspectives* 9(3): 15–32.

Frigenti, Laura, and Alberto Harth, with Rumana Huque. 1998. "Local Solutions to Regional Problems: The Growth of Social Funds and Public Works and Employment Projects in Sub-Saharan Africa." World Bank, Africa Region, Water and Urban 2 Division and Institutional and Social Policy Division, Washington, D.C.

Fukuyama, Francis. 1993. *The End of History and the Last Man.* New York: Avon Books.

———. 1995. *Trust: The Social Virtues and the Creation of Prosperity.* New York: Free Press.

Funaro-Curtis, Rita. 1982. *Natural Disasters and the Development Process: A Discussion of Issues.* Arlington, Va.: Evaluation Technologies.

Gaiha, Raghav, and Anil Deolalikar. 1993. "Persistent, Expected and Innate Poverty: Estimates for Semi-arid Rural South India, 1975–1984." *Cambridge Journal of Economics* 17(4): 409–21.

Galanter, Marc. 1972. "The Abolition of Disabilities: Untouchability and the Law." In Michael Mahar, ed., *The Untouchables in Contemporary India.* Tucson: University of Arizona Press.

Galasso, Emanuela, and Martin Ravallion. 2000. "Distributional Outcomes of a Decentralized Welfare Program." Policy Research Working Paper 2316. World Bank, Washington, D.C.

Galeotti, Marzio, and Alessandro Lanza. 1999. "Desperately Seeking (Environmental) Kuznets." Working paper. Fondazione Eni Enrico Mattei, Milan.

Gallup, John Luke. 1997. "Ethnicity and Earnings in Malaysia." Discussion Paper 593. Harvard Institute for International Development, Cambridge, Mass.

Gallup, John Luke, Steven Radelet, and Andrew Warner. 1998. "Economic Growth and the Income of the Poor." Harvard Institute for International Development, Cambridge, Mass.

Gallup, John Luke, Jeffrey Sachs, and Andrew Mellinger. 1999. "Geography and Economic Development." *International Regional Science Review* 22(2): 179–232.

Gardner, L. Bruce. 1995. "Policy Reform in Agriculture: An Assessment of the Results of Eight Countries." University of Maryland, Department of Agricultural and Resource Economics, College Park.

Garro, Alejandro. 1999. "Access to Justice for the Poor in Latin America." In Juan E. Mendez, Guillermo O'Donnell, and Paulo Sergio Pinheiro, eds., *The (Un)Rule of Law and the Underprivileged in Latin America.* Notre Dame, Ind.: University of Notre Dame.

Gatti, Roberta. 1999. "Corruption and Trade Tariffs, or a Case for Uniform Tariffs." Policy Research Working Paper 2216. World Bank, Washington, D.C.

Gaynor, Cathy. 1996. "Decentralization of Primary Education: Implications at School and Community Level—The Case of Nigeria and Tanzania." World Bank, Economic Development Institute, Washington, D.C.

———. 1998. *Decentralization of Education: Teacher Management.* Directions in Development Series. Washington, D.C.: World Bank.

Gereffi, Gary, and Martha Argelia Martinez. 1999. "Blue Jeans and Local Linkages: The Blue Jeans Boom in Torreón, Mexico." Background paper for *World Development Report 2000/2001.* World Bank, Washington, D.C.

German, Tony, and Judith Randel. 1998. "Targeting the End of Absolute Poverty: Trends in Development Cooperation." In Judith Randel and Tony German, eds., *The Reality of Aid, 1998/1999: An Independent Review of Poverty Reduction and Development Assistance.* London: Earthscan.

Gertler, Paul. 2000. "Insuring the Economic Costs of Illness." In Nora Lustig, ed., *Shielding the Poor: Social Protection in the Developing World.* Washington, D.C.: Brookings Institution and Inter-American Development Bank.

Gertler, Paul, and Paul Glewwe. 1989. *The Willingness to Pay for Education in Developing Countries: Evidence from Rural Peru.* Living Standards Measurement Study Working Paper 54. Washington, D.C.: World Bank.

Gertler, Paul, and Jonathan Gruber. 1997. "Insuring Consumption against Illness." NBER Working Paper 6035. National Bureau of Economic Research, Cambridge, Mass.

Gertler, Paul, and Jeffrey Hammer. 1997. "Policies for Pricing Publicly Provided Health Services." Policy Research Working Paper 1762. World Bank, Washington, D.C.

Gertler, Paul, and Orville Solon. 1998. "Who Benefits from Social Health Insurance in Low-Income Countries?" University of California at Berkeley, Haas School of Business.

Gertler, Paul, and Jacques van der Gaag. 1990. *The Willingness to Pay for Medical Care: Evidence from Two Developing Countries.* Baltimore, Md.: Johns Hopkins University Press.

Ghana Statistical Service. 1999. "Poverty Trends in Ghana in the 1990s." Report prepared by government of Ghana for the tenth consultative group meeting, 23–24 November, Accra.

Ghatak, Maitreesh. 1999. "Group Lending, Local Information and Peer Selection." *Journal of Development Economics* 60(1): 27–50.

Gibbs, Christopher, Claudia Fumo, and Thomas Kuby. 1999. *Nongovernmental Organizations in World Bank–Supported Projects: A Review.* Washington, D.C.: World Bank.

Gilbert, Alan. 1998a. "A Home Is for Ever? Residential Mobility and Home Ownership in Self-Help Settlements." *Environment and Planning* 31(6): 1073–91.

———. 1998b. "Market Efficiency and the Secondary Housing Market in Third World Cities." Report for U.K. Department for International Development. London.

Gilbert, Alan, Oscar O. Camacho, Rene Coulomb, and Andres Necochea. 1993. *In Search of a Home: Rental and Shared Housing in Latin America.* Tucson: University of Arizona Press.

Gilson, Lucy. 1998. "The Lessons of User Fee Experience in Africa." In Alison Beattie, Jan Doherty, Lucy Gilson, Eyitayo Lambo, and Paul Shaw, eds., *Sustainable Health Care Financing in Southern Africa: Papers from an EDI Health Policy Seminar held in Johannesburg, South Africa, June 1996.* Washington, D.C.: World Bank.

Girishankar, Navin. 1999a. "Reforming Institutions for Service Delivery." Policy Research Working Paper 2039. World Bank, Washington, D.C.

———. 1999b. "Securing the Public Interest under Pluralistic Institutional Design." World Bank, Operations Evaluation Department, Washington, D.C.

Girishankar, Navin, and Nicholas P. Manning. 1999. "Toolkit for Assessing Constraints on Frontline Delivery in Decentralized Settings." World Bank, Poverty Reduction and Economic Management Network, Washington, D.C.

Gittell, Ross, and Avis Vidal. 1998. *Community Organizing: Building Social Capital as a Development Strategy.* Newbury Park, Calif.: Sage.

Glaeser, Edward, David Laibson, and Bruce Sacerdote. 2000. "The Economic Approach to Social Capital." NBER Working Paper 7728. National Bureau of Economic Research, Cambridge, Mass.

Glewwe, Paul. 1991. "Investigating the Determinants of Household Welfare in Côte d'Ivoire." *Journal of Development Economics* 35: 307–37.

Glewwe, Paul, and Dennis de Tray. 1989. *The Poor in Latin America during Adjustment: A Case Study of Peru.* Living Standards Measurement Study Working Paper 56. Washington, D.C.: World Bank.

Glewwe, Paul, and Gilette Hall. 1998. "Are Some Groups More Vulnerable to Macroeconomic Shocks than Others? Hypothesis Tests Based on Panel Data from Peru." *Journal of Development Economics* 56: 181–206.

Glewwe, Paul, Michele Gragnolati, and Hassan Zaman. 2000. "Who Gained from Vietnam's Boom in the 1990s? An Analysis of Poverty and Inequality Trends." Policy Research Working Paper 2275. World Bank, Washington, D.C.

Gokcekus, Omer, Ranjana Mukherjee, and Nick Manning. 2000. "Institutional Arrangements Affect Performance." World Bank, Poverty Reduction and Economic Management Network, Washington, D.C.

Goldstein, Anne. 1999. "Thinking Outside Pandora's Box." Background paper for forthcoming World Bank Policy Research Report *EnGendering Development.* World Bank, Washington, D.C.

Goldstein, Morris, Graciela Kaminsky, and Carmen Reinhart. 2000. *Assessing Financial Vulnerability: An Early Warning System for Emerging Markets.* Washington, D.C.: Institute for International Economics.

Gonzales de Olarte, Efraín, and Pilar Gavilano Llosa. 1999. "Does Poverty Cause Domestic Violence? Some Answers from Lima." In Andrew Morrison and Maria Loreto Biehl, eds., *Too Close to Home: Domestic Violence in the Americas.* Washington, D.C.: Inter-American Development Bank.

Goodin, Robert E., Bruce Headey, Ruud Muffels, and Henk-Jan Dirven. 1999. *The Real Worlds of Welfare Capitalism.* Cambridge: Cambridge University Press.

Goody, Jack. 1976. *Production and Reproduction: A Comparative Study of the Domestic Domain.* Cambridge: Cambridge University Press.

———. 1990. *The Oriental, the Ancient and the Primitive: Systems of Marriage and the Family in the Pre-industrial Societies of Eurasia.* Cambridge: Cambridge University Press.

Gopal, Gita. 1999. *Gender-Related Legal Reform and Access to Economic Resources in Eastern Africa.* World Bank Discussion Paper 405. Washington, D.C.

Gragnolati, Michele. 1999. "Children's Growth and Poverty in Rural Guatemala." Policy Research Working Paper 2193. World Bank, Washington, D.C.

Graham, Carol. 1992. "Politics of Protecting the Poor during Adjustment: Bolivia's Emergency Social Fund." *World Development* 20: 1233–51.

———. 1994. *Safety Nets, Politics, and the Poor: Transitions to Market Economies.* Washington, D.C.: Brookings Institution.

———. 1996. *Gender Issues in Poverty Alleviation: Recent Experiences with Demand-Based Programs in Latin America, Africa and Eastern Europe.* Development and Technical Cooperation Department. Geneva: International Labour Office.

Grandin, Barbara, and P. Lembuya. 1992. "Amboseli National Park, the Surrounding Group Ranches and Community Conservation." African Wildlife Foundation, Nairobi.

Grandvoinnet, Helene. 2000. "Rule of Law and Poverty Reduction: Some Issues." In Asbjørn Kjønstad and Peter Robson, eds., *Poverty and Law.* London: Hart.

Grandvoinnet, Helene, and Pauline Tamesis. 2000. "Fighting Corruption: The Case of the Philippines." In Helene Grandvoinnet, Irene Hors, and Pauline Tamesis, eds., *Fighting Corruption: Comparative Country Case Studies in Five Developing Countries.* Paris: Organisation for Economic Co-operation and Development, Development Center; and United Nations Development Programme.

Granovetter, Mark. 1994. "Business Groups." In Neil Smelser and Richard Swedberg, eds., *The Handbook of Economic Sociology.* Princeton, N.J.: Princeton University Press.

Gray, Cheryl, and Daniel Kaufmann. 1998. "Corruption and Development." *Finance and Development* 35(3): 7–10.

Gray, Leslie, and Michael Kevane. 1996. *Land Tenure Status of African Women.* Washington, D.C.: World Bank.

Gray, William, Christopher Landsea, Paul Mielke, and Kenneth Berry. 1999. "Summary of 1999 Atlantic Tropical Cyclone Activity and Verification of Author's Seasonal Activity Prediction." Colorado State University, Atmospheric Science Faculty, Fort Collins.

Greenland, David J. 1997. "International Agricultural Research and the CGIAR System: Past, Present, and Future." *Journal of International Development* 9: 449–58.

Greenwald, Bruce C., and Joseph E. Stiglitz. 1990. "Asymmetric Information and the New Theory of the Firm: Financial Constraints and Risk Behavior." NBER Working Paper 3359. National Bureau of Economic Research, Cambridge, Mass.

Greif, Avner. 1994. "Cultural Beliefs and the Organization of Society: A Historical and Theoretical Reflection on Collectivist and Individualist Societies." *Journal of Political Economy* 102: 912–50.

Grimard, Franque. 1997. "Household Consumption Smoothing through Ethnic Ties: Evidence from Côte d'Ivoire." *Journal of Development Economics* 53: 391–422.

Grindle, Merilee. 1996. *Challenging the State: Crisis and Innovation in Latin America and Africa.* New York: Cambridge University Press.

———. 1997. *Getting Good Government: Capacity Building in the Public Sectors of Developing Countries.* Cambridge, Mass.: Harvard University Press.

Grootaert, Christiaan. 1997. "Social Capital: The Missing Link?" In World Bank, *Expanding the Measure of Wealth: Indicators of Environmentally Sustainable Development.* Washington, D.C.

———. 1998. "Child Labor in Côte d'Ivoire: Incidence and Determinants." Policy Research Working Paper 1905. World Bank, Washington, D.C.

———. 1999a. "Does Social Capital Help the Poor? A Synthesis of Findings from the Local Level Institutions Studies in Bolivia, Burkina Faso and Indonesia." World Bank, Social Development Department, Washington, D.C.

———. 1999b. "Social Capital, Household Welfare and Poverty in Indonesia." Local Level Institutions Working Paper 6. World Bank, Social Development Department, Washington, D.C.

Grootaert, Christiaan, and Jeanine Braithwaite. 1998. "Poverty Correlates and Indicator-Based Targeting in Eastern Europe and the Former Soviet Union." Policy Research Working Paper 1942. World Bank, Washington, D.C.

Grootaert, Christiaan, and Ravi Kanbur. 1995a. "Child Labor: A Review." Policy Research Working Paper 1454. World Bank, Washington, D.C.

———. 1995b. "The Lucky Few amidst Economic Decline: Distributional Change in Côte d'Ivoire as Seen through Panel Data Sets." *Journal of Development Studies* 31(4): 603–19.

Grootaert, Christiaan, and Deepa Narayan. 2000. "Local Institutions, Poverty and Household Welfare in Bolivia." Local Level Institutions Working Paper 9. World Bank, Social Development Department, Washington, D.C.

Grootaert, Christiaan, and Harry Anthony Patrinos, eds. 1999. *The Policy Analysis of Child Labor: A Comparative Study.* New York: St. Martin's.

Grootaert, Christiaan, Ravi Kanbur, and Gi-Taik Oh. 1997. "The Dynamics of Welfare Gains and Losses: An African Case Study." *Journal of Development Studies* 33(5): 635–57.

Grootaert, Christiaan, Gi-Taik Oh, and Anand Swamy. 1999. "Social Capital and Development Outcomes in Burkina Faso." Local Level Institutions Working Paper 7. World Bank, Social Development Department, Washington, D.C.

Grosh, Margaret. 1994. *Administering Targeted Social Programs in Latin America: From Platitudes to Practice.* Regional and Sectoral Studies Series. Washington, D.C.: World Bank.

Grosh, Margaret, and Paul Glewwe, eds. 2000. *Designing Household Survey Questionnaires for Developing Countries: Lessons from 15 Years of the Living Standards Measurement Study.* Washington, D.C.: World Bank.

Guillaumont, Patrick, and Lisa Chauvet. 1999. *Aid and Perfor-*

mance: A Reassessment. Clermant-Ferrand: Centre d'Etudes Recherches le Development International.

Guillaumont, Patrick, Sylviane Guillaumont Jeanneney, and Jean-François Brun. 1999. "How Instability Lowers African Growth." *Journal of African Economies* 8(1): 87–107.

Gupta, Dipankar, ed. 1991. *Social Stratification.* New Delhi: Oxford University Press.

Gupta, Sanjeev, Hamid Davoodi, and Rosa Alonso-Terme. 1998. "Does Corruption Affect Income Inequality and Poverty?" IMF Working Paper 98/76. International Monetary Fund, Washington, D.C.

Gupta, Sanjeev, Jerald Schiff, and Benedict Clements. 1996. "Worldwide Military Spending, 1990–95." IMF Working Paper 96/64. International Monetary Fund, Washington, D.C.

———. 1998. "Public Spending on Human Development." *Finance and Development* 35(3): 10–13.

Gupta, Sanjeev, Calvin McDonald, Christian Schiller, Marijin Verhoeven, Želco Bogetić, and G. Schwartz. 1998. "Mitigating the Social Cost of the Economic Crisis and the Reform Programs in Asia." Paper on Policy Analysis and Assessment 98/7. International Monetary Fund, Washington, D.C.

Gurr, Ted Robert, Barbara Harff, Monty G. Marshall, and James R. Scarritt. 1993. *Minorities at Risk: A Global View of Ethnopolitical Conflicts.* Washington, D.C.: Institute of Peace Press.

Gwatkin, Davidson R., Michel Guillot, and Patrick Heuveline. 2000. *The Burden of Disease among the Global Poor: Current Situation, Future Trends, and Implications for Strategy.* Washington, D.C.: World Bank.

Gwatkin, Davidson R., Shea Rutstein, Kiersten Johnson, Rohini Pande, and Adam Wagstaff. 2000. *Socioeconomic Differences in Health, Nutrition and Population.* Washington, D.C.: World Bank. [www.worldbank.org/poverty/health/data/index.htm].

Haan, Hans Christian, Adrian Coad, and Inge Lardinois. 1998. *Municipal Solid Waste Management: Involving Micro and Small Enterprises.* Turin: International Labour Office.

Haddad, Lawrence, and Ravi Kanbur. 1990. "Are Better-off Households More Unequal or Less Unequal?" Policy Research and External Affairs Working Paper 373. World Bank, Washington, D.C.

Haddad, Lawrence, and Thomas Reardon. 1993. "Gender Bias in the Allocation of Resources within Households in Burkina Faso: A Disaggregated Outlay Equivalent Analysis." *Journal of Development Studies* 29(2): 260–76.

Haddad, Lawrence, Marie J. Ruel, and James L. Garrett. 1999. "Are Urban Poverty and Undernutrition Growing? Some Newly Assembled Evidence." Food Consumption and Nutrition Division Discussion Paper 63. International Food Policy Research Institute, Washington, D.C.

Haggard, Stephan. 1998. "Institutions and Growth in Korea and Taiwan: The Bureaucracy." *Journal of Development Studies* 34: 87–111.

Haggard, Stephan, and Steven B. Webb. 1993. "What Do We Know about the Political Economy of Economic Policy Reform?" *World Bank Research Observer* 8(2): 143–68.

Haggard, Stephan, Eliza Willis, and Christopher da C.B. Garman.

1999. "Politics of Decentralization in Latin America." *Latin American Research Review* 34(1): 7–56.

Hallberg, Kristin. 1999. *Small and Medium-Scale Enterprises: A Framework for Intervention.* Washington, D.C.: World Bank.

Haltiwanger, John, and Manisha Singh. 1999. "Cross-Country Evidence on Public Sector Retrenchment." *World Bank Economic Review* 13(1): 23–66.

Haltiwanger, John, and Milan Vodopivec. 1999. "Gross Worker and Job Flows in a Transition Economy: An Analysis of Estonia." Policy Research Working Paper 2082. World Bank, Washington, D.C.

Hammer, Jeffrey. 1997. "Economic Analysis for Health Projects." *World Bank Research Observer* 12(1): 47–72.

Hamoudi, Amar, and Jeffrey Sachs. 1999. "Economic Consequences of Health Status: A Review of Evidence." Harvard University, Center for International Development, Cambridge, Mass.

Hanmer, Lucia. 1994. "What Happens to Welfare When User Fees Finance Health Care? The Impact of Gender on Policy Outcomes: Theory and Evidence from Zimbabwe." Institute of Social Studies Working Paper Series, no. 180. The Hague, Netherlands.

Hanmer, Lucia, and Felix Naschold. 1999. "Are the International Development Targets Attainable?" Overseas Development Institute, Portland House, London.

Hansen, Henrik, and Finn Tarp. 2000. "Aid Effectiveness Disputed." In Finn Tarp, ed., *Foreign Aid and Development: Lessons Learnt and Directions for the Future.* London: Routledge.

Hanson, Gordon, and Ann Harrison. 1999. "Trade and Wage Inequality in Mexico." *Industrial and Labor Relations Review* 52(2): 271–88.

Hanushek, Eric, and Dennis D. Kimko. Forthcoming. "Schooling, Labor Force Quality and the Growth of Nations." *American Economic Review.*

Haque, Nadeem Ul, and Jahangir Aziz. 1997. "The Quality of Governance: 'Second Generation' Civil Service Reform in Africa." *Journal of African Economics* 8(1): 68–106.

Haque, Nadeem Ul, and Ali Khan. 1997. "Institutional Development: Skill Transference through a Reversal of 'Human Capital Flight' or Technical Assistance." IMF Working Paper 97/89. International Monetary Fund, Washington, D.C.

Harberger, Arnold. 1998. "A Vision of the Growth Process." *American Economic Review* 88: 1–32.

Harrison, Ann, and Gordon Hanson. 1999. "Who Gains from Trade Reform? Some Remaining Puzzles." NBER Working Paper 6915. National Bureau of Economic Research, Cambridge, Mass.

Harriss, John. 1999. "How Much Difference Does Politics Make? Regime Differences across Indian States and Rural Poverty Reduction." London School of Economics and Political Science.

Harriss, John, Janet Hunter, and Colin M. Lewis. 1995. *The New Institutional Economics and Third World Development.* London: Routledge.

Harris-White, Barbara. 1996. "The Political Economy of Disability and Development, with Special Reference to India." United Nations Research Institute for Social Development Discussion Paper 73. Geneva.

Harrold, Peter, and associates. 1995. *The Broad Sector Approach to Investment Lending: Sector Investment Programs.* World Bank Discussion Paper 302. Washington, D.C.

Harvey, Pharis J., Terry Collingsworth, and Bama Athreya. 1998. "Developing Effective Mechanisms for Implementing Labor Rights in the Global Economy." International Labor Rights Fund, Washington, D.C.

Hashemi, Syed M., and Sidney R. Schuler. 1997. "Sustainable Banking with the Poor: A Case Study of the Grameen Bank." John Snow Inc. Research and Training Institute Working Paper 10. Arlington, Va.

Hausmann, Ricardo, and Michael Gavin. 1995. "Overcoming Volatility in Latin America." Seminar Series, 95-34. International Monetary Fund, Washington, D.C.

Heath, Julia A. 1998. "The Financing and Provisioning of Education and Health Services in Developing Countries: A Review Article." *Economics of Education Review* 17(3): 359–62.

Heggie, Ian G., and Piers Vickers. 1998. *Commercial Management and Financing of Roads.* World Bank Technical Paper 409. Washington, D.C.

Helleiner, Gerry K. 2000a. "Developing Countries in Global Economic Governance and Negotiation Processes." Paper prepared for World Institute for Development and Economic Research project New Roles and Functions for the United Nations and the Bretton Woods Institutions. University of Toronto, Department of Economics.

———. 2000b. "External Conditionality, Local Ownership, and Development." In Jim Freedman, ed., *Transforming Development.* Toronto: University of Toronto Press.

Heller, Patrick. 1996. "Social Capital as a Product of Class Mobilization and State Intervention: Industrial Workers in Kerala, India." *World Development* 24(6): 1055–71.

Hellman, Joel, Geraint Jones, Daniel Kaufmann, and Mark Schankerman. 2000. "Measuring Governance, Corruption, and State Capture: How Firms and Bureaucrats Shape the Business Environment in Transition Economies." Policy Research Working Paper 2312. World Bank Institute, Governance, Regulation, and Finance; and European Bank for Reconstruction and Development, the Chief Economist's Office, Washington, D.C.

Hentschel, Jesko, and Jesse Bump. 2000. "Urban Income Poverty: Some Cross-Country Comparisons." World Bank, Poverty Group, Washington, D.C.

Herbst, Jeffrey. 1999. "The Role of Citizenship Laws in Multiethnic Societies: Evidence from Africa." In Richard Joseph, ed., *State, Conflict and Democracy in Africa.* Boulder, Colo.: Lynne Rienner.

Herrera, Javier. 1999. *Dynamique de la pauvrete et de l'inegalite au Perou, 1997–1998.* Paris: Institute for Resource Development/DIAL.

Herring, Ronald J. 1999. "Political Conditions for Agrarian Reform and Poverty Alleviation." Background paper for *World Development Report 2000/2001.* World Bank, Washington, D.C.

Herring, Ronald J., and Rex Edwards. 1983. "Guaranteeing Employment to the Rural Poor: Social Functions and Class Interests in Employment Guarantee Schemes in Western India." *World Development* 11: 575–92.

Hertel, Thomas, and Will Martin. 1999a. "Developing Country Interests in Liberalizing Manufactures Trade." Purdue University, Agricultural Economics Department, West Lafayette, Ind.; and World Bank, Washington, D.C.

———. 1999b. "Would Developing Countries Gain from Inclusion of Manufactures in the WTO Negotiations?" Paper presented at conference on the WTO and the Millennium Round, 20–21 September, Geneva.

Herzog, Henry W. 1997. "Ethnicity and Job Tenure in a Segmented Labour Market: The Case for New Zealand." *Australian Economic Review* 30(2): 167–84.

Hicks, David. 1993. *An Evaluation of the Zimbabwe Drought Relief Program, 1992–1993: The Roles of Household-Level Response and Decentralized Decision Making.* Harare: World Food Programme.

Hicks, Norman, and Quentin Wodon. 2000. "Economic Shocks, Safety Nets, and Fiscal Constraints: Social Protection for the Poor in Latin America." XII Seminario Regional de Politica Fiscal: Compendio de Documentos 2000, Economic Commission for Latin America and the Caribbean, United Nations, Santiago.

Hill, Anne, and Elizabeth King. 1995. "Women's Education and Economic Well-Being." *Feminist Economics* 1(2): 1–26.

Hino, Toshiko. 1993. "Community Participation in 'Programme de restructuration de l'hydraulique villageoise' in Côte d'Ivoire." World Bank, Washington, D.C.

Hirsch, Aaron. 1999. "Report on the Internet Center in Wa, Northern Ghana." World Bank, Washington, D.C.

Hirschman, Albert. 1968. *Journeys toward Progress: Studies of Economic Policy-Making in Latin America.* New York: Greenwood.

———. 1984. *Getting Ahead Collectively: Grass-Roots Organizations in Latin America.* New York: Pergamon.

Hobcraft, John. 1993. "Women's Education, Child Welfare and Child Survival: A Review of the Evidence." *Health Transition Review* 3: 159–75.

Hoddinott, John, and Lawrence Haddad. 1995. "Does Female Income Share Influence Household Expenditures? Evidence from Côte d'Ivoire." *Oxford Bulletin of Economics and Statistics* 57(1): 77–96.

Hoddinott, John, and Bill Kinsey. 1998. "Child Growth in the Time of Drought." International Food Policy Research Institute, Washington, D.C.

———. 2000. "Adult Health in Time of Drought." Food Consumption and Nutrition Division Discussion Paper 79. International Food Policy Research Institute, Washington, D.C.

Hoff, Karla, Avishay Braverman, and Joseph E. Stiglitz, eds. 1993. *The Economics of Rural Organization: Theory, Practice, and Policy.* New York: Oxford University Press.

Holzer, Harry, and David Neumark. 1999. "Assessing Affirmative Action." NBER Working Paper 7323. National Bureau of Economic Research, Cambridge, Mass.

Holzmann, Robert, and Steen Lau Jorgensen. 1999. "Social Protection as Social Risk Management: Conceptual Understandings for the Social Protection Sector Strategy Paper." Social Protection Discussion Paper 9904. World Bank, Washington, D.C.

———. 2000. "Social Risk Management: A New Conceptual Framework for Social Protection and Beyond." Social Protection Discussion Paper 0006. World Bank, Human Development Network, Washington, D.C.

Holzmann, Robert, Truman Packard, and Jose Cuesta. 1999. "Extending Coverage in Multipillar Pension Systems: Constraints and Hypotheses, Preliminary Evidence and Future Research Agenda." Paper presented at World Bank conference on new ideas about old age security, 14–15 September, Washington, D.C.

Hopenhayn, Hugo, and Juan Pablo Nicolini. 1999. "Heterogeneity and Optimal Unemployment Insurance." Paper presented at conference on social protection and poverty, Inter-American Development Bank, February, Washington, D.C.

Horowitz, Donald. 1999. "Structure and Strategy in Ethnic Conflict: A Few Steps toward Synthesis." In Boris Pleskovic and Joseph E. Stiglitz, eds., Annual World Bank Conference on Development Economics 1998. Washington, D.C.: World Bank.

Horton, Sue, and Dipak Mazumdar. 1999. "Vulnerable Groups and Labor: The Aftermath of the Asian Financial Crisis." Paper presented at World Bank–International Labour Organization seminar on economic crisis, employment, and labor markets in East and Southeast Asia.

Hossain, Mahabub. 1988. "Credit for Alleviation of Rural Poverty: The Grameen Bank of Bangladesh." Research Report 65. International Food Policy Research Institute, Washington, D.C.

Hossain, Naomi, and Mick Moore, with Noushin Kalati, James Manor, and Elisa Reis. 1999. "Elites, Poverty and Development." Background paper for World Development Report 2000/2001. World Bank, Washington, D.C.

Hotchkiss, David. 1993. "The Role of Quality in the Demand for Health Care in Cebu, Philippines." University of North Carolina, Department of Economics, Chapel Hill.

Houtzager, Peter P., and Jonathan Pattenden. 1999. "Finding the Shape of the Mountain: When 'the Poor' Set the Agenda." Background paper for World Development Report 2000/2001. U.K. Department for International Development, London; and World Bank, Washington, D.C.

Hoy, M., and Emmanuel Jimenez. 1997. "The Impact on the Urban Environment of Incomplete Property Rights." World Bank, Development Research Group, Washington, D.C.

Hsiao, William. 1995. "The Chinese Health Care System: Lessons for Other Nations." Social Science and Medicine 41(8): 1047–55.

Hulme, David, and Paul Mosley. 1996. Finance against Poverty. New York: Routledge.

Humana, Charles. 1992. World Human Rights Guide. New York: Oxford University Press.

Humplick, Frannie, and Azadeh Moini-Araghi. 1996a. "Decentralized Structures for Providing Roads." Policy Research Working Paper 1658. World Bank, Washington, D.C.

———. 1996b. "Is There an Optimal Structure for Decentralized Provision of Roads?" Policy Research Working Paper 1657. World Bank, Washington, D.C.

Huntington, Samuel, and Joan Nelson. 1976. No Easy Choice: Political Participation in Developing Countries. Cambridge, Mass.: Harvard University Press.

Hutchinson, Paul. Forthcoming. "Combating Illness." In Ritva Reinikka and Paul Collier, eds., Uganda's Recovery: The Role of Farms, Firms and Government. Washington, D.C.: World Bank.

IDA (International Development Association). 1998. Additions to IDA Resources: Twelfth Replenishment—A Partnership for Poverty Reduction. Washington, D.C.: World Bank.

———. 2000. "Uganda: Poverty Reduction Strategy Paper and Joint World Bank–IMF Staff Assessment of the PRSP." World Bank, Washington, D.C.

IDB (Inter-American Development Bank). 1995. Overcoming Volatility: Economic and Social Progress in Latin America, 1995 Report. Washington, D.C.

———. 1997. Latin America after a Decade of Reforms. Washington, D.C.

———. 2000. Social Protection for Equity and Growth. Sustainable Development Department, Poverty and Inequality Advisory Unit, Washington, D.C.

———. Various years. Statistical and Social Database. Washington, D.C. [www.iadb.org/int/sta/ENGLISH/staweb/statshp.htm].

IDRC (International Development Research Centre). 1998. Acacia Page. [www.idrc.ca/acacia/engine/eng_6.htm].

IFC (International Finance Corporation) and FIAS (Foreign Investment Advisory Service). 1997. Foreign Direct Investment. Lessons of Experience 5. Washington, D.C.

ILO (International Labour Organization). 2000. "International Labour Standards and Human Rights." [www.ilo.org/public/english/standards/norm/index.htm].

Imber, Mark. 1996. "The Environment and the United Nations." In John Vogler and Mark Imber, eds., The Environment and International Relations. London: Routledge.

IMF (International Monetary Fund). 1995. International Financial Statistics. Washington, D.C.

———. 1999. "Military Spending Continues to Stabilize: Some Countries Increase Social Spending." International Monetary Fund Survey. Washington, D.C.

———. 2000. Progress in Strengthening the Architecture of the International Financial System. Washington, D.C.

IMF (International Monetary Fund) and IDA (International Development Association). 1999. Poverty Reduction Strategy Papers: Operational Issues. Washington, D.C.: International Development Association.

IMF (International Monetary Fund), OECD (Organisation for Economic Co-operation and Development), UN (United Nations), and World Bank. 2000. 2000: A Better World for All—Progress towards the International Development Goals. Washington, D.C. [www.paris21.org/betterworld/].

INADES Formation Tchad. 1999. "Synthèse de la consultation de la Banque Mondiale sur la pauvreté au Tchad." Background paper for World Development Report 2000/2001. World Bank, Washington, D.C.

Independent Review Team of Zambia's Health Sector. 1997. Comprehensive Review of the Zambian Health Reforms. Vol. 1, Main Report. Geneva: World Health Organization.

Independent Task Force. 1999. Safeguarding Prosperity in a Global

Financial System: The Future International Financial Architecture. Sponsored by the Council on Foreign Relations. Washington, D.C.: Institute for International Economics.

INEGI (Instituto Nacional de Estadística Geografía e Informática). 1992. *Encuesta nacional de ingresos y gastos de los hogares 1992.* Mexico City.

———. 1994. *Encuesta nacional de ingresos y gastos de los hogares 1994.* Mexico City.

———. 1996. *Encuesta nacional de ingresos y gastos de los hogares 1996.* Mexico City.

Instituto Nacional de Estadística y Censos. 1998. *Encuesta de condiciones de vida.* Quito, Ecuador.

Instituto Nacional de Estadística y Censos Argentina. 1991. "Census." [www.indec.mecon.ar/default.htm].

International Federation of Red Cross and Red Crescent Societies. 1993. *World Disaster Report 1993.* Geneva.

———. 1999. *World Disaster Report 1999.* Geneva.

International Institute for Environment and Development. 1992. "Special Issue on Applications of Wealth Ranking." Rapid Rural Appraisal Note 15. London.

International Task Force on Commodity Risk Management in Developing Countries. 1999. "Dealing with Commodity Price Volatility in Developing Countries: A Proposal for a Market-Based Approach." World Bank, Washington, D.C.

IRIS (Center for Institutional Reform and the Informal Sector) and USAID (U.S. Agency for International Development). 1996. *Governance and the Economy in Africa: Tools for Analysis and Reform of Corruption.* Washington, D.C.: USAID.

Irwin, Timothy. 1997. "Price Structures, Cross-Subsidies and Competition in Infrastructure." Viewpoint 108. World Bank, Finance, Private Sector, and Infrastructure Network, Washington, D.C.

Isham, Jonathan. 1999. "The Effect of Social Capital on Technology Adoption: Evidence from Rural Tanzania." Paper presented at Annual Meeting of American Economic Association, January, New York.

Isham, Jonathan, and Daniel Kaufmann. 1999. "The Forgotten Rationale for Policy Reform: The Productivity of Investment Projects." *Quarterly Journal of Economics* 114(1): 149–84.

Isham, Jonathan, Deepa Narayan, and Lant Pritchett. 1995. "Does Participation Improve Performance? Establishing Causality with Subjective Data." *World Bank Economic Review* 9(2): 175–200.

Izaguirre, Ada Karina. 1999. "Private Participation in Telecommunications: Recent Trends." Viewpoint 204. World Bank, Finance, Private Sector, and Infrastructure Network, Washington, D.C.

Jacoby, Hanan G., and Emmanuel Skoufias. 1997. "Risk, Financial Markets and Human Capital in a Developing Country." *Review of Economic Studies* 64(3): 311–35.

Jalan, Jyotsna, and Martin Ravallion. 1997a. "Are the Poor Less Well Insured? Evidence on Vulnerability to Income Risk in Rural China." *Journal of Development Economics* 58: 61–81.

———. 1997b. "Spatial Poverty Traps?" Policy Research Working Paper 1862. World Bank, Washington, D.C.

———. 1998a. "Behavioral Responses to Risk in Rural China."

Policy Research Working Paper 1978. World Bank, Washington, D.C.

———. 1998b. "Determinants of Transient and Chronic Poverty: Evidence from Rural China." Policy Research Working Paper 1936. World Bank, Washington, D.C.

———. 1999a. "China's Lagging Poor Areas." *American Economic Review* 89: 301–05.

———. 1999b. *Do Transient and Chronic Poverty in Rural China Share Common Causes?* Washington, D.C.: World Bank.

———. 1999c. "Income Gains to the Poor from Workfare: Estimates for Argentina's Trabajar Program." Policy Research Working Paper 2149. World Bank, Washington, D.C.

James, Estelle. 2000. "Old-Age Protection for the Uninsured: What Are the Issues?" In Nora Lustig, ed., *Shielding the Poor: Social Protection in the Developing World.* Washington, D.C.: Brookings Institution and Inter-American Development Bank.

Jamison, Dean T., Julio Frenk, and Felicia Knaul. 1998. "International Collective Action in Health: Objectives, Functions, and Rationale." *Lancet* 351: 514–17.

Jamison, Dean T., Jia Wang, Kenneth Hill, and Juan-Luis Londoño. 1996. "Income, Mortality and Fertility Control in Latin America: Country-Level Performance, 1960–90." World Bank, Latin America and the Caribbean Region, Washington, D.C.

Jayaraman, Rajshri. 1999. "Kerala and Uttar Pradesh: A Case Study." Background paper for *World Development Report 2000/2001.* World Bank, Washington, D.C.

Jejeebhoy, Shireen. 1995. *Women's Education, Autonomy, and Reproductive Behavior: Experience from Developing Countries.* New York: Oxford University Press.

Jensen, Robert. 1998. "Public Transfers, Private Transfers, and the 'Crowding Out' Hypothesis: Theory and Evidence from South Africa." John F. Kennedy School of Government Faculty Working Paper R98-08. Harvard University, Cambridge, Mass.

Jepma, Catrinus J. 1991. *The Tying of Aid.* Paris: Organisation for Economic Co-operation and Development.

Jha, Prabhat, and David Nalor. 1999. *A Fine Balance: Private and Public Health Care in Urban India.* Washington, D.C.: World Bank.

Jimenez, Emmanuel. 1986. "The Public Subsidization of Education and Health in Developing Countries: A Review of Equity and Efficiency." *World Bank Research Observer* 1(1): 111–29.

———. 1987. *Pricing Policy in the Social Sectors.* Baltimore, Md.: Johns Hopkins University Press.

Jimenez, Emmanuel, and Marlaine Lockheed. 1995. *Public and Private Secondary Education in Developing Countries: A Comparative Study.* World Bank Discussion Paper 309. Washington, D.C.

Jimenez, Emmanuel, and Vicente Paqueo. 1996. "Do Local Contributions Affect the Efficiency of Public Primary Schools?" *Economics of Education Review* 15(4): 377–86.

Jimenez, Emmanuel, and Yasuyuki Sawada. 1998. "Do Community-Managed Schools Work? An Evaluation of El Salvador's Educo Program." Impact Evaluation of Education Reforms Paper 8. World Bank, Development Research Group, Washington, D.C.

Jodha, Nerpat S. 1986. "Common Property Resources and the

Rural Poor in Dry Regions of India." *Economic and Political Weekly* 21(27): 1169–81.

Johansen, Frida. 1993. *Poverty Reduction in East Asia: The Silent Revolution.* World Bank Discussion Paper 203. Washington, D.C.

Johnson, Chalmers A. 1982. *MITI and the Japanese Miracle: The Growth of Industrial Policy, 1925–1975.* Stanford, Calif.: Stanford University Press.

Johnson, Simon, Daniel Kaufmann, and Pablo Zoido-Lobaton. 1998. "Regulatory Discretion and the Unofficial Economy." *American Economic Review* 88(2): 387–92.

Joint Commonwealth Secretariat–World Bank Task Force on the Small States. 2000. "Small States: Meeting Challenges in the Global Economy." Washington, D.C.

Jones, Patricia. 1998. "Skill Formation and Inequality in Poor Countries: How Much Do Ethnic Neighborhoods Matter?" *Journal of African Economies* 7(1): 62–90.

Jorgensen, Steen Lau, and Julie van Domelen. 1999. "Helping the Poor Manage Risk Better: The Role of Social Funds." Paper presented at Inter-American Development Bank Conference on Social Protection and Poverty, 4–5 February, Washington, D.C.

Joseph, Richard. 1999. *State, Conflict and Democracy in Africa.* Boulder, Colo.: Lynne Rienner.

Joshi, A., and Mick Moore. Forthcoming. "Rights, Institutions and Poverty." In Alison L. Booth and Paul Mosley, eds., *The New Poverty Strategies: What Have They Achieved?* London: Macmillan.

Joshi, Heather, Elizabeth Cooksey, Richard Wiggins, Andrew McCulloch, Georgia Verropoulou, and Lynda Clarke. 1999. "Diverse Family Living Situations and Child Development: Multilevel Analysis Comparing Longitudinal Evidence from Britain and the United States." *International Journal of Law, Policy and the Family* 13(3): 292–314.

Kabeer, Naila, and Subrahmanian Ramya. 1996. "Institutions, Relations and Outcomes: Framework and Tools for Gender-Aware Planning." Discussion Paper 357. Institute of Development Studies, Sussex University, Brighton.

Kähkönen, Satu, and Louis Pouliquen. 1999. "Institutions and Rural Infrastructure Delivery." World Bank, Department of Regional Economic and Social Policy, Washington, D.C.

Kakwani, Nanak. 1993. "Performance in Living Standards: An International Comparison." *Journal of Development Economics* 41: 307–36.

———. 1999. "Poverty and Inequality during the Economic Crisis in Thailand." National Economic and Social Development Board /Asian Development Bank. *Indicators of Well-Being and Policy Analysis* 3(1).

Kakwani, Nanak, and Jaroenjit Pothong. 1998. "Impact of Economic Crisis on the Standard of Living in Thailand." National Economic and Social Development Board /Asian Development Bank. *Indicators of Well-Being and Policy Analysis* 2(4).

Kakwani, Nanak, and Nicholas M. Prescott. 1999. "Impact of Economic Crisis on Poverty and Inequality in Korea." World Bank, East Asia and Pacific Region, Human Development Sector Unit, Washington, D.C.

Kalton, Graham. 1983. *Compensating for Missing Survey Data.* Ann Arbor: University of Michigan Press.

Kanbur, Ravi. 1986. "Structural Adjustment, Macroeconomic Adjustment and Poverty: A Methodology for Analysis." CEPR Discussion Paper 132. Centre for Economic Policy Research, London.

———. Forthcoming. "Income Distribution and Development." In Anthony B. Atkinson and François Bourguignon, eds., *Handbook of Income Distribution.* New York: North Holland-Elsevier.

Kanbur, Ravi, and Nora Lustig. 1999. "Why Is Inequality Back on the Agenda?" Department of Agricultural, Resource, and Managerial Economics Working Paper 99-14. Cornell University, Ithaca, N.Y.

Kanbur, Ravi, and Lyn Squire. 1999. "The Evolution of Thinking about Poverty: Exploring the Interactions." Department of Agricultural, Resource, and Managerial Economics Paper 99-24. Cornell University, Ithaca, N.Y.

Kanbur, Ravi, and Todd Sandler, with Kevin M. Morrison. 1999. *The Future of Development Assistance: Common Pools and International Public Goods.* Policy Essay 25. Washington, D.C.: Overseas Development Council.

Katakura, Yoko, and Alexander Bakalian. 1998. "PROSANEAR: People, Poverty and Pipes." United Nations Development Programme–World Bank Water and Sanitation Program, Washington, D.C.

Katz, Travis, and Jennifer Sara. 1998. "Rural Water Supply: Global Study." United Nations Development Programme–World Bank Water and Sanitation Program, Washington, D.C.

Kaufmann, Daniel, and Shang-jin Wei. 1999. "Does 'Grease Money' Speed Up the Wheels of Commerce?" NBER Working Paper 7093. National Bureau of Economic Research, Cambridge, Mass.

Kaufmann, Daniel, Aart Kraay, and Pablo Zoido-Lobaton. 1999. "Governance Matters." Policy Research Working Paper 2196. World Bank, Washington, D.C.

Kaufmann, Daniel, Pablo Zoido-Lobaton, and Young Lee. 2000. "Governance and Anticorruption: Empirical Diagnostic Study for Ecuador." World Bank, Washington, D.C.

Kaul, Inge, Isabelle Grunberg, and Marc Stern. 1999a. "Defining Global Public Goods." In Inge Kaul, Isabelle Grunberg, and Marc Stern, eds., *Global Public Goods: International Cooperation in the 21st Century.* New York: Oxford University Press.

———, eds. 1999b. *Global Public Goods: International Cooperation in the 21st Century.* New York: Oxford University Press.

Kawachi, Ichiro, and Lisa Berkman. 2000. "Social Cohesion, Social Capital and Health." In Lisa Berkman and Ichiro Kawachi, eds., *Social Epidemiology.* New York: Oxford University Press.

Kayani, Rogati, and Andrew Dymond. 1997. *Options for Rural Telecommunications Development.* World Bank Technical Paper 359. Washington, D.C.

KDP (Kecamatan Development Project) Secretariat. 1999. "Kecamatan Development Project: First Annual Report." Government of Indonesia, National Coordination Team, Jakarta.

Kelley, Allen C., and Robert M. Schmidt. 1994. *Population and*

Income Change: Recent Evidence. World Bank Discussion Paper 249. Washington, D.C.

Kemal, A.R. 1994. "Structural Adjustment, Employment, Income Distribution and Poverty." *Pakistan Development Review* 33: 901–11.

Kennedy, Bruce, Ichiro Kawachi, Roberta Glass, and Deborah Prothrow-Stith. 1998. "Income Distribution, Socioeconomic Status, and Self-Rated Health in the United States: Multilevel Analysis." *British Medical Journal* 317: 917–21.

Kenny, Charles. 1999. "Access to Telecommunications and Informatics Is of Great Benefit to the Poor, and This Has to Mean Public Access." Box for *World Development Report 2000/2001*. World Bank, Washington, D.C.

Kessides, Christine. 1997. "World Bank Experience with the Provision of Infrastructure Services for the Urban Poor: Preliminary Identification and Review of Best Practices." World Bank, Urban Development Division, Washington, D.C.

Khan, Naila, and Maureen Durkin. 1995. "Framework: Prevalence." In P. Zinkin and H. McConachie, eds., *Disabled Children and Developing Countries.* Cambridge: Cambridge University Press.

Khandker, Shahidur R. 1998. *Fighting Poverty with Microcredit: Experience in Bangladesh.* New York: Oxford University Press.

Khandker, Shahidur R., Baqui Khalily, and Zahed Khan, eds. 1996. *Credit Programs for the Poor: Household and Intrahousehold Impacts and Program Sustainability.* Washington, D.C.: World Bank and Bangladesh Institute of Development Studies.

Kiguel, Miguel. 1999. "The Argentine Currency Board." Documento de Trabajo 152. Universidad del CEMA, Buenos Aires.

KIHASA (Korea Institute for Health and Social Affairs) and UNDP (United Nations Development Programme). 1998. *Korea: Human Development Report 1998.* Seoul.

Killick, Tony. 1997. "Principals, Agents, and the Failings of Conditionality." *Journal of International Development* 9(4): 483–95.

Killick, Tony, with Rumani Gunatilaka and Ann Marr. 1998. *Aid and the Political Economy of Policy Change.* London: Overseas Development Institute.

Kim, Elim. 1991. *A Study of the Family Law and Its Reform Movement.* Seoul: Korean Women's Development Institute.

Kim, Jooseop, Harold Alderman, and Peter Orazem. 1998. "Can Private Schools Subsidies Increase Schooling for the Poor? The Quetta Urban Fellowship Program." Impact Evaluation of Education Reforms Paper 11. World Bank, Development Research Group, Washington, D.C.

Kim, Kwangkee, and Philip Moody. 1992. "More Resources, Better Health? A Cross-National Perspective." *Social Science and Medicine* 34(8): 837–42.

King, Elizabeth, and Peter Orazem. 1999. "Evaluating Education Reforms: Four Cases in Developing Countries." World Bank, Development Research Group, Washington, D.C.

King, Elizabeth, and Berk Ozler. 1998. "What's Decentralization Got to Do with Learning? The Case of Nicaragua's School Autonomy Reform." Impact Evaluation of Education Reforms Paper 9. World Bank, Development Research Group, Washington, D.C.

Kinsey, Bill, Kees Burger, and Jan W. Gunning. 1998. "Coping with Drought in Zimbabwe: Survey Evidence on Responses of Rural Households to Risk." *World Development* 26(1): 89–110.

Klasen, Stephan. 1994. " 'Missing Women' Reconsidered." *World Development* 22(7): 1061–71.

———. 1999. "Does Gender Inequality Reduce Growth and Development? Evidence from Cross-Country Regressions." Policy Research Report on Gender and Development Working Paper Series, no. 7. World Bank, Washington, D.C.

Klees, Rita, Joana Godinho, and Mercy Lawson Doe. 1999. "Health, Sanitation, and Hygiene in Rural Water Supply and Sanitation Projects and Other World Bank–Financed Projects." World Bank, Europe and Central Asia Regional Studies Program, Washington, D.C.

Klitgaard, Robert. 1990. *Tropical Gangsters.* New York: Basic Books.

———. 1997. "Cleaning Up and Invigorating the Civil Service." Report prepared for Operations Evaluation Department. World Bank, Washington, D.C.

Klugman, Jeni, and Jeanine Braithwaite. 1998. "Poverty in Russia during the Transition: An Overview." *World Bank Research Observer* 3(1): 37–58.

Knack, Stephen, and Philip Keefer. 1995. "Institutions and Economic Performance: Cross-Country Tests Using Alternative Institutional Measures." *Economics and Politics* 7: 207–27.

———. 1997. "Does Social Capital Have an Economic Payoff? A Cross-Country Investigation." *Quarterly Journal of Economics* 112: 1251–88.

Knack, Stephen, and Nick Manning. 2000. "Policy Volatility and Poverty." World Bank, Poverty Reduction and Economic Management Network, Washington, D.C.

Kochar, Anjini. 1995. "Explaining Household Vulnerability to Idiosyncratic Income Shocks." *American Economic Association Papers and Proceedings* 85(2): 159–64.

———. 1999. "Smoothing Consumption by Smoothing Income: Hours-of-Work Responses to Idiosyncratic Agricultural Shocks in Rural India." *Review of Economics and Statistics* 81(1): 50–61.

Kohli, Atul. 1987. *The State and Poverty in India: The Politics of Reform.* New York: Cambridge University Press.

Kormendi, Roger, and Philip McGuire. 1985. "Macroeconomic Determinants of Growth: Cross-Country Evidence." *Journal of Monetary Economics* 16(2): 141–63.

Kornai, János. 2000. "Ten Years after 'the Road to a Free Economy': The Author's Self-Evaluation." Paper presented at World Bank Annual Conference on Development Economics, 18–20 April, Washington, D.C.

Kozel, Valerie, and Barbara Parker. 2000. "Integrated Approaches to Poverty Assessment in India." In Michael Bamberger, ed., *Integrating Quantitative and Qualitative Research in Development Projects.* Washington, D.C.: World Bank.

Kreimer, Alcira. 1999. "Learning Lessons from the Earthquake in Turkey." Box for *World Development Report 2000/2001*. World Bank, Washington, D.C.

Kreimer, Alcira, and Edward Echeverria. 1991. "Case Study: Housing Reconstruction in Mexico City." In Alcira Kreimer and Mohan Munasinghe, eds., *Managing Natural Disaster and the Environment: Selected Materials from the Colloquium on the Environment and Natural Disaster Management.* Washington, D.C.: World Bank.

Kreimer, Alcira, Edward Echeverria, and Martha Preece. 1991. "Case Study: Reconstruction after North China's Earthquake." In Alcira Kreimer and Mohan Munasinghe, eds., *Managing Natural Disaster and the Environment: Selected Materials from the Colloquium on the Environment and Natural Disaster Management.* Washington, D.C.: World Bank.

Kreimer, Alcira, Margaret Arnold, Christopher Barham, Paul Freeman, Roy Gilbert, Frederick Krimgold, Rodney Lester, John D. Pollner, and Tom Vogt. 1999. *Managing Disaster Risk in Mexico: Market Incentives for Mitigation Investment.* Washington, D.C.: World Bank.

Kremer, Michael. 1999. "Purchase Pre-commitments for New Vaccines: Rationale and a Proposed Design." Harvard University, Department of Economics, Cambridge, Mass.; and Brookings Institution, Washington, D.C.

Krishna, Anirudh, Norman Uphoff, and Milton Esman, eds. 1997. *Reasons for Hope: Instructive Experiences in Rural Development.* West Hartford, Conn.: Kumarian.

Krueger, Alan B., and Michael Lindahl. 1999. "Education for Growth in Sweden and the World." *Swedish Economic Policy Review* 6(2): 289–339.

Krueger, Anne O. 1993. "East Asia: Lessons for Growth Theory." Paper presented at Fourth Annual East Asian Seminar on Economics, National Bureau of Economic Research, 17–19 June, San Francisco.

Krugman, Paul. 1998. "Saving Asia: It's Time to Get Radical." *Fortune* 138: 75–80.

Kruse, Sten-Erik, Timo Kyllönen, Satu Ojanperä, Roger C. Riddell, and Jean Vielajus. 1997. "Searching for Impact and Methods: NGO Evaluation Synthesis Study." Report prepared for Organisation for Economic Co-operation and Development, Development Assistance Committee Expert Group on Evaluation, Paris.

Kull, Steven, I.M. Destler, and Clay Ramsay. 1997. "The Foreign Policy Gap: How Policymakers Misread the Public." University of Maryland, Center for International and Security Studies, College Park.

Kunreuther, Howard. 1999. "Incentives for Mitigation Investments and More Effective Risk Management: The Need for Public-Private Partnerships." University of Pennsylvania, Operations and Information Department, Philadelphia.

Kurtz, Marcus. 1999. "The Political Economy of Pro-poor Policies in Chile and Mexico." Background paper for *World Development Report 2000/2001.* World Bank, Washington, D.C.

Lachaud, Jean-Pierre. 1999. "Pauvreté ménage et genre en Afrique sub-Saharienne: Nouvelles dimensions analytiques." Université Montesquieu-Bordeaux IV, Centre d'Economie du Développement, Bordeaux.

Lago, Ricardo. 1991. "The Illusion of Pursuing Redistribution through Macropolicy: Peru's Heterodox Experience, 1985–1990." In Rudiger Dornbusch and Sebastian Edwards, eds., *Macroeconomics of Populism.* Chicago: University of Chicago Press.

Lal, Deepak, I. Natarajan, and Rakesh Mohan. 2000. "Economic Reforms and Poverty Alleviation: A Tale of Two Sur-veys." University of California at Los Angeles, Department of Economics.

Lamontagne, Jacques. 1999. "National Minority Education in China: A Nationwide Survey across Counties." In Gerard A. Postiglione, ed., *China's National Minority Education: Culture, Schooling and Development.* London: Falmer.

Lampietti, Julian, Anthony Kolb, Sumila Gulyani, and Vahram Avenessian. 2000. "Pricing Services to Protect the Poor: Lessons from Armenia." World Bank, Europe and Central Asia Region, Washington, D.C.

Lanjouw, Jean Olson. 1997. "Demystifying Poverty Lines." Series on Poverty Reduction. United Nations Development Programme, New York.

Lanjouw, Peter, and Martin Ravallion. 1999. "Benefit Incidence and the Timing of Program Capture." *World Bank Economic Review* 13(2): 257–74.

Lanjouw, Peter, and Nicholas Stern. 1991. "Poverty in Palanpur." *World Bank Economic Review* 5(1): 23–56.

Larrain, Felipe, and Andres Velasco. 1999. "Exchange Rate Policy for Emerging Markets: One Size Does Not Fit All." Harvard University, Department of Economics, Cambridge, Mass.

Lavy, Victor, and Jean-Marc Germain. 1994. *Quality and Cost in Health Care Choice in Developing Countries.* Living Standards Measurement Study Working Paper 105. Washington, D.C.: World Bank.

Lavy, Victor, John Strauss, Duncan Thomas, and Philippe de Vreyer. 1996. "Quality of Care, Survival and Health Outcomes in Ghana." *Journal of Health Economics* 15: 333–57.

Leamer, Edward E., and Peter K. Schott. 1999. "Natural Resources as a Source of Latin American Income Inequality." Background paper for *World Development Report 2000/2001.* World Bank, Washington, D.C.

Legovini, Arianna, César Bouillón, and Nora Lustig. 1999. "Can Education Explain Income Inequality Changes in Mexico?" Inter-American Development Bank, Washington, D.C.

Lembuya, Peter. 1992. *Amboseli National Park, the Surrounding Group Ranches and Community Conservation.* Nairobi: African Wildlife Foundation.

Lensink, Robert, and Howard White. 1998. "Does the Revival of International Private Capital Flows Mean the End of Aid? An Analysis of Developing Countries' Access to Private Capital." *World Development* 26: 1221–34.

Leonard, David. 1987. "Political Realities of African Management." *World Development* 15: 899–910.

Lepkowski, James, Graham Kalton, and Daniel Kazprsyk. 1989. "Weighting Adjustments for Partial Non-response in the 1984 SIPP Panel." Paper presented at section on survey methods research, meeting of American Statistical Association.

Levav, Itzhak. 1999. "The Indivisible Face of Disaster." In World Bank, *Investing in Prevention: A Special Report on Disaster Risk Management.* Washington, D.C.

Levine, Ross. 1997. "Financial Development and Economic Growth: Views and an Agenda." *Journal of Economic Literature* 35(2): 688–726.

Levine, Ross, and David Renelt. 1992. "A Sensitivity Analysis of Cross-Country Regressions." *American Economic Review* 84(4): 942–63.

Levison, Deborah, Richard Anker, Shahid Ashraf, and Sandya Barge. Forthcoming. "Is Child Labor Really Necessary in India's Carpet Industry?" In Richard Anker and others, eds., *Economics of Child Labor in Selected Industries of India.* New Delhi: Hindustan.

Levy, Hernan. 1996. "Morocco Impact Evaluation Report: Socio-Economic Influence of Rural Roads—A Study of Rural Roads Financed under the World Bank's Fourth Highway Project." World Bank, Operations Evaluation Department, Washington, D.C.

Levy, Margaret. 1996. "Social and Unsocial Capital: A Review Essay on Robert Putnam's *Making Democracy Work.*" *Politics and Society* 24(1): 45–55.

Lewis, Maureen. 2000. "Informal Health Payments in Eastern Europe and Central Asia: Issues, Trends, and Policy Implications." World Bank, Europe and Central Asia Region, Washington, D.C.

Lewis, Maureen, Gunnar S. Eskeland, and Ximena Traa-Valerezo. Forthcoming. "Challenging El Salvador's Rural Health Care Strategy." Policy Research Working Paper 2164. World Bank, Washington, D.C.

Li, Guo, Diane Steele, and Paul Glewwe. 1999. "Distribution of Government Education Expenditures in Developing Countries." World Bank, Development Research Group, Washington, D.C.

Li, Hongyi, and Heng-fu Zou. 1998. "Income Inequality Is Not Harmful for Growth: Theory and Evidence." *Review of Development Economics* 2(3): 318–34.

Li, Hongyi, Lyn Squire, and Heng-fu Zou. 1998. "Explaining International Inequality and Intertemporal Variations in Income Inequality." *Economic Journal* 108: 26–43.

Liang, Xiaoyan. 1996. "Bangladesh Female Secondary School Assistance Project." World Bank, Human Development Department, Washington, D.C.

Lim, Young-Jae, and Robert Townsend. 1998. "General Equilibrium Models of Financial Systems: Theory and Measurement in Village Economies." *Review of Economic Dynamics* 1: 59–118.

Lin, Justin Yifu. 1995. "Commentary: Food Policy in China—In Retrospect and Prospect." *IFPRI Report* 17(3). International Food Policy Research Institute, Washington, D.C.

Lindauer, David. 1999. "Labor Market Reform and the Poor." Background paper for *World Development Report 2000/2001.* World Bank, Washington, D.C.; Wellesley College, Wellesley, Mass.; and Harvard Institute for International Development, Cambridge, Mass.

Lindauer, David, and Barbara Nunberg, eds. 1996. *Rehabilitating Government: Pay and Employment Reform in Africa.* Aldershot: Avebury.

Lipton, Michael. 1977. *Why Poor People Stay Poor: Urban Bias in World Development.* Canberra: Australian National University Press.

———. 1996. *Defining and Measuring Poverty: Conceptual Issues.* New York: United Nations Development Programme.

———. 1998. *Successes in Anti-Poverty.* Geneva: International Labour Office.

Lipton, Michael, and Martin Ravallion. 1995. "Poverty and Policy." In Jere R. Behrman and T.N. Srinivasan, eds., *Handbook of Development Economics.* Vol. 3. Amsterdam: North Holland.

Little, Roderick. 1988. "Missing-Data Adjustments in Large Surveys." *Journal of Business and Economic Statistics* 6(3): 287–96.

Litvack, Jennie, and Carol Bodart. 1993. "User Fees Plus Quality Equals Improved Access to Health Care: Results of a Field Experiment in Cameroon." *Social Science and Medicine* 37(3): 369–83.

Litvack, Jennie, and Dennis A. Rondinelli, eds. 1999. *Market Reform in Vietnam: Building Institutions for Development.* Westport, Conn.: Quorum Books.

Litvack, Jennie, and Jessica Seddon, eds. 1999. "Decentralization Briefing Notes." World Bank, Poverty Reduction and Economic Management Network, Washington, D.C.

Liu, Yuanli, William C. Hsiao, and Karen Eggleston. 1999. "Equity in Health and Health Care: The Chinese Experience." *Social Science and Medicine* 49: 1349–56.

Livi-Bacci, Massimo. 1997. "Population, Constraint, and Adaptation: A Historical Outlook." In Robert Dorfman and Peter Rogers, eds., *Science with a Human Face: Festschrift in Honour of Roger Randall Revelle.* Cambridge, Mass.: Harvard University Press.

Llavador, Humberto G., and John E. Roemer. 2000. "An Equal-Opportunity Approach to the Allocation of International Aid." Yale University, Department of Political Science, New Haven, Conn.

Lockheed, Marlaine, and Qinghua Zhao. 1993. "The Empty Opportunity: Local Control of Secondary Schools and Student Achievement in the Philippines." Policy Research Working Paper 825. World Bank, Washington, D.C.

Lockheed, Marlaine, Dean T. Jamison, and Lawrence Lau. 1980. "Farmer Education and Farm Efficiency: A Survey." *Economic Development and Cultural Change* 29: 37–134.

Lokshin, Michael, and Martin Ravallion. 2000a. "Short-Lived Shocks with Long-Lived Impacts? Household Income Dynamics in a Transition Economy." World Bank, Development Research Group, Washington, D.C.

———. 2000b. "Welfare Impact of Russia's 1998 Financial Crisis and the Response of the Public Safety Net." World Bank, Development Research Group, Washington, D.C.

Londoño, Juan Luis, and Miguel Székely. 1997. *Persistent Poverty and Excess Inequality: Latin America, 1970–1995.* Washington, D.C.: Inter-American Development Bank.

Lopez, Ramon, and Carla della Maggiora. Forthcoming. "Rural Poverty in Peru: Stylized Facts and Analytics for Policy." In Ramon Lopez and Alberto Valdes, eds., *Rural Poverty in Latin America: Analytics, New Empirical Evidence and Policy.* Washington, D.C.: World Bank.

Lopez, Ramon, and Alberto Valdes. Forthcoming. "Fighting Rural Poverty in Latin America: New Evidence and Policy." In Ramon Lopez and Alberto Valdes, eds., *Rural Poverty in Latin America: Analytics, New Empirical Evidence and Policy.* Washington, D.C.: World Bank.

Lopez, Ramon, T. Thomas, and Vinod Thomas. 1998. "Economic Growth and the Sustainability of Natural Resources." University of Maryland, Department of Agricultural and Resource Economics, College Park.

Lora, Eduardo, and Felipe Barrera. 1997. *Una década de reformas estructurales en América Latina: el crecimiento, la productividad y la inversión, ya no son como antes.* Inter-American Development Bank, Office of the Chief Economist, Washington, D.C.

Loury, Glenn C. 2000. "Social Exclusion and Ethnic Groups: The Challenge to Economics." Discussion Paper Series, no. 106. Boston University, Institute for Economic Development.

Lovei, Laszlo, Eugene Gurenko, Michael Haney, Philip O'Keefe, and Maria Shkaratan. 2000. "Maintaining Utility Services for the Poor: Policies and Practices in Central and Eastern Europe and the Former Soviet Union." World Bank, Europe and Central Asia Region, Washington, D.C.

Lowell, Peggy A., and Charles H. Wood. 1998. "Skin Color, Racial Identity and Life Chances in Brazil." *Latin American Perspectives* 25(3): 90–109.

Luckham, Robin. 1999. "Complex Political Emergencies and the State: Failure and the Fate of the State." *Third World Quarterly* 20(1): 27–50.

Lund, Frances, and Smita Srinivas. 1999a. "Learning from Experience: A Framework for Social Protection for Workers in the Informal Economy." Background paper for *World Development Report 2000/2001.* World Bank, Washington, D.C.

———. 1999b. "Learning from Experience: A Gendered Approach to Social Protection for Workers in the Informal Economy." Background paper for workshop on social protection for women in the informal sector, International Labour Organization, 6–8 December, Geneva.

Lundberg, Mattias, and Lyn Squire. 2000. "Inequality and Growth: Lessons for Policy." World Bank, Global Development Network, Washington, D.C.

Lundberg, Shelley, Robert A. Pollak, and Terence J. Wales. 1997. "Do Husbands and Wives Pool Their Resources? Evidence from the United Kingdom Child Benefit." *Journal of Human Resources* 32(3): 463–80.

Lustig, Nora. 1988. "From Structuralism to Neostructuralism: The Search for a Heterodox Paradigm." In Patricio Meller, ed., *The Latin American Development Debate.* Boulder, Colo.: Westview.

———. 1997. "The Safety Nets Which Are Not Safety Nets: Social Investment Funds in Latin America." Paper presented at Harvard Institute for International Development and United Nations Development Programme conference on governance, poverty eradication, and social policy, November, Cambridge, Mass.

———. 1998. *Mexico: The Remaking of an Economy.* 2d ed. Washington, D.C.: Brookings Institution.

———. Forthcoming. "Crises and the Poor: Socially Responsible Macroeconomics." *Economia, Journal of the Latin American and Caribbean Economic Association* 1(1).

———, ed. 1995. *Coping with Austerity: Poverty and Inequality in Latin America.* Washington, D.C.: Brookings Institution.

———, ed. Forthcoming. *Shielding the Poor: Social Protection in the Developing World.* Washington, D.C.: Brookings Institution.

Lustig, Nora, and Darryl McLeod. 1997. "Minimum Wages and Poverty in Developing Countries: Some Empirical Evidence." In Sebastian Edwards and Nora Lustig, eds., *Labor Markets in Latin America.* Washington, D.C.: Brookings Institution.

Lustig, Nora, and Miguel Székely. 1998. *Economic Trends, Poverty and Inequality in Mexico.* Washington, D.C.: Inter-American Development Bank.

Maddison, Angus. 1987. "Growth and the Slowdown in Advanced Capitalist Economies: Techniques of Quantitative Assessment." *Journal of Economic Literature* 25(2): 649–98.

———. 1995. "Monitoring the World Economy, 1820–92." Organisation for Economic Co-operation and Development, Development Centre, Paris.

Magalhaes, Antonio, and Michael H. Glantz. 1992. *Socioeconomic Impacts of Climate Variations and Policy Responses in Brazil.* Brasilia: Fundaçao Grupo Esquel Brasil.

Mahar, J. Michael, ed. 1972. *The Untouchables in Contemporary India.* Tucson: University of Arizona Press.

Maizels, Alfred, and Machiko K. Nissanke. 1984. "Motivations for Aid to Developing Countries." *World Development* 12: 879–900.

Mallick, Ross. 1998. *Development, Ethnicity and Human Rights in South Asia.* New Delhi: Sage.

Malmberg Calvo, Christina. 1998. *Options for Managing and Financing Rural Transport Infrastructure.* World Bank Technical Paper 411. Washington, D.C.

Malthus, Thomas. 1985 [1798]. *An Essay on the Principle of Population.* London: Penguin Classics.

Maluccio, John, Lawrence Haddad, and Julian May. 1999. "Social Capital and Income Generation in South Africa, 1993–98." International Food Policy Research Institute, Washington, D.C.

Mankiw, N. Gregory, David Romer, and David N. Weil. 1992. "A Contribution to the Empirics of Economic Growth." *Quarterly Journal of Economics* 107(2): 407–37.

Manning, Daniel S. 1999. "The Role of Legal Services Organizations in Attacking Poverty." Background paper for *World Development Report 2000/2001.* World Bank, Washington, D.C.

Manor, James. 1999. *The Political Economy of Democratic Decentralization.* Directions in Development Series. Washington, D.C.: World Bank.

Marchés Tropicaux et Méditerranéens. 1995. "Une évaluation de la crise des transports en Afrique sub-saharienne." 2612: 2629–31.

Marr, Ana. 1999. "The Poor and Their Money: What Have We Learned?" ODI Poverty Briefing 4. Overseas Development Institute, London.

Marshall, Adriana. 1998. "State Intervention, the Labor Market, and Inequality in Argentina." In Albert Berry, ed., *Poverty, Economic Reform and Income Distribution in Latin America.* London: Lynne Rienner.

Martin, Will, and Keith E. Maskus. 2000. "Core Labor Standards and Competitiveness: Implications for Global Trade Policy." World Bank, Development Research Group, Washington, D.C.; and University of Colorado, Boulder.

Maskus, Keith E. 1997. "Should Core Labor Standards Be Imposed through International Trade Policy?" Policy Research Working Paper 1817. World Bank, Washington, D.C.

———. 1999. "Comments on Core Labor Standards and International Trade Policy." Paper presented at World Bank symposium, 20 January, Washington, D.C.

————. 2000. "Regulatory Standards in the WTO: Comparing Intellectual Property Rights with Competition Policy, Environmental Protection, and Core Labor Standards." Working Paper 00-1. Institute for International Economics, Washington, D.C.

Massey, Douglas, and Karin Espinosa. 1997. "What's Driving Mexico-U.S. Migration? A Theoretical, Empirical, and Policy Analysis." *American Journal of Sociology* 102(4): 939–99.

Matin, Imran, David Hulme, and Stuart Rutherford. 1999. "Financial Services for the Poor and Poorest: Deepening Understanding to Improve Provision." Finance and Development Research Program Working Paper 9. University of Manchester, Institute for Development Policy and Management.

Mauro, Paolo. 1995. "Corruption and Growth." *Quarterly Journal of Economics* 110(3): 681–712.

————. 1998. "Corruption and the Composition of Government Expenditure." *Journal of Public Economics* 69: 263–79.

Maveneke, Taparandava N. 1998. "Local Participation as an Instrument for Natural Resources Management under the Communal Areas Management Programme for Indigenous Resources (CAMPFIRE) in Zimbabwe." Paper presented at international workshop on community-based natural resources management, World Bank, 10–14 May, Washington, D.C.

Mc Clymont, Mary, and Stephen Golub, eds. 2000. *Many Roads to Justice: The Law-Related Work of Ford Foundation Grantees around the World.* Washington, D.C.: Ford Foundation.

McCulloch, Andrew, and Heather Joshi. 1999. "Child Development and Family Resources: An Exploration of Evidence from the Second Generation of the 1958 British Birth Cohort." Working Paper 99-115. University of Essex, Institute for Social and Economic Research.

McDonald, Calvin, Christian Schiller, and Kenichi Ueda. 1999. "Income Distribution, Informal Safety Nets, and Social Expenditures in Uganda." IMF Working Paper 99/163. International Monetary Fund, Washington, D.C.

McGee, Rosemary. 1999. "Meeting the International Development Targets: What Are the Prospects and Key Challenges? Uganda Country Study." Christian Aid, London.

McGuire, Paul B., John Conroy, and Thapa Ganesh. 1998. *Getting the Framework Right: Policy and Regulation for Microfinance in Asia.* Brisbane: Foundation for Development Cooperation.

McKernan, Signe-Mary. 1996. "The Impact of Micro-Credit Programs on Self-Employment Profits: Do Non-credit Program Aspects Matter?" Brown University, Providence, R.I.

Meade, Donald C., and Carl Liedholm. 1998. "The Dynamics of Micro and Small Enterprises in Developing Countries." *World Development* 26(1): 61–74.

Mearns, Robin. 1999. "Access to Land in Rural India." Policy Research Working Paper 2123. World Bank, Washington, D.C.

Meerman, Jacob. 1997. *Reforming Agriculture: The World Bank Goes to Market.* Washington, D.C.: World Bank, Operations Evaluation Department.

————. 1999. "Slow Roads to Equality: A Study of Four Hard-Core Minorities—Issues from the Literature Review." Background paper for *World Development Report 2000/2001.* World Bank, Washington, D.C.

Meier, Gerald M., and Dudley Seers, eds. 1984. *Pioneers in Development.* New York: Oxford University Press.

Mejía, J. Antonio, and Rob Vos. 1997. "Poverty in Latin America and the Caribbean: An Inventory, 1980–95." Working Paper Series, no. I-4. Inter-American Development Bank, Washington, D.C.

Mellor, John W. 1999. "Pro-poor Growth: The Relation between Growth in Agriculture and Poverty Reduction." Abt Associates, Bethesda, Md.

Menard, Claude, and George Clarke. 2000. "Reforming Water Supply in Abidjan, Côte d'Ivoire: A Mild Reform in a Turbulent Environment." World Bank, Development Research Group, Washington, D.C.

Michalopoulos, Constantine. 1999. "Developing Countries' Participation in the World Trade Organization." *World Economy* 22(1): 117–44.

Milanovic, Branko. 1998. *Income, Inequality, and Poverty during the Transition from Planned to Market Economy.* New York: Oxford University Press.

————. 1999. "True World Income Distribution, 1988 and 1993." Policy Research Working Paper 2244. World Bank, Washington, D.C.

MIMAP (Micro Impacts of Macroeconomic Adjustment Policies). 1999a. "After the Crisis: A Look at the Elementary and Secondary Enrolment in the Philippines." *MIMAP Indicators* 6(2). [www.pins.ph.net/mimap/v620699c.htm].

————. 1999b. "An Analysis of the Social Impact of the Financial Crisis in the Philippines." *MIMAP Research Results* 6(1). [www.pins.ph.net/mimap/v610399a.htm].

————. 1999c. "National Statistics Office (NSO) in MIMAP Database." [www.pins.ph.net/mimap/eindune.htm].

Mingat, Alain, and Jee-Peng Tan. 1998. "The Mechanics of Progress in Education: Evidence from Cross-Country Data." Policy Research Working Paper 2015. World Bank, Washington, D.C.

Ministerio de Economía de Argentina. 1998. *Informe económico* 28. Buenos Aires.

Minot, Nicholas W. 1998. "Generating Disaggregated Poverty Maps: An Application to Vietnam." MSSD Discussion Paper 25. International Food Policy Research Institute, Washington, D.C.

MNA Live Database. "Human Development Indicators: Country at a Glance." World Bank, Washington, D.C.

Moctezuma, Esteban. 1999. Keynote address by Mexican Minister of Social Development, Inter-American Development Bank Conference on Social Protection and Poverty, February, Washington, D.C.

Molinas, Jose R. 1998. "The Impact of Inequality, Gender, External Assistance and Social Capital on Local-Level Cooperation." *World Development* 26(3): 413–31.

Monnet, Jean. 1988. *Memoires.* Paris: Fayard.

Moock, Peter. 1994. "Education and Agricultural Productivity." *International Encyclopedia of Education* 1. Oxford: Pergamon.

Moomaw, William, and Mark Tullis. 1999. "Population, Affluence or Technology? An Empirical Look at National Carbon Dioxide Production." In Barbara Sundberg Baudot and William Moomaw, eds., *People and Their Planet*. New York: St. Martin's.

Moore, Mick, and James Putzel. 1999. "Politics and Poverty." Background paper for *World Development Report 2000/2001*. Sussex University, Brighton; London School of Economics and Political Science, Development Studies Institute; and World Bank, Washington, D.C.

Moore, Mick, Jennifer Leavy, Peter P. Houtzager, and Howard White. 1999. "Polity Qualities: How Governance Affects Poverty." Background paper for *World Development Report 2000/2001*. World Bank, Washington, D.C.

Morduch, Jonathan. 1990. "Risk, Production, and Saving: Theory and Evidence from Indian Households." Harvard University, Department of Economics, Cambridge, Mass.

———. 1999a. "Between the Market and State: Can Informal Insurance Patch the Safety Net?" *World Bank Research Observer* 14(2): 187–207.

———. 1999b. "Does Microfinance Really Help the Poor? Evidence from Flagship Programs in Bangladesh." Princeton University, Department of Economics, Princeton, N.J.

———. 1999c. "The Microfinance Promise." *Journal of Economic Literature* 37(4): 1569–614.

———. 1999d. "The Role of Subsidies in Microfinance: Evidence from the Grameen Bank." *Journal of Development Economics* 60(1): 229–48.

Morley, Samuel A. 1994. *Poverty and Inequality in Latin America: Past Evidence and Future Prospects*. Policy Essay 13. Washington, D.C.: Overseas Development Council.

———. 1999. "Impact of Reforms on Equity in Latin America." Background paper for *World Development Report 2000/2001*. World Bank, Washington, D.C.

Morley, Samuel, and Carola Alvarez. 1992. "Recession and the Growth of Poverty in Argentina." Working Paper 92-W02. Vanderbilt University, Nashville, Tenn.

Morris, David. 1979. *Measuring the Conditions of the World's Poor: The Physical Quality of Life Index*. Oxford: Pergamon.

Morris, Saul, Oscar Neidecker-Gonzales, Calogero Carletto, Marcial Munguia, and Quentin Wodon. 2000. "Impact of Hurricane Mitch in the Poorest Communities of Honduras." International Food Policy Research Institute, Washington, D.C.

Morrison, Andrew, and Maria Beatriz Orlando. 1999. "Social and Economic Costs of Domestic Violence: Chile and Nicaragua." In Andrew Morrison and Maria Loreto Biehl, eds., *Too Close to Home: Domestic Violence in the Americas*. Washington, D.C.: Inter-American Development Bank.

Moser, Caroline. 1998. "The Asset Vulnerability Framework: Reassessing Urban Poverty Reduction Strategies." *World Development* 26(1): 1–19.

Mosley, Paul, and Marion J. Eeckhout. 2000. "From Project Aid to Programme Assistance." In Finn Tarp, ed., *Foreign Aid and Development: Lessons Learnt and Directions for the Future*. London: Routledge.

Mosley, Paul, Jane Harrigan, and John Toye. 1995. *Aid and Power*. London: Routledge.

Mukherjee, M., and G.S. Chatterjee. 1974. "On the Validity of NSS Estimates of Consumption Expenditure." In T.N. Srinivasan and P.K. Bardhan, eds., *Poverty and Income Distribution in India*. Calcutta: Indian Statistical Institute.

Murthi, Mamta, Anne-Catherine Guio, and Jean Drèze. 1995. "Mortality, Fertility and Gender Bias in India: A District-Level Analysis." Development Economic Research Discussion Paper 61. London School of Economics and Political Science.

Murty, Mamta. 1994. "Management of Common Property Resources: Limits to Voluntary Collective Action." *Environmental and Resource Economics* 4(6).

Musgrove, Philip. 1996. *Public and Private Roles in Health: Theory and Financing Patterns*. World Bank Discussion Paper 339. Washington, D.C.

Mwabu, Germano, Martha Ainsworth, and Andrew Nyamete. 1993. "Quality of Medical Care and Choice of Medical Treatment in Kenya: An Empirical Analysis." Africa Technical Department Technical Paper 9. World Bank, Washington, D.C.

Narayan, Deepa. 1998. "Participatory Rural Development." In Ernst Lutz, ed., *Agriculture and the Environment*. Washington, D.C.: World Bank.

———. 1999. "Bonds and Bridges: Social Capital and Poverty." Policy Research Working Paper 2167. World Bank, Washington, D.C.

Narayan, Deepa, and David Nyamwaya. 1996. "Learning from the Poor: A Participatory Poverty Assessment in Kenya." Environment Department Paper 034. Participation Series. World Bank, Washington, D.C.

Narayan, Deepa, and Lant Pritchett. 1999. "Cents and Sociability: Household Income and Social Capital in Rural Tanzania." *Economic Development and Cultural Change* 47(4): 871–97.

Narayan, Deepa, and Talat Shah. 1999. "Gender Inequity, Poverty and Social Capital." World Bank, Poverty Reduction and Economic Management Network, Washington, D.C.

Narayan, Deepa, Robert Chambers, Meera K. Shah, and Patti Petesch. 1999. "Global Synthesis: Consultations with the Poor." Paper presented at Global Synthesis Workshop, World Bank, Poverty Group, 22–23 September, Washington, D.C.

———. 2000. *Voices of the Poor: Crying Out for Change*. New York: Oxford University Press.

Narayan, Deepa, with Raj Patel, Kai Schafft, Anne Rademacher, and Sarah Koch-Schulte. 2000. *Voices of the Poor: Can Anyone Hear Us?* New York: Oxford University Press.

National Intelligence Council. 2000. "The Global Infectious Disease Threat and Its Implications for the United States." National Intelligence Estimate 99-17D. Washington, D.C.

Nelson, Joan. 1999. *Reforming Health and Education: The World Bank, the Inter-American Development Bank, and Complex Institutional Change*. Policy Essay 26. Washington, D.C.: Overseas Development Council.

Nepal, Department of Roads. 1997. "Environmental Management Guidelines." Geo-Environment Unit, Kathmandu.

Newman, John, Steen Jorgensen, and Menno Pradhan. 1991. *Workers' Benefits from Bolivia's Emergency Social Fund*. Living Standards Measurement Study Working Paper 77. Washington, D.C.: World Bank.

Ng, Francis, and Sandy Yeats. 1996. "Open Economies Work Better! Did Africa's Protectionist Policies Cause Its Marginalization in World Trade?" Policy Research Working Paper 1636. World Bank, Washington, D.C.

Nigerian Economic Society. 1997. *Poverty Alleviation in Nigeria. Selected Papers for the 1997 Annual Conference.* University of Ibadan.

Niles, Kimberly J. 1999. "Economic Adjustment and Targeted Social Spending: The Role of Political Institutions (Indonesia, Mexico, and Ghana)." Background paper for *World Development Report 2000/2001*. U.K. Department for International Development, London; and World Bank, Washington, D.C.

Nolan, Brian, and Vincent Turbat. 1995. *Cost Recovery in Public Health Services in Sub-Saharan Africa.* Economic Development Institute Technical Materials. Washington, D.C.: World Bank.

North, Douglass. 1990. *Institutions, Institutional Change, and Economic Performance.* New York: Cambridge University Press.

———. 1994. "Economic Performance through Time." *American Economic Review* 84(3): 359–68.

Norton, Seth. 1998. "Poverty, Property Rights and Human Well-Being: A Cross-National Study." *Cato Journal* 18(2): 233–450.

Nyonator, Frank, and Joseph Kutzin. 1999. "Health for Some? The Effects of User Fees in the Volta Region of Ghana." *Health Policy and Planning* 14(4): 329–41.

Oates, Wallace E. 1999. "An Essay on Fiscal Federalism." *Journal of Economic Literature* 37: 1120–49.

Ocampo, Jose Antonio, and Lance Taylor. 1998. "Trade Liberalization in Developing Economies: Modest Benefits but Problems with Productivity Growth, Macro Prices, and Income Distribution." Center for Economic Policy Analysis Working Paper 8. New School for Social Research, New York.

Odaka, Konosuke, and Juro Teranishi. 1998. *Markets and Government: In Search of Better Coordination.* Tokyo: Maruzen.

OECD (Organisation for Economic Co-operation and Development). 1996. *Trade, Employment, and Labor Standards: A Study of Core Workers' Rights and International Trade.* Paris.

———. 1999. *DAC Scoping Study of Donor Poverty Reduction Policies and Practices.* London: Overseas Development Institute.

OECD (Organisation for Economic Co-operation and Development), DAC (Development Assistance Committee). 1996. *Shaping the 21st Century: The Contribution of Development Cooperation.* Paris.

———. 1997. *DAC Guidelines on Conflict, Peace, and Development Cooperation.* Paris.

———. 1999. *Development Cooperation: Efforts and Policies of the Members of the Development Assistance Committee—1998 Report.* Paris.

———. 2000. "Development Cooperation: 1999 Report." *DAC Journal 2000* 1(1).

Ohiorhenuan, John. 1998. "Capacity Building Implications of Enhanced African Participation in Global Rules-Making and Arrangements." Paper prepared for the collaborative research project Africa and the World Trading System, African Economic Research Consortium, Nairobi.

Okrasa, Wlodzimierz. 1999. "Who Avoids and Who Escapes from Poverty during the Transition? Evidence from Polish Panel Data, 1993–96." Policy Research Working Paper 2218. World Bank, Washington, D.C.

Olinto, Pedro, Benjamin Davis, and Klaus Deininger. 1999. "Did the Poor Benefit from Land Market Liberalization in Mexico? Panel-Data Evidence of the Impact of the *Ejido* Reforms." World Bank, Latin America and the Caribbean Region and Development Research Group; and International Food Policy Research Institute, Washington, D.C.

Olson, Mancur. 1969. "The Principle of 'Fiscal Equivalence': The Division of Responsibilities among Different Levels of Government." *American Economic Review Papers and Proceedings* 59: 479–87.

———. 1982. *The Rise and Decline of Nations: Economic Growth, Stagflation, and Social Rigidities.* New Haven, Conn.: Yale University Press.

Olsson, Jonathan. 2000. "Mitigation Is the Cornerstone of Emergency Management in the United States." Box for *World Development Report 2000/2001*. World Bank, Washington, D.C.

"Openness, Macroeconomic Crisis and Poverty." 1999. Rapporteur's report of a dialogue and consultation on *World Development Report 2000/2001,* World Bank Institute and Institute of Strategic and International Studies Malaysia, May, Kuala Lumpur.

Osiptel (Organismo Supervisor de Inversión Privada en Telecomunicaciones). 1996. *La Apertura del mercado de las telecomunicaciones en el Peru.* Lima.

Ostrom, Elinor. 1997. "Investing in Capital, Institutions, and Incentives." In Christopher Clague, ed., *Institutions and Economic Development: Growth and Governance in Less-Developed and Post-Socialist Countries.* Baltimore, Md.: Johns Hopkins University Press.

———. Forthcoming. "The Puzzle of Counterproductive Property Rights Reforms: A Conceptual Analysis." In Alain de Janvry, Gustavo Gordillo, Jean-Philippe Platteau, and Elisabeth Sadoulet, eds., *Access to Land, Rural Poverty and Public Action.* New York: Oxford University Press.

Ostrom, Elinor, L. Schroeder, and S. Wynne. 1993. *Institutional Incentives and Sustainable Development: Infrastructure Policies in Perspective.* Boulder, Colo.: Westview.

Over, Mead. 1998. "The Effects of Societal Variables on Urban Rates of HIV Infection in Developing Countries: An Exploratory Analysis." In Martha Ainsworth, Lieve Fransen, and Mead Over, eds., *Confronting AIDS: Evidence from the Developing World.* Luxembourg: European Commission.

Owen, Daniel, and Julie van Domelen. 1998. "Getting an Earful: A Review of Beneficiary Assessments of Social Funds." Social Protection Discussion Paper 9816. World Bank, Washington, D.C.

Owens, Trudy. 2000. "The Determinants of Income Growth in Rural Households and the Role of Aid: A Case Study of Zimbabwe." Ph.D. diss. Oxford University.

Oxfam International. 1999. *Education Now: Break the Cycle of Poverty.* Oxford.

Oxford Analytica. 1998a. "Central America: Hurricane Impact." 10 November. [www.oxfam.com/index.html].

———. 1998b. "Indonesia: Ethnic-Chinese Plight." 15 July. [www.oxfam.com/index.html].

———. 1999. "Indonesia: New Management." 25 October. [www.oxfam.com/index.html].

Pack, Howard. 1999. "Poverty-Reducing Policy Reform." Paper presented at *World Development Report 2000/2001* Summer Workshop, World Bank, July, Washington, D.C.

Paerregaard, Karsten. 1998. "Alleviating Poverty in Latin America: Can Local Organizations Be of Any Help?" Working Paper 9810. Center for Development Research, Copenhagen.

PAHO (Pan American Health Organization). 1998. *Health in the Americas 1998.* Washington, D.C.

Palacios, Robert, and Montserrat Pallares-Miralles. 1999. "International Patterns of Pension Provision." Discussion paper. World Bank, Social Protection Department, Washington, D.C.

Palley, Thomas. 1999. "The Economic Case for International Labor Standards: Theory and Some Evidence." American Federation of Labor and Congress of Industrial Organizations (AFL-CIO), Washington, D.C.

Pande, Rohini. 1999. "Minority Representation and Policy Choices: The Significance of Legislator Identity." London School of Economics and Political Science.

Papageorgiou, Demetris, Armeane Choksi, and Michael Michaely. 1995. "Liberalizing Foreign Trade in Developing Countries: The Lessons of Experience." World Bank, Washington, D.C.

Park, Kyung Ae. 1990. "Women and Revolution in China: The Sources of Constraints on Women's Liberation." *Korea and World Affairs* 14(4).

Parker, Andrew, and Rodrigo Serrano. Forthcoming. *Promoting Good Local Governance through Social Funds and Decentralization.* Washington, D.C.: World Bank.

Parker, Edith A., Amy J. Schulz, Barbara A. Israel, and Rose Hollis. 1998. "Detroit's East Side Village Health Worker Partnership: Community-Based Lay Health Advisor Intervention in an Urban Area." *Health Education and Behaviour* 25(1): 24–45.

Parker, Roland, Randall Riopelle, and William Steel. 1995. *Small Enterprises Adjusting to Liberalization in Five African Countries.* World Bank Discussion Paper 271. Washington, D.C.

Parthasarthy, Gupta. 1991. "Lease Market, Poverty Alleviation and Policy Options." *Economic and Political Weekly* 26(13): A31–38.

Patrinos, Harry Anthony, and David Ariasingam. 1997. *Decentralization of Education: Demand-Side Financing.* Directions in Development Series. Washington, D.C.: World Bank.

Patten, Richard, and Jay Rosengard. 1991. *Progress with Profits: The Development of Rural Banking in Indonesia.* San Francisco: ICS Press.

Paugam, Serge, ed. 1996. *L'Exclusion l'etat des savoirs.* Paris: Editions La Découverte.

Paul, Samuel. 1998. "Making Voice Work: The Report Card on Bangalore's Public Services." Policy Research Working Paper 1921. World Bank, Washington, D.C.

Paul, Samuel, and M. Shan. 1997. "Corruption in Public Service Delivery." In Sanjivi Guhan and S. Paul, eds., *Corruption in India: Agenda for Action.* New Delhi: New Delhi Press.

Pawasuthipaisit, Anan, Sombat Sakuntasathien, and Robert M. Townsend. 1999. "Report to the Ford Foundation: Impact of the Thai Crisis." Background paper for *World Development Report 2000/2001.* World Bank, Washington, D.C.

Paxton, Julia, and Carlos Cuevas. 1996. *A Worldwide Inventory of Microfinance Institutions.* Sustainable Banking with the Poor Project. Washington, D.C.: World Bank.

Pearce, David, and others. 1996. "The Social Costs of Climate Change." In James Bruce, Hoesung Lee, and Erik Haites, eds., *Climate Change 1995: Economic and Social Dimensions of Climate Change—Contribution of Working Group III to the Second Assessment Report of the Intergovernmental Panel on Climate Change.* New York: Cambridge University Press.

Pencavel, John. 1997. "The Legal Framework for Collective Bargaining in Developing Countries." In Sebastian Edwards and Nora Lustig, eds., *Labor Markets in Latin America.* Washington, D.C.: Brookings Institution.

Perotti, Roberto. 1992. "Income Distribution: Politics and Growth." *American Economic Review* 82: 311–16.

———. 1993. "Political Equilibrium, Income Distribution, and Growth." *Review of Economic Studies* 60: 755–76.

———. 1996a. "Growth, Income Distribution, and Democracy: What the Data Say." *Journal of Economic Growth* 1: 149–87.

———. 1996b. "Redistribution and Non-consumption Smoothing in an Open Economy." *Review of Economic Studies* 63: 411–33.

Perry, Guillermo, and Daniel Lederman. 1999. *Adjustments after Speculative Attacks in Latin America and Asia: A Tale of Two Regions?* Washington, D.C.: World Bank.

Persley, Gabrielle J., and John J. Doyle. 1999. "Biotechnology for Developing-Country Agriculture: Problems and Opportunities—Overview." Focus 2, Brief 1. International Food Policy Research Institute, Washington, D.C.

Persson, Torsten, and Guido Tabellini. 1994. "Is Inequality Harmful for Growth?" *American Economic Review* 84: 600–21.

Pessino, Carola. 1997. "Argentina: The Labor Market during the Economic Transition." In Sebastian Edwards and Nora Lustig, eds., *Labor Markets in Latin America.* Washington, D.C.: Brookings Institution.

Pfaff, Alexander S.P. 1996. "What Drives Deforestation in the Brazilian Amazon? Evidence from Satellite and Socioeconomic Data." Columbia University, Department of Economics, New York.

Phipps, Shelley A., and Peter S. Burton. 1998. "What's Mine Is Yours? The Influence of Male and Female Incomes on Patterns of Household Expenditure." *Economica* 65: 599–613.

Piketty, Thomas. 1998. "Self-Fulfilling Beliefs about Social Status." *Journal of Public Economics* 70: 115–32.

———. Forthcoming. "Theories of Persistent Inequality and Intergenerational Mobility." In Anthony B. Atkinson and François Bourguignon, eds., *Handbook of Income Distribution.* New York: North Holland-Elsevier.

Pinstrup-Andersen, Per, Rajul Pandya-Lorch, and Mark Rosengrant. 1997. "The World Food Situation: Recent Developments, Emerging Issues, and Long-Term Prospects." Food Policy Report. International Food Policy Research Institute, Washington, D.C.

Pitt, Mark, and Shahidur Khandker. 1998. "The Impact of

Group-Based Credit Programs on Poor Households in Bangladesh: Does the Gender of Participants Matter?" *Journal of Political Economy* 106: 958–96.

Platteau, Jean-Philippe, and Jean Marie Baland. Forthcoming. "Impartible Inheritance versus Equal Division: A Comparative Perspective Centered on Europe and Sub-Saharan Africa." In Alain de Janvry, Gustavo Gordillo, Jean-Philippe Platteau, and Elisabeth Sadoulet, eds., *Access to Land, Rural Poverty and Public Action*. New York: Oxford University Press.

Polanyi, Karl. 1957. *The Great Transformation*. Boston: Beacon.

Poppele, Jessica, Sudarno Sumarto, and Lant Pritchett. 1999. "Social Impacts of the Indonesian Crisis: New Data and Policy Implications." SMERU Report. Social Monitoring and Early Response Unit, Jakarta.

Porter, Gareth, Raymond Clémençon, Waafas Ofosu-Amaah, and Michael Philips. 1998. *Study of GEF's Overall Performance*. Washington, D.C.: Global Environment Facility.

Portes, Alejandro. 1995. *The Economic Sociology of Immigration: Essays on Networks, Ethnicity and Entrepreneurship*. New York: Russell Sage Foundation.

———. 1998. "Social Capital: Its Origins and Applications in Contemporary Sociology." *Annual Review of Sociology* 24: 1–24.

Portes, Alejandro, and Patricia Landolt. 1996. "The Downside of Social Capital." *American Prospect* 26: 18–21, 94.

Portes, Alejandro, and Julia Sensenbrenner. 1993. "Embeddedness and Immigration: Notes on the Social Determinants of Economic Action." *American Journal of Sociology* 98(6): 1320–50.

Posner, Daniel. 1999. "Ethnic Fractionalization: How (Not) to Measure It? What Does (and Doesn't) It Explain?" Paper presented at annual meeting of American Political Science Association, Atlanta.

Posner, Richard. 1997. "Social Norms and the Law: An Economic Approach." *American Economic Review* 87(2): 365–69.

Postel, Sandra. 1999. "Water, Food and Population." In Barbara Sundberg Baudot and William R. Moomaw, eds., *People and Their Planet*. New York: St. Martin's.

Pottebaum, David A. 1999. *Economic and Social Implications of War and Conflict*. Cornell University, Agricultural Economics Department, Ithaca, N.Y.

Pouliquen, Louis Y. 1999a. "Infrastructure and Poverty." Background paper for *World Development Report 2000/2001*. World Bank, Washington, D.C.

———. 1999b. "Rural Infrastructure from a World Bank Perspective: A Knowledge Management Framework." World Bank, Environmentally and Socially Sustainable Development Network, Washington, D.C.

Pradhan, Sanjay. 1996. "Public-Private Partnerships for Service Provision." Background paper for *World Development Report 1997*. World Bank, Washington, D.C.

Prakash, S. 1997. "Poverty and Environment Linkages in Mountains and Uplands: Reflections on the 'Poverty Trap'." Collaborative Research in the Economics of the Environment and Development Working Paper Series, no. 12. International Instutute for Environment and Development, Environmental Economics Programme, London; Institute for Environmental Studies, Amsterdam; and Vrije Universiteit, Amsterdam.

Prasad, Kameshwar, Paolo Belli, and Monica Das Gupta. 1999. "Links between Poverty, Exclusion, and Health." Background paper for *World Development Report 2000/2001*. World Bank, Washington, D.C.

Preker, Alexander. 2000. "Partnership: Private Sector Role in Poverty and Health." Box for *World Development Report 2000/2001*. World Bank, Washington, D.C.

Preker, Alexander, and Richard Feachem. 1996. *Market Mechanisms and the Health Sector in Central and Eastern Europe*. World Bank Technical Paper 293. Washington, D.C.

Prennushi, Giovanna. 1999. "Nepal: Poverty at the Turn of the Twenty-First Century." South Asia Region Internal Discussion Paper 174. World Bank, Washington, D.C.

Prescott, Nicholas, and Menno Pradhan. 1999. "Coping with Catastrophic Health Shocks." Paper presented at Inter-American Development Bank conference on social protection and poverty, 4–5 February, Washington, D.C.

Preston, Samuel H., and Michael R. Haines. 1991. *Fatal Years: Child Mortality in Late-Nineteenth-Century America*. Princeton, N.J.: Princeton University Press.

Primo Braga, Carlos A., Carsten Fink, and Claudia Paz Sepulveda. 2000. *Intellectual Property Rights and Economic Development*. World Bank Discussion Paper 412. Washington, D.C.

Prince of Wales Business Leaders Forum. 1998. *Building Competitiveness and Communities*. London.

Pritchett, Lant. 1996a. "Mind Your P's and Q's: The Cost of Public Investment Is Not the Value of Public Capital." Policy Research Working Paper 1660. World Bank, Washington, D.C.

———. 1996b. "Where Has All the Education Gone?" Policy Research Working Paper 1581. World Bank, Washington, D.C.

———. 1997. "Divergence, Big Time." *Journal of Economic Perspectives* 11: 3–17.

Pritchett, Lant, and Lawrence Summers. 1994. "Desired Fertility and the Impact of Population Policies." *Population and Development Review* 20(1): 1–55.

———. 1996. "Wealthier Is Healthier." *Journal of Human Resources* 31(4): 841–68.

PROBE Team. 1999. *Public Report on Basic Education in India*. New Delhi: Oxford University Press.

Prunier, Gerard. 1997. *The Rwanda Crisis: History of a Genocide*. New York: Columbia University Press.

Przeworski, Adam, and Fernando Limongi. 1993. "Political Regimes and Economic Growth." *Journal of Economic Perspectives* 7: 51–69.

Psacharopoulos, George, and Harry Anthony Patrinos. 1994. *Indigenous People and Poverty in Latin America: An Empirical Analysis*. Washington, D.C.: World Bank.

Pulley, Robert V. 1989. *Making the Poor Creditworthy: A Case Study of the Integrated Rural Development Program of India*. World Bank Discussion Paper 58. Washington, D.C.

Putnam, Robert. 2000. *Bowling Alone: The Collapse and Revival of American Community*. New York: Simon and Schuster.

Putnam, Robert, with Robert Leonardi and Raffaella Nanetti. 1993. *Making Democracy Work: Civic Traditions in Modern Italy*. Princeton, N.J.: Princeton University Press.

Putzel, James. 1997. "Accounting for the 'Dark Side' of Social Capital: Reading Robert Putnam on Democracy." *Journal of International Development* 9(7): 939–49.

Qian, Yingyi, and Barry R. Weingast. 1996. "China's Transition to Markets: Market-Preserving Federalism, Chinese Style." *Journal of Policy Reform* 2: 149–85.

Quah, Danny. 1997. "Empirics of Growth and Distribution: Stratification, Polarization, and Convergence Clubs." Centre for Economic Performance Discussion Paper 324. London School of Economics and Political Science.

———. 1999. "6 x 10⁹: Some Dynamics of Global Inequality and Growth." Background paper for *World Development Report 2000/2001*. London School of Economics and Political Science, Suntory and Toyota International Centres for Economics and Related Disciplines; and World Bank, Washington, D.C.

Quisumbing, Agnes R. 1994. "Improving Women's Agricultural Productivity as Farmers and Workers." Education and Social Policy Department Discussion Paper 37. World Bank, Washington, D.C.

———. 1996. "Male-Female Differences in Agricultural Productivity: Methodological Issues and Empirical Evidence." *World Development* 24: 1579–95.

Quisumbing, Agnes R., and John A. Maluccio. 1999. "Intrahousehold Allocation and Gender Relations: New Empirical Evidence." Background paper for forthcoming World Bank Policy Research Report *EnGendering Development*. World Bank, Washington, D.C.

Ramamurti, R. 1999. "Why Haven't Developing Countries Privatized Deeper and Faster?" *World Development* 27: 137–56.

Ramey, Garey, and Valerie A. Ramey. 1995. "Cross-Country Evidence on the Link between Volatility and Growth." *American Economic Review* 85(5): 1138–51.

Ranis, Gustav. 1979. "Appropriate Technology in a Dual Economy: Reflection on Philippine and Taiwanese Experience." In Edward A. Robinson, ed., *Appropriate Technologies for Third World Development*. New York: St. Martin's.

Ranis, Gustav, and Frances Stewart. 1994. "Decentralization in Indonesia." *Bulletin of Indonesian Economic Studies* 30(3): 41–72.

Rao, J. Mohan. 1999. "Equity in a Global Public Goods Framework." In Inge Kaul, Isabelle Grunberg, and Marc Stern, eds., *Global Public Goods: International Cooperation in the 21st Century*. New York: Oxford University Press.

Rao, Vijayendra. 1998a. "Domestic Violence and Intra-household Resource Allocation in Rural India: An Exercise in Participatory Econometrics." In Maithreyi Krishnaraj, Ratna M. Sudarshan, and Abusaleh Shariff, eds., *Gender, Population and Development*. New York: Oxford University Press.

———. 1998b. "Wife-Abuse, Its Causes and Its Impact on Intra-household Resource Allocation in Rural Karnataka: A Participatory Econometric Analysis." In Maithreyi Krishnaraj, Ratna M. Sudarshan, and Abusaleh Shariff, eds., *Gender, Population and Development*. New York: Oxford University Press.

Rauch, James, and Peter Evans. 1999. "Bureaucratic Structure and Bureaucratic Performance in Developing Countries." Working Paper 99-06. University of California at San Diego, Department of Economics.

Rauch, James, and Vitor Trindade. 1999. "Ethnic Chinese Networks in International Trade." NBER Working Paper 7189. National Bureau of Economic Research, Cambridge, Mass.

Ravallion, Martin. 1988. "Expected Poverty under Risk-Induced Welfare Variability." *Economic Journal* 98: 1171–82.

———. 1991. "Reaching the Rural Poor through Public Employment: Arguments, Evidence and Lessons from South Asia." *World Bank Research Observer* 6(2): 153–76.

———. 1992. *Poverty Comparisons: A Guide to Concepts and Methods*. Living Standards Measurement Study Working Paper 88. Washington, D.C.: World Bank.

———. 1993. *Poverty Comparisons: Fundamentals of Pure and Applied Economics*. Chur, Switzerland: Harwood Academic.

———. 1997a. "Can High-Inequality Developing Countries Escape Absolute Poverty?" *Economics Letters* 56(1): 51–57.

———. 1997b. "Good and Bad Growth: The Human Development Reports." *World Development* 25: 631–38.

———. 1998. "Does Aggregation Hide the Harmful Effects of Inequality on Growth?" *Economics Letters* 61(1): 73–77.

———. 1999a. "Appraising Workfare." *World Bank Research Observer* 14(1): 31–48.

———. 1999b. " Is More Targeting Consistent with Less Spending?" *International Tax and Public Finance* 6(3): 411–19.

———. 1999c. "On Protecting the Poor from Fiscal Contractions." World Bank, Development Research Group, Washington, D.C.; and Université des Sciences Sociales, ARQADE, Toulouse.

———. 2000a. "How Long Before Most of the Poor Live in Urban Areas?" World Bank, Development Research Group, Washington, D.C.

———. 2000b. "Inequality Convergence." World Bank, Development Research Group, Washington, D.C.

———. Forthcoming. "Monitoring Targeting Performance When Decentralized Allocations to the Poor Are Unobserved." *World Bank Economic Review*.

Ravallion, Martin, and Shubham Chaudhuri. 1997. "Risk and Insurance in Village India: A Comment." *Econometrica* 65: 171–84.

Ravallion, Martin, and Shaohua Chen. 1997. "What Can New Survey Data Tell Us about Recent Changes in Distribution and Poverty?" *World Bank Economic Review* 11(2): 357–82.

Ravallion, Martin, and Gaurav Datt. 1996. "How Important to India's Poor Is the Sectoral Composition of Economic Growth?" *World Bank Economic Review* 10(1): 1–25.

———. 1999. "When Is Growth Pro-Poor? Evidence from the Diverse Experiences of India's States." Policy Research Working Paper 2263. World Bank, Washington, D.C.

Ravallion, Martin, and Binayak Sen. 1994. "The Impacts on Rural Poverty of Land-Based Targeting: Further Results for Bangladesh." *World Development* 22(6): 823–38.

Ravallion, Martin, and Dominique van de Walle. 1991. "Urban-Rural Cost-of-Living Differentials in a Developing Economy." *Journal of Urban Economics* 29(1): 113–27.

Ravallion, Martin, and Quentin Wodon. 1999. "Poor Areas, or Only Poor People?" *Journal of Regional Science* 39: 689–711.

———. 2000. "Does Child Labor Displace Schooling? Evidence on Behavioral Responses to an Enrollment Subsidy." *Economic Journal* 110: 158–75.

———. Forthcoming. "Banking on the Poor? Branch Placement and Nonfarm Rural Development in Bangladesh." *Review of Development Economics.*

Rawlings, Laura, Lynne Sherburne-Benz, and Julie van Domelen. Forthcoming. "Evaluating Social Fund Performance across Countries." World Bank, Human Development Network, Washington, D.C.

Reardon, Thomas. 1997. "Using Evidence of Household Income Diversification to Inform Study of the Rural Nonfarm Labor Market in Africa." *World Development* 25(5): 735–47.

Reardon, Thomas, and J. Edward Taylor. 1996. "Agroclimatic Shock, Income Inequality, and Poverty: Evidence from Burkina Faso." *World Development* 24(5): 901–14.

Reardon, Thomas, Christopher Delgado, and Peter Matlon. 1992. "Determinants and Effects of Income Diversification amongst Farm Households in Burkina Faso." *Journal of Development Studies* 28(2): 264–96.

Reardon, Thomas, J. Edward Taylor, Kostas Stamoulis, Peter Lanjouw, and Arsenio Balisacan. Forthcoming. "Effects of Non-farm Employment on Rural Income Inequality in Developing Countries: An Investment Perspective." *Journal of Agricultural Economics.*

Reinikka, Ritva, and Jakob Svensson. 1999. "Confronting Competition: Investment Response and Constraints in Uganda." Policy Research Working Paper 2242. World Bank, Washington, D.C.

Remenyi, Joe. 1991. *Where Credit Is Due: Income-Generating Programmes for the Poor in Developing Countries.* London: Intermediate Technologies.

Ren, X.S. 1996. "Regional Variation in Infant Survival in China." *Social Biology* 43(1–2): 1–19.

Renner, Michael. 1994. "Budgeting for Disarmament: The Costs of War and Peace." Worldwatch Paper 122. Worldwatch Institute, Washington, D.C.

Reno, William. 1998. *Warlord Politics and African States.* Boulder, Colo.: Lynne Rienner.

Revenga, Ana. 1997. "Employment and Wage Effects of Trade Liberalization: The Case of Mexican Manufacturing." *Journal of Labor Economics* 15(3): 20–43.

Reyes, Cecilia, and Anne Bernadette E. Mandap. 1999. "The Social Impact of the Regional Financial Crisis in the Philippines." Micro Impact of Macroeconomic and Adjustment Policies Research Paper Series, no. 41. Policy and Development Foundation, Manila.

Rhyne, Elisabeth, and Sharon Holt. 1994. *Women in Finance and Enterprise Development.* Washington, D.C.: World Bank.

Riddell, Roger C., and Mark Robinson, with John de Coninck, Ann Muir, and Sarah White. 1995. *Non-governmental Organizations and Rural Poverty Alleviation.* New York: Oxford University Press.

Rios-Rull, Jose Victor. 1994. "Population Changes and Capital Accumulation: The Aging of the Baby Boom." University of Pennsylvania, Department of Economics, Philadelphia.

Robbins, Donald J. 1995. "Should Educational Spending Be Re-distributed from Higher to Primary Education in LDCs? A Note with Application to Chile." *Revista de Analisis Economico* 10(1): 37–51.

———. 1996. "Evidence on Trade and Wages in the Developing World." Technical Paper 119. Organisation for Economic Co-operation and Development, Paris.

Robinson, James A. 1996. "When Is a State Predatory?" University of Southern California, Department of Economics, Los Angeles.

Robinson, Peter. 1993. "Economic Effects of the 1992 Drought on the Manufacturing Sector in Zimbabwe." Overseas Development Institute, London.

Robinson, Richard, and David Stiedl. 2000. "Decentralisation of Road Administration: Review of Experience." U.K. Department for International Development, London.

Rodgers, Gerry. 1979. "Income and Inequality as Determinants of Mortality: An International Cross-Section Analysis." *Population Studies* 33: 343–51.

Rodgers, Gerry, Charles G. Gore, and Jose B. Figueiredo. 1995. *Social Exclusion: Rhetoric, Reality, Responses.* Geneva: International Institute for Labor Studies.

Rodriguez, Francisco. 1999. "Inequality, Economic Growth and Economic Performance." Background paper for *World Development Report 2000/2001.* World Bank, Washington, D.C.

Rodriguez, Francisco, and Dani Rodrik. 1999. "Trade Policy and Economic Growth: A Skeptic's Guide to the Cross-National Evidence." University of Maryland, Department of Economics, College Park.

Rodrik, Dani. 1996. "Labor Standards in International Trade: Do They Matter and What Do We Do about Them?" In Robert Z. Lawrence, Dani Rodrik, and John Whalley, eds., *Emerging Agenda for Global Trade: High Stakes for Developing Countries.* Policy Essay 20. Washington, D.C.: Overseas Development Council.

———. 1997. "Trade Policy and Economic Performance in Sub-Saharan Africa." Harvard University, John F. Kennedy School of Government, Cambridge, Mass.

———. 1998. "Where Did All the Growth Go? External Shocks, Social Conflicts, and Growth Collapses." NBER Working Paper 6350. National Bureau of Economic Research, Cambridge, Mass.

———. 1999a. "Institutions for High-Quality Growth: What They Are and How to Acquire Them." Paper presented at International Monetary Fund conference on second-generation reforms, 8–9 November, Washington, D.C.

———. 1999b. *The New Global Economy and the Developing Countries: Making Openness Work.* Policy Essay 24. Washington, D.C.: Overseas Development Council.

———. 1999c. "Why Is There So Much Economic Insecurity in Latin America?" NBER Working Paper 6350. National Bureau of Economic Research, Cambridge, Mass.

———. 2000. "Institutions for High-Quality Growth: What They Are and How to Acquire Them." NBER Working Paper 7540. National Bureau of Economic Research, Cambridge, Mass.

Roemer, John E. 1996. *Theories of Distributive Justice.* Cambridge, Mass.: Harvard University Press.

———. 1998. *Equality of Opportunity.* Cambridge, Mass.: Harvard University Press.

Roger, Neil. 1999. "Recent Trends in Private Participation in Infrastructure." Viewpoint 196. World Bank, Finance, Private Sector, and Infrastructure Network, Washington, D.C.

Ros, Jaime. 2000. *Development Theory and the Economics of Growth.* Ann Arbor: University of Michigan Press.

Rose, Elaina. 1999. "Consumption Smoothing and Excess Female Mortality in Rural India." *Review of Economics and Statistics* 81(1): 41–49.

Rose, Richard. 1995. "Russia as an Hour-Glass Society: A Constitution without Citizens." *European Constitutional Review* 4(3): 34–42.

———. 1999. "Getting Things Done in Anti-modern Society: Social Capital Networks in Russia." Social Capital Initiative Working Paper 6. World Bank, Social Development Department, Washington, D.C.

Rose-Ackerman, Susan. 1997. "Corruption and Development." In Boris Pleskovic and Joseph E. Stiglitz, eds., *Annual World Bank Conference on Development Economics 1997.* Washington, D.C.: World Bank.

Rosen, George. 1993. *A History of Public Health.* Baltimore, Md.: Johns Hopkins University Press.

Rosenzweig, Mark. 1998. "Social Learning and Economic Growth: Empirical Evidence." Background paper for *World Development Report 1998/99.* World Bank, Washington, D.C.

Rosenzweig, Mark, and Hans Binswanger. 1993. "Wealth, Weather Risk and the Composition and Profitability of Agricultural Investment." *Economic Journal* 103: 56–78.

Rowntree, Benjamin Seebohm. 1901. *Poverty: A Study of Town Life.* London: Macmillan.

Royaume du Maroc, Ministère de la Prévision Economique et du Plan, Direction de la Statistique. 1999. "Enquête nationale sur les niveaux de vie des ménages 1998/99: Rapport de synthése."

Rozelle, Scott. 1996. "Stagnation without Equity: Patterns of Growth and Inequality in China's Rural Economy." *China Journal* 3: 63–91.

Rubin, Donald B. 1987. *Multiple Imputation for Nonresponse in Surveys.* New York: John Wiley & Sons.

Rubio, Mauricio. 1997. "Perverse Social Capital: Some Evidence from Colombia." *Journal of Economic Issues* 31(3): 805–16.

Rugalema, Gabriel. 1999. "Adult Mortality as Entitlement Failure: AIDS and the Crisis of Rural Livelihoods in a Tanzanian Village." Ph.D. diss. Institute of Social Studies, The Hague.

Ruprah, Inder. 1999. "Towards Fiscal Prudence, Transparency and Accountability in Peru: A Proposal." Inter-American Development Bank, Division 5 Regional Operations Department, Washington, D.C.

Ruprah, Inder, and Luis Marcano. 1998. "Poverty Alleviation in Venezuela: Who to Target and How Not to Adjust in a Crisis." Inter-American Development Bank, Division 5 Regional Operations Department, Washington, D.C.

———. 1999. "Digging a Hole: Income Inequality in Venezuela." Inter-American Development Bank, Division 5 Regional Operations Department, Washington, D.C.

Rutkowski, Michal. 1999. "Russia's Social Protection Malaise." Social Protection Discussion Paper 9909. World Bank, Washington, D.C.

Sable, Charles, Dara O'Rourke, and Archon Fung. 2000. "Ratcheting Labor Standards: Regulation for Continuous Improvement in the Global Workplace." World Bank, Human Development Network, Washington, D.C.

Sachs, Jeffrey. 1999. "Sachs on Development: Helping the World's Poorest." *Economist,* 14–20 August, pp. 17–20.

———. 2000. "Science, the Global Division of Labor, and International Public Policy." Keynote address at Annual World Bank Conference on Development Economics, 18–20 April, Washington, D.C.

Sachs, Jeffrey, and Andrew Warner. 1995. "Economic Reform and the Process of Global Integration." *Brookings Papers on Economic Activity* 1: 1–117.

Sachs, Jeffrey, Michael Kremer, and Amar Hamoudi. 1999. "The Case for a Vaccine Purchase Fund." Center for International Development Policy Paper 1. Harvard University, Cambridge, Mass.

Sachs, Jeffrey, Kwesi Botchwey, Maciej Cuchra, and Sara Sievers. 1999. "Implementing Debt Relief for the Highly Indebted Poor Countries." Center for International Development Policy Paper 2. Harvard University, Cambridge, Mass.

Sadoulet, Elisabeth, Rinku Murgai, and Alain de Janvry. Forthcoming. "Access to Land via Land Rental Markets." In Alain de Janvry, Gustavo Gordillo, Jean-Philippe Platteau, and Elisabeth Sadoulet, eds., *Access to Land, Rural Poverty and Public Action.* New York: Oxford University Press.

Sah, Raaj K. 1991. "Fallibility in Human Organizations and Political Systems." *Journal of Economic Perspectives* 5(2): 67–88.

Sahn, David E., and David C. Stifel. 1999. "Poverty Comparisons over Time and across Countries in Africa." Working Paper 95. Cornell University, Food and Nutrition Policy Program, Ithaca, N.Y.

Sahn, David E., Paul A. Dorosh, and Stephen D. Younger. 1997. *Structural Adjustment Reconsidered.* New York: Cambridge University Press.

Sahn, David E., David C. Stifel, and Stephen D. Younger. 1999. "Inter-temporal Changes in Welfare: Preliminary Results from Nine African Countries." Cornell University, Departments of Economics and Nutritional Science, Ithaca, N.Y.

Saito, Katrine, and Daphne Spurling. 1992. *Developing Agricultural Extension for Women Farmers.* World Bank Discussion Paper 156. Washington, D.C.

Saito, Katrine, Hailu Mekonen, and Daphne Spurling. 1994. *Raising the Productivity of Women Farmers in Sub-Saharan Africa.* World Bank Discussion Paper 230. Washington, D.C.

Sakurai, Takeshi. 1997. *Crop Production under Drought Risk and Estimation of Demand for Formal Drought Insurance in the Sahel.* Tokyo: Ministry of Agriculture, National Research Institute of Agricultural Economics, Forestry and Fisheries.

Salmen, Lawrence F. 1995. "Participatory Poverty Assessment: Incorporating Poor People's Perspectives into Poverty Assessment Work." World Bank, Environment Department, Washington, D.C.

Sampson, Robert, Jeffrey Morenhoff, and Felton Earls. 1999. "Beyond Social Capital: Spatial Dynamics of Collective Efficacy for Children." *American Sociological Review* 64(5): 633–60.

Sánchez, Susana. 2000. "Nicaragua Financial Markets." Background paper for *Nicaragua Poverty Assessment 2000*. World Bank, Latin America and the Caribbean Region, Washington, D.C.

Sandler, Todd. 1997. *Global Challenges: An Approach to Environmental, Political, and Economic Problems*. New York: Cambridge University Press.

———. 1998. "Global and Regional Public Goods: A Prognosis for Collective Action." *Fiscal Studies* 19(3): 221–47.

———. 1999. "Intergenerational Public Goods: Strategies, Efficiency, and Institutions." In Inge Kaul, Isabelle Grunberg, and Marc Stern, eds., *Global Public Goods: International Cooperation in the 21st Century*. New York: Oxford University Press.

Sara, Jennifer, and Travis Katz. 1997. "Making Rural Water Sustainable: Report on the Impact of Project Rules." United Nations Development Programme and World Bank Water and Sanitation Program, Washington, D.C.

Sarris, Alexander. 1994. "Household Welfare during Crisis and Adjustment in Ghana." *Journal of African Economies* 2(2): 195–237.

Satterthwaite, David. 2000. "Urban Upgrading and Water and Sanitation Services in Low-Income Areas." Box for *World Development Report 2000/2001*. World Bank, Washington, D.C.

Sauma, Pablo. 1997. "Costa Rica: A Public Approach." In Elaine Zuckerman and Emanuel de Kadt, eds., *The Public-Private Mix in Social Services: Health Care and Education in Chile, Costa Rica and Venezuela*. Washington, D.C.: Inter-American Development Bank.

Saunders, Robert J., Jeremy J. Warford, and Bjorn Wellenius. 1983. *Telecommunications and Economic Development*. Baltimore, Md.: Johns Hopkins University Press.

Savedoff, William, and Pablo Spiller. 1999. "Spilled Water: Institutional Commitment in the Provision of Water Services." Inter-American Development Bank, Washington, D.C.

Sawadogo, Kimseyinga. 1997. "La pauvrete au Burkina Faso: Une analyse critique des politiques et des strategies d'intervention locales." Working Paper 57. European Centre for Development Policy Management, Maastricht.

Scandizzo, Pasquale L. 1998. "Growth, Trade, and Agriculture: An Investigative Survey." FAO Economic and Social Development Paper 143. Food and Agriculture Organization of the United Nations, Rome.

Schalick, Lisa, Wilbur Hadden, Elsie Pamuk, Vicente Navarro, and Gregory Pappas. 2000. "The Widening Gap in Death Rates among Income Groups in the United States from 1967 to 1986." *International Journal of Health Services* 30(1): 13–26.

Schiavo-Campo, Salvatore, Giulio de Tommaso, and Amitabha Mukherjee. 1997a. "An International Statistical Survey of Government Employment and Wages." Policy Research Working Paper 1806. World Bank, Washington, D.C.

———. 1997b. "Government Employment and Pay: A Global and Regional Perspective." Policy Research Working Paper 1771. World Bank, Washington, D.C.

Schick, Allen. 1998. "Why Most Developing Countries Should Not Try New Zealand's Reforms." *World Bank Research Observer* 13(1): 123–31.

Schieber, George, ed. 1997. *Innovations in Health Care Financing: Proceedings of a World Bank Conference, March 10–11, 1997*. World Bank Discussion Paper 365. Washington, D.C.

Schieber, George, and Akiko Maeda. 1997. "A Curmudgeon's Guide to Financing Health Care in Developing Countries." In George Schieber, ed., *Innovations in Health Care Financing: Proceedings of a World Bank Conference, March 10–11, 1997*. World Bank Discussion Paper 365. Washington, D.C.

Schiff, Maurice. 1998. "Ethnic Diversity and Economic Reform in Sub-Saharan Africa." *Journal of African Economies* 7(2): 348–62.

Schilderman, Theo. 1993. "Disasters and Development: A Case Study from Peru." *Journal of International Development* 5: 415–23.

Schneider, Robert R. 1995. *Government and the Economy on the Amazon Frontier*. World Bank Environment Paper 11. Washington, D.C.

Schofield, Roger, David Reher, and Alain Bideau. 1991. *The Decline of Mortality in Europe*. Oxford: Clarendon.

Schraeder, Peter J., Steven Hook, and Bruce Taylor. 1998. "Clarifying the Foreign Aid Puzzle: A Comparison of American, Japanese, French, and Swedish Aid Flows." *World Politics* 50(2): 294–320.

Schuler, Margaret, and Sakuntala Kadirgamar-Rajasingham, eds. 1992. *Legal Literacy: A Tool for Women's Empowerment*. Washington, D.C.: OEF International, Women, Law, and Development.

Schultz, T. Paul. 1994. "Human Capital, Family Planning, and Their Effects on Population Growth." *American Economic Review* 84(2): 255–60.

———. 1999. "Preliminary Evidence of the Impact of Progresa on School Enrollment from 1997 and 1998." International Food Policy Research Institute, Washington, D.C.

Scoones, Ian. 1995. "Investigating Difference: Applications of Wealth Ranking and Household Survey Approaches among Farming Households in Southern Zimbabwe." *Development and Change* 26(1): 67–88.

Search, Leila. 1999. "Tanzania: Report on a Village Immersion." Box for *World Development Report 2000/2001*. World Bank, Washington, D.C.

Sebello Mendoza, Meyra, and Mark W. Rosegrant. 1995. *Pricing Behavior in Philippine Corn Markets: Implications for Market Efficiency*. Washington, D.C.: International Food Policy Research Institute.

Sebstad, Jennefer, and Monique Cohen. 1999. "Microfinance, Risk Management and Poverty." Background paper for *World Development Report 2000/2001*. U.S. Agency for International Development and World Bank, Washington, D.C.

Secretaría de Programación Económica y Regional. 1998. *Caracterización y evolución del gasto público social*. Buenos Aires: Ministerio de Economía y Obras y Servicios.

Sell, Susan. 1996. "North-South Environmental Bargaining: Ozone, Climate Change, and Biodiversity." *Global Governance* 2: 97–118.

Sen, Amartya. 1984. "Poor, Relatively Speaking." In Amartya Sen, ed., *Resources, Values and Development.* New York: Basil Blackwell.

——. 1992. "Missing Women." *British Medical Journal* 304(6827): 587–88.

——. 1993. "Capability and Well-Being." In Martha Nussbaum and Amartya Sen, eds., *The Quality of Life.* Oxford: Clarendon.

——. 1997a. "Development Thinking at the Beginning of the 21st Century." New Series, DERP-2. London School of Economics and Political Science.

——. 1997b. *Inequality Reexamined.* Cambridge, Mass.: Harvard University Press.

——. 1997c. *On Economic Inequality.* Oxford: Clarendon.

——. 1999. *Development as Freedom.* New York: Knopf.

Sen, Amartya, and Jean Dréze. 1989. *Hunger and Public Action.* Oxford: Clarendon.

Serageldin, Ismail, and Christiaan Grootaert. 2000. "Defining Social Capital: An Integrating View." In Partha Dasgupta and Ismail Serageldin, eds., *Social Capital: A Multifaceted Perspective.* Washington, D.C.: World Bank.

Serieux, John E. 1999. "Reducing the Debt of the Poorest: Challenges and Opportunities." North-South Institute, Ottawa.

SEWA (Self-Employed Women's Association). 1997. *Liberalizing for the Poor.* Ahmedabad.

Seymour, Frances J., and Navroz K. Dubash, with Jake Brunner, François Ekoko, Colin Filer, Hariadi Kartodihardjo, and John Mugabe. 2000. *The Right Conditions: The World Bank, Structural Adjustment, and Forest Policy Reform.* Washington, D.C.: World Resources Institute.

Shah, Anwar. 1999. "Balance, Accountability and Responsiveness: Lessons about Decentralization." Policy Research Working Paper 2021. World Bank, Washington, D.C.

Shah, Shekhar. 1999. "Coping with Natural Disasters: The 1998 Floods in Bangladesh." Paper presented at *World Development Report 2000/2001* Summer Workshop, World Bank, July, Washington, D.C.

Sharma, Naresh, and Jean Drèze. 1996. "Sharecropping in a North Indian Village." *Journal of Development Studies* 27(2): 277–92.

Shaw, R. Paul, and Martha Ainsworth, eds. 1995. *Financing Health Services through User Fees and Insurance: Case Studies from Sub-Saharan Africa.* World Bank Discussion Paper 294. Washington, D.C.

Shkolnikov, Vladimir, Giovanni Andrea Cornia, David A. Leon, and France Mesle. 1998. "Causes of the Russian Mortality Crisis: Evidence and Interpretations." *World Development* 26(11): 1995–2011.

Siegel, Paul, and Jeffrey Alwang. 1999. "An Asset-Based Approach to Social Risk Management: A Conceptual Framework." Social Protection Discussion Paper 9926. World Bank, Washington, D.C.

Silver, Hilary. 1994. "Social Exclusion and Social Solidarity: Three Paradigms." *International Labour Review* 133(5–6): 531–78.

Sindzingre, Alice. 2000. "A Comparative Analysis of African and East Asian Corruption." In Arnold J. Heidenheimer and Michael Johnston, eds., *Political Corruption.* London: Transaction.

——. Forthcoming. "Dimensions economiques des reformes de l'etat en Afrique sub-saharienne." In Comi Toulabor and Dominique Darbon, eds., *Reforme de l'etat: Reconstruction institutionnelle et modes de regulation.* Paris: Karthala.

Singerman, Diane. 1995. *Avenues of Participation: Family, Politics, and Networks in Urban Quarters of Cairo.* Princeton, N.J.: Princeton University Press.

Singh, Balmiki Prasad. 1999. "Democracy, Ecology and Culture: The Indian Experience." Sardar Patel Memorial Lecture, 31 October, New Delhi.

Sinha, Saurabh, and Michael Lipton. 1999. "Damaging Fluctuations, Risk and Poverty: A Review." Background paper for *World Development Report 2000/2001.* Sussex University, Poverty Research Unit, Brighton; and World Bank, Washington, D.C.

Skocpol, Theda. 1992. *Protecting Soldiers and Mothers: The Political Origins of Social Policy in the United States.* Cambridge, Mass.: Harvard University Press.

Skoufias, Emmanuel, Benjamin Davis, and Jere R. Behrman. 1999. "An Evaluation of the Selection of Beneficiary Households in the Education, Health, and Nutrition Program (Progresa) of Mexico." International Food Policy Research Institute, Washington, D.C.

Smale, Melinda, and Paul Heisey. 1994. "Maize Research in Malawi Revisited: An Emerging Success Story?" *Journal of International Development* 6(6): 689–706.

Snodgrass, Donald R., and Richard H. Patten. 1989. "Reform of Rural Credit in Indonesia: Inducing Bureaucracies to Behave Competitively." Development Discussion Paper 315. Harvard Institute for International Development, Cambridge, Mass.

Solo, Tova Maria. 1998a. "Competition in Water and Sanitation: The Role of Small-Scale Entrepreneurs." Viewpoint 165. World Bank, Finance, Private Sector, and Infrastructure Network, Washington, D.C.

——. 1998b. "Keeping Paraguay's *Aguateros* on Stream." *Wall Street Journal,* 27 November.

——. 1999. "West African Businesses Pioneer Water and Sanitation Services to the Poor." Box for *World Development Report 2000/2001.* World Bank, Washington, D.C.

Solow, Robert. 1956. "A Contribution to the Theory of Economic Growth." *Quarterly Journal of Economics* 70: 65–94.

Soobader, Mah-Jabeen, and Felicia LeClere. 1999. "Aggregation and the Measurement of Income Inequality: Effects on Morbidity." *Social Science and Medicine* 48: 733–44.

Spohr, Chris. 2000. "Essays on Household and the Workforce in Taiwan." Massachusetts Institute of Technology, Department of Economics, Cambridge, Mass.

Srinivas, Mysore. 1987. "The Dominant Caste in Rampura." In Mysore Srinivas, ed., *The Dominant Caste and Other Essays.* New Delhi: Oxford University Press.

Srinivasan, T.N. 2000. "Growth, Poverty Reduction, and Inequality." Paper presented at Annual World Bank Conference on Development Economics in Europe, World Bank, 26–28 June, Paris.

Srinivasan, T.N., and Pranab K. Bardhan. 1974. *Poverty and In-*

come Distribution in India. Calcutta: Statistical Publishing Society.

Steele, Claude M. 1999. "Thin Ice: 'Stereotype Threat' and Black College Students." *Atlantic Monthly* 284(2): 44–54.

Stein, Ernesto. 1999. "Fiscal Discipline and Social Protection: Are They Compatible?" Inter-American Development Bank, Research Department, Washington, D.C.

Stein, Howard. 1999. "The Development of the Developmental State in Africa: A Theoretical Enquiry." Paper presented at African Studies Association meeting, 11–14 November, University of Pennsylvania, Philadelphia.

Steward, Fred. 1978. *Technology and Underdevelopment.* London: Macmillan.

Stewart, Frances. 1995. "The Social Impacts of Globalization and Marketization." In Üner Kirdar and Leonard Silk, eds., *People: From Impoverishment to Empowerment.* New York: New York University Press.

Stewart, Frances, Frank P. Humphreys, and Nick Lea. 1997. "Civil Conflict in Developing Countries over the Last Quarter of a Century: An Empirical Overview of Economic and Social Consequences." *Oxford Development Studies* 25(1): 11–41.

Stiglitz, Joseph E. 1998a. "Gender and Development: The Role of the State." Paper presented at gender and development workshop, 2 April, World Bank, Washington, D.C.

———. 1998b. "The Role of International Financial Institutions in the Current Global Economy." Address to Chicago Council on Foreign Relations, February, Chicago.

———. 1998c. "Towards a New Paradigm for Development: Strategies, Policies, and Processes." Prebisch Lecture at United Nations Conference on Trade and Development, October, Geneva.

———. 1999. "Quis Custodiet Ipsos Custodes? Corporate Governance Failure in the Transition." Keynote address at Annual World Bank Conference on Development Economics in Europe, World Bank, 21–23 June, Paris.

Stiglitz, Joseph E., and Hirofumi Uzawa. 1969. *Readings in the Modern Theory of Economic Growth.* Cambridge, Mass.: MIT Press.

Stock, Elisabeth, and Jan de Veen. 1996. *Expanding Labor-Based Methods for Road Works in Africa.* World Bank Technical Paper 347. Washington, D.C.

Strauss, John, and Duncan Thomas. 1998. "Health, Nutrition, and Economic Development." *Journal of Economic Literature* 36: 766–817.

Streeten, Paul. 1984. "Basic Needs: Some Unsettled Questions." *World Development* 12: 973–82.

Streeten, Paul, Shahid J. Burki, Mahbub ul Haq, Norman Hicks, and Frances Stewart. 1981. *First Things First: Meeting Basic Human Needs in the Developing Countries.* Oxford: Oxford University Press.

Subbarao, Kalanidhi. 1997. "Public Works as an Anti-poverty Program: An Overview of Cross-Country Experience." *American Journal of Agricultural Economics* 79: 678–83.

———. 1998. "Namibia's Social Safety Net: Issues and Options for Reform." Policy Research Working Paper 1996. World Bank, Washington, D.C.

Subbarao, Kalanidhi, Aniruddha Bonnerjee, Jeanine Braithwaite,

Soniya Carvalho, Kene Ezemenari, Carol Graham, and Alan Thompson. 1997. *Safety Net Programs and Poverty Reduction: Lessons from Cross-Country Experience.* Directions in Development Series. Washington, D.C.: World Bank.

Summers, Lawrence H. 1992. "Investing in All the People." *Pakistan Development Review* 31: 367–93.

———. 1993. "Foreword." In Elizabeth M. King and M. Anne Hill, eds., *Women's Education in Developing Countries: Barriers, Benefits, and Policies.* Baltimore, Md.: Johns Hopkins University Press.

Summers, Robert, and Alan Heston. 1991. "The Penn World Table (Mark 5): An Expanded Set of International Comparisons, 1950–1988." *Quarterly Journal of Economics* 106(2): 327–68.

Suryahadi, Asep, Sudarno Sumarto, Yusuf Suharso, and Lant Pritchett. 1999. "The Evolution of Poverty during the Crisis in Indonesia, 1996 to 1999." World Bank, Washington, D.C.; and Social Monitoring and Early Response Unit, Jakarta.

Swamy, Anand V., Steve Knack, Young Lee, and Omar Azfar. 1999. "Gender and Corruption." University of Maryland, Center on Institutional Reform and the Informal Sector, College Park.

Sweden, Ministry for Foreign Affairs. 1999. "Making Partnerships Work on the Ground." Report of a workshop, 30–31 August, Ulvsunda Castle, Stockholm.

Szekély, Miguel, Nora Lustig, Jose Antonio Mejia, and Martin Cumpa. Forthcoming. *How Many Poor People in Latin America Are There Really?* Washington, D.C.: Inter-American Development Bank.

Szreter, Simon. 1997. "Economic Growth, Disruption, Deprivation, Disease and Death: On the Importance of the Politics of Public Health." *Population and Development Review* 23(4): 693–728.

———. Forthcoming. "Social Capital, the Economy and Education in Historical Perspective." In Stephen Baron, John Field, and Tom Schuller, eds., *Social Capital: Critical Perspectives.* Oxford: Oxford University Press.

Tacoli, Cecilia. 1998. "Rural-Urban Interactions: A Guide to the Literature." *Environment and Urbanization* 10(1): 147–66.

Tanzi, Vito. 1998. "Fundamental Determinants of Inequality and the Role of Government." IMF Working Paper 98/178. International Monetary Fund, Washington, D.C.

———. 1999. "The Quality of the Public Sector." Paper presented at International Monetary Fund conference on second-generation reforms, 8–9 November, Washington, D.C.

Tanzi, Vito, and Hamid Davoodi. 1997. "Corruption, Public Investment, and Growth." IMF Working Paper 97/139. International Monetary Fund, Washington, D.C.

Temple, Jonathan. 1998. "Initial Conditions, Social Capital, and Growth in Africa." *Journal of African Economics* 73(3): 309–47.

———. 1999. "The New Growth Evidence." *Journal of Economic Literature* 37: 112–56.

Temple, Jonathan, and Paul A. Johnson. 1998. "Social Capability and Economic Growth." *Quarterly Journal of Economics* 113(3): 965–90.

Tendler, Judith. 1993. *New Lessons from Old Projects: The Workings of Rural Development in Northeast Brazil.* Operations

Evaluation Study. Washington, D.C.: World Bank.

———. 1997. *Good Governance in the Tropics.* Baltimore, Md.: Johns Hopkins University Press.

Tendler, Judith, and Sara Freedheim. 1994. "Trust in a Rent-Seeking World: Health and Government Transformed in Northeast Brazil." *World Development* 22(12): 1771–91.

Teranish, Juro. 1996. "Sectoral Resource Transfer, Conflict and Macro-Stability in Economic Development: A Comparative Analysis." In Masahiko Aoki, Hyung-Ki Kim, and Masahiro Okuno-Fujiwara, eds., *The Role of Government in East Asian Economic Development: Comparative Institutional Analysis.* New York: Oxford University Press.

Ter-Minassian, Teresa. 1997. *Fiscal Federalism in Theory and Practice.* Washington, D.C.: International Monetary Fund.

TGNP (Tanzania Gender Networking Programme). 1999. *Budgeting with a Gender Focus.* Dar es Salaam.

Thomas, Duncan. 1990. "Intrahousehold Resource Allocation: An Inferential Approach." *Journal of Human Resources* 25: 635–64.

———. 1997. "Incomes, Expenditures, and Health Outcomes: Evidence on Intrahousehold Resource Allocation." In Lawrence Haddad, John Hoddinott, and Harold Alderman, eds., *Intrahousehold Resource Allocation in Developing Countries: Models, Methods, and Policy.* Baltimore, Md.: Johns Hopkins University Press.

———. 1999. "Economic Crisis and Poverty: Evidence from Indonesia." University of California at Los Angeles, Department of Economics.

Thomas, Duncan, Victor Lavy, and John Strauss. 1996. "Public Policy and Anthropometric Outcomes in the Côte d'Ivoire." *Journal of Public Economics* 61: 155–92.

Thomas, Vinod, and Yan Wang. 1998. "Missing Lessons of East Asia: Openness, Education, and the Environment." Paper presented at Annual Bank Conference on Development in Latin America and the Caribbean, World Bank, June, Montevideo.

Thorbecke, Erik. 1985. "The Social Accounting Matrix and Consistency-Type Planning Models." In Graham Pyatt and Jeffrey I. Round, eds., *Social Accounting Matrices: A Basis for Planning.* Washington, D.C.: World Bank.

———. 1991. "Adjustment, Growth and Income Distribution in Indonesia." *World Development* 19(11): 1595–614.

———. 2000. "The Evolution of the Development Doctrine and the Role of Foreign Aid, 1950–2000." In Finn Tarp, ed., *Foreign Aid and Development: Lessons Learnt and Directions for the Future.* London: Routledge.

Thorbecke, Erik, and Hong-Sang Jung. 1996. "A Multiplier Decomposition Method to Analyze Poverty Alleviation." *Journal of Development Economics* 48: 279–300.

Timmer, C. Peter. 1997. "How Well Do the Poor Connect to the Growth Process?" Consulting Assistance on Economic Reform Discussion Paper 178. Harvard Institute for International Development, Cambridge, Mass.

Timmer, Marcel P., and Adam Szirmai. 1997. "Growth and Divergence in Manufacturing Performance in South and East Asia." Research Memorandum Gd-37. University of Groningen, Groningen Growth and Development Centre.

Tomich, Thomas P., and Meine van Noodwijk, eds. 1998. *Alternatives to Slash-and-Burn in Indonesia: Summary Report and Synthesis of Phase II.* Bogor: International Centre for Research in Agroforestry.

Tommasi, Mariano. 1999. "On High Inflation and the Allocation of Resources." *Journal of Monetary Economics* 44: 401–21.

Tommasi, Mariano, and Andrés Velasco. 1996. "Where Are We in the Political Economy of Reform?" *Journal of Policy Reform* 1(2): 187–238.

Tommasi, Mariano, and Federico Weischelbaum. 1999. "A Principal-Agent Building Block for the Study of Decentralization and Integration." Harvard University, Cambridge, Mass.

Townsend, Peter. 1979. *Poverty in the United Kingdom: A Survey of Household Resources and Standards of Living.* London: Allen Lane.

———. 1985. "Sociological Approach to the Measurement of Poverty: A Rejoinder to Professor Amartya Sen." *Oxford Economic Papers* 37: 659–68.

Townsend, Robert. 1994. "Risk and Insurance in Village India." *Econometrica* 62(3): 539–91.

———. 1995. "Consumption Insurance: An Evaluation of Risk-Bearing Systems in Low-Income Economies." *Journal of Economic Perspectives* 9: 83–102.

Treisman, Daniel. 1998. "The Causes of Corruption: A Cross-National Study." University of California at Los Angeles, Department of Political Science.

Tsui, Kay Yuen. 1995. "Multidimensional Generalizations of the Relative and Absolute Indices: The Atkinson-Kolm-Sen Approach." *Journal of Economic Theory* 67: 251–65.

———. 1997. "Multidimensional Poverty Indices." Chinese University of Hong Kong, Department of Economics.

Tuck, Laura, and Kathy Lindert. 1996. *From Universal Food Subsidies to a Self-Targeted Program: A Case Study in Tunisian Reform.* World Bank Discussion Paper 351. Washington, D.C.

Tummala, Krishna K. 1999. "Policy of Preference: Lessons from India, the United States, and South Africa." *Public Administration Review* 59(6): 495–509.

Turok, Ben. 1999. "South Africa: From Exclusion to Integration." Background paper for *World Development Report 2000/2001.* World Bank, Washington, D.C.

Turton, David, ed. 1997. *War and Ethnicity: Global Connections and Local Violence.* Rochester, N.Y.: University of Rochester Press.

Tzannatos, Zafiris. 1998. "Child Labor and School Enrollment in Thailand in the 1990s." Social Protection Paper 9818. World Bank, Washington, D.C.

Uberoi, Patricia. 1999. "Gender and State Policies in India, 1950–2000." World Bank, Washington, D.C.

Uddin, Sharif. 1999. "The 'Village Phone': Bringing Universal Service to Rural Areas in Bangladesh." Paper presented at National Telephone Cooperative Association's First International Conference on Rural Telecommunications, November, Washington, D.C.

Udry, Christopher. 1991. "Credit Markets in Northern Nigeria: Credit as Insurance in a Rural Economy." *World Bank Economic Review* 4(3): 251–71.

———. 1996. "Gender, Agricultural Production, and the Theory of the Household." *Journal of Political Economy* 104(5): 1010–46.

———. 1999. "Poverty, Risk and Households." Paper presented at *World Development Report 2000/2001* Summer Workshop, World Bank, July, Washington, D.C.

Udry, Christopher, John Hoddinott, Harold Alderman, and Lawrence Haddad. 1995. "Gender Differentials in Farm Productivity: Implications for Household Efficiency and Agricultural Policy." *Food Policy* 20(5): 407–23.

UN (United Nations). 1998. *Poverty Reduction Strategies: A Review.* New York.

UNAIDS (Joint United Nations Programme on HIV/AIDS). 1998. *AIDS Epidemic Update.* Geneva.

———. 2000. *Report on the Global HIV/AIDS Epidemic.* Geneva.

UNDP (United Nations Development Programme). 1995. *Human Development Report 1995.* New York: Oxford University Press.

———. 1996. *Human Development Report 1996.* New York: Oxford University Press.

———. 1997. *Human Development Report 1997.* New York: Oxford University Press.

———. 1998. *Overcoming Human Poverty.* New York: United Nations.

———. 1999a. *Human Development Report 1999.* New York: Oxford University Press.

———. 1999b. *United Nations Development Projects Programming Manual.* New York: United Nations.

UNESCO (United Nations Educational, Scientific, and Cultural Organization). *Database.* [unescostat.unesco.org/en/stats/stats0.htm].

UNFPA (United Nations Population Fund) and Australian National University. 1998. "South East Asian Populations in Crisis: Challenges to the Implementation of the ICPD Programme of Action." UNFPA, New York.

Unger, Danny. 1998. *Building Social Capital in Thailand: Fibers, Finance, and Infrastructure.* New York: Cambridge University Press.

UNICEF (United Nations Children's Fund). 1994. *Children at Work.* East Asia and Pacific Regional Office. Bangkok.

UNICEF (United Nations Children's Fund) and Oxfam International. 1999. "Debt Relief and Poverty Reduction: Meeting the Challenge." Paper presented at Heavily Indebted Poor Countries Review Seminar, United Nations Commission for Africa, July, Addis Ababa. [www.worldbank.org/hipc].

United Kingdom, Secretary of State for International Development. 1997. *Eliminating World Poverty: A Challenge for the 21st Century.* White Paper on International Development. London: Her Majesty's Stationery Office.

Uphoff, Norman. 1992. *Learning from Gal Oya: Possibilities for Participatory Development and Post-Newtonian Social Science.* Ithaca, N.Y.: Cornell University Press.

———. 1993. "Grassroots Organizations and NGOs in Rural Development: Opportunities with Diminishing States and Expanding Markets." *World Development* 21(4): 607–22.

———. 1998. "Community-Based Natural Resources Management: Connecting Micro and Macro Processes, and People with Their Environments." Plenary presentation at International Workshop on Community-Based Natural Resources Management, World Bank, 10–14 May, Washington, D.C.

USAID (U.S. Agency for International Development), OFDA (Of-

fice of U.S. Foreign Disaster Assistance). 1999. *International Disaster Database.* Washington, D.C.

U.S. Census Bureau. 1999. *Poverty in the United States 1998.* Washington, D.C.: U.S. Department of Commerce.

Uvin, Peter. 1995. "Fighting Hunger at the Grassroots: Paths to Scaling Up." *World Development* 23: 927–39.

Valdes, Alberto. 1994. "Agricultural Reforms in Chile and New Zealand: A Review." *Journal of Agricultural Economics* 45(2): 189–201.

———. 1999. "A Rural Poverty Profile of the Region." In Ramon Lopez and Alberto Valdes, eds., *Rural Poverty in Latin America: Analytics, New Empirical Evidence and Policy.* Washington, D.C.: World Bank.

van de Walle, Dominique. 1995. "Toward a Synthesis." In Dominique van de Walle and Kimberly Nead, eds., *Public Spending and the Poor: Theory and Evidence.* Baltimore, Md.: Johns Hopkins University Press.

———. 1996. *Infrastructure and Poverty in Vietnam.* Living Standards Measurement Study Working Paper 121. Washington, D.C.: World Bank.

———. 2000a. "Are Returns to Investment Lower for the Poor? Human and Physical Capital Interactions in Rural Vietnam." World Bank, Development Research Group, Washington, D.C.; and University of Toulouse, Department of Economics.

———. 2000b. "Choosing Pro-poor Rural Road Investments." World Bank, Development Research Group, Washington, D.C.

———. 2000c. "Human Capital and Labor Market Constraints in Developing Countries: A Case Study of Irrigation in Vietnam." World Bank, Development Research Group, Washington, D.C.

van de Walle, Dominique, and Dileni Gunewardena. 2000. "Sources of Ethnic Inequality in Viet Nam." Policy Research Working Paper 2297. World Bank, Washington, D.C.

van de Walle, Dominique, and Kimberly Nead, eds. 1995. *Public Spending and the Poor: Theory and Evidence.* Baltimore, Md.: Johns Hopkins University Press.

van de Walle, Nicolas. Forthcoming. *The Politics of Permanent Crisis: Managing African Economies, 1979–1999.* New York: Cambridge University Press.

van de Walle, Nicolas, and Timothy Johnston. 1996. *Improving Aid to Africa.* Policy Essay 21. Washington, D.C.: Overseas Development Council.

van der Gaag, Jacques. 1995. *Private and Public Initiatives Working Together for Health and Education.* Directions in Development Series. Washington, D.C.: World Bank.

van Dijk, Meine Pieter, and Roberta Rabellotti. 1997. *Enterprise Clusters and Networks in Developing Countries.* London: Frank Cass.

van Domelen, Julie, and Daniel Owen. 1998. "Getting an Earful: A Review of Beneficiary Assessments of Social Funds." Social Protection Discussion Paper 9816. World Bank, Washington, D.C.

van Doorslaer, Eddy, and Adam Wagstaff. 1997. "Income-Related Inequalities in Health: Some International Comparisons." *Journal of Health Economics* 16: 93–112.

van Ginneken, Wouter, ed. 1999. *Social Security for the Excluded Majority*. Geneva: International Labour Office.

van Nieuwkoop, Martien, and Jorge E. Uquillas. 2000. "Defining Ethnodevelopment in Operational Terms: Lessons from the Ecuador Indigenous and Afro-Ecuadoran Peoples Development Project." Sustainable Development Working Paper 6. World Bank, Latin America and the Caribbean Region, Washington, D.C.

van Rijckeghem, Caroline, and Beatrice Weder. 1997. "Corruption and the Rate of Temptation: Do Low Wages in Civil Service Cause Corruption?" IMF Working Paper 97/73. International Monetary Fund, Washington, D.C.

van Rooy, Alison, ed. 1998. *Civil Society and the Aid Industry*. London: Earthscan.

van Trotsenburg, Axel, and Alan MacArthur. 1999. "The HIPC Initiative: Delivering Debt Relief to Poor Countries." [www.worldbank.org/hipc/related-papers/related-papers.html].

Varian, Hall R. 1990. "Monitoring Agents with Other Agents." *Journal of Institutional and Theoretical Economics* 146: 153–74.

Varma, Keshav. 1999. "City of Ahmedabad Slum Networking Project." Self-Employed Women's Association, Ahmedabad.

Varshney, Ashutosh. 1999a. "Democracy and Poverty." Background paper for *World Development Report 2000/2001*. World Bank, Washington, D.C.

———. 1999b. "Mass Politics or Elite Politics? India's Economic Reforms in Comparative Perspective." In Jeffrey Sachs, Ashutosh Varshney, and Nirupam Bajpai, eds., *India in the Era of Economic Reforms*. New Delhi: Oxford University Press.

———. 2000. *Ethnic Conflict and Civic Life: Hindus and Muslims in India*. New Haven, Conn.: Yale University Press.

Vatsa, Krishna. 1999. "Community Participation in Postdisaster Reconstruction: Lessons Learned from the Maharashtra Emergency Earthquake Rehabilitation Program." Box for *World Development Report 2000/2001*. World Bank, Washington, D.C.

Vélez, Carlos Eduardo, Adriana Kugler, and César Bouillón. 1999. "A Microeconomic Decomposition of the Inequality U-turn in Urban Colombia: Labor Market Forces and Beyond." Inter-American Development Bank, Poverty and Inequality Advisory Unit, Washington, D.C.

Vella, Venanzio. 1997. "Health and Nutritional Aspects of Well-Being." In Jeni Klugman, ed., *Poverty in Russia: Public Policy and Private Responses*. Washington, D.C.: World Bank.

Venkataraman, Arjunamurthy, and Julia Falconer. 1999. "Rejuvenating India's Decimated Forests through Joint Action: Lessons from Andhra Pradesh." Project Brief. World Bank, Rural Development Department, Washington, D.C.

Vietnam, General Statistics Office. 1998. *Vietnam Living Standards Survey 1998*. Hanoi.

Villagran, Eduardo. 2000. "Key Drivers of Improved Access: Off-Grid Service." In Energy Sector Management Assistance Programme, *Energy and Development Report 2000: Energy Services for the World's Poor*. Washington, D.C.: World Bank.

Visaria, Pravin. 2000. "Poverty in India during 1994–98: Alternative Estimates." Institute of Economic Growth, Dehli.

von Pischke, J.D., Dale W. Adams, and Gordon Donald, eds. 1984. *Rural Financial Markets in Developing Countries: Their Use and Abuse*. Baltimore, Md.: Johns Hopkins University Press.

Vos, Rob, Margarita Velasco, and Edgar de Labastida. 1999. "Economic and Social Effects of El Niño in Ecuador, 1997–1998." Inter-American Development Bank, Washington, D.C.

Waddington, Catriona, and K.A. Enyimayew. 1989. "Price to Pay: The Impact of User Charges in Asante-Akim District, Ghana." *International Journal of Health Planning and Management* 4(1): 17–47.

———. 1990. "A Price to Pay, Part 2: The Impact of User Charges in the Volta Region of Ghana." *International Journal of Health Planning and Management* 5(4): 287–312.

Wade, Robert. 1985. "The Market for Public Office: Why the Indian State Is Not Better at Development." *World Development* 13(April): 467–97.

———. 1987. *Village Republics: Economic Conditions for Collective Action in South India*. New York: Cambridge University Press.

———. 1991. *Governing the Market: Economic Theory and the Role of Government in East Asian Industrialization*. Princeton, N.J.: Princeton University Press.

———. 1992. "How to Make Street-Level Bureaucracies Work Better: India and Korea." *International Development Studies Bulletin* 23: 51–54.

Wagstaff, Adam. 1999. *Inequalities in Child Mortality in the Developing World: How Large Are They? How Can They Be Reduced?* Washington, D.C.: World Bank, Human Development Network.

———. 2000. "Socioeconomic Inequalities in Child Mortality: Comparisons across Nine Developing Countries." *Bulletin of the World Health Organization* 78(1).

———. Forthcoming a. *If the Health of the Poor Matters More: Child Survival Inequalities in Nine Developing Countries*. Washington, D.C.: World Bank, Human Development Network.

———. Forthcoming b. *Inequalities in Child Health*. Washington, D.C.: World Bank, Human Development Network.

Wagstaff, Adam, and Eddy van Doorslaer. 2000. "Income Inequality and Health: What Does the Literature Tell Us?" *Annual Review of Public Health* 21: 543–67.

Wagstaff, Adam, and Naoko Watanabe. 2000. "Socioeconomic Inequalities in Child Malnutrition in the Developing World." World Bank, Health, Nutrition, and Population Team, Washington, D.C.

Waldmann, Robert. 1992. "Income Distribution and Infant Mortality." *Quarterly Journal of Economics* 107: 1283–302.

Walker, Ian, Rafael del Cid, Fidel Ordonez, and Florencia Rodriguez. 1999. "Ex-post Evaluation of the Honduran Social Investment Fund." World Bank, Washington, D.C.

Walker, Ian, Margarita Velasquez, Francisco Ordonez, and Florencia Rodriguez. 1997. "Regulation, Organization and Incentives: The Political Economy of Potable Water Services in Honduras." Working Paper R-314. Inter-American Development Bank, Washington, D.C.

Walker, Thomas, and James Ryan. 1990. *Village and Household Economies in India's Semi-arid Tropics*. Baltimore, Md.: Johns Hopkins University Press.

Wallsten, Scott J. 1999. "An Empirical Analysis of Competition,

Privatization, and Regulation in Africa and Latin America." Policy Research Working Paper 2136. World Bank, Washington, D.C.

Walt, Gill, Enrico Pavignani, Lucy Gilson, and Kent Buse. 1999. "Managing External Resources in the Health Sector: Are There Lessons for SWAps?" *Health Policy and Planning* 14(3): 273–84.

Ward-Batts, Jennifer. 1998. "Modeling Family Expenditures to Test Income Pooling." Paper presented at 1998 Population Association of America Meetings, 2–4 April, Chicago.

Waterbury, John. 1973. "Endemic and Planned Corruption in a Monarchical Regime." *World Politics* 25(4): 533–55.

Webb, Michael, and David Ehrhardt. 1998. "Improving Water Services through Competition." World Bank, Finance, Private Sector, and Infrastructure Network, Washington, D.C.

Weber, Eugene J. 1976. *Peasants into Frenchmen: The Modernization of Rural France, 1870–1914.* Stanford, Calif.: Stanford University Press.

Wei, Shang-Jin. 1999a. *Corruption and Poverty: New Evidence.* Washington, D.C.: World Bank.

———. 1999b. "Corruption in Economic Development: Beneficial Grease, Minor Annoyance, or Major Obstacle?" Policy Research Working Paper 2048. World Bank, Washington, D.C.

Weidenbaum, Murray, and Samuel Hughes. 1996. *The Bamboo Network: How Expatriate Chinese Entrepreneurs Are Creating a New Economic Superpower in Asia.* New York: Free Press.

Weiner, David. 1999. "At Seattle, Start the Trade and Labor Dialogue." ODC Viewpoint. Overseas Development Council, Washington, D.C.

Weiner, Myron. 1991. *The Child and the State in India: Child Labor and Education Policy in Comparative Perspective.* Princeton, N.J.: Princeton University Press.

Wellenius, Bjorn. 1997. "Extending Telecommunications Service to Rural Areas: The Chilean Experience." Viewpoint 105. World Bank, Finance, Private Sector, and Infrastructure Network, Washington, D.C.

Whang, In-Joun. 1981. *Management of Rural Change in Korea.* Seoul: National University Press.

White, Judy. 1997. "Evaluation Synthesis of Rural Water and Sanitation Projects." Evaluation Report EV596. U.K. Department for International Development, London.

Whitehead, Laurence, and George Gray-Molina. 1999. "The Long-Term Politics of Pro-poor Policies." Background paper for *World Development Report 2000/2001.* World Bank, Washington, D.C.

Whittington, Dale, Donald T. Lauria, and Xinming Mu. 1989. "Paying for Urban Services: A Study of Water Vending and Willingness to Pay for Water in Onitsha, Nigeria." Report INU40. World Bank, Infrastructure and Urban Development Department, Washington, D.C.

WHO (World Health Organization). 1980. *International Classification of Impairments, Disabilities and Handicaps.* Geneva.

———. 1998. *TB: A Crossroad—WHO Report on the Global Tuberculosis Epidemic 1998.* Geneva.

———. 1999a. *Removing Obstacles to Healthy Development: WHO Report on Infectious Diseases.* Geneva.

———. 1999b. *World Health Report 1999: Making a Difference.* Geneva.

Wilkinson, Richard. 1996. *Unhealthy Societies: The Afflictions of Inequality.* London: Routledge.

Williamson, John. 1990. *Latin American Adjustment: How Much Has Happened?* Washington, D.C.: Institute for International Economics.

———. 1993. "Democracy and the 'Washington Consensus'." *World Development* 21: 1329–36.

Wilson, William Julius. 1996. *When Work Disappears: The World of the New Urban Poor.* New York: Knopf.

Winters, L. Alan. 1999. "Trade, Trade Policy, and Poverty: What Are the Links?" Background paper for *World Development Report 2000/2001.* Sussex University, Economics Department, Brighton; and World Bank, Washington, D.C.

Wodon, Quentin. 1997. "Food Energy Intake and Cost of Basic Needs: Measuring Poverty in Bangladesh." *Journal of Development Studies* 34: 66–101.

———. 1999. "Growth, Inequality, and Poverty: A Regional Panel for Bangladesh." Policy Research Working Paper 2072. World Bank, Washington, D.C.

———. 2000a. "Extreme Poverty and Human Rights: Essays on Joseph Wresinski." Background paper for *World Development Report 2000/2001.* World Bank, Washington, D.C.

———. 2000b. "Income Mobility and Risk during the Business Cycle." World Bank, Poverty Reduction and Economic Management Network, Washington, D.C.

———. 2000c. "Public Works Employment and Workfare Programs: Optimizing the Timing of Benefits for Poverty Reduction." World Bank, Poverty Reduction and Economic Management Network, Washington, D.C.

———. Forthcoming. "Micro Determinants of Consumption, Poverty, Growth, and Inequality in Bangladesh." *Applied Economics.*

Wodon, Quentin, and Norman Hicks. 1999. "Protecting the Poor during Crisis through Public Spending? Framework and Application to Argentina and Mexico." World Bank, Poverty Reduction and Economic Management Network, Washington, D.C.

Wodon, Quentin, and Mari Minowa. 2000. "Training for the Urban Unemployed: A Reevaluation of Mexico's Probecat." World Bank, Poverty Reduction and Economic Management Network, Washington, D.C.

Wodon, Quentin, Norman Hicks, Bernadette Ryan, and Gabriel Gonzalez. 2000. "Are Governments Pro-poor but Short-Sighted? Targeted and Social Spending for the Poor during Booms and Busts." World Bank, Poverty Reduction and Economic Management Network and Latin America and the Caribbean Region, Washington, D.C.

Wodon, Quentin, Robert Ayres, Matias Barenstein, Kihoon Lee, Pia Peeters, Corinne Siaens, and Shlomo Yitzhaki. 2000. *Poverty and Policy in Latin America and the Caribbean.* World Bank Technical Paper 467. Washington, D.C.

Wolf, Margery. 1985. *Revolution Postponed: Women in Contemporary China.* Stanford, Calif.: Stanford University Press.

Wolfensohn, James D. 1999. "A Proposal for a Comprehensive Development Framework: A Discussion Draft." World Bank, Office of the President, Washington, D.C.

Woo-Cumings, Meredith, ed. 1999. *The Developmental State.* Ithaca, N.Y.: Cornell University Press.

Woods, Ngaire. 1999. "Good Governance in International Organizations." *Global Governance* 5: 39–61.

Woolcock, Michael. 1998. "Social Capital and Economic Development: Toward a Theoretical Synthesis and Policy Framework." *Theory and Society* 27(2): 151–208.

———. 1999. "Learning from Failures in Microfinance." *American Journal of Economics and Sociology* 58(1): 17–42.

———. 2000. "Managing Risk, Shocks, and Opportunities in Developing Economies: The Role of Social Capital." In Gustav Ranis, ed., *Dimensions of Development.* New Haven, Conn.: Yale Center Press.

———. Forthcoming. *Using Social Capital: Getting the Social Relations Right in the Theory and Practice of Economic Development.* Princeton, N.J.: Princeton University Press.

Woolcock, Michael, and Deepa Narayan. Forthcoming. "Social Capital: Implications for Development Theory, Research and Policy." *World Bank Research Observer.*

Woolcock, Michael, Lant Pritchett, and Jonathan Isham. 1999. "The Social Foundations of Poor Economic Growth in Resource-Rich Countries." Paper prepared for United Nations University–World Institute for Development Economics Research project on natural resources and economic growth, Helsinki.

World Bank. 1980. *World Development Report 1980.* New York: Oxford University Press.

———. 1989. "Nepal Hill Community Forestry." South Asia Region, Washington, D.C.

———. 1990. *World Development Report 1990: Poverty.* New York: Oxford University Press.

———. 1991a. *Jordan: Public Expenditure Review.* Washington, D.C.

———. 1991b. "A Symposium Issue on the Analysis of Poverty and Adjustment." *World Bank Economic Review* 5(2): 177–393.

———. 1991c. *World Development Report 1991: The Challenge of Development.* New York: Oxford University Press.

———. 1992a. "Effective Implementation: Key to Development Impact." Report of Portfolio Management Task Force. Washington, D.C.

———. 1992b. *World Development Report 1992: Development and the Environment.* New York: Oxford University Press.

———. 1993a. "Area Development Projects." Lessons and Practices 3. Operations Evaluation Department, Washington, D.C.

———. 1993b. *The East Asian Miracle: Economic Growth and Public Policy.* Policy Research Report. New York: Oxford University Press.

———. 1993c. *Uganda: Social Sectors.* Country Study. Washington, D.C.

———. 1993d. *World Development Report 1993: Investing in Health.* New York: Oxford University Press.

———. 1994a. *Adjustment in Africa: Reforms, Results, and the Road Ahead.* New York: Oxford University Press.

———. 1994b. *Averting the Old Age Crisis.* Policy Research Report. New York: Oxford University Press.

———. 1994c. "Hashemite Kingdom of Jordan: Poverty Assessment." Vol. 1. Report 12675-JO. Washington, D.C.

———. 1994d. "Republic of Turkey—Second Health Project: Essential Health Services and Management Development in Eastern and Southeastern Anatolia." Staff Appraisal Report 12765-TU. Washington, D.C.

———. 1994e. *World Development Report 1994: Infrastructure for Development.* New York: Oxford University Press.

———. 1995a. "Argentina: Argentina's Poor—A Profile." Sector Report 13318. Washington, D.C.

———. 1995b. *Priorities and Strategies for Education: A World Bank Review.* Washington, D.C.

———. 1995c. *World Development Report 1995: Workers in an Integrating World.* New York: Oxford University Press.

———. 1996a. "Access to Education and Health Care in Uganda." Eastern Africa Department and Poverty and Social Policy Department, Washington, D.C.

———. 1996b. "Democratic and Popular Participation in the Public Field: The Experience of the Participative Budget in Porto Alegre (1989–1995)." Economic Development Institute, Washington, D.C.

———. 1996c. *Mexico: Rural Poverty.* Washington, D.C.

———. 1996d. *Poverty Reduction and the World Bank: Progress and Challenges in the 1990s.* Washington, D.C.

———. 1996e. "Technical Assistance." Lessons and Practices 7. Operations Evaluation Department, Washington, D.C.

———. 1996f. *World Development Report 1996: From Plan to Market.* New York: Oxford University Press.

———. 1997a. *Can the Environment Wait? Priorities for East Asia.* Washington, D.C.

———. 1997b. *China 2020: Sharing Rising Incomes.* Washington, D.C.

———. 1997c. *Clear Water, Blue Skies: China's Environment in the New Century.* Washington, D.C.

———. 1997d. *Confronting AIDS: Public Priorities in a Global Epidemic.* Policy Research Report. New York: Oxford University Press.

———. 1997e. *Expanding the Measure of Wealth: Indicators of Environmentally Sustainable Development.* Environmentally and Socially Sustainable Development Studies and Monographs Series, no. 17. Washington, D.C.

———. 1997f. "Health, Nutrition and Population." Sector Strategy Paper. Human Development Network, Washington, D.C.

———. 1997g. *India: Achievements and Challenges in Reducing Poverty.* Country Study. Washington, D.C.

———. 1997h. "India: Andhra Pradesh Hazard Mitigation and Emergency Cyclone Recovery Project." Memorandum and Recommendation of the President P7100. Washington, D.C.

———. 1997i. "Romania Poverty and Social Policy Report." Europe and Central Asia Region, Washington, D.C.

———. 1997j. *Rural Development: From Vision to Action—A Sector Strategy.* Environmentally and Socially Sustainable Development Studies and Monographs Series, no. 12. Washington, D.C.

———. 1997k. "Social Funds Portfolio Review." Social Funds Thematic Group, Washington, D.C.

———. 1997l. *World Development Report 1997: The State in a Changing World.* New York: Oxford University Press.

———. 1998a. "Africa Region Findings: Listening to Farmers—Participatory Assessment of Policy Reform in Zambia's Agricultural Sector." Report 105. Africa Region, Washington, D.C.

———. 1998b. *Assessing Aid: What Works, What Doesn't, and Why.* Policy Research Report. New York: Oxford University Press.

———. 1998c. "Bangladesh Emergency Flood Recovery Project." Report P7264. South Asia Region, Washington, D.C.

———. 1998d. *Bangladesh: From Counting the Poor to Making the Poor Count.* Country Study. Washington, D.C.

———. 1998e. "Cambodia Poverty Assessment." East Asia and Pacific Region, Poverty Reduction and Economic Management Unit and Human Development Sector Unit, Washington, D.C.

———. 1998f. *East Asia: The Road to Recovery.* Washington, D.C.

———. 1998g. *El Salvador Rural Development Study.* Country Study. Washington, D.C.

———. 1998h. *Ethiopia: Social Sector Report.* Country Study. Washington, D.C.

———. 1998i. *Global Economic Prospects and the Developing Countries 1998/1999.* Washington, D.C.

———. 1998j. "Honduras: Hurricane Emergency Project." Memorandum and Recommendation of the President P7280. Washington, D.C.

———. 1998k. *The Impact of Public Expenditure Reviews: An Evaluation.* Washington, D.C.

———. 1998l. "Indonesia: Education in Indonesia, from Crisis to Recovery." Education Sector Unit Report 18651-IND. East Asia and Pacific Region, Washington, D.C.

———. 1998m. "Nicaragua Basic Education Project." Staff Appraisal Report. Latin America and the Caribbean Region, Human and Social Development Group, Washington, D.C.

———. 1998n. "Pakistan Public Expenditure Review: Reform Issues and Options." Poverty Reduction and Economic Management Report 18432. East Asia and Pacific Region, Washington, D.C.

———. 1998o. "Philippines Local Government Units Urban Water and Sanitation Project." Project Appraisal and Supervision Document. East Asia and Pacific Region, Washington, D.C.

———. 1998p. "Philippines Social Expenditure Priorities." Sector Report 18562-PH. East Asia and Pacific Region, Washington, D.C.

———. 1998q. "Post-conflict Reconstruction: The Role of the World Bank." Environmentally and Socially Sustainable Development Network, Washington, D.C.

———. 1998r. "Rapid Social Assessments, January–April 1998." In *Social Impact of the East Asian Financial Crisis.* Washington, D.C.

———. 1998s. "Recent Experience with Involuntary Resettlement: Overview." Report 17538. Operations Evaluation Department, Washington, D.C.

———. 1998t. "Reducing Poverty in India: Options for More Effective Public Services." Report 17881-IN. Washington, D.C.

———. 1998u. "Road Sector Investment Program—Zambia." Africa Technical Department, Washington, D.C.

———. 1998v. "Rwanda Poverty Note: Rebuilding an Equitable Society—Poverty and Poverty Reduction after the Genocide." World Development Sources Report 17792-RW. Washington, D.C.

———. 1998w. "Security, Poverty Reduction and Sustainable Development Challenges for the New Millennium." Social Development Department, Washington, D.C.

———. 1998x. *Social Impact of the East Asian Financial Crisis.* Washington, D.C.

———. 1998y. "Thailand Economic Monitor." Departmental Working Paper 18936. Thailand Resident Unit, Bangkok.

———. 1998z. "The World Bank and Climate Change: East Asia." Global Environment Unit, Washington, D.C.

———. 1998aa. *World Development Report 1998/99: Knowledge for Development.* New York: Oxford University Press.

———. 1999a. "Access to Justice: The English Experience with Small Claims." PREM Note 40. Poverty Reduction and Economic Management Network, Legal Institutions Thematic Group, Washington, D.C.

———. 1999b. "Africa Region." Community Action Program Working Group Notes. Africa Region, Washington, D.C.

———. 1999c. "Argentina: The Flood Rehabilitation Project." Implementation Completion Report 18769. Washington, D.C.

———. 1999d. "Bolivia: Implementing the Comprehensive Development Framework." Report 19326-BO. Bolivia, Paraguay, and Peru Country Management Unit, Washington, D.C.

———. 1999e. "Brazil: Rio Flood Reconstruction and Prevention Project." Performance Audit Report 19497. Washington, D.C.

———. 1999f. "Cities without Slums: Action Plan for Moving Slum Upgrading to Scale." Urban Development Division, Washington, D.C.

———. 1999g. "Coping with the Crisis in Education and Health." In *Thailand Social Monitor* 2. Washington, D.C.

———. 1999h. "Country Assessments and IDA Allocations." Washington, D.C. [www.worldbank.org/ida/idalloc.htm].

———. 1999i. *Global Development Finance 1999.* Washington, D.C.

———. 1999j. *Global Economic Prospects and the Developing Countries 2000.* Washington, D.C.

———. 1999k. *Greening Industry: New Roles for Communities, Markets, and Governments.* Policy Research Report. New York: Oxford University Press.

———. 1999l. "Honduras: Country Assistance Strategy." Report 19893-HO. Latin America and the Caribbean Region, Washington, D.C.

———. 1999m. *Intensifying Action against HIV/AIDS in Africa: Responding to a Development Crisis.* Washington, D.C.

———. 1999n. "Managing the Social Dimensions of Crises: Good Practices in Social Policy." Human Development Network, Washington, D.C.

———. 1999o. "Moldova: Poverty Assessment Technical Papers." Report 19846. Europe and Central Asia Region, Washington, D.C.

———. 1999p. *Peru: Improving Health Care for the Poor.* Country Study. Washington, D.C.

———. 1999q. "Poverty Alleviation in Jordan in the 1990s: Lessons for the Future." Report 19869-JO. Middle East and North Africa Region, Washington, D.C.

———. 1999r. "Poverty and Policy in Latin America and the Caribbean." Latin America and the Caribbean Region, Office of the Chief Economist, Regional Studies Program, Washington, D.C.

———. 1999s. *Poverty and Social Development in Peru, 1994–1997.* Washington D.C.

———. 1999t. "Poverty Trends and the Voices of the Poor." Poverty Reduction and Economic Management Network, Washington, D.C.

———. 1999u. "Progress Report to the World Bank's Executive Board." Washington, D.C.

———. 1999v. "Public Expenditure Reviews: Progress and Potential." PREM Note 20. Poverty Reduction and Economic Management Network, Public Expenditure Thematic Group, Washington, D.C.

———. 1999w. "Republic of Korea: Establishing a New Foundation for Sustained Growth." Washington, D.C.

———. 1999x. "A Review of World Bank Participatory Poverty Assessments." Poverty Reduction and Economic Management Network, Washington, D.C.

———. 1999y. "A Strategic View of Urban and Local Government Issues: Implications for the Bank." Transportation, Water, and Urban Development Department, Washington, D.C.

———. 1999z. "Sub-national Database of the World's Largest Countries." Sub-national Regional Economics Thematic Group, Washington, D.C.

———. 1999aa. "Turkey: Economic Reforms, Living Standards and Social Welfare Study." Europe and Central Asia Region, Washington, D.C.

———. 1999bb. "Vietnam—Development Report 2000: Attacking Poverty." Country Economic Memorandum. Washington, D.C.

———. 1999cc. *World Development Indicators 1999.* Washington, D.C.

———. 1999dd. *World Development Report 1999/2000: Entering the 21st Century.* New York: Oxford University Press.

———. 1999ee. "Zambia: Road Sector Investment Program Supervision Reports." Africa Region, Washington, D.C.

———. 2000a. "Accelerating an AIDS Vaccine for Developing Countries: Recommendations for the World Bank." AIDS Vaccine Task Force, Washington, D.C.

———. 2000b. *Can Africa Claim the 21st Century?* Washington, D.C.

———. 2000c. "China: Overcoming Rural Poverty." East Asia and Pacific Region, Washington, D.C.

———. 2000d. "East Asia and the Pacific Quarterly Brief." Washington, D.C.

———. 2000e. *East Asia: Recovery and Beyond.* Washington, D.C.

———. 2000f. "Ecuador: Crisis, Poverty and Social Services." Washington, D.C.

———. 2000g. *Global Development Finance 2000.* Washington, D.C.

———. 2000h. "Health, Nutrition, Population, and Poverty Country Information Sheets." Health, Nutrition, and Population Department, Washington, D.C.

———. 2000i. "India—Policies to Reduce Poverty and Accelerate Sustainable Development." Sector Report. South Asia Region, Washington, D.C.

———. 2000j. "Kingdom of Morocco: Poverty Update." Human Development Group, Washington, D.C. Draft. 28 June.

———. 2000k. "Maintaining Utility Services for the Poor." Washington, D.C.

———. 2000l. *Making Transition Work for Everyone: Poverty and Inequality in Europe and Central Asia.* Europe and Central Asia Region, Washington, D.C.

———. 2000m. "Nicaragua: Rainfall Risk Management." Project Appraisal Document. Washington, D.C.

———. 2000n. "A Note on Economic Reforms and Performance in Sub-Saharan Africa." Africa Region, Office of the Chief Economist, Washington, D.C.

———. 2000o. "Philippines Poverty Assessment." East Asia and Pacific Region, Washington, D.C.

———. 2000p. *The Quality of Growth.* New York: Oxford University Press.

———. 2000q. "Social Protection Sector Strategy: From Safety Net to Trampoline." Human Development Network, Social Protection Team, Washington, D.C.

———. 2000r. "Water, Sanitation and Poverty." Poverty Reduction Strategy Paper. Washington, D.C.

———. 2000s. *World Development Indicators 2000.* Washington, D.C.

———. Forthcoming a. *EnGendering Development.* Policy Research Report. New York: Oxford University Press.

———. Forthcoming b. *Poverty Reduction Strategy Sourcebook.* Washington, D.C.

———. Forthcoming c. *Sourcebook on Community-Driven Development in the Africa Region.* Washington, D.C.

World Bank and IMF (International Monetary Fund). 2000a. "Progress Report on Poverty Reduction Strategy Papers." Paper prepared for meeting of Joint Ministerial Committee of the Boards of Governors of the Bank and the Fund on the Transfer of Real Resources to Developing Countries (Development Committee), World Bank and International Monetary Fund, 31 March, Washington, D.C.

———. 2000b. "Trade, Development, and Poverty Reduction." Issues paper prepared for meeting of Joint Ministerial Committee of the Boards of Governors of the Bank and the Fund on the Transfer of Real Resources to Developing Countries (Development Committee), World Bank and International Monetary Fund, 31 March, Washington, D.C.

World Bank Partnerships Group. 1998a. "Partnership for Development: From Vision to Action." Briefing to Board of Executive Directors, September, Washington, D.C.

———. 1998b. "Partnership for Development: Proposed Actions for the World Bank." Discussion paper. Washington, D.C.

World Faiths Development Dialogue. 1999. "A Different Perspective on Poverty and Development." Comment on *World Development Report 2000/2001.* London.

———. 2000. "A New Direction for World Development? Comment on the First Full Version of the *World Development Report 2000/2001.*" Occasional Paper 3. London.

Wuyts, Marc. 1996. "Foreign Aid, Structural Adjustment, and Public Management: The Mozambican Experience." *Development and Change* 27(4): 717–49.

Yao, Shujie. 1999. "Economic Growth, Income Inequality and Poverty in China under Economic Reforms." *Journal of Development Studies* 35(6): 104–30.

Yaqub, Shahin. 1999. "How Equitable Is Public Spending on Health and Education?" Background paper for *World Development Report 2000/2001.* Sussex University, Poverty Research Unit, Brighton; and World Bank, Development Research Group, Washington, D.C.

Yaron, Jacob. 1992. *Successful Rural Finance Institutions.* World Bank Discussion Paper 150. Washington, D.C.

Yaron, Jacob, McDonald Benjamin Jr., and Stephanie Charitonenko. 1998. "Promoting Efficient Rural Financial Intermediation." *World Bank Research Observer* 13(2): 147–70.

Yaron, Jacob, McDonald Benjamin Jr., and Gerda Piprek. 1997. *Rural Finance: Issues, Design and Best Practices.* Environmentally and Socially Sustainable Development Studies and Monographs Series, no. 14. Washington, D.C.: World Bank.

Yepes, Guillermo. 1999. "Do Cross-Subsidies Help the Poor to Benefit from Water and Wastewater Services? Lessons from Guayaquil." Water Supply and Sanitation Program Working Paper. United Nations Development Programme and World Bank, Washington, D.C.

Yost, Carol. 1999. "Gender and Law: Challenges and Opportunities for Development." Remarks at World Bank seminar on Gender and Law, June, Washington, D.C.

Young, Alwyn. 1995. "The Tyranny of Numbers: Confronting the Statistical Realities of East Asian Growth." *Quarterly Journal of Economics* 110(3): 641–80.

Younger, Stephen. 1996. "Labor Market Consequences of Retrenchment for Civil Servants in Ghana." In David E. Sahn, ed., *Economic Reform and the Poor in Africa.* Oxford: Clarendon.

Zaman, Hassan. 1999. "Assessing the Impact of Microcredit on Poverty and Vulnerability in Bangladesh." Policy Research Working Paper 2145. World Bank, Washington, D.C.

Zeller, Manfred. 1999. "The Role of Microfinance for Income and Consumption Smoothing." Paper presented at Inter-American Development Bank conference on social protection and poverty, 4–5 February, Washington, D.C.

Zeng Yi, Tu Ping, Gu Baochang, Xu Yi, Li Bohua, and Li Yongping. 1993. "Causes and Implications of the Recent Increase in the Reported Sex Ratio at Birth in China." *Population and Development Review* 19(2): 283–302.

Zimmerman, Frederic, and Michael R. Carter. 1999. "Asset Smoothing, Consumption Smoothing and the Reproduction of Inequality under Risk and Subsistence Constraints." Department of Agricultural and Applied Economics Staff Paper 402. University of Wisconsin, Madison.

Selected World Development Indicators

Introduction to the Selected World Development Indicators

The Selected World Development Indicators provides a core set of standard indicators drawn from the World Bank's development databases. The layout of the 21 tables retains the tradition of presenting comparative socioeconomic data for more than 130 economies for the most recent year for which data are available and for an earlier year. An additional table presents basic indicators for 74 economies with sparse data or with populations of less than 1.5 million.

The indicators presented here are a selection from more than 500 included in the World Bank's *World Development Indicators 2000*. Published annually, the *World Development Indicators* reflects a comprehensive view of the development process. Its opening chapter reports on the record of and the prospects for social and economic progress in developing countries, measured against seven international development goals. Its five main sections recognize the contribution of a wide range of factors: human capital development, environmental sustainability, macroeconomic performance, private sector development, and the global links that influence the external environment for development. A separately published CD-ROM database gives access to more than 1,000 data tables and 500 time-series indicators for 223 countries and regions.

Organization of the Selected World Development Indicators

Tables 1–2, *World View,* offer an overview of key development issues: How rich or poor are the people in each economy? What is their real level of welfare as reflected in child malnutrition and mortality rates? What is the life expectancy of newborns? What percentage of adults are illiterate?

Tables 3–7, *People,* show the rate of progress in social development during the past decade. They include data on population growth, labor force participation, and income distribution. They also provide measures of well-being such as health status, poverty rates, school enrollment and achievement, and gender differences in educational attainment.

Tables 8–10, *Environment,* bring together key indicators on land use and agricultural output, deforestation and protected areas, water resources, energy consumption, and carbon dioxide emissions.

Tables 11–15, *Economy,* present information on the structure and growth of the world's economies, including government finance statistics and a summary of the balance of payments.

Tables 16–19, *States and Markets,* focus on the roles of the public and private sectors in creating the necessary infrastructure for economic growth. These tables present information on private investment, stock markets, the economic activities of the state (including military expenditure), information technology, and research and development.

Tables 20–21, *Global Links,* contain information on trade and financial flows, including aid and lending to developing countries.

Because the World Bank's primary business is providing lending and policy advice to its low- and middle-income members, the issues covered in these tables focus mainly on these economies. Where available, information on the high-income economies is also provided for comparison. Readers may wish to refer to national statistical publications and publications of the Organisation for Economic Cooperation and Development (OECD) and the European Union for more information on the high-income economies.

Classification of economies

As in the rest of the report, the main criterion used in the Selected World Development Indicators to classify economies and broadly distinguish stages of economic development is GNP per capita. Economies are classified into three categories according to income. The classification used in this edition has been updated to reflect the World Bank's current operational guidelines. The GNP per capita cutoff levels are as follows: low income, $755 or less in 1999; middle income, $756–9,265; and high income, $9,266 or more. A further division at $2,995 is made between lower-middle-income and upper-middle-income economies. Economies are further classified by region. See the table on classification of economies at the end of this volume for a list of economies in each group (including those with populations of less than 1.5 million).

From time to time an economy's classification is revised because of changes in the above cutoff values or in the economy's measured GNP per capita. When such changes occur, aggregates based on those classifications are recalculated for the past period so that a consistent time series is maintained. Between 1999 and 2000 several large countries changed classification, resulting in significant changes in the income and regional aggregates. For example, revisions to estimates of China's GNP per capita have caused that economy to be reclassified from low to lower middle income. The following changes are also reflected: Turkey moved from upper middle income to lower middle income; Georgia, Ukraine, and Uzbekistan from lower middle income to low income; Dominica and South Africa from lower middle income to upper middle income; and Honduras from low income to lower middle income.

Data sources and methodology

The socioeconomic and environmental data presented here are drawn from several sources: primary data collected by the World Bank, member country statistical publications, research institutes, and such international organizations as the OECD, the International Monetary Fund (IMF), and the United Nations and its specialized agencies (see the Data Sources following the Technical Notes for a complete listing). Although international standards of coverage, definition, and classification apply to most statistics reported by countries and international agencies, there are inevitably differences in timeliness and reliability arising from differences in the capabilities and resources devoted to basic data collection and compilation. For some topics, competing sources of data require review by World Bank staff to ensure that the most reliable data available are presented. In some instances, where available data are deemed too weak to provide reliable measures of levels and trends or do not adequately adhere to international standards, the data are not shown.

The data presented are generally consistent with those in *World Development Indicators 2000,* though data have been revised and updated wherever new information has become available. Differences may also reflect revisions to historical series and changes in methodology. Thus data of different vintages may be published in different editions of World Bank publications. Readers are advised not to compile data series from different publications or different editions of the same publication. Consistent time-series data are available on the *World Development Indicators 2000* CD-ROM.

All dollar figures are in current U.S. dollars unless otherwise stated. The various methods used to convert from national currency figures are described in the Technical Notes.

Summary measures

The summary measures at the bottom of each table are totals (indicated by *t* if the aggregates include estimates for missing data and nonreporting countries, or by an *s* for simple sums of the data available), weighted averages (*w*), or median values (*m*) calculated for groups of economies. Data for the countries excluded from the main tables (those presented in table 1a) have been included in the summary measures, where data are available, or by assuming that they follow the trend of reporting countries. This gives a more consistent aggregated measure by standardizing country coverage for each period shown. Where missing information accounts for a third or more of the overall estimate, however, the group measure is reported as not available. The section on statistical methods in the Technical Notes provides further information on aggregation methods. Weights used to construct the aggregates are listed in the technical notes for each table.

Terminology and country coverage

The term *country* does not imply political independence but may refer to any territory for which authorities report separate social or economic statistics. Data are shown for economies as they were constituted in 1999, and historical data are revised to reflect current political arrangements. Throughout the tables, exceptions are noted.

On 1 July 1997 China resumed its exercise of sovereignty over Hong Kong. On 20 December 1999 China resumed its exercise of sovereignty over Macao. Unless otherwise noted, data for China do not include data for Hong Kong, China; Taiwan, China; or Macao, China. Data for the Democratic Republic of the Congo (Congo, Dem. Rep., in the table listings) refer to the former Zaire. For clarity, this edition also uses the formal name of the Republic of Congo (Congo, Rep., in the table listings). Data are shown whenever possible for the individual countries formed from the former Czechoslovakia—the Czech Republic and the Slovak Republic. On 25 October 1999 the United Nations Transitional Administration for East Timor (UNTAET) assumed responsibility for the administration of East Timor. Data for Indonesia include East Timor. Data are shown for Eritrea whenever possible, but in most cases before 1992 Eritrea is included in the data for Ethiopia. Data for Germany refer to the unified Germany unless otherwise noted. Data for Jordan refer to the East Bank only unless otherwise noted. In 1991 the Union of Soviet Socialist Republics was dissolved into 15 countries (Armenia, Azerbaijan, Belarus, Estonia, Georgia, Kazakhstan, the Kyrgyz Republic, Latvia, Lithuania, Moldova, the Russian Federation, Tajikistan, Turkmenistan, Ukraine, and Uzbekistan). Whenever possible, data are shown for the individual countries. Data for the Republic of Yemen refer to that country from 1990 onward; data for previous years refer to aggregated data for the former People's Democratic Republic of Yemen and the former Yemen Arab Republic unless otherwise noted. In December 1999 the official name of Venezuela was changed to República Bolivariana de Venezuela (Venezuela, RB, in the table listings). Whenever possible, data are shown for the individual countries formed from the former Socialist Federal Republic of Yugoslavia—Bosnia and Herzegovina, Croatia, the former Yugoslav Republic of Macedonia, Slovenia, and the Federal Republic of Yugoslavia. All references to the Federal Republic of Yugoslavia in the tables are to the Federal Republic of Yugoslavia (Serbia/Montenegro) unless otherwise noted.

Technical notes

Because data quality and intercountry comparisons are often problematic, readers are encouraged to consult the Technical Notes, the table on classification of economies, and the footnotes to the tables. For more extensive documentation, see *World Development Indicators 2000*. The Data Sources section following the Technical Notes lists sources that contain more comprehensive definitions and descriptions of the concepts used.

For more information about the Selected World Development Indicators and the World Bank's other statistical publications, please contact:

Information Center, Development Data Group
The World Bank
1818 H Street N.W.
Washington, D.C. 20433
Hotline: 800-590-1906 or 202-473-7824
Fax: 202-522-1498
Email: info@worldbank.org
Web site: www.worldbank.org/wdi

To order World Bank publications, email your request to books@worldbank.org, write to World Bank Publications at the address above, or call 202-473-1155.

The World by Income

This map presents economies classified according to World Bank estimates of 1999 GNP per capita.
Not shown on the map because of space constraints are French Polynesia (high income);
American Samoa (upper middle income); Fiji, Kiribati, Samoa, and Tonga (lower middle income);
and Tuvalu (no data).

Legend:
- **Low** $755 or less
- **Lower middle** $756–2,995
- **Upper middle** $2,996–9,265
- **High** $9,266 or more
- **No data**

IBRD 30988
JULY 2000

Table 1. Size of the economy

Economy	Population Millions 1999	Surface area Thousands of sq. km 1999	Population density People per sq. km 1999	Gross national product (GNP) Billions of dollars 1999[b]	Rank 1999	Avg. annual growth rate (%) 1998–99	GNP per capita Dollars 1999[b]	Rank 1999	Avg. annual growth rate (%) 1998–99	GNP measured at PPP[a] Billions of dollars 1999	Per capita Dollars 1999	Rank 1999
Albania	3	29	123	2.9	134	1.0	870	136	−0.1	9.8	2,892	137
Algeria	30	2,382	13	46.5	52	2.8	1,550	115	1.3	142.3 [c]	4,753 [c]	101
Angola	12	1,247	10	2.7	136	−35.5	220	194	−37.4	7.8 [c]	632 [c]	199
Argentina	37	2,780	13	277.9	17	−2.9	7,600	55	−4.1	414.1	11,324	56
Armenia	4	30	135	1.9	151	2.7	490	158	2.3	8.4	2,210	150
Australia	19	7,741	2	380.8	15	3.8	20,050	26	2.5	426.4	22,448	20
Austria	8	84	98	210.0	21	2.3	25,970	12	2.2	192.5	23,808	15
Azerbaijan	8	87	92	4.4	116	6.9	550	152	6.0	18.5	2,322	146
Bangladesh	128	144	981	47.0	50	5.0	370	167	3.3	188.3	1,475	168
Belarus	10	208	49	26.8	61	3.4	2,630	92	3.7	66.5	6,518	79
Belgium	10	33	312	250.6	19	1.9	24,510	16	1.7	247.4	24,200	13
Benin	6	113	55	2.3	141	5.1	380	165	2.2	5.4	886	189
Bolivia	8	1,099	8	8.2	92	2.2	1,010	132	−0.2	17.8	2,193	151
Botswana	2	582	3	5.1	108	4.7	3,240	84	3.0	9.6	6,032	84
Brazil	168	8,547	20	742.8	8	−2.0	4,420	70	−3.2	1,061.7	6,317	81
Bulgaria	8	111	74	11.3	81	3.0	1,380	121	3.5	40.4	4,914	99
Burkina Faso	11	274	40	2.6	138	5.2	240	190	2.7	9.9 [c]	898 [c]	187
Burundi	7	28	260	0.8	174	−0.5	120	204	−2.5	3.7 [c]	553 [c]	204
Cambodia	12	181	67	3.0	133	4.5	260	186	2.2	15.1 [c]	1,286 [c]	176
Cameroon	15	475	32	8.5	90	5.0	580	150	2.2	21.2	1,444	169
Canada	31	9,971	3	591.4	9	3.8	19,320	29	2.8	726.1	23,725	16
Central African Republic	4	623	6	1.0	168	3.7	290	181	1.9	4.0 [c]	1,131 [c]	180
Chad	7	1,284	6	1.6	156	−1.5	200	196	−4.1	6.1 [c]	816 [c]	190
Chile	15	757	20	71.1	43	−1.4	4,740	67	−2.6	125.7	8,370	68
China	1,250	9,597 [d]	134	980.2	7	7.2	780	140	6.3	4,112.2	3,291	128
Hong Kong, China	7	1	6,946	161.7 [e]	24	2.9	23,520 [e]	20	0.1	144.0	20,939	26
Colombia	42	1,139	40	93.6	37	−1.9	2,250	99	−3.6	237.2 [c]	5,709 [c]	88
Congo, Dem. Rep.	50	2,345	22	..	..	..	.. [f]	..	..	..	..	..
Congo, Rep.	3	342	8	1.9	150	7.7	670	147	4.8	2.6	897	188
Costa Rica	4	51	70	9.8	85	1.5	2,740	89	−0.3	20.7	5,770 [c]	87
Côte d'Ivoire	15	322	46	10.4	84	2.8	710	146	1.1	22.8	1,546	163
Croatia	4	57	80	20.4	62	−0.3	4,580	69	0.5	30.9	6,915	78
Czech Republic	10	79	133	52.0	48	−0.5	5,060	65	−0.3	126.3	12,289	52
Denmark	5	43	125	170.3	23	1.3	32,030	7	1.0	129.1	24,280	12
Dominican Republic	8	49	174	16.1	74	8.1	1,910	103	6.2	39.1 [c]	4,653 [c]	103
Ecuador	12	284	45	16.2	72	−12.5	1,310	124	−14.2	32.3	2,605	141
Egypt, Arab Rep.	62	1,001	63	87.5	38	5.7	1,400	120	4.0	206.2	3,303	127
El Salvador	6	21	299	11.8	79	2.1	1,900	104	−0.1	25.1 [c]	4,048 [c]	114
Eritrea	4	118	40	0.8	176	3.7	200	196	0.8	4.0 [c]	1,012 [c]	183
Estonia	1	45	34	5.0	110	1.9	3,480	80	2.4	11.3	7,826	74
Ethiopia	63	1,104	63	6.6	100	7.4	100	206	4.8	37.6 [c]	599 [c]	200
Finland	5	338	17	122.9	30	3.7	23,780	19	3.5	109.6	21,209	25
France	59	552	107	1,427.2 [g]	4	2.4	23,480 [g]	21	2.0	1,293.8	21,897	24
Georgia	5	70	78	3.4	128	4.0	620	149	3.8	19.7	3,606	122
Germany	82	357	235	2,079.2	3	1.2	25,350	13	1.2	1,837.8	22,404	21
Ghana	19	239	83	7.4	96	4.8	390	164	2.1	34.0 [c]	1,793 [c]	157
Greece	11	132	82	124.0	29	3.3	11,770	45	3.1	153.8	14,595	50
Guatemala	11	109	102	18.4	69	3.2	1,660	110	0.5	39.0 [c]	3,517 [c]	125
Guinea	7	246	29	3.7	124	3.2	510	155	0.9	12.8	1,761	158
Haiti	8	28	283	3.6	125	3.1	460	161	1.0	11.0 [c]	1,407 [c]	170
Honduras	6	112	57	4.8	112	−1.3	760	141	−3.9	14.3 [c]	2,254 [c]	148
Hungary	10	93	109	46.8	51	5.3	4,650	68	5.8	105.5	10,479	60
India	998	3,288	336	442.2	11	6.9	450	162	4.9	2,144.1 [c]	2,149 [c]	153
Indonesia	207	1,905	114	119.5	32	1.9	580	150	0.3	505.0	2,439	143
Iran, Islamic Rep.	63	1,633	39	110.5	33	2.1	1,760	107	0.5	325.2	5,163	95
Ireland	4	70	54	71.4	42	8.6	19,160	30	8.0	71.5	19,180	34
Israel	6	21	296	..	..	..	.. [h]	..	..	..	..	..
Italy	58	301	196	1,136.0	6	1.0	19,710	28	0.9	1,196.3	20,751	29
Jamaica	3	11	240	6.0	103	0.1	2,330	97	−0.7	8.5	3,276	129
Japan	127	378	336	4,078.9	2	1.0	32,230	6	0.8	3,042.9	24,041	14
Jordan	5	89	53	7.0	97	0.8	1,500	119	−2.0	16.6	3,542	124
Kazakhstan	15	2,717	6	18.9	68	0.6	1,230	125	1.6	68.0	4,408	106
Kenya	29	580	52	10.6	83	0.5	360	170	0.1	28.7	975	185
Korea, Rep.	47	99	475	397.9	13	11.0	8,490	51	10.1	685.7	14,637	49
Kuwait	2	18	108	..	..	..	.. [h]	..	..	..	..	..
Kyrgyz Republic	5	199	25	1.4	159	2.6	300	180	1.7	10.5	2,223	149
Lao PDR	5	237	22	1.4	160	4.0	280	184	1.5	8.8	1,726	161
Latvia	2	65	39	6.0	104	0.5	2,470	94	1.3	14.4	5,938	85
Lebanon	4	10	418	15.8	75	1.0	3,700	76	−0.4	17.6	4,129	113
Lesotho	2	30	69	1.2	164	−0.8	550	152	−3.0	4.3	2,058	155
Lithuania	4	65	57	9.7	86	−4.1	2,620	93	−4.0	22.5	6,093	83
Macedonia, FYR	2	26	79	3.4	127	2.9	1,690	109	2.3	8.8	4,339	108
Madagascar	15	587	26	3.7	123	5.5	250	187	2.3	11.5	766	192
Malawi	11	118	115	2.0	146	6.9	190	199	4.4	6.3	581	203
Malaysia	23	330	69	77.3	41	4.3	3,400	82	1.9	180.8	7,963	72

WORLD VIEW

Economy	Population Millions 1999	Surface area Thousands of sq. km 1999	Population density People per sq. km 1999	Gross national product (GNP) Billions of dollars 1999[b]	Rank 1999	Avg. annual growth rate (%) 1998–99	GNP per capita Dollars 1999[b]	Rank 1999	Avg. annual growth rate (%) 1998–99	GNP measured at PPP[a] Billions of dollars 1999	Per capita Dollars 1999	Rank 1999
Mali	11	1,240	9	2.6	137	5.8	240	190	2.7	7.6	693	196
Mauritania	3	1,026	3	1.0	169	4.8	380	165	2.0	4.0 c	1,522 c	164
Mexico	97	1,958	51	428.8	12	4.1	4,400	71	2.4	752.0	7,719	75
Moldova	4	34	130	1.6	155	16.5	370	167	17.0	10.1	2,358	144
Mongolia	3	1,567	2	0.9	171	2.7	350	171	1.2	3.9	1,496	166
Morocco	28	447	63	33.8	57	0.6	1,200	126	−1.0	90.1	3,190	131
Mozambique	17	802	22	3.9	119	8.6	230	193	6.6	13.8 c	797 c	191
Myanmar	45	677	68	..	..	..	.. f	..	..	..	..	..
Namibia	2	824	2	3.2	130	3.0	1,890	105	0.6	9.1 c	5,369 c	92
Nepal	23	147	164	5.1	109	4.6	220	194	2.2	28.5	1,219	177
Netherlands	16	41	466	384.3	14	3.0	24,320	18	2.3	364.3	23,052	17
New Zealand	4	271	14	52.7	47	2.7	13,780	41	1.9	63.3	16,566	42
Nicaragua	5	130	41	2.1	143	8.0	430	163	5.3	10.6 c	2,154 c	152
Niger	10	1,267	8	2.0	147	2.3	190	199	−1.1	7.6 c	727 c	194
Nigeria	124	924	136	37.9	54	3.0	310	179	0.5	92.2	744	193
Norway	4	324	15	146.4	27	0.6	32,880	5	0.1	118.1	26,522	8
Pakistan	135	796	175	64.0	44	3.6	470	160	1.2	236.8	1,757	159
Panama	3	76	38	8.6	89	1.7	3,070	87	0.1	14.1	5,016	98
Papua New Guinea	5	463	10	3.7	122	3.8	800	138	1.6	10.6 c	2,263 c	147
Paraguay	5	407	13	8.5	91	−1.5	1,580	113	−4.1	22.5 c	4,193 c	111
Peru	25	1,285	20	60.3	45	3.4	2,390	95	1.7	110.7	4,387	107
Philippines	77	300	258	78.0	40	3.6	1,020	131	1.4	292.9	3,815	118
Poland	39	323	127	153.1	25	3.4	3,960	73	3.3	305.5	7,894	73
Portugal	10	92	109	105.9	34	3.1	10,600	47	2.9	151.3	15,147	45
Romania	22	238	97	34.2	56	−3.0	1,520	117	−2.8	126.8	5,647	89
Russian Federation	147	17,075	9	332.5	16	1.3	2,270	98	1.6	928.8	6,339	80
Rwanda	8	26	337	2.1	145	7.5	250	187	4.8	..	..	..
Saudi Arabia	21	2,150	10	..	..	..	.. i	59	..	..	..	..
Senegal	9	197	48	4.7	113	5.1	510	155	2.3	12.4	1,341	173
Sierra Leone	5	72	69	0.7	179	−8.1	130	203	−9.8	2.0	414	206
Singapore	3	1	5,283	95.4	36	5.6	29,610	9	3.6	87.1	27,024	7
Slovak Republic	5	49	112	19.4	66	1.0	3,590	78	0.9	52.9	9,811	64
Slovenia	2	20	98	19.6	64	3.5	9,890	49	3.5	29.8	15,062	47
South Africa	42	1,221	34	133.2	28	0.8	3,160	86	−0.9	350.2 c	8,318 c	69
Spain	39	506	79	551.6	10	3.7	14,000	40	3.6	659.3	16,730	41
Sri Lanka	19	66	294	15.7	76	3.8	820	137	2.7	58.0	3,056	136
Sweden	9	450	22	221.8	20	3.9	25,040	15	3.8	184.4	20,824	28
Switzerland	7	41	180	273.1	18	1.4	38,350	3	1.2	195.7	27,486	6
Syrian Arab Republic	16	185	85	15.2	77	−1.5	970	134	−3.9	43.2	2,761	139
Tajikistan	6	143	44	1.8	153	3.7	290	181	2.0	6.1	981	184
Tanzania	33	945	37	8.0 j	94	5.6	240 j	190	3.1	15.7	478	205
Thailand	62	513	121	121.0	31	4.9	1,960	102	4.1	345.4	5,599	90
Togo	5	57	84	1.5	157	2.1	320	176	−0.3	6.1 c	1,346 c	172
Tunisia	9	164	61	19.9	63	6.2	2,100	101	4.9	51.8	5,478	91
Turkey	64	775	84	186.3	22	−6.4	2,900	88	−7.8	394.1	6,126	82
Turkmenistan	5	488	10	3.2	132	14.9	660	148	13.5	14.8	3,099	134
Uganda	21	241	108	6.8	99	7.7	320	176	4.8	24.4 c	1,136 c	179
Ukraine	50	604	86	37.5	55	−1.2	750	143	−0.4	156.8	3,142	133
United Kingdom	59	245	245	1,338.1	5	1.7	22,640	22	1.6	1,234.4	20,883	27
United States	273	9,364	30	8,351.0	1	4.1	30,600	8	3.1	8,350.1	30,600	4
Uruguay	3	177	19	19.5	65	−3.4	5,900	63	−4.1	27.4	8,280	70
Uzbekistan	25	447	59	17.6	70	3.9	720	145	1.5	51.5	2,092	154
Venezuela, RB	24	912	27	87.0	39	−6.8	3,670	77	−8.6	124.9	5,268	94
Vietnam	78	332	238	28.2	60	4.2	370	167	2.9	136.1	1,755	160
Yemen, Rep.	17	528	32	5.9	105	−1.3	350	171	−3.9	11.7	688	197
Zambia	10	753	13	3.2	131	2.6	320	176	0.4	6.8	686	198
Zimbabwe	12	391	32	6.1	102	0.0	520	154	−1.8	29.4	2,470	142
World	**5,975 s**	**133,572 s**	**46 w**	**29,232.1 t**		**2.7 w**	**4,890 w**		**1.3 w**	**38,804.9 t**	**6,490 w**	
Low income	2,417	34,227	73	987.6		4.4	410		2.5	4,315.1	1,790	
Middle income	2,667	67,258	40	5,323.2		2.6	2,000		1.5	13,022.0	4,880	
Lower middle income	2,094	44,751	48	2,512.5		3.3	1,200		2.3	8,298.2	3,960	
Upper middle income	573	22,507	26	2,810.7		2.0	4,900		0.7	4,769.2	8,320	
Low and middle income	**5,084**	**101,487**	**51**	**6,310.8**		**2.9**	**1,240**		**1.4**	**17,323.9**	**3,410**	
East Asia & Pacific	1,837	16,385	115	1,832.6		7.2	1,000		6.0	6,423.8	3,500	
Europe & Central Asia	475	24,209	20	1,022.2		0.0	2,150		−0.1	2,654.1	5,580	
Latin America & Caribbean	509	20,461	25	1,954.9		−0.9	3,840		−2.4	3,197.1	6,280	
Middle East & North Africa	291	11,024	26	599.3		..	2,060		..	1,337.5	4,600	
South Asia	1,329	5,140	278	581.1		6.2	440		4.2	2,695.0	2,030	
Sub-Saharan Africa	642	24,267	27	320.6		2.0	500		−0.3	929.3	1,450	
High income	**891**	**32,087**	**29**	**22,921.3**		**2.6**	**25,730**		**2.1**	**21,763.4**	**24,430**	

Note: For data comparability and coverage, see the Technical Notes. Figures in italics are for years other than those specified. Rankings are based on 206 economies, including 74 listed in table 1a. See the Technical Notes.

a. Purchasing power parity; see the Technical Notes. b. Preliminary World Bank estimates calculated using the World Bank Atlas method. c. The estimate is based on regression; others are extrapolated from the latest International Comparison Programme benchmark estimates. d. Includes Taiwan, China. e. GNP data refer to GDP. f. Estimated to be low income ($755 or less). g. GNP and GNP per capita estimates include the French overseas departments French Guiana, Guadeloupe, Martinique, and Réunion. h. Estimated to be high income ($9,266 or more). i. Estimated to be upper middle income ($2,996–9,265). j. Data refer to mainland Tanzania only.

Table 2.   Quality of life

Economy	Growth of private consumption per capita Avg. annual growth rate (%), 1980–98	Distribution-corrected	Prevalence of child malnutrition % of children under age 5 1992–98[a]	Under-5 mortality rate Per 1,000 1980	1998	Life expectancy at birth Years 1998 Males	Females	Adult illiteracy rate % of people 15 and above 1998 Males	Females	Urban population % of total 1980	1999	Access to sanitation in urban areas % of urban pop. with access 1990–96[a]
Albania	..	..	8	57	31	69	75	9	24	34	41	97
Algeria	−2.3	−1.5	13	139	40	69	72	24	46	44	60	..
Angola	−9.5	..	..	261	204	45	48	..	..	21	34	34
Argentina	..	..	2	38	22	70	77	3	3	83	90	80
Armenia	..	..	3	..	18	71	78	1	3	66	70	..
Australia	1.7	1.1	0	13	6	76	82	..	..	86	85	..
Austria	2.0	1.5	..	17	6	75	81	..	..	65	65	100
Azerbaijan	..	..	10	..	21	68	75	..	..	53	57	67
Bangladesh	2.1	1.4	56	211	96	58	59	49	71	14	24	77
Belarus	−2.7	−2.1	..	..	14	63	74	0	1	57	71	..
Belgium	1.6	1.2	..	15	6	75	81	..	..	95	97	100
Benin	−0.4	..	29	214	140	52	55	46	77	27	42	54
Bolivia	0.1	0.1	8	170	78	60	64	9	22	46	62	77
Botswana	3.0	..	..	94	105	45	47	27	22	15	50	91
Brazil	0.7	0.3	6	80	40	63	71	16	16	66	81	74
Bulgaria	−0.8	−0.5	..	25	15	67	75	1	2	61	69	100
Burkina Faso	0.4	0.2	33	..	210	43	45	68	87	9	18	78
Burundi	−0.9	−0.6	..	193	196	41	44	45	63	4	9	60
Cambodia	..	..	..	330	143	52	55	43	80	12	16	..
Cameroon	−2.0	..	22	173	150	53	56	20	33	31	48	73
Canada	1.4	0.9	..	13	7	76	82	..	..	76	77	..
Central African Republic	−0.8	−0.3	23	..	162	43	46	43	68	35	41	..
Chad	..	..	39	235	172	47	50	51	69	19	23	74
Chile	4.0	1.7	1	35	12	72	78	4	5	81	85	82
China	7.2	4.3	16	65	36	68	72	9	25	20	32	58
Hong Kong, China	4.8	..	..	..	..	76	82	4	11	92	100	..
Colombia	1.2	0.5	8	58	28	67	73	9	9	64	73	76
Congo, Dem. Rep.	−4.5	..	34	210	141	49	52	29	53	29	30	23
Congo, Rep.	0.2	..	..	125	143	46	51	14	29	41	62	15
Costa Rica	0.8	0.4	5	29	15	74	79	5	5	43	48	100
Côte d'Ivoire	−2.2	−1.4	24	170	143	46	47	47	64	35	46	59
Croatia	..	..	1	23	10	69	77	1	3	50	57	71
Czech Republic	..	..	1	19	6	71	78	..	..	75	75	..
Denmark	1.8	1.4	..	10	6	73	78	..	..	84	85	100
Dominican Republic	0.0	0.0	6	92	47	69	73	17	17	51	64	76
Ecuador	−0.2	−0.1	..	101	37	68	73	8	11	47	64	87
Egypt, Arab Rep.	2.0	1.4	12	175	59	65	68	35	58	44	45	20
El Salvador	3.0	1.4	11	120	36	67	72	19	25	42	46	78
Eritrea	..	..	44	..	90	49	52	34	62	14	18	12
Estonia	−1.0	−0.7	..	25	12	64	75	..	..	70	69	..
Ethiopia	−0.4	−0.3	48	213	173	42	44	58	70	11	17	..
Finland	1.4	1.1	..	9	5	74	81	..	..	60	67	100
France	1.6	1.1	..	13	5	75	82	..	..	73	75	100
Georgia	..	..	..	..	20	69	77	..	..	52	60	..
Germany	..	..	..	16	6	74	80	..	..	83	87	..
Ghana	0.2	0.2	27	157	96	58	62	22	40	31	38	53
Greece	1.9	1.3	..	23	8	75	81	2	5	58	60	100
Guatemala	0.2	0.1	27	..	52	61	67	25	40	37	39	91
Guinea	1.0	0.6	..	299	184	46	47	..	..	19	32	..
Haiti	..	..	28	200	116	51	56	50	54	24	35	42
Honduras	−0.1	−0.1	25	103	46	67	72	27	27	35	52	81
Hungary	−0.1	−0.1	..	26	12	66	75	1	1	57	64	100
India	2.7	1.7	..	177	83	62	64	33	57	23	28	46
Indonesia	4.6	2.9	34	125	52	64	67	9	20	22	40	73
Iran, Islamic Rep.	0.5	..	16	126	33	70	72	18	33	50	61	89
Ireland	2.9	1.9	..	14	7	73	79	..	..	55	59	100
Israel	3.3	2.1	..	19	8	76	80	2	6	89	91	100
Italy	2.1	1.6	..	17	6	75	82	1	2	67	67	100
Jamaica	1.3	0.8	10	39	24	73	77	18	10	47	56	89
Japan	2.8	2.1	..	11	5	77	84	..	..	76	79	..
Jordan	−1.5	−1.0	5	..	31	69	73	6	17	60	74	..
Kazakhstan	..	..	8	..	29	59	70	..	..	54	56	..
Kenya	0.4	0.2	23	115	124	50	52	12	27	16	32	69
Korea, Rep.	6.5	4.4	..	27	11	69	76	1	4	57	81	100
Kuwait	..	..	2	35	13	74	80	17	22	90	97	100
Kyrgyz Republic	..	..	11	..	41	63	71	..	..	38	34	87
Lao PDR	..	..	40	200	..	52	55	38	70	13	23	70
Latvia	..	..	..	26	19	64	76	0	0	68	69	90
Lebanon	..	..	3	..	30	68	72	9	21	74	89	100
Lesotho	0.8	0.4	16	168	144	54	57	29	7	13	27	..
Lithuania	..	..	..	24	12	67	77	0	1	61	68	..
Macedonia, FYR	..	..	..	69	18	70	75	..	..	54	62	68
Madagascar	−2.2	−1.2	40	216	146	56	59	28	42	18	29	50
Malawi	0.8	..	30	265	229	42	42	27	56	9	24	70
Malaysia	2.9	1.5	20	42	12	70	75	9	18	42	57	100

WORLD VIEW

Economy	Growth of private consumption per capita Avg. annual growth rate (%), 1980–98		Prevalence of child malnutrition % of children under age 5 1992–98a	Under-5 mortality rate Per 1,000		Life expectancy at birth Years 1998		Adult illiteracy rate % of people 15 and above 1998		Urban population % of total		Access to sanitation in urban areas % of urban pop. with access 1990–96a
		Distribution-corrected		1980	1998	Males	Females	Males	Females	1980	1999	
Mali	−1.0	−0.5	27	..	218	49	52	54	69	19	29	58
Mauritania	0.8	0.5	23	175	140	52	55	48	69	27	56	44
Mexico	0.2	0.1	..	74	35	69	75	7	11	66	74	81
Moldova	..	..	..	..	22	63	70	1	2	40	46	96
Mongolia	..	..	9	..	60	65	68	28	49	52	63	..
Morocco	1.9	1.2	10	152	61	65	69	40	66	41	55	69
Mozambique	−1.0	−0.6	26	..	213	44	47	42	73	13	39	53
Myanmar	..	..	43	134	118	58	62	11	21	24	27	42
Namibia	−1.4	..	26	114	112	54	55	18	20	23	30	77
Nepal	2.0	1.3	57	180	107	58	58	43	78	7	12	34
Netherlands	1.6	1.1	..	11	7	75	81	..	..	88	89	100
New Zealand	0.8	0.4	..	16	7	75	80	..	..	83	86	..
Nicaragua	−2.2	−1.1	12	143	42	66	71	34	31	50	56	34
Niger	−2.2	−1.1	50	317	250	44	48	78	93	13	20	71
Nigeria	−4.2	−2.1	39	196	119	52	55	30	48	27	43	61
Norway	1.6	1.2	..	11	6	76	81	..	..	71	75	100
Pakistan	2.0	1.4	38	161	120	61	63	42	71	28	36	53
Panama	2.4	1.2	6	36	25	72	76	8	9	50	56	99
Papua New Guinea	−0.6	−0.3	30	..	76	57	59	29	45	13	17	82
Paraguay	1.7	0.7	..	61	27	68	72	6	9	42	55	20
Peru	−0.4	−0.2	8	126	47	66	71	6	16	65	72	62
Philippines	0.8	0.4	30	81	40	67	71	5	5	38	58	88
Poland	..	..	..	..	11	69	77	0	0	58	65	100
Portugal	3.1	2.0	..	31	8	72	79	6	11	29	63	100
Romania	0.4	0.3	6	36	25	66	73	1	3	49	56	81
Russian Federation	..	..	3	..	20	61	73	0	1	70	77	..
Rwanda	−1.0	−0.7	29	..	205	40	42	29	43	5	6	..
Saudi Arabia	..	..	..	85	26	70	74	17	36	66	85	100
Senegal	−0.6	−0.4	22	..	121	51	54	55	74	36	47	83
Sierra Leone	−3.1	−1.2	..	336	283	36	39	..	..	24	36	17
Singapore	4.8	..	..	13	6	75	79	4	12	100	100	100
Slovak Republic	−2.1	−1.7	..	23	10	69	77	..	..	52	57	..
Slovenia	..	..	..	18	7	71	79	0	0	48	50	100
South Africa	−0.1	0.0	9	91	83	61	66	15	16	48	52	79
Spain	2.2	1.5	..	16	7	75	82	2	4	73	77	100
Sri Lanka	2.9	1.9	38	48	18	71	76	6	12	22	23	33
Sweden	0.7	0.5	..	9	5	77	82	..	..	83	83	100
Switzerland	0.5	0.3	..	11	5	76	82	..	..	57	68	100
Syrian Arab Republic	0.9	..	13	73	32	67	72	13	42	47	54	77
Tajikistan	..	..	..	..	33	66	71	1	1	34	28	83
Tanzania	0.0	0.0	31	176	136	46	48	17	36	15	32	97
Thailand	5.1	3.0	..	58	33	70	75	3	7	17	21	98
Togo	−0.1	..	25	188	144	47	50	28	62	23	33	57
Tunisia	1.1	0.7	9	100	32	70	74	21	42	52	65	100
Turkey	2.6	1.5	10	133	42	67	72	7	25	44	74	99
Turkmenistan	..	..	..	..	44	63	70	..	..	47	45	70
Uganda	1.9	1.2	26	180	170	42	41	24	46	9	14	75
Ukraine	..	..	..	..	17	62	73	0	1	62	68	70
United Kingdom	2.6	1.6	..	14	7	75	80	..	..	89	89	100
United States	1.9	1.1	1	15	..	74	80	..	..	74	77	..
Uruguay	2.6	1.5	4	42	19	70	78	3	2	85	91	56
Uzbekistan	5.5	3.7	19	..	29	66	73	7	17	41	37	46
Venezuela, RB	−0.8	−0.4	5	42	25	70	76	7	9	79	87	64
Vietnam	..	..	40	105	42	66	71	5	9	19	20	43
Yemen, Rep.	..	..	46	198	96	55	56	34	77	19	24	40
Zambia	−3.6	−1.8	24	149	192	43	43	16	31	40	40	40
Zimbabwe	0.4	0.2	16	108	125	50	52	8	17	22	35	99
World	**1.3 w**		**30 w**	**123 w**	**75 w**	**65 w**	**69 w**	**18 w**	**32 w**	**40 w**	**46 w**	**.. w**
Low income	1.4		..	177	107	59	61	30	49	24	31	56
Middle income	2.2		14	79	38	67	72	10	20	38	50	..
Lower middle income	3.6		15	83	39	67	72	10	23	31	43	59
Upper middle income	1.5		..	66	35	67	74	9	11	64	76	..
Low and middle income	1.9		..	135	79	63	67	18	33	32	41	..
East Asia & Pacific	5.6		22	82	43	67	71	9	22	22	34	61
Europe & Central Asia	..		8	..	26	65	74	2	5	59	67	..
Latin America & Caribbean	0.6		8	78	38	67	73	11	13	65	75	..
Middle East & North Africa	..		15	136	55	66	69	26	48	48	58	..
South Asia	2.6		51	180	89	62	63	35	59	22	28	46
Sub-Saharan Africa	−1.2		33	188	151	49	52	32	49	23	34	..
High income	2.2		..	15	6	75	81	..	..	75	77	..

Note: For data comparability and coverage, see the Technical Notes. Figures in italics are for years other than those specified.
a. Data are for most recent year available.

Table 3.   Population and labor force

| | Population | | | | | | Labor force | | | | | | | |
| Economy | Total Millions | | Avg. annual growth rate (%) | | Ages 15–64 Millions | | Total Millions | | Avg. annual growth rate (%) | | Female % of labor force | | Children ages 10–14 % of age group | |
	1980	1999	1980–90	1990–99	1980	1999	1980	1999	1980–90	1990–99	1980	1999	1980	1999
Albania	2.7	3.4	2.1	0.3	2	2	1	2	2.7	0.8	39	41	4	1
Algeria	18.7	30.5	2.9	2.2	9	18	5	10	3.7	4.0	21	27	7	1
Angola	7.0	12.4	2.7	3.2	4	6	3	6	2.3	3.0	47	46	30	26
Argentina	28.1	36.6	1.5	1.3	17	23	11	15	1.5	1.9	28	33	8	3
Armenia	3.1	3.8	1.4	0.8	2	3	1	2	1.6	1.3	48	48	0	0
Australia	14.7	19.0	1.5	1.2	10	13	7	10	2.3	1.4	37	43	0	0
Austria	7.6	8.1	0.2	0.5	5	6	3	4	0.4	0.7	41	40	0	0
Azerbaijan	6.2	8.0	1.5	1.2	4	5	3	4	1.0	1.7	48	44	0	0
Bangladesh	86.7	127.7	2.4	1.6	44	74	41	66	2.2	3.0	42	42	35	29
Belarus	9.6	10.2	0.6	−0.1	6	7	5	5	0.4	−0.1	50	49	0	0
Belgium	9.8	10.2	0.1	0.3	6	7	4	4	0.1	0.8	34	41	0	0
Benin	3.5	6.1	3.1	2.8	2	3	2	3	2.5	2.8	47	48	30	27
Bolivia	5.4	8.1	2.0	2.4	3	5	2	3	2.6	2.6	33	38	19	13
Botswana	0.9	1.6	3.4	2.4	0	1	0	1	3.4	2.4	50	45	26	15
Brazil	121.7	168.1	2.0	1.4	70	110	47	79	3.2	2.2	28	35	19	15
Bulgaria	8.9	8.2	−0.2	−0.7	6	6	5	4	−0.4	−0.7	45	48	0	0
Burkina Faso	7.0	11.0	2.4	2.4	3	6	4	5	1.9	1.9	48	47	71	47
Burundi	4.1	6.7	2.8	2.2	2	3	2	4	2.6	2.2	50	49	50	49
Cambodia	6.8	11.8	2.9	2.8	4	6	4	6	2.6	2.8	55	52	27	24
Cameroon	8.7	14.7	2.8	2.7	5	8	4	6	2.3	3.0	37	38	34	24
Canada	24.6	30.6	1.2	1.1	17	21	12	17	1.8	1.3	40	46	0	0
Central African Republic	2.3	3.5	2.4	2.1	1	2	..	..	..	..	..	..	..	..
Chad	4.5	7.5	2.5	2.9	2	3	2	4	2.1	2.9	43	45	42	37
Chile	11.1	15.0	1.6	1.5	7	10	4	6	2.7	2.4	26	33	0	0
China	981.2	1,249.7	1.5	1.1	586	844	540	750	2.2	1.3	43	45	30	9
Hong Kong, China	5.0	6.9	1.2	2.1	3	5	2	4	1.6	2.5	34	37	6	0
Colombia	28.4	41.5	2.1	1.9	16	26	9	18	4.0	2.7	26	38	12	6
Congo, Dem. Rep.	27.0	49.8	3.2	3.2	14	25	12	20	2.8	2.9	45	43	33	29
Congo, Rep.	1.7	2.9	2.9	2.8	1	1	1	1	2.9	2.5	42	43	27	26
Costa Rica	2.3	3.6	2.7	2.0	1	2	1	1	3.5	2.6	21	31	10	5
Côte d'Ivoire	8.2	14.7	3.5	2.6	4	8	3	6	3.0	3.2	32	33	28	19
Croatia	4.6	4.5	0.4	−0.8	3	3	2	2	0.4	−0.8	40	44	0	0
Czech Republic	10.2	10.3	0.1	−0.1	6	7	5	6	0.3	0.5	47	47	0	0
Denmark	5.1	5.3	0.0	0.4	3	4	3	3	0.8	0.0	44	46	0	0
Dominican Republic	5.7	8.4	2.2	1.9	3	5	2	4	3.0	2.9	25	30	25	14
Ecuador	8.0	12.4	2.5	2.1	4	8	3	5	3.4	3.3	20	28	9	5
Egypt, Arab Rep.	40.9	62.4	2.5	1.9	23	38	14	24	2.5	2.9	27	30	18	10
El Salvador	4.6	6.2	1.1	2.1	2	4	2	3	2.2	3.5	27	36	17	14
Eritrea	2.4	4.0	2.8	2.7	..	2	1	2	2.6	2.7	47	47	44	39
Estonia	1.5	1.4	0.6	−0.9	1	1	1	1	0.4	−0.7	51	49	0	0
Ethiopia	37.7	62.8	3.1	2.8	20	32	17	27	3.1	1.8	42	41	46	42
Finland	4.8	5.2	0.4	0.4	3	3	2	3	0.8	0.0	47	48	0	0
France	53.9	59.1	0.5	0.5	34	39	24	27	0.5	0.7	40	45	0	0
Georgia	5.1	5.5	0.7	0.0	3	4	3	3	0.5	0.0	49	47	0	0
Germany	78.3	82.0	0.1	0.4	52	56	38	41	0.6	0.4	40	42	0	0
Ghana	10.7	18.9	3.3	2.7	6	10	5	9	3.3	2.7	51	51	16	13
Greece	9.6	10.5	0.5	0.4	6	7	4	5	1.0	0.9	28	38	5	0
Guatemala	6.8	11.1	2.5	2.6	3	6	2	4	2.8	3.2	22	28	19	15
Guinea	4.5	7.2	2.5	2.6	2	4	2	3	2.1	2.1	47	47	41	32
Haiti	5.4	7.8	1.9	2.1	3	4	3	3	1.5	1.8	45	43	33	24
Honduras	3.6	6.3	3.1	2.9	2	3	1	2	3.1	3.8	25	31	14	8
Hungary	10.7	10.1	−0.3	−0.3	7	7	5	5	−0.8	0.1	43	45	0	0
India	687.3	997.5	2.1	1.8	394	609	302	439	1.7	2.3	34	32	21	13
Indonesia	148.3	207.0	1.8	1.7	83	133	58	99	3.0	2.6	35	41	13	9
Iran, Islamic Rep.	39.1	63.0	3.3	1.6	20	38	12	20	3.0	2.4	20	27	14	3
Ireland	3.4	3.7	0.3	0.7	2	2	1	2	0.3	2.1	28	34	1	0
Israel	3.9	6.1	1.8	3.0	2	4	1	3	2.4	4.1	34	41	0	0
Italy	56.4	57.6	0.1	0.2	36	39	23	26	0.8	0.7	33	38	2	0
Jamaica	2.1	2.6	1.2	0.9	1	2	1	1	2.0	1.5	46	46	0	0
Japan	116.8	126.6	0.6	0.3	79	87	57	68	1.2	0.7	38	41	0	0
Jordan	2.2	4.7	3.7	4.4	1	3	1	1	4.9	5.2	15	24	4	0
Kazakhstan	14.9	15.4	0.9	−0.6	9	10	7	8	0.9	−0.2	48	47	0	0
Kenya	16.6	30.0	3.5	2.7	8	16	8	15	3.7	3.3	46	46	45	40
Korea, Rep.	38.1	46.8	1.2	1.0	24	33	16	24	2.3	2.1	39	41	0	0
Kuwait	1.4	1.9	4.4	−1.1	1	1	0	1	5.9	−1.6	13	31	0	0
Kyrgyz Republic	3.6	4.7	1.9	0.8	2	3	2	2	1.4	1.4	48	47	0	0
Lao PDR	3.2	5.1	2.3	2.6	2	3	..	..	..	..	..	..	31	26
Latvia	2.5	2.4	0.5	−1.0	2	2	1	1	0.3	−1.0	51	50	0	0
Lebanon	3.0	4.3	1.9	1.8	2	3	1	1	2.9	3.1	23	29	5	0
Lesotho	1.3	2.1	2.5	2.2	1	1	1	1	2.0	2.5	38	37	28	21
Lithuania	3.4	3.7	0.9	−0.1	2	2	2	2	0.7	−0.1	50	48	0	0
Macedonia, FYR	1.9	2.0	0.1	0.7	1	1	1	1	0.5	1.2	36	42	1	0
Madagascar	8.9	15.1	2.7	2.9	5	8	4	7	2.3	2.9	45	45	40	35
Malawi	6.2	10.8	3.2	2.6	3	6	3	5	3.0	2.4	51	49	45	33
Malaysia	13.8	22.7	2.8	2.5	8	14	5	9	3.1	3.0	34	38	8	3

PEOPLE

	Population						Labor force								
	Total Millions		Avg. annual growth rate (%)		Ages 15–64 Millions		Total Millions		Avg. annual growth rate (%)		Female % of labor force		Children ages 10–14 % of age group	
Economy	1980	1999	1980–90	1990–99	1980	1999	1980	1999	1980–90	1990–99	1980	1999	1980	1999
Mali	6.6	10.9	2.5	2.8	3	5	3	5	2.3	2.6	47	46	61	52
Mauritania	1.6	2.6	2.7	2.8	1	1	1	1	2.0	3.0	45	44	30	23
Mexico	67.6	97.4	2.1	1.8	35	60	22	40	3.2	2.9	27	33	9	6
Moldova	4.0	4.3	0.9	–0.2	3	3	2	2	0.3	0.0	50	49	3	0
Mongolia	1.7	2.6	2.9	1.9	1	2	1	1	2.9	2.8	46	47	4	2
Morocco	19.4	28.2	2.2	1.8	10	18	7	11	2.4	2.7	34	35	21	3
Mozambique	12.1	17.3	1.6	2.2	6	9	7	9	1.2	2.0	49	48	39	33
Myanmar	33.8	45.0	1.8	1.2	19	30	17	24	1.8	1.6	44	43	28	24
Namibia	1.0	1.7	2.7	2.6	1	1	0	1	2.5	2.3	40	41	34	19
Nepal	14.5	23.4	2.6	2.4	8	13	7	11	2.2	2.4	39	40	56	43
Netherlands	14.2	15.8	0.6	0.6	9	11	6	7	1.9	0.9	32	40	0	0
New Zealand	3.1	3.8	1.0	1.2	2	2	1	2	2.3	1.6	34	45	0	0
Nicaragua	2.9	4.9	2.7	2.8	1	3	1	2	3.3	4.0	28	35	19	13
Niger	5.6	10.5	3.2	3.4	3	5	3	5	3.0	2.9	45	44	48	44
Nigeria	71.1	123.9	3.0	2.8	36	66	29	50	2.8	2.8	36	36	29	25
Norway	4.1	4.5	0.4	0.5	3	3	2	2	0.8	1.0	41	46	0	0
Pakistan	82.7	134.8	2.7	2.5	44	74	29	50	2.9	2.8	23	28	23	16
Panama	2.0	2.8	2.1	1.8	1	2	1	1	3.2	2.6	30	35	6	3
Papua New Guinea	3.1	4.7	2.2	2.3	2	3	2	2	2.2	2.3	42	42	28	18
Paraguay	3.1	5.4	3.0	2.7	2	3	1	2	2.8	3.3	27	30	15	7
Peru	17.3	25.2	2.2	1.7	9	15	5	9	3.1	2.7	24	31	4	2
Philippines	48.3	76.8	2.6	2.3	27	46	19	32	2.8	2.8	35	38	14	6
Poland	35.6	38.7	0.7	0.2	23	26	19	20	0.1	0.6	45	46	0	0
Portugal	9.8	10.0	0.1	0.1	6	7	5	5	0.5	0.5	39	44	8	1
Romania	22.2	22.5	0.4	–0.4	14	15	11	11	–0.2	0.1	46	44	0	0
Russian Federation	139.0	146.5	0.6	–0.1	95	101	76	78	0.1	0.1	49	49	0	0
Rwanda	5.2	8.3	3.0	2.0	3	4	3	4	3.2	2.4	49	49	43	41
Saudi Arabia	9.4	21.4	5.2	3.4	5	12	3	7	6.5	3.1	8	15	5	0
Senegal	5.5	9.3	2.8	2.6	3	5	3	4	2.6	2.6	42	43	43	29
Sierra Leone	3.2	4.9	2.1	2.4	2	3	1	2	1.6	2.4	36	37	19	15
Singapore	2.3	3.2	1.7	1.9	2	2	1	2	2.7	1.7	35	39	2	0
Slovak Republic	5.0	5.4	0.6	0.2	3	4	2	3	0.8	0.9	45	48	0	0
Slovenia	1.9	2.0	0.5	–0.1	1	1	1	1	0.3	0.3	46	46	0	0
South Africa	27.6	42.1	2.4	2.0	16	26	10	17	2.7	2.3	35	38	1	0
Spain	37.4	39.4	0.4	0.2	23	27	14	17	1.4	0.9	28	37	0	0
Sri Lanka	14.7	19.0	1.4	1.2	9	13	5	8	2.2	2.0	27	36	4	2
Sweden	8.3	8.9	0.3	0.4	5	6	4	5	0.9	0.4	44	48	0	0
Switzerland	6.3	7.1	0.6	0.7	4	5	3	4	1.6	0.9	37	40	0	0
Syrian Arab Republic	8.7	15.7	3.3	2.8	4	9	2	5	3.3	4.0	24	27	14	4
Tajikistan	4.0	6.2	2.9	1.8	2	3	2	2	2.1	2.7	47	45	0	0
Tanzania	18.6	32.9	3.2	2.9	9	17	9	17	3.3	2.6	50	49	43	38
Thailand	46.7	61.7	1.7	1.2	26	42	24	37	2.7	1.7	47	46	25	14
Togo	2.6	4.6	2.9	2.9	1	2	1	2	2.5	2.7	39	40	36	28
Tunisia	6.4	9.5	2.4	1.6	3	6	2	4	2.7	2.8	29	31	6	0
Turkey	44.5	64.4	2.3	1.5	25	43	19	31	2.6	2.8	36	37	21	9
Turkmenistan	2.9	4.8	2.5	2.9	2	3	1	2	2.5	3.5	47	46	0	0
Uganda	12.8	21.5	2.4	3.0	6	11	7	11	2.2	2.6	48	48	49	44
Ukraine	50.0	49.9	0.4	–0.4	33	34	27	25	–0.2	–0.2	50	49	0	0
United Kingdom	56.3	59.1	0.2	0.3	36	39	27	30	0.6	0.3	39	44	0	0
United States	227.2	272.9	0.9	1.0	151	179	109	139	1.3	1.2	41	46	0	0
Uruguay	2.9	3.3	0.6	0.7	2	2	1	2	1.6	1.2	31	42	4	1
Uzbekistan	16.0	24.5	2.5	2.0	9	14	6	10	2.3	2.8	48	47	0	0
Venezuela, RB	15.1	23.7	2.6	2.2	8	15	5	9	3.4	3.0	27	34	4	0
Vietnam	53.7	77.5	2.1	1.8	28	48	26	40	2.7	1.8	48	49	22	7
Yemen, Rep.	8.5	17.0	3.3	4.0	4	8	2	5	3.6	4.7	33	28	26	19
Zambia	5.7	9.9	3.0	2.7	3	5	2	4	2.8	2.9	45	45	19	16
Zimbabwe	7.0	11.9	3.3	2.2	3	7	2	3	3.5	2.2	44	44	37	28
World	4,430.2 s	5,974.7 s	1.7 w	1.0 w	2,595 s	3,761 s	2,035 s	2,892 s	1.9 w	1.7 w	39 w	41 w	20 w	12 w
Low income	1,612.9	2,417.0	2.3	2.0	890	1,417	709	1,085	2.1	2.4	38	38	24	19
Middle income	2,027.9	2,666.8	1.7	1.2	1,199	1,748	970	1,374	2.1	1.5	40	42	21	7
Lower middle income	1,607.9	2,093.7	1.6	1.1	955	1,379	805	1,121	2.0	1.4	42	43	24	7
Upper middle income	419.9	573.1	1.8	1.4	245	369	165	253	2.4	2.1	33	36	9	6
Low and middle income	3,641.0	5,083.8	1.9	1.6	2,090	3,166	1,679	2,459	2.1	1.9	39	40	23	13
East Asia & Pacific	1,397.8	1,836.9	1.6	1.3	820	1,220	719	1,038	2.3	1.5	43	45	26	9
Europe & Central Asia	425.8	475.3	0.9	0.2	274	318	214	238	0.5	0.6	47	46	3	1
Latin America & Caribbean	360.3	509.2	2.0	1.7	201	319	130	219	3.0	2.5	28	35	13	9
Middle East & North Africa	174.0	290.9	3.1	2.2	91	171	54	97	3.1	3.1	24	27	14	5
South Asia	902.6	1,329.3	2.2	1.9	508	797	392	585	1.8	2.5	34	33	23	16
Sub-Saharan Africa	380.5	642.3	2.9	2.6	195	340	170	282	2.7	2.6	42	42	35	30
High income	789.1	890.9	0.6	0.6	505	596	357	433	1.1	0.9	38	43	0	0

Note: For data comparability and coverage, see the Technical Notes. Figures in italics are for years other than those specified.

Table 4.   Poverty

Economy	National poverty lines							International poverty lines				
	Survey year	Population below the poverty line (%)			Survey year	Population below the poverty line (%)			Survey year	Population below $1 a day %	Poverty gap at $1 a day %	Population below $2 a day %	Poverty gap at $2 a day %
		Rural	Urban	National		Rural	Urban	National					
Albania													
Algeria	1988	16.6	7.3	12.2	1995	30.3	14.7	22.6	1995	<2	<0.5	15.1	3.6
Angola													
Argentina	1991	..	..	25.5	1993	..	..	17.6		..	..	..	..
Armenia		..	..	..		..	..	..		..	..	..	..
Australia		..	..	..		..	..	..		..	..	..	..
Austria		..	..	..		..	..	..		..	..	..	..
Azerbaijan	1995	..	..	68.1		..	..	..		..	..	..	..
Bangladesh	1991–92	46.0	23.3	42.7	1995–96	39.8	14.3	35.6	1996	29.1	5.9	77.8	31.8
Belarus	1995	..	..	22.5		..	..	..	1998	<2	<0.5	<2	0.1
Belgium		..	..	..		..	..	..		..	..	..	..
Benin	1995	..	..	33.0		..	..	..		..	..	..	..
Bolivia	1993	..	29.3	..	1995	79.1	..	..	1990	11.3	2.2	38.6	13.5
Botswana									1985–86	33.3	12.5	61.4	30.7
Brazil	1990	32.6	13.1	17.4					1997	5.1	1.3	17.4	6.3
Bulgaria		..	..	..		..	..	..	1995	<2	<0.5	7.8	1.6
Burkina Faso		..	..	..		..	..	..	1994	61.2	25.5	85.8	50.9
Burundi	1990	..	..	36.2		..	..	..		..	..	..	..
Cambodia	1993–94	43.1	24.8	39.0	1997	40.1	21.1	36.1		..	..	..	..
Cameroon	1984	32.4	44.4	40.0		..	..	..		..	..	..	..
Canada		..	..	..		..	..	..		..	..	..	..
Central African Republic		..	..	..		..	..	..	1993	66.6	38.1	84.0	58.4
Chad	1995–96	67.0	63.0	64.0		..	..	..		..	..	..	..
Chile	1992	..	..	21.6	1994	..	..	20.5	1994	4.2	0.7	20.3	5.9
China	1996	7.9	<2	6.0	1998	4.6	<2	4.6	1998	18.5	4.2	53.7	21.0
Hong Kong, China		..	..	..		..	..	..		..	..	..	..
Colombia	1991	29.0	7.8	16.9	1992	_31.2_	8.0	17.7	1996	11.0	3.2	28.7	11.6
Congo, Dem. Rep.		..	..	..		..	..	..		..	..	..	..
Congo, Rep.		..	..	..		..	..	..		..	..	..	..
Costa Rica		..	..	..		..	..	..	1996	9.6	3.2	26.3	10.1
Côte d'Ivoire		..	..	..		..	..	..	1995	12.3	2.4	49.4	16.8
Croatia		..	..	..		..	..	..		..	..	..	..
Czech Republic		..	..	..		..	..	..	1993	<2	<0.5	<2	<0.5
Denmark		..	..	..		..	..	..		..	..	..	..
Dominican Republic	1989	27.4	23.3	24.5	1992	29.8	10.9	20.6	1996	3.2	0.7	16.0	5.0
Ecuador	1994	47.0	25.0	35.0		..	..	..	1995	20.2	5.8	52.3	21.2
Egypt, Arab Rep.	1995–96	23.3	22.5	22.9		..	..	..	1995	3.1	0.3	52.7	11.4
El Salvador	1992	55.7	43.1	48.3		..	..	..	1996	25.3	10.4	51.9	24.7
Eritrea		..	..	..		..	..	..		..	..	..	..
Estonia	1995	14.7	6.8	8.9		..	..	..	1995	4.9	1.2	17.7	6.0
Ethiopia		..	..	..		..	..	..	1995	31.3	8.0	76.4	32.9
Finland		..	..	..		..	..	..		..	..	..	..
France		..	..	..		..	..	..		..	..	..	..
Georgia	1997	9.9	12.1	11.1		..	..	..		..	..	..	..
Germany		..	..	..		..	..	..		..	..	..	..
Ghana	1992	34.3	26.7	31.4		..	..	..		..	..	..	..
Greece		..	..	..		..	..	..		..	..	..	..
Guatemala	1989	71.9	33.7	57.9		..	..	..	1989	39.8	19.8	64.3	36.6
Guinea	1994	..	..	40.0		..	..	..		..	..	..	..
Haiti	1987	..	..	65.0	1995	66.0	..	..		..	..	..	..
Honduras	1992	46.0	56.0	50.0	1993	51.0	57.0	53.0	1996	40.5	17.5	68.8	36.9
Hungary	1989	..	..	1.6	1993	..	..	8.6	1993	<2	<0.5	4.0	0.9
India	1992	43.5	33.7	40.9	1994	36.7	30.5	35.0	1997	44.2	12.0	86.2	41.4
Indonesia	1996	12.3	9.7	11.3	1998	22.0	17.8	20.3	1999	15.2	2.5	66.1	22.6
Iran, Islamic Rep.		..	..	..		..	..	..		..	..	..	..
Ireland		..	..	..		..	..	..		..	..	..	..
Israel		..	..	..		..	..	..		..	..	..	..
Italy		..	..	..		..	..	..		..	..	..	..
Jamaica	1992	..	..	34.2		..	..	..	1996	3.2	0.7	25.2	6.9
Japan		..	..	..		..	..	..		..	..	..	..
Jordan	1991	..	..	15.0	1997	..	..	11.7	1997	<2	<0.5	7.4	1.4
Kazakhstan	1996	39.0	30.0	34.6		..	..	..	1996	1.5	0.3	15.3	3.9
Kenya	1992	46.4	29.3	42.0		..	..	..	1994	26.5	9.0	62.3	27.5
Korea, Rep.		..	..	..		..	..	..	1993	<2	<0.5	<2	<0.5
Kuwait		..	..	..		..	..	..		..	..	..	..
Kyrgyz Republic	1993	48.1	28.7	40.0	1997	64.5	28.5	51.0		..	..	..	..
Lao PDR	1993	53.0	24.0	46.1		..	..	..		..	..	..	..
Latvia		..	..	..		..	..	..	1998	<2	<0.5	8.3	2.0
Lebanon		..	..	..		..	..	..		..	..	..	..
Lesotho	1993	53.9	27.8	49.2		..	..	..	1993	43.1	20.3	65.7	38.1
Lithuania		..	..	..		..	..	..	1996	<2	<0.5	7.8	2.0
Macedonia, FYR		..	..	..		..	..	..		..	..	..	..
Madagascar	1993–94	77.0	47.0	70.0		..	..	..	1993	60.2	24.5	88.8	51.3
Malawi	1990–91	..	..	54.0		..	..	..		..	..	..	..
Malaysia	1989	..	..	15.5		..	..	..		..	..	..	..

PEOPLE

Economy	National poverty lines							International poverty lines				
	Survey year	Population below the poverty line (%)			Survey year	Population below the poverty line (%)			Survey year	Population below $1 a day %	Poverty gap at $1 a day %	Population below $2 a day %	Poverty gap at $2 a day %
		Rural	Urban	National		Rural	Urban	National					
Mali		..	..	..		..	..	..	1994	72.8	37.4	90.6	60.5
Mauritania	1989–90	..	..	57.0		..	..	..	1995	3.8	1.0	22.1	6.6
Mexico	1988	..	..	10.1		..	..	..	1995	17.9	6.1	42.5	18.1
Moldova	1997	26.7	..	23.3		..	..	..	1992	7.3	1.3	31.9	10.2
Mongolia	1995	33.1	38.5	36.3		..	..	..	1995	13.9	3.1	50.0	17.5
Morocco	1990–91	18.0	7.6	13.1	1998–99	27.2	12.0	19.0	1990–91	<2	<0.5	7.5	1.3
Mozambique		..	..	..		..	..	..	1996	37.9	12.0	78.4	36.8
Myanmar		..	..	..		..	..	..		..	..	..	..
Namibia		..	..	..		..	..	..	1993	34.9	14.0	55.8	30.4
Nepal	1995–96	44.0	23.0	42.0		..	..	..	1995	37.7	9.7	82.5	37.5
Netherlands		..	..	..		..	..	..		..	..	..	..
New Zealand		..	..	..		..	..	..		..	..	..	..
Nicaragua	1993	76.1	31.9	50.3		..	..	..		..	..	..	..
Niger	1989–93	66.0	52.0	63.0		..	..	..	1995	61.4	33.9	85.3	54.8
Nigeria	1985	49.5	31.7	43.0	1992–93	36.4	30.4	34.1	1997	70.2	34.9	90.8	59.0
Norway		..	..	..		..	..	..		..	..	..	..
Pakistan	1991	36.9	28.0	34.0		..	..	..	1996	31.0	6.2	84.7	35.0
Panama	1997	64.9	15.3	37.3		..	..	..	1997	10.3	3.2	25.1	10.2
Papua New Guinea		..	..	..		..	..	..		..	..	..	..
Paraguay	1991	28.5	19.7	21.8		..	..	..	1995	19.4	8.3	38.5	18.8
Peru	1994	67.0	46.1	53.5	1997	64.7	40.4	49.0	1996	15.5	5.4	41.4	17.1
Philippines	1994	53.1	28.0	40.6	1997	51.2	22.5	40.6		..	..	..	..
Poland	1993	..	..	23.8		..	..	..	1993	5.4	4.3	10.5	6.0
Portugal		..	..	..		..	..	..	1994	<2	<0.5	<2	<0.5
Romania	1994	27.9	20.4	21.5		..	..	..	1994	2.8	0.8	27.5	6.9
Russian Federation	1994	..	..	30.9		..	..	..	1998	7.1	1.4	25.1	8.7
Rwanda	1993	..	..	51.2		..	..	..	1983–85	35.7	7.7	84.6	36.7
Saudi Arabia		..	..	..		..	..	..		..	..	..	..
Senegal		..	..	..		..	..	..	1995	26.3	7.0	67.8	28.2
Sierra Leone	1989	76.0	53.0	68.0		..	..	..	1989	57.0	39.5	74.5	51.8
Singapore		..	..	..		..	..	..		..	..	..	..
Slovak Republic		..	..	..		..	..	..	1992	<2	<0.5	<2	<0.5
Slovenia		..	..	..		..	..	..	1993	<2	<0.5	<2	<0.5
South Africa		..	..	..		..	..	..	1993	11.5	1.8	35.8	13.4
Spain		..	..	..		..	..	..		..	..	..	..
Sri Lanka	1985–86	45.5	26.8	40.6	1990–91	38.1	28.4	35.3	1995	6.6	1.0	45.4	13.5
Sweden		..	..	..		..	..	..		..	..	..	..
Switzerland		..	..	..		..	..	..		..	..	..	..
Syrian Arab Republic		..	..	..		..	..	..		..	..	..	..
Tajikistan		..	..	..		..	..	..		..	..	..	..
Tanzania	1991	..	..	51.1		..	..	..	1993	19.9	4.8	59.7	23.0
Thailand	1990	..	..	18.0	1992	15.5	10.2	13.1	1998	<2	<0.5	28.2	7.1
Togo	1987–89	..	..	32.3		..	..	..		..	..	..	..
Tunisia	1985	29.2	12.0	19.9	1990	21.6	8.9	14.1	1990	<2	<0.5	11.6	2.9
Turkey		..	..	..		..	..	..	1994	2.4	0.5	18.0	5.0
Turkmenistan		..	..	..		..	..	..	1993	20.9	5.7	59.0	23.3
Uganda	1993	..	..	55.0		..	..	..	1992	36.7	11.4	77.2	35.8
Ukraine	1995	..	..	31.7		..	..	..	1996	<2	<0.5	23.7	4.4
United Kingdom		..	..	..		..	..	..		..	..	..	..
United States		..	..	..		..	..	..		..	..	..	..
Uruguay		..	..	..		..	..	..	1989	<2	<0.5	6.6	1.9
Uzbekistan		..	..	..		..	..	..	1993	3.3	0.5	26.5	7.3
Venezuela, RB	1989	..	..	31.3		..	..	..	1996	14.7	5.6	36.4	15.7
Vietnam	1993	57.2	25.9	50.9		..	..	..		..	..	..	..
Yemen, Rep.	1992	19.2	18.6	19.1		..	..	..	1998	5.1	0.9	35.5	10.1
Zambia	1991	88.0	46.0	68.0	1993	..	..	86.0	1996	72.6	37.7	91.7	61.2
Zimbabwe	1990–91	31.0	10.0	25.5		..	..	..	1990–91	36.0	9.6	64.2	29.4

Note: For data comparability and coverage, see the Technical Notes. Figures in italics are for years other than those specified.

Table 5.   Distribution of income or consumption

Economy	Survey year	Gini index	Percentage share of income or consumption						
			Lowest 10%	Lowest 20%	Second 20%	Third 20%	Fourth 20%	Highest 20%	Highest 10%
Albania	..	..	..	..	..	..	..	..	..
Algeria	1995[a,b]	35.3	2.8	7.0	11.6	16.1	22.7	42.6	26.8
Angola	..	..	..	..	..	..	..	..	..
Argentina	..	..	..	..	..	..	..	..	..
Armenia	..	..	..	..	..	..	..	..	..
Australia	1994[c,d]	35.2	2.0	5.9	12.0	17.2	23.6	41.3	25.4
Austria	1987[c,d]	23.1	4.4	10.4	14.8	18.5	22.9	33.3	19.3
Azerbaijan	..	..	..	..	..	..	..	..	..
Bangladesh	1995–96[a,b]	33.6	3.9	8.7	12.0	15.7	20.8	42.8	28.6
Belarus	1998[a,b]	21.7	5.1	11.4	15.2	18.2	21.9	33.3	20.0
Belgium	1992[c,d]	25.0	3.7	9.5	14.6	18.4	23.0	34.5	20.2
Benin	..	..	..	..	..	..	..	..	..
Bolivia	1990[c,d]	42.0	2.3	5.6	9.7	14.5	22.0	48.2	31.7
Botswana	..	..	..	..	..	..	..	..	..
Brazil	1996[c,d]	60.0	0.9	2.5	5.5	10.0	18.3	63.8	47.6
Bulgaria	1995[a,b]	28.3	3.4	8.5	13.8	17.9	22.7	37.0	22.5
Burkina Faso	1994[a,b]	48.2	2.2	5.5	8.7	12.0	18.7	55.0	39.5
Burundi	1992[a,b]	33.3	3.4	7.9	12.1	16.3	22.1	41.6	26.6
Cambodia	1997[a,b]	40.4	2.9	6.9	10.7	14.7	20.1	47.6	33.8
Cameroon	..	..	..	..	..	..	..	..	..
Canada	1994[c,d]	31.5	2.8	7.5	12.9	17.2	23.0	39.3	23.8
Central African Republic	1993[a,b]	61.3	0.7	2.0	4.9	9.6	18.5	65.0	47.7
Chad	..	..	..	..	..	..	..	..	..
Chile	1994[c,d]	56.5	1.4	3.5	6.6	10.9	18.1	61.0	46.1
China	1998[c,d]	40.3	2.4	5.9	10.2	15.1	22.2	46.6	30.4
Hong Kong, China	..	..	..	..	..	..	..	..	..
Colombia	1996[c,d]	57.1	1.1	3.0	6.6	11.1	18.4	60.9	46.1
Congo, Dem. Rep.	..	..	..	..	..	..	..	..	..
Congo, Rep.	..	..	..	..	..	..	..	..	..
Costa Rica	1996[c,d]	47.0	1.3	4.0	8.8	13.7	21.7	51.8	34.7
Côte d'Ivoire	1995[a,b]	36.7	3.1	7.1	11.2	15.6	21.9	44.3	28.8
Croatia	1998[a,b]	26.8	4.0	9.3	13.8	17.8	22.9	36.2	21.6
Czech Republic	1996[c,d]	25.4	4.3	10.3	14.5	17.7	21.7	35.9	22.4
Denmark	1992[c,d]	24.7	3.6	9.6	14.9	18.3	22.7	34.5	20.5
Dominican Republic	1996[c,d]	48.7	1.7	4.3	8.3	13.1	20.6	53.7	37.8
Ecuador	1995[a,b]	43.7	2.2	5.4	9.4	14.2	21.3	49.7	33.8
Egypt, Arab Rep.	1995[a,b]	28.9	4.4	9.8	13.2	16.6	21.4	39.0	25.0
El Salvador	1996[c,d]	52.3	1.2	3.4	7.5	12.5	20.2	56.5	40.5
Eritrea	..	..	..	..	..	..	..	..	..
Estonia	1995[c,d]	35.4	2.2	6.2	12.0	17.0	23.1	41.8	26.2
Ethiopia	1995[a,b]	40.0	3.0	7.1	10.9	14.5	19.8	47.7	33.7
Finland	1991[c,d]	25.6	4.2	10.0	14.2	17.6	22.3	35.8	21.6
France	1995[c,d]	32.7	2.8	7.2	12.6	17.2	22.8	40.2	25.1
Georgia	..	..	..	..	..	..	..	..	..
Germany	1994[c,d]	30.0	3.3	8.2	13.2	17.5	22.7	38.5	23.7
Ghana	1997[a,b]	32.7	3.6	8.4	12.2	15.8	21.9	41.7	26.1
Greece	1993[c,d]	32.7	3.0	7.5	12.4	16.9	22.8	40.3	25.3
Guatemala	1989[c,d]	59.6	0.6	2.1	5.8	10.5	18.6	63.0	46.6
Guinea	1994[a,b]	40.3	2.6	6.4	10.4	14.8	21.2	47.2	32.0
Haiti	..	..	..	..	..	..	..	..	..
Honduras	1996[c,d]	53.7	1.2	3.4	7.1	11.7	19.7	58.0	42.1
Hungary	1996[c,d]	30.8	3.9	8.8	12.5	16.6	22.3	39.9	24.8
India	1997[a,b]	37.8	3.5	8.1	11.6	15.0	19.3	46.1	33.5
Indonesia	1996[c,d]	36.5	3.6	8.0	11.3	15.1	20.8	44.9	30.3
Iran, Islamic Rep.	..	..	..	..	..	..	..	..	..
Ireland	1987[c,d]	35.9	2.5	6.7	11.6	16.4	22.4	42.9	27.4
Israel	1992[c,d]	35.5	2.8	6.9	11.4	16.3	22.9	42.5	26.9
Italy	1995[c,d]	27.3	3.5	8.7	14.0	18.1	22.9	36.3	21.8
Jamaica	1996[a,b]	36.4	2.9	7.0	11.5	15.8	21.8	43.9	28.9
Japan	1993[c,d]	24.9	4.8	10.6	14.2	17.6	22.0	35.7	21.7
Jordan	1997[a,b]	36.4	3.3	7.6	11.4	15.5	21.1	44.4	29.8
Kazakhstan	1996[a,b]	35.4	2.7	6.7	11.5	16.4	23.1	42.3	26.3
Kenya	1994[a,b]	44.5	1.8	5.0	9.7	14.2	20.9	50.2	34.9
Korea, Rep.	1993[a,b]	31.6	2.9	7.5	12.9	17.4	22.9	39.3	24.3
Kuwait	..	..	..	..	..	..	..	..	..
Kyrgyz Republic	1997[c,d]	40.5	2.7	6.3	10.2	14.7	21.4	47.4	31.7
Lao PDR	1992[a,b]	30.4	4.2	9.6	12.9	16.3	21.0	40.2	26.4
Latvia	1998[c,d]	32.4	2.9	7.6	12.9	17.1	22.1	40.3	25.9
Lebanon	..	..	..	..	..	..	..	..	..
Lesotho	1986–87[a,b]	56.0	0.9	2.8	6.5	11.2	19.4	60.1	43.4
Lithuania	1996[a,b]	32.4	3.1	7.8	12.6	16.8	22.4	40.3	25.6
Macedonia, FYR	..	..	..	..	..	..	..	..	..
Madagascar	1993[a,b]	46.0	1.9	5.1	9.4	13.3	20.1	52.1	36.7
Malawi	..	..	..	..	..	..	..	..	..
Malaysia	1995[c,d]	48.5	1.8	4.5	8.3	13.0	20.4	53.8	37.9

PEOPLE

Economy	Survey year	Gini index	Percentage share of income or consumption						
			Lowest 10%	Lowest 20%	Second 20%	Third 20%	Fourth 20%	Highest 20%	Highest 10%
Mali	1994[a,b]	50.5	1.8	4.6	8.0	11.9	19.3	56.2	40.4
Mauritania	1995[a,b]	38.9	2.3	6.2	10.8	15.4	22.0	45.6	29.9
Mexico	1995[c,d]	53.7	1.4	3.6	7.2	11.8	19.2	58.2	42.8
Moldova	1992[c,d]	34.4	2.7	6.9	11.9	16.7	23.1	41.5	25.8
Mongolia	1995[a,b]	33.2	2.9	7.3	12.2	16.6	23.0	40.9	24.5
Morocco	1998–99[a,b]	39.5	2.6	6.5	10.6	14.8	21.3	46.6	30.9
Mozambique	1996–97[a,b]	39.6	2.5	6.5	10.8	15.1	21.1	46.5	31.7
Myanmar		..	..	..	..	..	..	..	..
Namibia		..	..	..	..	..	..	..	..
Nepal	1995–96[a,b]	36.7	3.2	7.6	11.5	15.1	21.0	44.8	29.8
Netherlands	1994[c,d]	32.6	2.8	7.3	12.7	17.2	22.8	40.1	25.1
New Zealand	1991[c,d]	43.9	0.3	2.7	10.0	16.3	24.1	46.9	29.8
Nicaragua	1993[a,b]	50.3	1.6	4.2	8.0	12.6	20.0	55.2	39.8
Niger	1995[a,b]	50.5	0.8	2.6	7.1	13.9	23.1	53.3	35.4
Nigeria	1996–97[a,b]	50.6	1.6	4.4	8.2	12.5	19.3	55.7	40.8
Norway	1995[c,d]	25.8	4.1	9.7	14.3	17.9	22.2	35.8	21.8
Pakistan	1996–97[a,b]	31.2	4.1	9.5	12.9	16.0	20.5	41.1	27.6
Panama	1997[a,b]	48.5	1.2	3.6	8.1	13.6	21.9	52.8	35.7
Papua New Guinea	1996[a,b]	50.9	1.7	4.5	7.9	11.9	19.2	56.5	40.5
Paraguay	1995[d]	59.1	0.7	2.3	5.9	10.7	18.7	62.4	46.6
Peru	1996[c,d]	46.2	1.6	4.4	9.1	14.1	21.3	51.2	35.4
Philippines	1997[a,b]	46.2	2.3	5.4	8.8	13.2	20.3	52.3	36.6
Poland	1996[c,d]	32.9	3.0	7.7	12.6	16.7	22.1	40.9	26.3
Portugal	1994–95[c,d]	35.6	3.1	7.3	11.6	15.9	21.8	43.4	28.4
Romania	1994[c,d]	28.2	3.7	8.9	13.6	17.6	22.6	37.3	22.7
Russian Federation	1998[a,b]	48.7	1.7	4.4	8.6	13.3	20.1	53.7	38.7
Rwanda	1983–85[a,b]	28.9	4.2	9.7	13.2	16.5	21.6	39.1	24.2
Saudi Arabia		..	..	..	..	..	..	..	..
Senegal	1995[a,b]	41.3	2.6	6.4	10.3	14.5	20.6	48.2	33.5
Sierra Leone	1989[a,b]	62.9	0.5	1.1	2.0	9.8	23.7	63.4	43.6
Singapore		..	..	..	..	..	..	..	..
Slovak Republic	1992[c,d]	19.5	5.1	11.9	15.8	18.8	22.2	31.4	18.2
Slovenia	1995[c,d]	26.8	3.2	8.4	14.3	18.5	23.4	35.4	20.7
South Africa	1993–94[a,b]	59.3	1.1	2.9	5.5	9.2	17.7	64.8	45.9
Spain	1990[c,d]	32.5	2.8	7.5	12.6	17.0	22.6	40.3	25.2
Sri Lanka	1995[a,b]	34.4	3.5	8.0	11.8	15.8	21.5	42.8	28.0
Sweden	1992[c,d]	25.0	3.7	9.6	14.5	18.1	23.2	34.5	20.1
Switzerland	1992[c,d]	33.1	2.6	6.9	12.7	17.3	22.9	40.3	25.2
Syrian Arab Republic		..	..	..	..	..	..	..	..
Tajikistan		..	..	..	..	..	..	..	..
Tanzania	1993[a,b]	38.2	2.8	6.8	11.0	15.1	21.6	45.5	30.1
Thailand	1998[a,b]	41.4	2.8	6.4	9.8	14.2	21.2	48.4	32.4
Togo		..	..	..	..	..	..	..	..
Tunisia	1990[a,b]	40.2	2.3	5.9	10.4	15.3	22.1	46.3	30.7
Turkey	1994[a,b]	41.5	2.3	5.8	10.2	14.8	21.6	47.7	32.3
Turkmenistan	1998[a,b]	40.8	2.6	6.1	10.2	14.7	21.5	47.5	31.7
Uganda	1992–93[a,b]	39.2	2.6	6.6	10.9	15.2	21.3	46.1	31.2
Ukraine	1996[a,b]	32.5	3.9	8.6	12.0	16.2	22.0	41.2	26.4
United Kingdom	1991[c,d]	36.1	2.6	6.6	11.5	16.3	22.7	43.0	27.3
United States	1997[c,d]	40.8	1.8	5.2	10.5	15.6	22.4	46.4	30.5
Uruguay	1989[c,d]	42.3	2.1	5.4	10.0	14.8	21.5	48.3	32.7
Uzbekistan	1993[c,d]	33.3	3.1	7.4	12.0	16.7	23.0	40.9	25.2
Venezuela, RB	1996[c,d]	48.8	1.3	3.7	8.4	13.6	21.2	53.1	37.0
Vietnam	1998[a,b]	36.1	3.6	8.0	11.4	15.2	20.9	44.5	29.9
Yemen, Rep.	1992[a,b]	39.5	2.3	6.1	10.9	15.3	21.6	46.1	30.8
Zambia	1996[a,b]	49.8	1.6	4.2	8.2	12.8	20.1	54.8	39.2
Zimbabwe	1990–91[a,b]	56.8	1.8	4.0	6.3	10.0	17.4	62.3	46.9

Note: For data comparability and coverage, see the Technical Notes. Figures in italics are for years other than those specified.
a. Refers to consumption shares by percentiles of population. b. Ranked by per capita consumption. c. Refers to income shares by percentiles of population. d. Ranked by per capita income.

Table 6.   Education

Economy	Public expenditure on education % of GNP		Net enrollment ratio[a] % of relevant age group				Percentage of cohort reaching grade 5				Expected years of schooling			
			Primary		Secondary		Males		Females		Males		Females	
	1980	1997	1980	1997	1980	1997	1980	1996	1980	1996	1980	1997	1980	1997
Albania	..	3.1	..	..	..	..	..	81	..	83	..	..	..	..
Algeria	7.8	5.1	82	96	43	69	90	94	85	95	10	12	7	10
Angola	..	..	83	35	81	31	..	..	..	..	8	9	7	7
Argentina	2.7	3.5	97	100	59	77	..	..	..	..	..	..	..	..
Armenia	..	2.0	..	..	..	..	..	..	..	..	..	..	..	..
Australia	5.5	5.4	100	100	81	96	..	..	..	..	12	17	12	17
Austria	5.5	5.4	100	100	91	97	..	..	..	..	11	15	11	14
Azerbaijan	..	3.0	..	..	..	..	..	..	..	..	..	..	..	..
Bangladesh	1.1	2.2	60	75	18	22	18	..	26	..	5	..	3	..
Belarus	..	5.9	..	85	..	..	..	..	..	..	..	..	..	..
Belgium	6.0	3.1	100	100	96	100	..	..	..	..	14	17	13	17
Benin	..	3.2	53	68	25	28	59	64	62	57	..	..	..	..
Bolivia	4.4	4.9	79	97	34	40	..	..	..	..	..	..	..	..
Botswana	6.0	8.6	76	80	40	89	80	87	84	93	7	12	8	12
Brazil	3.6	5.1	80	97	46	66	..	..	..	..	..	..	..	..
Bulgaria	4.5	3.2	98	98	75	78	..	93	..	90	11	12	11	12
Burkina Faso	2.2	1.5	15	32	5	13	77	74	74	77	2	3	1	2
Burundi	3.4	4.0	20	36	8	17	100	..	96	..	3	5	2	4
Cambodia	..	2.9	100	100	15	39	..	51	..	46	..	..	..	..
Cameroon	3.8	..	71	62	40	40	70	..	70	..	8	..	6	..
Canada	6.9	6.9	100	100	84	95	..	..	..	..	15	17	15	17
Central African Republic	..	..	57	46	27	19	63	..	50	..	..	..	..	..
Chad	..	1.7	26	48	13	18	..	62	..	53	..	..	..	..
Chile	4.6	3.6	93	90	70	85	94	100	97	100	..	13	..	13
China	2.5	2.3	84	100	63	70	..	93	..	94	..	..	..	..
Hong Kong, China	2.4	2.9	98	91	67	69	98	..	99	..	12	12	11	12
Colombia	1.9	4.1	73	89	60	76	36	70	39	76	..	..	..	..
Congo, Dem. Rep.	2.6	..	71	58	44	37	56	..	59	..	..	7	..	4
Congo, Rep.	7.0	6.1	97	78	98	84	81	40	83	78	..	..	..	..
Costa Rica	7.8	5.4	89	89	39	40	77	86	82	89	10	..	10	..
Côte d'Ivoire	7.2	5.0	55	58	39	34	86	77	79	71	..	..	..	..
Croatia	..	5.3	100	100	80	72	..	98	..	98	..	11	..	12
Czech Republic	..	5.1	95	100	93	100	..	..	..	..	..	13	..	13
Denmark	6.7	8.1	96	100	89	95	99	100	99	99	14	15	13	15
Dominican Republic	2.2	2.3	99	91	50	79	..	..	..	..	..	11	..	11
Ecuador	5.6	3.5	92	100	66	51	..	84	..	86	..	..	..	..
Egypt, Arab Rep.	5.7	4.8	72	95	43	75	92	..	88	..	..	12	..	10
El Salvador	3.9	2.5	70	89	23	36	46	76	48	77	..	10	..	10
Eritrea	..	1.8	..	29	..	38	..	73	..	67	..	5	..	4
Estonia	..	7.2	100	100	100	86	..	96	..	97	..	12	..	13
Ethiopia	3.1	4.0	28	35	19	25	50	51	51	50	..	..	..	..
Finland	5.3	7.5	100	100	87	95	..	100	..	100	..	15	..	17
France	5.0	6.0	100	100	94	99	..	..	..	..	..	15	..	16
Georgia	..	5.2	93	89	97	76	..	..	..	..	..	11	..	11
Germany	..	4.8	100	100	82	95	..	..	..	..	..	16	..	16
Ghana	3.1	4.2	..	..	..	..	..	..	..	..	..	..	..	..
Greece	2.0	3.1	100	100	75	91	99	..	98	..	13	14	12	14
Guatemala	1.8	1.7	59	74	28	35	..	52	..	47	..	..	..	..
Guinea	..	1.9	30	46	20	15	59	85	41	68	..	..	..	..
Haiti	1.5	..	..	..	..	..	33	..	34	..	..	..	..	..
Honduras	3.2	3.6	79	88	44	36	..	..	..	..	..	..	..	..
Hungary	4.7	4.6	95	98	71	97	96	..	97	..	..	13	..	13
India	3.0	3.2	65	77	41	60	..	62	..	55	..	..	..	..
Indonesia	1.7	1.4	89	99	42	56	..	88	..	88	..	10	..	10
Iran, Islamic Rep.	7.5	4.0	72	90	50	81	..	92	..	89	..	12	..	11
Ireland	6.3	6.0	100	100	90	100	..	99	..	100	11	14	12	14
Israel	8.2	7.6	..	..	..	..	..	..	..	..	..	..	..	..
Italy	..	4.9	100	100	70	95	99	98	99	99	..	..	..	..
Jamaica	7.0	7.4	98	96	71	70	91	..	91	..	..	11	..	11
Japan	5.8	3.6	100	100	93	100	100	100	100	100	14	..	13	..
Jordan	6.6	6.8	73	68	53	41	100	..	98	..	12	..	12	..
Kazakhstan	..	4.4	..	..	..	..	..	..	..	..	..	..	..	..
Kenya	6.8	6.5	91	65	55	61	60	..	62	..	..	..	..	..
Korea, Rep.	3.7	3.7	100	100	76	100	94	98	94	99	12	15	11	14
Kuwait	2.4	5.0	85	65	81	63	..	..	..	..	12	9	12	9
Kyrgyz Republic	..	5.3	100	100	100	78	..	..	..	..	..	..	..	..
Lao PDR	..	2.1	72	73	53	63	..	57	..	54	..	..	..	..
Latvia	3.3	6.3	100	100	90	81	..	..	..	..	..	12	..	13
Lebanon	..	2.5	..	76	..	..	..	..	..	..	..	..	..	..
Lesotho	5.1	8.4	67	69	69	73	50	72	68	87	7	9	10	10
Lithuania	..	5.4	..	..	..	81	..	..	..	..	..	..	..	..
Macedonia, FYR	..	5.1	..	95	..	56	..	95	..	95	..	11	..	11
Madagascar	4.4	1.9	..	61	..	..	..	49	..	33	..	..	..	..
Malawi	3.4	5.4	43	99	39	73	48	..	40	..	..	..	..	..
Malaysia	6.0	4.9	92	100	48	64	97	98	97	100	..	..	..	..

PEOPLE

Economy	Public expenditure on education % of GNP		Net enrollment ratio[a] % of relevant age group				Percentage of cohort reaching grade 5				Expected years of schooling			
			Primary		Secondary		Males		Females		Males		Females	
	1980	1997	1980	1997	1980	1997	1980	1996	1980	1996	1980	1997	1980	1997
Mali	3.7	2.2	20	38	10	18	48	92	42	70	..	..	..	..
Mauritania	..	5.1	..	57	..	..	..	61	..	68	..	..	..	..
Mexico	4.7	4.9	98	100	67	66	..	85	..	86	..	..	..	..
Moldova	3.4	10.6	..	..	..	..	..	..	..	..	..	..	..	..
Mongolia	..	5.7	100	85	89	56	..	..	..	..	..	7	..	9
Morocco	6.1	5.0	62	77	36	38	79	76	78	74	8	..	5	..
Mozambique	3.1	..	35	40	40	22	..	52	..	39	5	4	4	3
Myanmar	1.7	1.2	71	99	38	54	..	..	..	..	..	..	..	..
Namibia	1.5	9.1	86	91	67	81	..	76	..	82	..	..	..	..
Nepal	1.8	3.2	66	78	26	55	..	..	..	..	..	..	..	..
Netherlands	7.7	5.1	100	100	93	100	94	..	98	..	13	16	13	16
New Zealand	5.8	7.3	100	100	85	93	97	..	97	..	14	16	13	17
Nicaragua	3.4	3.9	71	79	51	51	40	52	47	57	..	9	..	9
Niger	3.2	2.3	22	24	7	9	74	72	72	74	..	3	..	2
Nigeria	6.4	0.7	..	..	..	..	..	..	..	..	..	..	..	..
Norway	6.5	7.4	99	100	84	98	100	100	100	100	13	15	13	16
Pakistan	2.1	2.7	..	..	..	..	..	..	..	..	..	..	..	..
Panama	4.9	5.1	89	90	65	71	74	..	79	..	11	..	12	..
Papua New Guinea	..	..	..	..	..	..	..	..	..	..	..	..	..	..
Paraguay	1.5	4.0	91	96	37	61	59	77	58	80	..	10	..	10
Peru	3.1	2.9	87	94	80	84	78	..	74	..	11	..	10	..
Philippines	1.7	3.4	95	100	72	78	68	..	73	..	11	..	11	..
Poland	..	7.5	99	99	73	87	..	..	..	..	12	13	12	13
Portugal	3.8	5.8	99	100	45	90	..	..	..	..	..	14	..	15
Romania	3.3	3.6	91	100	100	76	..	..	..	..	..	12	..	12
Russian Federation	3.5	3.5	92	100	98	88	..	..	..	..	..	..	..	..
Rwanda	2.7	..	59	..	..	..	69	..	74	..	..	..	..	..
Saudi Arabia	4.1	7.5	49	60	37	59	82	87	86	92	7	10	5	9
Senegal	..	3.7	37	60	19	20	89	89	82	85	..	..	..	..
Sierra Leone	3.5	..	..	..	..	..	..	..	..	..	..	..	..	..
Singapore	2.8	3.0	100	91	66	76	100	..	100	..	..	..	..	..
Slovak Republic	..	5.0	..	..	..	..	..	..	..	..	..	..	..	..
Slovenia	..	5.7	..	95	..	..	..	..	..	..	..	..	..	..
South Africa	..	7.9	68	100	62	95	..	72	..	79	..	14	..	14
Spain	2.3	5.0	100	100	79	92	95	..	94	..	13	..	13	..
Sri Lanka	2.7	3.4	96	100	59	76	92	..	91	..	..	14	..	15
Sweden	9.0	8.3	100	100	83	100	98	97	99	97	12	14	13	14
Switzerland	4.7	5.4	100	100	80	84	..	..	..	..	13	15	12	14
Syrian Arab Republic	4.6	3.1	90	95	48	42	93	93	88	94	11	10	8	9
Tajikistan	..	2.2	..	..	..	..	..	..	..	..	..	..	..	..
Tanzania	..	..	68	48	..	..	89	78	90	84	10	..	7	..
Thailand	3.4	4.8	92	88	25	48	..	..	..	..	..	..	..	..
Togo	5.6	4.5	79	82	65	58	59	79	45	60	..	..	..	..
Tunisia	5.4	7.7	83	100	40	74	89	90	84	92	10	..	7	..
Turkey	2.2	2.2	81	100	42	58	..	93	..	96	..	11	..	9
Turkmenistan	..	..	..	..	..	..	..	..	..	..	..	..	..	..
Uganda	1.3	2.6	..	..	..	..	82	..	73	..	..	..	..	..
Ukraine	5.6	7.3	..	..	..	..	..	..	..	..	..	..	..	..
United Kingdom	5.6	5.3	100	100	88	92	..	..	..	..	13	16	13	17
United States	6.7	5.4	90	100	94	96	..	..	..	..	14	16	15	16
Uruguay	2.3	3.3	87	94	70	84	..	97	..	99	..	..	..	..
Uzbekistan	..	7.7	..	..	..	..	..	..	..	..	..	..	..	..
Venezuela, RB	4.4	5.2	83	83	24	49	..	86	..	92	..	10	..	11
Vietnam	..	3.0	96	100	47	55	..	..	..	..	..	..	..	..
Yemen, Rep.	..	7.0	..	..	..	..	..	..	..	..	..	..	..	..
Zambia	4.5	2.2	77	72	35	42	88	..	82	..	..	8	..	7
Zimbabwe	5.3	..	72	93	20	59	82	78	76	79	..	..	..	..
World	**3.9 m**	**4.8 m**	**81 w**	**90 w**	**60 w**	**68 w**	**.. w**	**.. w**	**.. w**	**.. w**				
Low income	3.4	3.3	66	76	38	51	..	..	..	..				
Middle income	3.8	4.8	86	97	63	71	..	..	..	..				
Lower middle income	3.5	4.8	85	98	64	70	..	92	..	92				
Upper middle income	4.0	5.0	88	96	59	75	..	..	..	..				
Low and middle income	3.5	4.1	78	89	53	63	..	..	..	..				
East Asia & Pacific	2.5	2.9	86	99	59	67	..	93	..	93				
Europe & Central Asia	..	5.1	92	100	84	81	..	..	..	..				
Latin America & Caribbean	3.8	3.6	85	94	55	66	..	..	..	..				
Middle East & North Africa	5.0	5.2	74	87	46	66	88	..	84	..				
South Asia	2.0	3.1	64	77	38	55	..	62	..	55				
Sub-Saharan Africa	3.8	4.1	..	..	..	..	..	..	..	..				
High income	5.6	5.4	97	100	87	96	..	..	..	..				

Note: For data comparability and coverage, see the Technical Notes. Figures in italics are for years other than those specified.
a. UNESCO enrollment estimates and projections as assessed in 1999.

Table 7.   Health

Economy	Public expenditure on health % of GDP 1990–98a	Access to improved water source % of population with access 1982–85a	1990–96a	Access to sanitation % of population with access 1982–85a	1990–96a	Infant mortality rate Per 1,000 live births 1980	1998	Contraceptive prevalence rate % of women ages 15–49 1990–98a	Total fertility rate Births per woman 1980	1998	Maternal mortality ratio Per 100,000 live births 1990–98a
Albania	2.7	92	76	..	58	47	25	..	3.6	2.5	..
Algeria	3.3	..	..	..	..	98	35	51	6.7	3.5	..
Angola	3.9	28	32	18	16	154	124	..	6.9	6.7	..
Argentina	4.0	55	65	69	75	35	19	..	3.3	2.6	38 b
Armenia	3.1	..	..	..	..	26	15	..	2.3	1.3	35 b
Australia	5.5	99	99	99	86	11	5	..	1.9	1.8	..
Austria	6.0	99	..	..	100	14	5	..	1.6	1.3	..
Azerbaijan	1.2	..	..	..	36	30	17	..	3.2	2.0	37 b
Bangladesh	1.6	40	84	4	35	132	73	49	6.1	3.1	440 c
Belarus	4.9	..	..	..	..	16	11	..	2.0	1.3	22 d
Belgium	6.8	98	..	..	100	12	6	..	1.7	1.6	..
Benin	1.6	14	50	10	20	116	87	16	7.0	5.7	500 c
Bolivia	1.1	53	55	36	41	118	60	49	5.5	4.1	390 c
Botswana	2.7	..	70	36	55	71	62	..	6.1	4.2	330 d
Brazil	3.4	75	72	24	67	70	33	77	3.9	2.3	160 c
Bulgaria	3.2	85	..	..	99	20	14	..	2.0	1.1	15 d
Burkina Faso	1.2	35	..	9	18	121	104	12	7.5	6.7	..
Burundi	0.6	23	52	..	51	122	118	..	6.8	6.2	..
Cambodia	0.6	..	13	..	..	201	102	..	4.7	4.5	..
Cameroon	1.0	36	41	36	40	103	77	19	6.4	5.0	430 c
Canada	6.4	100	99	85	95	10	5	..	1.7	1.6	..
Central African Republic	1.9	..	19	19	46	117	98	14	5.8	4.8	1,100 c
Chad	2.4	..	24	14	21	123	99	4	6.9	6.4	830 c
Chile	2.4	86	85	67	..	32	10	..	2.8	2.2	23 b
China	2.0	..	90	..	21	42	31	85	2.5	1.9	65 c
Hong Kong, China	2.1	..	..	..	..	11	3	..	2.0	1.1	..
Colombia	4.9	..	78	68	83	41	23	72	3.9	2.7	80 b
Congo, Dem. Rep.	1.2	..	27	..	9	112	90	..	6.6	6.3	..
Congo, Rep.	1.8	..	47	..	9	89	90	..	6.3	6.0	..
Costa Rica	6.9	..	92	95	97	19	13	..	3.6	2.6	29 c
Côte d'Ivoire	1.4	20	72	17	54	108	88	11	7.4	5.0	600 c
Croatia	8.1	..	63	67	61	21	8	..	..	1.5	12 b
Czech Republic	6.4	100	..	..	..	16	5	69	2.1	1.2	9 d
Denmark	6.7	100	..	..	100	8	5	..	1.5	1.8	10 d
Dominican Republic	1.6	49	71	66	78	76	40	64	4.2	2.9	..
Ecuador	2.5	58	70	57	64	74	32	57	5.0	2.9	160 c
Egypt, Arab Rep.	1.8	90	64	..	11	120	49	48	5.1	3.2	170 c
El Salvador	2.6	51	55	62	68	84	31	60	4.9	3.3	..
Eritrea	2.9	..	7	..	..	..	61	8	..	5.7	1,000 c
Estonia	5.1	..	..	..	..	17	9	..	2.0	1.2	50 d
Ethiopia	1.7	..	27	..	8	155	107	4	6.6	6.4	..
Finland	5.7	95	98	100	100	8	4	..	1.6	1.8	6 d
France	7.1	98	100	..	96	10	5	71	1.9	1.8	10 d
Georgia	0.7	..	..	..	..	25	15	..	2.3	1.3	70 b
Germany	8.3	..	..	..	..	12	5	..	1.4	1.4	8 d
Ghana	1.8	..	56	26	42	94	65	20	6.5	4.8	..
Greece	5.3	85	..	..	96	18	6	..	2.2	1.3	1 d
Guatemala	1.5	58	67	54	67	84	42	32	6.3	4.4	190 c
Guinea	1.2	20	62	12	14	185	118	2	6.1	5.4	..
Haiti	1.3	..	28	19	24	123	71	18	5.9	4.3	..
Honduras	2.7	50	65	32	65	70	36	50	6.5	4.2	220 d
Hungary	4.1	87	..	..	94	23	10	73	1.9	1.3	15 d
India	0.6	54	81	8	16	115	70	41	5.0	3.2	410 c
Indonesia	0.6	39	62	30	51	90	43	57	4.3	2.7	450 c
Iran, Islamic Rep.	1.7	71	83	65	67	87	26	73	6.7	2.7	37 c
Ireland	4.9	97	..	..	100	11	6	60	3.2	1.9	6 d
Israel	7.0	100	99	..	100	16	6	..	3.2	2.7	5 d
Italy	5.3	99	..	..	100	15	5	..	1.6	1.2	7 d
Jamaica	2.3	96	70	91	74	33	21	65	3.7	2.6	..
Japan	5.9	99	96	99	100	8	4	..	1.8	1.4	8 d
Jordan	3.7	89	89	91	95	41	27	50	6.8	4.1	41 b
Kazakhstan	2.1	..	..	..	..	33	22	59	2.9	2.0	70 e
Kenya	2.2	27	53	44	77	75	76	39	7.8	4.6	590 c
Korea, Rep.	2.5	83	83	100	100	26	9	..	2.6	1.6	20 d
Kuwait	2.9	100	100	100	100	27	12	..	5.3	2.8	5 d
Kyrgyz Republic	2.7	..	81	..	..	43	26	60	4.1	2.8	65 b
Lao PDR	1.2	..	39	..	24	127	96	25	6.7	5.5	650 b
Latvia	4.0	..	..	..	..	20	15	..	2.0	1.1	45 d
Lebanon	3.0	92	100	75	100	48	27	..	4.0	2.4	100 c
Lesotho	3.7	18	52	12	8	119	93	23	5.5	4.6	..
Lithuania	7.2	..	..	..	..	20	9	..	2.0	1.4	18 d
Macedonia, FYR	7.8	..	..	..	..	54	16	..	2.5	1.8	11 b
Madagascar	1.1	31	29	..	15	119	92	19	6.6	5.7	490 c
Malawi	2.8	32	45	60	53	169	134	22	7.6	6.4	620 c
Malaysia	1.3	71	89	75	94	30	8	..	4.2	3.1	39 b

PEOPLE

Economy	Public expenditure on health % of GDP 1990–98[a]	Access to improved water source % of population with access 1982–85[a]	1990–96[a]	Access to sanitation % of population with access 1982–85[a]	1990–96[a]	Infant mortality rate Per 1,000 live births 1980	1998	Contraceptive prevalence rate % of women ages 15–49 1990–98[a]	Total fertility rate Births per woman 1980	1998	Maternal mortality ratio Per 100,000 live births 1990–98[a]
Mali	2.0	..	37	21	31	184	117	7	7.1	6.5	580 [c]
Mauritania	1.8	37	64	..	32	120	90	..	6.3	5.4	
Mexico	2.8	82	83	57	66	51	30	65	4.7	2.8	48 [c]
Moldova	4.8	..	56	..	50	35	18	74	2.4	1.7	42 [d]
Mongolia	4.3	..	..	..	..	82	50	..	5.3	2.5	150 [d]
Morocco	1.3	32	52	50	40	99	49	59	5.4	3.0	230 [c]
Mozambique	2.1	9	32	10	21	145	134	6	6.5	5.2	
Myanmar	0.2	27	38	24	41	109	78	..	4.9	3.1	230 [c]
Namibia	3.8	..	57	..	34	90	67	29	5.9	4.8	230 [c]
Nepal	1.3	24	44	1	6	132	77	29	6.1	4.4	540 [c]
Netherlands	6.1	100	100	..	100	9	5	75	1.6	1.6	7 [d]
New Zealand	5.9	100	..	88	..	13	5	..	2.0	1.9	15 [d]
Nicaragua	4.4	50	81	27	31	84	36	60	6.3	3.7	150 [b]
Niger	1.3	37	53	9	15	135	118	8	7.4	7.3	590 [c]
Nigeria	0.2	36	39	..	36	99	76	6	6.9	5.3	
Norway	6.2	99	100	..	100	8	4	..	1.7	1.8	6 [d]
Pakistan	0.9	38	60	16	30	127	91	24	7.0	4.9	
Panama	6.0	82	84	81	90	32	21	..	3.7	2.6	85 [d]
Papua New Guinea	2.6	..	28	..	22	78	59	26	5.8	4.2	
Paraguay	2.6	23	39	49	32	50	24	59	5.2	3.9	190 [c]
Peru	2.2	53	80	48	44	81	40	64	4.5	3.1	270 [c]
Philippines	1.7	65	83	57	77	52	32	47	4.8	3.6	170 [c]
Poland	4.2	82	..	..	100	26	10	..	2.3	1.4	8 [d]
Portugal	4.7	66	82	..	100	24	8	..	2.2	1.5	8 [d]
Romania	2.9	71	62	..	44	29	21	57	2.4	1.3	41 [d]
Russian Federation	4.5	..	..	..	..	22	17	34	1.9	1.2	50 [b]
Rwanda	2.1	..	..	..	..	128	123	21	8.3	6.1	..
Saudi Arabia	6.4	91	93	86	86	65	20	..	7.3	5.7	
Senegal	2.6	44	50	..	58	117	69	13	6.8	5.5	560 [c]
Sierra Leone	1.7	24	34	13	11	190	169	..	6.5	6.0	..
Singapore	1.1	100	100	85	100	12	4	..	1.7	1.5	6 [d]
Slovak Republic	5.2	..	..	46	51	21	9	..	2.3	1.4	9 [d]
Slovenia	6.8	..	98	80	98	15	5	..	2.1	1.2	11 [d]
South Africa	3.2	..	70	..	46	67	51	69	4.6	2.8	
Spain	5.6	99	..	..	100	12	5	..	2.2	1.2	6 [d]
Sri Lanka	1.4	37	46	..	52	34	16	..	3.5	2.1	60 [d]
Sweden	7.2	100	..	..	100	7	4	..	1.7	1.5	5 [d]
Switzerland	7.1	100	100	..	100	9	4	..	1.5	1.5	5 [d]
Syrian Arab Republic	..	71	85	45	56	56	28	40	7.4	3.9	
Tajikistan	6.6	..	69	..	62	58	23	..	5.6	3.4	65 [b]
Tanzania	1.3	52	49	..	86	108	85	18	6.7	5.4	530 [c]
Thailand	1.7	66	89	47	96	49	29	72	3.5	1.9	44 [c]
Togo	1.1	35	63	14	26	100	78	24	6.8	5.1	480 [c]
Tunisia	3.0	89	99	52	96	69	28	60	5.2	2.2	70 [b]
Turkey	2.9	69	..	..	94	109	38	..	4.3	2.4	
Turkmenistan	3.5	..	60	..	60	54	33	..	4.9	2.9	110 [b]
Uganda	1.8	16	34	13	57	116	101	15	7.2	6.5	510 [c]
Ukraine	4.1	..	55	..	49	17	14	..	2.0	1.3	25 [b]
United Kingdom	5.9	100	100	..	100	12	6	..	1.9	1.7	7 [d]
United States	6.5	..	..	98	..	13	7	76	1.8	2.0	8 [b]
Uruguay	1.9	83	89	59	61	37	16	..	2.7	2.4	21 [b]
Uzbekistan	3.3	..	57	..	18	47	22	56	4.8	2.8	21 [b]
Venezuela, RB	3.0	84	79	45	58	36	21	..	4.2	2.9	65 [c]
Vietnam	0.4	..	36	..	21	57	34	75	5.0	2.3	160 [c]
Yemen, Rep.	2.1	..	39	..	19	141	82	21	7.9	6.3	350 [c]
Zambia	2.3	48	43	47	23	90	114	26	7.0	5.5	650 [c]
Zimbabwe	3.1	52	77	26	66	80	73	48	6.4	3.7	400 [d]
World	**2.5 w**	**.. w**	**.. w**	**.. w**	**.. w**	**80 w**	**54 w**	**49 w**	**3.7 w**	**2.7 w**	
Low income	1.3	..	..	..	24	97	68	24	4.3	3.1	
Middle income	3.1	..	..	..	..	60	31	53	3.7	2.5	
Lower middle income	3.0	..	..	..	..	62	35	53	3.7	2.5	
Upper middle income	3.3	77	..	51	..	57	26	65	3.7	2.4	
Low and middle income	1.9	..	..	..	29	87	59	48	4.1	2.9	
East Asia & Pacific	1.7	..	84	..	29	55	35	52	3.0	2.1	
Europe & Central Asia	4.0	..	..	..	..	41	22	67	2.5	1.6	
Latin America & Caribbean	3.3	72	..	46	..	61	31	59	4.1	2.7	
Middle East & North Africa	2.4	68	..	..	..	95	45	55	6.2	3.5	
South Asia	0.8	52	77	7	16	119	75	49	5.3	3.4	
Sub-Saharan Africa	1.5	..	..	..	..	115	92	21	6.6	5.4	
High income	6.2	..	..	..	..	12	6	75	1.8	1.7	

Note: For data comparability and coverage, see the Technical Notes. Figures in italics are for years other than those specified.
a. Data are for most recent year available. b. Official estimate. c. Estimate based on survey data. d. Estimate by the World Health Organization and Eurostat. e. Estimate by UNICEF.

Table 8.   Land use and agricultural productivity

Economy	Land under permanent crops % of land area		Irrigated land % of cropland		Arable land Hectares per capita		Agricultural machinery Tractors per thousand agricultural workers		Agricultural productivity Agr. value added per agricultural worker 1995 dollars		Food production index 1989–91 = 100	
	1980	1997	1979–81	1995–97	1979–81	1995–97	1979–81	1995–97	1979–81	1996–98	1979–81	1996–98
Albania	4.3	4.6	53.0	48.4	0.22	0.18	15	11	1,219	1,841	..	..
Algeria	0.3	0.2	3.4	6.9	0.37	0.26	27	41	1,411	1,943	67.6	129.4
Angola	0.4	0.4	2.2	2.1	0.41	0.27	4	3	..	123	91.9	130.0
Argentina	0.8	0.8	5.8	6.3	0.89	0.71	132	190	7,375	9,597	92.0	125.9
Armenia	..	2.3	..	51.5	..	0.13	..	68	..	4,886	..	76.8
Australia	0.0	0.0	3.5	5.1	2.97	2.75	751	700	20,880	30,904	91.3	130.4
Austria	1.2	1.0	0.2	0.3	0.20	0.17	945	1,567	9,761	16,070	92.2	102.3
Azerbaijan	..	3.0	..	74.9	..	0.21	..	33	..	776	..	60.6
Bangladesh	2.0	2.5	17.1	43.4	0.10	0.06	0	0	212	276	79.2	110.8
Belarus	..	0.7	..	1.8	..	0.60	..	124	..	3,666	..	65.9
Belgium[a]	0.4	0.5	1.7	3.8	0.08	0.07	917	1,156	18,192	34,929	88.5	113.0
Benin	0.8	1.4	0.3	0.8	0.39	0.26	0	0	311	534	63.5	140.6
Bolivia	0.2	0.2	6.6	4.1	0.35	0.23	4	4	..	..	70.9	134.1
Botswana	0.0	0.0	0.5	0.3	0.44	0.23	9	20	630	666	87.2	98.7
Brazil	1.2	1.4	3.3	4.8	0.32	0.33	31	57	2,047	4,081	69.5	125.7
Bulgaria	3.2	1.8	28.3	18.0	0.43	0.51	66	63	2,754	5,135	105.5	67.8
Burkina Faso	0.1	0.2	0.4	0.7	0.39	0.33	0	0	134	161	62.1	127.8
Burundi	10.1	12.9	0.7	1.3	0.22	0.12	0	0	177	141	80.3	95.8
Cambodia	0.4	0.6	5.8	7.1	0.29	0.34	0	0	..	408	48.9	130.6
Cameroon	2.2	2.6	0.2	0.3	0.68	0.44	0	0	866	1,054	83.0	120.2
Canada	0.0	0.0	1.3	1.6	1.86	1.53	824	1,642	..	..	79.8	117.7
Central African Republic	0.1	0.1	..	..	0.81	0.58	0	0	377	440	79.7	127.9
Chad	0.0	0.0	0.2	0.4	0.70	0.47	0	0	155	217	90.8	139.1
Chile	0.3	0.4	31.1	54.3	0.34	0.14	43	49	3,174	5,039	71.5	129.6
China	0.4 [b]	1.2 [b]	45.1	37.7	0.10	0.10	2	1	161	307	60.9	153.5
Hong Kong, China	1.0	1.0	37.5	30.2	0.00	0.00	0	0	..	..	97.4	25.9
Colombia	1.4	2.4	7.7	23.7	0.13	0.05	8	6	3,034	3,448	76.0	109.7
Congo, Dem. Rep.	0.4	0.5	0.1	0.1	0.25	0.15	0	0	270	285	71.7	95.9
Congo, Rep.	0.1	0.1	0.6	0.5	0.08	0.05	2	1	385	492	81.1	112.1
Costa Rica	4.4	5.5	12.1	24.7	0.12	0.07	22	22	3,160	4,409	73.0	128.6
Côte d'Ivoire	7.2	13.8	1.0	1.0	0.24	0.21	1	1	1,074	1,011	70.8	128.5
Croatia	..	2.2	..	0.2	..	0.27	..	14	..	8,521	..	59.4
Czech Republic	..	3.1	..	0.7	..	0.30	..	164	..	4,677	..	79.7
Denmark	0.3	0.2	14.5	20.5	0.52	0.44	973	1,116	21,321	..	83.2	103.0
Dominican Republic	7.2	9.9	11.7	17.2	0.19	0.13	3	4	1,839	2,599	85.2	105.4
Ecuador	3.3	5.2	19.4	8.1	0.20	0.13	6	7	1,206	1,795	77.4	143.6
Egypt, Arab Rep.	0.2	0.5	100.0	99.8	0.06	0.05	4	11	721	1,189	68.0	139.7
El Salvador	11.7	12.1	13.7	14.5	0.12	0.10	5	5	1,925	1,679	90.8	111.3
Eritrea	..	0.0	..	7.0	..	0.11	..	0	..	..	..	114.6
Estonia	..	0.4	..	0.3	..	0.77	..	495	..	3,519	..	47.0
Ethiopia	..	0.6	..	1.8	..	0.17	..	0	..	..	..	123.7
Finland	..	0.0	..	3.0	0.50	0.42	721	1,147	16,995	28,231	93.5	90.7
France	2.5	2.1	4.6	8.5	0.32	0.31	737	1,236	14,956	36,889	93.8	105.4
Georgia	..	4.1	..	43.3	..	0.14	..	29	..	2,120	..	85.2
Germany	1.4	0.7	3.7	3.9	0.15	0.14	624	991	..	22,759	91.2	92.3
Ghana	7.5	7.5	0.2	0.2	0.18	0.16	1	1	670	542	68.7	144.1
Greece	7.9	8.5	24.2	34.5	0.30	0.27	120	277	8,804	..	91.2	99.0
Guatemala	4.4	5.0	5.0	6.6	0.19	0.13	3	2	2,143	2,075	69.7	124.1
Guinea	1.8	2.4	7.9	6.4	0.16	0.13	0	0	..	271	96.3	137.4
Haiti	12.5	12.7	7.9	9.9	0.10	0.08	0	0	578	396	101.3	94.4
Honduras	1.8	3.1	4.1	3.6	0.44	0.29	5	7	694	1,018	88.2	113.0
Hungary	3.3	2.5	3.6	4.2	0.47	0.47	59	156	3,390	4,771	90.8	76.3
India	1.8	2.7	22.8	32.4	0.24	0.17	2	6	275	406	68.1	119.9
Indonesia	4.4	7.2	16.2	15.5	0.12	0.09	0	1	610	749	62.8	120.4
Iran, Islamic Rep.	0.5	1.0	35.5	37.7	0.36	0.29	17	40	2,570	4,089	61.1	144.7
Ireland	0.0	0.0	..	..	0.33	0.37	606	978	..	..	83.3	106.2
Israel	4.3	4.2	49.3	45.5	0.08	0.06	294	322	..	..	85.4	107.0
Italy	10.0	9.0	19.3	24.9	0.17	0.14	370	913	9,993	20,031	101.4	101.2
Jamaica	9.7	9.2	13.4	12.0	0.06	0.07	9	11	894	1,291	86.0	120.1
Japan	1.6	1.0	62.6	62.8	0.04	0.03	209	637	15,698	31,094	94.0	95.2
Jordan	0.4	1.5	11.0	19.5	0.14	0.06	48	34	1,176	1,431	57.3	152.5
Kazakhstan	..	0.1	..	7.2	..	1.95	..	91	..	1,450	..	57.2
Kenya	0.8	0.9	0.9	1.5	0.23	0.14	1	1	262	228	67.7	104.9
Korea, Rep.	1.4	2.0	59.6	60.6	0.05	0.04	1	41	3,800	11,657	77.6	122.2
Kuwait	..	0.1	..	75.4	0.00	0.00	3	14	..	..	93.2	161.2
Kyrgyz Republic	..	0.4	..	77.3	..	0.29	..	39	..	..	..	102.0
Lao PDR	0.1	0.2	15.4	18.6	0.21	0.17	0	0	..	548	70.8	126.7
Latvia	..	0.5	..	1.1	..	0.70	..	312	..	2,505	..	48.1
Lebanon	8.9	12.5	28.3	36.0	0.07	0.04	28	100	..	27,409	59.2	138.2
Lesotho	..	..	..	..	0.22	0.16	6	6	723	533	90.0	111.1
Lithuania	..	0.9	..	0.3	..	0.79	..	263	..	3,245	..	69.2
Macedonia, FYR	..	1.9	..	8.7	..	0.31	..	381	..	2,215	..	97.0
Madagascar	0.9	0.9	21.5	35.0	0.28	0.19	1	1	197	186	84.4	108.7
Malawi	0.9	1.3	1.3	1.6	0.20	0.16	0	0	102	138	91.1	109.7
Malaysia	11.6	17.6	6.7	4.5	0.07	0.09	4	23	3,275	6,061	55.4	125.2

ENVIRONMENT

Economy	Land under permanent crops % of land area		Irrigated land % of cropland		Arable land Hectares per capita		Agricultural machinery Tractors per thousand agricultural workers		Agricultural productivity Agr. value added per agricultural worker 1995 dollars		Food production index 1989–91 = 100	
	1980	1997	1979–81	1995–97	1979–81	1995–97	1979–81	1995–97	1979–81	1996–98	1979–81	1996–98
Mali	0.0	0.0	2.9	2.1	0.31	0.42	0	1	241	271	77.9	114.5
Mauritania	0.0	0.0	22.8	9.7	0.14	0.21	1	1	285	433	86.5	104.7
Mexico	0.8	1.1	20.3	22.8	0.34	0.27	16	20	1,882	2,164	83.8	120.2
Moldova	..	12.1	..	14.1	..	0.41	..	85	..	1,474	..	53.2
Mongolia	..	0.0	..	6.4	0.71	0.53	32	21	932	1,151	88.1	88.5
Morocco	1.1	1.9	15.2	13.1	0.38	0.33	7	10	1,146	1,836	55.9	107.2
Mozambique	0.3	0.3	2.1	3.4	0.24	0.18	1	1	..	127	100.1	130.9
Myanmar	0.7	0.9	10.4	15.4	0.28	0.22	1	0	..	..	87.7	138.1
Namibia	0.0	0.0	0.6	0.9	0.64	0.52	10	11	862	1,233	107.4	123.5
Nepal	0.2	0.5	22.5	38.2	0.16	0.13	0	0	162	189	65.9	117.2
Netherlands	0.9	1.0	58.5	61.0	0.06	0.06	561	631	21,663	..	86.5	99.0
New Zealand	3.7	6.4	5.2	8.7	0.80	0.42	619	437	..	..	90.7	124.6
Nicaragua	1.5	2.4	6.0	3.2	0.39	0.54	6	7	1,620	1,821	117.0	122.7
Niger	0.0	0.0	0.7	1.3	0.62	0.53	0	0	222	195	101.4	127.8
Nigeria	2.8	2.8	0.7	0.7	0.39	0.25	1	2	414	624	57.9	142.5
Norway	..	..	..	..	0.20	0.22	824	1,276	17,044	32,600	92.1	100.9
Pakistan	0.4	0.7	72.7	80.8	0.24	0.17	5	13	394	626	66.4	136.2
Panama	1.6	2.1	5.0	4.9	0.22	0.19	27	20	2,122	2,512	85.6	99.6
Papua New Guinea	1.1	1.3	..	..	0.01	0.01	1	1	716	798	86.2	107.8
Paraguay	0.3	0.2	3.4	2.9	0.52	0.44	14	25	2,618	3,448	60.6	120.0
Peru	0.3	0.4	32.8	42.0	0.19	0.15	5	3	1,348	1,663	77.3	140.5
Philippines	14.8	14.8	14.0	16.3	0.09	0.07	1	1	1,347	1,352	86.0	125.8
Poland	1.1	1.2	0.7	0.7	0.41	0.37	112	281	..	1,751	87.9	88.2
Portugal	7.8	8.2	20.1	21.8	0.25	0.22	72	208	..	..	71.9	97.0
Romania	2.9	2.6	21.9	31.3	0.44	0.41	39	84	..	3,101	112.8	95.9
Russian Federation	..	0.1	..	4.0	..	0.86	..	106	..	2,476	..	64.4
Rwanda	10.3	12.2	0.4	0.3	0.15	0.12	0	0	371	249	89.7	79.1
Saudi Arabia	0.0	0.1	28.9	42.3	0.20	0.19	2	12	2,167	10,742	26.7	78.8
Senegal	0.0	0.2	2.6	3.1	0.42	0.26	0	0	341	320	74.2	100.4
Sierra Leone	0.7	0.8	4.1	5.3	0.14	0.11	0	0	368	411	84.5	99.5
Singapore	9.8	..	..	..	0.00	0.00	3	18	13,937	41,673	154.3	31.8
Slovak Republic	..	2.6	..	12.5	..	0.28	..	92	..	3,378	..	74.7
Slovenia	..	2.7	..	0.7	..	0.12	..	3,082	..	26,517	..	100.3
South Africa	0.7	0.8	8.4	7.9	0.45	0.38	94	68	2,899	3,958	92.6	100.8
Spain	9.9	9.7	14.8	18.1	0.42	0.38	200	546	..	13,499	82.1	110.1
Sri Lanka	15.9	15.8	28.3	30.7	0.06	0.05	4	2	649	726	98.3	109.1
Sweden	..	..	..	..	0.36	0.32	715	958	..	..	100.1	100.8
Switzerland	0.5	0.6	6.2	5.8	0.06	0.06	494	627	..	..	95.8	95.8
Syrian Arab Republic	2.5	4.1	9.6	20.5	0.60	0.33	29	66	1,743	..	94.2	148.7
Tajikistan	..	0.9	..	79.7	..	0.13	..	38	..	396	..	59.0
Tanzania	1.0	1.0	3.8	3.8	0.12	0.10	1	1	..	174	76.9	100.0
Thailand	3.5	6.6	16.4	23.9	0.35	0.28	1	7	634	932	80.4	112.6
Togo	6.6	6.6	0.3	0.3	0.76	0.49	0	0	345	539	77.0	135.9
Tunisia	9.7	12.9	4.9	7.6	0.51	0.32	30	39	1,743	2,959	67.6	121.4
Turkey	4.1	3.4	9.6	14.7	0.57	0.42	38	58	1,860	1,858	75.8	111.3
Turkmenistan	..	0.1	..	..	..	0.35	..	82	..	..	..	101.7
Uganda	8.0	8.8	0.1	0.1	0.32	0.26	0	1	..	345	70.4	107.1
Ukraine	..	1.7	..	7.4	..	0.65	..	89	..	1,454	..	52.3
United Kingdom	0.3	0.2	2.0	1.7	0.12	0.10	726	883	..	..	92.0	99.7
United States	0.2	0.2	10.8	12.0	0.83	0.67	1,230	1,484	..	39,001	94.5	117.9
Uruguay	0.3	0.3	5.4	10.7	0.48	0.39	171	173	6,821	9,826	86.9	130.8
Uzbekistan	..	0.9	..	88.3	..	0.19	..	59	..	2,113	..	109.8
Venezuela, RB	0.9	1.0	3.6	5.7	0.19	0.12	50	59	4,041	5,036	80.3	114.4
Vietnam	1.9	4.7	24.1	31.0	0.11	0.08	1	4	..	230	63.8	140.5
Yemen, Rep.	0.2	0.2	19.9	31.3	0.16	0.09	3	2	..	338	75.0	120.7
Zambia	0.0	0.0	0.4	0.9	0.89	0.57	3	2	328	209	74.0	104.5
Zimbabwe	0.3	0.3	3.1	4.7	0.36	0.27	7	7	307	347	81.9	101.9
World	**0.9 w**	**1.0 w**	**17.8 w**	**19.2 w**	**0.24 w**	**0.24 w**	**18 w**	**20 w**	**.. w**	**.. w**	**75.7 w**	**130.3 w**
Low income	1.0	1.4	19.9	25.5	0.22	0.19	..	..	..	..	71.3	124.3
Middle income	1.0	1.0	23.9	19.4	0.18	0.23	..	..	..	..	71.8	143.8
Lower middle income	1.1	0.9	32.1	22.3	0.14	0.21	..	..	..	..	69.8	151.1
Upper middle income	1.0	1.2	10.1	11.4	0.32	0.29	..	..	..	..	79.1	118.5
Low and middle income	1.0	1.2	21.9	21.9	0.20	0.21	4	8	..	568	71.6	134.7
East Asia & Pacific	1.5	2.6	37.0	36.3	0.11	0.11	2	2	..	..	67.0	152.1
Europe & Central Asia	3.2	0.4	11.6	10.4	0.14	0.60	..	101	..	2,186	..	..
Latin America & Caribbean	1.1	1.3	11.6	13.5	0.32	0.28	25	35	..	..	80.4	123.9
Middle East & North Africa	0.4	0.7	25.8	35.5	0.29	0.21	12	25	..	..	70.1	138.0
South Asia	1.5	2.1	28.7	39.7	0.23	0.16	2	5	265	356	70.4	122.1
Sub-Saharan Africa	0.7	0.9	4.0	4.2	0.32	0.25	3	2	418	379	78.8	124.3
High income	0.5	0.5	9.8	11.2	0.46	0.41	520	906	..	..	93.1	107.5

Note: For data comparability and coverage, see the Technical Notes. Figures in italics are for years other than those specified.
a. Includes Luxembourg. b. Includes Taiwan, China.

Table 9. Water use, deforestation, and protected areas

Economy	Freshwater resources Cu. meters per capita 1998	Annual freshwater withdrawals Billion cu. m[a]	% of total resources[a]	% for agriculture[b]	% for industry[b]	% for domestic use[b]	Access to improved water source % of pop. with access 1996[c] Urban	Rural	Annual deforestation 1990–95 Square kilometers	Avg. annual % change	Nationally protected areas 1996 Thousand square km	% of total land area
Albania	12,758 d	1.4	3.3 d	71	0	29	97	70	0	0.0	0.8	2.9
Algeria	485 d	4.5	31.5 d	60 e	15 e	25 e	..	..	234	1.2	58.9	2.5
Angola	15,783	0.5	0.3	76 e	10 e	14 e	69	15	2,370	1.0	81.8	6.6
Argentina	27,865 d	28.6	2.8 d	75	9	16	71	24	894	0.3	46.6	1.7
Armenia	2,767 d	2.9	27.9 d	66	4	30	..	..	−84	−2.7	2.1	7.4
Australia	18,772	15.1	4.3	33	2	65	..	..	−170	0.0	563.9	7.3
Austria	10,399 d	2.2	2.7 d	9	60	31	..	..	0	0.0	23.4	28.3
Azerbaijan	3,831 d	16.5	54.6 d	70	25	5	..	..	0	0.0	4.8	5.5
Bangladesh	9,636 d	14.6	1.2 d	86	2	12	47	85	88	0.8	1.0	0.8
Belarus	5,665 d	2.7	4.7 d	35	43	22	..	..	−688	−1.0	8.6	4.1
Belgium	1,228 d	9.0	72.2 d	4	85	11	..	..	..	..	0.8	..
Benin	4,337 d	0.2	0.6 d	67 e	10 e	23 e	41	53	596	1.2	7.8	7.1
Bolivia	38,625	1.4	0.4	48	20	32	..	..	5,814	1.2	156.0	14.4
Botswana	9,413 d	0.1	0.7 d	48 e	20 e	32 e	100	53	708	0.5	105.0	18.5
Brazil	42,459 d	54.9	0.5 d	61	18	21	..	..	25,544	0.5	355.5	4.2
Bulgaria	24,663 d	13.9	6.8 d	22	76	3	..	..	−6	0.0	4.9	4.4
Burkina Faso	1,671	0.4	2.2	81 e	0 e	19 e	..	..	320	0.7	28.6	10.5
Burundi	561	0.1	2.8	64 e	0 e	36 e	..	..	14	0.4	1.4	5.5
Cambodia	41,407	0.5	0.1	94	1	5	20	12	1,638	1.6	28.6	16.2
Cameroon	18,737	0.4	0.1	35 e	19 e	46 e	71	24	1,292	0.6	21.0	4.5
Canada	92,142	45.1	1.6	9	80	11	..	..	−1,764	−0.1	921.0	10.0
Central African Republic	41,250	0.1	0.0	73 e	6 e	21 e	..	..	1,282	0.4	51.1	8.2
Chad	5,904 d	0.2	0.4 d	82 e	2 e	16 e	48	17	942	0.8	114.9	9.1
Chile	32,007	21.4	3.6	84	11	5	..	..	292	0.4	141.3	18.9
China	2,285	525.5	18.6	77	18	5	93	89	866	0.1	598.1	6.4
Hong Kong, China	..	..	..	..	..	..	..	..	..	..	0.4	40.4
Colombia	26,722	8.9	0.5	37	4	59	88	48	2,622	0.5	93.6	9.0
Congo, Dem. Rep.	21,134	0.4	0.0	23 e	16 e	61 e	..	..	..	..	101.9	4.5
Congo, Rep.	298,963 d	0.0	0.0 d	11 e	27 e	62 e	50	8	416	0.2	15.4	4.5
Costa Rica	27,425	5.8	1.4	80	7	13	..	..	414	3.0	7.0	13.7
Côte d'Ivoire	5,362	0.7	0.9	67 e	11 e	22 e	59	81	308	0.6	19.9	6.3
Croatia	15,863	0.1	0.1	..	50	50	75	41	0	0.0	3.7	6.6
Czech Republic	1,554	2.5	15.8	2	57	41	..	..	−2	0.0	12.2	15.8
Denmark	2,460 d	0.9	9.2 d	43	27	30	..	..	0	0.0	13.7	32.3
Dominican Republic	2,467	8.3	14.9	89	1	11	74	67	264	1.6	12.2	25.2
Ecuador	26,305	17.0	1.8	82	6	12	82	55	1,890	1.6	119.3	43.1
Egypt, Arab Rep.	949 d	55.1	94.5 d	86 e	8 e	6 e	82	50	0	0.0	7.9	0.8
El Salvador	3,197	0.7	5.3	46	20	34	78	37	38	3.3	0.1	0.5
Eritrea	2,269	..	..	..	..	..	..	..	0	0.0	5.0	5.0
Estonia	8,829	0.2	1.3 d	5	39	56	..	..	−196	−1.0	5.1	12.1
Ethiopia	1,795	2.2	2.0	86 e	3 e	11 e	90	20	624	0.5	55.2	5.5
Finland	21,347	2.4	2.2 d	3	85	12	100	85	166	0.1	18.2	6.0
France	3,246 d	40.6	21.3 d	12	73	15	100	100	−1,608	−1.1	58.8	10.7
Georgia	11,632 d	3.5	5.5 d	59	20	21	..	..	0	0.0	1.9	2.7
Germany	2,169 d	46.3	26.0 d	0	86	14	..	..	0	0.0	94.2	27.0
Ghana	2,882 d	0.3 f	0.6 d	52 e	13 e	35 e	70	49	1,172	1.3	11.0	4.8
Greece	6,562 d	7.0	10.2 d	81	3	16	..	..	−1,408	−2.3	3.1	2.4
Guatemala	11,030	1.2	0.6	74	17	9	97	48	824	2.0	18.2	16.8
Guinea	31,910	0.7	0.3	87 e	3 e	10 e	61	62	748	1.1	1.6	0.7
Haiti	1,468	1.0	0.4	94	1	5	37	23	8	3.4	0.1	0.4
Honduras	9,258	1.5	2.7	91	5	4	81	53	1,022	2.3	11.1	9.9
Hungary	11,865 d	6.3	5.2 d	36	55	9	..	..	−88	−0.5	6.3	6.8
India	1,947 d	500.0	26.2 d	92	3	5	85	79	−72	0.0	142.9	4.8
Indonesia	12,625	74.3	0.7	93	1	6	78	54	10,844	1.0	192.3	10.6
Iran, Islamic Rep.	1,339	70.0	85.8	92	2	6	..	..	284	1.7	83.0	5.1
Ireland	14,035 d	1.2	2.3 d	10	74	16	..	..	−140	−2.7	0.6	0.9
Israel	184 d	1.7	155.5 d	64 e	7 e	29 e	100	95	0	0.0	3.1	15.0
Italy	2,909 d	57.5	34.4 d	45	37	18	..	..	−58	−0.1	21.5	7.3
Jamaica	3,250	0.9	3.9	77	7	15	92	48	158	7.2	0.0	0.0
Japan	3,402	91.4	21.3	64	17	19	..	..	132	0.1	25.5	6.8
Jordan	198 d	1.0	51.1 d	75	3	22	..	..	12	2.5	3.0	3.4
Kazakhstan	7,029 d	33.7	30.7 d	81	17	2	..	..	−1,928	−1.9	73.4	2.7
Kenya	1,031 d	2.1	6.8 d	76 e	4 e	20 e	67	49	34	0.3	35.0	6.1
Korea, Rep.	1,501	23.7	34.0	63	11	26	93	77	130	0.2	6.8	6.9
Kuwait	0	0.5	2,700.0	60	2	37	100	100	0	0.0	0.3	1.7
Kyrgyz Republic	10,049	10.1	94.9	94	3	3	93	42	0	0.0	6.9	3.6
Lao PDR	56,638	1.0	0.4	82	10	8	40	39	..	..	0.0	0.0
Latvia	14,455 d	0.3	0.8 d	13	32	55	92	..	−250	−0.9	7.8	12.6
Lebanon	1,140	1.3	26.9	68	4	28	100	100	52	7.8	0.0	0.0
Lesotho	2,527	0.1	1.0	56 e	22 e	22 e	14	64	0	0.0	0.1	0.3
Lithuania	6,724 d	0.3	1.0 d	3	16	81	..	..	−112	−0.6	6.5	10.0
Macedonia, FYR	3,483	..	..	..	..	..	..	..	2	0.0	1.8	7.1
Madagascar	23,094	19.7	5.8	99 e	0 e	1 e	83	10	1,300	0.8	11.2	1.9
Malawi	1,775 d	0.9	5.0 d	86 e	3 e	10 e	52	44	546	1.6	10.6	11.3
Malaysia	21,046	12.7	2.1	76	13	11	100	86	4,002	2.4	14.8	4.5

ENVIRONMENT

Economy	Freshwater resources Cu. meters per capita 1998	Annual freshwater withdrawals Billion cu. m[a]	% of total resources[a]	% for agriculture[b]	% for industry[b]	% for domestic use[b]	Access to improved water source % of pop. with access 1996[c] Urban	Rural	Annual deforestation 1990–95 Square kilometers	Avg. annual % change	Nationally protected areas 1996 Thousand square km	% of total land area
Mali	9,438	1.4	1.4	97 e	1 e	2 e	*36*	*38*	1,138	1.0	45.3	3.7
Mauritania	4,508 d	16.3	143.0 d	92	2	6	87	41	0	0.0	17.5	1.7
Mexico	4,779	77.8	17.0	78	5	17	91	62	5,080	0.9	71.0	3.7
Moldova	2,722	3.0	25.3 d	26	65	9	98	18	0	0.0	0.4	1.2
Mongolia	9,677	0.4	2.2	53	27	20	..	..	0	0.0	161.3	10.3
Morocco	1,080	11.1	36.8	92 e	3 e	5 e	*98*	*14*	118	0.3	3.2	0.7
Mozambique	12,746 d	0.6	0.3 d	89	2 e	9 e	*17*	*40*	1,162	0.7	47.8	6.1
Myanmar	23,515	4.0	0.4	90	3	7	*36*	*39*	3,874	1.4	1.7	0.3
Namibia	27,373 d	0.3	0.5 d	68 e	3 e	29 e	..	..	420	0.3	106.2	12.9
Nepal	9,199	29.0	13.8	99	0	1	..	..	548	1.1	11.1	7.8
Netherlands	5,797 d	7.8	8.6	34	61	5	*100*	*100*	0	0.0	2.4	7.1
New Zealand	86,053	2.0	100.0	44	10	46	..	..	−434	−0.6	63.3	23.6
Nicaragua	37,467	1.3	0.5	84	2	14	*81*	*27*	1,508	2.5	9.0	7.4
Niger	3,204 d	0.5	1.5 d	82 e	2 e	16 e	*46*	*55*	0	0.0	96.9	7.6
Nigeria	2,318 d	4.0	1.4 d	54 e	15 e	31 e	*63*	*26*	1,214	0.9	30.2	3.3
Norway	88,673 d	2.0	0.5 d	8	72	20	100	100	−180	−0.2	93.7	30.5
Pakistan	1,938 d	155.6	61.0 d	97	2	2	*77*	*52*	550	2.9	37.2	4.8
Panama	52,961	1.6	0.9	70	2	28	99	73	636	2.1	14.2	19.1
Papua New Guinea	177,940	0.1	0.0	49	22	29	*84*	*17*	1,332	0.4	0.1	0.0
Paraguay	61,750	0.4	0.1 d	78	7	15	70	6	3,266	2.6	14.0	3.5
Peru	1,641	19.0	15.3	86	7	7	..	..	2,168	0.3	34.6	2.7
Philippines	4,393	55.4	9.1	88	4	8	91	81	2,624	3.5	14.5	4.9
Poland	1,629 d	12.1	19.2 d	11	76	13	..	..	−120	−0.1	29.1	9.6
Portugal	7,223 d	7.3	10.1 d	48	37	15	..	..	−240	−0.9	5.9	6.4
Romania	9,222 d	26.0	12.5 d	59	33	8	*69*	*10*	12	0.0	10.7	4.6
Russian Federation	30,619 d	77.1	1.7 d	20	62	19	..	..	0	0.0	516.7	3.1
Rwanda	798	0.8	12.2	94 e	1 e	5 e	..	44	4	0.2	3.6	14.6
Saudi Arabia	116	17.0	708.3	90	1	9	..	..	18	0.8	49.6	2.3
Senegal	4,359 d	1.5	3.8 d	92 e	3 e	5 e	*82*	*28*	496	0.7	21.8	11.3
Sierra Leone	32,957	0.4	0.2	89 e	4 e	7 e	*58*	*21*	426	3.0	0.8	1.1
Singapore	193	*0.2*	31.7	4	51	45	100	..	0	0.0	0.0	0.0
Slovak Republic	15,396	1.4	1.7	..	..	..	..	..	−24	−0.1	10.5	21.8
Slovenia	9,334	0.5	2.7	..	50	50	*100*	*97*	0	0.0	1.1	5.5
South Africa	1,208 d	13.3	26.6 d	72 e	11 e	17 e	..	..	150	0.2	65.8	5.4
Spain	2,847 d	35.5	31.7 d	62	26	12	..	..	0	0.0	42.2	8.4
Sri Lanka	2,329	9.8	14.6	96	2	2	..	..	202	1.1	8.6	13.3
Sweden	20,109 d	2.7	1.5 d	9	55	36	..	..	24	0.0	36.2	8.8
Switzerland	7,458 d	2.6	4.9 d	0	58	42	*100*	*100*	0	0.0	7.1	18.0
Syrian Arab Republic	2,926	14.4	32.2	94	2	4	*92*	*78*	52	2.2	0.0	0.0
Tajikistan	13,017	11.9	14.9	92	4	4	*86*	*32*	0	0.0	5.9	4.2
Tanzania	2,770 d	1.2	1.3 d	89 e	2 e	9 e	*65*	*45*	3,226	1.0	138.2	15.6
Thailand	6,698 d	33.1	8.1 d	91	4	5	94	88	3,294	2.6	70.7	13.8
Togo	2,692 d	0.1	0.8 d	25 e	13 e	62 e	..	..	186	1.4	4.3	7.9
Tunisia	439 d	2.8	69.0 d	86 e	2 e	13 e	..	..	30	0.5	0.4	0.3
Turkey	3,213 d	35.5	17.4 d	73 e	11 e	16 e	..	..	0	0.0	10.7	1.4
Turkmenistan	9,644 d	23.8	52.3 d	98	1	1	*80*	*5*	0	0.0	19.8	4.2
Uganda	3,158 d	0.2	0.3 d	60	8	32	*47*	*32*	592	0.9	19.1	9.6
Ukraine	2,776 d	26.0 f	18.6 d	30	52	18	*77*	*12*	−54	−0.1	9.0	1.6
United Kingdom	2,489	9.3	6.4	3	77	20	*100*	*100*	−128	−0.5	50.6	20.9
United States	9,168 d	447.7	18.1 d	27 e	65 e	8 e	..	..	−5,886	−0.3	1,226.7	13.4
Uruguay	37,971 d	4.2	0.5 d	91	3	6	99	..	4	0.0	0.5	0.3
Uzbekistan	5,476 d	58.1	63.4 d	94	2	4	*72*	*46*	−2,260	−2.7	8.2	2.0
Venezuela, RB	57,821 d	4.1	0.3 d	46	10	44	..	..	5,034	1.1	319.8	36.3
Vietnam	11,647	54.3	6.1	86	10	4	*53*	*32*	1,352	1.4	9.9	3.0
Yemen, Rep.	254	2.9	71.5	92	1	7	74	14	0	0.0	0.0	0.0
Zambia	12,001 d	1.7	1.5 d	77 e	7 e	16 e	*64*	*27*	2,644	0.8	63.6	8.6
Zimbabwe	1,711 d	1.2	6.1 d	79 e	7 e	14 e	*99*	*64*	500	0.6	30.7	7.9
World	**8,354 w**	..	..	**70 w**	**22 w**	**8 w**	**.. w**	**.. w**	**101,724 s**	**0.3 w**	**8,543.5 s**	**6.6 w**
Low income	5,538	..	..	87	8	5	..	..	45,130	0.7	1,852.4	5.6
Middle income	9,333	..	..	74	13	12	..	..	68,288	0.3	3,396.9	5.1
Lower middle income	6,227	..	..	75	15	10	*90*	*84*	25,214	0.2	2,095.5	4.8
Upper middle income	..	..	..	73	10	17	..	..	43,074	0.5	1,301.4	5.9
Low and middle income	8,114	..	..	82	10	7	..	..	113,418	0.4	5,249.3	5.3
East Asia & Pacific	..	..	..	80	14	6	*89*	*82*	29,956	0.8	1,102.2	6.9
Europe & Central Asia	14,341	..	..	63	26	11	..	..	−5,798	−0.1	768.0	3.2
Latin America & Caribbean	27,393	..	..	74	9	18	..	..	57,766	0.6	1,456.3	7.3
Middle East & North Africa	1,045	..	..	89	4	6	..	..	800	0.9	242.1	2.2
South Asia	4,088	..	..	93	2	4	*83*	*75*	1,316	0.2	213.0	4.5
Sub-Saharan Africa	8,441	..	..	87	4	9	..	..	29,378	0.7	1,467.7	6.2
High income	..	..	..	30	59	11	..	..	−11,694	−0.2	3,294.2	10.8

Note: For data comparability and coverage, see the Technical Notes. Figures in italics are for years other than those specified.
a. Refers to any year from 1980 to 1998, unless otherwise noted. b. Unless otherwise noted, percentages are estimated for 1987. c. Data refer to the most recent year available in 1990–96. d. Total water resources include river flows from other countries. e. Data refer to a year other than 1987 (see the primary data documentation table in *World Development Indicators 2000*). f. Data refer to a year before 1980 (see the primary data documentation table in *World Development Indicators 2000*).

Table 10. Energy use and emissions

	Commercial energy use					GDP per unit of energy use		Net energy imports[a]		Carbon dioxide emissions			
	Thousand metric tons of oil equivalent		Per capita			PPP$ per kg of oil equivalent		% of commercial energy use		Total Million metric tons		Per capita Metric tons	
			Kg of oil equivalent		Avg. annual % growth								
Economy	1990	1997	1990	1997	1990-97	1990	1997	1990	1997	1990	1996	1990	1996
Albania	2,567	1,048	782	317	-10.4	3.4	8.5	8	13	8.4	1.9	2.6	0.6
Algeria	23,959	26,497	958	912	-1.8	4.7	5.3	-332	-374	80.4	94.3	3.2	3.3
Angola	5,617	6,848	609	587	-0.7	3.1	2.6	-414	-505	4.6	5.1	0.5	0.5
Argentina	43,313	61,710	1,332	1,730	3.7	5.6	6.9	-9	-30	109.7	129.9	3.4	3.7
Armenia	7,941	1,804	2,240	476	-23.2	1.5	4.3	98	70	*3.7*	3.7	*1.0*	1.0
Australia	87,155	101,626	5,107	5,484	1.3	3.2	4.0	-80	-96	266.0	306.6	15.6	16.7
Austria	25,699	27,761	3,326	3,439	0.2	5.5	6.7	67	71	57.4	59.3	7.4	7.4
Azerbaijan	22,841	11,987	3,191	1,529	-10.7	1.5	1.3	11	-17	*47.1*	30.0	*6.4*	3.9
Bangladesh	20,936	24,327	190	197	1.0	5.0	6.8	10	10	15.4	23.0	0.1	0.2
Belarus	43,050	25,142	4,196	2,449	-9.3	1.6	2.4	91	87	*94.3*	61.7	*9.1*	6.0
Belgium	48,426	57,125	4,858	5,611	1.7	3.8	4.1	74	77	97.4	106.0	9.8	10.4
Benin	1,678	2,182	354	377	1.0	1.9	2.3	-6	13	0.6	0.7	0.1	0.1
Bolivia	2,896	4,254	441	548	2.5	4.0	4.1	-69	-40	5.5	10.1	0.8	1.3
Botswana	..	..	..	..	..	..	..	..	..	2.2	2.1	1.7	1.4
Brazil	136,131	172,030	920	1,051	2.0	5.8	6.5	27	30	202.6	273.4	1.4	1.7
Bulgaria	27,126	20,616	3,111	2,480	-1.2	1.7	1.9	64	52	75.3	55.3	8.6	6.6
Burkina Faso	..	..	..	..	..	..	..	..	..	1.0	1.0	0.1	0.1
Burundi	..	..	..	..	..	..	..	..	..	0.2	0.2	0.0	0.0
Cambodia	..	..	..	..	..	..	..	..	..	0.5	0.5	0.0	0.0
Cameroon	5,058	5,756	441	413	-0.8	3.5	3.6	-149	-95	1.5	3.5	0.1	0.3
Canada	209,712	237,983	7,546	7,930	1.0	2.6	3.0	-31	-52	409.6	409.4	14.7	13.8
Central African Republic	..	..	..	..	..	..	..	..	..	0.2	0.2	0.1	0.1
Chad	..	..	..	..	..	..	..	..	..	0.1	0.1	0.0	0.0
Chile	13,876	23,012	1,059	1,574	5.7	4.5	5.7	46	65	36.3	48.8	2.8	3.4
China	866,666	1,113,050	763	907	2.9	1.8	3.3	-3	1	2,401.7	3,363.5	2.1	2.8
Hong Kong, China	10,455	14,121	1,833	2,172	2.2	8.7	10.6	100	100	26.2	23.1	4.6	3.7
Colombia	26,762	30,481	765	761	0.7	7.4	8.2	-80	-122	55.9	65.3	1.6	1.7
Congo, Dem. Rep.	11,858	14,539	317	311	-0.2	4.5	2.7	-1	1	4.1	2.3	0.1	0.1
Congo, Rep.	1,117	1,242	503	459	-1.5	2.0	2.2	-706	-990	2.0	5.0	0.9	1.9
Costa Rica	2,025	2,663	676	769	2.0	6.8	7.7	49	57	2.9	4.7	1.0	1.4
Côte d'Ivoire	4,596	5,597	395	394	-0.2	3.5	4.0	26	12	9.9	13.1	0.9	0.9
Croatia	..	7,650	..	1,687	9.6	..	4.0	..	48	..	17.5	..	3.9
Czech Republic	45,020	40,576	4,344	3,938	-0.1	2.8	3.3	13	22	*141.7*	126.7	*13.7*	12.3
Denmark	18,282	21,107	3,557	3,994	1.8	5.0	6.0	45	4	50.7	56.6	9.9	10.7
Dominican Republic	3,973	5,453	559	673	2.5	5.6	6.6	74	74	9.4	12.9	1.3	1.6
Ecuador	6,558	8,513	639	713	1.9	4.1	4.6	-150	-168	16.6	24.5	1.6	2.1
Egypt, Arab Rep.	31,895	39,581	608	656	0.8	3.9	4.7	-72	-47	75.4	97.9	1.4	1.7
El Salvador	2,695	4,095	527	691	3.9	5.5	5.9	30	35	2.6	4.0	0.5	0.7
Eritrea	..	..	..	..	..	..	..	..	..	..	..	..	..
Estonia	10,163	5,556	6,469	3,811	-7.4	1.2	2.0	47	32	*21.4*	16.4	*13.8*	11.2
Ethiopia	15,208	17,131	297	287	-0.3	1.6	2.1	7	5	3.0	3.4	0.1	0.1
Finland	28,813	33,075	5,779	6,435	1.5	3.0	3.2	59	54	51.1	59.2	10.2	11.5
France	227,600	247,534	4,012	4,224	0.6	4.3	5.0	51	48	353.2	361.8	6.2	6.2
Georgia	10,590	2,295	1,940	423	-24.2	4.3	7.9	87	70	15.2	3.0	2.8	0.5
Germany	355,732	347,272	4,478	4,231	-0.6	*4.3*	5.2	48	60	*889.2*	861.2	*11.1*	10.5
Ghana	5,233	6,896	352	383	1.7	4.0	4.5	16	15	3.5	4.0	0.2	0.2
Greece	22,056	25,556	2,171	2,435	1.6	5.1	5.7	60	62	72.2	80.6	7.1	7.7
Guatemala	4,377	5,633	500	536	0.9	5.5	6.5	24	21	5.1	6.8	0.6	0.7
Guinea	..	..	..	..	..	..	..	..	..	1.0	1.1	0.2	0.2
Haiti	1,585	1,779	245	237	0.2	6.5	5.9	21	27	1.0	1.1	0.2	0.1
Honduras	2,442	3,182	501	532	0.8	4.1	4.7	31	37	2.6	4.0	0.5	0.7
Hungary	28,463	25,311	2,746	2,492	-1.0	3.3	4.0	50	50	64.1	59.5	6.2	5.8
India	359,846	461,032	424	479	1.9	3.3	4.2	7	12	675.3	997.4	0.8	1.1
Indonesia	98,846	138,779	555	693	3.1	3.4	4.5	-69	-60	165.2	245.1	0.9	1.2
Iran, Islamic Rep.	72,342	108,289	1,330	1,777	3.7	2.9	3.0	-151	-108	212.4	266.7	3.9	4.4
Ireland	10,463	12,491	2,984	3,412	2.0	3.8	6.0	68	77	29.8	34.9	8.5	9.6
Israel	11,923	17,591	2,559	3,014	2.9	5.1	5.8	96	97	34.6	52.3	7.4	9.2
Italy	153,316	163,315	2,703	2,839	0.5	6.3	7.3	84	82	398.9	403.2	7.0	7.0
Jamaica	3,037	3,963	1,264	1,552	3.6	2.5	2.2	85	85	8.0	10.1	3.3	4.0
Japan	438,797	514,898	3,552	4,084	2.2	5.4	6.0	83	79	1,070.7	1,167.7	8.7	9.3
Jordan	3,445	4,795	1,087	1,081	0.3	2.1	3.3	97	96	..	..	..	..
Kazakhstan	106,028	38,418	6,486	2,439	-11.6	1.0	1.8	15	-69	*292.7*	173.8	*17.7*	10.9
Kenya	12,479	14,138	530	494	-1.2	1.8	2.0	18	18	5.8	6.8	0.2	0.2
Korea, Rep.	91,402	176,351	2,132	3,834	8.9	4.0	3.9	76	86	241.2	408.1	5.6	9.0
Kuwait	13,132	16,165	6,180	8,936	12.9	..	..	-409	-618	..	..	..	..
Kyrgyz Republic	1,875	2,793	427	603	-4.5	8.3	3.8	-27	50	*11.8*	6.1	*2.6*	1.3
Lao PDR	..	..	..	..	..	..	..	..	..	0.2	0.3	0.1	0.1
Latvia	3,274	4,460	1,226	1,806	-1.1	6.6	3.1	88	63	*13.1*	9.3	*5.0*	3.7
Lebanon	2,297	5,244	632	1,265	10.3	3.2	3.3	94	96	9.1	14.2	2.5	3.5
Lesotho	..	..	..	..	..	..	..	..	..	..	..	..	..
Lithuania	17,224	8,806	4,628	2,376	-10.2	..	2.6	72	55	*21.4*	13.8	*5.7*	3.7
Macedonia, FYR	..	..	..	..	..	..	..	..	..	..	12.7	..	6.4
Madagascar	..	..	..	..	..	..	..	..	..	0.9	1.2	0.1	0.1
Malawi	..	..	..	..	..	..	..	..	..	0.6	0.7	0.1	0.1
Malaysia	23,974	48,473	1,317	2,237	6.4	4.0	4.0	-104	-53	55.3	119.1	3.0	5.6

ENVIRONMENT

Economy	Commercial energy use — Thousand metric tons of oil equivalent 1990	1997	Per capita — Kg of oil equivalent 1990	1997	Avg. annual % growth 1990–97	GDP per unit of energy use PPP$ per kg of oil equivalent 1990	1997	Net energy imports[a] % of commercial energy use 1990	1997	Carbon dioxide emissions — Total Million metric tons 1990	1996	Per capita Metric tons 1990	1996
Mali	..	..	..	..	..	..	..	..	..	0.4	0.5	0.0	0.0
Mauritania	..	..	..	..	..	..	..	..	..	2.6	2.9	1.3	1.2
Mexico	124,187	141,520	1,492	1,501	–0.3	4.2	5.1	–57	–58	295.0	348.1	3.5	3.8
Moldova	9,959	4,436	2,283	1,029	–11.2	2.0	2.1	100	98	21.8	12.1	5.0	2.8
Mongolia	..	..	..	..	..	..	..	..	..	10.0	8.9	4.5	3.6
Morocco	6,745	9,275	281	340	2.9	9.9	9.5	89	88	23.5	27.9	1.0	1.0
Mozambique	7,318	7,664	517	461	–1.7	1.0	1.6	6	9	1.0	1.0	0.1	0.1
Myanmar	10,787	13,009	266	296	1.6	..	..	–1	6	4.1	7.3	0.1	0.2
Namibia	..	..	..	..	..	..	..	..	..	..	..	..	..
Nepal	5,834	7,160	311	321	0.6	2.8	3.7	3	8	0.6	1.6	0.0	0.1
Netherlands	66,593	74,910	4,454	4,800	1.1	3.8	4.6	10	13	138.9	155.2	9.3	10.0
New Zealand	14,157	16,679	4,120	4,435	0.9	3.4	4.0	14	15	23.6	29.8	6.9	8.0
Nicaragua	2,174	2,573	568	551	–0.8	2.8	3.9	31	41	2.6	2.9	0.7	0.6
Niger	..	..	..	..	..	..	..	..	..	1.0	1.1	0.1	0.1
Nigeria	70,905	88,652	737	753	0.2	1.0	1.1	–112	–115	88.7	83.3	0.9	0.7
Norway	21,456	24,226	5,059	5,501	1.0	3.6	4.8	–460	–778	47.7	67.0	11.2	15.3
Pakistan	43,238	56,818	400	442	1.7	3.3	3.9	21	26	67.9	94.3	0.6	0.8
Panama	1,535	2,328	640	856	4.0	5.8	6.1	61	65	3.1	6.7	1.3	2.5
Papua New Guinea	..	..	..	..	..	..	..	..	..	2.4	2.4	0.6	0.5
Paraguay	3,097	4,191	734	824	2.1	5.3	5.5	–48	–66	2.3	3.7	0.5	0.7
Peru	11,549	15,127	535	621	2.4	5.3	7.3	–6	19	22.2	26.2	1.0	1.1
Philippines	28,294	38,251	452	520	2.3	6.8	7.2	44	57	44.3	63.2	0.7	0.9
Poland	100,114	105,155	2,626	2,721	0.8	2.1	2.7	1	4	347.6	356.8	9.1	9.2
Portugal	16,419	20,400	1,659	2,051	2.9	6.6	7.1	87	89	42.3	47.9	4.3	4.8
Romania	61,117	44,135	2,634	1,957	–2.6	2.3	3.2	35	30	155.1	119.3	6.7	5.3
Russian Federation	906,433	591,982	6,112	4,019	–6.2	1.6	1.7	–40	–57	1,954.4	1,579.5	13.1	10.7
Rwanda	..	..	..	..	..	..	..	..	..	0.5	0.5	0.1	0.1
Saudi Arabia	63,275	98,449	4,004	4,906	1.7	2.5	2.1	–483	–395	177.1	267.8	11.2	13.8
Senegal	2,213	2,770	302	315	0.5	3.8	4.1	38	40	2.9	3.1	0.4	0.4
Sierra Leone	..	..	..	..	..	..	..	..	..	0.3	0.4	0.1	0.1
Singapore	13,357	26,878	4,938	8,661	8.4	2.8	2.9	..	100	41.9	65.8	15.5	21.6
Slovak Republic	21,363	17,216	4,044	3,198	–2.7	2.1	3.0	75	73	43.0	39.6	8.1	7.4
Slovenia	5,250	..	2,627	..	3.6	..	4.4	..	55	..	13.0	..	6.5
South Africa	91,229	107,220	2,592	2,636	0.3	3.1	3.3	–26	–33	291.1	292.7	8.3	7.3
Spain	90,552	107,328	2,332	2,729	2.0	5.3	5.9	62	71	211.7	232.5	5.5	5.9
Sri Lanka	5,476	7,159	322	386	2.4	6.2	7.6	23	39	3.9	7.1	0.2	0.4
Sweden	47,747	51,934	5,579	5,869	1.0	3.1	3.5	38	36	48.5	54.1	5.7	6.1
Switzerland	24,998	26,218	3,724	3,699	–0.3	6.2	6.9	61	58	42.7	44.2	6.4	6.3
Syrian Arab Republic	11,928	14,642	984	983	–0.3	2.4	3.0	–89	–124	35.8	44.3	3.0	3.1
Tajikistan	3,268	3,384	616	562	–8.0	4.0	1.6	43	63	21.3	5.8	3.8	1.0
Tanzania	12,529	14,258	492	455	–1.1	0.9	1.0	6	5	2.3	2.4	0.1	0.1
Thailand	43,706	79,963	786	1,319	8.5	4.9	4.7	39	42	95.7	205.4	1.7	3.4
Togo	..	..	..	..	..	..	..	..	..	0.7	0.8	0.2	0.2
Tunisia	5,683	6,805	697	738	1.1	5.5	7.2	–7	2	13.3	16.2	1.6	1.8
Turkey	52,498	71,273	935	1,142	2.9	5.0	5.7	51	61	143.8	178.3	2.6	2.9
Turkmenistan	18,923	12,181	5,159	2,615	–6.7	1.1	1.0	–293	–54	34.2	34.2	8.5	7.4
Uganda	..	..	..	..	..	..	..	..	..	0.8	1.0	0.1	0.1
Ukraine	252,631	150,059	4,868	2,960	–7.5	1.3	1.1	46	46	631.1	397.3	12.1	7.8
United Kingdom	213,090	227,977	3,702	3,863	0.7	4.4	5.3	2	–18	563.3	557.0	9.8	9.5
United States	1,925,680	2,162,190	7,720	8,076	0.6	2.9	3.6	14	22	4,824.0	5,301.0	19.3	20.0
Uruguay	2,233	2,883	719	883	2.2	8.2	9.7	48	62	3.9	5.6	1.3	1.7
Uzbekistan	43,697	42,553	2,130	1,798	–3.1	1.1	1.1	12	–15	106.5	95.0	5.0	4.1
Venezuela, RB	40,851	57,530	2,095	2,526	1.3	2.4	2.4	–221	–255	113.6	144.5	5.8	6.5
Vietnam	24,451	39,306	369	521	4.9	2.7	3.2	–1	–11	22.5	37.6	0.3	0.5
Yemen, Rep.	2,665	3,355	224	208	–1.8	3.0	3.5	–267	–469	..	..	..	..
Zambia	5,220	5,987	671	634	–1.0	1.1	1.2	8	7	2.4	2.4	0.3	0.3
Zimbabwe	8,934	9,926	917	866	–1.2	2.6	3.1	9	18	16.6	18.4	1.7	1.6
World	8,608,414 t	9,431,190 t	1,705 w	1,692 w	0.0 w	.. w	.. w	.. w	.. w	16,183.1 t	22,690.1 t	3.3 w	4.0 w
Low income	1,122,683	1,194,696	607	563	–1.2	..	..	–17	–9	1,376.8	2,433.8	0.7	1.1
Middle income	3,297,830	3,523,253	1,397	1,368	–0.2	..	..	–28	–33	5,772.8	9,524.1	2.7	3.7
Lower middle income	2,426,917	2,384,856	1,302	1,178	–1.2	..	..	–18	–20	3,721.6	6,734.6	2.2	3.3
Upper middle income	870,913	1,138,397	1,753	2,068	2.2	..	..	–63	–65	2,051.2	2,789.6	4.3	5.1
Low and middle income	4,420,513	4,717,949	1,049	1,005	–0.6	..	..	–26	–28	7,150.8	11,959.5	1.8	2.5
East Asia & Pacific	1,188,126	1,647,182	743	942	3.8	..	..	..	..	3,289.6	4,717.5	2.0	2.7
Europe & Central Asia	1,799,838	1,240,586	3,966	2,690	–5.6	1.8	2.2	–5	–13	924.8	3,448.9	9.1	7.3
Latin America & Caribbean	457,439	575,389	1,057	1,181	1.4	..	..	–31	–35	966.4	1,207.5	2.2	2.5
Middle East & North Africa	266,687	374,375	1,134	1,354	2.1	3.3	3.3	–266	–225	737.6	987.2	3.3	3.9
South Asia	435,330	556,496	394	443	1.9	..	..	9	15	765.9	1,125.1	0.7	0.9
Sub-Saharan Africa	273,093	323,921	705	695	–0.2	..	..	..	..	465.3	471.7	0.9	0.8
High income	4,187,901	4,713,241	4,996	5,369	1.1	..	..	23	24	9,033.5	10,732.1	11.9	12.3

Note: For data comparability and coverage, see the Technical Notes. Figures in italics are for years other than those specified.
a. A negative value indicates that a country is a net exporter.

Table 11. Growth of the economy

| | \multicolumn{13}{c}{Average annual % growth} |
| | Gross domestic product | | GDP implicit deflator | | Agriculture value added | | Industry value added | | Services value added | | Exports of goods and services | | Gross domestic investment |
Economy	1980–90	1990–99	1980–90	1990–99	1980–90	1990–99	1980–90	1990–99	1980–90	1990–99	1980–90	1990–99	1990–99
Albania	1.5	2.3	–0.4	51.5	1.9	6.2	2.1	–4.6	–0.4	5.0	..	13.6	22.4
Algeria	2.7	1.6	8.1	19.0	4.6	3.0	2.3	–0.1	3.6	3.1	4.1	2.2	0.2
Angola	3.4	0.8	5.9	813.8	0.5	–3.1	6.4	4.2	1.8	–3.4	2.2	8.2	12.9
Argentina	–0.7	4.9	391.1	6.2	0.7	3.1	–1.3	4.8	0.0	4.8	3.8	8.7	9.1
Armenia	..	–3.1	..	269.5	..	–0.3	..	–9.0	..	–6.2	..	–21.5	–29.5
Australia	3.4	3.8	7.3	1.6	3.3	1.1	2.9	2.5	3.8	4.4	6.9	7.9	6.1
Austria	2.2	2.0	3.3	2.3	1.1	–0.7	1.9	1.3	2.5	2.2	4.9	4.5	2.9
Azerbaijan	..	–9.0	..	249.5	..	–0.5	..	9.3	..	–0.7	..	12.6	14.7
Bangladesh	4.3	4.8	9.5	3.9	2.7	2.3	4.9	3.9	5.2	6.3	7.7	13.2	7.0
Belarus	..	–4.3	..	449.9	..	–5.4	..	–5.6	..	–2.4	..	–11.1	–10.0
Belgium	1.9	1.7	4.4	2.2	2.0	1.7	2.2	1.1	1.9	1.4	4.3	4.2	0.3
Benin	2.5	4.7	1.7	9.4	5.1	5.3	3.4	3.8	0.7	4.4	–2.4	1.9	5.3
Bolivia	–0.2	4.2	327.2	9.4	..	..	..	..	..	..	1.0	4.9	10.1
Botswana	10.3	4.3	13.6	10.0	3.3	0.3	10.2	2.8	11.7	6.3	10.6	2.5	–1.3
Brazil	2.7	2.9	284.0	264.3	2.8	3.0	2.0	3.2	3.3	2.7	7.5	4.9	3.1
Bulgaria	3.4	–2.7	1.8	111.8	–2.1	0.3	5.2	–4.4	4.5	–2.3	–3.5	0.3	–0.9
Burkina Faso	3.6	3.8	3.3	6.2	3.1	3.5	3.8	3.9	4.6	3.5	–0.4	0.4	4.8
Burundi	4.4	–2.9	4.4	11.7	3.1	–2.0	4.5	–6.7	5.6	–2.5	3.4	2.4	–12.4
Cambodia	..	4.8	..	28.7	..	2.1	..	9.6	..	6.9	..	..	..
Cameroon	3.4	1.3	5.6	5.5	2.2	5.3	5.9	–2.0	2.1	0.1	5.9	2.7	0.0
Canada	3.3	2.3	4.5	1.3	1.2	1.1	3.1	2.2	3.6	1.9	6.3	8.8	2.6
Central African Republic	1.4	1.8	7.9	4.9	1.6	3.7	1.4	0.4	1.0	–0.7	–1.2	6.7	–1.7
Chad	6.1	2.3	1.4	7.6	2.3	4.9	8.1	2.2	6.7	0.8	6.5	5.0	4.4
Chile	4.2	7.2	20.7	8.6	5.9	1.3	3.5	6.3	2.9	7.5	6.9	9.7	11.4
China	10.1	10.7	5.9	8.2	5.9	4.3	11.1	14.4	13.5	9.2	19.3	13.0	12.8
Hong Kong, China	6.9	3.9	7.7	5.2	..	..	..	..	..	..	14.4	8.4	6.3
Colombia	3.6	3.3	24.8	20.5	2.9	–2.6	5.0	2.3	3.1	6.3	7.5	5.2	7.5
Congo, Dem. Rep.	1.6	–5.1	62.9	1,423.1	2.5	2.9	0.9	–11.7	1.3	–15.2	9.6	–5.5	–3.5
Congo, Rep.	3.3	0.9	0.5	7.1	3.4	1.7	5.2	–0.2	2.1	1.5	5.1	4.3	4.7
Costa Rica	3.0	4.1	23.6	16.8	3.1	2.5	2.8	3.7	3.1	4.9	6.1	9.7	3.4
Côte d'Ivoire	0.7	3.7	2.8	8.0	0.3	1.8	4.4	5.9	–0.3	3.9	1.9	4.7	17.6
Croatia	..	–0.4	..	131.2	..	–3.3	..	–4.8	..	1.4	..	..	..
Czech Republic	1.7	0.9	2.6	13.7	..	2.6	..	–0.1	..	1.1	..	9.0	6.3
Denmark	2.3	2.8	5.6	1.7	3.1	1.7	2.9	1.9	2.3	1.5	4.3	3.8	4.8
Dominican Republic	3.1	5.7	21.6	9.8	0.4	3.8	3.6	6.8	3.5	5.7	4.5	7.5	7.4
Ecuador	2.0	2.2	36.4	33.7	4.4	2.0	1.2	2.7	1.7	1.9	5.4	4.4	1.1
Egypt, Arab Rep.	5.4	4.4	13.7	9.1	2.7	3.1	5.2	4.7	6.6	4.3	5.2	3.1	6.7
El Salvador	0.2	4.9	16.3	8.1	–1.1	0.9	0.1	5.6	0.7	5.6	–3.4	11.7	7.2
Eritrea	..	5.2	..	9.7	..	..	..	..	..	..	..	0.5	..
Estonia	2.2	–1.3	2.3	62.7	..	–3.4	..	–4.5	..	1.4	..	10.2	–1.8
Ethiopia[a]	1.1	4.8	4.6	7.4	0.2	2.5	0.4	6.3	3.1	6.7	2.4	9.3	13.4
Finland	3.3	2.5	6.8	1.8	–0.2	0.2	3.3	2.1	3.7	0.1	2.2	9.6	–3.2
France	2.3	1.7	6.0	1.5	2.0	0.5	1.1	0.6	3.0	1.7	3.7	4.9	–1.6
Georgia	0.4	–10.3	1.9	513.0	..	2.5	..	3.4	..	15.4	..	9.8	51.2
Germany[b]	2.2	1.5	..	2.0	1.7	0.5	1.2	..	2.9	1.8	..	4.1	0.5
Ghana	3.0	4.3	42.1	27.2	1.0	3.4	3.3	4.8	5.7	5.0	2.5	10.8	4.2
Greece	1.8	1.9	18.0	10.1	–0.1	2.0	1.3	–0.5	2.7	1.8	7.2	3.3	1.3
Guatemala	0.8	4.2	14.6	10.7	1.2	2.7	–0.2	4.1	0.9	4.9	–1.8	6.4	5.0
Guinea	..	4.2	..	6.2	..	4.5	..	4.5	..	3.2	..	4.7	2.4
Haiti	–0.2	–1.7	7.5	23.3	–0.1	–4.3	–1.7	–1.0	0.9	–0.3	1.2	2.4	1.7
Honduras	2.7	3.2	5.7	19.8	2.7	1.8	3.3	3.6	2.5	3.7	1.1	2.0	6.0
Hungary	1.3	1.0	8.9	20.7	1.7	–3.2	0.2	2.4	2.1	0.6	3.6	8.2	8.4
India	5.8	6.1	8.0	8.6	3.1	3.8	7.0	6.7	6.9	7.7	5.9	11.3	7.4
Indonesia	6.1	4.7	8.5	14.4	3.4	2.6	6.9	7.8	7.0	5.4	2.9	9.2	5.1
Iran, Islamic Rep.	1.7	3.4	14.4	26.7	4.5	3.8	3.3	3.7	–1.0	5.8	6.9	0.2	1.4
Ireland	3.2	7.9	6.6	2.0	..	..	..	..	..	..	9.0	13.3	4.8
Israel	3.5	5.1	101.1	10.6	..	..	..	..	..	..	5.5	9.1	5.5
Italy	2.4	1.2	10.0	4.1	0.1	1.1	2.0	0.9	2.8	1.2	4.1	7.2	–1.0
Jamaica	2.0	0.1	18.6	25.8	0.6	2.3	2.4	–0.6	1.8	0.3	5.4	0.1	3.9
Japan	4.0	1.4	1.7	0.1	1.3	–1.3	4.2	1.1	3.9	2.3	4.5	5.1	1.1
Jordan	2.5	4.8	4.3	3.2	6.8	–4.6	1.7	6.2	2.0	5.5	5.9	7.4	3.4
Kazakhstan	..	–5.9	..	255.7	..	–12.2	..	–8.0	..	1.2	..	4.3	–11.7
Kenya	4.2	2.2	9.1	14.8	3.3	1.4	3.9	1.9	4.9	3.3	4.4	0.4	4.9
Korea, Rep.	9.4	5.7	6.1	5.8	2.8	2.1	12.0	6.2	8.9	5.8	12.0	15.6	1.6
Kuwait	1.3	..	–2.8	..	14.7	..	1.0	..	2.1	..	–2.3	..	..
Kyrgyz Republic	..	–7.4	..	157.3	..	–1.5	..	–15.3	..	–8.2	..	6.7	12.6
Lao PDR	3.7	6.4	37.6	22.9	3.5	4.6	6.1	11.8	3.3	7.4	..	..	..
Latvia	3.7	–4.8	–0.2	58.8	2.8	–7.6	4.6	–10.0	3.4	1.7	..	0.7	–4.4
Lebanon	..	7.7	..	24.0	..	..	..	..	..	..	..	15.6	18.4
Lesotho	4.6	4.4	12.1	9.6	2.8	2.0	5.5	6.3	4.0	5.2	4.9	11.3	2.3
Lithuania	..	–3.9	..	90.4	..	–1.5	..	–9.9	..	–0.4	..	2.9	8.8
Macedonia, FYR	..	1.9	..	13.5	..	3.1	..	–2.1	..	–2.6	..	1.2	6.7
Madagascar	1.1	1.7	17.1	20.6	2.5	1.5	0.9	1.9	0.3	1.9	–1.7	3.6	0.9
Malawi	2.5	4.0	14.6	33.5	2.0	9.0	2.9	1.7	3.6	0.7	2.5	4.9	–7.5
Malaysia	5.3	6.3	1.7	5.0	3.8	1.1	7.2	9.4	4.2	7.6	10.9	11.0	6.2

ECONOMY

	Gross domestic product		GDP implicit deflator		Agriculture value added		Industry value added		Services value added		Exports of goods and services		Gross domestic investment
					Average annual % growth								
Economy	1980–90	1990–99	1980–90	1990–99	1980–90	1990–99	1980–90	1990–99	1980–90	1990–99	1980–90	1990–99	1990–99
Mali	0.8	3.6	4.5	8.5	3.3	2.8	4.3	6.4	1.9	2.7	4.8	9.6	–0.8
Mauritania	1.8	4.1	8.4	6.1	1.7	5.2	4.9	2.8	0.4	4.8	2.1	1.6	6.8
Mexico	1.1	2.7	71.5	19.3	0.8	1.3	1.1	3.6	1.4	2.4	7.0	14.3	3.9
Moldova	3.0	–11.5	..	142.5	..	–6.2	..	–11.8	..	–14.8	..	4.8	–20.0
Mongolia	5.4	0.7	–1.6	66.5	1.4	2.9	6.6	–1.8	5.9	0.8	..	..	..
Morocco	4.2	2.3	7.1	3.2	6.7	0.0	3.0	3.1	4.2	2.5	5.7	3.0	1.5
Mozambique	–0.1	6.3	38.3	36.4	6.6	5.2	–4.5	9.9	9.1	5.5	–6.8	13.4	13.1
Myanmar	0.6	6.3	12.2	25.9	0.5	4.9	0.5	10.1	0.8	6.6	1.9	7.5	14.7
Namibia	1.3	3.4	13.7	9.8	1.9	3.8	–0.6	2.5	2.3	3.4	0.7	4.3	2.5
Nepal	4.6	4.8	11.1	8.6	4.0	2.3	8.7	7.0	3.9	6.0	3.9	14.3	5.7
Netherlands	2.3	2.7	1.6	2.1	3.4	3.7	1.6	1.2	2.6	2.3	4.5	4.8	1.5
New Zealand	1.7	2.9	10.8	1.5	3.8	2.6	1.1	3.5	1.8	3.4	4.0	5.4	8.1
Nicaragua	–1.9	3.2	422.3	38.8	–2.2	5.4	–2.3	4.1	–1.5	1.1	–3.9	10.3	12.6
Niger	–0.1	2.5	1.9	6.4	1.7	3.3	–1.7	1.9	–0.7	1.9	–2.9	1.7	5.4
Nigeria	1.6	2.4	16.7	34.8	3.3	2.9	–1.1	1.7	3.7	3.1	–0.3	2.5	5.8
Norway	2.8	3.7	5.6	1.8	–0.2	4.1	3.3	5.5	2.7	3.2	5.2	6.1	5.1
Pakistan	6.3	4.0	6.7	10.7	4.3	4.3	7.3	4.9	6.8	4.6	8.4	2.7	2.1
Panama	0.5	4.2	1.9	2.0	2.5	1.7	–1.3	5.5	0.7	4.2	–0.9	0.0	12.1
Papua New Guinea	1.9	4.0	5.3	7.8	1.8	2.3	1.9	6.9	2.0	2.8	3.3	9.5	6.8
Paraguay	2.5	2.4	24.4	13.7	3.6	2.8	0.3	2.8	3.1	2.0	12.2	5.1	1.5
Peru	–0.3	5.4	231.3	28.7	2.7	5.8	–0.9	6.7	–0.7	4.0	–1.6	9.0	9.0
Philippines	1.0	3.2	14.9	8.4	1.0	1.5	–0.9	3.4	2.8	3.9	3.5	9.6	4.1
Poland	2.2	4.7	53.5	24.5	–0.4	0.0	0.3	6.3	2.8	3.8	6.6	10.8	11.9
Portugal	3.1	2.5	18.0	5.3	..	–0.4	..	0.7	..	2.2	8.7	5.6	3.5
Romania	0.5	–1.2	2.5	105.5	..	–0.5	..	–1.6	..	–1.0	..	6.1	–11.8
Russian Federation	..	–6.1	..	189.6	..	–6.3	..	–9.8	..	–1.8	..	2.3	–13.3
Rwanda	2.2	–1.5	4.0	16.3	0.5	–3.9	2.5	2.0	5.5	–1.2	3.4	–6.0	2.1
Saudi Arabia	0.0	1.6	–4.9	1.4	13.4	0.7	–2.3	1.5	1.3	2.0	..	..	..
Senegal	3.1	3.2	6.5	5.2	2.8	1.6	4.3	4.6	2.8	3.4	3.7	2.6	3.1
Sierra Leone	1.2	–4.8	62.8	31.2	3.1	1.6	1.7	–7.1	–2.7	–5.3	0.2	–12.2	–10.3
Singapore	6.7	8.0	1.9	1.6	–6.2	0.4	5.3	7.9	7.6	8.0	..	..	8.5
Slovak Republic	2.0	1.9	1.8	10.8	1.6	–0.2	2.0	–4.9	0.8	8.0	..	12.0	4.6
Slovenia	..	2.4	..	23.5	..	–0.1	..	2.0	..	3.8	..	–0.5	10.2
South Africa	1.0	1.9	15.5	10.2	2.9	1.0	0.7	0.9	2.4	2.4	1.9	5.3	3.0
Spain	3.0	2.2	9.3	4.0	..	–2.5	..	..	..	..	5.7	10.9	–0.5
Sri Lanka	4.0	5.3	11.0	9.7	2.2	1.5	4.6	7.4	4.7	5.6	4.9	8.4	6.2
Sweden	2.3	1.5	7.4	2.1	1.5	..	2.8	..	2.2	..	4.3	8.3	–2.2
Switzerland	2.0	0.5	3.4	1.5	..	..	..	..	..	..	3.5	2.2	–0.4
Syrian Arab Republic	1.5	5.7	15.3	8.7	–0.6	..	6.6	..	0.1	..	7.3	4.7	7.9
Tajikistan	..	–9.8	..	300.0	..	–12.2	..	–17.2	..	–10.7	..	..	..
Tanzania[c]	..	3.1	..	23.2	..	3.6	..	2.6	..	2.5	..	9.5	–1.7
Thailand	7.6	4.7	3.9	4.6	3.9	2.7	9.8	6.7	7.3	5.5	14.1	9.4	–2.9
Togo	1.7	2.5	4.8	8.3	5.6	4.5	1.1	2.9	–0.3	0.5	0.1	1.5	11.6
Tunisia	3.3	4.6	7.4	4.7	2.8	2.1	3.1	4.5	3.5	5.3	5.6	5.1	3.4
Turkey	5.4	4.1	45.2	77.9	1.3	1.6	7.8	4.8	4.4	4.3	..	11.9	4.6
Turkmenistan	..	–3.5	..	622.8	..	..	..	..	..	..	..	..	..
Uganda	2.9	7.2	113.8	13.7	2.1	3.7	5.0	12.7	2.8	8.1	1.8	16.3	9.9
Ukraine	..	–10.8	..	440.0	..	–5.8	..	–15.5	..	–3.1	..	–3.6	–24.8
United Kingdom	3.2	2.2	5.7	2.9	..	..	..	..	..	..	3.9	6.0	1.8
United States	3.0	3.4	4.2	1.8	..	2.5	..	4.9	..	2.1	4.7	9.3	7.0
Uruguay	0.4	3.7	61.3	36.0	0.0	4.3	–0.2	1.7	0.8	4.5	4.3	7.0	8.9
Uzbekistan	..	–2.0	..	356.7	..	–1.0	..	–5.1	..	–1.1	..	..	..
Venezuela, RB	1.1	1.7	19.3	47.6	3.0	0.7	1.6	2.6	0.5	0.8	2.8	5.6	2.9
Vietnam	4.6	8.1	210.8	16.8	4.3	4.9	..	13.0	..	8.6	..	27.7	25.5
Yemen, Rep.	..	3.0	..	26.0	..	5.0	..	7.8	..	–1.8	..	10.2	7.7
Zambia	1.0	1.0	42.2	56.9	3.6	–4.4	0.8	–4.3	–1.5	10.6	–3.4	1.8	11.3
Zimbabwe	3.6	2.4	11.6	23.8	3.1	4.3	3.2	–1.2	3.1	3.6	4.3	11.0	–0.7
World	**3.2 w**	**2.5 w**			**2.7 w**	**1.6 w**	**.. w**	**3.0 w**	**.. w**	**2.5 w**	**5.2 w**	**6.9 w**	**2.9 w**
Low income	4.4	2.4			3.0	2.5	5.4	1.1	5.7	4.7	3.3	5.3	–1.4
Middle income	3.2	3.5			3.5	2.0	3.6	4.4	3.5	3.6	7.3	8.8	4.0
Lower middle income	4.0	3.4			4.0	2.0	6.1	5.2	5.3	3.7	7.6	6.7	3.5
Upper middle income	2.5	3.6			2.8	1.9	2.3	3.9	2.8	3.6	7.0	10.8	4.4
Low and middle income	3.4	3.3			3.4	2.2	3.8	3.9	3.8	3.7	6.6	8.2	3.0
East Asia & Pacific	8.0	7.4			4.4	3.4	9.5	9.8	8.7	6.6	11.1	12.6	7.0
Europe & Central Asia	2.4	–2.7			..	–3.0	..	–3.5	..	0.5	..	4.4	–7.0
Latin America & Caribbean	1.7	3.4			2.2	2.0	1.3	3.6	1.8	3.4	5.4	8.7	4.9
Middle East & North Africa	2.0	3.0			5.5	2.5	0.3	2.1	2.2	3.5	..	..	..
South Asia	5.7	5.7			3.2	3.7	6.8	6.3	6.6	7.0	6.5	9.6	6.8
Sub-Saharan Africa	1.7	2.4			2.5	2.5	1.2	1.5	2.4	2.5	2.4	4.4	3.6
High income	3.1	2.4			..	0.8	..	2.6	..	2.2	5.0	6.5	2.6

Note: For data comparability and coverage, see the Technical Notes. Figures in italics are for years other than those specified.
a. Data prior to 1992 include Eritrea. b. Data prior to 1990 refer to the Federal Republic of Germany before unification. c. Data cover mainland Tanzania only.

Table 12.   Structure of output

| | Gross domestic product | | Value added as % of GDP | | | | | | | |
| | Millions of dollars | | Agriculture | | Industry | | Manufacturing | | Services | |
Economy	1990	1999	1990	1999	1990	1999	1990	1999	1990	1999
Albania	2,102	3,058	37	54	47	25	..	..	16	21
Algeria	61,902	47,015	14	13	45	54	12	11	41	33
Angola	10,260	5,861	18	7	41	70	5	63	41	23
Argentina	141,352	281,942	8	6	36	32	27	22	56	61
Armenia	4,124	1,911	17	33	52	32	33	22	31	35
Australia	297,204	389,691	3	..	29	..	15	..	67	..
Austria	159,499	208,949	3	..	32	..	23	..	65	..
Azerbaijan	9,837	4,457	..	19	..	43	..	6	..	38
Bangladesh	29,855	45,779	28	21	24	27	15	17	48	52
Belarus	34,911	25,693	24	13	47	46	39	39	29	40
Belgium	196,134	245,706	2	1	30	28	21	18	68	71
Benin	1,845	2,402	36	38	13	14	8	8	51	48
Bolivia	4,868	8,516	15	16	30	31	17	17	54	54
Botswana	3,766	5,996	5	4	56	45	5	5	39	51
Brazil	464,989	760,345	8	9	39	29	25	23	53	62
Bulgaria	20,726	12,103	18	18	51	27	..	20	31	55
Burkina Faso	2,765	2,643	32	32	22	27	16	21	45	41
Burundi	1,132	701	56	52	19	17	13	9	25	30
Cambodia	1,115	3,117	56	51	11	15	5	6	33	35
Cameroon	11,152	8,781	25	44	29	20	15	11	46	36
Canada	572,673	612,049	3	..	33	..	18	..	64	..
Central African Republic	1,488	1,053	48	55	20	20	11	9	33	25
Chad	1,739	1,574	29	38	18	14	14	11	53	48
Chile	30,307	71,092	8	8	39	33	19	16	53	59
China	354,644	991,203	27	17	42	50	33	24	31	33
Hong Kong, China	74,784	158,611	0	0	25	15	18	6	74	85
Colombia	46,907	88,596	19	14	31	24	15	12	51	61
Congo, Dem. Rep.	9,348	6,964	30	58	28	17	11	..	42	25
Congo, Rep.	2,799	2,273	13	10	41	48	8	6	46	42
Costa Rica	5,713	11,076	16	14	24	22	19	17	60	64
Côte d'Ivoire	10,796	11,223	32	24	23	24	21	20	44	52
Croatia	13,370	21,752	10	9	34	32	28	21	56	59
Czech Republic	34,880	56,379	8	4	45	39	..	..	48	57
Denmark	133,361	174,363	4	..	27	..	18	..	69	..
Dominican Republic	7,074	17,125	13	11	31	35	18	16	55	54
Ecuador	10,686	18,712	13	12	38	33	19	22	49	55
Egypt, Arab Rep.	43,130	92,413	19	17	29	33	24	27	52	50
El Salvador	4,807	12,229	17	10	26	28	22	22	57	61
Eritrea	437	670	29	16	19	27	13	14	52	57
Estonia	6,760	5,101	17	6	50	27	42	16	34	66
Ethiopia[a]	6,842	6,534	49	49	13	7	8	..	38	44
Finland	134,806	126,130	6	..	35	..	23	..	58	..
France	1,195,438	1,410,262	3	2	29	26	21	19	67	72
Georgia	12	4,192	32	22	33	13	24	12	35	65
Germany	1,719,510	2,081,202	1	1	..	..	29	24	34	36
Ghana	5,886	7,606	45	36	17	25	10	9	38	39
Greece	82,914	123,934	11	..	22	..	13	..	67	..
Guatemala	7,650	18,016	26	23	20	19	15	13	54	58
Guinea	2,818	3,693	24	23	33	36	5	4	43	41
Haiti	2,981	3,871	33	30	22	20	16	7	45	50
Honduras	3,049	5,342	22	18	26	30	16	18	51	52
Hungary	33,056	48,355	15	6	39	34	23	25	46	60
India	322,737	459,765	31	28	27	25	17	16	42	46
Indonesia	114,426	140,964	19	20	39	45	21	25	41	35
Iran, Islamic Rep.	120,404	101,073	24	..	29	..	12	..	48	..
Ireland	45,527	84,861	8	..	..	..	..	..	53	..
Israel	52,490	99,068	..	..	..	..	..	..	..	..
Italy	1,093,947	1,149,958	3	3	33	31	22	20	63	67
Jamaica	4,239	6,134	6	8	43	33	20	15	50	59
Japan	2,970,043	4,395,083	3	2	41	37	28	24	56	61
Jordan	4,020	7,616	8	2	28	27	15	15	64	71
Kazakhstan	40,304	15,594	27	10	45	30	9	23	29	60
Kenya	8,533	10,603	29	27	19	17	12	11	52	56
Korea, Rep.	252,622	406,940	9	5	43	44	29	32	48	51
Kuwait	18,428	29,572	1	..	52	..	12	..	47	..
Kyrgyz Republic	..	1,629	35	44	36	22	28	19	29	35
Lao PDR	865	1,373	61	53	15	22	10	17	24	25
Latvia	12,490	6,664	22	5	46	33	34	22	32	63
Lebanon	2,838	17,229	..	12	..	27	..	17	..	61
Lesotho	622	874	23	18	34	38	..	..	43	44
Lithuania	13,264	10,454	27	10	31	33	21	19	42	57
Macedonia, FYR	2,635	3,445	14	11	32	28	..	..	54	60
Madagascar	3,081	3,733	32	30	14	14	12	11	53	56
Malawi	1,803	1,820	45	38	29	18	19	14	26	45
Malaysia	42,775	74,634	19	14	40	44	26	35	41	43

ECONOMY

Economy	Gross domestic product Millions of dollars		Value added as % of GDP Agriculture		Industry		Manufacturing		Services	
	1990	1999	1990	1999	1990	1999	1990	1999	1990	1999
Mali	2,421	2,714	46	47	16	17	9	4	39	37
Mauritania	1,020	959	30	25	29	29	10	10	42	46
Mexico	262,710	474,951	7	5	26	27	19	21	67	68
Moldova	10,583	1,092	43	21	33	24	..	18	24	55
Mongolia	..	905	15	33	41	28	..	..	44	40
Morocco	25,821	35,238	18	17	32	32	18	17	50	51
Mozambique	2,512	4,169	37	32	18	24	10	13	44	44
Myanmar	..	..	57	53	11	9	8	6	32	38
Namibia	2,340	3,075	12	13	38	33	14	15	50	55
Nepal	3,628	4,904	52	41	16	22	6	9	32	37
Netherlands	283,672	384,766	4	..	29	..	19	..	67	..
New Zealand	43,103	53,622	7	..	26	..	18	..	67	..
Nicaragua	1,009	2,302	31	26	21	21	17	14	48	53
Niger	2,481	2,067	35	40	16	17	7	6	49	43
Nigeria	28,472	43,286	33	41	41	62	6	5	26	-3
Norway	115,453	145,449	3	2	31	32	12	11	66	66
Pakistan	40,010	59,880	26	26	25	25	17	17	49	49
Panama	5,313	9,606	10	8	16	18	10	9	73	74
Papua New Guinea	3,221	3,571	29	21	30	15	9	8	41	64
Paraguay	5,265	8,065	28	26	25	22	17	16	47	52
Peru	32,802	57,318	7	8	38	39	27	24	55	54
Philippines	44,331	75,350	22	17	34	31	25	21	44	52
Poland	61,197	154,146	8	4	48	33	..	20	44	63
Portugal	69,132	107,716	6	..	37	..	27	..	57	..
Romania	38,299	33,750	20	16	50	40	..	30	30	44
Russian Federation	579,068	375,345	17	7	48	34	..	..	35	58
Rwanda	2,584	1,956	33	46	25	20	19	12	42	34
Saudi Arabia	104,670	128,892	6	7	50	48	8	10	43	45
Senegal	5,698	4,791	20	18	19	25	13	17	61	57
Sierra Leone	897	669	47	44	20	24	4	4	33	32
Singapore	36,638	84,945	0	0	35	36	27	26	65	64
Slovak Republic	15,485	19,307	7	4	59	32	..	23	33	64
Slovenia	12,673	20,653	6	4	46	39	35	28	49	57
South Africa	111,997	131,127	5	4	40	32	24	19	55	64
Spain	491,938	562,245	5	..	35	..	23	..	60	..
Sri Lanka	8,032	15,707	26	21	26	28	15	17	48	51
Sweden	229,756	226,388	3	..	34	..	22	..	63	..
Switzerland	228,415	260,299	..	..	..	..	..	..	..	..
Syrian Arab Republic	12,309	19,380	29	..	24	..	..	..	48	..
Tajikistan	4,857	1,778	27	6	34	30	..	..	39	65
Tanzania[b]	4,220	8,777	48	48	16	14	9	7	36	38
Thailand	85,345	123,887	12	13	37	40	27	32	50	49
Togo	1,628	1,506	34	43	23	21	10	9	44	36
Tunisia	12,291	21,188	16	13	30	28	17	18	54	59
Turkey	150,721	188,374	18	18	30	26	20	16	52	56
Turkmenistan	6,333	2,708	32	25	30	42	..	29	38	34
Uganda	4,304	6,349	57	44	11	18	6	9	32	38
Ukraine	91,327	42,415	26	14	45	34	36	29	30	51
United Kingdom	975,512	1,373,612	2	..	35	..	23	..	63	..
United States	5,554,100	8,708,870	2	2	28	26	19	18	70	72
Uruguay	8,355	20,211	11	9	32	29	26	19	57	62
Uzbekistan	23,673	16,844	33	31	33	27	..	13	34	42
Venezuela, RB	48,593	103,918	5	5	50	24	20	12	44	71
Vietnam	6,472	28,567	37	26	23	33	19	..	40	42
Yemen, Rep.	4,660	6,769	27	17	30	49	10	11	43	34
Zambia	3,288	3,325	18	17	45	26	32	11	37	57
Zimbabwe	8,784	5,716	16	19	33	24	23	17	50	56
World	**21,390,644 t**	**30,211,993 t**	**6 w**	**4 w**	**34 w**	**32 w**	**22 w**	**21 w**	**60 w**	**61 w**
Low income	889,723	1,067,242	29	27	31	30	18	18	41	43
Middle income	3,525,445	5,488,604	13	10	39	36	25	23	47	55
Lower middle income	1,820,097	2,575,942	21	15	39	40	26	23	40	46
Upper middle income	1,722,041	2,918,403	8	7	39	32	24	24	53	61
Low and middle income	4,413,061	6,557,913	16	12	38	35	23	22	46	54
East Asia & Pacific	925,765	1,888,729	20	13	40	46	29	28	40	41
Europe & Central Asia	1,240,214	1,093,237	17	10	43	32	..	..	40	58
Latin America & Caribbean	1,146,895	2,055,025	9	8	36	29	23	21	56	63
Middle East & North Africa	402,799	590,253	15	..	38	..	13	..	47	..
South Asia	410,341	595,915	30	28	26	25	17	16	44	47
Sub-Saharan Africa	297,397	332,744	18	18	34	32	17	17	48	50
High income	16,967,888	23,662,676	3	2	33	30	22	21	64	64

Note: For data comparability and coverage, see the Technical Notes. Figures in italics are for years other than those specified.
a. Data prior to 1992 include Eritrea. b. Data cover mainland Tanzania only.

Table 13. Structure of demand

	Percentage of GDP											
	Private consumption		General government consumption		Gross domestic investment		Gross domestic savings		Exports of goods and services		Resource balance	
Economy	1990	1999	1990	1999	1990	1999	1990	1999	1990	1999	1990	1999
Albania	61	96	19	10	29	16	21	−7	15	9	−8	−23
Algeria	56	59	16	11	29	27	27	30	23	26	−2	3
Angola	36	14	34	38	12	23	30	48	39	84	18	25
Argentina	77	73	3	11	14	18	20	16	10	10	6	−1
Armenia	46	103	18	11	47	19	36	−14	35	19	−11	−33
Australia	61	62	17	17	21	22	21	21	17	21	0	−1
Austria	56	56	19	19	24	25	25	25	40	42	1	−1
Azerbaijan	..	84	..	11	..	34	..	5	..	29	..	−29
Bangladesh	85	80	4	6	19	20	11	14	6	14	−7	−6
Belarus	45	60	26	19	27	26	29	20	46	62	2	−6
Belgium	64	63	14	14	20	18	22	22	68	73	2	5
Benin	84	82	11	11	14	18	5	8	22	21	−9	−10
Bolivia	77	73	12	16	13	18	11	11	23	15	−1	−7
Botswana	39	58	24	28	32	20	37	14	55	28	5	−6
Brazil	59	64	19	16	20	21	21	20	8	10	1	−1
Bulgaria	60	76	18	12	26	16	22	12	33	38	−4	−4
Burkina Faso	77	77	15	13	21	27	8	10	13	12	−13	−17
Burundi	95	85	11	14	15	10	−5	1	8	9	−20	−9
Cambodia	91	86	7	9	8	15	2	5	6	34	−7	−10
Cameroon	67	71	13	10	18	19	21	19	20	24	3	0
Canada	57	59	23	20	21	20	21	21	26	41	0	2
Central African Republic	86	81	15	12	12	14	−1	7	15	17	−13	−7
Chad	97	89	10	11	7	18	−6	0	13	17	−15	−18
Chile	62	68	10	9	25	24	28	23	35	27	3	0
China	50	50	12	8	35	40	38	42	18	22	3	2
Hong Kong, China	57	60	7	10	27	25	36	30	134	132	8	4
Colombia	65	69	11	12	20	17	25	19	20	18	4	2
Congo, Dem. Rep.	79	83	12	8	9	8	9	9	30	24	0	2
Congo, Rep.	62	45	14	10	16	26	24	45	54	79	8	19
Costa Rica	61	51	18	17	27	28	21	32	35	73	−7	4
Côte d'Ivoire	72	65	17	10	7	19	11	25	32	44	5	6
Croatia	74	60	24	26	10	23	2	14	78	40	−8	−9
Czech Republic	49	52	23	19	25	30	28	29	45	60	3	−1
Denmark	49	51	26	25	20	21	25	24	36	36	5	3
Dominican Republic	80	73	5	10	25	26	15	16	34	32	−10	−10
Ecuador	69	70	9	10	17	15	23	20	33	58	5	5
Egypt, Arab Rep.	73	77	11	9	29	23	16	14	20	15	−13	−8
El Salvador	89	87	10	11	14	16	1	2	19	25	−13	−14
Eritrea	98	72	33	48	5	45	−31	−20	20	17	−37	−65
Estonia	62	64	16	19	30	28	22	17	60	83	−8	−11
Ethiopia[a]	74	80	19	15	12	19	7	4	8	14	−5	−14
Finland	53	53	21	21	28	17	26	26	23	40	−2	9
France	60	60	18	19	22	17	22	21	23	27	0	4
Georgia	65	98	10	8	31	7	25	−6	40	17	−6	−13
Germany	57	58	20	19	23	21	23	23	25	27	0	2
Ghana	85	85	9	11	14	22	5	4	17	32	−9	−18
Greece	73	73	15	15	23	20	11	12	17	16	−11	−8
Guatemala	84	88	7	6	14	16	10	6	21	18	−4	−10
Guinea	70	76	12	7	18	18	18	17	31	23	0	−1
Haiti	93	100	8	7	12	11	−1	−7	16	11	−13	−18
Honduras	66	79	14	13	23	26	20	9	36	42	−3	−17
Hungary	61	57	11	15	25	30	28	28	31	55	3	−3
India	67	69	11	11	25	24	22	20	7	11	−3	−3
Indonesia	58	70	9	6	31	14	33	24	26	54	2	10
Iran, Islamic Rep.	62	65	11	19	29	16	27	16	22	14	−2	0
Ireland	58	49	15	13	21	20	27	37	59	80	6	18
Israel	56	60	30	30	25	20	14	10	35	36	−11	−10
Italy	61	62	18	16	21	18	21	22	20	27	0	4
Jamaica	62	60	14	21	28	32	24	19	52	52	−4	−13
Japan	58	60	9	10	32	29	33	30	11	11	1	1
Jordan	74	65	25	29	32	27	1	6	62	49	−31	−21
Kazakhstan	52	68	18	17	32	15	30	15	74	43	−1	0
Kenya	67	77	19	16	20	15	14	7	26	25	−5	−8
Korea, Rep.	53	56	10	10	38	27	37	34	29	42	−1	7
Kuwait	57	50	39	27	18	12	4	22	45	47	−13	10
Kyrgyz Republic	71	93	25	17	24	10	4	−11	29	37	−20	−21
Lao PDR	..	71	..	5	..	25	..	24	11	4	−13	−1
Latvia	53	68	9	22	40	20	39	10	48	44	−1	−10
Lebanon	140	98	25	15	18	28	−64	−13	18	11	−82	−40
Lesotho	137	115	14	20	53	47	−51	−35	17	27	−104	−82
Lithuania	57	63	19	25	33	24	24	12	52	47	−9	−12
Macedonia, FYR	68	75	17	18	14	23	15	7	48	41	1	−16
Madagascar	86	88	8	8	17	12	6	5	17	25	−11	−8
Malawi	75	80	16	12	20	15	10	7	25	30	−10	−8
Malaysia	50	46	14	8	34	32	36	45	76	124	2	13

ECONOMY

	Private consumption		General government consumption		Gross domestic investment		Gross domestic savings		Exports of goods and services		Resource balance	
	\multicolumn{12}{c}{Percentage of GDP}
Economy	1990	1999	1990	1999	1990	1999	1990	1999	1990	1999	1990	1999
Mali	80	80	14	12	23	20	6	8	17	22	−17	−12
Mauritania	69	73	26	15	20	22	5	12	46	39	−15	−10
Mexico	70	70	8	7	23	24	22	23	19	31	−1	−1
Moldova	63	92	14	12	25	18	23	−4	49	49	−2	−21
Mongolia	57	63	30	18	34	26	13	20	21	50	−21	−6
Morocco	69	67	15	15	25	23	16	18	19	29	−10	−5
Mozambique	101	79	12	10	16	35	−12	11	8	13	−28	−24
Myanmar	89	89	.. b	.. b	13	12	11	11	3	1	−2	−1
Namibia	51	64	31	26	34	20	18	9	52	53	−16	−11
Nepal	83	80	9	10	18	19	8	11	11	22	−11	−9
Netherlands	59	59	15	14	22	20	27	27	54	56	5	7
New Zealand	63	63	17	15	19	21	20	21	28	29	1	1
Nicaragua	59	85	43	14	19	37	−2	1	25	37	−21	−36
Niger	84	83	15	13	8	10	1	4	15	15	−7	−6
Nigeria	56	88	15	12	15	11	29	0	43	17	15	−11
Norway	49	48	21	20	23	25	30	32	41	41	7	7
Pakistan	74	78	15	11	19	15	11	11	16	15	−8	−4
Panama	60	59	18	16	17	34	21	25	38	34	5	−9
Papua New Guinea	59	48	25	15	24	36	16	37	41	66	−8	1
Paraguay	78	73	5	10	22	19	16	17	23	41	−6	−2
Peru	70	65	8	15	21	22	22	20	12	14	0	−2
Philippines	72	68	10	16	24	21	18	16	28	56	−6	−5
Poland	50	74	19	9	25	28	32	18	28	20	7	−10
Portugal	63	64	16	19	29	26	21	17	34	31	−7	−9
Romania	66	81	13	9	30	15	21	10	17	29	−9	−5
Russian Federation	49	57	21	14	30	14	30	29	18	48	0	15
Rwanda	84	89	10	13	15	14	6	−1	6	6	−8	−16
Saudi Arabia	40	41	31	32	20	21	30	26	46	36	10	5
Senegal	76	76	15	10	14	21	9	14	25	34	−5	−7
Sierra Leone	82	93	10	13	9	5	8	−2	24	14	−1	−8
Singapore	46	39	10	10	37	33	44	52	202	..	7	19
Slovak Republic	54	50	22	22	33	39	24	28	27	64	−9	−11
Slovenia	55	56	19	21	17	25	26	24	84	57	9	−1
South Africa	63	63	20	19	12	16	18	18	24	25	6	3
Spain	62	62	16	16	25	21	22	22	17	28	−3	1
Sri Lanka	76	71	10	10	22	25	14	19	30	36	−8	−6
Sweden	51	53	27	26	21	14	22	21	30	44	0	7
Switzerland	57	61	14	14	28	20	29	25	36	40	1	4
Syrian Arab Republic	70	70	14	11	15	29	16	18	28	29	0	−11
Tajikistan	65	..	21	..	23	..	14	..	..	..	−10	..
Tanzania c	84	72	17	13	23	18	−1	14	12	20	−23	−4
Thailand	57	57	9	11	41	21	34	32	34	57	−8	12
Togo	71	83	14	12	27	14	15	6	33	32	−12	−8
Tunisia	58	63	16	12	32	28	25	24	44	42	−7	−3
Turkey	69	68	11	11	24	24	20	21	13	26	−4	−3
Turkmenistan	49	..	23	..	40	..	28	..	..	7	−13	..
Uganda	92	84	8	10	13	17	1	6	7	11	−12	−12
Ukraine	57	56	17	26	27	21	26	18	28	40	−1	−3
United Kingdom	63	64	21	20	19	16	17	15	24	29	−3	0
United States	67	68	18	15	17	19	15	17	10	12	−1	−1
Uruguay	69	78	14	9	11	14	17	13	26	19	6	−1
Uzbekistan	61	59	25	22	32	19	13	19	29	22	−19	0
Venezuela, RB	62	77	8	6	10	15	29	17	39	21	19	3
Vietnam	86	71	8	8	13	29	6	21	26	44	−7	−7
Yemen, Rep.	73	72	18	15	15	21	9	13	15	37	−6	−8
Zambia	64	85	19	10	17	17	17	6	36	29	−1	−11
Zimbabwe	63	69	19	16	17	18	17	15	23	46	0	−2
World	**61 w**	**62 w**	**15 w**	**15 w**	**24 w**	**22 w**	**23 w**	**23 w**	**19 w**	**22 w**	**0 w**	**0 w**
Low income	66	70	12	11	24	20	21	19	17	27	−3	−1
Middle income	59	62	14	12	26	24	27	26	21	28	1	1
Lower middle income	57	59	13	11	31	27	30	30	21	32	−1	3
Upper middle income	60	65	15	12	23	22	25	23	21	25	2	0
Low and middle income	60	63	14	12	26	24	26	25	21	26	0	1
East Asia & Pacific	54	53	11	10	35	33	35	37	26	39	0	5
Europe & Central Asia	55	64	18	12	28	20	26	23	23	38	−1	4
Latin America & Caribbean	65	68	13	13	19	21	22	20	14	16	2	−1
Middle East & North Africa	58	60	20	21	24	22	22	19	33	25	−2	−3
South Asia	69	71	11	10	23	22	19	19	9	12	−4	−4
Sub-Saharan Africa	66	69	18	16	15	17	16	14	27	27	2	−2
High income	62	62	16	15	23	21	23	22	19	22	0	1

Note: For data comparability and coverage, see the Technical Notes. Figures in italics are for years other than those specified.
a. Data prior to 1992 include Eritrea. b. General government consumption figures are not available separately; they are included in private consumption. c. Data cover mainland Tanzania only.

Table 14. Central government finances

| | Percentage of GDP | | | | | | | | | | Percentage of total expenditure[b] | | | |
| Economy | Current tax revenue | | Current nontax revenue | | Current expenditure | | Capital expenditure | | Overall deficit/surplus[a] | | Goods and services | | Social services[c] | |
	1990	1998	1990	1998	1990	1998	1990	1998	1990	1998	1990	1998	1990	1998
Albania	..	14.8	..	4.5	..	25.1	..	4.7	..	–8.5	..	16.5	..	28.8
Algeria	..	30.7	..	1.5	..	21.5	..	7.7	..	2.9	..	..	..	..
Angola	..	..	..	..	..	..	..	..	..	..	..	..	..	..
Argentina	9.4	12.4	1.0	1.2	10.1	14.1	0.5	1.2	–0.4	–1.5	29.7	21.4	57.1	63.6
Armenia	..	..	..	..	..	..	..	..	..	..	..	..	..	..
Australia	23.8	22.9	2.1	1.6	22.2	23.3	2.1	1.3	2.1	2.9	27.4	30.6	50.7	66.3
Austria	31.4	34.8	3.0	2.5	34.8	37.9	3.3	2.6	–4.5	–2.7	24.5	22.6	68.4	68.2
Azerbaijan	..	18.2	..	1.1	..	19.8	..	5.3	..	–3.9	..	34.6	..	37.6
Bangladesh	..	..	..	..	..	..	..	..	..	..	..	..	..	..
Belarus	30.6	28.7	0.5	2.1	31.7	27.5	5.9	4.7	–5.1	–0.9	36.2	25.4	57.2	43.7
Belgium	41.5	43.3	1.5	0.7	45.8	44.4	2.3	2.2	–5.6	–2.0	18.4	19.1	..	..
Benin	..	..	..	..	..	..	..	..	..	..	..	..	..	..
Bolivia	8.4	15.1	5.2	2.4	13.9	18.5	2.5	3.4	–1.7	–2.3	63.2	40.0	38.1	51.2
Botswana	27.7	14.7	23.4	29.5	26.5	28.5	7.3	6.8	11.3	8.4	41.4	46.8	33.9	42.7
Brazil	19.0	..	3.7	..	46.1	..	0.7	..	–5.8	..	14.7	..	33.0	..
Bulgaria	34.5	27.0	12.6	6.9	53.5	30.5	1.6	3.0	–8.2	2.8	33.5	32.9	30.3	45.0
Burkina Faso	10.1	..	0.8	..	11.6	..	3.4	..	–1.3	..	60.3	..	26.5	..
Burundi	16.3	12.7	1.9	1.0	14.2	17.3	11.8	3.7	–3.3	–5.5	33.0	55.2	22.3	23.0
Cambodia	..	..	..	..	..	..	..	..	..	..	..	..	..	..
Cameroon	10.8	..	4.3	..	14.7	..	5.5	..	–5.9	..	51.0	..	30.1	..
Canada	18.3	..	2.7	..	25.3	..	0.5	..	–4.9	..	21.3	..	47.7	..
Central African Republic	..	..	..	..	..	..	..	..	..	..	..	..	..	..
Chad	6.1	..	0.5	..	9.5	..	12.3	..	–4.7	..	41.4	..	..	..
Chile	16.3	18.4	4.3	3.6	18.1	18.0	2.3	3.6	0.8	0.4	28.5	28.8	63.9	71.3
China	4.0	5.7	2.4	0.2	..	..	..	..	–1.9	–1.5	..	..	2.5	2.5
Hong Kong, China	..	..	..	..	..	..	..	..	..	..	..	..	..	..
Colombia	8.8	10.1	2.1	1.4	7.7	12.8	2.2	3.2	3.4	–4.7	25.1	20.4	32.1	45.2
Congo, Dem. Rep.	9.4	4.3	0.7	1.0	15.7	9.9	3.1	0.5	–6.5	–0.8	72.6	94.5	6.1	0.5
Congo, Rep.	14.7	6.6	7.8	22.8	34.8	33.9	0.8	4.1	–14.1	–8.6	54.4	49.7	..	..
Costa Rica	19.7	23.1	3.3	3.2	22.7	27.2	2.9	2.9	–3.1	–3.8	55.4	47.1	58.7	59.6
Côte d'Ivoire	19.9	21.0	2.1	0.6	24.5	17.1	0.0	7.1	–2.9	–1.3	68.8	44.0	38.0	..
Croatia	31.9	43.3	1.1	2.1	36.4	40.8	1.2	4.8	–4.6	0.6	53.9	48.7	63.8	63.5
Czech Republic	..	31.6	..	1.1	..	32.0	..	3.0	..	–1.6	..	14.3	..	67.1
Denmark	32.3	..	5.5	..	37.7	..	1.3	..	–0.7	..	20.3	..	50.5	..
Dominican Republic	10.8	15.5	1.2	1.4	6.5	11.6	5.1	4.3	0.6	0.4	38.9	43.3	44.0	44.2
Ecuador	17.8	..	0.4	..	11.9	..	2.6	..	3.7	..	41.5	..	32.1	..
Egypt, Arab Rep.	16.7	16.6	6.2	9.7	23.0	23.3	4.8	7.4	–5.7	–2.0	37.2	40.9	32.1	23.6
El Salvador	..	..	..	..	..	..	..	..	..	..	..	..	..	..
Eritrea	..	..	..	..	..	..	..	..	..	..	..	..	..	..
Estonia	25.6	29.9	0.6	1.8	21.9	30.1	1.8	2.8	0.4	–0.1	22.3	42.9	48.7	55.5
Ethiopia[d]	12.2	..	5.1	..	24.6	..	4.4	..	–9.8	..	75.3	..	21.6	..
Finland	28.3	28.1	2.8	3.9	28.7	34.2	2.1	1.1	0.2	–2.5	19.6	19.0	60.8	55.3
France	37.6	39.2	2.8	2.6	40.0	44.6	2.5	2.0	–2.1	–3.5	25.7	23.6	68.2	..
Georgia	..	4.6	..	1.0	..	8.2	..	0.4	..	–2.5	..	45.5	..	26.1
Germany	27.0	26.6	1.4	5.1	28.2	31.6	1.9	1.4	–2.2	–0.9	32.0	31.8	65.0	69.8
Ghana	11.4	..	1.0	..	10.7	..	2.5	..	0.2	..	48.2	..	46.4	..
Greece	26.0	20.6	2.3	2.4	48.9	28.4	4.1	4.3	–23.2	–8.4	31.5	29.3	32.1	35.0
Guatemala	..	..	..	..	..	..	..	..	..	..	..	..	..	..
Guinea	11.5	10.0	4.6	0.4	10.8	10.0	12.1	5.6	–3.3	–4.1	36.7	34.0	..	..
Haiti	..	..	..	..	..	..	..	..	..	..	..	..	..	..
Honduras	..	..	..	..	..	..	..	..	..	..	..	..	..	..
Hungary	44.7	31.4	8.2	4.2	50.2	39.4	1.9	4.0	0.8	–6.1	26.5	16.0	46.5	46.6
India	9.9	8.6	2.4	3.0	14.2	12.8	1.8	1.6	–7.5	–5.2	19.2	20.1	8.1	9.2
Indonesia	17.8	15.6	1.0	1.2	10.4	12.2	8.0	5.7	0.4	–2.4	22.9	18.9	13.2	26.2
Iran, Islamic Rep.	7.2	11.2	10.8	15.3	15.0	17.7	4.9	8.8	–1.8	0.3	53.0	54.5	49.3	41.8
Ireland	32.8	31.6	2.4	1.6	36.3	32.2	2.8	3.2	–2.1	–0.4	18.8	18.1	55.3	58.8
Israel	33.7	35.8	5.7	6.4	47.3	45.1	3.0	3.0	–5.3	–1.2	37.4	33.2	39.2	57.6
Italy	37.3	38.6	1.2	2.9	43.8	42.2	4.0	2.4	–10.3	–3.3	16.5	19.2	..	..
Jamaica	..	..	..	..	..	..	..	..	..	..	..	..	..	..
Japan	13.7	..	0.8	..	13.7	..	2.0	..	–1.6	..	13.6	..	52.0	..
Jordan	18.6	19.8	7.5	6.7	30.1	28.3	5.8	5.7	–3.5	–3.3	54.5	62.6	36.6	44.6
Kazakhstan	..	..	..	..	..	..	..	..	..	..	..	..	..	..
Kenya	20.2	23.5	2.2	3.7	22.0	25.6	5.5	3.4	–3.8	–0.9	49.7	44.5	28.5	29.6
Korea, Rep.	15.9	17.3	1.7	2.7	13.8	13.7	2.4	3.8	–0.7	–1.3	30.1	21.6	27.8	27.8
Kuwait	1.5	1.5	..	..	45.1	44.0	10.2	6.6	..	..	..	..	..	..
Kyrgyz Republic	..	..	..	..	..	..	..	..	..	..	..	..	..	..
Lao PDR	..	..	..	..	..	..	..	..	..	..	..	..	..	..
Latvia	..	28.0	..	3.8	..	30.6	..	2.5	..	0.1	..	29.8	..	58.4
Lebanon	..	12.7	..	4.3	..	26.0	..	6.1	..	–15.1	..	29.7	..	19.4
Lesotho	34.7	34.9	4.3	9.8	28.3	40.6	22.8	9.7	–1.0	–3.7	39.2	75.6	34.3	35.7
Lithuania	29.3	25.4	2.6	1.3	23.1	27.2	5.9	3.1	1.4	–0.4	11.7	54.5	..	60.1
Macedonia, FYR	..	..	..	..	..	..	..	..	..	..	..	..	..	..
Madagascar	9.4	8.5	2.1	0.2	9.1	10.5	6.9	6.8	–0.9	–1.3	35.3	24.6	22.4	16.5
Malawi	18.0	..	2.7	..	20.2	..	6.4	..	–1.7	..	54.6	..	22.4	..
Malaysia	19.6	18.9	7.5	4.1	23.3	15.2	7.3	4.5	–2.1	2.9	42.6	40.5	35.6	42.5

ECONOMY

| Economy | Percentage of GDP | | | | | | | | | | Percentage of total expenditure[b] | | | |
| | Current tax revenue | | Current nontax revenue | | Current expenditure | | Capital expenditure | | Overall deficit/surplus[a] | | Goods and services | | Social services[c] | |
	1990	1998	1990	1998	1990	1998	1990	1998	1990	1998	1990	1998	1990	1998
Mali	..	..	..	..	..	..	..	..	..	..	..	..	..	..
Mauritania	..	..	..	..	..	..	..	..	..	..	..	..	..	..
Mexico	13.7	13.0	1.6	1.7	15.5	14.3	2.5	1.9	−2.5	−1.1	24.7	23.5	30.6	48.1
Moldova	..	..	..	..	..	..	..	..	..	..	..	..	..	..
Mongolia	15.6	13.5	2.7	6.0	18.7	19.8	2.9	3.2	−6.0	−10.8	24.2	23.6	24.7	25.4
Morocco	22.9	..	3.5	..	20.8	..	8.0	..	−2.2	..	47.9	..	27.0	..
Mozambique	..	..	..	..	..	..	..	..	..	..	..	..	..	..
Myanmar	6.2	4.5	4.3	3.3	11.4	4.3	4.6	4.5	−5.1	−0.9	..	..	35.7	15.5
Namibia	27.4	..	4.0	..	28.4	..	5.1	..	−1.2	..	71.7	..	..	..
Nepal	7.0	8.8	1.4	1.8	..	..	..	..	−6.8	−4.7	..	..	24.4	28.9
Netherlands	42.8	42.7	4.2	3.0	48.6	46.0	3.0	1.7	−4.5	−1.7	15.2	15.4	64.6	63.9
New Zealand	36.3	32.1	6.2	2.1	43.1	32.5	0.9	0.9	4.0	0.5	22.1	50.9	69.2	71.0
Nicaragua	29.3	..	4.3	..	68.9	..	3.1	..	−35.6	..	42.6	..	36.2	..
Niger	..	..	..	..	..	..	..	..	..	..	..	..	..	..
Nigeria	..	..	..	..	..	..	..	..	..	..	..	..	..	..
Norway	32.3	34.1	10.2	9.1	39.2	34.1	2.1	1.6	0.5	0.7	18.8	17.3	44.0	42.1
Pakistan	13.3	12.6	5.8	3.3	19.8	18.8	2.6	2.5	−5.4	−6.3	38.7	46.5	..	..
Panama	17.7	18.4	7.9	7.0	23.3	25.0	0.4	2.0	3.0	0.2	67.3	54.9	66.7	65.2
Papua New Guinea	20.1	..	5.2	..	31.0	..	3.7	..	−3.5	..	58.7	..	30.4	..
Paraguay	9.2	..	3.1	..	7.8	..	1.6	..	2.9	..	54.2	..	31.5	..
Peru	9.4	13.7	0.6	2.3	15.1	13.8	1.3	2.6	−6.4	−0.2	30.0	41.8	..	..
Philippines	14.1	17.0	2.1	2.0	16.5	16.3	3.1	2.2	−3.5	0.1	42.4	51.1	22.5	26.5
Poland	..	32.8	..	2.9	..	35.7	..	2.0	..	−1.0	..	25.2	..	69.6
Portugal	28.4	32.1	4.0	3.6	34.3	35.6	4.5	5.2	−4.6	−2.1	38.0	39.5	..	..
Romania	30.9	24.4	3.5	2.1	27.9	29.1	5.9	2.9	0.9	−3.9	25.6	30.1	42.9	49.0
Russian Federation	..	..	..	..	..	..	..	..	..	..	..	..	..	..
Rwanda	9.5	..	1.3	..	12.7	..	6.3	..	−5.3	..	52.9	..	..	..
Saudi Arabia	..	..	..	..	..	..	..	..	..	..	..	..	..	..
Senegal	..	..	..	..	..	..	..	..	..	..	..	..	..	..
Sierra Leone	3.9	9.9	0.2	0.3	5.8	13.0	0.5	4.2	−1.8	−5.8	76.2	39.0	25.8	..
Singapore	15.4	16.2	11.5	8.4	16.4	11.8	5.1	5.1	10.8	11.8	49.8	36.7	32.2	23.2
Slovak Republic	..	..	..	..	..	..	..	..	..	..	..	..	..	..
Slovenia	..	..	..	..	..	..	..	..	..	..	..	..	..	..
South Africa	24.3	24.5	2.0	1.7	27.0	28.4	3.1	1.2	−4.1	−2.9	51.9	26.6	..	..
Spain	28.8	28.1	1.6	2.0	30.6	34.2	3.2	1.9	−3.2	−5.5	18.7	15.9	50.6	48.3
Sri Lanka	19.0	14.5	2.0	2.7	22.3	19.7	6.1	5.3	−7.8	−8.0	30.2	37.1	27.5	30.0
Sweden	38.4	35.8	5.8	4.5	39.8	41.7	1.0	1.1	1.0	−1.6	13.7	14.5	61.8	53.2
Switzerland	19.4	22.0	1.4	1.7	22.1	27.0	1.2	1.0	−0.9	−1.3	29.9	29.1	66.4	72.9
Syrian Arab Republic	16.7	16.4	5.1	7.8	16.0	15.5	5.8	9.1	0.3	−0.2	..	..	12.6	16.4
Tajikistan	..	..	..	..	..	..	..	..	..	..	..	..	..	..
Tanzania	..	..	..	..	..	..	..	..	..	..	..	..	..	..
Thailand	17.1	14.4	1.5	1.8	11.5	11.7	2.6	6.7	4.6	−3.4	59.2	51.2	32.2	38.3
Togo	..	..	..	..	..	..	..	..	..	..	..	..	..	..
Tunisia	24.0	24.8	6.7	4.8	27.0	25.9	7.6	6.7	−5.4	−3.1	31.7	37.9	36.9	46.6
Turkey	11.6	19.1	2.1	2.8	15.1	26.5	2.3	3.4	−3.0	−8.4	52.0	32.8	26.3	25.7
Turkmenistan	..	..	..	..	..	..	..	..	..	..	..	..	..	..
Uganda	..	..	..	..	..	..	..	..	..	..	..	..	..	..
Ukraine	..	..	..	..	..	..	..	..	..	..	..	..	..	..
United Kingdom	33.3	36.3	3.2	2.0	34.2	36.3	3.8	1.5	0.6	0.6	31.1	28.3	52.8	57.5
United States	18.0	20.4	1.5	1.4	21.7	20.4	1.8	0.6	−3.9	0.9	27.4	21.9	43.4	53.8
Uruguay	25.2	30.0	1.3	2.3	24.0	31.6	1.9	1.7	0.4	−0.8	34.6	31.7	61.6	75.8
Uzbekistan	..	..	..	..	..	..	..	..	..	..	..	..	..	..
Venezuela, RB	18.4	12.8	5.3	4.6	17.4	16.0	3.3	3.8	0.0	−2.8	27.2	23.9	..	..
Vietnam	..	15.8	..	2.4	..	14.3	..	5.8	..	−1.1	..	..	..	30.5
Yemen, Rep.	11.2	13.7	8.3	23.1	22.8	31.2	9.6	6.8	−9.1	−2.3	61.9	43.5	21.9	22.4
Zambia	..	..	..	..	..	..	..	..	..	..	..	..	..	..
Zimbabwe	21.7	26.4	2.4	3.0	24.5	33.6	2.8	2.1	−5.3	−5.0	51.2	48.5	..	55.3

Note: For data comparability and coverage, see the Technical Notes. Figures in italics are for years other than those specified.
a. Includes grants. b. Total expenditure includes lending minus repayments. c. Refers to education, health, social security, welfare, housing, and community amenities. d. Data prior to 1992 include Eritrea.

Table 15.   Balance of payments current account and international reserves

Millions of dollars

Economy	Goods and services Exports 1990	Exports 1998	Imports 1990	Imports 1998	Net income 1990	Net income 1998	Net current transfers 1990	Net current transfers 1998	Current account balance 1990	Current account balance 1998	Gross international reserves 1990	reserves 1999
Albania	354	295	485	941	−2	77	15	504	−118	−65	..	369
Algeria	13,462	10,809	10,106	9,119	−2,268	−2,332	333	..	1,420	..	2,703	4,526
Angola	3,992	3,879	3,385	4,546	−765	−1,317	−77	208	−236	−1,776	..	496
Argentina	14,800	31,125	6,846	38,573	−4,400	−7,335	998	509	4,552	−14,274	6,222	26,252
Armenia	..	360	..	988	..	60	..	177	..	−390	1	319
Australia	49,843	72,027	53,056	78,487	−13,158	−11,474	358	−107	−16,013	−18,042	19,319	21,212
Austria	63,694	95,173	61,580	96,641	−942	−1,227	−6	−1,914	1,166	−4,609	17,228	15,120
Azerbaijan	392	1,010	348	2,425	0	−13	106	64	150	−1,364	0	673
Bangladesh	1,903	5,879	4,156	8,049	−122	−100	802	2,017	−1,574	−253	660	1,604
Belarus	3,661	7,957	3,557	8,964	−1	−78	79	140	182	−945	..	299
Belgium[a]	138,605	191,640	135,098	180,988	2,316	5,936	−2,197	−4,420	3,627	12,168	23,789	10,937
Benin	364	545	454	771	−25	−17	139	86	24	−157	69	400
Bolivia	977	1,358	1,086	2,201	−249	−162	159	330	−199	−675	511	917
Botswana	2,005	2,316	1,987	2,506	−106	120	69	240	−19	170	3,385	6,299
Brazil	35,170	58,767	28,184	74,415	−11,608	−19,617	799	1,436	−3,823	−33,829	9,200	34,796
Bulgaria	6,950	5,981	8,027	5,989	−758	−284	125	230	−1,710	−62	670	3,083
Burkina Faso	349	399	758	783	0	−36	332	187	−77	−233	305	295
Burundi	89	72	318	172	−15	−12	174	59	−69	−53	112	48
Cambodia	314	815	507	1,286	−21	−50	120	297	−93	−224	..	393
Cameroon	2,251	2,306	1,931	2,176	−478	−469	−39	105	−196	−235	37	4
Canada	149,538	248,161	149,118	240,290	−19,388	−19,618	−796	534	−19,764	−11,213	23,530	28,126
Central African Republic	220	149	410	255	−22	−20	123	69	−89	−57	123	136
Chad	271	326	488	581	−21	−3	192	179	−46	−132	132	95
Chile	10,221	18,953	9,166	21,583	−1,737	−1,972	198	463	−485	−4,139	6,784	14,407
China*	57,374	207,584	46,706	165,894	1,055	−16,644	274	4,279	11,997	29,325	34,476	157,728
Hong Kong, China	100,413	208,519	94,084	207,729	0	904	..	..	6,329	−4,987	24,656	96,236
Colombia	8,679	13,516	6,858	17,531	−2,305	−1,725	1,026	447	542	−5,293	4,453	7,644
Congo, Dem. Rep.	2,557	1,446	2,497	1,385	−770	−752	−27	33	−738	−658	261	..
Congo, Rep.	1,488	1,493	1,282	1,539	−460	−168	3	−20	−251	−252	10	39
Costa Rica	1,963	6,876	2,346	6,974	−233	−468	192	105	−424	−460	525	1,460
Côte d'Ivoire	3,172	5,022	3,120	4,095	−988	−695	−164	−438	−1,100	−207	21	632
Croatia	..	8,569	..	10,663	..	−164	..	708	..	−1,551	167	3,025
Czech Republic	..	33,908	..	34,713	..	−994	..	408	..	−1,392	..	12,806
Denmark	48,902	62,766	41,415	59,501	−5,708	−3,791	−408	−1,481	1,372	−2,007	11,226	22,287
Dominican Republic	1,832	7,482	2,233	8,917	−249	−887	371	1,986	−280	−336	69	689
Ecuador	3,262	5,007	2,365	6,409	−1,364	−1,543	107	776	−360	−2,169	1,009	1,642
Egypt, Arab Rep.	9,151	13,502	13,710	21,807	−912	1,140	4,836	4,403	−634	−2,762	3,620	14,484
El Salvador	973	2,741	1,624	4,266	−132	−66	631	1,507	−152	−84	595	2,004
Eritrea	88	109	278	597	0	4	171	249	−19	−234	..	..
Estonia	664	4,170	711	4,715	−13	−81	97	148	36	−478	198	853
Ethiopia[b]	672	1,037	1,069	1,815	−67	−91	220	349	−244	−520	55	459
Finland	31,180	50,153	33,456	38,705	−3,735	−3,083	−952	−994	−6,962	7,371	10,415	8,207
France	285,389	387,123	283,238	342,244	−3,896	4,380	−8,199	−9,097	−9,944	40,161	68,291	39,701
Georgia	..	720	..	1,437	..	117	..	211	..	−389	..	132
Germany	474,713	623,416	423,497	587,353	20,832	−9,203	−23,745	−30,303	48,303	−3,443	104,547	61,039
Ghana	983	1,989	1,506	2,887	−111	−136	411	684	−223	−350	309	454
Greece	13,018	14,863	19,564	25,601	−1,709	−1,632	4,718	7,510	−3,537	−4,860	4,721	18,122
Guatemala	1,568	3,487	1,812	5,047	−196	−184	227	705	−213	−1,039	362	1,189
Guinea	829	804	953	962	−149	−81	70	121	−203	−119	80	122
Haiti	318	479	515	1,021	−18	−12	193	516	−22	−38	10	83
Honduras	1,032	2,387	1,127	2,736	−237	−176	280	367	−51	−158	47	1,258
Hungary	12,035	25,657	11,017	27,101	−1,427	−1,878	787	1,018	379	−2,304	1,185	10,954
India	23,028	47,419	31,485	59,138	−1,757	−3,546	2,069	10,280	−8,145	−4,984	5,637	32,667
Indonesia	29,295	54,850	27,511	43,903	−5,190	−8,189	418	379	−2,988	4,096	8,657	26,445
Iran, Islamic Rep.	19,741	14,297	22,292	16,189	378	−502	2,500	497	327	−1,897	..	..
Ireland	26,786	71,749	24,576	61,713	−4,955	−10,718	2,384	1,488	−361	806	5,362	5,346
Israel	17,276	32,021	20,228	36,022	−1,975	−2,984	5,088	6,143	161	−842	6,598	22,605
Italy	219,971	310,121	218,573	270,320	−14,712	−12,318	−3,164	−7,485	−16,479	19,998	88,595	22,425
Jamaica	2,217	3,383	2,390	3,970	−430	−304	291	635	−312	−255	168	555
Japan	323,692	436,456	297,306	363,488	22,492	56,570	−4,800	−8,842	44,078	120,696	87,828	286,916
Jordan	2,511	3,636	3,754	5,200	−215	−138	1,046	1,712	−411	9	1,139	2,629
Kazakhstan	5,758	6,735	5,862	7,716	−175	−298	168	78	−111	−1,201	..	1,479
Kenya	2,228	2,851	2,705	3,695	−418	−173	368	654	−527	−363	236	792
Korea, Rep.	73,295	156,701	76,360	114,446	−87	−5,049	1,149	3,352	−2,003	40,558	14,916	73,987
Kuwait	8,268	11,376	7,169	13,197	7,738	5,867	−4,951	−1,520	3,886	2,527	2,929	4,824
Kyrgyz Republic	285	598	400	936	0	−76	..	50	..	−365	..	230
Lao PDR	102	487	212	602	−1	−35	56	74	−55	−77	8	101
Latvia	1,090	3,120	997	3,947	2	53	96	125	191	−650	..	840
Lebanon	511	1,817	2,836	8,717	622	323	1,818	2,689	115	−3,888	4,210	7,776
Lesotho	100	247	754	918	433	234	286	157	65	−280	72	500
Lithuania	..	5,071	..	6,348	..	−255	..	235	..	−1,298	107	1,195
Macedonia, FYR	..	1,449	..	2,019	..	−45	..	327	..	−288	..	430
Madagascar	471	829	809	1,128	−161	−78	234	88	−265	−289	92	171
Malawi	443	563	549	1,076	−80	−97	99	..	−86	..	142	251
Malaysia	32,665	71,900	31,765	60,200	−1,872	0	102	−1,094	−870	−4,792	10,659	30,588
* Taiwan, China	74,175	126,946	67,015	124,031	4,361	2,049	−601	−1,527	10,920	3,437	77,653	106,200

ECONOMY

Millions of dollars

Economy	Goods and services — Exports		Goods and services — Imports		Net income		Net current transfers		Current account balance		Gross international reserves	
	1990	1998	1990	1998	1990	1998	1990	1998	1990	1998	1990	1999
Mali	420	637	830	899	−37	−45	225	126	−221	−178	198	350
Mauritania	471	393	520	471	−46	−32	86	187	−10	77	59	224
Mexico	48,805	129,523	51,915	138,441	−8,316	−13,056	3,975	6,014	−7,451	−15,960	10,217	31,782
Moldova	..	765	..	1,228	..	33	..	83	..	−347	0	186
Mongolia	493	540	1,096	671	−44	0	7	56	−640	−75	23	136
Morocco	6,239	9,970	7,783	11,358	−988	−1,101	2,336	2,345	−196	−144	2,338	5,689
Mozambique	229	531	996	1,132	−97	−141	448	313	−415	−429	232	654
Myanmar	641	1,634	1,182	2,789	−61	38	77	515	−526	−602	410	265
Namibia	1,220	1,605	1,584	1,908	37	61	354	403	28	162	50	305
Nepal	379	1,108	761	1,646	71	13	60	103	−251	−421	354	843
Netherlands	160,447	224,762	147,652	200,897	−631	8,905	−2,943	−7,185	9,221	25,585	34,401	10,098
New Zealand	11,683	16,017	11,699	15,859	−1,576	−3,093	138	338	−1,453	−2,596	4,129	4,455
Nicaragua	392	761	682	1,656	−217	−151	202	..	−305	..	166	510
Niger	533	332	728	479	−54	−24	14	−22	−236	−192	226	39
Nigeria	14,550	9,855	6,909	13,377	−2,738	−2,291	85	1,570	4,988	−4,244	4,129	6,485
Norway	47,078	54,768	38,911	54,440	−2,700	−898	−1,476	−1,591	3,992	−2,161	15,788	20,400
Pakistan	6,217	10,017	9,351	12,819	−966	−2,330	2,748	3,430	−1,352	−1,702	1,046	1,511
Panama	4,438	8,023	4,193	8,869	−255	−525	219	159	209	−1,212	344	823
Papua New Guinea	1,381	2,091	1,509	1,872	−103	−259	156	87	−76	47	427	205
Paraguay	1,609	3,893	2,094	4,277	260	61	55	58	−171	−265	675	987
Peru	4,120	7,488	4,086	10,494	−1,733	−1,484	316	..	−1,384	..	1,891	8,730
Philippines	11,430	36,973	13,967	39,631	−872	3,510	714	435	−2,695	1,287	2,036	13,230
Poland	19,037	43,387	15,095	52,007	−3,386	−1,178	2,511	2,897	3,067	−6,901	4,674	24,535
Portugal	21,554	34,621	27,146	45,323	−96	−579	5,507	4,031	−181	−7,250	20,579	8,427
Romania	6,380	9,519	9,901	12,798	161	−392	106	753	−3,254	−2,918	1,374	2,690
Russian Federation	53,883	87,734	48,915	74,078	−4,500	−12,000	..	−415	468	1,241	..	8,457
Rwanda	145	112	359	482	−17	−8	145	236	−86	−143	44	174
Saudi Arabia	47,445	43,551	43,939	44,417	7,979	2,768	−15,637	−15,053	−4,152	−13,150	13,437	16,997
Senegal	1,453	1,319	1,840	1,627	−129	−37	153	264	−363	−81	22	404
Sierra Leone	210	75	215	161	−71	−15	7	..	−69	..	5	39
Singapore	67,489	128,706	64,953	113,698	1,006	3,783	−421	−1,177	3,122	17,614	27,748	76,843
Slovak Republic	..	13,012	..	15,346	..	−158	..	366	..	−2,126	..	3,371
Slovenia	7,900	11,143	6,930	11,405	−38	146	46	112	978	−4	112	3,168
South Africa	27,119	34,526	21,017	32,687	−4,096	−3,029	60	−746	2,065	−1,936	2,583	6,353
Spain	83,595	161,294	100,870	160,165	−3,533	−7,513	2,799	3,249	−18,009	−3,135	57,238	33,115
Sri Lanka	2,293	5,648	2,965	6,661	−167	−178	541	903	−298	−288	447	1,636
Sweden	70,560	103,130	70,490	89,268	−4,473	−5,785	−1,936	−3,438	−6,339	4,639	20,324	15,019
Switzerland	96,926	120,542	96,402	108,277	8,746	16,018	−2,329	−3,736	6,941	24,547	61,284	36,321
Syrian Arab Republic	5,030	4,930	2,955	4,788	−401	−606	88	523	1,762	59	..	..
Tajikistan	..	604	..	731	..	−38	..	57	..	−107	..	..
Tanzania	538	1,144	1,474	2,353	−185	−139	562	560	−559	−788	193	775
Thailand	29,229	65,903	35,870	48,704	−853	−3,566	213	414	−7,281	14,048	14,258	34,063
Togo	663	693	847	823	−32	7	132	..	−84	..	358	122
Tunisia	5,203	8,482	6,039	9,131	−455	−857	828	831	−463	−675	867	2,262
Turkey	21,042	54,541	25,652	55,412	−2,508	−2,985	4,493	5,727	−2,625	1,871	7,626	23,340
Turkmenistan	1,238	614	857	1,608	0	33	66	27	447	−934	..	1,513
Uganda	246	634	676	1,871	−77	−9	78	539	−429	−706	44	763
Ukraine	..	17,621	..	18,828	..	−871	..	782	..	−1,296	469	1,046
United Kingdom	238,568	372,594	263,985	386,529	−818	23,589	−7,624	−10,754	−33,859	−1,100	43,146	29,834
United States	536,058	933,906	615,992	1,098,181	28,431	−12,209	−27,821	−44,075	−79,324	−220,559	173,094	60,500
Uruguay	2,158	4,225	1,659	4,507	−321	−185	8	67	186	−400	1,446	2,587
Uzbekistan	..	3,148	..	3,182	..	−61	..	43	..	−52	..	..
Venezuela, RB	18,806	19,021	9,451	19,870	−774	−1,559	−302	−154	8,279	−2,562	12,733	12,277
Vietnam	1,913	11,974	1,901	13,507	−412	−689	49	951	−351	−1,271	429	2,002
Yemen, Rep.	1,490	1,708	2,170	2,771	−454	−422	1,872	1,256	739	−228	441	1,010
Zambia	1,360	1,057	1,897	1,140	−437	−485	380	..	−594	..	201	45
Zimbabwe	2,012	2,535	2,001	2,742	−263	−346	112	..	−140	..	295	268
World	4,251,942 t	6,766,816 t	4,257,615 t	6,696,346 t								
Low income	130,884	209,252	148,102	243,846								
Middle income	699,711	1,374,233	666,224	1,356,708								
Lower middle income	289,307	634,614	302,617	610,185								
Upper middle income	409,317	739,691	365,852	746,047								
Low and middle income	829,625	1,583,740	814,842	1,603,017								
East Asia & Pacific	239,776	614,457	240,892	497,263								
Europe & Central Asia	188,731	340,843	187,584	363,280								
Latin America & Caribbean	169,084	335,772	146,919	393,251								
Middle East & North Africa	134,093	131,866	134,828	154,797								
South Asia	34,113	70,684	49,041	89,001								
Sub-Saharan Africa	80,330	89,935	74,324	104,277								
High income	3,418,264	5,183,326	3,430,033	5,096,364								

Note: For data comparability and coverage, see the Technical Notes. Figures in italics are for years other than those specified.
a. Includes Luxembourg. b. Data prior to 1992 include Eritrea.

Table 16.   Private sector finance

Economy	Private investment % of gross domestic fixed investment		Stock market capitalization Millions of dollars		Listed domestic companies		Interest rate spread (lending minus deposit rate) Percentage points		Domestic credit provided by the banking sector % of GDP	
	1990	1997	1990	1999	1990	1999	1990	1999	1990	1999
Albania	..	..	..	..	..	..	2.1	8.7	..	47.2
Algeria	..	..	..	..	..	..	..	2.5	74.7	45.8
Angola	..	..	..	..	..	..	..	7.5	..	−10.4
Argentina	67.4	92.6	3,268	83,887	179	129	..	3.0	32.4	34.8
Armenia	..	..	..	25	..	95	..	11.5	58.7	10.8
Australia	74.2	80.1	107,611	427,683	1,089	1,217	4.5	2.9	103.5	93.7
Austria	..	..	11,476	33,025	97	97	..	3.4	123.0	132.1
Azerbaijan	..	..	..	4	..	2	..	..	57.2	10.6
Bangladesh	50.1	67.2	321	865	134	211	4.0	5.4	24.1	33.4
Belarus	..	..	..	..	..	..	..	27.2	..	37.4
Belgium	..	..	65,449	184,942	182	172	6.9	4.3	70.9	147.9
Benin	44.8	59.5	..	..	..	..	9.0	..	22.4	6.6
Bolivia	39.3	59.7	..	116	..	18	18.0	23.1	30.7	66.2
Botswana	..	..	261	1,052	9	15	1.8	5.2	−46.4	−69.7
Brazil	76.7	80.6	16,354	227,962	581	478	..	..	89.8	50.5
Bulgaria	3.6	42.2	..	706	..	860	8.9	9.6	0.1	0.0
Burkina Faso	..	..	..	..	..	..	9.0	..	13.7	13.2
Burundi	..	..	..	..	..	..	..	..	23.2	30.7
Cambodia	86.0	73.9	..	..	..	..	..	10.2	..	7.4
Cameroon	..	..	..	..	..	..	11.0	17.0	31.2	17.7
Canada	86.3	88.5	241,920	800,914	1,144	3,767	1.3	1.5	85.8	100.9
Central African Republic	..	..	..	..	..	..	11.0	17.0	12.9	11.7
Chad	..	54.1	..	..	..	..	11.0	17.0	11.5	12.0
Chile	79.5	80.8	13,645	68,228	215	285	8.6	4.1	73.0	68.8
China	33.8	47.5	2,028	330,703	14	950	0.7	3.6	90.0	130.4
Hong Kong, China	..	..	83,397	609,090	284	695	3.3	4.0	156.3	141.1
Colombia	61.5	55.9	1,416	11,590	80	145	8.8	9.1	30.8	40.5
Congo, Dem. Rep.	..	..	..	..	..	..	..	..	25.3	..
Congo, Rep.	..	..	..	..	..	..	11.0	17.0	29.1	19.7
Costa Rica	78.9	73.2	475	2,303	82	22	11.4	11.4	29.9	38.3
Côte d'Ivoire	57.9	70.2	549	1,514	23	38	9.0	..	44.5	25.9
Croatia	..	..	..	2,584	2	59	499.3	10.6	..	48.4
Czech Republic	..	..	..	11,796	..	164	..	4.2	..	65.1
Denmark	..	..	39,063	105,293	258	233	6.2	4.7	63.0	57.1
Dominican Republic	73.1	82.9	..	141	..	6	15.2	9.0	31.5	37.0
Ecuador	78.3	82.9	69	415	65	28	−6.0	15.1	17.2	87.0
Egypt, Arab Rep.	62.3	68.6	1,765	32,838	573	1,032	7.0	3.7	106.8	96.3
El Salvador	81.5	77.3	..	2,141	..	40	3.2	4.7	32.0	44.4
Eritrea	..	..	..	..	..	..	..	..	..	..
Estonia	..	..	..	1,789	..	25	..	4.5	65.0	34.9
Ethiopia	..	..	..	..	..	..	3.6	4.2	50.4	51.3
Finland	..	..	22,721	349,409	73	147	4.1	3.5	84.3	57.5
France	..	..	314,384	1,475,457	578	968	6.1	3.7	106.1	103.1
Georgia	..	..	..	..	..	..	..	18.8	..	13.1
Germany	..	..	355,073	1,432,190	413	933	4.5	6.4	108.5	146.9
Ghana	..	..	76	916	13	22	..	..	13.2	36.8
Greece	49.8	..	15,228	204,213	145	281	8.1	6.3	73.3	65.4
Guatemala	79.9	79.8	..	215	..	5	5.1	11.6	17.4	17.1
Guinea	..	..	..	..	..	..	0.2	..	5.4	6.8
Haiti	..	..	..	..	..	..	..	15.5	32.9	24.1
Honduras	..	..	40	458	26	71	8.3	10.2	40.9	28.5
Hungary	..	..	505	16,317	21	66	4.1	3.1	105.5	52.2
India	56.7	70.1	38,567	184,605	2,435	5,863	..	..	50.6	44.9
Indonesia	67.5	77.2	8,081	64,087	125	277	3.3	1.9	45.5	61.1
Iran, Islamic Rep.	53.6	55.5	34,282	21,830	97	295	..	..	62.1	49.4
Ireland	..	..	..	42,458	..	84	5.0	3.2	57.3	100.0
Israel	..	..	3,324	63,820	216	644	12.0	5.0	106.2	85.3
Italy	..	..	148,766	728,273	220	241	7.3	4.0	90.1	93.5
Jamaica	..	..	911	2,530	44	46	6.6	16.0	34.8	49.1
Japan	79.4	70.9	2,917,679	4,546,937	2,071	2,470	3.4	2.0	266.8	142.4
Jordan	..	..	2,001	5,827	105	152	2.2	3.2	110.0	90.1
Kazakhstan	..	..	..	2,260	..	17	..	..	..	11.1
Kenya	41.8	56.0	453	1,409	54	57	5.1	12.8	52.9	50.1
Korea, Rep.	79.9	73.4	110,594	308,534	669	725	0.0	1.4	57.2	85.2
Kuwait	..	..	..	18,814	..	76	0.4	2.8	217.6	116.8
Kyrgyz Republic	..	..	..	..	..	..	..	25.3	..	20.0
Lao PDR	..	..	..	..	..	..	2.5	18.6	5.1	10.7
Latvia	..	..	..	391	..	70	..	9.2	..	18.8
Lebanon	..	..	..	1,921	..	13	23.1	7.0	132.6	134.9
Lesotho	..	..	..	..	..	..	7.4	11.6	27.4	−0.2
Lithuania	..	..	..	1,138	..	54	..	8.1	..	13.1
Macedonia, FYR	..	..	..	8	..	2	..	9.1	..	19.0
Madagascar	46.5	46.9	..	..	..	..	5.3	19.0	26.2	15.8
Malawi	51.8	27.7	..	..	..	..	8.9	20.4	17.8	7.3
Malaysia	64.5	72.8	48,611	145,445	282	757	1.3	3.2	77.9	160.5

STATES AND MARKETS

Economy	Private investment % of gross domestic fixed investment		Stock market capitalization Millions of dollars		Listed domestic companies		Interest rate spread (lending minus deposit rate) Percentage points		Domestic credit provided by the banking sector % of GDP	
	1990	1997	1990	1999	1990	1999	1990	1999	1990	1999
Mali	..	..	..	..	..	..	9.0	..	13.7	16.1
Mauritania	46.2	49.4	..	..	..	..	5.0	..	54.7	0.3
Mexico	76.0	81.4	32,725	154,044	199	188	..	16.3	36.6	29.1
Moldova	..	..	..	38	..	58	..	8.0	62.8	30.8
Mongolia	..	..	..	32	..	418	..	17.9	68.5	11.6
Morocco	68.3	67.9	966	13,695	71	55	0.5	6.2	43.0	83.8
Mozambique	..	..	..	..	..	..	..	11.8	15.6	6.2
Myanmar	..	..	..	..	..	..	2.1	5.1	32.8	29.1
Namibia	61.7	62.2	21	691	3	14	10.6	7.7	20.4	53.7
Nepal	..	..	..	418	..	108	2.5	4.0	28.9	41.4
Netherlands	87.3	86.9	119,825	695,209	260	344	8.4	0.7	107.4	131.5
New Zealand	74.7	86.8	8,835	28,352	171	114	4.4	3.9	81.6	121.3
Nicaragua	54.7	62.0	..	..	..	..	12.5	11.9	206.6	144.8
Niger	..	..	..	..	..	..	9.0	..	16.2	9.2
Nigeria	..	..	1,372	2,940	131	194	5.5	13.1	23.7	15.4
Norway	65.8	..	26,130	63,696	112	195	4.6	2.8	67.4	60.8
Pakistan	51.7	58.3	2,850	6,965	487	765	..	..	50.9	47.0
Panama	86.9	84.0	226	3,584	13	31	3.6	3.1	52.7	93.6
Papua New Guinea	79.7	79.9	..	..	..	..	6.9	3.4	35.8	31.0
Paraguay	86.7	67.0	..	423	..	55	8.1	10.5	14.9	27.1
Peru	83.1	84.5	812	13,392	294	242	2,335.0	14.5	16.2	24.9
Philippines	81.8	80.1	5,927	48,105	153	226	4.6	3.6	23.2	64.1
Poland	41.2	53.4	144	29,577	9	221	462.5	6.3	18.8	36.5
Portugal	..	..	9,201	66,488	181	125	7.8	2.8	71.8	107.9
Romania	9.8	35.4	..	873	..	5,825	..	..	79.7	18.8
Russian Federation	..	..	244	72,205	13	207	..	26.0	..	35.0
Rwanda	..	..	..	..	..	..	6.3	..	17.1	13.2
Saudi Arabia	..	..	48,213	60,440	59	73	..	..	14.4	46.6
Senegal	..	..	..	..	..	..	9.0	..	33.8	22.8
Sierra Leone	..	..	..	..	..	..	12.0	17.3	26.3	50.1
Singapore	..	..	34,308	198,407	150	355	2.7	4.1	62.2	83.7
Slovak Republic	..	..	..	723	..	845	..	6.7	..	67.5
Slovenia	..	..	..	2,180	24	28	142.0	5.1	36.8	40.1
South Africa	65.6	72.7	137,540	262,478	732	668	2.1	5.8	97.8	73.4
Spain	..	..	111,404	431,668	427	718	5.4	2.1	110.8	114.4
Sri Lanka	..	..	917	1,584	175	239	−6.4	−4.8	43.1	31.9
Sweden	79.9	79.7	97,929	373,278	258	277	6.8	3.9	145.5	122.1
Switzerland	..	..	160,044	693,127	182	239	−0.9	2.7	179.0	184.1
Syrian Arab Republic	..	..	..	..	..	..	..	..	56.6	28.9
Tajikistan	..	..	..	..	..	..	..	..	..	..
Tanzania	..	..	..	181	..	4	..	22.1	39.2	13.9
Thailand	84.8	65.9	23,896	58,365	214	392	2.2	4.3	91.1	126.0
Togo	..	..	..	..	..	..	9.0	..	21.3	22.2
Tunisia	50.5	50.8	533	2,706	13	44	..	..	62.5	69.2
Turkey	68.2	77.6	19,065	112,716	110	285	..	..	25.9	36.6
Turkmenistan	..	..	..	..	..	..	..	..	..	26.6
Uganda	..	..	..	..	..	..	7.4	12.8	17.8	7.6
Ukraine	..	..	..	1,121	..	125	..	34.3	83.2	24.3
United Kingdom	83.6	87.0	848,866	2,933,280	1,701	1,945	2.2	2.7	123.0	129.1
United States	84.9	85.8	3,059,434	16,635,114	6,599	7,651	..	..	114.7	170.1
Uruguay	71.5	72.0	..	168	36	17	76.6	39.0	60.1	43.2
Uzbekistan	..	..	..	119	..	4	..	..	..	..
Venezuela, RB	34.8	43.6	8,361	7,471	76	87	7.7	10.8	37.4	16.5
Vietnam	..	..	..	..	..	..	..	5.3	15.9	21.9
Yemen, Rep.	..	..	..	..	..	..	..	..	62.8	32.2
Zambia	..	..	..	291	..	8	9.5	20.1	67.8	63.5
Zimbabwe	..	..	2,395	2,514	57	70	2.9	16.9	41.7	32.8
World	**78.1 w**	**76.0 w**	**9,398,391 s**	**36,030,808 s**	**25,424 s**	**49,640 s**			**125.1 w**	**136.4 w**
Low income	48.1	56.5	54,588	268,082	3,446	8,332			43.7	42.7
Middle income	72.2	74.8	430,570	2,159,249	4,914	16,560			62.1	80.2
Lower middle income	..	..	58,226	751,775	1,833	11,451			63.4	92.5
Upper middle income	73.8	77.9	372,344	1,407,474	3,081	5,109			60.2	60.3
Low and middle income	64.5	66.9	485,158	2,427,331	8,360	24,892			58.4	72.2
East Asia & Pacific	63.3	56.9	197,109	955,379	1,443	3,754			71.0	112.5
Europe & Central Asia	..	..	19,065	265,207	110	9,000			..	33.5
Latin America & Caribbean	74.3	79.8	78,470	584,985	1,748	1,938			58.7	27.6
Middle East & North Africa	..	..	5,265	151,562	817	1,863			54.3	72.2
South Asia	55.9	68.9	42,655	194,475	3,231	7,199			48.3	44.1
Sub-Saharan Africa	..	..	142,594	275,723	1,011	1,138			55.6	43.2
High income	81.9	79.2	8,913,233	33,603,476	17,064	24,748			140.1	139.0

Note: For data comparability and coverage, see the Technical Notes. Figures in italics are for years other than those specified.

Table 17.   Role of government in the economy

Economy	Subsidies and other current transfers % of total expenditure		Value added by state-owned enterprises % of GDP		Military expenditures % of GNP		Composite ICRG risk rating[a]	Institutional Investor credit rating[a]	Highest marginal tax rate[b] Individual		Corporate %
									%	On income over (dollars)	
	1990	1997	1985–90	1990–97	1992	1997	March 2000	March 2000	1999	1999	1999
Albania	..	45	..	..	4.7	1.4	62.5	12.6	..	..	..
Algeria	27	26	..	..	1.8	3.9	56.8	27.7	..	..	..
Angola	..	..	..	..	24.2	20.5	45.0	12.6	..	..	..
Argentina	57	58	2.7	1.3	1.9	1.2	71.0	43.0	35	200,000	35
Armenia	..	..	..	..	3.5	3.5	57.5	..	..	..	..
Australia	56	61	..	..	2.5	2.2	83.5	78.3	47	30,579	36
Austria	57	62	..	..	1.0	0.9	82.0	89.4	50	59,590	34
Azerbaijan	28	44	..	..	2.9	1.9	59.3	..	40	3,704	30
Bangladesh	..	..	2.3	2.5	1.3	1.4	62.3	25.5	..	..	..
Belarus	46	54	..	..	1.9	1.7	59.3	12.7	..	..	..
Belgium	56	60	2.8	..	1.8	1.5	80.3	85.6	55	69,993	39
Benin	..	..	..	..	1.3	1.3	..	17.3	..	..	..
Bolivia	16	40	13.4	11.4	2.2	1.9	68.3	31.1	13	..	25
Botswana	25	31	5.6	5.5	4.4	5.1	83.5	57.0	30	17,960	15
Brazil	39	..	7.7	7.4	1.1	1.8	64.8	38.5	28	17,881	15
Bulgaria	52	37	..	..	3.3	3.0	70.8	32.5	40	9,403	27
Burkina Faso	11	..	..	..	2.4	2.8	62.8	19.2	..	..	..
Burundi	10	11	7.3	..	2.7	6.1	..	9.6	..	..	..
Cambodia	..	..	..	..	4.9	4.1	..	..	20	39,915	20
Cameroon	13	13	18.0	8.5	1.6	3.0	60.5	18.0	60	13,321	39
Canada	56	62	..	..	2.0	1.3	85.5	85.1	29	38,604	38
Central African Republic	..	..	4.1	..	2.0	3.9	..	..	..	..	..
Chad	3	..	..	..	4.0	2.7	..	12.4	..	..	..
Chile	51	52	14.4	8.3	2.5	3.9	74.5	62.6	45	6,526	15
China	..	..	..	..	2.8	2.2	72.3	56.6	45	12,079	30
Hong Kong, China	..	..	..	..	..	..	79.3	60.8	17	13,583	16
Colombia	42	40	7.0	..	2.4	3.7	57.0	42.6	35	32,221	35
Congo, Dem. Rep.	4	1	..	..	3.0	5.0	45.3	8.0	..	..	..
Congo, Rep.	20	5	15.1	..	5.7	4.1	50.5	7.1	50	14,210	45
Costa Rica	20	23	8.1	..	1.4	0.6	76.5	42.7	25	14,185	30
Côte d'Ivoire	30	9	..	..	1.5	1.1	55.3	25.2	10	4,263	35
Croatia	42	38	..	..	7.7	6.3	69.8	41.8	35	5,556	..
Czech Republic	64	74	..	..	2.7	1.9	76.3	59.1	40	36,979	35
Denmark	61	64	..	..	2.0	1.7	86.0	86.3	59	..	32
Dominican Republic	13	23	..	..	0.9	1.1	71.8	31.9	25	14,309	25
Ecuador	16	..	10.2	..	3.5	4.0	49.8	19.1	0	..	0
Egypt, Arab Rep.	26	15	..	..	3.7	2.8	70.5	45.4	32	14,706	40
El Salvador	..	..	1.8	..	2.1	0.9	76.0	38.3	..	..	..
Eritrea	..	..	..	..	..	7.8	..	..	..	..	..
Estonia	73	47	..	..	0.5	1.5	74.3	49.4	26	..	26
Ethiopia	9	..	..	..	3.7	1.9	57.5	15.9	..	..	..
Finland	70	67	..	..	2.2	1.7	88.8	85.6	38	61,164	28
France	63	65	11.2	..	3.4	3.0	80.3	91.7	..	..	33
Georgia	..	28	..	..	2.4	1.4	..	11.1	..	..	..
Germany	58	58	..	..	2.1	1.6	83.3	92.9	53	66,690	30
Ghana	20	..	8.5	..	0.8	0.7	57.8	31.0	35	7,102	35
Greece	41	22	11.5	..	4.4	4.6	75.8	62.5	45	56,271	35
Guatemala	..	..	1.9	2.0	1.5	1.4	69.8	31.0	25	26,740	28
Guinea	4	..	..	..	1.4	1.5	59.8	14.4	..	..	..
Haiti	..	..	..	..	1.5	..	56.3	10.1	..	..	..
Honduras	..	..	5.5	..	1.4	1.3	63.0	19.3	..	..	..
Hungary	64	48	..	..	2.1	1.9	74.3	59.2	40	4,566	18
India	43	40	13.4	13.4	2.5	2.8	64.3	45.3	30	3,538	35
Indonesia	21	36	14.5	..	1.4	2.3	50.3	28.3	30	6,623	30
Iran, Islamic Rep.	22	14	..	..	3.0	3.0	66.3	29.2	54	174,171	54
Ireland	55	60	..	..	1.4	1.2	86.0	84.8	46	14,799	32
Israel	37	48	..	..	11.7	9.7	69.8	57.6	50	57,789	36
Italy	54	58	..	..	2.1	2.0	79.5	82.0	46	81,665	37
Jamaica	..	..	..	..	1.0	0.9	68.8	29.5	25	2,712	33
Japan	54	..	..	..	1.0	1.0	82.0	86.9	50	259,291	35
Jordan	11	9	..	..	8.8	9.0	70.8	38.6	..	..	..
Kazakhstan	..	..	..	..	2.9	1.3	64.8	30.2	30	..	30
Kenya	10	18	11.6	..	3.0	2.1	56.8	26.6	33	382	33
Korea, Rep.	46	49	10.3	..	3.7	3.4	80.0	58.8	40	66,236	28
Kuwait	20	20	..	..	77.0	7.5	80.5	59.8	0	..	0
Kyrgyz Republic	..	..	..	..	0.7	1.6	..	17.6	..	..	30
Lao PDR	..	..	..	..	9.8	3.4	..	..	40	1,064	..
Latvia	59	61	..	..	1.6	0.9	72.3	43.4	25	..	25
Lebanon	18	12	..	..	4.0	3.0	58.5	35.0	..	..	..
Lesotho	5	9	..	..	3.6	2.5	..	26.9	..	..	..
Lithuania	67	41	..	..	0.7	0.8	71.3	40.8	33	..	29
Macedonia, FYR	..	..	..	..	2.2	2.5	..	..	..	..	..
Madagascar	9	8	..	..	1.1	1.5	62.5	..	..	..	..
Malawi	8	..	4.3	..	1.1	1.0	61.3	19.5	38	948	38
Malaysia	16	24	..	..	3.2	2.2	75.3	54.9	30	39,474	28

STATES AND MARKETS

Economy	Subsidies and other current transfers % of total expenditure 1990	1997	Value added by state-owned enterprises % of GDP 1985–90	1990–97	Military expenditures % of GNP 1992	1997	Composite ICRG risk rating[a] March 2000	Institutional Investor credit rating[a] March 2000	Highest marginal tax rate[b] Individual % 1999	On income over (dollars) 1999	Corporate % 1999
Mali	..	..	..	..	2.3	1.7	66.3	17.2	..	..	..
Mauritania	..	..	..	..	3.5	2.3	..	..	..	..	..
Mexico	17	51	6.7	4.9	0.5	1.1	70.5	49.8	40	200,000	35
Moldova	..	..	..	..	0.5	1.0	53.3	16.0	..	..	..
Mongolia	56	44	..	..	2.6	1.9	64.0	..	..	..	..
Morocco	8	12	16.8	..	4.5	4.3	72.8	45.6	44	6,445	35
Mozambique	..	..	..	..	7.6	2.8	56.3	19.2	20	792	35
Myanmar	..	..	..	..	8.3	7.6	58.8	16.9	30		30
Namibia	10	..	..	..	2.2	2.7	78.3	39.7	40	16,129	40
Nepal	..	..	..	..	1.0	0.8	..	26.8	..	..	..
Netherlands	70	72	..	..	2.5	1.9	87.0	92.1	60	56,075	35
New Zealand	64	38	..	..	1.6	1.3	80.3	75.5	33	18,134	33
Nicaragua	14	25	..	..	3.1	1.5	50.3	13.4	30	18,083	30
Niger	..	..	5.1	..	1.3	1.1	62.8	14.6	..	..	..
Nigeria	..	..	..	..	2.6	1.4	53.3	18.3	25	1,395	28
Norway	69	70	..	..	3.1	2.1	89.3	89.5	..	..	..
Pakistan	20	8	..	..	7.4	5.7	54.3	18.8	..	..	..
Panama	26	27	7.6	7.3	1.3	1.4	74.0	42.7	30	200,000	30
Papua New Guinea	18	..	..	..	1.5	1.3	62.5	30.9	47	48,251	25
Paraguay	19	..	4.8	4.6	1.8	1.3	63.8	31.7	0		30
Peru	24	36	6.4	5.1	1.8	2.1	66.8	38.8	30	47,985	30
Philippines	7	18	2.3	2.2	1.9	1.5	70.8	46.7	33	12,773	33
Poland	61	62	..	..	2.3	2.3	76.0	58.5	40	15,192	34
Portugal	33	38	15.1	..	2.7	2.4	80.8	79.7	40	36,478	34
Romania	57	50	..	..	3.3	2.4	62.5	27.5	45	4,080	38
Russian Federation	49	..	..	..	8.0	5.8	54.8	19.6	35	6,036	35
Rwanda	16	..	..	..	4.4	4.4	..	..	..	..	..
Saudi Arabia	..	..	..	..	26.8	14.5	73.0	55.1	0		45
Senegal	..	..	6.9	..	2.8	1.6	62.5	23.2	50	22,469	35
Sierra Leone	1	24	..	..	3.2	5.9	37.5	7.1	..	..	..
Singapore	12	8	..	..	5.2	5.7	89.0	80.4	28	240,964	26
Slovak Republic	..	..	..	..	2.2	2.1	72.3	42.9	42	29,258	40
Slovenia	..	..	..	..	2.1	1.7	79.8	63.1	..	..	..
South Africa	23	49	14.9	..	3.2	1.8	70.5	45.2	45	20,391	30
Spain	63	66	..	..	1.6	1.5	75.8	80.4	40	77,139	35
Sri Lanka	23	20	..	..	3.8	5.1	60.3	35.4	35	4,405	35
Sweden	72	71	..	..	2.6	2.5	83.8	83.9	..	..	28
Switzerland	61	64	..	..	1.8	1.4	88.3	93.8	..	..	45
Syrian Arab Republic	..	..	..	..	9.7	5.6	71.0	23.2	..	..	..
Tajikistan	..	..	..	..	0.3	1.7	..	12.9	..	..	..
Tanzania	..	..	9.0	..	2.2	1.3	59.0	19.1	35	12,335	30
Thailand	9	7	..	..	2.6	2.3	74.8	48.8	37	108,430	30
Togo	..	..	..	..	2.9	2.0	60.0	17.4	..	..	..
Tunisia	35	29	..	..	2.4	2.0	73.5	49.7	..	..	..
Turkey	16	29	6.5	5.0	3.8	4.0	54.5	39.0	40	159,898	30
Turkmenistan	..	..	..	..	..	4.6	..	17.1	..	..	..
Uganda	..	..	..	..	2.4	4.2	63.0	22.9	30	3,578	30
Ukraine	..	..	..	..	1.9	3.7	58.3	18.1	40	5,953	30
United Kingdom	52	58	3.6	2.8	3.8	2.7	85.3	91.1	40	46,589	31
United States	50	60	..	..	4.8	3.3	80.0	92.9	40	283,150	35
Uruguay	50	62	5.0	..	2.3	1.4	73.3	49.1	..	..	30
Uzbekistan	..	..	..	..	2.7	2.5	..	18.0	45	2,400	33
Venezuela, RB	37	48	22.3	..	2.6	2.2	64.0	34.9	34	78,500	34
Vietnam	..	..	..	..	3.4	2.8	67.3	29.1	..	..	32
Yemen, Rep.	6	35	..	..	9.4	8.1	62.5	..	..	..	..
Zambia	..	..	32.2	..	3.3	1.1	58.8	15.1	30	742	35
Zimbabwe	18	26	8.6	9.2	3.8	3.8	56.0	24.1	50	20,455	35
World	**23 m**	**37 m**			**3.2 w**	**2.5 w**	**68.7 m**	**32.5 m**			
Low income	..	..			2.7	2.9	57.8	17.4			
Middle income	23	40			4.0	2.9	70.5	39.0			
Lower middle income	18	26			4.2	3.2	67.6	31.7			
Upper middle income	32	48			3.8	2.8	73.3	49.3			
Low and middle income	..	..			3.8	2.9	62.9	27.7			
East Asia & Pacific	19	..			2.9	2.5	67.3	38.8			
Europe & Central Asia	..	46			5.2	4.0	63.7	27.5			
Latin America & Caribbean	24	31			1.4	1.8	68.6	36.6			
Middle East & North Africa	11	14			14.4	7.0	70.5	36.8			
South Asia	23	20			3.1	3.1	61.3	26.1			
Sub-Saharan Africa	10	..			3.1	2.3	58.9	18.7			
High income	56	60			3.1	2.4	82.0	84.3			

Note: For data comparability and coverage, see the Technical Notes. Figures in italics are for years other than those specified.
a. This copyrighted material is reprinted with permission from the following data providers: PRS Group, 6320 Fly Road, Suite 102, P.O. Box 248, East Syracuse, NY 13057; and Institutional Investor, Inc., 488 Madison Avenue, New York, NY 10022. b. These data are from PricewaterhouseCoopers's *Individual Taxes: Worldwide Summaries 1999–2000* and *Corporate Taxes: Worldwide Summaries 1999–2000*, copyright 1999 by PricewaterhouseCoopers by permission of John Wiley & Sons, Inc.

Table 18.   Power and transportation

| Economy | Electric power | | | | Paved roads % of total | | Goods transported by road Millions of ton-km hauled | | Goods transported by rail Ton-km per $ million of GDP (PPP) | | Air passengers carried Thousands |
| | Consumption per capita Kilowatt-hours | | Transmission and distribution losses % of output | | | | | | | | |
	1990	1997	1990	1997	1990	1998	1990	1998	1990	1998	1998
Albania	810	851	18	53	..	30.0	1,195	1,830	67,204	2,029	21
Algeria	449	566	14	15	67.0	68.9	14,000	..	23,449	..	3,382
Angola	60	64	25	28	25.0	25.0	..	..	..	..	553
Argentina	1,123	1,634	17	17	28.5	29.5	..	..	31,570	..	8,447
Armenia	2,545	1,141	16	21	99.2	100.0	..	213	419,134	53,150	365
Australia	7,572	8,307	7	6	35.0	38.7	..	..	76,786	..	30,186
Austria	5,587	6,051	6	6	100.0	100.0	13,300	15,700	86,340	79,889	5,872
Azerbaijan	2,584	1,631	13	23	..	92.3	..	706	..	..	669
Bangladesh	43	76	34	15	7.2	9.5	..	..	6,543	5,148	1,153
Belarus	3,700	2,607	11	15	95.8	95.6	..	9,747	1,094,182	469,369	226
Belgium	5,817	7,055	5	5	81.2	80.7	25,000	36,000	45,390	32,071	8,748
Benin	37	43	214	76	20.0	20.0	..	..	..	..	91
Bolivia	271	391	15	11	4.3	5.5	..	..	47,053	..	2,116
Botswana	..	..	..	..	32.0	23.5	..	..	..	..	124
Brazil	1,425	1,743	14	17	9.7	9.3	..	..	51,486	31,663	28,091
Bulgaria	4,046	3,203	11	14	91.6	92.0	13,823	307	303,350	154,935	828
Burkina Faso	..	..	..	..	16.6	16.0	..	..	..	..	102
Burundi	..	..	..	..	..	..	..	..	..	..	12
Cambodia	..	..	..	..	7.5	7.5	..	1,200	..	78,146	..
Cameroon	204	181	13	20	10.5	12.5	..	..	37,699	37,719	278
Canada	14,972	15,829	7	4	35.0	35.3	54,700	72,240	411,103	440,137	24,653
Central African Republic	..	..	..	..	..	2.7	144	60	..	..	91
Chad	..	..	..	..	0.8	0.8	..	..	..	..	98
Chile	1,178	2,011	11	9	13.8	13.8	..	..	23,140	7,959	5,150
China	471	714	7	8	..	..	..	..	667,164	304,775	53,234
Hong Kong, China	4,178	4,959	11	14	100.0	100.0	..	..	..	..	12,254
Colombia	751	885	21	22	11.9	12.0	6,227	..	2,113	1,945	9,290
Congo, Dem. Rep.	122	120	13	3	..	..	..	..	32,460	..	..
Congo, Rep.	254	197	0	1	9.7	9.7	..	..	189,871	..	241
Costa Rica	1,111	1,353	8	8	15.3	21.0	2,243	3,070	..	..	1,170
Côte d'Ivoire	158	181	18	16	8.7	9.7	..	..	15,674	19,827	162
Croatia	2,765	2,429	18	19	..	..	..	..	201,699	60,241	828
Czech Republic	4,649	4,817	7	8	100.0	100.0	..	33,912	..	143,684	1,601
Denmark	5,650	6,027	6	5	100.0	100.0	13,700	14,700	18,759	12,268	5,947
Dominican Republic	437	620	25	28	44.7	49.4	..	..	..	..	34
Ecuador	467	611	23	23	13.4	16.8	2,638	3,753	..	..	1,919
Egypt, Arab Rep.	697	803	12	12	72.0	78.1	31,400	31,500	21,444	20,062	3,895
El Salvador	358	537	16	13	14.4	19.8	..	..	..	..	1,694
Eritrea	..	..	..	..	19.4	21.8	..	..	..	..	..
Estonia	4,332	3,466	7	16	51.8	22.1	..	3,791	354,541	519,698	297
Ethiopia	21	21	1	1	15.0	15.0	..	..	2,120	..	790
Finland	11,822	13,689	5	4	61.0	64.0	26,300	25,400	97,605	92,017	6,771
France	5,321	6,060	7	6	..	100.0	190,500	237,200	51,687	43,309	42,232
Georgia	2,711	1,142	18	16	93.8	93.5	..	98	272,478	146,315	110
Germany	5,729	5,626	4	4	99.0	99.1	182,800	301,800	..	..	49,280
Ghana	301	276	1	0	19.6	24.1	..	..	6,191	..	210
Greece	2,802	3,493	8	9	91.7	91.8	78,900	96,200	5,763	2,196	6,403
Guatemala	242	404	16	13	24.9	27.6	..	..	..	..	506
Guinea	..	..	..	..	15.2	16.5	..	..	..	..	36
Haiti	61	42	31	43	21.9	24.3	..	..	..	..	..
Honduras	365	411	20	24	21.1	20.3	..	..	..	..	..
Hungary	3,048	2,840	14	13	50.4	43.4	1,836	14	177,696	74,713	1,749
India	254	363	18	18	47.3	45.7	..	..	199,742	137,082	16,521
Indonesia	156	329	15	12	46.0	46.3	..	..	9,570	9,125	12,614
Iran, Islamic Rep.	829	1,163	19	22	..	50.0	..	..	44,931	46,269	9,200
Ireland	3,385	4,559	9	8	94.0	94.1	5,100	5,500	14,784	4,875	10,401
Israel	3,902	5,069	5	9	100.0	100.0	..	..	16,931	9,605	3,699
Italy	3,784	4,315	8	7	100.0	100.0	177,900	207,200	20,143	18,885	27,463
Jamaica	686	2,170	18	11	64.0	70.7	..	..	..	..	1,454
Japan	6,125	7,241	4	4	69.2	74.9	274,444	306,263	11,356	7,854	101,701
Jordan	959	1,196	8	10	100.0	100.0	..	..	102,326	40,974	1,187
Kazakhstan	5,905	2,595	9	15	55.1	86.5	..	4,637	3,964,805	1,498,375	566
Kenya	115	127	16	17	12.8	13.9	..	..	80,740	41,917	1,138
Korea, Rep.	2,202	4,847	5	4	71.5	74.5	31,841	74,504	37,095	20,362	27,109
Kuwait	6,875	12,886	9	..	72.9	80.6	..	..	..	..	2,241
Kyrgyz Republic	1,900	1,372	8	34	90.0	91.1	..	350	..	..	620
Lao PDR	..	..	..	..	24.0	13.8	120	..	..	..	124
Latvia	3,281	1,758	18	29	13.4	38.6	..	4,108	854,603	788,435	229
Lebanon	369	1,930	7	13	95.0	95.0	..	..	..	..	716
Lesotho	..	..	..	..	18.0	17.9	..	..	..	..	28
Lithuania	3,228	1,818	5	11	81.8	91.0	..	5,611	..	346,800	259
Macedonia, FYR	..	..	..	..	58.9	63.8	1,708	1,210	62,004	47,137	489
Madagascar	..	..	..	..	15.4	11.6	..	..	..	..	601
Malawi	..	..	..	..	22.0	19.0	..	..	15,207	11,185	158
Malaysia	1,096	2,352	10	9	70.0	75.1	..	..	15,555	7,339	13,654

STATES AND MARKETS

Economy	Electric power Consumption per capita Kilowatt-hours 1990	1997	Transmission and distribution losses % of output 1990	1997	Paved roads % of total 1990	1998	Goods transported by road Millions of ton-km hauled 1990	1998	Goods transported by rail Ton-km per $ million of GDP (PPP) 1990	1998	Air passengers carried Thousands 1998
Mali	..	..	..	..	10.9	*12.1*	..	..	53,612	*34,053*	91
Mauritania	..	..	..	..	11.0	*11.3*	..	..	..	..	250
Mexico	1,204	1,459	12	14	35.1	*29.7*	108,884	*154,083*	68,768	62,102	17,717
Moldova	2,279	1,217	8	27	87.1	*87.3*	..	*780*	..	..	118
Mongolia	..	..	..	..	10.2	3.4	1,871	123	1,351,705	*653,947*	240
Morocco	340	423	9	4	49.1	*52.3*	2,638	*2,086*	67,356	*49,613*	3,012
Mozambique	35	47	16	31	16.8	*18.7*	..	*110*	..	..	201
Myanmar	43	57	26	35	10.9	*12.2*	..	..	..	..	333
Namibia	..	..	..	..	10.8	*8.3*	..	..	285,327	*129,941*	214
Nepal	28	39	29	28	37.5	*41.5*	..	..	..	..	754
Netherlands	4,917	5,736	4	4	88.0	90.0	31,800	*45,000*	12,187	*9,938*	18,676
New Zealand	8,087	8,380	11	11	57.0	*58.1*	..	..	49,742	51,977	8,655
Nicaragua	284	286	18	26	10.5	*10.1*	..	..	..	..	51
Niger	..	..	..	..	29.0	*7.9*	..	..	..	..	91
Nigeria	77	84	38	32	30.0	*30.9*	..	..	3,359	*4,834*	313
Norway	22,824	23,499	6	8	69.0	74.5	7,940	*11,838*	..	..	14,292
Pakistan	267	333	21	24	54.0	57.0	352	90,268	41,763	*26,278*	5,414
Panama	883	1,152	24	22	32.0	28.1	..	..	..	..	860
Papua New Guinea	..	..	..	..	3.2	3.5	..	..	..	..	1,110
Paraguay	470	759	0	2	8.5	9.5	..	..	..	..	222
Peru	491	607	18	16	9.9	12.9	..	..	8,138	*4,757*	2,775
Philippines	336	432	13	17	..	19.8	..	..	65	4	6,732
Poland	2,525	2,451	8	12	61.6	65.6	49,800	69,543	395,542	209,664	2,213
Portugal	2,379	3,206	11	10	..	..	12,200	*13,500*	13,550	13,975	7,023
Romania	2,337	1,704	9	12	*51.0*	67.6	13,800	15,785	345,140	146,252	908
Russian Federation	5,821	3,981	8	10	74.2	..	..	..	1,726,768	*1,042,132*	15,224
Rwanda	..	..	..	..	9.0	*9.1*	..	..	..	..	..
Saudi Arabia	3,181	4,085	9	8	40.6	30.1	..	..	4,324	*3,843*	11,816
Senegal	94	107	14	17	27.2	29.3	..	..	61,227	35,183	121
Sierra Leone	..	..	..	..	10.6	8.0	..	..	..	..	0
Singapore	4,792	7,944	3	4	97.1	97.3	..	..	..	..	13,331
Slovak Republic	4,432	4,243	8	9	98.7	99.0	4,180	4,750	..	224,788	107
Slovenia	4,875	4,955	6	5	72.0	90.6	3,440	325	*120,357*	92,945	460
South Africa	3,676	3,800	6	8	29.8	11.8	..	..	362,402	*283,262*	6,480
Spain	3,239	3,899	9	9	74.0	*99.0*	10,900	*16,500*	22,227	17,569	31,594
Sri Lanka	153	227	17	17	*32.0*	95.0	19	*30*	5,077	*2,035*	1,213
Sweden	14,061	14,042	6	7	71.0	77.5	26,500	*33,100*	122,858	99,690	11,878
Switzerland	6,997	6,885	6	6	..	..	10,400	13,250	..	..	14,299
Syrian Arab Republic	683	776	26	..	*72.0*	23.1	..	..	41,508	26,484	685
Tajikistan	3,346	2,177	9	12	71.6	82.7	..	..	..	..	592
Tanzania	51	54	20	14	37.0	4.2	..	..	*77,249*	71,671	220
Thailand	690	1,360	11	9	55.3	97.5	..	..	15,903	8,835	15,015
Togo	..	..	..	..	21.2	31.6	..	..	..	..	91
Tunisia	532	709	11	11	76.1	78.9	..	..	52,684	*42,976*	1,859
Turkey	801	1,275	12	18	..	28.0	..	152,210	30,183	20,310	9,949
Turkmenistan	2,293	934	8	11	73.5	*81.2*	..	..	..	..	521
Uganda	..	..	..	..	..	..	..	..	13,470	4,990	100
Ukraine	4,308	2,449	7	16	93.7	96.5	..	18,266	1,476,624	987,824	1,066
United Kingdom	4,768	5,241	8	7	100.0	100.0	133,000	*152,500*	17,203	..	61,940
United States	10,558	11,822	9	6	58.2	*58.8*	1,073,100	*1,534,430*	358,829	213,751	588,171
Uruguay	1,220	1,710	14	19	74.0	*90.0*	..	..	11,124	*6,290*	557
Uzbekistan	2,383	1,645	9	9	79.0	*87.3*	..	..	..	317,391	1,560
Venezuela, RB	2,307	2,488	18	21	35.6	*33.6*	..	..	..	*354*	3,737
Vietnam	94	203	24	18	23.5	25.1	..	..	*18,124*	11,367	2,304
Yemen, Rep.	108	93	12	26	9.1	*8.1*	..	..	..	..	765
Zambia	503	563	11	11	16.6	..	..	..	81,810	57,858	49
Zimbabwe	933	919	6	13	14.0	47.4	..	..	215,462	*140,231*	789
World	**1,928 w**	**2,053 w**	**8 w**	**8 w**	**39.0 m**	**43.1 m**					**1,466,869 s**
Low income	373	357	13	17	17.4	*18.8*					53,586
Middle income	1,243	1,340	9	11	50.5	*49.7*					292,223
Lower middle income	1,061	1,042	9	11	50.5	*43.7*					153,612
Upper middle income	1,926	2,434	10	12	50.4	*47.1*					138,611
Low and middle income	860	896	10	12	28.8	*29.5*					345,809
East Asia & Pacific	465	771	8	8	23.5	*17.4*					133,490
Europe & Central Asia	3,853	2,693	8	12	74.2	*86.5*					41,165
Latin America & Caribbean	1,131	1,402	14	16	21.9	*26.0*					89,378
Middle East & North Africa	920	1,159	13	13	67.0	*50.2*					40,144
South Asia	228	324	19	18	37.5	*57.0*					25,390
Sub-Saharan Africa	446	446	9	10	16.6	*15.0*					16,242
High income	7,294	8,238	7	6	86.3	93.9					1,121,061

Note: For data comparability and coverage, see the Technical Notes. Figures in italics are for years other than those specified.

Table 19. Communications, information, and science and technology

| Economy | Per 1,000 people | | | | | | Internet hosts[b] Per 10,000 people January 2000 | Scientists and engineers in R&D Per million people 1987–97[d] | High-technology exports % of mfg. exports 1998 | Patent applications filed[c] 1997 | |
	Daily newspapers 1996	Radios 1997	Television sets[a] 1998	Telephone mainlines[a] 1998	Mobile telephones[a] 1998	Personal computers[a] 1998				Residents	Nonresidents
Albania	36	217	109	31	1	..	0.24	..	1	..	26,005
Algeria	38	241	105	53	1	4.2	0.01	..	1	34	206
Angola	11	54	14	6	1	0.8	0.00	..	..	..	..
Argentina	123	681	289	203	78	44.3	38.48	660	5	824	5,035
Armenia	23	224	218	157	2	4.2	2.11	1,485	5	63	25,059
Australia	293	1,376	639	512	286	411.6	567.30	3,357	11	8,937	39,274
Austria	296	753	516	491	282	233.4	338.73	1,627	12	2,681	108,543
Azerbaijan	27	23	254	89	8	..	0.16	2,791	..	..	24,308
Bangladesh	9	50	6	3	1	..	0.00	52	0	70	156
Belarus	174	296	314	241	1	..	0.89	2,248	4	755	25,280
Belgium	160	793	510	500	173	286.0	313.44	2,272	8	1,687	84,958
Benin	2	108	10	7	1	0.9	0.04	176	..	..	..
Bolivia	55	675	116	69	27	7.5	1.14	172	8	17	106
Botswana	27	156	20	65	15	25.5	13.90	..	..	1	92
Brazil	40	444	316	121	47	30.1	26.22	168	9	36	31,947
Bulgaria	257	543	398	329	15	14.50	14.50	1,747	4	400	27,600
Burkina Faso	1	33	9	4	0	0.7	0.19	17	..	..	..
Burundi	3	71	4	3	0	..	0.00	33	..	1	4
Cambodia	2	127	123	2	6	0.9	0.13	..	..	..	..
Cameroon	7	163	32	5	0	..	0.00	..	2	..	..
Canada	159	1,077	715	634	176	330.0	540.17	2,719	15	4,192	50,254
Central African Republic	2	83	5	3	0	..	0.02	56	0	..	..
Chad	0	242	1	1	0	..	0.01	..	..	..	..
Chile	98	354	232	205	65	48.2	26.42	445	4	189	1,771
China	..	333	272	70	19	8.9	0.57	454	15	12,786	48,596
Hong Kong, China	792	684	431	558	475	254.2	162.82	..	21	26	2,359
Colombia	46	581	217	173	49	27.9	9.59	..	9	87	1,172
Congo, Dem. Rep.	3	375	135	0	0	..	0.00	..	..	2	27
Congo, Rep.	8	124	12	8	1	..	0.01	..	..	..	..
Costa Rica	94	271	387	172	28	39.1	20.47	532	13	..	..
Côte d'Ivoire	17	164	70	12	6	3.6	0.42	..	..	..	..
Croatia	115	336	272	348	41	111.6	31.65	1,916	8	273	439
Czech Republic	254	803	447	364	94	97.3	109.78	1,222	8	601	29,976
Denmark	309	1,141	585	660	364	377.4	631.80	3,259	18	2,658	106,403
Dominican Republic	52	178	95	93	31	..	7.89	..	1	..	..
Ecuador	70	419	293	78	25	18.5	1.52	146	4	8	302
Egypt, Arab Rep.	40	324	122	60	1	9.1	0.73	459	0	504	706
El Salvador	48	464	675	80	18	..	1.54	20	8	3	64
Eritrea	..	91	14	7	0	..	0.01	..	..	..	..
Estonia	174	693	480	343	170	34.4	206.81	2,017	9	18	26,626
Ethiopia	1	195	5	3	0	..	0.01	..	..	4[e]	..
Finland	455	1,496	640	554	572	349.2	1,218.42	2,799	22	4,061	105,376
France	218	937	601	570	188	207.8	131.47	2,659	23	18,669	93,962
Georgia	..	555	473	115	11	..	1.71	..	..	265	26,561
Germany	311	948	580	567	170	304.7	207.62	2,831	14	62,052	113,543
Ghana	14	238	99	8	1	1.6	0.06	..	7	..	34,103
Greece	153	477	466	522	194	51.9	73.84	773	7	53	82,390
Guatemala	33	79	126	41	10	8.3	1.56	104	7	4	131
Guinea	..	47	41	5	3	2.6	0.00	..	..	3	6
Haiti	3	55	5	8	0	..	0.00	..	4	3	6
Honduras	55	386	90	38	5	7.6	0.18	..	1	10	126
Hungary	186	689	437	336	105	58.9	113.38	1,099	21	774	29,331
India	..	121	69	22	1	2.7	0.23	149	5	10,155[e]	..
Indonesia	24	156	136	27	5	8.2	1.00	182	10	..	4,517
Iran, Islamic Rep.	28	265	157	112	6	31.9	0.09	560	..	418[e]	..
Ireland	150	699	403	435	257	271.7	159.17	2,319	45	946	82,484
Israel	290	520	318	471	359	217.2	225.10	..	20	1,796	28,548
Italy	104	878	486	451	355	173.4	114.42	1,318	8	2,574	88,836
Jamaica	62	480	182	166	22	39.4	1.40	..	0	..	..
Japan	578	955	707	503	374	237.2	208.06	4,909	26	351,487	66,487
Jordan	58	287	52	86	12	8.7	1.27	94	..	..	..
Kazakhstan	..	384	231	104	2	..	2.45	..	9	1,171	24,998
Kenya	9	104	21	9	0	2.5	0.20	..	4	25	49,935
Korea, Rep.	393	1,033	346	433	302	156.8	60.03	2,193	27	92,798	37,184
Kuwait	374	660	491	236	138	104.9	20.50	230	0	..	..
Kyrgyz Republic	15	112	45	76	0	..	5.02	584	16	152	24,951
Lao PDR	4	143	4	6	1	1.1	0.00	..	..	..	..
Latvia	247	710	492	302	68	..	57.33	1,049	4	163	26,860
Lebanon	107	906	352	194	157	39.2	10.93	..	..	..	..
Lesotho	8	49	25	10	5	..	0.23	..	..	..	49,483
Lithuania	93	513	459	300	72	54.0	34.40	2,028	3	125	26,673
Macedonia, FYR	21	200	250	199	15	..	7.20	1,335	1	66	26,087
Madagascar	5	192	21	3	1	1.3	0.22	12	1	..	26,174
Malawi	3	249	2	3	1	..	0.00	..	..	2	49,932
Malaysia	158	420	166	198	99	58.6	25.43	93	54	179	6,272

STATES AND MARKETS

Economy	Per 1,000 people						Internet hosts[b] Per 10,000 people January 2000	Scientists and engineers in R&D Per million people 1987–97[d]	High-technology exports % of mfg. exports 1998	Patent applications filed[c] 1997	
	Daily newspapers 1996	Radios 1997	Television sets[a] 1998	Telephone mainlines[a] 1998	Mobile telephones[a] 1998	Personal computers[a] 1998				Residents	Nonresidents
Mali	1	54	12	3	0	0.7	0.01	..	..	..	..
Mauritania	0	151	91	6	0	5.5	0.22	..	..	..	..
Mexico	97	325	261	104	35	47.0	40.88	214	19	429	35,503
Moldova	60	740	297	150	2	6.4	2.97	330	7	295	25,030
Mongolia	27	151	63	37	1	5.4	0.19	910	1	186	26,197
Morocco	26	241	160	54	4	2.5	0.33	..	0	90	237
Mozambique	3	40	5	4	0	1.6	0.09	..	6	..	..
Myanmar	10	95	7	5	0	..	0.00	..	..	..	..
Namibia	19	144	37	69	12	18.6	11.74	..	..	..	..
Nepal	11	38	6	8	0	..	0.12	..	..	..	..
Netherlands	306	978	543	593	213	317.6	517.03	2,219	30	5,227	85,402
New Zealand	216	990	508	479	203	282.1	703.33	1,663	..	1,735	33,402
Nicaragua	30	285	190	31	4	7.8	2.04	..	4	..	..
Niger	0	69	27	2	0	0.2	0.03	..	..	..	..
Nigeria	24	223	66	4	0	5.7	0.01	15	..	..	..
Norway	588	915	579	660	474	373.4	899.48	3,664	16	1,518	30,489
Pakistan	23	98	88	19	1	3.9	0.34	72	0	16	782
Panama	62	299	187	151	29	27.1	4.33	..	0	31	142
Papua New Guinea	15	97	24	11	1	..	0.70	..	..	..	..
Paraguay	43	182	101	55	41	9.6	3.02	..	2	..	..
Peru	0	273	144	67	30	18.1	3.60	233	3	48	756
Philippines	79	159	108	37	22	15.1	1.58	157	71	125	3,440
Poland	113	523	413	228	50	43.9	47.26	1,358	3	2,401	30,137
Portugal	75	304	542	413	309	81.3	90.67	1,182	4	92	106,595
Romania	300	319	233	162	29	10.2	11.02	1,387	2	1,709	27,346
Russian Federation	105	418	420	197	5	40.6	14.69	3,587	12	15,277	32,943
Rwanda	0	102	0	2	1	..	0.30	35	..	..	..
Saudi Arabia	57	321	262	143	31	49.6	1.28	..	1	57	1,001
Senegal	5	142	41	16	2	11.4	0.32	3	..	..	..
Sierra Leone	4	253	13	4	0	..	0.15	..	..	..	9,506
Singapore	360	822	348	562	346	458.4	452.25	2,318	59	8,188	29,467
Slovak Republic	185	580	402	286	87	65.1	47.96	1,866	3	234	27,973
Slovenia	199	406	356	375	84	250.9	103.71	2,251	4	285	27,162
South Africa	32	317	125	115	56	47.4	39.17	1,031	9	..	..
Spain	100	333	506	414	179	144.8	105.36	1,305	7	2,856	110,911
Sri Lanka	29	209	92	28	9	4.1	0.63	191	..	81	26,322
Sweden	445	932	531	674	464	361.4	670.83	3,826	20	7,893	107,107
Switzerland	337	1,000	535	675	235	421.8	429.01	3,006	16	5,814	107,038
Syrian Arab Republic	20	278	70	95	0	1.7	0.00	30	..	..	..
Tajikistan	20	142	285	37	0	..	0.35	666	..	23	24,742
Tanzania	4	279	21	4	1	1.6	0.06	..	0	..	..
Thailand	63	232	236	84	32	21.6	6.46	103	31	238	5,205
Togo	4	218	18	7	2	6.8	0.26	98	..	..	..
Tunisia	31	223	198	81	4	14.7	0.10	125	2	46	128
Turkey	111	180	286	254	53	23.2	13.92	291	2	233	27,985
Turkmenistan	..	276	201	82	1	..	0.92	..	..	52	24,584
Uganda	2	128	27	3	1	1.5	0.06	21	..	..	49,760
Ukraine	54	884	490	191	2	13.8	5.39	2,171	..	4,692	28,036
United Kingdom	329	1,436	645	557	252	263.0	321.39	2,448	28	26,591	121,618
United States	215	2,146	847	661	256	458.6	1,939.97	3,676	33	125,808	110,884
Uruguay	293	607	241	250	60	91.2	76.09	..	2	32	370
Uzbekistan	3	465	275	65	1	..	0.08	1,763	..	817	26,490
Venezuela, RB	206	468	185	117	87	43.0	5.91	209	3	201	2,323
Vietnam	4	107	47	26	2	6.4	0.02	..	..	30	27,410
Yemen, Rep.	15	64	29	13	1	1.2	0.02	..	..	..	..
Zambia	12	121	137	9	1	..	0.53	..	..	..	96
Zimbabwe	19	93	30	17	4	9.0	1.71	..	2	3	21,966
World	.. w	418 w	247 w	146 w	55 w	70.6 w	120.02 w	.. w	22 w	798,007 s	3,602,785 s
Low income	..	157	76	23	2	3.2	0.37	..	..	16,764	680,497
Middle income	..	359	257	109	31	22.9	9.96	668	18	133,150	784,961
Lower middle income	..	322	250	90	18	13.6	2.83	763	15	34,272	445,265
Upper middle income	89	493	285	176	76	53.1	35.88	660	20	98,878	339,696
Low and middle income	..	263	172	69	17	15.6	5.40	..	17	149,914	1,465,458
East Asia & Pacific	..	302	228	70	25	14.1	2.69	492	28	106,342	184,288
Europe & Central Asia	102	442	353	200	23	34.6	18.87	2,534	8	31,081	685,716
Latin America & Caribbean	71	420	255	123	45	33.9	22.33	..	12	1,708	175,004
Middle East & North Africa	33	274	135	81	8	9.9	0.55	..	1	509	1,207
South Asia	..	112	61	19	1	2.9	0.22	137	4	10,236	26,322
Sub-Saharan Africa	12	198	52	14	5	7.5	2.73	..	..	38	392,921
High income	286	1,286	661	567	256	311.2	777.22	3,166	33	648,093	2,137,327

Note: For data comparability and coverage, see the Technical Notes. Figures in italics are for years other than those specified.
a. Data are from the International Telecommunication Union's (ITU) *World Telecommunication Development Report 1999.* Please cite the ITU for third-party use of these data. b. Data are from the Internet Software Consortium (www.isc.org). c. Other patent applications filed in 1997 include those filed under the auspices of the African Intellectual Property Organization (31 by residents, 26,057 by nonresidents), African Regional Industrial Property Organization (7 by residents, 25,724 by nonresidents), European Patent Office (44,604 by residents, 53,339 by nonresidents), and Eurasian Patent Organization (258 by residents, 26,207 by nonresidents). The original information was provided by the World Intellectual Property Organization (WIPO). The International Bureau of WIPO assumes no liability or responsibility with regard to the transformation of these data. d. Data are for the most recent year available. e. Total for residents and nonresidents.

Table 20.   Global trade

Economy	Merchandise exports Millions of dollars 1990	1998	Mfg. % of total 1990	1998	Exports of commercial services Millions of dollars 1990	1998	Merchandise imports Millions of dollars 1990	1998	Mfg. % of total 1990	1998	Imports of commercial services Millions of dollars 1990	1998
Albania	230	210	..	68	32	83	380	840	..	67	29	119
Algeria	11,330	10,300	3	3	479	..	9,715	9,320	68	62	1,155	..
Angola	3,910	2,880	0	..	65	226	1,578	2,120	..	..	1,288	1,738
Argentina	12,353	26,441	29	35	2,264	4,494	4,076	31,404	78	89	2,876	8,714
Armenia	..	225	..	54	..	118	..	895	..	39	..	175
Australia	39,752	55,900	16	29	9,833	15,809	42,032	64,630	80	87	13,388	16,928
Austria	41,265	62,584	88	83	22,755	31,817	49,146	68,028	81	84	14,104	30,035
Azerbaijan	..	605	..	13	..	320	..	1,075	..	75	..	692
Bangladesh	1,671	3,831	77	91	296	252	3,598	6,974	56	69	554	1,180
Belarus	..	7,015	..	76	..	935	..	8,510	..	57	..	444
Belgium[a]	117,703	178,811	77	78	24,690	36,076	119,702	166,798	68	78	24,298	34,104
Benin	288	420	..	..	109	102	265	671	..	..	113	170
Bolivia	926	1,103	5	30	133	238	687	1,983	85	86	291	423
Botswana	1,784	1,948	..	..	183	241	1,946	2,387	..	..	371	517
Brazil	31,414	51,120	52	55	3,706	7,083	22,524	60,730	56	76	6,733	15,743
Bulgaria	5,030	4,300	..	61	837	1,766	5,100	4,980	49	50	600	1,398
Burkina Faso	152	315	..	..	34	..	536	750	..	..	196	..
Burundi	75	65	..	..	7	3	231	158	..	..	59	33
Cambodia	86	320	..	..	50	99	164	680	..	..	64	185
Cameroon	2,002	1,870	9	8	369	..	1,400	1,520	78	67	1,018	..
Canada	127,629	214,710	59	66	18,350	30,281	123,244	206,066	81	85	27,479	35,249
Central African Republic	120	160	..	43	17	..	154	280	..	61	166	..
Chad	188	270	..	..	23	..	285	255	..	..	223	..
Chile	8,372	14,830	11	17	1,786	4,030	7,678	18,779	75	81	1,983	4,077
China*	62,091	183,809	72	87	5,748	24,040	53,345	140,237	80	81	4,113	28,775
Hong Kong, China	82,390[b]	174,863[b]	95	95	18,128	34,523	84,725[b]	186,759[b]	85	89	11,018	22,788
Colombia	6,766	10,852	25	32	1,548	1,999	5,590	14,635	77	79	1,683	3,462
Congo, Dem. Rep.	999	600	..	..	127	..	887	322	..	..	689	..
Congo, Rep.	981	1,250	..	..	65	45	621	470	..	..	748	553
Costa Rica	1,448	5,511	27	56	583	1,315	1,990	6,230	66	86	540	1,168
Côte d'Ivoire	3,072	4,575	..	..	385	451	2,097	2,991	..	56	1,375	1,314
Croatia	..	4,541	..	76	..	3,964	..	8,384	..	75	..	1,889
Czech Republic	12,170	26,350	..	88	..	7,366	12,880	28,790	..	82	..	5,665
Denmark	36,870	48,173	60	65	12,731	14,830	33,333	46,086	73	77	10,106	15,460
Dominican Republic	735	795	78	8	1,086	2,421	2,062	4,716	..	..	435	1,300
Ecuador	2,714	4,203	2	10	508	757	1,861	5,576	84	76	601	1,178
Egypt, Arab Rep.	2,585	3,130	42	44	4,813	7,832	9,216	16,166	56	59	3,327	5,886
El Salvador	582	1,263	38	47	301	277	1,263	3,112	63	68	296	539
Eritrea	..	..	..	..	..	..	..	..	..	..	..	..
Estonia	..	3,240	..	66	..	1,476	..	4,785	..	71	..	814
Ethiopia	..	561	..	..	261	348	1,081	1,450	..	..	348	405
Finland	26,571	43,145	83	86	4,562	6,703	27,001	32,338	76	77	7,432	7,679
France	216,588	305,362	77	80	66,274	84,627	234,436	289,421	74	80	50,455	65,420
Georgia	..	190	..	..	..	278	..	1,055	..	..	..	335
Germany	421,100	542,812	88	86	51,605	78,903	355,686	470,656	74	73	79,214	125,039
Ghana	897	1,700	8	..	79	162	1,205	1,850	70	..	226	433
Greece	8,105	10,765	54	54	6,514	9,224	19,777	28,754	70	73	2,756	4,196
Guatemala	1,163	2,582	24	33	313	581	1,649	4,651	69	77	363	759
Guinea	671	800	..	..	91	66	723	1,090	..	..	243	274
Haiti	160	175	85	84	43	178	332	797	..	..	71	370
Honduras	831	1,575	9	17	121	361	935	2,500	71	74	213	396
Hungary	10,000	22,995	63	82	2,677	4,870	10,340	25,705	70	84	2,264	3,941
India	17,975	33,626	71	74	4,609	11,067	23,642	42,742	51	55	5,943	14,192
Indonesia	25,675	48,847	35	45	2,488	4,340	21,837	27,337	77	69	5,898	11,744
Iran, Islamic Rep.	16,870	13,100	..	..	343	902	15,716	12,500	..	..	3,703	2,392
Ireland	23,743	64,380	70	84	3,286	6,586	20,669	44,526	76	81	5,145	20,005
Israel	12,080	22,993	87	92	4,546	8,980	16,793	29,342	77	82	4,825	9,626
Italy	170,304	242,348	88	89	48,579	66,621	181,968	215,576	64	72	46,602	62,887
Jamaica	1,135	1,312	69	70	976	1,727	1,859	2,997	61	65	667	1,233
Japan	287,581	387,927	96	94	41,384	61,795	235,368	280,484	44	58	84,281	110,705
Jordan	1,064	1,800	51	42	1,430	1,810	2,600	3,836	51	58	1,118	1,588
Kazakhstan	..	5,340	..	23	..	897	..	4,240	..	70	..	1,128
Kenya	1,031	2,008	29	24	774	638	2,125	3,197	66	64	598	603
Korea, Rep.	65,016	132,313	94	91	9,155	23,843	69,844	93,282	63	61	10,050	23,523
Kuwait	7,042	9,554	6	14	1,054	1,496	3,972	8,619	79	81	2,805	4,243
Kyrgyz Republic	..	515	..	38	..	58	..	840	..	48	..	177
Lao PDR	78	370	..	..	11	116	201	553	..	..	25	92
Latvia	..	1,810	..	58	290	1,035	..	3,190	..	74	120	717
Lebanon	494	662	..	..	..	..	2,529	7,070	..	..	..	..
Lesotho	59	194	..	..	34	46	672	863	..	..	48	50
Lithuania	..	3,710	..	61	..	1,096	..	5,795	..	69	..	816
Macedonia, FYR	..	..	..	72	..	130	..	..	..	47	..	297
Madagascar	319	243	14	28	129	264	571	514	69	61	172	326
Malawi	417	528	5	..	37	..	581	637	78	..	268	..
Malaysia	29,416	73,305	54	79	3,769	11,296	29,258	58,326	82	85	5,394	13,230
* Taiwan, China	67,142	110,518	93	93	6,937	16,660	54,831	104,946	69	73	13,923	23,240

GLOBAL LINKS

Economy	Merchandise exports Millions of dollars		Mfg. % of total		Exports of commercial services Millions of dollars		Merchandise imports Millions of dollars		Mfg. % of total		Imports of commercial services Millions of dollars	
	1990	1998	1990	1998	1990	1998	1990	1998	1990	1998	1990	1998
Mali	359	556	2	..	71	*62*	619	750	53	..	352	*324*
Mauritania	469	448	..	..	14	24	387	319	..	..	126	130
Mexico	40,711	117,500	43	85	7,222	11,937	43,548	130,811	75	85	10,063	12,621
Moldova	..	635	..	25	..	117	..	1,025	..	57	..	191
Mongolia	660	370	..	*10*	48	75	924	472	..	*65*	155	142
Morocco	4,265	7,266	52	*49*	1,871	2,558	6,800	10,276	61	*58*	940	1,414
Mozambique	126	210	..	*17*	103	286	878	910	..	*62*	206	396
Myanmar	325	1,065	*10*	..	93	529	270	2,666	*81*	..	72	429
Namibia	1,085	1,460	..	..	106	315	1,163	1,680	..	..	341	449
Nepal	210	474	83	90	166	433	686	1,245	67	42	159	189
Netherlands	131,775	201,001	59	70	29,621	51,706	126,098	187,357	71	77	28,995	46,506
New Zealand	9,488	12,071	23	32	2,415	3,651	9,501	12,495	81	81	3,251	4,508
Nicaragua	330	573	8	8	34	151	638	1,492	59	69	73	264
Niger	282	298	..	..	22	..	388	377	..	..	209	..
Nigeria	13,670	9,729	*1*	*2*	965	884	5,627	10,002	*67*	75	1,901	4,054
Norway	34,047	39,645	33	30	12,452	13,953	27,231	36,193	82	*83*	12,247	15,211
Pakistan	5,589	8,594	79	84	1,240	*1,473*	7,546	9,415	54	55	1,897	*2,468*
Panama	340	784	21	17	907	1,563	1,539	3,350	70	78	666	1,129
Papua New Guinea	1,144	1,772	10	..	198	318	1,193	1,232	73	..	393	794
Paraguay	959	1,021	10	*15*	404	469	1,352	3,200	77	*69*	361	535
Peru	3,230	5,735	18	24	715	1,653	3,470	9,840	61	73	1,071	2,191
Philippines	8,068	29,414	38	90	2,897	7,465	13,041	31,496	53	80	1,721	10,087
Poland	14,320	28,230	59	77	3,200	10,890	11,570	47,055	63	80	2,847	6,559
Portugal	16,417	24,177	80	87	5,054	8,512	25,263	36,912	71	77	3,772	6,708
Romania	4,960	8,300	73	81	610	1,192	7,600	11,835	39	73	787	1,838
Russian Federation	..	74,200	..	28	..	12,937	..	59,100	..	44	..	16,127
Rwanda	110	60	60	..	31	31	288	285	..	..	96	115
Saudi Arabia	44,417	39,775	7	88	3,031	*4,421*	24,069	30,013	81	78	12,694	8,678
Senegal	761	965	23	..	356	329	1,219	1,407	51	..	368	*389*
Sierra Leone	138	7	..	..	45	..	149	95	..	..	67	..
Singapore	52,752 [b]	109,895 [b]	72	86	12,719	18,243	60,899 [b]	101,496 [b]	73	84	8,575	17,884
Slovak Republic	..	10,775	..	84	..	2,275	..	13,005	..	77	..	2,272
Slovenia	..	9,048	..	90	..	2,045	..	10,110	..	80	..	1,520
South Africa	23,549	26,362	22	54	3,442	5,109	18,399	29,242	77	70	4,096	5,278
Spain	55,642	109,037	75	78	27,649	48,729	87,715	132,799	71	76	15,197	27,495
Sri Lanka	1,983	4,735	54	..	425	888	2,685	5,917	65	..	620	1,325
Sweden	57,540	84,705	83	82	13,453	17,675	54,264	68,177	79	81	16,959	21,620
Switzerland	63,784	78,876	94	93	18,232	25,795	69,681	80,094	84	85	11,086	15,273
Syrian Arab Republic	4,212	2,890	36	*10*	740	1,551	2,400	3,895	62	*69*	702	1,297
Tajikistan	..	600	..	..	..	..	..	770	..	..	..	..
Tanzania	415	676	..	*10*	131	534	1,027	1,453	..	*66*	288	885
Thailand	23,070	54,456	63	74	6,292	13,074	33,379	42,971	75	78	6,160	11,874
Togo	268	230	9	..	114	..	581	623	67	..	217	..
Tunisia	3,526	5,750	69	82	1,575	2,662	5,542	8,338	72	79	682	1,153
Turkey	12,959	26,974	68	77	7,882	23,161	22,302	45,921	61	76	2,794	9,441
Turkmenistan	..	920	..	..	..	*269*	..	980	..	81	..	*669*
Uganda	147	501	..	..	*21*	*165*	213	1,414	..	..	195	*693*
Ukraine	..	12,635	..	..	..	3,922	..	14,675	..	..	..	2,545
United Kingdom	185,172	272,832	79	85	53,172	99,097	222,977	315,145	75	82	44,608	78,219
United States	393,592	682,497	74	82	132,184	239,957	516,987	942,645	73	81	97,940	165,827
Uruguay	1,693	2,769	39	39	460	1,382	1,343	3,808	69	79	363	866
Uzbekistan	..	2,390	..	..	..	..	..	2,750	..	..	..	..
Venezuela, RB	17,497	17,193	10	19	1,121	1,297	7,335	15,727	77	82	2,390	4,824
Vietnam	2,404	9,361	..	..	182	*2,530*	2,752	11,494	..	..	126	*3,153*
Yemen, Rep.	692	1,496	*1*	..	82	166	1,571	2,167	*31*	..	493	510
Zambia	1,309	740	..	..	94	..	1,220	700	..	..	370	..
Zimbabwe	1,726	2,111	31	*32*	253	..	1,847	2,772	73	77	460	..
World	**3,328,357 t**	**5,253,926 t**	**72 w**	**79 w**	**754,507 s**	**1,279,291 s**	**3,408,529 t**	**5,383,645 t**	**71 w**	**77 w**	**783,538 s**	**1,266,754 s**
Low income	110,592	165,177	*48*	52	16,955	31,453	118,035	177,252	*64*	*63*	30,934	57,435
Middle income	613,527	1,124,846	54	71	104,602	236,330	572,952	1,147,658	70	74	131,347	243,647
Lower middle income	281,205	499,085	59	66	57,873	122,664	297,148	508,531	70	73	63,395	116,077
Upper middle income	332,321	625,765	51	74	46,729	113,666	275,891	639,025	70	76	67,952	127,570
Low and middle income	724,243	1,290,207	54	69	121,557	267,783	692,669	1,327,018	70	74	162,281	301,082
East Asia & Pacific	220,817	537,290	68	81	31,420	88,106	230,492	413,466	73	75	34,539	104,151
Europe & Central Asia	140,625	248,210	..	57	31,466	79,758	143,083	300,176	..	67	37,865	59,067
Latin America & Caribbean	141,932	272,768	34	49	26,660	49,114	120,241	336,683	69	80	33,386	64,007
Middle East & North Africa	126,139	109,391	17	*19*	15,626	24,438	101,726	125,552	69	*69*	27,525	28,711
South Asia	27,790	51,606	71	77	6,838	12,970	39,339	67,217	54	56	9,317	19,272
Sub-Saharan Africa	66,763	70,732	*20*	*36*	9,547	13,397	56,115	81,867	..	71	19,649	25,874
High income	2,604,220	3,963,915	77	82	632,950	1,011,508	2,717,343	4,058,694	71	78	621,257	965,672

Note: For data comparability and coverage, see the Technical Notes. Figures in italics are for years other than those specified.
a. Includes Luxembourg. b. Includes reexports.

Table 21.   Aid and financial flows

| | Net private capital flows (Millions of dollars) | | Foreign direct investment (Millions of dollars) | | External debt Total (Millions of dollars) | | Present value % of GNP | Official development assistance | | | |
| | | | | | | | | Dollars per capita | | % of GNP | |
Economy	1990	1998	1990	1998	1990	1998	1998	1990	1998	1990	1998
Albania	31	42	0	45	349	821	20	3	73	0.5	7.8
Algeria	−424	−1,321	0	5	27,877	30,665	66	10	13	0.4	0.9
Angola	235	40	−335	360	8,594	12,173	279	29	28	3.3	8.1
Argentina	−203	18,899	1,836	6,150	62,730	144,050	52	5	2	0.1	0.0
Armenia	0	232	0	232	0	800	29	1	36	0.1	7.1
Australia	..	..	7,465	6,165	..	..	..	..	..	..	..
Austria	..	..	653	6,034	..	..	..	..	..	..	..
Azerbaijan	..	1,081	..	1,023	..	693	13	1	11	0.1	2.2
Bangladesh	70	288	3	308	12,769	16,376	22	19	10	6.9	2.7
Belarus	..	122	..	149	..	1,120	4	18	3	0.5	0.1
Belgium	..	..	..	..	..	..	..	..	..	..	..
Benin	1	34	1	34	1,292	1,647	46 [a]	57	35	14.8	9.2
Bolivia	3	860	27	872	4,275	6,078	59 [a]	83	79	11.8	7.5
Botswana	77	91	95	95	563	548	10	115	68	4.0	2.3
Brazil	562	54,385	989	31,913	119,877	232,004	29	1	2	0.0	0.0
Bulgaria	−42	498	4	401	10,890	9,907	78	2	28	0.1	1.9
Burkina Faso	0	0	0	0	834	1,399	32 [a]	37	37	12.0	15.5
Burundi	−5	2	1	1	907	1,119	72	48	12	23.6	8.8
Cambodia	0	118	0	121	1,854	2,210	62	5	29	3.7	11.9
Cameroon	−125	1	−113	50	6,679	9,829	98	39	30	4.2	5.0
Canada	..	..	7,581	16,515	..	..	..	..	..	..	..
Central African Republic	0	5	1	5	699	921	55	85	34	17.1	11.6
Chad	−1	16	0	16	524	1,091	38	55	23	18.1	10.0
Chile	2,098	9,252	590	4,638	19,227	36,302	50	8	7	0.4	0.1
China	8,107	42,676	3,487	43,751	55,301	154,599	15	2	2	0.6	0.3
Hong Kong, China	..	..	..	..	..	..	..	7	1	0.1	0.0
Colombia	345	3,630	500	3,038	17,222	33,263	32	3	4	0.2	0.2
Congo, Dem. Rep.	−24	1	−12	1	10,270	12,929	196	24	3	10.5	2.0
Congo, Rep.	−100	4	0	4	4,953	5,119	280	98	23	9.4	3.9
Costa Rica	23	800	163	559	3,756	3,971	37	76	8	4.2	0.3
Côte d'Ivoire	57	181	48	435	17,251	14,852	122 [a]	59	55	7.5	7.6
Croatia	..	1,666	..	873	..	8,297	31	..	9	..	0.2
Czech Republic	876	3,331	207	2,554	6,383	25,301	45	1	43	0.0	0.8
Denmark	..	..	1,132	6,373	..	..	..	..	..	..	..
Dominican Republic	130	771	133	691	4,372	4,451	28	14	15	1.5	0.8
Ecuador	183	584	126	831	12,109	15,140	75	16	14	1.6	0.9
Egypt, Arab Rep.	698	1,385	734	1,076	32,947	31,964	29	104	31	12.9	2.3
El Salvador	8	242	2	12	2,148	3,633	27	68	30	7.4	1.5
Eritrea	..	0	..	0	..	149	11	..	41	..	19.7
Estonia	104	714	82	581	58	782	13	10	62	0.3	1.8
Ethiopia	−45	6	12	4	8,634	10,352	135	20	11	15.0	10.0
Finland	..	..	812	12,029	..	..	..	..	..	..	..
France	..	..	13,183	27,998	..	..	..	..	..	..	..
Georgia	21	57	..	50	79	1,674	36	..	30	..	4.6
Germany	..	..	2,532	18,712	..	..	..	..	..	..	..
Ghana	−5	42	15	56	3,881	6,884	55 [a]	38	38	9.7	9.6
Greece	..	..	1,005	984	..	..	..	4	..	0.0	..
Guatemala	44	621	48	673	3,080	4,565	23	23	22	2.7	1.2
Guinea	−1	−9	18	1	2,476	3,546	69	51	51	11.0	9.8
Haiti	8	11	8	11	889	1,048	16	26	53	5.7	10.5
Honduras	77	193	44	84	3,724	5,002	64	92	52	16.2	6.3
Hungary	−308	4,683	0	1,936	21,277	28,580	64	6	21	0.2	0.5
India	1,873	6,151	162	2,635	83,717	98,232	20	2	2	0.4	0.4
Indonesia	3,235	−3,759	1,093	−356	69,872	150,875	169	10	6	1.6	1.5
Iran, Islamic Rep.	−392	588	−362	24	9,021	14,391	12	2	3	0.1	0.1
Ireland	..	..	627	2,920	..	..	..	..	..	..	..
Israel	..	..	129	1,850	..	..	..	294	179	2.7	0.9
Italy	..	..	6,411	2,635	..	..	..	..	..	..	..
Jamaica	92	586	138	369	4,671	3,995	61	113	7	7.1	0.3
Japan	..	..	1,777	3,268	..	..	..	..	..	..	..
Jordan	254	207	38	310	8,177	8,485	110	280	89	23.3	5.7
Kazakhstan	117	1,983	100	1,158	35	5,714	25	7	13	0.4	1.0
Kenya	122	−57	57	11	7,058	7,010	45	50	16	14.7	4.2
Korea, Rep.	1,056	7,644	788	5,415	34,986	139,097	43	1	−1	0.0	0.0
Kuwait	..	..	..	59	..	..	..	3	3	0.0	0.0
Kyrgyz Republic	..	108	..	109	4	1,148	53	1	46	..	13.8
Lao PDR	6	46	6	46	1,768	2,437	92	37	57	17.3	23.0
Latvia	43	366	29	357	65	756	12	1	40	0.0	1.6
Lebanon	12	1,740	6	200	1,779	6,725	41	71	56	7.5	1.5
Lesotho	17	281	17	265	396	692	42	82	32	13.8	5.7
Lithuania	−3	983	..	926	56	1,950	17	1	34	..	1.2
Macedonia, FYR	..	190	..	118	..	2,392	66	..	46	..	2.8
Madagascar	7	15	22	16	3,701	4,394	89	34	34	13.6	13.5
Malawi	2	24	0	1	1,558	2,444	77 [a]	59	41	28.6	24.4
Malaysia	769	8,295	2,333	5,000	15,328	44,773	69	26	9	1.1	0.3

GLOBAL LINKS

Economy	Net private capital flows (Millions of dollars) 1990	1998	Foreign direct investment (Millions of dollars) 1990	1998	External debt Total (Millions of dollars) 1990	1998	Present value % of GNP 1998	Official development assistance Dollars per capita 1990	1998	% of GNP 1990	1998
Mali	−8	17	−7	17	2,467	3,202	84 [a]	57	33	20.0	13.5
Mauritania	6	3	7	5	2,096	2,589	148	117	68	22.0	17.8
Mexico	8,253	23,188	2,634	10,238	104,431	159,959	39	2	0	0.1	0.0
Moldova	..	62	..	85	39	1,035	58	2	8	0.3	2.0
Mongolia	28	7	2	19	350	739	49	6	79	..	20.6
Morocco	341	965	165	322	24,458	20,687	54	44	19	4.2	1.5
Mozambique	35	209	9	213	4,653	8,208	74 [a]	71	61	42.4	28.2
Myanmar	153	153	161	70	4,695	5,680	..	4	1	..	..
Namibia	..	..	6	12	..	..	..	90	108	5.1	5.8
Nepal	−8	−1	6	12	1,640	2,646	31	23	18	11.5	8.3
Netherlands	..	..	12,352	33,346	..	..	..	..	..	..	..
New Zealand	..	..	1,735	2,657	..	..	..	..	..	..	..
Nicaragua	21	171	0	184	10,708	5,968	262 [a]	87	117	33.7	28.1
Niger	9	−23	−1	1	1,726	1,659	55 [a]	51	29	16.4	14.4
Nigeria	467	1,028	588	1,051	33,440	30,315	74	3	2	1.0	0.5
Norway	..	..	1,003	3,597	..	..	..	..	..	..	..
Pakistan	182	806	244	500	20,663	32,229	41	10	8	2.9	1.6
Panama	127	1,459	132	1,206	6,679	6,689	78	41	8	2.0	0.3
Papua New Guinea	204	230	155	110	2,594	2,692	69	107	78	13.3	10.4
Paraguay	67	236	76	256	2,104	2,305	25	13	15	1.1	0.9
Peru	59	2,724	41	1,930	20,067	32,397	55	19	20	1.3	0.8
Philippines	639	2,587	530	1,713	30,580	47,817	66	20	8	2.9	0.9
Poland	71	9,653	89	6,365	49,366	47,708	28	35	23	2.4	0.6
Portugal	..	..	2,610	1,783	..	..	..	..	..	..	..
Romania	4	1,826	0	2,031	1,140	9,513	23	10	16	0.6	0.9
Russian Federation	5,562	19,346	..	2,764	59,797	183,601	62	2	7	..	0.4
Rwanda	6	7	8	7	712	1,226	34	42	43	11.3	17.3
Saudi Arabia	..	..	..	..	..	..	..	3	1	0.0	0.0
Senegal	42	24	57	40	3,732	3,861	58	112	56	14.9	10.8
Sierra Leone	36	5	32	5	1,151	1,243	126	15	22	7.9	16.2
Singapore	..	..	5,575	7,218	..	..	..	−1	1	0.0	0.0
Slovak Republic	278	1,480	0	562	2,008	9,893	45	1	29	0.0	0.8
Slovenia	..	..	..	165	..	..	..	..	20	..	0.2
South Africa	..	783	..	550	..	24,712	18	..	12	..	0.4
Spain	..	..	13,984	11,392	..	..	..	..	..	..	..
Sri Lanka	54	325	43	193	5,863	8,526	41	43	26	9.3	3.2
Sweden	..	..	1,982	19,413	..	..	..	..	..	..	..
Switzerland	..	..	4,961	5,488	..	..	..	..	..	..	..
Syrian Arab Republic	18	76	71	80	17,068	22,435	136	56	10	5.9	1.0
Tajikistan	..	−3	..	18	10	1,070	49	2	17	0.4	5.9
Tanzania	4	157	0	172	6,438	7,603	71 [b]	46	31	29.3	12.5
Thailand	4,399	7,825	2,444	6,941	28,165	86,172	79	14	11	0.9	0.6
Togo	0	0	0	0	1,275	1,448	68	74	29	16.3	8.6
Tunisia	−122	694	76	650	7,691	11,078	56	48	16	3.3	0.8
Turkey	1,782	1,641	684	940	49,424	102,074	49	22	0	0.8	0.0
Turkmenistan	..	473	..	130	..	2,266	78	1	4	0.1	0.6
Uganda	16	198	0	200	2,583	3,935	35 [a]	41	23	15.8	7.0
Ukraine	369	2,087	..	743	551	12,718	30	6	8	0.3	0.9
United Kingdom	..	..	32,518	67,481	..	..	..	..	..	..	..
United States	..	..	48,954	193,373	..	..	..	..	..	..	..
Uruguay	−192	496	0	164	4,415	7,600	36	17	7	0.7	0.1
Uzbekistan	40	592	40	200	60	3,162	17	0	6	0.0	0.8
Venezuela, RB	−126	6,866	451	4,435	33,170	37,003	40	4	2	0.2	0.0
Vietnam	16	832	16	1,200	23,270	22,359	76	3	15	2.4	4.3
Yemen, Rep.	30	−210	−131	−210	6,345	4,138	56	34	19	8.8	5.5
Zambia	194	40	203	72	6,916	6,865	181	62	36	16.0	11.4
Zimbabwe	85	−217	−12	76	3,247	4,716	69	35	24	4.0	4.7
World	.. s	.. s	193,382 s	619,258 s	.. s	.. s		13 w	9 w	.. w	0.6 w
Low income	6,648	12,231	2,201	10,674	418,922	579,545		9	7	2.6	1.3
Middle income	35,959	255,469	21,929	160,267	1,041,421 [c]	1,956,501 [c]		18	12	0.7	0.4
Lower middle income	..	..	..	..	..	..		24	16	1.2	1.0
Upper middle income	..	..	..	..	..	..		10	6	0.4	
Low and middle income	42,606	267,700	24,130	170,942	1,460,343 [c]	2,536,046 [c]		11	8	1.2	0.7
East Asia & Pacific	18,720	67,249	11,135	64,162	274,071	667,522		4	4	..	0.5
Europe & Central Asia	7,649	53,342	1,051	24,350	220,428	480,539		13	14	0.6	0.6
Latin America & Caribbean	12,412	126,854	8,188	69,323	475,867	786,019		11	9	0.4	0.2
Middle East & North Africa	369	9,223	2,458	5,054	183,205	208,059		42	18	2.1	1.0
South Asia	2,174	7,581	464	3,659	129,899	163,775		5	4	1.5	0.9
Sub-Saharan Africa	1,283	3,452	834	4,364	176,873	230,132		36	21	9.9	4.1
High income			169,252	448,316				..	..	..	..

Note: For data comparability and coverage, see the Technical Notes. Figures in italics are for years other than those specified.
a. Data are from debt sustainability analyses undertaken as part of the Heavily Indebted Poor Countries (HIPC) Initiative. Present value estimate covers public and publicly guaranteed debt only. b. Data refer to mainland Tanzania only. c. Includes data for Gibraltar not included in other tables.

Table 1a. Key indicators for other economies

Economy	Population Thousands 1999	Surface area Thousands of sq. km 1999	Population density People per sq. km 1999	GNP Millions of dollars 1999[b]	GNP Avg. annual growth rate (%) 1998–99	GNP per capita Dollars 1999[b]	GNP per capita Avg. annual growth rate (%) 1998–99	GNP at PPP[a] Millions of dollars 1999	GNP at PPP[a] Per capita (dollars) 1999	Life expectancy at birth Years 1998	Adult illiteracy rate % of people 15 and above 1998	Carbon dioxide emissions Thousands of tons 1996
Afghanistan	25,869	652.1	40	..	..	.. [c]	..	..	..	46	65	1,176
American Samoa	63	0.2	317	..	..	.. [d]	..	..	..	..	..	282
Andorra	*65*	0.5	*144*	..	..	.. [e]	..	..	..	..	..	..
Antigua and Barbuda	67	0.4	153	..	..	.. [d]	..	..	..	75	..	322
Aruba	*94*	0.2	*495*	..	..	.. [e]	..	..	..	..	..	1,517
Bahamas, The	298	13.9	30	..	..	.. [e]	..	..	..	74	5	1,707
Bahrain	665	0.7	963	..	..	.. [d]	..	..	..	73	14	10,578
Barbados	267	0.4	620	..	..	.. [d]	..	..	..	76	..	835
Belize	247	23.0	11	673	4.7	2,730	1.1	1,109	4,492	75	7	355
Bermuda	64	0.1	1,280	..	..	.. [e]	..	..	..	..	..	462
Bhutan	782	47.0	17	399	6.0	510	2.9	1,169 [f]	1,496 [f]	61	..	260
Bosnia and Herzegovina	3,881	51.1	76	..	6.1	.. [g]	3.0	..	..	73	..	3,111
Brunei	322	5.8	61	..	..	.. [e]	..	..	..	76	9	5,071
Cape Verde	429	4.0	106	569	8.3	1,330	5.1	1,499 [f]	3,497 [f]	68	27	121
Cayman Islands	*36*	0.3	*138*	..	..	.. [e]	..	..	..	..	..	282
Channel Islands	149	0.3	480	..	..	.. [e]	..	..	..	79	..	55
Comoros	544	2.2	244	189	-1.4	350	-3.8	740 [f]	1,360 [f]	60	42	
Cuba	11,150	110.9	102	..	..	.. [g]	..	..	..	76	4	31,170
Cyprus	760	9.3	82	9,086	4.2	11,960	3.3	13,977 [f]	18,395 [f]	78	3	5,379
Djibouti	648	23.2	28	511	..	790	..	..	..	50	38	366
Dominica	73	0.8	97	231	-0.1	3,170	-0.1	352	4,825	76	..	81
Equatorial Guinea	443	28.1	16	516	8.5	1,170	5.7	..	..	50	19	143
Faeroe Islands	*44*	1.4	*31*	..	..	.. [e]	..	..	..	..	..	630
Fiji	801	18.3	44	1,771	7.8	2,210	6.4	3,634	4,536	73	8	762
French Polynesia	231	4.0	63	..	..	.. [e]	..	..	..	72	..	561
Gabon	1,208	267.7	5	4,043	-3.9	3,350	-6.2	6,435	5,325	53	..	3,690
Gambia, The	1,251	11.3	125	430	5.2	340	2.2	1,867 [f]	1,492 [f]	53	65	216
Greenland	56	341.7	0	..	..	.. [e]	..	..	..	68	..	509
Grenada	97	0.3	285	335	7.5	3,450	6.6	567	5,847	72	..	161
Guam	151	0.6	275	..	..	.. [e]	..	..	..	77	..	4,078
Guinea-Bissau	1,185	36.1	42	195	4.9	160	2.8	705 [f]	595 [f]	44	63	231
Guyana	856	215.0	4	653	3.0	760	2.2	2,774 [f]	3,242 [f]	64	2	953
Iceland	277	103.0	3	8,109	6.0	29,280	4.9	7,280	26,283	79	..	2,195
Iraq	22,797	438.3	52	..	..	.. [g]	..	..	..	59	46	91,387
Isle of Man	*76*	0.6	*129*	..	..	.. [d]	..	..	..	..	..	..
Kiribati	88	0.7	121	81	-16.5	910	-18.7	282 [f]	3,186 [f]	61	..	22
Korea, Dem. Rep.	23,414	120.5	194	..	..	.. [c]	..	..	..	63	..	254,326
Liberia	3,044	111.4	32	..	..	.. [c]	..	..	..	47	49	326
Libya	5,419	1,759.5	3	..	..	.. [d]	..	..	..	70	22	40,579
Liechtenstein	*32*	0.2	*200*	..	..	.. [e]	..	..	..	..	..	..
Luxembourg	432	2.6	167	19,285	5.1	44,640	3.8	16,523	38,247	77	..	8,281
Macao, China	469	0.0	23,450	..	..	.. [e]	..	..	..	78	..	1,407
Maldives	278	0.3	925	322	7.2	1,160	3.3	984 [f]	3,545 [f]	67	4	297
Malta	379	0.3	1,184	3,492	3.5	9,210	2.9	5,710 [f]	15,066 [f]	77	9	1,751
Marshall Islands	64	0.2	353	100	0.5	1,560	-2.6	..	..	..	..	..
Mauritius	1,170	2.0	576	4,203	4.9	3,590	4.0	10,123	8,652	71	16	1,744
Mayotte	*128*	0.4	*341*	..	..	.. [d]	..	..	..	..	..	..
Micronesia, Fed. Sts.	116	0.7	165	210	0.3	1,810	-1.9	..	..	67	..	..
Monaco	*32*	0.0	*16,410*	..	..	.. [e]	..	..	..	..	..	..
Netherlands Antilles	215	0.8	268	..	..	.. [e]	..	..	..	76	4	6,430
New Caledonia	213	18.6	12	..	..	.. [e]	..	..	..	73	..	1,751
Northern Mariana Islands	*68*	0.5	*143*	..	..	.. [e]	..	..	..	..	..	..
Oman	2,348	212.5	11	..	..	.. [d]	..	..	..	73	31	15,143
Palau	*19*	0.5	*40*	..	..	.. [d]	..	..	..	71	..	245
Puerto Rico	3,890	9.0	439	..	..	.. [d]	..	..	..	76	7	15,806
Qatar	757	11.0	69	..	..	.. [e]	..	..	..	74	20	29,121
Samoa	170	2.8	60	181	1.0	1,060	0.5	666 [f]	3,915 [f]	69	20	132
São Tomé and Principe	145	1.0	151	40	5.2	270	2.9	193 [f]	1,335 [f]	64	..	77
Seychelles	80	0.5	177	520	-3.0	6,540	-4.1	826 [f]	10,381 [f]	72	..	169
Solomon Islands	429	28.9	15	320	-0.4	750	-3.4	836 [f]	1,949 [f]	71	..	161
Somalia	9,388	637.7	15	..	..	.. [c]	..	..	..	48	..	15
St. Kitts and Nevis	41	0.4	114	262	2.1	6,420	2.0	401	9,801	70	..	103
St. Lucia	154	0.6	253	581	3.1	3,770	1.5	775	5,022	72	..	191
St. Vincent and the Grenadines	114	0.4	293	307	4.0	2,700	3.2	532	4,667	73	..	125
Sudan	28,993	2,505.8	12	9,435	6.0	330	3.6	37,641 [f]	1,298 [f]	55	44	3,473
Suriname	413	163.3	3	..	..	.. [g]	..	..	..	70	..	2,099
Swaziland	1,018	17.4	59	1,379	2.0	1,360	-0.9	4,274	4,200	56	22	341
Tonga	100	0.8	138	172	2.2	1,720	1.2	427 [f]	4,281 [f]	71	..	117
Trinidad and Tobago	1,293	5.1	252	5,661	4.5	4,390	3.9	9,388	7,262	73	7	22,237
United Arab Emirates	2,815	83.6	34	..	..	.. [e]	..	..	..	75	25	81,843
Vanuatu	189	12.2	16	221	-2.0	1,170	-5.2	525 [f]	2,771 [f]	65	..	62
Virgin Islands (U.S.)	*120*	0.3	352	..	..	.. [e]	..	..	..	77	..	12,912
West Bank and Gaza	2,839	6.2	446	4,559	5.2	1,610	1.3	..	..	71	..	..
Yugoslavia, FR (Serb./Mont.)	10,616	102.2	104	..	..	.. [g]	..	..	..	72	..	36,197

Note: Figures in italics are for years other than those specified.

a. Purchasing power parity; see the Technical Notes. b. Calculated using the World Bank Atlas method. c. Estimated to be low income ($755 or less). d. Estimated to be upper middle income ($2,996–9,265). e. Estimated to be high income ($9,266 or more). f. The estimate is based on regression; others are extrapolated from the latest International Comparison Programme benchmark estimates. g. Estimated to be lower middle income ($756–2,995).

Technical Notes

T hese technical notes discuss the sources and methods used to compile the 149 indicators included in this year's Selected World Development Indicators. The notes follow the order in which the indicators appear in the tables.

Sources

The data published in the Selected World Development Indicators are taken from *World Development Indicators 2000*. Where possible, however, revisions reported since the closing date of that edition have been incorporated. In addition, newly released estimates of population and GNP per capita for 1999 are included in table 1.

The World Bank draws on a variety of sources for the statistics published in the *World Development Indicators*. Data on external debt are reported directly to the World Bank by developing member countries through the Debtor Reporting System. Other data are drawn mainly from the United Nations and its specialized agencies, from the International Monetary Fund (IMF), and from country reports to the World Bank. Bank staff estimates are also used to improve currentness or consistency. For most countries, national accounts estimates are obtained from member governments through World Bank economic missions. In some instances these are adjusted by staff to ensure conformity with international definitions and concepts. Most social data from national sources are drawn from regular administrative files, special surveys, or periodic census inquiries. The Data Sources section following the Technical Notes lists the principal international sources used (as well as the sources cited in the Technical Notes).

Data consistency and reliability

Considerable effort has been made to standardize the data, but full comparability cannot be assured, and care must be taken in interpreting the indicators. Many factors affect data availability, comparability, and reliability: statistical systems in many developing economies are still weak; statistical methods, coverage, practices, and definitions differ widely; and cross-country and intertemporal comparisons involve complex technical and conceptual problems that cannot be unequivocally

resolved. For these reasons, although the data are drawn from the sources thought to be most authoritative, they should be construed only as indicating trends and characterizing major differences among economies rather than offering precise quantitative measures of those differences. Also, national statistical agencies tend to revise their historical data, particularly for recent years. Thus data of different vintages may be published in different editions of World Bank publications. Readers are advised not to compile such data from different editions. Consistent time-series data are available on the *World Development Indicators 2000* CD-ROM.

Ratios and growth rates

For ease of reference, the tables usually show ratios and rates of growth rather than the simple underlying values. Values in their original form are available on the *World Development Indicators 2000* CD-ROM. Unless otherwise noted, growth rates are computed using the least-squares regression method (see the section on statistical methods below). Because this method takes into account all available observations during a period, the resulting growth rates reflect general trends that are not unduly influenced by exceptional values. To exclude the effects of inflation, constant price economic indicators are used in calculating growth rates. Data in italics are for a year or period other than that specified in the column heading—up to two years before or after for economic indicators, and up to three years for social indicators, which tend to be collected less regularly and to change less dramatically over short periods.

Constant price series

An economy's growth is measured by the increase in value added produced by the individuals and enterprises operating in that economy. Thus measuring real growth requires estimates of GDP and its components valued in constant prices. The World Bank collects constant price national accounts series in national currencies and recorded in the country's original base year. To obtain comparable series of constant price data, it rescales GDP and value added by industrial origin to a common reference year, currently 1995. This process gives rise to a discrepancy between the rescaled GDP and the sum of the rescaled components. Because allocating the discrepancy would give rise to distortions in the growth rate, it is left unallocated.

Summary measures

The summary measures for regions and income groups, presented at the end of most tables, are calculated by simple addition when they are expressed in levels. Aggregate growth rates and ratios are usually computed as weighted averages. The summary measures for social indicators are weighted by population or subgroups of population, except for infant mortality, which is weighted by the number of births. See the notes on specific indicators for more information.

For summary measures that cover many years, calculations are based on a uniform group of economies so that the composition of the aggregate does not change over time. Group measures are compiled only if the data available for a given year account for at least two-thirds of the full group, as defined for the 1995 benchmark year. As long as this criterion is met, economies for which data are missing are assumed to behave like those for which there are estimates. Readers should keep in mind that the summary measures are estimates of representative aggregates for each topic and that nothing meaningful can be deduced about behavior at the country level by working back from group indicators. In addition, the weighting process may result in discrepancies between subgroup and overall totals.

Table 1. Size of the economy

Population is based on the de facto definition, which counts all residents, regardless of legal status or citizenship, except for refugees not permanently settled in their country of asylum, who are generally considered part of the population of their country of origin. The indicators shown are midyear estimates (see the technical note for table 3).

Surface area is a country's total area, including areas under inland bodies of water and coastal waterways.

Population density is midyear population divided by land area. Land area is a country's total area excluding areas under inland bodies of water and coastal waterways. Density is calculated using the most recently available data on land area.

Gross national product (GNP), the broadest measure of national income, measures total value added from domestic and foreign sources claimed by residents. GNP comprises gross domestic product (GDP) plus net receipts of primary income from non-resident sources. Data are converted from national currency to current U.S. dollars using the World Bank Atlas method. This involves using a three-year average of exchange rates to smooth the effects of transitory exchange rate fluctuations. (See the section on statistical methods below for further discussion of the Atlas method.) **Average annual growth rate of GNP** is calculated from constant price GNP in national currency units.

GNP per capita is GNP divided by midyear population. It is converted into current U.S. dollars by the Atlas method. The World Bank uses GNP per capita in U.S. dollars to classify economies

for analytical purposes and to determine borrowing eligibility. **Average annual growth rate of GNP per capita** is calculated from constant price GNP per capita in national currency units.

Because nominal exchange rates do not always reflect international differences in relative prices, table 1 also shows GNP converted into international dollars using purchasing power parity (PPP) exchange rates. **GNP measured at PPP** is GNP converted to international dollars by the PPP exchange rate. At the PPP rate, one international dollar has the same purchasing power over domestic GNP that the U.S. dollar has over U.S. GNP. PPP rates allow a standard comparison of real price levels between countries, just as conventional price indexes allow comparison of real values over time. The PPP conversion factors used here are derived from the most recent round of price surveys conducted by the International Comparison Programme, a joint project of the World Bank and the regional economic commissions of the United Nations. This round of surveys, completed in 1996 and covering 118 countries, is based on a 1993 reference year. Estimates for countries not included in the survey are derived from statistical models using available data.

Rankings are based on 206 economies and include the 74 economies with sparse data or populations of less than 1.5 million from table 1a. Range estimates for GNP and GNP per capita have been used to rank many of these 74 economies—such as Liechtenstein, which ranks second in GNP per capita.

Table 2. Quality of life

Growth of private consumption per capita is the average annual rate of change in private consumption divided by the midyear population. (See the definition of private consumption in the technical note to table 13.) The distribution-corrected growth rate is 1 minus the Gini index (see the technical note to table 5) multiplied by the annual rate of growth of private consumption. Growth in private consumption per capita is generally associated with a reduction in poverty, but where the distribution of income or consumption is highly unequal, the poor may not share in that growth. The relationship between the rate of poverty reduction and the distribution of income or consumption, as measured by an index such as the Gini index, is complicated. But Ravallion and Chen (1997) have found that the rate of poverty reduction is, on average, proportional to the distribution-corrected rate of growth of private consumption.

Prevalence of child malnutrition is the percentage of children under age 5 whose weight for age is less than minus 2 standard deviations from the median of the reference population, which is based on children from the United States, assumed to be well nourished. Weight for age is a composite indicator of both weight for height (wasting) and height for age (stunting). Estimates of child malnutrition are from the World Health Organization.

Under-5 mortality rate is the probability that a child born in the indicated year will die before reaching age 5, if the child is subject to current age-specific mortality rates. The probability is expressed as a rate per 1,000.

Life expectancy at birth is the number of years a newborn infant would live if patterns of mortality prevailing at its birth were to stay the same throughout its life.

Age-specific mortality data such as infant and child mortality rates, along with life expectancy at birth, are probably the best general indicators of a community's current health status and are often cited as overall measures of a population's welfare or quality of life. The main sources of mortality data are vital registration systems and direct or indirect estimates based on sample surveys or censuses. Because civil registers with relatively complete vital registration systems are fairly uncommon, estimates must be obtained from sample surveys or derived by applying indirect estimation techniques to registration, census, or survey data. Indirect estimates rely on estimated actuarial ("life") tables, which may be inappropriate for the population concerned. Life expectancy at birth and age-specific mortality rates are generally estimates based on the most recently available census or survey; see the primary data documentation table in *World Development Indicators 2000*.

Adult illiteracy rate is the percentage of people age 15 and above who cannot, with understanding, read and write a short, simple statement about their everyday life. The definition here is based on the concept of functional literacy: a person's ability to use reading and writing skills effectively in the context of his or her society. Measuring literacy using such a definition requires census or sample survey measurements under controlled conditions. In practice, many countries estimate the number of illiterate adults from self-reported data or from estimates of school completion rates. Because of these differences in method, comparisons across countries—and even over time within countries—should be made with caution.

Urban population is the share of the population living in areas defined as urban by each country.

Access to sanitation in urban areas is the percentage of the urban population served by connections to public sewers or household systems such as pit privies, pour flush latrines, septic tanks, communal toilets, or other such facilities.

Table 3. Population and labor force

Total population includes all residents regardless of legal status or citizenship, except for refugees not permanently settled in their country of asylum, who are generally considered part of the population of their country of origin. The indicators shown are midyear estimates. Population estimates are usually based on national censuses. Intercensal estimates are interpolations or extrapolations based on demographic models. Errors and undercounting occur even in high-income economies; in developing countries such errors may be substantial because of limits on transportation, communication, and the resources required to conduct a full census. Moreover, the international comparability of population indicators is limited by differences in the concepts, definitions, data collection procedures, and estimation methods used by national statistical agencies and other organizations that collect population data. The data in table 3 are provided by national statistical offices or by the United Nations Population Division.

Average annual population growth rate is the exponential rate of change for the period (see the section on statistical methods below).

Population ages 15–64 is a commonly accepted measure of the number of people who are potentially economically active. In many developing countries, however, children under age 15 work full or part time, and in some high-income economies many workers postpone retirement past age 65.

Total labor force comprises people who meet the definition established by the International Labour Organization (ILO) for the economically active population: all people who supply labor for the production of goods and services during a specified period. It includes both the employed and the unemployed. Although national practices vary, in general the labor force includes the armed forces and first-time job seekers but excludes homemakers and other unpaid caregivers and workers in the informal sector. Data on the labor force are compiled by the ILO from census or labor force surveys. Despite the ILO's efforts to encourage the use of international standards, labor force data are not fully comparable because of differences among countries, and sometimes within countries, in definitions and in methods of collection, classification, and tabulation. The labor force estimates reported in table 3 were calculated by applying activity rates from the ILO database to the World Bank's population estimates to create a labor force series consistent with those estimates. This procedure sometimes results in estimates that differ slightly from those published in the ILO's *Yearbook of Labour Statistics*.

Average annual labor force growth rate is calculated using the exponential endpoint method (see the section on statistical methods below).

Females as a percentage of the labor force show the extent to which women are active in the labor force. Estimates are from the ILO database. These estimates are not comparable internationally because in many countries large numbers of women assist on farms or in other family enterprises without pay, and countries use different criteria to determine the extent to which such workers are to be counted in the labor force.

Children ages 10–14 in the labor force are the share of that age group that is active in the labor force. Reliable estimates of child labor are difficult to obtain. In many countries child labor is illegal or officially presumed not to exist and is therefore not reported or included in surveys nor recorded in official data. Data are also subject to underreporting because they do not include children engaged in agricultural or household activities with their families.

Table 4. Poverty

Survey year is the year in which the underlying data were collected.

Rural population below the national poverty line is the percentage of the rural population living below the rural poverty line determined by national authorities. **Urban population below the national poverty line** is the percentage of the urban population living below the urban poverty line determined by national authorities. **Total population below the national poverty line** is the percentage of the total population living below the national poverty line. National estimates are based on population-weighted subgroup estimates from household surveys.

Population below $1 a day and **population below $2 a day** are the percentages of the population living below those levels of consumption or income at 1993 prices, adjusted for purchasing power parity.

Poverty gap at $1 a day and **poverty gap at $2 a day** are calculated as the mean shortfall below the poverty line (counting the nonpoor as having zero shortfall), expressed as a percentage of the poverty line. This measure reflects the depth of poverty as well as its prevalence.

International comparisons of poverty data entail both conceptual and practical problems. Different countries have different definitions of poverty, and consistent comparisons between countries based on the same definition can be difficult. National poverty lines tend to have greater purchasing power in rich countries, where more generous standards are used than in poor countries.

International poverty lines attempt to hold the real value of the poverty line constant between countries. The standard of $1 a day, measured in 1985 international prices and adjusted to local currency using PPP conversion factors, was chosen for *World Development Report 1990: Poverty* because it is typical of poverty lines in low-income economies. For this year's report, the standard has been updated to $1.08 a day, measured in 1993 international prices. PPP conversion factors are used because they take into account the local prices of goods and services that are not traded internationally. However, these factors were designed not for making international poverty comparisons but for comparing aggregates in the national accounts. As a result, there is no certainty that an international poverty line measures the same degree of need or deprivation across countries.

Problems can arise in comparing poverty measures within countries as well as between them. For example, the cost of food staples—and the cost of living generally—are typically higher in urban than in rural areas. So the nominal value of the urban poverty line should be higher than the rural poverty line. But the difference between urban and rural poverty lines found in practice does not always reflect the difference in the cost of living. For some countries the urban poverty line in common use has a higher real value—meaning that it allows poor people to buy more commodities for consumption—than does the rural poverty line. Sometimes the difference has been so large as to imply that the incidence of poverty is greater in urban than in rural areas, even though the reverse is found when adjustments are made only for differences in the cost of living.

Other issues arise in measuring household living standards. The choice between income and consumption as a welfare indicator is one. Incomes are generally more difficult to measure accurately, and consumption accords better with the idea of a standard of living than does income, which can vary over time even if the standard of living does not. But consumption data are not always available, and when they are not, there is little choice but to use income. There are still other problems. Household survey questionnaires can differ widely, for example, in the number of distinct categories of consumer goods they identify. Survey quality varies, and even similar surveys may not be strictly comparable.

Comparisons across countries at different levels of development also pose a potential problem because of differences in the relative importance of consumption of nonmarket goods. The local market value of all consumption in kind (including consumption from a household's own production, particularly important in underdeveloped rural economies) should be included in the measure of total consumption expenditure. Similarly, the imputed profit from production of nonmarket goods should be included in income. This is not always done, although such omissions were a far bigger problem in surveys before the 1980s than today. Most survey data now include valuations for consumption or income from own production. Nonetheless, valuation methods vary: for example, some surveys use the price at the nearest market, whereas others use the average farm-gate selling price.

Whenever possible, consumption has been used as the welfare indicator for deciding who is poor. The international poverty measures in table 4 are based on the most recent PPP estimates of consumption in 1993 prices from the World Bank. When only household income is available, average income has been adjusted to accord with either a survey-based estimate of mean consumption (when available) or an estimate based on consumption data from national accounts. This procedure adjusts only the mean, however; nothing can be done to correct for the difference between the Lorenz (income distribution) curves for consumption and income.

Empirical Lorenz curves were weighted by household size, so they are based on percentiles of population, not of households. In all cases the measures of poverty have been calculated from primary data sources (tabulations or household data) rather than existing estimates. Estimates from tabulations require an interpolation method; the method chosen is Lorenz curves with flexible functional forms, which have proved reliable in past work.

Table 5. Distribution of income or consumption

Survey year is the year in which the underlying data were collected.

Gini index measures the extent to which the distribution of income (or, in some cases, consumption expenditure) among individuals or households within an economy deviates from a perfectly equal distribution. The Gini index measures the area between the Lorenz curve (described in the technical note to table 4) and a hypothetical line of absolute equality, expressed as a percentage of the maximum area under the line. As defined here, a Gini index of zero would represent perfect equality, and an index of 100 would imply perfect inequality.

Percentage share of income or consumption is the share that accrues to deciles or quintiles of the population ranked by income or consumption. Percentage shares by quintiles may not add up to 100 because of rounding.

Data on personal or household income or consumption come from nationally representative household surveys. The data in the table refer to different years between 1985 and 1999. Footnotes to the survey year indicate whether the rankings are based on income or consumption. Distributions are based on percentiles of population, not of households. Where the original data from the household survey were available, they have been used to directly calculate the income or consumption shares by quintile. Otherwise, shares have been estimated from the best available grouped data.

The distribution indicators have been adjusted for household size, providing a more consistent measure of income or consumption per capita. No adjustment has been made for differences in the cost of living in different parts of the same country because the necessary data are generally unavailable. For further details on the estimation method for low- and middle-income economies, see Ravallion and Chen (1996).

Because the underlying household surveys differ in method and in the type of data collected, the distribution indicators are not strictly comparable across countries. These problems are diminishing as survey methods improve and become more standardized, but strict comparability is still impossible. The income distributions and Gini indexes for the high-income economies are calculated directly from the Luxembourg Income Study database using an estimation method consistent with that applied for developing countries.

The following sources of noncomparability should be noted. First, the surveys can differ in many respects, including whether they use income or consumption expenditure as the living standard indicator. Income is typically more unequally distributed than consumption. In addition, the definitions of income used in surveys are usually very different from the economic definition of income (the maximum level of consumption consistent with keeping productive capacity unchanged). Consumption is usually a much better welfare indicator, particularly in developing countries. Second, households differ in size (number of members) and in the extent of income sharing among members. Individuals differ in age and in consumption needs. Differences between countries in these respects may bias distribution comparisons.

Table 6. Education

Public expenditure on education is the percentage of GNP accounted for by public spending on public education plus subsidies to private education at the primary, secondary, and tertiary levels. It may exclude spending on religious schools, which play a significant role in many developing countries. Data for some countries and for some years refer to spending by the ministry of education of the central government only and thus exclude education expenditures by other central government ministries and departments, local authorities, and others.

Net enrollment ratio is the ratio of the number of children of official school age (as defined by the education system) who are enrolled in school to the population of the corresponding official school age. Enrollment data are based on annual enrollment surveys, typically conducted at the beginning of the school year. They do not reflect actual attendance or dropout rates during the school year. Problems affecting cross-country comparisons of enrollment data stem from inadvertent or deliberate misreporting of age and from errors in estimates of school-age populations. Age structures from censuses or vital registration systems, the primary sources of data on school-age populations, are commonly subject to underenumeration, especially of young children.

Percentage of cohort reaching grade 5 is the share of students enrolled in the first grade of primary school who eventually reach fifth grade. Because tracking data for individual students are not available, aggregate student flows from one grade to the next are estimated using data on enrollment and repetition by grade for two consecutive years. This procedure, called the reconstructed cohort method, makes three simplifying assumptions: that dropouts never return to school; that promotion, repetition, and dropout rates remain constant over the entire period in which the cohort is enrolled; and that the same rates apply to all pupils enrolled in a given grade, regardless of whether they previously repeated a grade.

Expected years of schooling are the average years of formal schooling that a child is expected to receive, including university education and years spent in repetition. This indicator may also be interpreted as an indicator of the total education resources, measured in school years, that a child will require over the course of his or her "lifetime" in school.

Data on education are compiled by the United Nations Educational, Scientific, and Cultural Organization (UNESCO) from official responses to surveys and from reports provided by education authorities in each country. Because coverage, definitions, and data collection methods vary across countries and over time within countries, data on education should be interpreted with caution.

Table 7. Health

Public expenditure on health consists of recurrent and capital spending from government (central and local) budgets, external borrowings and grants (including donations from international agencies and nongovernmental organizations), and social (or compulsory) health insurance funds. Because few developing countries have national health accounts, compiling estimates of public health expenditure is complicated in countries where state, provincial, and local governments are involved in health care financing. Such data are not regularly reported and, when reported, are often of poor quality. The data on health expenditure in table 7 are the product of an effort to collect all available information on health expenditures from national and local government budgets, national accounts, household surveys, insurance publications, international donors, and existing tabulations.

Access to improved water source refers to the percentage of the population with reasonable access to an adequate amount of water (including treated surface water and untreated but uncontaminated water, such as from springs, sanitary wells, and protected boreholes). In urban areas the source may be a public fountain or standpipe located not more than 200 meters from the residence. In rural areas the definition implies that household members do not have to spend a disproportionate part of the day fetching water. An "adequate" amount of water is that needed to satisfy metabolic, hygienic, and domestic requirements, usually about 20 liters per person per day.

Access to sanitation is the percentage of the population with disposal facilities that can effectively prevent human, animal, and insect contact with excreta. Suitable facilities range from simple but protected pit latrines to flush toilets with sewerage. To be effective, all facilities must be correctly constructed and properly maintained.

Infant mortality rate is the number of infants who die before reaching 1 year of age, expressed per 1,000 live births in a given year (see the discussion of age-specific mortality rates in the technical note to table 2).

Contraceptive prevalence rate is the percentage of women who are practicing, or whose sexual partners are practicing, any form of contraception. It is usually measured for married women aged 15–49 only. Contraceptive prevalence includes all methods: ineffective traditional methods as well as highly effective modern methods. Unmarried women are often excluded from the surveys, and this may bias the estimate. The rates are obtained mainly from demographic and health surveys and contraceptive prevalence surveys.

Total fertility rate is the number of children who would be born to a woman if she were to live to the end of her childbearing years and bear children in accordance with current age-specific fertility rates. Data are from vital registration systems or, in their absence, from censuses or sample surveys. Provided that the censuses or surveys are fairly recent, the estimated rates are considered reliable. As with other demographic data, international comparability is affected by differences in definitions, data collection, and estimation methods.

Maternal mortality ratio is the number of women who die during pregnancy or childbirth, per 100,000 live births. Household surveys such as the demographic and health surveys attempt to measure maternal mortality by asking respondents about survivorship of sisters. The main disadvantage of this method is that the estimates of maternal mortality that it produces pertain to 12 years or so before the survey, making them unsuitable for monitoring recent changes or observing the impact of interventions. In addition, measurement of maternal mortality is subject to many types of errors. Even in high-income countries with vital registration systems, misclassification of maternal deaths has been found to lead to serious underestimation. The data in the table are official estimates based on national surveys or derived from official community and hospital records. Some reflect only births in hospitals and other medical institutions. In some cases smaller private and rural hospitals are excluded, and sometimes even primitive local facilities are included. Thus the coverage is not always comprehensive, and cross-country comparisons should be made with extreme caution.

Table 8. Land use and agricultural productivity

Land under permanent crops is land cultivated with crops that occupy the land for long periods and do not need to be replanted after each harvest, excluding trees grown for wood or timber. **Irrigated land** refers to areas purposely provided with water, including land irrigated by controlled flooding. **Arable land** includes land defined by the Food and Agriculture Organization (FAO) as land under temporary crops (double-cropped areas are counted once), temporary meadows for mowing or for pasture, land under market or kitchen gardens, and land temporarily fallow. Land abandoned as a result of shifting cultivation is not included.

The comparability of land use data from different countries is limited by variations in definitions, statistical methods, and the quality of data collection. For example, countries may define land use differently. The FAO, the primary compiler of these data, occasionally adjusts its definitions of land use categories and sometimes revises earlier data. Because the data thus reflect changes in data reporting procedures as well as actual changes in land use, apparent trends should be interpreted with caution.

Agricultural machinery refers to wheel and crawler tractors (excluding garden tractors) in use in agriculture at the end of the calendar year specified or during the first quarter of the following year. **Agricultural productivity** refers to agricultural value added per agricultural worker, measured in constant 1995 U.S. dollars. Agricultural value added includes that from forestry and fishing. Thus interpretations of land productivity should be made with caution. To smooth annual fluctuations in agricultural activity, the indicators have been averaged over three years.

Food production index covers food crops that are considered edible and that contain nutrients. Coffee and tea are excluded because, although edible, they have no nutritive value. The food production index is prepared by the FAO, which obtains data from official and semiofficial reports of crop yields, area under production, and livestock numbers. Where data are not available, the FAO makes estimates. The index is calculated using the Laspeyres formula: the production quantities of each commodity are weighted by average international commodity prices in the base period and summed for each year. The FAO's index may differ from those of other sources because of differences in coverage, weights, concepts, time periods, calculation methods, and use of international prices.

Table 9. Water use, deforestation, and protected areas

Freshwater resources refer to total renewable resources, which include flows of rivers and groundwater from rainfall in the country and river flows from other countries. Freshwater resources per capita are calculated using the World Bank's population estimates.

Data on freshwater resources are based on estimates of runoff into rivers and recharge of groundwater. These estimates are based on different sources and refer to different years, so cross-country comparisons should be made with caution. Because they are collected intermittently, the data may hide significant variations in total renewable water resources from one year to the next. These annual averages also obscure large seasonal and interannual variations in water availability within countries. Data for small countries and countries in arid and semiarid zones are less reliable than those for larger countries and countries with more rainfall.

Annual freshwater withdrawals refer to total water withdrawals, not counting evaporation losses from storage basins. They also include water from desalination plants in countries where these are a significant source of water. Withdrawal data are for single years between 1980 and 1998 unless otherwise indicated. Caution is advised in comparing data on annual freshwater withdrawals, which are subject to variations in collection and estimation methods. Withdrawals can exceed 100 percent of renewable supplies when extraction from nonrenewable aquifers or desalination plants is considerable or when there is significant reuse of water. Withdrawals for agriculture and industry are total withdrawals for irrigation and livestock production and for direct industrial use (including withdrawals for cooling thermoelectric plants). Withdrawals for domestic use include drinking water, municipal use or supply, and use for public services, commercial establishments, and homes. For most countries, sectoral withdrawal data are estimated for 1987–95.

Access to improved water source refers to the percentage of the population with reasonable access to an adequate amount of water (including treated surface water and untreated but uncontaminated water, such as from springs, sanitary wells, and protected boreholes; see table 7). While information on access to water is widely used, it is extremely subjective, and such terms as "adequate" may have very different meanings in different countries. Even in high-income countries treated water may not always be safe to drink. Although access to an improved source is often equated with connection to a public supply system, this does not take account of variations in the quality and cost (broadly defined) of the service once connected. Thus cross-country comparisons must be made cautiously. Changes over time within countries may result from changes in definitions or measurements.

Annual deforestation refers to the permanent conversion of forest area (land under natural or planted stands of trees) to other uses, including shifting cultivation, permanent agriculture, ranching, settlements, and infrastructure development. Deforested areas do not include areas logged but intended for regeneration or areas degraded by fuelwood gathering, acid precipitation, or forest fires. Negative numbers indicate an increase in forest area.

Estimates of forest area are from the FAO's *State of the World's Forests 1999*, which provides information on forest cover as of 1995 and revised estimates of forest cover in 1990. Forest cover data for developing countries are based on country assessments that were prepared at different times and that, for reporting purposes, had to be adapted to the standard reference years of 1990 and 1995. This adjustment was made with a deforestation model designed to correlate forest cover change over time with certain ancillary variables, including population change and density, initial forest cover, and ecological zone of the forest area under consideration.

Nationally protected areas refer to totally or partially protected areas of at least 1,000 hectares that are designated as national parks, natural monuments, nature reserves, wildlife sanctuaries, protected landscapes and seascapes, or scientific reserves with limited public access. The indicator is calculated as a percentage of total area. For small countries whose protected areas may be smaller than 1,000 hectares, this limit will result in an underestimate of the extent and number of protected areas. The data do not include sites protected under local or provincial law.

Data on protected areas are compiled from a variety of sources by the World Conservation Monitoring Centre, a joint venture of the United Nations Environment Programme, the World Wide Fund for Nature, and the World Conservation Union. Because of differences in definitions and reporting practices, cross-country comparability is limited. Compounding these problems, the data available cover different periods. Designating land as a protected area does not necessarily mean, moreover, that protection is in force.

Table 10. Energy use and emissions

Commercial energy use is measured as apparent consumption, which is equal to indigenous production plus imports and stock changes, minus exports and fuels supplied to ships and aircraft engaged in international transportation. The International Energy Agency (IEA) and the United Nations Statistics Division (UNSD) compile energy data. IEA data for countries that are not members of the Organisation for Economic Co-operation and Development

(OECD) are based on national energy data that have been adjusted to conform with annual questionnaires completed by OECD member governments. UNSD data are compiled primarily from responses to questionnaires sent to national governments, supplemented by official national statistical publications and by data from intergovernmental organizations. When official data are not available, the UNSD bases its estimates on the professional and commercial literature. The variety of the sources affects the cross-country comparability of data.

Commercial energy use refers to domestic primary energy use before transformation to other end-use energy sources (such as electricity and refined petroleum products). It includes energy from combustible renewables and waste. All forms of commercial energy—primary energy and primary electricity—are converted into oil equivalents. To convert nuclear electricity into oil equivalents, a notional thermal efficiency of 33 percent is assumed; for hydroelectric power, 100 percent efficiency is assumed.

GDP per unit of energy use is the PPP GDP per kilogram of oil equivalent of commercial energy use. PPP GDP is gross domestic product converted to international dollars using purchasing power parity rates. An international dollar has the same purchasing power as a U.S. dollar has in the United States.

Net energy imports are calculated as energy use less production, both measured in oil equivalents. A negative value indicates that the country is a net exporter of energy.

Carbon dioxide emissions refer to those stemming from the burning of fossil fuels and the manufacture of cement. These emissions include carbon dioxide produced during consumption of solid, liquid, and gas fuels and from gas flaring.

The Carbon Dioxide Information Analysis Center (CDIAC), sponsored by the U.S. Department of Energy, calculates annual anthropogenic emissions of carbon dioxide. These calculations are based on data on fossil fuel consumption from the World Energy Data Set maintained by the UNSD, and data on world cement manufacturing from the Cement Manufacturing Data Set maintained by the U.S. Bureau of Mines. Each year the CDIAC recalculates the entire time series from 1950 to the present, incorporating its most recent findings and the latest corrections to its database. Estimates exclude fuels supplied to ships and aircraft engaged in international transportation because of the difficulty of apportioning these fuels among the countries benefiting from that transport.

Table 11. Growth of the economy

Gross domestic product is gross value added, at purchaser prices, by all resident producers in the economy plus any taxes and minus any subsidies not included in the value of the products. It is calculated without deducting for depreciation of fabricated assets or for depletion or degradation of natural resources. Value added is the net output of a sector after adding up all outputs and subtracting intermediate inputs. The industrial origin of value added is determined by the International Standard Industrial Classification (ISIC) revision 3.

GDP implicit deflator reflects changes in prices for all final demand categories, such as government consumption, capital formation, and international trade, as well as the main component, private final consumption. It is derived as the ratio of current to constant price GDP. The GDP deflator may also be calculated explicitly as a Paasche price index in which the weights are the current period quantities of output.

Agriculture value added corresponds to ISIC divisions 1–5 and includes forestry and fishing. **Industry value added** comprises the following sectors: mining (ISIC divisions 10–14), manufacturing (15–37), construction (45), and electricity, gas, and water supply (40 and 41). **Services value added** corresponds to ISIC divisions 50–99.

Exports of goods and services represent the value of all goods and services provided to the rest of the world. Included is the value of merchandise, freight, insurance, travel, transport, and other services such as communications and financial services. Factor and property income (formerly called factor services), such as investment income, interest, and labor income, is excluded, as are transfer payments.

Gross domestic investment consists of outlays on additions to the fixed assets of the economy plus net changes in the level of inventories. Additions to fixed assets include land improvements (fences, ditches, drains, and so on); plant, machinery, and equipment purchases; and the construction of buildings, roads, railways, and the like, including commercial and industrial buildings, offices, schools, hospitals, and private dwellings. Inventories are stocks of goods held by firms to meet temporary or unexpected fluctuations in production or sales.

Growth rates are annual averages calculated using constant price data in local currency. Growth rates for regional and income groups are calculated after converting local currencies to U.S. dollars at the average official exchange rate reported by the International Monetary Fund (IMF) for the year shown or, occasionally, using an alternative conversion factor determined by the World Bank's Development Data Group. Alternative conversion factors and methods of computing growth rates are described in the section on statistical methods below. For additional information on the calculation of GDP and its sectoral components, see the technical note to table 12.

Table 12. Structure of output

Gross domestic product represents the sum of value added by all producers in the economy (see the technical note to table 11 for a more detailed definition and for definitions of **agriculture, industry, manufacturing,** and **services value added**). Since 1968 the United Nations' System of National Accounts (SNA) has called for estimates of GDP by industrial origin to be valued at producer prices (including taxes on factors of production, but excluding indirect taxes on final output). Some countries, however, report such data at basic prices—the prices at which final sales are made (including indirect taxes)—and this may affect estimates of the distribution of output. Total GDP as shown in this table is measured at purchaser prices. GDP components are measured at either basic or producer prices.

Among the difficulties faced by compilers of national accounts is the extent of unreported economic activity in the informal or secondary economy. In developing countries a large share of agricultural output is either not exchanged (because it is consumed within the household) or not exchanged for money. Financial transactions also may go unrecorded. As a result, agricultural production often must be estimated indirectly, using a combination of methods involving estimates of inputs, yields, and area under cultivation.

The output of industry ideally should be measured through regular censuses and surveys of firms. But in most developing countries such surveys are infrequent and quickly go out of date, so many results must be extrapolated. The choice of sampling unit, which may be the enterprise (where responses may be based on financial records) or the establishment (where production units may be recorded separately), also affects the quality of the data. Moreover, much industrial production is organized not in firms but in unincorporated or owner-operated ventures not captured by surveys aimed at the formal sector. Even in large industries, where regular surveys are more likely, evasion of excise and other taxes lowers the estimates of value added. Such problems become more acute as countries move from state control of industry to private enterprise because new firms go into business and growing numbers of established firms fail to report. In accordance with the SNA, output should include all such unreported activity as well as the value of illegal activities and other unrecorded, informal, or small-scale operations. Data on these activities need to be collected using techniques other than conventional surveys.

In industries dominated by large organizations and enterprises, data on output, employment, and wages are usually readily available and reasonably reliable. But in the service industry the many self-employed workers and one-person businesses are sometimes difficult to locate, and their owners have little incentive to respond to surveys, let alone report their full earnings. Compounding these problems are the many forms of economic activity that go unrecorded, including the work that women and children do for little or no pay. For further discussion of the problems encountered in using national accounts data, see Srinivasan (1994) and Heston (1994).

Table 13. Structure of demand

Private consumption is the market value of all goods and services, including durable products (such as cars, washing machines, and home computers), purchased or received as income in kind by households and nonprofit institutions. It excludes purchases of dwellings but includes imputed rent for owner-occupied dwellings. In practice, it may include any statistical discrepancy in the use of resources relative to the supply of resources.

Private consumption is often estimated as a residual, by subtracting from GDP all other known expenditures. The resulting aggregate may incorporate fairly large discrepancies. When private consumption is calculated separately, the household surveys providing the basis for a large part of the estimates tend to be one-year studies with limited coverage. Thus the estimates quickly become outdated and must be supplemented by price- and quantity-based statistical estimating procedures. Complicating the issue, in many developing countries the distinction between cash outlays for personal business and those for household use may be blurred.

General government consumption includes all current spending for purchases of goods and services (including wages and salaries) by all levels of government, excluding most government enterprises. It also includes most expenditure on national defense and security, some of which is now considered part of investment in the 1993 SNA.

Gross domestic investment consists of outlays on additions to the fixed assets of the economy plus net changes in the level of inventories. For definitions of fixed assets and inventories, see the technical note to table 11. Under the 1993 SNA guidelines, gross domestic investment also includes capital outlays on defense establishments that may be used by the general public, such as schools, hospitals, and certain types of private housing for family use. All other defense expenditures are treated as current spending.

Investment data may be estimated from direct surveys of enterprises and administrative records or based on the commodity flow method, using data from trade and construction activities. The quality of public fixed investment data depends on the quality of government accounting systems, which tend to be weak in developing countries. Measures of private fixed investment—particularly capital outlays by small, unincorporated enterprises—are usually very unreliable.

Estimates of changes in inventories are rarely complete but usually include the most important activities or commodities. In some countries these estimates are derived as a composite residual along with aggregate private consumption. According to national accounts conventions, adjustments should be made for appreciation of inventory value due to price changes, but this is not always done. In economies where inflation is high, this element can be substantial.

Gross domestic savings are the difference between GDP and total consumption.

Exports of goods and services represent the value of all goods and services (including freight, transport, travel, and other services such as communications, insurance, and financial services) provided to the rest of the world. Data on exports and imports are compiled from customs returns and from balance of payments data obtained from central banks. Although data on exports and imports from the payments side provide reasonably reliable records of cross-border transactions, they may not adhere strictly to the appropriate valuation and timing definitions of balance of payments accounting or, more important, correspond to the change-of-ownership criterion. (In conventional balance of payments accounting, a transaction is recorded as occurring when ownership changes hands.) This issue has assumed greater significance with the increasing globalization of business. Neither customs nor balance of payments data capture the illegal transactions that occur in many countries. Goods carried by travelers across borders in legal but unreported shuttle trade may further distort trade statistics.

Resource balance is the difference between exports of goods and services and imports of goods and services.

Table 14. Central government finances

Current tax revenue comprises compulsory, unrequited, nonrepayable receipts collected by central governments for public purposes. It includes interest collected on tax arrears and penalties collected on nonpayment or late payment of taxes. It is shown net of refunds and other corrective transactions.

Current nontax revenue includes requited, nonrepayable receipts for public purposes, such as fines, administrative fees, or entrepreneurial income from government ownership of property, and voluntary, unrequited, nonrepayable current government receipts other than from government sources. This category does not include grants, borrowing, repayment of previous lending, or sales of fixed capital assets or of stocks, land, or intangible assets, nor does it include gifts from nongovernment sources for capital purposes. Together, tax and nontax revenue make up the current revenue of the government.

Current expenditure includes requited payments other than for capital assets or for goods or services to be used in the production of capital assets. It also includes unrequited payments for purposes other than permitting the recipients to acquire capital assets, compensating the recipients for damage to or destruction of capital assets, or increasing the financial capital of the recipients. Current expenditure does not include government lending or repayments to the government, or government acquisition of equity for public policy purposes.

Capital expenditure is nonmilitary spending to acquire fixed capital assets, land, intangible assets, and strategic and emergency stocks. Also included are unrequited capital transfers for acquiring capital assets or to increase the financial capital of recipients.

Overall deficit/surplus is current and capital revenue and official grants received, less total expenditure and lending minus repayment.

Goods and services expenditure comprises all government payments in exchange for goods and services, including wages and salaries.

Social services expenditure comprises expenditure on health, education, housing, welfare, social security, and community amenities. It also covers compensation for loss of income to the sick and temporarily disabled; payments to the elderly, the permanently disabled, and the unemployed; family, maternity, and child allowances; and the cost of welfare services such as care of the aged, the disabled, and children. Many expenditures relevant to environmental protection, such as pollution abatement, water supply, sanitation, and refuse collection, are included indistinguishably in this category.

Data on government revenues and expenditures are collected by the IMF, through questionnaires distributed to member governments, and by the OECD. In general, the definition of government excludes nonfinancial public enterprises and public financial institutions (such as the central bank). Despite the IMF's efforts to systematize and standardize the collection of public finance data, statistics on public finance are often incomplete, untimely, and noncomparable. Inadequate statistical coverage precludes the presentation of subnational data, making cross-country comparisons potentially misleading.

Total central government expenditure as presented in the IMF's *Government Finance Statistics Yearbook* is a more limited measure of general government consumption than that shown in the national accounts because it excludes consumption expenditure by state and local governments. At the same time, the IMF's concept of central government expenditure is broader than the national accounts definition because it includes government gross domestic investment and transfer payments.

Central government finances can refer to one of two accounting concepts: consolidated or budgetary. For most countries central government finance data have been consolidated into one account, but for others only budgetary central government accounts are available. Countries reporting budgetary data are noted in the primary data documentation table in *World Development Indicators 2000*. Because budgetary accounts do not necessarily include all central government units, the picture they provide of central government activities is usually incomplete. A key issue is the failure to include the quasi-fiscal operations of the central bank. Central bank losses arising from monetary operations and subsidized financing can result in sizable quasi-fiscal deficits. Such deficits may also result from the operations of other financial intermediaries, such as public development finance institutions. Also missing from the data are governments' contingent liabilities for unfunded pension and insurance plans.

Table 15. Balance of payments current account and international reserves

Goods and services exports and **goods and services imports** together comprise all transactions between residents of a country and the rest of the world involving a change in ownership of general merchandise, goods sent for processing and repairs, nonmonetary gold, and services.

Net income refers to compensation earned by workers in an economy other than the one in which they are resident, for work performed for and paid for by a resident of that economy, and investment income (receipts and payments on direct investment, portfolio investment, and other investment, and receipts on reserve assets). Income derived from the use of intangible assets is recorded under business services.

Net current transfers consist of transactions in which residents of an economy provide or receive goods, services, income, or financial items without a quid pro quo. All transfers not considered to be capital transfers are current transfers.

Current account balance is the sum of net exports of goods and services, income, and current transfers.

Gross international reserves comprise holdings of monetary gold, special drawing rights, reserves of IMF members held by the IMF, and holdings of foreign exchange under the control of monetary authorities. The gold component of these reserves is valued at year-end London prices ($385.00 an ounce in 1990 and $290.25 an ounce in 1999).

The balance of payments is divided into two groups of accounts. The current account records transactions in goods and services, income, and current transfers. The capital and financial account records capital transfers, the acquisition or disposal of nonproduced, nonfinancial assets (such as patents), and transactions in financial assets and liabilities. Gross international reserves are recorded in a third set of accounts, the international investment position, which records the stocks of assets and liabilities.

The balance of payments is a double-entry accounting system that shows all flows of goods and services into and out of an economy; all transfers that are the counterpart of real resources or financial claims provided to or by the rest of the world without a quid pro quo, such as donations and grants; and all changes in residents' claims on, and liabilities to, nonresidents that arise from economic transactions. All transactions are recorded twice: once as a credit and once as a debit. In principle the net balance should be zero, but in practice the accounts often do not balance. In these cases a balancing item, called net errors and omissions, is included in the capital and financial account.

Discrepancies may arise in the balance of payments because there is no single source for balance of payments data and no way to ensure that data from different sources are fully consistent. Sources include customs data, monetary accounts of the banking system, external debt records, information provided by enterprises, surveys to estimate service transactions, and foreign exchange records. Differences in recording methods—for example, in the timing of transactions, in definitions of residence and ownership, and in the exchange rate used to value transactions—contribute to net errors and omissions. In addition, smuggling and other illegal or quasi-legal transactions may be unrecorded or misrecorded.

The concepts and definitions underlying the data in table 15 are based on the fifth edition of the IMF's *Balance of Payments Manual*. That edition redefined as capital transfers some transactions previously included in the current account, such as debt forgiveness, migrants' capital transfers, and foreign aid to acquire capital goods. Thus the current account balance now more accurately reflects net current transfer receipts in addition to transactions in goods, services (previously nonfactor services), and income (previously factor income). Many countries still maintain their data collection systems according to the concepts and definitions in the fourth edition. Where necessary, the IMF converts data reported in earlier systems to conform with the fifth edition (see the primary data documentation table in *World Development Indicators 2000*). Values are in U.S. dollars converted at market exchange rates.

Table 16. Private sector finance

Private investment covers gross outlays by the private sector (including private nonprofit agencies) on additions to its fixed domestic assets. When direct estimates of private gross domestic fixed investment are not available, such investment is estimated as the difference between total gross domestic investment and consolidated public investment. No allowance is made for the depreciation of assets. Because private investment is often estimated as the difference between two estimated quantities—domestic fixed investment and consolidated public investment—private investment may be undervalued or overvalued and subject to errors over time.

Stock market capitalization (also called market value) is the sum of the market capitalizations of all firms listed on domestic stock exchanges, where each firm's market capitalization is its share price at the end of the year times the number of shares outstanding. Market capitalization, presented as one measure for gauging a country's level of stock market development, may not be strictly comparable across countries as a result of conceptual and statistical weaknesses such as inaccurate reporting and differences in accounting standards.

Listed domestic companies refer to the number of domestically incorporated companies listed on the country's stock exchanges at the end of the year. Excluded are investment companies, mutual funds, and other collective investment vehicles. Data on stock market capitalization and listed domestic companies are from Standard & Poor's *Emerging Stock Markets Factbook 2000.*

Interest rate spread (also known as the intermediation margin) is the difference between the interest rate charged by banks on short- and medium-term loans to the private sector and the interest rate offered by banks to resident customers for demand, time, or savings deposits. Interest rates should reflect the responsiveness of financial institutions to competition and price incentives. However, the interest rate spread may not be a reliable measure of a banking system's efficiency, to the extent that information about interest rates is inaccurate, that banks do not monitor all bank managers, or that the government sets deposit and lending rates.

Domestic credit provided by the banking sector includes all credit to various sectors on a gross basis, with the exception of credit to the central government, which is net. The banking sector includes monetary authorities, deposit money banks, and other banking institutions for which data are available (including institutions that do not accept transferable deposits but do incur such liabilities as time and savings deposits). Examples of other banking institutions include savings and mortgage loan institutions and building and loan associations.

In general, the indicators reported in table 16 do not capture the activities of the informal sector, which remains an important source of finance in developing economies.

Table 17. Role of government in the economy

Subsidies and other current transfers include all unrequited, nonrepayable transfers on current account to private and public enterprises and the cost to the public of covering the cash operating deficits on sales to the public by departmental enterprises.

Value added by state-owned enterprises is estimated as sales revenue minus the cost of intermediate inputs, or as the sum of these enterprises' operating surplus (balance) and their wage payments. State-owned enterprises are government-owned or -controlled economic entities that generate most of their revenue by selling goods and services. This definition encompasses commercial enterprises directly operated by a government department and those in which the government holds a majority of shares directly or indirectly through other state enterprises. It also includes enterprises in which the state holds a minority of shares, if the distribution of the remaining shares leaves the government with effective control. It excludes public sector activity—such as education, health services, and road construction and maintenance—that is financed in other ways, usually from the government's general revenue. Because financial enterprises are of a different nature, they have generally been excluded from the data.

Military expenditures for members of the North Atlantic Treaty Organization (NATO) are based on the NATO definition, which covers military-related expenditures of the defense ministry (including recruiting, training, construction, and the purchase of military supplies and equipment) and other ministries. Civilian-type expenditures of the defense ministry are excluded. Military assistance is included in the expenditures of the donor country. Purchases of military equipment on credit are included at the time the debt is incurred, not at the time of payment. Data for countries that are not members of NATO generally cover expenditures of the ministry of defense; excluded are expenditures on public order and safety, which are classified separately.

Definitions of military spending differ depending on whether they include civil defense, reserves and auxiliary forces, police and paramilitary forces, dual-purpose forces such as military and civilian police, military grants in kind, pensions for military personnel, and social security contributions paid by one part of government to another. Official government data may omit some military spending, disguise financing through extrabudgetary accounts or unrecorded use of foreign exchange receipts, or fail to include military assistance or secret imports of military equipment. Current spending is more likely to be reported than capital spending. In some cases a more accurate estimate of military spending can be obtained by adding the value of estimated arms imports and nominal military expenditures. This method may understate or overstate spending in a particular year, however, because payments for arms may not coincide with deliveries.

The data on military expenditures in table 17 are from the U.S. Department of State's Bureau of Arms Control. The IMF's *Government Finance Statistics Yearbook* is a primary source for data on defense spending. It uses a consistent definition of defense spending based on the NATO definition and the United Nations' classification of the functions of government. The IMF checks data on defense spending for broad consistency with other macroeconomic data reported to it, but it is not always able to verify the accuracy and completeness of such data. Moreover, country coverage is affected by delays or failure to report data. Thus most researchers supplement the IMF's data with assessments by other organizations such as the Bureau of Arms Control, the Stockholm International Peace Research Institute, and the International Institute for Strategic Studies. However, these agencies rely heavily on reporting by governments, on confidential intelligence estimates of varying quality, on sources that they do not or cannot reveal, and on one another's publications.

Composite ICRG risk rating is an overall index of investment risk in a country, taken from the PRS Group's *International Country Risk Guide.* The index is based on 22 components of risk. The PRS Group collects information on each component, groups these components into three major categories (political, financial, and economic), and converts the information into a single numerical risk assessment ranging from 0 to 100. Ratings below 50 indicate very high risk and those above 80 very low risk. Ratings are updated every month.

Institutional Investor credit rating ranks, from 0 to 100, the probability of a country's default. A high number indicates a low probability of default. Institutional Investor country credit ratings are based on information provided by leading international banks. Responses are weighted using a formula that gives more importance to responses from banks with greater worldwide exposure and more sophisticated country analysis systems. Ratings are updated every six months.

Risk ratings may be highly subjective, reflecting external perceptions that do not always capture a country's actual situation. But these subjective perceptions are the reality that policymakers face in the climate they create for foreign private inflows. Countries not rated favorably by credit risk rating agencies typically do not attract registered flows of private capital. The risk ratings presented here are not endorsed by the World Bank but are included for their analytical usefulness.

Highest marginal tax rate is the highest rate shown on the schedule of tax rates applied to the taxable income of individuals and corporations. The table also presents the income threshold above which the highest marginal tax rate applies for individuals.

Tax collection systems are often complex, containing many exceptions, exemptions, penalties, and other inducements that affect the incidence of taxation and thus influence the decisions of workers, managers, entrepreneurs, investors, and consumers. A potentially important influence on both domestic and international investors is the tax system's progressivity, as reflected in the highest marginal tax rate on individual and corporate income. Marginal tax rates for individuals generally refer to employment income. For some countries the highest marginal tax rate is also the basic or flat rate, and other surtaxes, deductions, and the like may apply.

Table 18. Power and transportation

Electric power consumption per capita measures the production of power plants and combined heat and power plants less transmission, distribution, and transformation losses and own use by heat and power plants. **Electric power transmission and distribution losses** are losses in transmission between sources of supply and points of distribution, and in distribution to consumers, including pilferage.

The International Energy Agency collects data on electric power production and consumption from national energy agencies and adjusts those data to meet international definitions—for example, to account for self-production by establishments that, in addition to their main activities, generate electricity wholly or partly for their own use. In some countries self-production by households and small entrepreneurs is substantial because of their remoteness or because public power sources are unreliable, and in these cases adjustments may not adequately reflect actual output.

Although power plants' own consumption and transmission losses are netted out, electric power consumption includes consumption by auxiliary stations, losses in transformers that are considered integral parts of those stations, and electricity produced by pumping installations. Where data are available, consumption covers electricity generated by all primary sources of energy: coal, oil, gas, nuclear, hydroelectric, geothermal, wind, tide and wave, and combustible renewables. Neither production nor consumption data capture the reliability of supplies, including the frequency of outages, breakdowns, and load factors.

Paved roads are those surfaced with crushed stone (macadam) and hydrocarbon binder or bituminized agents, with concrete, or with cobblestones, as a percentage of all the country's roads, measured in length. **Goods transported by road** are the volume of goods hauled by road vehicles, measured in millions of metric tons

times kilometers traveled. **Goods transported by rail** are the tonnage of goods transported times kilometers traveled per million dollars of GDP measured in PPP terms. **Air passengers carried** include those on both domestic and international passenger routes.

Data for most transport sectors are not internationally comparable because—unlike for demographic statistics, national income accounts, and international trade data—the collection of infrastructure data has not been "internationalized." Data on roads are collected by the International Road Federation (IRF), and data on air transportation by the International Civil Aviation Organization. National road associations are the primary source of IRF data; in countries where such an association is lacking or does not respond, other agencies are contacted, such as road directorates, ministries of transportation or public works, or central statistical offices. As a result, the compiled data are of uneven quality.

Table 19. Communications, information, and science and technology

Daily newspapers are the number of copies distributed of newspapers published at least four times a week, per 1,000 people. **Radios** are the estimated number of radio receivers in use for broadcasts to the general public, per 1,000 people. Data on these two indicators are obtained from statistical surveys carried out by UNESCO. In some countries definitions, classifications, and methods of enumeration do not entirely conform to UNESCO standards. For example, some countries report newspaper circulation as the number of copies printed rather than the number distributed. In addition, many countries impose radio license fees to help pay for public broadcasting, discouraging radio owners from declaring ownership. Because of these and other data collection problems, estimates of the number of newspapers and radios vary widely in reliability and should be interpreted with caution.

Television sets are the estimated number of sets in use, per 1,000 people. Data on television sets are supplied to the International Telecommunication Union (ITU) through annual questionnaires sent to national broadcasting authorities and industry associations. Some countries require that television sets be registered. To the extent that households do not register some or all of their sets, the number of licensed sets may understate the true number of sets in use.

Telephone mainlines are all telephone lines that connect a customer's equipment to the public switched telephone network, per 1,000 people. **Mobile telephones** refer to users of portable telephones subscribing to an automatic public mobile telephone service using cellular technology that provides access to the public switched telephone network, per 1,000 people. The ITU compiles data on telephone mainlines and mobile phones through annual questionnaires sent to telecommunications authorities and operating companies. The data are supplemented by annual reports and statistical yearbooks of telecommunications ministries, regulators, operators, and industry associations.

Personal computers are the estimated number of self-contained computers designed to be used by a single person, per 1,000 people. Estimates by the ITU of the number of personal computers are derived from an annual questionnaire, supplemented by other sources. In many countries mainframe computers are used extensively, and thousands of users may be connected to a single mainframe computer; in such cases the number of personal computers understates the total use of computers.

Internet hosts are computers connected directly to the worldwide network; many computer users can access the Internet through a single host. Hosts are assigned to countries on the basis of their country code, though this code does not necessarily indicate that the host is physically located in that country. All hosts lacking a country code identification are assigned to the United States. The Internet Software Consortium changed the methods used in its Internet domain survey beginning in July 1998. The new survey is believed to be more reliable and to avoid the problem of undercounting that occurs when organizations restrict download to their domain data. Nevertheless, some measurement problems remain, so the number of Internet hosts shown for each country should be considered an approximation.

Scientists and engineers in research and development (R&D) are the number of people trained to work in any field of science who are engaged in professional research and development activity (including administrators), per million people. Most such jobs require completion of tertiary education.

UNESCO collects data on scientists, engineers, and R&D expenditure from its member states, mainly from official replies to UNESCO questionnaires and special surveys, as well as from official reports and publications, supplemented by information from other national and international sources. UNESCO reports either the stock of scientists and engineers or the number of economically active persons qualified to be scientists and engineers. Stock data generally come from censuses and are less timely than measures of the economically active population. UNESCO supplements these data with estimates of the number of qualified scientists and engineers by counting the number of people who have completed education at ISCED (International Standard Classification of Education) levels 6 and 7. The data on scientists and engineers, normally calculated in terms of full-time-equivalent staff, cannot take into account the considerable variations in the quality of training and education.

High-technology exports are products with high R&D intensity. They include high-technology products in aerospace, computers, pharmaceuticals, scientific instruments, and electrical machinery.

The methodology used for determining a country's high-technology exports was developed by the OECD in collaboration with Eurostat (the Statistical Office of the European Communities). Termed the "product approach" to distinguish it from a "sectoral approach," the method is based on the calculation of R&D intensity (R&D expenditure divided by total sales) for groups of products from six countries (Germany, Italy, Japan, the Netherlands, Sweden, and the United States). Because industrial sectors characterized by a few high-technology products may also produce many low-technology products, the product approach is more appropriate for analyzing international trade than is the sectoral approach. To construct a list of high-technology manufactured products (services are excluded), the R&D intensity was calculated for products classified at the three-digit level of the Standard International Trade Classification (SITC) revision 3. The final list was determined at the four- and five-digit level. At this level, because no R&D data were available, final selection was based on patent data and expert opinion. This methodology takes only R&D intensity into account. Other characteristics of high technology are also important, such as know-how, scientific and technical personnel, and technology embodied in patents; considering these characteristics would result in a different list (see Hatzichronoglou 1997).

Patent applications filed are the number of documents, issued by a government office, that describe an invention and create a legal situation in which the patented invention can normally be exploited (made, used, sold, imported) only by, or with the authorization of, the patentee. The protection of inventions is limited in time (generally 20 years from the filing date of the application for the grant of a patent). Information on patent applications filed is shown separately for residents and nonresidents of the country. Data on patents are from the World Intellectual Property Organization, which estimates that at the end of 1996 about 3.8 million patents were in force in the world.

Table 20. Global trade

Merchandise exports show the f.o.b. (free on board) value, in U.S. dollars, of goods provided to the rest of the world. **Merchandise imports** show the c.i.f. (cost plus insurance and freight) value, in U.S. dollars, of goods purchased from the rest of the world. **Manufactured exports and imports** refer to commodities in Standard International Trade Classification (SITC) sections 5 (chemicals), 6 (basic manufactures), 7 (machinery), and 8 (miscellaneous manufactured goods), excluding division 68 (nonferrous metals) and group 891 (arms and ammunition). **Commercial services** comprise all trade in services, including transportation, communication, and business services, excluding government services, which comprise services associated with government sectors (such as expenditures on embassies and consulates) and with regional and international organizations.

Data on merchandise exports and imports are derived from customs records and may not fully conform to the concepts and definitions in the fifth edition of the IMF's *Balance of Payments Manual.* The value of exports is recorded as the cost of the goods delivered to the frontier of the exporting country for shipment—the f.o.b. value. Many countries collect and report trade data in U.S. dollars. When countries report in local currency, the value is converted at the average official exchange rate for the period. The value of imports is generally recorded as the cost of the goods when purchased by the importer plus the cost of transport and insurance to the frontier of the importing country—the c.i.f. value. Data on imports of goods are derived from the same sources as data on exports. In principle, world exports and imports should be identical. Similarly, exports from an economy should equal the sum of imports by the rest of the world from that economy. But differences in timing and definition result in discrepancies in reported values at all levels.

The data in table 20 were compiled by the World Trade Organization (WTO). Data on merchandise trade come from the IMF's *International Financial Statistics Yearbook,* supplemented by data from the Commodity Trade (COMTRADE) database maintained by the United Nations Statistics Division and from national publications for countries that do not report to the IMF. Data on trade in manufactures come from the COMTRADE database. Where data were not available from the WTO, World Bank staff estimated shares of manufactures using the most recent information available from the COMTRADE database. Wherever available, WTO reports merchandise trade data on the basis of the general system of trade, which includes goods imported for reexport. Two economies with substantial reexports, Hong Kong (China) and Singapore, are noted in the table. Goods transported through a country en route to another are not included. Data on trade in commercial services are drawn from the IMF's Balance of Payments database, supplemented by national publications from countries that do not report to the IMF.

Table 21. Aid and financial flows

Net private capital flows consist of private debt and nondebt flows. Private debt flows include commercial bank lending, bonds, and other private credits; private nondebt flows are foreign direct investment and portfolio equity investment. **Foreign direct investment** is net inflows of investment to acquire a lasting management interest (10 percent or more of voting stock) in an enterprise operating in an economy other than that of the investor. It is the sum of equity capital flows, reinvestment of earnings, other long-term capital flows, and short-term capital flows as shown in the balance of payments.

The data on foreign direct investment are based on balance of payments data reported by the IMF, supplemented by data on net foreign direct investment reported by the OECD and official national sources. The internationally accepted definition of foreign direct investment is that provided in the fifth edition of the IMF's *Balance of Payments Manual.* The OECD has also published a definition, in consultation with the IMF, Eurostat, and the United Nations. Because of the multiplicity of sources and differences in definitions and reporting methods, more than one estimate of foreign direct investment may exist for a country, and data may not be comparable across countries.

Foreign direct investment data do not give a complete picture of international investment in an economy. Balance of payments data on foreign direct investment do not include capital raised in the host economies, which has become an important source of financing for investment projects in some developing countries. There is also increasing awareness that foreign direct investment data are limited because they capture only cross-border investment flows involving equity participation and omit nonequity cross-border transactions such as intrafirm flows of goods and services. For a detailed discussion of the data issues, see the World Bank's *World Debt Tables 1993–94* (volume 1, chapter 3).

Total external debt is debt owed to nonresidents repayable in foreign currency, goods, or services. It is the sum of public, publicly guaranteed, and private nonguaranteed long-term debt, use of IMF credit, and short-term debt. Short-term debt includes all debt having an original maturity of one year or less and interest in arrears on long-term debt. **Present value of external debt** is the sum of short-term external debt plus the discounted sum of total debt service payments due on public, publicly guaranteed, and private nonguaranteed long-term external debt over the life of existing loans.

Data on the external debt of low- and middle-income economies are gathered by the World Bank through its Debtor Reporting System. World Bank staff calculate the indebtedness of developing countries using loan-by-loan reports submitted by these countries on long-term public and publicly guaranteed borrowing, along with information on short-term debt collected by the countries or from creditors through the reporting systems of the Bank for International Settlements and the OECD. These data are supplemented by information on loans and credits from major multilateral banks and loan statements from official lending agencies in major creditor countries, and by estimates from World Bank country economists and IMF desk officers. In addition, some countries provide data on private nonguaranteed debt. In 1996, 34 countries reported their private nonguaranteed debt to the World Bank; estimates were made for 28 additional countries known to have significant private debt.

The present value of external debt provides a measure of future debt service obligations that can be compared with such indicators as GNP. It is calculated by discounting debt service (interest plus amortization) due on long-term external debt over the life of existing loans. Short-term debt is included at its face value. Data on debt are in U.S. dollars converted at official exchange rates. The discount rate applied to long-term debt is determined by the currency of repayment of the loan and is based on the OECD's commercial interest reference rates. Loans from the International Bank for Reconstruction and Development and credits from the International Development Association are discounted using a reference rate for special drawing rights, as are obligations to the IMF. When the discount rate is greater than the interest rate of the loan, the present value is less than the nominal sum of future debt service obligations.

Official development assistance (ODA) consists of disbursements of loans (net of repayments of principal) and grants made on concessional terms by official agencies of the members of the Development Assistance Committee (DAC), by multilateral institutions, and by certain Arab countries to promote economic development and welfare in recipient economies listed by DAC as developing. Loans with a grant element of more than 25 percent are included in ODA, as are technical cooperation and assistance. Also included are aid flows (net of repayments) from official donors to the transition economies of Eastern Europe and the former Soviet Union and to certain higher-income developing countries and territories as determined by DAC. These flows are sometimes referred to as official aid and are provided under terms and conditions similar to those for ODA. Data for aid as a share of GNP are calculated using values in U.S. dollars converted at official exchange rates.

The data cover bilateral loans and grants from DAC countries, multilateral organizations, and certain Arab countries. They do not reflect aid given by recipient countries to other developing countries. As a result, some countries that are net donors (such as Saudi Arabia) are shown in the table as aid recipients.

The data do not distinguish among different types of aid (program, project, or food aid; emergency assistance; peacekeeping assistance; or technical cooperation), each of which may have a very different effect on the economy. Technical cooperation expenditures do not always directly benefit the recipient economy, to the extent that they defray costs incurred outside the country for salaries and benefits of technical experts and for overhead of firms supplying technical services.

Because the aid data in table 21 are based on information from donors, they are not consistent with information recorded by recipients in the balance of payments, which often excludes all or some technical assistance—particularly payments to expatriates made directly by the donor. Similarly, grant commodity aid may not always be recorded in trade data or in the balance of payments. Although estimates of ODA in balance of payments statistics are meant to exclude purely military aid, the distinction is sometimes blurred. The definition used by the country of origin usually prevails.

Statistical methods

This section describes the calculation of the least-squares growth rate, the exponential (endpoint) growth rate, the Gini index, and the World Bank's Atlas method for calculating the conversion factor used to estimate GNP and GNP per capita in U.S. dollars.

Least-squares growth rate

Least-squares growth rates are used wherever there is a sufficiently long time series to permit a reliable calculation. No growth rate is calculated if more than half the observations in a period are missing.

The least-squares growth rate, r, is estimated by fitting a linear regression trend line to the logarithmic annual values of the variable in the relevant period. The regression equation takes the form

$$\ln X_t = a + bt,$$

which is equivalent to the logarithmic transformation of the compound growth equation,

$$X_t = X_0 (1 + r)^t.$$

In this equation X is the variable, t is time, and $a = \ln X_0$ and $b = \ln (1 + r)$ are the parameters to be estimated. If b^* is the least-squares estimate of b, the average annual growth rate, r, is obtained as $[\exp(b^*) - 1]$ and is multiplied by 100 to express it as a percentage.

The calculated growth rate is an average rate that is representative of the available observations over the entire period. It does not necessarily match the actual growth rate between any two periods.

Exponential growth rate

The growth rate between two points in time for certain demographic data, notably labor force and population, is calculated from the equation

$$r = \ln (p_n / p_1) / n,$$

where p_n and p_1 are the last and first observations in the period, n is the number of years in the period, and ln is the natural logarithm operator. This growth rate is based on a model of continuous, exponential growth between two points in time. It does not take into account the intermediate values of the series. Nor does it correspond to the annual rate of change measured at a one-year interval, which is given by $(p_n - p_{n-1})/p_{n-1}$.

The Gini index

The Gini index measures the extent to which the distribution of income (or, in some cases, consumption expenditure) among individuals or households within an economy deviates from a perfectly equal distribution. A Lorenz curve plots the cumulative percentages of total income received against the cumulative percentage of recipients, starting with the poorest individual or household. The Gini index measures the area between the Lorenz curve and a hypothetical line of absolute equality, expressed as a percentage of the maximum area under the line. Thus a Gini index of zero represents perfect equality, and an index of 100 perfect inequality.

The World Bank uses a numerical analysis program, POVCAL, to estimate values of the Gini index; see Chen, Datt, and Ravallion (1993).

World Bank Atlas method

In calculating GNP and GNP per capita in U.S. dollars for certain operational purposes, the World Bank uses a synthetic exchange rate commonly called the Atlas conversion factor. The purpose of the Atlas conversion factor is to reduce the impact of exchange rate fluctuations in the cross-country comparison of national incomes.

The Atlas conversion factor for any year is the average of a country's exchange rate (or alternative conversion factor) for that year and its exchange rates for the two preceding years, adjusted for the difference between the rate of inflation in the country and that in the Group of Five (G-5) countries (France, Germany, Japan, the United Kingdom, and the United States). A country's inflation rate is measured by the change in its GNP deflator.

The inflation rate for the G-5 countries, representing international inflation, is measured by the change in the SDR deflator. (Special drawing rights, or SDRs, are the IMF's unit of account.) The SDR deflator is calculated as a weighted average of the G-5 countries' GDP deflators in SDR terms, the weights being the amount of each country's currency in one SDR unit. Weights vary over time because both the composition of the SDR and the relative exchange rates for each currency change. The SDR deflator is calculated in SDR terms first and then converted to U.S. dollars using the SDR to dollar Atlas conversion factor. The Atlas conversion factor is then applied to a country's GNP. The resulting GNP in U.S. dollars is divided by the midyear population for the latest of the three years to derive GNP per capita.

When official exchange rates are deemed to be unreliable or unrepresentative during a period, an alternative estimate of the exchange rate is used in the Atlas formula (see below).

The following formulas describe the calculation of the Atlas conversion factor for year t:

$$e_t^* = \frac{1}{3}\left[e_{t-2}\left(\frac{p_t}{p_{t-2}}\Big/\frac{p_t^{S\$}}{p_{t-2}^{S\$}}\right) + e_{t-1}\left(\frac{p_t}{p_{t-1}}\Big/\frac{p_t^{S\$}}{p_{t-1}^{S\$}}\right) + e_t\right]$$

and the calculation of GNP per capita in U.S. dollars for year t:

$$Y_t^\$ = (Y_t/N_t)/e_t^*,$$

where e_t^* is the Atlas conversion factor (national currency to the U.S. dollar) for year t, e_t is the average annual exchange rate (national currency to the U.S. dollar) for year t, pt is the GNP deflator for year t, $p_t^{S\$}$ is the SDR deflator in U.S. dollar terms for year t, $Y_t^\$$ is the Atlas GNP in U.S. dollars in year t, Y_t is current GNP (local currency) for year t, and N_t is the midyear population for year t.

Alternative conversion factors

The World Bank systematically assesses the appropriateness of official exchange rates as conversion factors. An alternative conversion factor is used when the official exchange rate is judged to diverge by an exceptionally large margin from the rate effectively applied to domestic transactions of foreign currencies and traded products. This is the case for only a small number of countries (see the primary data documentation table in *World Development Indicators 2000*). Alternative conversion factors are used in the Atlas method and elsewhere in the Selected World Development Indicators as single-year conversion factors.

Data Sources

Ahmad, Sultan. 1992. "Regression Estimates of Per Capita GDP Based on Purchasing Power Parities." Policy Research Working Paper 956. World Bank, International Economics Department, Washington, D.C.

———. 1994. "Improving Inter-Spatial and Inter-Temporal Comparability of National Accounts." *Journal of Development Economics* 4: 53–75.

Ball, Nicole. 1984. "Measuring Third World Security Expenditure: A Research Note." *World Development* 12(2): 157–64.

Chen, Shaohua, Gaurav Datt, and Martin Ravallion. 1993. "Is Poverty Increasing in the Developing World?" Policy Research Working Paper. World Bank, Washington, D.C.

Council of Europe. Various years. *Recent Demographic Developments in Europe and North America.* Strasbourg: Council of Europe Press.

Eurostat (Statistical Office of the European Communities). 1999. *EU Transport in Figures.* Luxembourg.

———. Various years. *Demographic Statistics.* Luxembourg.

———. Various years. *Statistical Yearbook.* Luxembourg.

FAO (Food and Agriculture Organization of the United Nations). 1999. *State of the World's Forests 1999.* Rome.

———. Various years. *Production Yearbook.* FAO Statistics Series. Rome.

Hatzichronoglou, Thomas. 1997. "Revision of the High-Technology Sector and Product Classification." STI Working Paper 1997/2. Organisation for Economic Co-operation and Development (OECD) Directorate for Science, Technology, and Industry. Paris.

Heston, Alan. 1994. "A Brief Review of Some Problems in Using National Accounts Data in Level of Output Comparisons and Growth Studies." *Journal of Development Economics* 44: 29–52.

ICAO (International Civil Aviation Organization). 1999. *Civil Aviation Statistics of the World: 1998.* ICAO Statistical Yearbook. 23rd ed. Montreal.

IEA (International Energy Agency). Various years. *Energy Balances of OECD Countries.* Paris.

———. Various years. *Energy Statistics and Balances of Non-OECD Countries.* Paris.

———. Various years. *Energy Statistics of OECD Countries.* Paris.

IFC (International Finance Corporation). 1999. *Trends in Private Investment in Developing Countries 1999.* Washington, D.C.

ILO (International Labour Organization). 1999. *Key Indicators of the Labour Market.* Geneva.

———. Various years. *Yearbook of Labour Statistics.* Geneva.

IMF (International Monetary Fund). 1986. *A Manual on Government Finance Statistics.* Washington, D.C.

———. 1993. *Balance of Payments Manual.* 5th ed. Washington, D.C.

———. Various years. *Direction of Trade Statistics Yearbook.* Washington, D.C.

———. Various years. *Government Finance Statistics Yearbook.* Washington, D.C.

———. Various years. *International Financial Statistics Yearbook.* Washington, D.C.

Institutional Investor. 2000. March. New York.

Internet Software Consortium. 2000. *Internet Domain Survey.* January. [www.isc.org].

IRF (International Road Federation). 1999. *World Road Statistics 1999.* Geneva.

ITU (International Telecommunication Union). 1999. *World Telecommunication Development Report 1999.* Geneva.

OECD (Organisation for Economic Co-operation and Development). Various years. *Geographical Distribution of Financial Flows to Aid Recipients: Disbursements, Commitments, Country Indicators.* Paris.

———. Various years. *National Accounts.* Vol. 1, *Main Aggregates.* Paris.

———. Various years. *National Accounts.* Vol. 2, *Detailed Tables.* Paris.

OECD (Organisation for Economic Co-operation and Development), DAC (Development Assistance Committee). Various years. *Development Co-operation.* Paris.

PricewaterhouseCoopers. 1999a. *Corporate Taxes: Worldwide Summaries 1999–2000.* New York.

———. 1999b. *Individual Taxes: Worldwide Summaries 1999–2000.* New York.

PRS Group. 2000. *International Country Risk Guide.* March. East Syracuse, N.Y.

Ravallion, Martin, and Shaohua Chen. 1996. "What Can New Survey Data Tell Us about the Recent Changes in Living Standards in Developing and Transitional Economies?" Policy Research Working Paper 1694. World Bank, Washington, D.C.

———. 1997. "Can High-Inequality Developing Countries Escape Absolute Poverty?" *Economic Letters* 56: 51–57.

Srinivasan, T.N. 1994. "Database for Development Analysis: An Overview." *Journal of Development Economics* 44(1): 3–28.

Standard & Poor's. 2000. *Emerging Stock Markets Factbook 2000.* New York.

UN (United Nations). 1968. *A System of National Accounts: Studies and Methods.* Series F, no. 2, rev. 3. New York.

———. 1999a. *World Population Prospects: The 1998 Revision.* New York.

———. 1999b. *World Urbanization Prospects: The 1998 Revision.* New York.

———. Various issues. *Monthly Bulletin of Statistics.* Statistics Division. New York.

———. Various years. *Energy Statistics Yearbook.* Statistics Division. New York.

———. Various years. *National Income Accounts.* Statistics Division. New York.

———. Various years. *Population and Vital Statistics Report.* Statistics Division. New York.

———. Various years. *Statistical Yearbook.* Statistics Division. New York.

———. Various years. *Update on the Nutrition Situation.* Administrative Committee on Coordination, Subcommittee on Nutrition. Geneva.

UNCTAD (United Nations Conference on Trade and Development). Various years. *Handbook of International Trade and Development Statistics.* Geneva.

UNESCO (United Nations Educational, Scientific, and Cultural Organization). 1999a. *Statistical Yearbook.* Paris.

———. 1999b. *World Education Report.* Paris.

UNICEF (United Nations Children's Fund). Various years. *The State of the World's Children.* New York: Oxford University Press.

UNIDO (United Nations Industrial Development Organization). Various years. *International Yearbook of Industrial Statistics.* Vienna.

U.S. Department of State, Bureau of Arms Control. 1999. *World Military Expenditures and Arms Transfers 1998.* Washington, D.C.

WHO (World Health Organization). 1997. *Coverage of Maternity Care.* Geneva.

———. Various years. *World Health Report.* Geneva.

———. Various years. *World Health Statistics Annual.* Geneva.

World Bank. 1993a. *Purchasing Power of Currencies: Comparing National Incomes Using ICP Data.* Washington, D.C.

———. 1993b. *World Debt Tables 1993–94.* Vol. 1. Washington, D.C.

———. 2000a. *Global Development Finance 2000.* Washington, D.C.

———. 2000b. *World Development Indicators 2000.* Washington, D.C.

World Intellectual Property Organization. 1999. *Industrial Property Statistics.* Publication A. Geneva.

World Resources Institute, in collaboration with UNEP (United Nations Environment Programme) and UNDP (United Nations Development Programme). Various years. *World Resources: A Guide to the Global Environment.* New York: Oxford University Press.

WTO (World Trade Organization). Various years. *Annual Report.* Geneva.

Classification of Economies by Income and Region, 2000

Income group	Subgroup	Sub-Saharan Africa		Asia		Europe and Central Asia		Middle East and North Africa		Americas
		East and Southern Africa	West Africa	East Asia and Pacific	South Asia	Eastern Europe and Central Asia	Rest of Europe	Middle East	North Africa	
Low income		Angola Burundi Comoros Congo, Dem. Rep. Eritrea Ethiopia Kenya Lesotho Madagascar Malawi Mozambique Rwanda Somalia Sudan Tanzania Uganda Zambia Zimbabwe	Benin Burkina Faso Cameroon Central African Republic Chad Congo, Rep. Côte d'Ivoire Gambia, The Ghana Guinea Guinea-Bissau Liberia Mali Mauritania Niger Nigeria São Tomé and Principe Senegal Sierra Leone Togo	Cambodia Indonesia Korea, Dem. Rep. Lao PDR Mongolia Myanmar Solomon Islands Vietnam	Afghanistan Bangladesh Bhutan India Nepal Pakistan	Armenia Azerbaijan Georgia Kyrgyz Republic Moldova Tajikistan Turkmenistan Ukraine Uzbekistan		Yemen, Rep.		Haiti Nicaragua
Middle income	Lower	Namibia Swaziland	Cape Verde Equatorial Guinea	China Fiji Kiribati Marshall Islands Micronesia, Fed. Sts. Papua New Guinea Philippines Samoa Thailand Tonga Vanuatu	Maldives Sri Lanka	Albania Belarus Bosnia and Herzegovina Bulgaria Kazakhstan Latvia Lithuania Macedonia, FYR[a] Romania Russian Federation Yugoslavia, Fed. Rep.[b]	Turkey	Iran, Islamic Rep. Iraq Jordan Syrian Arab Republic West Bank and Gaza	Algeria Djibouti Egypt, Arab Rep. Morocco Tunisia	Belize Bolivia Colombia Costa Rica Cuba Dominican Republic Ecuador El Salvador Guatemala Guyana Honduras Jamaica Paraguay Peru St. Vincent and the Grenadines Suriname
	Upper	Botswana Mauritius Mayotte Seychelles South Africa	Gabon	American Samoa Korea, Rep. Malaysia Palau		Croatia Czech Republic Estonia Hungary Poland Slovak Republic	Isle of Man	Bahrain Lebanon Oman Saudi Arabia	Libya Malta	Antigua and Barbuda Argentina Barbados Brazil Chile Dominica Grenada Mexico Panama Puerto Rico St. Kitts and Nevis St. Lucia Trinidad and Tobago Uruguay Venezuela, RB
Subtotal	157	25	23	23	8	26	2	10	7	33

| Income group | Subgroup | Sub-Saharan Africa | | Asia | | Europe and Central Asia | | Middle East and North Africa | | Americas |
		East and Southern Africa	West Africa	East Asia and Pacific	South Asia	Eastern Europe and Central Asia	Rest of Europe	Middle East	North Africa	
High income	OECD			Australia Japan New Zealand			Austria Belgium Denmark Finland France[c] Germany Greece Iceland Ireland Italy Luxembourg Netherlands Norway Portugal Spain Sweden Switzerland United Kingdom			Canada United States
	Non-OECD			Brunei French Polynesia Guam Hong Kong, China[d] Macao, China[e] New Caledonia N. Mariana Islands Singapore Taiwan, China		Slovenia	Andorra Channel Islands Cyprus Faeroe Islands Greenland Liechtenstein Monaco	Israel Kuwait Qatar United Arab Emirates		Aruba Bahamas, The Bermuda Cayman Islands Netherlands Antilles Virgin Islands (U.S.)
Total	157	25	23	35	8	27	27	14	7	41

a. Former Yugoslav Republic of Macedonia. b. Federal Republic of Yugoslavia (Serbia/Montenegro). c. The French overseas departments French Guiana, Guadeloupe, Martinique, and Réunion are included in France.
d. On 1 July 1997 China resumed its exercise of sovereignty over Hong Kong. e. On 20 December 1999 China resumed its exercise of sovereignty over Macao.
Source: World Bank data.

The World Bank classifies economies for operational and analytical purposes primarily by GNP per capita. Every economy is classified as low income, middle income (subdivided into lower middle and upper middle), or high income. Other analytical groups, based on geographic regions and levels of external debt, are also used.

Low-income and middle-income economies are sometimes referred to as developing economies. The term is used for convenience; it does not imply that all such economies are experiencing similar development or that other economies have reached a pre-ferred or final stage of development. Nor does classification by income necessarily reflect development status.

This table classifies all World Bank member economies as well as all other economies with populations of more than 30,000. Economies are divided among income groups according to 1999 GNP per capita, calculated using the World Bank Atlas method. The groups are as follows: low income, $755 or less; lower middle income, $756–2,995; upper middle income, $2,996–9,265; and high income, $9,266 or more.

DISTRIBUTORS AND BOOKSELLERS OF WORLD BANK GROUP PUBLICATIONS

Prices and credit terms vary from country to country. Please consult your local distributor or bookseller before placing an order.

DISTRIBUTORS

ARGENTINA
World Publications SA
Av. Cordoba 1877
1120 Buenos Aires
Tel: (54 11) 4815 8156
Fax: (54 11) 4815 8156
Email: wpbooks@infovia.com.ar

AUSTRALIA, PAPUA NEW GUINEA, FIJI, SOLOMON ISLANDS, VANUATU, AND SAMOA
D.A. Information Services
648 Whitehorse Road
Mitcham 3132
Victoria, Australia
Tel: (61 3) 9210 7777
Fax: (61 3) 9210 7788
Email: service@dadirect.com.au
URL: www.dadirect.com.au

AUSTRIA
Gerold and Co.
Weihburggasse 26
A-1010 Wien
Tel: (43 1) 512 47310
Fax: (43 1) 512 473129
Email: buch@gerold.telecom.at

BANGLADESH
Micro Industries Development
Assistance Society (MIDAS)
House 5, Road 16
Dhanmondi R/Area
Dhaka 1209
Tel: (880 2) 326427
Fax: (880 2) 8111188
Email: midas@fsbd.net

BELGIUM
Jean de Lannoy
Av. du Roi 202
1060 Brussels
Tel: (32 2) 538 5169
Fax: (32 2) 538 0841
Email: jean.de.lannoy@infoboard.be
URL: www.jean-de-lannoy.be

BOSNIA AND HERZEGOVINA
Book Trading Company
"Sahinpasic"
Marsala Tita 29/II
71000 Sarajevo
Tel: (387 33) 21 05 20
Fax: (387 33) 66 88 56
Email: tajib@btcsahinpasic.com
URL: www.btcsahinpasic.com

BRAZIL
Publicacoes Tecnicas Interna-
cionais Ltda.
Rua Peixoto Gomide, 209
Bela Vista
01409-901 Sao Paulo, SP
Tel: (55 11) 259 6644
Fax: (55 11) 258 6990
Email: webmaster@pti.com.br
URL: www.pti.com.br

CANADA
Renouf Publishing Co. Ltd.
5369 Canotek Road
Ottawa, Ontario K1J 9J3
Tel: (613) 745-2665
Fax: (613) 745-7660
Email: order.dept@renoufbooks.com
URL: www.renoufbooks.com

CHINA
Chinese Corporation for
Promotion and Humanities
15, Ding Hui Dong Li,
Kun Lan Hotal
Haidian District 100036
Beijing
Tel: (86 10) 88117711
Fax: (86 10) 88129871
Email: wangjiang99@yahoo.com

China Book Import Centre
P.O. Box 2825
Beijing

China Financial & Economic
Publishing House
8, Da Fo Si Dong Jie
Beijing
Tel: (86 10) 6401 7365
Fax: (86 10) 6401 7365

COLOMBIA
Infoenlace Ltda./An IHS Group
Company
Calle 72 No. 13-23 - Piso 3
Edificio Nueva Granada
Santafé de Bogotá, D.C.
Tel: (57 1) 260 9474, 260 9480
Fax: (57 1) 248 0808
Email: infoenlace@andinet.com

COTE D'IVOIRE
Centre d'Edition et de Diffu-
sion Africaines (CEDA)
04 B.P. 541
Abidjan 04
Tel: (225) 24 6510
Fax: (225) 25 0567
Email: info@ceda-ci.com
URL: www.ceda-ci.com

CYPRUS
Center for Applied Research
6, Diogenes Street, Engomi
P.O. Box 2006
Nicosia
Tel: (357 2) 59 0730
Fax: (357 2) 66 2051
Email: ttzitzim@sting.
cycollege.ac.cy

CZECH REPUBLIC
Management Press, NT
Publishing, s.r.o.
Nam. W. Churchilla 2
130 59 Prague 3
Tel: (420 2) 2446 2232, 2446 2254
Fax: (420 2) 2446 2242
Email: mgmtpress@
mgmtpress.cz
URL: www.mgmtpress.cz

USIS, NIS Prodejna
Havelkova 22
130 00 Prague 3
Tel: (42 2) 2423 1486
Fax: (42 2) 2423 1114
Email: posta@usiscr.cz
URL: www.usiscr.cz

DENMARK
Samfundslitteratur
Solbjerg Plads 3
DK-2000 Frederiksberg
Tel: (45 38) 153870
Fax: (45 38) 153856
Email: ck@sl.cbs.dk
URL: www.sl.cbs.dk

ECUADOR
Libri Mundi - Libreria Internacional
Juan Leon Mera 851
P.O. Box 17-01-3029
Quito
Tel: (593 2) 521 606
Fax: (593 2) 504 209
Email: librimu1@librimundi.com.ec

CODEU
Ruiz de Castilla 763, Edif.
Expocolor
Primer piso, Of. #2
Quito
Tel: (593 2) 507-383
Fax: (593 2) 507-383
Email: codeu@impsat.net.ec

EGYPT, ARAB REPUBLIC OF
Al Ahram Distribution Agency
Al Galaa Street
Cairo
Tel: (20 2) 578 60 83
Fax: (20 2) 575 93 88

MERIC (Middle East Readers
Information Center)
2 Bahrat Aly St.
Building "D" 1st Floor, Apt. 24
Cairo
Tel: (20 2) 341 3824
Fax: (20 2) 341 9355
Email: order@meric-co.com
URL: www.meobserver.com.eg

For subscription orders and
publications in French only:
Middle East Observer
41, Sherif Street
11111 Cairo
Tel: (20 2) 392 6919
Fax: (20 2) 393 9732
Email:
inquiry@meobserver.com
URL: www.meobserver.com

FINLAND
Akateeminen Kirjakauppa
PL 128 (Keskuskatu 1)
FIN-00101 Helsinki
Tel: (358 9) 121 4385
Fax: (358 9) 121 4450
Email: akatilaus@akateeminen.com
URL: www.akateeminen.com

FRANCE
Editions Eska; DJB/Offilib
12, rue du Quatre-Septembre
75002 Paris
Tel: (33 1) 42 86 58 88
Fax: (33 1) 42 60 45 35
Email: offilib@offilib.fr
URL: www.offilib.fr

GERMANY
UNO-VERLAG
Am Hofgarten 10
D-53113 Bonn
Tel: (49 228) 949 020
Fax: (49 228) 949 0222
Email: unoverlag@aol.com
URL: www.uno-verlag.de

GHANA
Epp Books Services
Post Office Box 44
TUC
Accra
Tel: (233 21) 778 843
Fax: (233 21) 779 099
Email: epp@africaonline.com.gh

GREECE
Papasotiriou S.A.,
International Technical
Bookstore
35, Stournara Str.
106 82 Athens
Tel: (30 1) 364 1826
Fax: (30 1) 364 8254

Email: pap4@ioa.forthnet.gr
URL: www.papasotiriou.gr

HAITI
Culture Diffusion
Mr. Yves Clément Jumelle
5, Rue Capois
C.P. 257
Port-au-Prince
Tel: (509) 23 9260
Fax: (509) 23 4858

HONG KONG, CHINA; MACAU
Asia 2000 Ltd.
Sales & Circulation Department
302 Seabird House
22–28 Wyndham Street, Central
Hong Kong, China
Tel: (852) 2530 1409
Fax: (852) 2526 1107
Email: sales@asia2000.com.hk
URL: www.asia2000.com.hk

HUNGARY
Euro Info Service
Hungexpo Europa Haz (Pf. 44)
H-1441 Budapest
Tel: (36 1) 264 8270; 264 8271
Fax: (36 1) 264 8275
Email: euroinfo@euroinfo.hu
URL: www.euroinfo.hu

INDIA
Allied Publishers Ltd.
751 Mount Road
Madras 600 002
Tel: (91 44) 852 3938
Fax: (91 44) 852 0649
Email: allied.mds@smb.
sprintrpg.ems.vsnl.net.in

INDONESIA
Pt. Indira Limited
Jalan Borobudur 20
PO Box 181
Jakarta 10320
Tel: (62 21) 390 4290
Fax: (62 21) 390 4289
Email:

PF Book
J1. dr. Setia Budhi No. 274
Bandung 40143
Tel: (62 22) 2011 149
Fax: (62 22) 2012 840
Email: pfbook@bandung.
wasantara.net.id

IRAN
Ketab Sara Co. Publishers
P.O. Box 15745-733
Tehran 15117
Tel: (98 21) 871 6104
Fax: (98 21) 871 2479
Email: ketab-sara@neda.net.ir

Kowkab Publishers
P.O. Box 19575-511
Tehran
Tel: (98 21) 258 3723
Fax: (98 21) 258 3723
Email: kowkabpub@tavana.net

ISRAEL
Yozmot Literature Ltd.
P.O. Box 56055
3 Yohanan Hasandlar St.
Tel Aviv 61560
Tel: (972 3) 5285 397
Fax: (972 3) 5285 397

ITALY
Licosa Libreria Commissionaria
Sansoni S.P.A.
Via Duca di Calabria 1/1
50125 Firenze
Tel: (39 55) 648 31
Fax: (39 55) 641 257
Email: licosa@ftbcc.it
URL: www.ftbcc.it/licosa

JAMAICA
Ian Randle Publishers Ltd
206 Old Hope Road
Kingston 6
Tel: (876) 927 2085
Fax: (876) 977 0243
Email: irpl@colis.com

JAPAN
Eastern Book Service (EBS)
3-13 Hongo 3-chome, Bunkyo-ku
Tokyo 113
Tel: (81 3) 3818 0861
Fax: (81 3) 3818 0864
Email: orders@svt-ebs.co.jp
URL: www.svt-ebs.co.jp

KENYA
Legacy Books
Loita House
P.O. Box 68077
Nairobi
Tel: (254 2) 330 853
Fax: (254 2) 330 854
Email: legacy@form-net.com

Africa Book Service (E.A.) Ltd.
Quaran House, Mfangano
Street
P.O. Box 45245
Nairobi
Tel: (254 2) 223 641
Fax: (254 2) 330 272

KOREA, REPUBLIC OF
Eulyoo Publishing Co., Ltd.
46-1, Susong-Dong
Jongro-Gu
Seoul
Tel: (82 2) 734 3515
Fax: (82 2) 732 9154
Email: eulyoo@chollian.net

Dayang Books Trading Co.
International Division
954-22, Bangbae-Dong,
Socho-ku
Seoul
Tel: (82 2) 582 3588
Fax: (82 2) 521 8827
Email: dico3@chollian.net

LEBANON
Librairie du Liban
P.O. Box 11-9232
Beirut
Tel: (961 9) 217 944
Fax: (961 9) 217 434
Email: hsageh@cyberia.net.lb
URL: www.librairie-du-
liban.com.lb

MALAYSIA
University of Malaya Coopera-
tive Bookshop, Limited
P.O. Box 1127, Jalan Pantai Baru
59700 Kuala Lumpur
Tel: (60 3) 756 5000
Fax: (60 3) 755 4424
Email: umkoop@tm.net.my

MEXICO
INFOTEC
Av. San Fernando No. 37
Col. Toriello Guerra
14050 Mexico D.F.
Tel: (52 5) 624 2800
Fax: (52 5) 624 2822
Email: infotec@rtn.net.mx
URL: www.rtn.net.mx

Mundi-Prensa Mexico, S.A.
de C.V.
c/Rio Panuco, 141 - Colonia
Cuauhtemoc
06500 Mexico DF
Tel: (52 5) 533 56 58
Fax: (52 5) 514 67 99
Email: 1015245.2361@
compuserve.com

MOROCCO
Librarie Internationale
70, Rue T'ssoule
P.O. Box 302
Rabat (Souissi) MA 10001
Tel: (212 7) 75 01 83
Fax: (212 7) 75 86 61

NEPAL
Everest Media International
Services (P.) Ltd.
GPO Box 5443
Kathmandu
Tel: (977 1) 416 026
Fax: (977 1) 250 176
Email: emispltd@wlink.com.np

NETHERLANDS
De Lindeboom/Internationale
Publikaties b.v.
M.A. de Ruyterstraat 20A
7482 BZ Haaksbergen
Tel: (31 53) 574 0004
Fax: (31 53) 572 9296
Email: books@delindeboom.com
URL: www.delindeboom.com

NEW ZEALAND
EBSCO NZ Ltd.
Private Mail Bag 99914
New Market
Auckland
Tel: (64 9) 524 8119
Fax: (64 9) 524 8067
Email: WGent%ess-nz.ebsco@
iss.ebsco.com

Oasis Official
P.O. Box 3627
Wellington
Tel: (64 4) 4991551
Fax: (64 4) 499 1972
Email: oasis@actix.gen.nz
URL: www.oasisbooks.co.nz

NIGERIA
University Press Plc
Three Crowns Building Jericho
Private Mail Bag 5095
Ibadan
Tel: (234 22) 411356
Fax: (234 22) 412056
Email: unipress@skannet.com

PAKISTAN
Oxford University Press
5 Bangalore Town, Sharae
Faisal
P.O. Box 13033
Karachi 75350
Tel: (92 21) 446307; 449032;
440532
Fax: (92 21) 4547640;449032
Email: ouppak@theoffice.net
URL: www.oup.com.pk

Pak Book Corporation
Aziz Chambers 21
Queen's Road
Lahore
Tel: (92 42) 636 3222; 636 0885
Fax: (92 42) 636 2328
Email: pbc@brain.net.pk

Mirza Book Agency
65, Shahrah-e-Quaid-e-Azam
Lahore 54000
Tel: (92 42) 7353601
Fax: (92 42) 576 3714
Email: merchant@brain.net.pk

PERU
Editorial Desarrollo SA
Apartado 3824
Ica 242, OF. 106
Lima 1
Tel: (51 14) 285 380
Fax: (51 14) 286 628

PHILIPPINES
International Booksource
Center, Inc.
1127-A Antipolo St.
Barangay, Venezuela
Makati City
Tel: (63 2) 896 6501
Fax: (63 2) 896 6497

POLAND
International Publishing Service
Ul. Piekna 31/37
00 677 Warsaw
Tel: (48 2) 628 6089
Fax: (48 2) 621 7255
Email: books%ips@ikp.atm.com.pl
URL: www.ips.com.pl

PORTUGAL
Livraria Portugal
Apartado 2681
Rua Do Carmo 70-74
1200 Lisbon
Tel: (351 1) 347 4982
Fax: (351 1) 347 0264

ROMANIA
Compani De Librarii Bucuresti s.a.
Str. Lipscani nr. 26, sector 3
Bucharest
Tel: (40 1) 313 9645
Fax: (40 1) 312 4000

RUSSIAN FEDERATION
Izdatelstvo << Ves Mir >>
Moscow 101831
Tel: (7 95) 917 8749
Fax: (7 95) 917 9259
Email: ozimarin@glasnet.ru
URL: www.vesmir.tsx.org

SENEGAL
Librairie Clairafrique
2, Rue El Hadj Mbaye Gueye
Place de l'Independance
B.P. 2005
Dakar
Tel: (221) 822 21 69
Fax: (221) 821 84 09

**SINGAPORE; TAIWAN, CHINA,
MYANMAR; BRUNEI**
Hemisphere Publishing Services
Golden Wheel Building
41 Kallang Pudding Road, #04-03
Singapore 349316
Tel: (65) 741 5166
Fax: (65) 742 9356
Email: info@hemisphere.com.sg

SLOVAK REPUBLIC
Slovart G.T.G. Ltd.
Krupinská 4
P.O. Box 152
852 99 Bratislava 5
Tel: (42 7) 839 471; 472; 473
Fax: (42 7) 839 485
Email: gtg@internet.sk

SLOVENIA
Gospodarski vestnik Publishing Group
Dunajska cesta 5
1000 Ljubljana
Tel: (386 61) 133 83 47
Fax: (386 61) 133 80 30
Email: repansekj@gvestnik.si
URL: www.gvestnik.si/
EUROPA/index.htm

SOUTH AFRICA, BOTSWANA
For single titles:
Oxford University Press
Southern Africa
P.O. Box 12119
N1 City 7463
Cape Town, South Africa
Tel: (27 21) 595 4400
Fax: (27 21) 595 4430
Email: oxford@oup.co.za

For subscription orders:
International Subscription Service
P.O. Box 41095
Craighall
Johannesburg 2024, South Africa
Tel: (27 11) 880 1448
Fax: (27 11) 880 6248
Email: iss@is.co.za

SPAIN
Mundi-Prensa Libros, s.a.
Castello 37
28001 Madrid
Tel: (34 91) 436 37 00
Fax: (34 91) 575 39 98
Email: libreria@mundiprensa.es
URL: www.mundiprensa.es

Mundi-Prensa Barcelona
Consell de Cent No. 391
08009 Barcelona
Tel: (34 3) 488 3492
Fax: (34 3) 487 7659
Email: barcelona@mundiprensa.es

SRI LANKA, THE MALDIVES
Lake House Bookshop
P.O. Box 244
100, Sir Chittampalam Gardiner Mawatha
Colombo 2, Sri Lanka
Tel: (94 1) 32 104
Fax: (94 1) 432 104
Email: LHL@sri.lanka.net

SWEDEN
For periodicals and serials only:
Wennergren-Williams
Informations Service AB
P.O. Box 1305
S-171 25 Solna
Tel: (46 8) 705 9750
Fax: (46 8) 27 0071
Email: mail@wwi.se

SWITZERLAND
Librarie Payot S.A.
Service Institutionnel
Côtes-de-Montbenon 30
1002 Lausanne
Tel: (41 21) 341 3229
Fax: (41 21) 341 3235
Email: institutionnel@payot-libraire.ch

ADECO Van Diermen Editions
Techniques
Ch. de Lacuez 41
CH-1807 Blonay
Tel: (41 21) 943 2673
Fax: (41 21) 943 3605

TANZANIA
TEPUSA
The Network of Technical
Publications in Africa
P.O. Box 22638
Dar es Salaam
Tel: (255 51) 114 876
Fax: (255 51) 112 434
Email: tepusa@intafrica.com

THAILAND
Centrac International Ltd.
ATTN: Central Books Distribution Co., Ltd.
Sinnrat Bldg. 13th Floor
3388/42-45 Rama 4 Rd.
Klong-Teoy
Bangkok 10110
Tel: (66 2) 367-5030-41 X178
Fax: (66 2) 3675049

**TRINIDAD & TOBAGO AND
THE CARIBBEAN**
Systematics Studies Ltd.
St. Augustine Shopping Center
Eastern Main Road

St. Augustine
Tel: (868) 645 8466
Fax: (868) 645 8467
Email: tobe@trinidad.net

UGANDA
Gustro Limited
P.O. Box 9997
Madhvani Building
Plot 16/4, Jinja Road
Kampala
Tel: (256 41) 251467
Fax: (256 41) 251468
Email: gus@swiftuganda.com

UKRAINE
LIBRA Publishing House
Ms. Sophia Ghemborovskaya
53/80 Saksahanskoho Str.
252033, Kiev 33
Tel: (7 44) 227 62 77
Fax: (7 44) 227 62 77

UNITED KINGDOM
Microinfo Ltd.
P.O. Box 3, Omega Park
Alton
Hampshire GU34 2 PG
Tel: (44 1420) 86 848
Fax: (44 1420) 89 889
Email: wbank@microinfo.co.uk
URL: www.microinfo.co.uk

The Stationery Office
51 Nine Elms Lane
London SW8 5DR
Tel: (44 20) 7 873 8372
Fax: (44 20) 7 873 8242
Email: chris.allen@theso.co.uk
URL: www.the-stationery-office.co.uk/ai/

VENEZUELA, R.B. de
Tecni-Ciencia Libros, S.A.
Sr. Luis Fernando Ramirez,
Director
Centro Cuidad Comercial
Tamanaco
Nivel C-2
Caracas
Tel: (58 2) 959 5547
Fax: (58 2) 959 5636
Email: lfrg001@ibm.net

VIETNAM
FAHASA (The Book Distribution Co. of Hochiminh City)
246 Le Thanh Ton Street
District 1
Hochiminh City
Tel: (84 8) 829 7638, 822 5446
Fax: (84 8) 822 5795
Email: fahasa-sg@hcm.vnn.vn
URL: www.tlnet.com.vn/fahasa

ZAMBIA
University Bookshop, University of Zambia
Great East Road Campus
P.O. Box 32379
Lusaka
Tel: (260 1) 252576
Fax: (260 1) 253952
Email: hunene@admin.unza.zm

ZIMBABWE
Academic and Baobab Books
(Pvt.) Ltd.
4 Conald Road
Graniteside
P.O. Box 567
Harare
Tel: (263 4) 755 035
Fax: (263 4) 759 052
Email: Academic@Africaon-line.Co.Zw

BOOKSELLERS

CHINA
China National Publications
Import
& Export Corporation
16 Gongti East Road
Post Code 100020
Beijing

HUNGARY
Foundation for Market Economy
112 Pf 249
1519 Budapest
Tel: (36 1) 204 2951; 2948
Fax: (36 1) 204 2953
Email: ipargazd@hungary.net

INDIA
Bookwell
Head Office: 2/72, Nirankari Colony
Delhi - 110009
Tel: (91 11) 725 1283
Sales Office: 24/4800, Ansari Road, Darya Ganj
New Delhi-110002
Tel: (91 11) 326 8786, 325 7264
Fax: (91 11) 328 1315
Email: bkwell@nde.vsnl.net.in

JORDAN
Global Development Forum
(GDF)
P.O. Box 941488
Amman 11194
Tel: (962 6) 465 6123
Fax: (962 6) 465 6123
Email: gdf@index.com.jo

KOREA, REPUBLIC OF
Sejong Books, Inc.
81-4 Neung-dong
Kwangjin-ku
Seoul 143-180
Tel: (82 2) 498 0300
Fax: (82 2) 3409 0321
Email: danielchoi@sejong
books.com
URL: http: www.sejong
books.com

MALAYSIA
MDC Publishers Printers SDN
BHD
MDC Building
2718, Jalan Permata Empat
Taman Permata, Ulu Kelang
53300 Kuala Lumpur
Tel: (60 3) 408 6600
Fax: (60 3) 408 1506
Email: mdcpp@2mws.com.my
URL: www.2mws.com.my/mdc

NEPAL
Bazaar International
228 Sanchaya Kosh Building
GPO Box 2480, Tridevi Marg
Kathmandu
Tel: (977 1) 255 125
Fax: (977 1) 229 437
Email: bazaar@mos.com.np

NIGERIA
Mosuro Booksellers
5 Oluware Obasa Street (Near
Awolowo Ave.)
P.O. Box 30201
Ibadan
Tel: (234 2) 810-2560
Fax: (234 2) 810-2042
Email: Kmosuro@linkserve.com.ng

POLAND
A.B.E. Marketing
Ul. Grzybowska 37A
00-855 Warsaw
Tel: (48 22) 654 06 75

Fax: (48 22) 682 22 33; 682 17 24
Email: abe@ikp.atm.com.pl

TAIWAN, CHINA
Tycoon Information, Inc.
Ms. Eileen Chen
5 Floor, No. 500
Chang-Chun Road
Taipei 105, Taiwan
Tel: (866 2) 8712 8886
Fax: (886 2) 8712 4747; 8712 4777
Email: eiutpe@ms21.hinet.net

THAILAND
Chulalongkorn University Book
Center
Phyathai Road
Bangkok 10330
Tel: (66 2) 235 5400
Fax: (66 2) 255 4441

Book Link Co. Ltd.
118/4 Ekamai Soi 28
Vadhana
Bangkok 10110
Tel: (662) 711 4392
Fax: (662) 711 4103
Email: bbatpt@au.ac.th

TURKEY
Dünya Infotel A.Ş.
"Globus" Dünya Basinevi
100, Yil Mahallesi
34440 Bagcilar-Istanbul
Tel: (90 212) 629 08 08
Fax: (90 212) 629 46 89; 629 46 27
Email: dunya@dunya-gazete.com.tr
URL: http: www.dunya.com

UNITED ARAB EMIRATES
Al Rawdha Bookshop
P.O. Box 5027
Sharjah
Tel: (971 6) 734 687
Fax: (971 6) 384 473
Email: alrawdha@hotmail.com

URUGUAY
Librería Técnica Uruguaya
Colonia 1543, Piso 7, Of. 702
Casilla de Correo 1518
Montevideo 11000, Uruguay
Tel: (598 2) 490072
Fax: (598 2) 41 34 48
Email: ltu@cs.com.uy